REMOTE EDUCATION AND INFORMATICS: TELETEACHING

IFIP TC 3 International Conference on
Remote Education and Informatics: Teleteaching '86
Budapest, Hungary, 20–25 October, 1986

NORTH-HOLLAND
AMSTERDAM · NEW YORK · OXFORD · TOKYO

REMOTE EDUCATION
AND INFORMATICS:
TELETEACHING

Proceedings of the IFIP TC 3 International Conference on
Remote Education and Informatics: Teleteaching '86
Budapest, Hungary, 20–25 October, 1986

edited by

Frank LOVIS
Computing Discipline
Faculty of Mathematics
The Open University
U.K.

LC
5803
.C65
I35
1986
West

1988

NORTH-HOLLAND
AMSTERDAM · NEW YORK · OXFORD · TOKYO

Arizona State Univ. West Campus Library

© IFIP, 1988

All rights reserved. No part of this publication may be reproduced, stored in a retrieval system, or transmitted, in any form or by any means, electronic, mechanical, photocopying, recording or otherwise, without the prior permission of the copyright owner.

ISBN: 0 444 70418 3

Published by:
ELSEVIER SCIENCE PUBLISHERS B.V.
P.O. Box 1991
1000 BZ Amsterdam
The Netherlands

Sole distributors for the U.S.A. and Canada:
ELSEVIER SCIENCE PUBLISHING COMPANY, INC.
52 Vanderbilt Avenue
New York, N.Y. 10017
U.S.A.

LIBRARY OF CONGRESS
Library of Congress Cataloging-in-Publication Data

IFIP TC 3 International Conference on Remote Education and
   Informatics: Teleteaching '86 (1986 : Budapest, Hungary)
   Remote education and informatics : teleteaching : proceedings of
the IFIP TC 3 International Conference on Remote Education and
Informatics: Teleteaching '86, Budapest, Hungary, 20-25 October 1986
/ edited by Frank Lovis.
      p.   cm.
   ISBN 0-444-70418-3 (U.S.)
   1. Distance education--Computer assisted instruction--Congresses.
2. Electronic data processing--Study and teaching--Congresses.
I. Lovis, F. B. (Frank B.) II. IFIP Technical Committee 3,
Education. III. Title.
LC5803.C65I35 1986
371.3'9445--dc19   88-7218
                                                           CIP

PRINTED IN THE NETHERLANDS

'For I departed into the future far as human eye could see.
Saw the vision of the world, and all the wonder that would be.'
(Tennyson)

PREFACE

I read with pleasure reports written by the first computer-constructors, the well-known old of formatics. I am particularly interested in their way of thinking about future development: whether they could imagine at that time this fast spread of computers that we experience today.

I found that computer experts in the 1950's and 60's could see, or rather guess that computers would bring about a revolution in the history of sciences and would influence the economic life, due to the ability of doing the kind of mathematical calculations and estimations which could not have been done before, through lack of computers of appropriate output.

On the other hand, they did not think that computers would revolutionize human sciences, medicine, biology and other non-mathematical sciences. The first computer-constructors did not suppose, not even in the slightest degree, that their machines would be used in such a personal activity as education.

Education meant a special relationship between the old and the young for centuries. The old handed over all the experience and information to the young. The emergence of computers and informatics overthrew this order for it was relatively quick and influenced mainly young people. At the same time, informatics seemed to work well in almost every field, so 'unfortunately' old people also need to learn how to apply computers.

The whole society has become interested in studying computer sciences, so the task is to render these studies possible for everyone in the near future.

The fact that a new world is being formed where the knowledge once obtained can be used for a rather short time, might be the consequence of the quick technical development. There are always more and more new and important pieces of information and that is the reason why we all have to learn continually. Studies lasting for a lifetime mean a new way of life for the majority of people. Obviously, this kind of education can be successful neither with the traditional methods, nor with the present system of institutions, and these are particularly inconvenient for teaching computing sciences, which should be widely used in a few years. Demonstration has always been applied to increase the efficiency of teaching, for it helps both teachers to explain and students to understand the subject. Nearly all of the inventions, like photographs, films, television and video have soon become useful in education. Usually, they mean a passive medium, for this kind of demonstration cannot be applied without the teacher's explanation.

The fact that computers are gaining ground has resulted in a quality-change of teaching. With the help of computers it is possible to create such interactive and intelligent systems which are not only used for an easier explanation, but also for new tasks, such as controlling the lesson and measuring knowledge.

The planning of these intelligent teaching-learning systems, which also presumes thorough pedagogical and methodical knowledge, is apparently far more difficult than the shooting of a documentary film, for instance. Education technology has been making good use of computers for some years, in most cases exploiting them together with other media such as television, creating thus a rich variety of instruments and systems for distance-teaching.

The only way of teaching informatics to adults which seems to be possible is by distance-education. Our purpose at the Teleteaching '86 Conference, in Budapest was mainly to prove this statement. The participants of the conference surveyed recent reforms in education technology; lecturers presented the choice of hardware and course-ware that we possess today and also talked about theoretical problems. An exhibition of new distance-teaching instruments (videodisk, videotex, local computer systems, etc.) made a presentation possible in practice.

A proposition to set up a new IFIP working group (W.G. 3.6) was made at the closing session of the conference. This working group would be called the 'Distance-learning' W.G., thus expressing exactly what the forty expert-members intend to deal with.

The W.G. decided to hold the next conference (Teleteaching '88) in Thailand. Experts from the Sukhothai Thammathirat Open University (STOU) have engaged themselves for the organization of the event.

We do hope that the initiative taken in the field of distance-teaching is not only accepted by IFIP, but that it will also have the possibility of further development. The conference in Bangkok is to prove how much IFIP will grow rich if the distance-teaching of computing sciences as a new technology in education becomes widely used.

Gy. Kovács
Chairman of the Program Committee   *January, 1987*

CONTENTS

x *Contents*

Section 1
Remote Education — General

Remote Education and Informatics: Teleteaching
F. Lovis (Editor)
Elsevier Science Publishers B.V. (North-Holland)
© IFIP, 1988

TELETEACHING AS THE MOST IMPORTANT MEANS OF THE
INFORMATIZATION OF THE SOCIETY

Győző KOVÁCS*

BASE-SITUATION

The eighties are regarded - especially in popular scientific
writings - as the epoch leading to the age of informatics.

It would be an interesting investigation task to examine and define the characteristics of the age of informatics. I don't even
try to do it in the frame of this short paper, but try to define
the features of the transitional period instead, and by taking
them all into account I'll try to summarize the conclusions concerning the training of informatics.

HARDWARE

- Cheap computers of relatively great performance appeared in an
ever growing number not only at work-places but also in schools
and households.

- Data-networks over the whole world were established not only
for serving business affairs but also to cope with the requirements of the private spheres (e.g. Videotex).

- More and more products have been made - from the telephone sets
and cameras to the motorcars - which function by means of connecting them to computers; these products even may be built together
with simple or complicated intelligent electronic constructions.
Thus, willingly or unwillingly, nearly all members of the society
will gradually get in touch with informatics.

SOFTWARE

- The conditions of software development changed as the equipments were getting cheaper and cheaper; thus, they might be
accessible to anyone. Amateurism grew stronger and the experts of
software development were hereby constrained to enter into competition.

- At the same time, the demand for ready software products was
steadily increasing. In order to meet the requirements, the software industry established itself, and, to assure the conditions
of quality, the software technology was brought about. The process was similar to, but essentially faster than the development
that lead from craftmanship to the establishment of modern great
industry. The latter lasted for nearly two centuries (18th and
19th cent.), whereas producing the software industry, the mass
production and technology took only three decades (circa 1950-
-1980).

- The software products appeared and consequently a market

* J.v.Neumann Society for Computing Sciences

for them was called into existence. The mass-production was started, keeping up the possibility of producing tailored software, too.
This dualism has also been reflected in the software prices.While
the mass-products can be bought at a price of a few tens of dollars, the price of the tailored software is many times ten
thousand dollars.

SOCIETY

- Writings about the social effect of informatics appeared in an
ever growing number in the course of recent years. Nowadays, not
only the experts of informatics but those of education and naturally also the experts of social sciences are more intensively
dealing with this subject.

For a long time, computers could be bought only by the economically prosperous great enterprises, national institutions and
concerns; therefore, the effect of these systems could only be
noticed within the institutions mentioned above. Then, one could
not practically speak of the social effect, or in certain regards only. Only the experts trained in informatics could get in
direct touch with these enterprise-systems. The user gave only
the basic data, i.e. received the results of calculations from
the computer center.

Having put into operation the systems of many terminals in the
late sixties and early seventies, the social effect could be
first noticed. Terminals connected with great mainframes could
also be used by people untrained in informatics in the fields of
input, controlling partial results, i.e. printing them out. Thus,
the person-machine contact was established in a very simple form
which was, however, very important as regards the ensuing development.

The first cheap equipments of informatics (personal computers)
appeared on the market in the late seventies. Nearly all the
spheres of economy were conquered by them in the course of a few
years. Their cheap prices and the low running costs resulted in
the ever growing use of the personal computers by institutions
(belonging, e.g., to public health, education, etc.) that - apart
from some privileged ones - couldn't even think earlier of the
general use of the information processing. One of the most important consequences - producing a lot of problems - was that
more and more people were getting in direct touch with the systems of informatics and the possible work by means of computers
hardened hereby to an obligatory one.

In several countries, among them ours, it was the education that
first came to the right conclusion to announce the schools-in-
formatics-program. In Hungary, e.g., all the secondary schools got
computers in the course of a few years, and supplying primary
schools with computers has been started, too. The social effect
of this rule, which is of great importance as regards the development of the future generation, has surprised even the experts, and in my opinion, it is promoting the success of the
society-informatization program. The wide spread use of computers
hasn't had only positive effects, it causes often social problems,
it even becomes sometimes the source of generation problems.

- The school-informatics program has caused problems in the family; more urgent, ones than for instance the teaching of mathematics based on new theories has caused. A great number of parents simply refuse to get acquainted with computers and the
learning of informatical methods with the remark: I am too old
to do it.

- There is often discrepancy between the young people knowing informatics and the senior experts. Having finished the university
studies or the secondary school training, the young meet the
seniors who, having gained experience during their working of
more decades, can't learn the new technology, or don't want to
do it.

- Perhaps the greatest conflict came about between the youth re-
ceptive to informatics and teachers not willing to apply informatics. This conflict has often caused the decrease in the
teachers' respect or led to grave educational troubles.

EDUCATION

The social conflicts of the age of informatics can only be solved
by a society-wide education program.

There is a Hungarian proverb: a hair of the dog that bites you.
Informatics, being the cause of conflicts, also offers the tools
and methods of the social-wide training of informatics through
which all these problems can be solved.

The key-person of the traditional training is the teacher, because

- he is compiling and elaborating the matter of instruction,

- he is the interpreter while explaining and teaching,

- and finally it is he again who examines the level of the acquired knowledge in the course of questioning the students.

As the teacher has the most important role in all phases of the
course of training, he can therefore also be the weakest point
in traditional education. The efficiency of teaching can mostly
be spoilt by a bad pedagogue. The authorities responsible for
education can only intervene efficiently at one point in the
course of teaching and that is by providing the school with an
instruction material compiled and controlled many times by the
centre of education. Teacher and his questioning the students can
only be controlled from time to time, as it is not possible to
appoint an inspector to every teacher, and it would be in vain,
as all bad teachers couldn't be replaced by good ones.

The other problem of the traditional training is that it is very
difficult to change the instruction matter elaborated by the educational center. New school-books, new tools for testing should
be given to all schools. In the FRG*, e.g., publishing the new
- - - - - -
*Brenel B: Die vielgeforderte "Qualifizierungsoffensive" darf
sich nicht nur auf die Arbeitslosen beschranken. Handelsblatt
18.02.1986.

subject matter of informatics takes at least five years which is
a very long period in case of the informatics knowledge. Experience proves that the knowledge matter necessary in informatics
must - due to the fast development - be renewed in 3 - 4 years.

TELETEACHING - MASS EDUCATION

According to the information coming from the FRG, 70 % of the
workers must acquire   the knowledge of informatics in about
five years.

It means that up to 1990, altogether about 20-25 millions of
people must be educated in informatics, i.e. 3-5 million workers
per year. In case of accepting the "knowledge refreshing" to be
obligatory in every third year, the above figures will redouble.
As this estimation refers only to the retraining of the adult
working people, therefore, the number of the students of public
education and universities must still be added.

I think, it isn't necessary to continue arguing in order to convince all competent people that this demand for informatics re-
education can't be met by means of the traditional education
system either in the FRG or elsewhere.

The only solution is teleteaching, or, in other terms, the education aided by machines (not only by computers).

I couldn't find a precise definition for teleteaching, therefore,
I should like to characterize it shortly as follows: Teleteaching, or remote teaching, is the form of teaching in which it is
the teacher's task to elaborate the subject matter satisfying all
special demands, and to organize the systems of teaching and
examinations. The subject matter (courseware) reaches the student
by means of technical tools. During the course of training,
teacher and student, in general, do not meet each other directly.

In traditional teaching, the teacher has the only role, and not-
withstanding he is charged in teleteaching, too, with the stressed task of elaborating the training system, the courseware, the
computer as intermediator and the medium carrying the information
are also very important elements of the remote teaching.

- The ancient, classical teleteaching media are written matters,
books, notes and letters. In point of fact, they answer all necessary training demands, they are cheap and easy to handle, the
subject matter can be repeated as many times the students want
to do it. The book is a passive teaching system element, as one
can learn by means of it, but it is not able to examine the
acquired knowledge.

- The educational film was perhaps the first teleteaching medium
operating by means of pictures. Videos and records belong to this
category, too. As a matter of fact, each of them is a passive
teaching-system element, too; the pupil has to look at or listen
to them while he doesn't know the matter. The system doesn't examine the knowledge.

- Also, radios and televisions belong to this category. It is
evident that the teleteaching system organized to be transmitted
by means of them is the cheapest, but it is efficient only if

it is combined with the use of videos, records or even of programmed text-books, as the training matter can't otherwise be repeated.

Up to the present, the computer is the only active teaching instrument. It stores the matter of training in form of texts,
images, and graphics (magnetic band, magnetic disc, recently also
optical disc, etc.), and is teaching the students in accordance
with the stored subject matter, repeating it as many times as it
is needed. It even poses questions to the students, and where it
finds a lack of knowledge, it is doing the repetition. Thus, the
computer is fit to do the examination, too.

- Collective systems of computer teaching: the star network for
teaching a smaller learning group, local networks within one
school, or connecting more schools, national teaching network
(e.g. videotex), computer and terminal networks of educational
aims linked to the international data networks.

Highly developed countries, developing countries and teleteaching.

It is generally believed and said very often that teleteaching
was discovered in the industrially developed countries (U.K.,
France, GFR, Austria, USA, Japan etc.) and is chiefly employed
in these countries. Because of the relatively high prices of the
necessary computers, there is no perspective in the less developed countries and in the developing ones for applying this teaching form.

It was mentioned, too, that the courseware elaborated in countries disposing of developed teaching traditions could hardly be
used in the developing countries even in the case of an existing
teleteaching system, because the matter of courses couldn't be
understood by the pupils.

I think that after a bit more meditating upon this subject, I
could mention at least ten new counter-arguments in connection
with teleteaching, but each of them would be a weaker argument
than that one which says that there is no development without
teaching informatics at the level of the whole society; and in
the lack of it, the economic, scientific and cultural distances
between the developed and developing countries will continue to
increase.

The country that neglects the effort of making the tools and
methods of informatics familiar to every active member of the
working staff makes impossible

- its joining to the worldsize information change,

- its getting in touch with developed countries in the fields of
  equal rank science and commerce, and

- to produce competitive goods without the possibilities granted
  by informatics,

- to organize the optimal production lacking informatics, therefore:

- the production costs are more and more increasing, i.e. the
production is getting more and more expensive. Thus:

- the realization of the products doesn't assure any profit,

- the country becomes defenceless, because without the knowledge
of informatics it has to charge foreign experts, who are qualified but often very expensive, with the care of its connections,
etc.

The list of the arguments and counter-arguments could be a very
long one, but the final result wouldn't be changed by it. The
great and important step leading the whole society to informatics
must be taken by all nations.

The informatized society can only be established by qualified,
educated people, and this task can only be solved - within an
acceptable period - by an efficient educational system, i.e. by
T E L E T E A C H I N G. There is no alternative.

Remote Education and Informatics: Teleteaching
F. Lovis (Editor)
Elsevier Science Publishers B.V. (North-Holland)
© IFIP, 1988

REMOTE EDUCATION WITH ONLINE COMMUNICATIONS AND LABORATORIES

Dr. G.Schlageter
Dr.H-W.Six
W. Stern
Dr. C. Unger

University of Hagen (FernUniversität)
Postfach 940
5800 Hagen
West-Germany

This report is based upon a project which is funded by the German "Bundesminister für Bildung und Wissenschaft" (Project No. M0538.00). The authors are responsible for the contents of this publication.

CHAPTER 1   INTRODUCTION

The "FernUniversität Hagen" is the only university in Germany which offers remote education for several subjects, e.g. computer science. Our students may enrol for a full diploma degree in computer science, for a certificate covering a specific area of computer science, or even for individual courses.

Students are mainly living remote from the university and, at the time being, are chiefly taught via written course material, written exercises, etc. They usually communicate with their supervisors via mail or phone, only for rather compact seminars and computer laboratories they have to be present at Hagen.

Though many of our students have their own computer at home or have access to terminals or computers (e.g. at their employers), there is not yet any overall concept to use these computers for learning, training, experimenting and communicating in the course of distant education.

In contrast to "normal" universities, our students are faced with several specific problems due to their remoteness:

- the communication and cooperation among students and between students and the university is rather limited
- only for a few weeks a year, most of the students can use computers and their course related software

- as during the past years the number of students in computer
  sciences at Hagen increased in an unforeseeable rate, a
  poor ratio of the number of students and the size of the
  teaching staff additionally makes individual tutoring
  almost impossible.

To overcome these problems, the department of Mathematics and
Computer Science has started a project to develop courseware based
on electronic media for distant learning and education. This
project is partly supported by the German Government.

The main goal of the project is to develop attractive 'electronic
courses' for continued education. The students can use their
personal computers as learner-stations to work through an
electronic course. All the advantages of computer-support can be
integrated into such a concept:

- *graphic presentation and animation*
  'Learning by reading' is complemented by 'learning by
  intuition'.
- *interaction and electronic laboratories*
  Electronic question/answer technics and course related
  tools are integrated into a course allowing the student to
  deepen his actual knowledge by testing and trying-out.
- *communication*
  Students are integrated into a national-wide communication
  system allowing a fast and comprehensive communication
  among students and between students and the university.

In this paper we present prime ideas and concepts concerning the
project. After this introductional chapter the general concept is
described in *chapter 2*. The problem of communication for remote
working students is discussed in *chapter 3* and possible solutions
are presented. *Chapter 4* introduces the concept of electronic
courseware. Electronic laboratories are dealt with in *chapter 5*.

CHAPTER 2   GENERAL CONCEPT

The main goal of the project is to develop an attractive program
for continued education.

The salient features of this program are:

- the student can work at home at an electronic station
  (personal computer)
- the student's workstation is connected to a communication
  network
- the courseware is of "electronic" form
- the electronic courses are presented in an attractive and
  motivating form
- the idea of "learning by doing" is achieved by consequently
  integrating electronic laboratory sessions into the courses
- the courses will cover actual topics of computer science

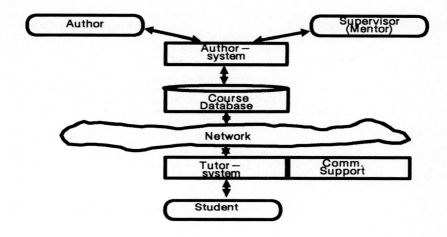

(Figure 1: The General Concept of the Learning System)

The functions of the different modules within this system are as follows (fig. 1):

1) *Author System*
The author and the mentor of a course use the author system to develop, edit and structure an electronic course. It also supports testing of a course (student's view).

2) *Central Course Base*
All offered courses are stored in a central course database. This database also includes the programs that realize the electronic laboratories.

3) *Tutor System*
The tutor system acts as a tutor to the student. It includes the following components:
  Presentation:
  Shows the contents of a course to a student
  Tutoring:
  Leads the student through a course with many learning-supporting functions
  Laboratory:
  Enables to "trying-out" the currently learned material.

4) *Communication Support*
This module supports the use of a connected communication network. There are two main applications:
  a) *distributed learning system*
  As the student workstations are geographically distributed all over Germany, the access to the course database must be realized efficiently and at low costs.

   b) dialogue/mailing
       Messages can be sent to other students or to the uni-
       versity in a convenient way.

   At the moment videotex (in Germany called BILDSCHIRMTEXT
   (BTX)) seems to be the most appropriate network which
   satisfies the required functions.
   Furthermore, BTX provides high quality graphic support,
   thus non-intelligent videotex-decoders can be used as
   learning stations, too. In this case the tutor program has
   to be run in the central computer.

CHAPTER 3   THE COMMUNICATION FACILITIES

A major problem of a remote teaching system is the lack of communication facilities between students or between students and the
university.

At a conventional university students mostly are working in
groups. They learn to solve problems or develop projects by doing
teamwork. The possibility to discuss problems with the professor
or an assistant is a very important part of the study.

Since the students of the University of Hagen are only temporary
on the campus so far

       - students can discuss problems with the mentor of a course
         only by telephone
       - only for a short period, students of computer science may
         work on (software-) projects in Hagen

Unfortunately, students are still isolated while studying at home.

This disadvantage can be solved in an electronic learning system
by integrating *comfortable mailing functions*.

We are planning a system which allows to send mail to specified
groups of receivers (students or mentors), which can be actually
defined by the sender of the message.

As an example, a message may be sent to

       - a specified student
       - the mentor of a specified course
       - all students who currently are participating in a specified
         course
       - all students living close to Hagen

Using such a system students can try to solve their problems by
contacting other students, but also to interchange some important
"background" information (e.g.: "Who knows about inexpensive
hotels in Hagen?").

For the first time a form of teamworking, based on an electronic
mail system, becomes feasible without the need for meeting
physically.

Integrated Exercises

These exercises are fully integrated into, and controlled by, their electronic courses. They are limited in scope and size. The solution provided by the student as well as the final results can be controlled and be checked by the tutor-system. This kind of exercise can be used to monitor the student and, dependent on his progress, repeat parts of the course or branch into different paths of the lecture. Multiple choice tests, or to apply a given algorithm to a given data structure, are examples for this kind of exercise.

Written Exercises

During his electronic lecture, at certain predefined points, the student is asked to solve a given problem using paper and pencil. The student's solution cannot be checked on automatically by the courseware tutor, the student himself has to compare it with the standard model solution provided by the courseware. In some cases the student may be asked to type the final results of his solution into his computer for monitoring purposes. If the student is not able to either match his solution with the given one or to find and fix errors within his solution, he may use the communication system mentioned above to directly contact his -human- supervisor.

Proving a theorem or solving a complex numerical problem are examples for this kind of exercise.

Tools and Laboratories

Efficient exercises for courses on programming, compilers, data bases, simulation, expert systems, etc, usually require large-scale software tools which cannot be produced for each course and be integrated into it individually.

There are three main approaches how an existing tool can be used for an electronic course. It can either be used separately, loosely be coupled with the courseware, or fully be integrated into the courseware.

In the first approach the student himself has explicitly to switch between the courseware and the tool, details depending on the students computer, the underlying operating system etc. In the worst case he may even have to struggle with several floppy disks; in the most convenient one, he may just have to switch between two concurrent processes (sidekick).

CHAPTER 4   ELECTRONIC COURSEWARE

Possibilities and limitations of the new medium[1]

Before developing electronic courseware one has carefully to
examine the possibilities and limitations of the computer-driven
screen. They are summarized as "able to show dynamic processes in
such a way that the viewer can interact and control the process
being displayed". The computer-driven screen replaces the one-to-
many type of monologue of a teacher in a conventional setting or
of the paperbased courseware of the FernUniversität Hagen by a
one-to-one type of interaction which support individual activities
of various kinds. Moreover, controlling the lectures' running off
enables the students to proceed at their own pace rather than
being locked into some predefined schedule.

Graphic and animation capabilities of the computer-driven screen
are the most powerful demonstration aid in education history so
far. In contrast to conventional educational films, for example,
the computer may serve as a simulation machine displaying
processes under user-driven initial conditions and user-controlled
speed.

A general inquiry among students taking their first programming
course, partly on the PLATO CAI System /2/ and partly in the conventional lecture mode, showed that more than 80 percent of the students preferred the PLATO System. Stated advantages were:

    - the possibility to use the PLATO System nearly 24 hours a
      day
    - proceeding at one's pace
    - the personal freedom in the PLATO classrooms (as opposed to
      the discipline required in the lecture halls).

Most of the advantages stated in the PLATO inquiry already hold
for the remote education system of the FernUniversität Hagen.

The limitations of the new medium can easily be characterized by
the fact that one partner of the dialog is a machine and not a
human being. The man-machine dialog is not symmetric, the dialog
machine is devoid of creativity and intuition. A wide-ranging
dialog over the why's and how's   quickly brings up an idea
outside the scope of the program and finally ends up in a situation of complete misunderstanding.

Courseware topics

Before explaining the topics of the intended courseware in more
detail, we introduce the audience in mind.

For the time being, we mainly think of students having already
reasonable knowledge in computer sciences, e.g. people who have a
later stage diplomas in computer sciences or who are employed with

---

[1] The basic ideas of this chapter are taken from /1/.

the computer industry. We want to address people, who have an academic diploma in any discipline which covers sufficient knowledge in mathematics enabling them to understand basic courseware of applied computer sciences.

We start our project with experienced computer sciences students mainly for two reasons. Firstly, these students usually have easy access to appropriate hardware and communication network facilities and hence need not spend money for the technical equipment. Secondly, discussions with industrial companies have shown that especially the computer industry and companies with big computer departments are heavily interested in continued education in computer sciences.

Since we address people of the computer science community, we are going to develop "high-tech" courseware for topics like

- introduction to artificial intelligence
- expert systems
- PROLOG
- SMALLTALK
- ADA
- UNIX

The contents of each course is comparable with the contents of a 2-hour lesson at a conventional university. In addition to each electronic course, a written documentation is delivered containing a table of contents, references, eventually a list of frames with important definitions or formulas, and a general introduction to the material similar to the foreword of a textbook. An electronic course usually follows a generally accepted textbook. On the one hand this surely improves the selection of material and overall-organization of the electronic courseware. On the other hand, regarding electronic courseware as the natural counterpart of the conventional classroom teaching, we are convinced that one or more appropriate textbooks must be available to the students for further reading, preparation of examinations, etc.

As mentioned before, in a second step we want to develop courseware on more elementary topics like introduction to computer programming, data structures and algorithms, introduction to operating systems, data base systems, and software engineering. This courseware will be dedicated to non-computer scientists with appropriate educational background.

CHAPTER 5   ELECTRONIC EXERCISES AND LABORATORIES

The efficiency of learning, especially in the case of remote education, highly depends on the extent the student is enabled to apply the subjects taught to specific exercises and problems. Thus, in addition to textbooks and electronic course material, the student has to be provided with various kinds of exercises and laboratories, differing in their level of complexity, sophistication, and integration into the courseware.

In the following paragraph, the major classes of exercises and laboratories are dealt with in more detail.

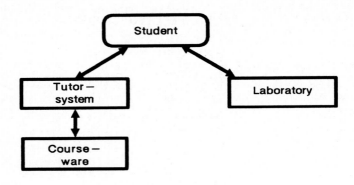

Figure 2: Independent Courseware and Laboratories

In the second approach both the courseware as well as the tool are controlled by a simple tutor which

- switches between both modules
- assists the user in providing input for the tool
- controls and evaluates the use of the tool.

This approach still leaves the tool unchanged by 'just' encapsulating it into a new shell (fig. 3).

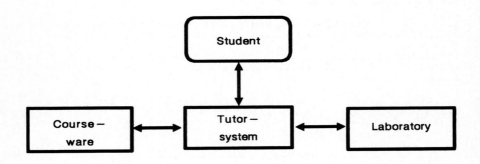

Figure 3: Loosely coupled Courseware and Laboratories

By providing a standard interface for courseware communication as well as for laboratory communication, the same, generic, tutor can be used for different courses and tools. This approach also allows coupling courseware created by an author system with an existing tool.

The third approach is   to fully integrate the tool as well as
the courseware into a sophisticated tutor system (fig. 4)

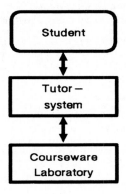

Figure 4: Integrated Laboratories

In case of a compiler course, this approach, for example, would
allow using   different modules of an Ada compiler, e.g. scanner,
parser, front-end, back-end, etc., in different parts of the
course.

This approach usually cannot be realized without significant
changes to the existing tools as well as courseware, and thus for
the time being seems most unrealistic.

The idea of course related tools very smoothly leads to the idea
of laboratories for individual courses, allowing the student to
continuously work and experiment with course related tools at his
own computer. Figures 2 and 3 apply to this situation as well, the
courseware being mainly employed as an assistant and helper for
the use of the laboratory.

If possible, the tools actually needed are dynamically loaded into
the student's local computer via the communication system. Large-
scale tools, running at the central computers only, can be used by
the student via the same communication network:

  - In case of independent courseware and tools, the access to
    the - from the student's point of view - remote tool can be
    achieved by a - from the central computer's point of view -
    remote login of the student.
  - In case of loosely coupled or integrated courseware and
    tools, a remote procedure call protocol is to be used.

The situation becomes even more complex if single tools or parts
of them are run on different computers, either local or remote. An
example for such a distributed laboratory is given in the next
paragraph.

Distributed Laboratories

Present diploma students have to pass a one term computer laboratory, for which they have to be present at Hagen for three weeks. In groups of eight, they have to work at a joint complex problem, involving problem analysis, modularization, interface design, programming implementation testing and documentation.

In the future this kind of laboratory is to be replaced by a remote distributed laboratory, which at least has to meet the following requirements:

- The communication system, mentioned above, has to make available sophisticated facilities for electronic mail, teleconferencing, distributed documentation etc.
- Each student's computer as well as the central computers involved have to provide the same programming environment, including a unified user interface to the underlying operating system.

The Portable Common Tool Environment (PCTE) may be good candidate for this environment. PCTE is based upon UNIX and is presently being developed as a common environment for all ESPRIT projects and is being implemented on different computers of various size.

Conclusion

At a first glance, remote education might seem to exclusively benefit from the concept of electronic exercises and laboratories. Thus some critical comments seem to be advisable:

- With regard to exercises, the present concept of external control, correcting and rating is highly replaced by a concept of individual control, correcting and rating by the student himself. This may lead to a lower performance and incentive of some students and, consequently, to poorer final exams. This situation may be compensated for by additional 'realtime' tests and pre-exams, controlled individually by the supervisors.
- It seems to be questionable, if important and intended side effects of programming laboratories like group behavior, group dynamics etc. can sufficiently be induced by teleconferencing, distributed testing, etc, as well.

LITERATURE

/1/ J. Nievergelt, A. Ventura, H. Hinterberger: Interactive
       Computer Programs for Education, Addison-Wesley 1986.
/2/ Bitzer, D.L., P. Braunfeld, W. Lichtenberger: PLATO: An
       Automatic Teaching Device, IRE Trans. Education, Vol. E-
       4, Dec 1961, pp. 157-161.

Remote Education and Informatics: Teleteaching
F. Lovis (Editor)
Elsevier Science Publishers B.V. (North-Holland)
© IFIP, 1988

THE EDUCATION INDUSTRY

Neil Spoonley

International Management Institute, Geneva, Switzerland

1. INTRODUCTION

This paper presents a picture of the education industry, where
the educational activities are the customers for technological
products. This has been the case in the past for books and many
other items, but the level of expenditure is now substantially
higher. Computer companies are deliberately targeting their activities towards the education market in search of profits. This
paper considers the issues in a broad context, looking for aspects which will improve the overall usefulness of investing in
technology.

2. THE EDUCATIONAL OBJECTIVE

It should be without question that the purpose of spending money
on a computer (or indeed, any other purchase), which is to be
installed in the school, should only be done on the basis of
improving the educational process. For small purchases this
question rarely arises, but when computers are bought it is only
reasonable to ask if their use will improve the quality of education in some relevant way. But, how many of the educational
institutions can give a clear description of their objectives and
precisely where the computer fits in? As we shall see, not all
the elements of the educational industry have the same objective
and it is worthwhile for the customers to appreciate this.

3. THE INDUSTRY

Later in this paper there is more detailed consideration of each
of the elements below, but firstly let us consider the functions
of the industry with particular reference to the use of technology.

The "customers" of technology for serving education are within
the educational system itself. They may be in the schools, or
the parents, or perhaps in the Education Authority which mana-
ges them. They, above all, should be looking at the reasons for
purchase and for ensuring that they only buy products which enhance the process.

Although the schools have been considered in this context as the
customers, it is also true that they are, of course, the principal producers of the industry. They create a product, namely,
a better educated individual and they consume other products and
services in so doing.

Like all production systems, the quality of the raw materials and
additives is vital for the quality of the end product. Thus, it
is essential that we know what the computers are for and how
they should be used to achieve their purpose.

The principal "suppliers" to the industry are the hardware manufacturers and the software creators. Their objective is to make
profit from sales of their products.

Some software producers only sell to the hardware manufacturers
and their software becomes part of a package available from the
latter.

In between are the various means of publishing and distributing
both hardware and software. For the former, there are generally
well proven ways of arranging licences or agencies. However, for
software, it seems to be a different picture.

Finally, there are all those organizations that influence the
level of activity. It is often through these that specific go-
vernmental actions are channelled. It is possible that there is a
greater range of ways to do this than may be realised.

Thus, we have the elements of the industry. To a large extent,
the success of each element in achieving its objectives lies with
the others. Money flows out of one pocket into another and the
level of investment in any area needs to take the success of the
other areas into account.

4. THE EDUCATION SYSTEM AS "CUSTOMERS"

As suggested above, the education system should be clear as to
why it is buying computers. They are not, in general, experts
in computing and there is no reason why most people who touch
one should ever be so. However, they can be expected to be expert in the process of education and therefore, their objectives
for using a computer ought to be expressed in such terms.

A recent study in the U.K. (1) showed very clearly that not only
was there no clear understanding of the uses of computers but,
there was no collective approach, as to how to express the usage.
The need for such information may not be fully apparent to
teachers but, they must recognize that the suppliers of such
computers need market studies, intelligence, etc., on which they
base their plans. The absence of such information deprives them
of a basic tool for product design and leaves them only considering the commercial market potential for their design criteria.

The following types of usage are therefore proposed as a check
for ascertaining current usage and as a way of ensuring that in
planning for the use of computers, it is clear as to why they
are being bought.

A. Teacher (School) Administration Efficiency

The computer is used to help in all conceivable ways to aid
the efficient operation of the staff and other resources. It
includes timetabling, record keeping, management tasks, examinations, etc. Different members of staff may see the computer
in different ways; some may use it for drill and practice for
the student, whilst others will see it as a file for notes.

B. Teaching Enhancement

The computer is used to teach a topic. Generally, the use would
be independent of teachers, but under their control. They may
adjust the parameters of lessons to make them more complex or
limit their use. In a sense, the teachers are using the computer to extend their own range of capabilities.

C. Information Resource and Management

To a large extent, this particularly applies to the use by a
student. In some subjects, the computer will be used like a
calculator or a typewriter. But, as database, spreadsheets and
graphics become more available, so will the use multiply.

D. Teaching of Computing or Information Science

Here computers are needed for the topic itself, to teach
programming, design and other aspects which require an intimate
knowledge of the device.

Each of these categories of use has value for the suppliers, particularly of software, and it is vital that they understand, not
only the existing pattern of use, but that which can be forecast
or is intended.

In the U.K., there appears to be a general consensus from the recent study that:

1. There is a definitive move in the secondary sector to Category
C. usage.

2. Over the next few years Category D. will decline in importance.

3. Category B. will not play a major role for many years to come.

4. Category A. use will increase with the need to meet the multi-
grading and assessment criteria of the new examinations (GCSE),
from 1988 onwards.

These suggestions are made in a context where there is no specific change in the syllabus of any topic to accommodate the new
opportunities that computer availability offers. For example, it
does not include the use of databases for history teaching, the
use of simulations, the use of spreadsheets for "what if" explora-
tions, etc. Should a country take specific action to bring these
possibilities into the syllabus and the examination system, then
new patterns of use may occur.

It is an interesting point to consider, as to where in an educational system there is the trigger that sets a new initiative in motion. In the U.K., it seems that the examination system governs the
intentions of most teaching. The syllabus is, however, agreed on a
regional basis, mainly by subject committees of teachers. There is
thus an in-built conservative approach which will generally consider any change with regard to the use of computers as some
"trendy thing". Of course, there are exceptions where there are
quite exciting developments, but they tend to be alongside the
examination system, rather that within it. Thus, we have the local
school enthusiast and the computer clubs which make the news about
the use of computers.

An influential aspect of the education system is the support
structure that may have been created to assist in development of
the use of computers. Some authorities in the U.K. have created
effective support units to advise on purchase and, even, to develop software. Others have set standards or trained teachers.

5. THE SUPPLIES

Most personal computers and many of the lower end of the business
computer range can be found in schools across the world. Few of
these computers can be said to have been specifically designed
for the education sector. In the U.K., we have had the RML and
Acorn/BBC computers which have been primarily targetted toward
this sector, but both would agree that it does not offer a large
enough market to create the investment to design machines just
to meet educational needs.

There seems to be no escape from the fact that the education
sector is not a major influence on the development of hardware
and, in the manufacturing world, they see little evidence that
it will ever be so. It is interesting to speculate on the pattern
of purchase in the U.K. of 8-bit versus 16-bit machines in the
future. There are many in the schools and local authorities who
would wish to continue to increase their investment in computers
by buying more of the same, i.e. 8-bit machines. But, for the
suppliers, this is the opposite of what they wish. The business
community do not wish to buy them and it is now cheaper to make
the 16-bit machines. Thus, it is in their interest to encourage
the 16-bit machines to be bought, even to the extent of increasing
the price of the 8-bit to well above the going price for the newer computers.

This will generate more resentment in the schools, particularly
for those people who have written useful packages that only work
on the old machines. It will also accentuate the pressure to use
the software in Category C. usage, i.e. spreadsheet, databases,
etc.

What must be accepted by the schools is that there is going to
be a range of hardware as time passes and each school must
develop its strategy for making most use of all of it, whether
it is old or new. Computers do not wear out that easily now and
most of them can be useful for up to 10 years.

The problem is now being recognized and we are seeing the networks
where many varying computers can be linked to a common source of
programmes, databases, etc. The first thought is to insist on
upward compatibility so that all the machines can run all the
work that can be done on the lowest machine. The suppliers will
not be hamstrung by this and it will not happen. Thus, again the
schools will find that they will have to define the limits of use
of each range of machines and fit them within their overall
objectives.

In the U.K., there is an annual spend by the schools on hardware
that is over 10M pounds. By contrast, the spend on software is
about 1.5M pounds.

The software suppliers have different problems. Those who create commercial software, which is delivered to a user via the hardware suppliers, are isolated from the educational world. These suppliers, providing the tools like Visicalc, Dbase II, GEM, Wordstar, etc, design their products for the commercial world and then let the hardware suppliers package them and bundle them in the hardware product. It seems to the school as though they are getting it all for free. It is highly unlikely that this trend will change, particularly as many educational and commercial customers buy in bulk and are only too happy to have an easy way of accepting an imposed "standard". However, it can be said that in the educational context, so many of the packages are so sufficiently similar that is really does not matter which they use.

But there are also the software developers for educational software itself, especially developed for the schools. There are three categories of developer.

1. Commercial Developers

    They develop the software with the intention of making a profit out of its sale.

2. Subsidised Development

    This is often done by units which exist in the schools system, perhaps associated with a local authority. They develop the software and then either give it away, or charge some notional sum for it in their local area with a scale of cost recovery charges for elsewhere.

3. The Shadow Developers

    Most of this is done by enthusiastic teachers or others and it is passed on by hand, or word of mouth. Generally, it is of poor quality (but there are exceptions), poorly documented and rarely achieves little purpose.

Predominantly, the second category undermines the hope for a lively industry of creative software developers. The subsidies have allowed the schools to undervalue the good software and to have a price expectation that is totally unrealistic for profit earning. Thus, not only is it impossible for companies to make a profit, it is equally unlikely that an investment organization will finance such activity.

The consequence is that there is little development of good educational material and little sign that the situation will change. The free market approach demands that the buyer appreciates the value in meeting their objectives and is prepared to pay appropriately. At present, it would seem that not only do few people appreciate the benefit of the use of computers but, even if they did, they would not have the money to spend.

However, in one area things are clear and that is in Category D. usage where computing is the subject being taught. There are definitive needs like languages that have to be served but, even here, there is still much confusion as to whether we are teaching computing as a subject or making people aware of the role of the computers which is something sompletely different. For the latter, there have been some large sales of software but that period, in the U.K., seems to be over.

6. DISTRIBUTION AND PUBLISHING

Generally, the educational software developers have scorned the publishers as a means of taking their wares to the buyers. It seems that there is considerable ignorance of each other's intentions. The software people have seen the publishers as just an another intermediary that they have no need for, and they do not appear to understand software. Meanwhile, the publishers have dabbled a little and some have lost their investment.

Let us consider the assets of a publisher:

- They know where to find subject matter experts (authors) and they know how to motivate them to produce with royalties, up-front money, etc.

- They know how to take a prototype (script) and productise it for the market, sub-contracting most of the activity.

- They know where the markets are, have channels to them and can set them in motion.

- They know how to establish licences, publishing rights, and set up relationships with foreign companies.

- They do not have large investment capability and have few tangible assets to borrow against.

The above is generally true of the book or magazine publishers but it is the function itself that seems to be missing in the educational computing industry. For publishers do several most important things:

- They discriminate and remove from the market the poorest material.

- They set standards by ensuring that their products meet some common quality.

- They invest in marketing their products, helping the buyer to see the benefits.

The above has been done for many years by the educational book publishers and now they face the opportunity of adding a new dimension to their business as long as they can accept the new parameters of this new business. For them to be seriously involved and to work for profit, they must recognize that software publishing

- demands capital at a level which is substantially above the book business;

- requires negotiation with a development team and not single authors;

- produces an item which is not in itself attractive and is far less tangible, but can rapidly be reproduced to meet demand;

- creates a balance sheet that is markedly different from their traditional form.

Despite all the above issues, there is one over-riding problem and that is the pride that the schools are prepared to pay for the software products. It has been pointed out that the schools have been able to obtain heavily subsidised software. That has led them to see the typical price in the same range as that for computer games. However, the markets are very different, with game sales being in the 100,000s and the education software in numbers well below 10,000. The latter is often achieved over years and the former over several months.

There is a need to increase the revenue earned for the effort put into creating good software, by perhaps 10-fold, before we can expect to see a flourishing business of serving education with an ever widening range of excellent material.

7. STRATEGIES

It is worthwhile repeating that the sole purpose in installing computers in schools is to meet some pre-declared educational objective. It is not to support a local industry, or promote employment or exports. If these latter intentions predominate, it is highly unlikely that the education system will benefit and ultimately the demand will cease and destroy the suppliers who had become dependent on it.

For any country now coming to terms with the possible uses of technology, it is vital that it has the correct priorities within its strategy. A most important aspect is to ensure that the appropriate motivation is provided in each part of the industry. The educational needs are paramount and then the category of application or use is vital in being able to specify clearly the intended purpose. Without this understanding, it is impossible to train the teaching staff to use the machines effectively. We have seen so far, too little education of the teachers into an understanding of how to apply the computers to meeting educational objectives and too few teachers given the material to work with.

The examination or certification system must be a part of the planning process. Without their involvement, there is really little incentive for the teaching staff to take on the additional load of understanding about the benefits of using computers. For the present, there is no simple way to introduce the benefits without the investment of time on the part of the teaching staff.

We must recognize that there are some things that you can do with one computer per class as, perhaps, in a primary school; but as the number rises to scheduled occasions where we have one computer per student, there are totally different capabilities in the syllabus.

We must recognize the existence of a hierarchy of capabilities in the equipment. As years go by, it is essential that we do not discard the continuing capabilities of the earlier machines.

All this demands an overall strategic approach which ensures that
all the actions are compatible and consistent with a declared aim.
The experiences gained in countries like the U.K. can be invaluable,
particularly in assisting countries in looking at all the issues.
We were in the field at the beginning and have learnt some hard
lessons. There have been many different approaches taken by the
various local educational authorities and these can be considered
in the light of other local objectives. It seems that the various
elements of the industry have surprisingly limited vision over the
whole range of inter-relationships and the suppliers, in particular,
cannot offer much strategic help. In the engineering profession,
we saw the development of the role of the "consulting engineer".
They worked across the world, assisting many countries to develop
new industries, build bridges, etc. We need the same for our
education industry where such organizations can assist in setting
the use of computers in education on to a solid foundation across
the world.

References:

1. A Study of the Potential Benefits of Standardisation in
   Educational Computing, by the National Computing Centre for
   the U.K. Dept. of Trade and Industry, March 1986.

Section 2
Educational Strategies

Remote Education and Informatics: Teleteaching
F. Lovis (Editor)
Elsevier Science Publishers B.V. (North-Holland)
IFIP, 1988

KNOWLEDGE-BASED SYSTEMS IN TELETEACHING

Martinez V., Maté L., Pazos J.

Facultad de Informática.
Universidad Politécnica de Madrid
Carretera de Valencia, km. 7, 28031 Madrid

In this article, after presentation of present-day teaching problems at all levels, the use of a combination of
communication networks and Knowledge-Based Systems is proposed as a solution, with a possible structure for same.

1. PRESENT-DAY PROBLEMS: DIAGNOSIS

If there is something in this world on which there exists complete
agreement among all human beings, without regard to race, sex, age,
religious beliefs or political ideas, it is the lack of quality in
present-day instruction at all levels.

The reasons for having reached the present situation would seem
to be multiple and various, in accordance with different countries
and historic cultural circumstances. However, there seem to be
three which stand out as most visible and important. The first is
the reluctance of teachers and politico-administrative persons
responsible for instruction to apply the new technological advances
to education. In effect, if an analysis is made of an operating-
theatre of 100 years ago and a present-day one, it will be observed
that any resemblance between the two is mere coincidence. The
technological resources presently used in operating theatres are
of such calibre, both in quality and quantity, that without their
aid it would be well-nigh impossible for the operations carried
out there to be successful. However if a look is taken at a
classroom of 200 or 300 years ago and a present-day one, it will
be observed that their differences are minimal. In spite of
everything, as we shall demostrate below, the possibility of using
new technology in teaching is more than a possibility, and should
become a necessity.

The second is determined by the great growth of instruction, at
least in the developed countries, and the lack of resources,
fundamentally human ones, who can adequately transmit their knowledge to these pupils.

In all the advanced countries, schooling is obligatory up to 14
or 16 years; in these conditions it is impossible to have a
sufficient number of competent teachers available to teach all
these pupils within an adequate pupil/teacher relationship, with
the aggravation that it is precisely in the first years of schooling where pupils are most numerous and, on the contrary, where
pedagogical and formation requirements for teachers in this
educational period are fewer. In spite of everything, world-wide
there exists a sufficient number of teachers so that, if adequate
advantage was taken of their pedagogical capabilities and their
knowledge, the previous problem, in the worst case,would be
alleviated.

Finally, the third reason giving rise to the problem is the speed with which discoveries are produced and the vertiginous increase in knowledge. A new teaching method is necessary, based on fewer subjects, better selected and less descriptive. Otherwise it will be impossible for students to be capable, not only of applying, but of understanding the new know-how. And with the aggravation that the new formative knowledge acquired in the initial phases of education, quickly becomes obsolete, due to the rapid evolution of knowledge itself. In fact, the majority are being forced to learn, badly, many things they will use only a little. This is a waste of time, energy and money that, apart from uselessly tiring the pupil, lessens the time and desire to carry out a more productive and gratifying work. The words of Einstein in this respect are very clarifying: "as a consequence of a brief period during which I had to remain at school preparing a degree exam, I felt incapable of carrying out any creative work at all for several years."

Said in other words, on the one hand, it is necessary to reduce to the minimum the memorization aspect presented by teaching nowadays and, on the other, achieve an adequate reduction of the transmission function of know-how, for the sake of a better learn- ing organization by the pupil, that is of self-learning and permanent formation.

Faced with this accumulation of difficulties one could, as Goethe said, lose everything but hope. If, during good times, certain licences can be permitted, when difficult moments arise the only advisable thing is to do things well. Nowadays, doing things well consists in using in a rational and efficient way the pedagogical facilities offered by the new technologies and, in particular, communications and expert systems.

2. THERAPY

Once the diagnosis of the present state of education has been established it is possible to prescribe a therapy which, at least, may alleviate the pernicious effects that the bad health of present-day education might produce.

In the first place, since there are few conveniently trained teachers, use them as efficiently as possible. One way of achieving this would be to transmit their classes live, using present means of communication (satellites, laser, optical fibres, etc.). On a second plane, there is no sense in not using computers joined to projectors as new "blackboards". The flexibility and versatility that this provides makes the use of conventional means seem inadequate and antediluvian. Further- more, permitting the pupils' reception of the contents of the lecture through a magnetic or conventional support means that they do not have to be copying what the lecturer is explaining, both in writing and aloud, which allows them to give full attention to the lecturer's explanations.

Finally, present reality permits the affirmation that computers facilitate memorization, and the handling of information. This implies a new concept of learning. Facilities for the memorization, re-structure and reinterpretation of data and information, and

we are in the course of doing the same with knowledge, have
multiplied in such a way that human memoristic capacities for
reaching learning are reduced. In consequence the necessity arises
for other different skills in order to make knowledge available.
An "ideographic" knowledge, as description of individual events
occurring in the past, is no longer convenient, if ever it was,
but a "nomothetic" knowledge is;   that is, a formulator of laws
or relationships within a concept structure of a theory.

This necessity of new skills, in order to make knowledge available,
is beginning to be satisfied through the application of Knowledge-
Based Systems, obtained by means of advances carried out in the
area of Artificial Intelligence, the use of which, as we shall see,
not only favours self-learning and permanent formation, but is
also an extraordinary help in achieving individualized instruction.
These systems, which are authentic knowledge distributors, allow
the solution of, or themselves solve, cognitive problems, as well
as helping to understand, point out, clarify, save time, generate,
maintain and increase the attention, increase the motivation and
give life to facts in such a way that information becomes formation
and so knowledge.

What is intended by the use of this technology is that the pupil
should acquire methodology, developing a spirit of criticism and
initiative, forming his capacity for synthesis and analysis,
obtaining a decisive and imaginative character and reaching a
capacity for group communication and work. The difficulty of
reaching these objectives is no secret, but without them there
is no direction, and to navigate without it across a stormy ocean
of knowledge, daily more numerous, profound and varied, is to go
adrift.

Our opinion is that the joint use of communication networks, and
Knowledge-Based Systems will contribute to alleviate the problems
set forth above.

3. KNOWLEDGE-BASED SYSTEMS

The generic name of "Knowledge-Based Systems" designates a set of
programs, constructed through the use of principles, methods and
tools of artificial intelligence, whose contributions depend more
on the explicit presence of an ample body of knowledge, than on
the possession of ingenious and/or potent computational methods.
In other terms, it is the step from the power pattern to the
knowledge pattern. In effect, for a long time, AI (Artificial
Intelligence) centred its attention almost exclusively in the
development of methods of "intelligent" inference; which was
known as the power pattern. But the power of expert systems is
knowledge, which is what is known as the knowledge pattern.

Knowledge-Based Systems, as shown in Figure 1, have two essential
parts: the knowledge base, broken down in turn into fact and/or
data base, and rules base; and the deductive machine or inferences
motor, which permits making inferences and reaching conclusions
by logically analyzing combinations of rules. By taking advantage
of this architectural principle, which is shared by Knowledge-
Based Systems, the following step was to separate these two
functions.

The fact that in order to construct these systems it is necessary
to design and construct separately the knowledge base of the
inferences motor, holds a strategic implication of the highest
order that is frequently, passed over. In effect in a certain
sense, the bases of knowledge are something like a form of storage
of human knowledge in an active way that is not only accesible
for the machine, but that, and this is important, can be understood
by the machine.

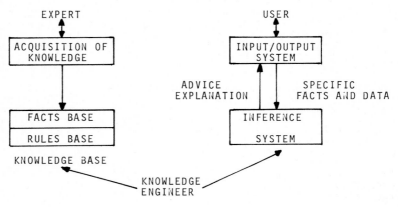

Figure 1

This is particularly profound and transcendental if one thinks
that this gives rise, neither more nor less, to building a knowledge industry in which the modules of knowledge and experience
are created and sold, perhaps even under patented names. It is
difficult to imagine the impact that such an industry would have
on society, given the enormous influence that passive information
has had. The capacity of passing on knowledge from one generation
to the next one will be without a doubt a similar achievement to,
but greater than, the appearance of the first graphics in the era
of the Sumerians or the invention of the printing press.

But we should not deceive ourselves, knowledge and experience
continue to be scarce and precious resources, of great
intrinsic value, whose refinement and reproduction create riches.
This justifies delicate and, at the present time expensive
"mining" operations to extract them from humans and place them in
a computable form. These operations require efficient and effective
instruments and technologies in order to convert them into an
industrial and commercial product, making reality of the dream of
their synthetic reproduction. In such a way that, by wider and
better use of the knowledge that is patrimony of entire mankind,
the degree of happiness and wellbeing of the individual increases,
and as a result, of all peoples.

At the present time a Knowledge-Based type of system is being used
to achieve tele-teaching that eliminates the deficiencies of
conventional computer-assisted instruction methods, among which
the following are to be found: impossibility, on the student's

part, of raising questions, incapacity for adequately treating
unforeseen replies, lack of any kind of knowledge on a concrete
subject, and lack of friendly communication in a natural language
with the students. These systems present the following as main
components:

1. Resolver Expert Problems which have as tasks:
    a) To generate problems.
    b) To evaluate the correction of the proposed solutions.
    c) To represent knowledge, which goes beyond storing information,
       in order to obtain some way of joining the stored facts of
       interrelated knowledge. This can be done as:
       - Semantic Networks.
       - Production Networks.
       - Procedural.

The expert component of a teleteaching system is called
"transparent" or "articulate" if it can explain each decision in
the solution of a problem in terms that correspond, to some
abstract level, to those of a human resolvent. Teleteaching
systems separate teaching strategies from the subject to be
taught; they are conceptually very similar to representing the
matter itself or the language used in discussing it.

The introduction of a new knowledge or of a fresh theme is
organized by using trees or reticles showing the interaction of
the pre-requisites.

2. Student model. That is, some method of identifying what things
a student is capable of understanding and what mistaken conceptions
or errors are to be found in the student's thinking or in his
strategies to resolve problems. The computer needs to follow the
track of what the student knows and what he needs to know. By
posing him questions, the computer can imagine what the student
does not know and supply him with this knowledge. It is an
advantage for the system to be capable of recognizing alternative
ways of resolving problems, including the incorrect methods the
student may use as a result of his wrong systematic conceptions
of the problem or of the use of inefficient strategies.

In this way, the use of AI techniques to model the student's
knowledge includes:

a) Recognition of Forms applied to the history of the student's
   answers.
b) Signals in the semantic network or in the rule base,
   representing the areas dominated by the student.

The student model is formed by comparing the behaviour of the
student with that of the "expert", based on the computer, in the
same circumstances. The modelling component marks each piece of
knowledge according to whether the evidence indicates that the
student knows the material or not.

Other information that can be accumulated in the student model
includes: the means preferred by the student to interact with
the program, a "gross" characterization of his capacity level, a
consideration of what he appears to forget as time goes by, and
an indication of what his goals are and plans for learning the
subject matter.

The main sources of evidence for maintaining the student model
can be classified as:

    a) Implicit, of the student's behaviour in resolving problems.
    b) Explicit, from the questions posed directly by the student.
    c) Historic, from the suppositions based on the student's
       experience.
    d) Structural, from suppositions based on some measure of
       difficulty of the theme.

3. Tutorial Module. It must integrate knowledge about dialogues
in natural language, teaching methods and the subject matter. It
is the module that communicates with the student, selects problems
for him, watches over and criticises his contributions, gives
help on request and selects revision material.

Teaching methods explored are based on the "diagnostic modelling"
in which the program filters the student's understanding by setting
him tasks and evaluating his replies. From the program feedback,
it is hoped that the student will learn what knowledge he is using
incorrectly, what he is not using but ought to use in order to
improve, etc. At the present time, work is being carried out on
the possibility of telling the student correctly exactly what
he should do, in such a way that he perceives his own errors and
turns to a better method.

Another focus is to provide a circumstance that encourages the
student to think in terms of filtering his own knowledge. The
possibility is suggested of fomenting the capacity of constructing
hypotheses and verifying them by establishing problems in which
the student first makes a probably incorrect guess, and in this
way centres his attention on how to detect what is wrong and how
to revise it.

Another very successful teaching strategy is that called
"preceptor". In this case, no attempt is made to cover a
determined plan of lessons within a fixed time. Rather, its goal
is to encourage the acquisition of general abilities and capacities
for resolving problems by tying the student to some activity,
which could be a computer game. The tutorship arises when the
computer, observing the game being carried out by the student,
interrupts him and offers him new information or suggests fresh
strategies.

4. THE PROPOSED SYSTEM

The system proposed is the following:

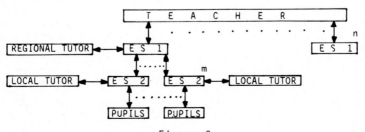

Figure 2

In this the following levels for each communication node can be distinguished:

Level 1. This is where the TEACHER is found, so naming the person who has shown him/herself to be not only an expert, in the determined area explained, but also the person having a high pedagogical level to put over its instructions.

This TEACHER is inter-related with Level 2. by means of an expert system.

Level 2. Expert System (ES) 1. and the Regional Tutor are found on this level. ES 1. receives the lessons from the TEACHER, passing them on to the other members of the network; this ES is modified and brought up-to-date not only with the knowledge from the TEACHER but also with that from the Regional Tutor; this Tutor will try to resolve the problems brought up by the different lower levels, passing the question on to the TEACHER if it cannot resolve same.

The Regional Tutor, together with the ES 1, will control a geographical zone, more or less extensive according to the interests and needs, and conveniently this region should have the same spoken language.

Level 3. The ES 2, local Tutors and Pupils are to be found on this level. The ES 2, receives the TEACHER's lessons from the ES 1, passing them on to the Local Tutors and Pupils, and receiving consultations from both which, where required, will have access to the ES 1, Regional Tutor and, finally, the TEACHER if necessary.

The compass of these ES 2, Local Tutors and Pupils, will, if possible, be that of a country unless its area, number of consultations or other causes, advise otherwise.

5. CONCLUSIONS

The architectural separation of Knowledge-Based Systems between, on the one hand, knowledge base (that is, assertive or declarative facts, or knowledge and operative rules or knowledge) and on the other hand, the inferences motor, together with its modular flexibility which makes them easy to modify, favouring both supervised learning (that is, with a monitor) and non-supervised learning and its transparency or, what is the same, its explanatory capacity, makes the focus of Artificial Intelligence, applied to remote instruction, differ substantially from other conventional focuses.

It is quite true that even with this process, the problems of "distance" existing in education are not resolved, the excessive nearness between teacher and pupil (habitual instruction) provokes a defensive attitude on the pupil's part, and the distance (remote education) provokes a desire for help and warmth.

In any case, Artificial Intelligence is and will continue to be the most promising field of investigation and development in remote education. For this reason, educators should be wary of indiscriminately accepting and using all Artificial Intelligence

realizations, since the interests of one and the other are
distinct and the methods, languages and applications
frequently even appear incompatible. The proposal here made
is that educators should understand the possibilities of what
Artificial Intelligence is and make an effective use of same.

6. BIBLIOGRAPHY

1.   Alonso-Matías, A. and others: "I Jornadas Fuerzas Armadas,
      Universidad Politécnica de Madrid", Madrid, 1.984.
2.   Barr, A, and Feigenbaum, E.: "The Handbook of Artificial
      Intelligence", Vol. II, Pitman, London, 1.982.
3.   Gercke-Brandau, Oscar.: "Gestión Informática y su enseñanza
      apoyada en algunos métodos participativos", Madrid, 1.986.
4.   Llorente-Gomez, E.: "La calidad Educativa Universitaria
      ante las nuevas tecnologias", Real Academia de Doctores,
      Madrid, 1.985.
5.   Martinez-Ora , V., y Pazos-Sierra, J.: "Sistemas Basados
      en el Conocimiento: Una aplicación de la Inteligencia Arti-
      ficial", Madrid, 1.985
6.   Sleeman, D. and Brown, J.S.: "Intelligent Tutoring Systems"
      Academia Press, New York, 1.982.
7.   Wyer, J.A.: "New Bird on the Branch: Artificial Intelligence
      and Computer-Assisted Instruction", Program. Learn. and
      Educ. Technology Vol. 21, Part. 3, 1.984.

Remote Education and Informatics: Teleteaching
F. Lovis (Editor)
Elsevier Science Publishers B.V. (North-Holland)
© IFIP, 1988

SIGN-MANIPULATION RESULTING FROM NEW ECOLOGICAL CONDITIONS
PRODUCED BY THE MEDIA

DR. RUDOLF A.M. MAYER, GERMAN YOUTH INSTITUTE, SAARSTR. 7,
8000 MÜNCHEN 40, WEST GERMANY
INSTITUTE FOR THEATRICAL SCIENCE, UNIVERSITY OF MUNICH

0   INTRODUCTION

Sign-manipulation or manipulation by signs? Questions like this are
surely tautological, for, in the face of manipulative employment of
information, the signs themselves remain neutral units used by the media for transmission. It all depends on the theory, then. This allows
one to ask if we are not, in fact, concerned with manipulation by means
of the theory of signs itself. That would constitute a meta-level for
the question of manipulation through, and by means of, signs.

Let us assume that the basic suppositions of semiotic theory are formal. In our (pragmatic) context the structure of the theoretical
statement is this: the pragmatic is one among many aspects of signs
and, according to the questions asked, is either a point of departure
or a subsequent point of view. This has to be determined in each individual case (Klaus, Morris, Eco).

Neuro-psychological research (Guttmann), new psychotherapies (Watzlawick, Bandler, etc.) and applied constructivism (von Foerster, etc.)
have shown that the lasting effectiveness of signs - measured by behavioural disposition and memory ability - depends more on the form
and structure of signs and their combinations than on the content and
statements they transmit. What does that mean? Perhaps that in the beginning was the form, to which content adapts itself - realising the
form, as it were. In linguistic terms this would mean syntax taking
precedence as a statement over semantic explanation and decoding.

I leave these questions open. Semiotics should be on the lookout for
new models explaining the exchange of signs between communication
partners.

1   LEARNING TO INTERPRET SIGNS

Symbolic Interactionism (Mead, Rose, Brumlik) provides a socio-psycho-
logical behaviorist model for explaining the socialization process.
With the help of symbols - which with Mead and his followers are almost invariably synonymous with signs - human beings learn in their

earliest childhood the meaning of things and events as well as their value and
evaluation. As a rule, evaluation is derived from the context. The context may
be conditioned by function (water is necessary for a bath, warm water is pleasant, water that is too hot or too cold is not pleasant) or, where functional
evidence is lacking, may be complemented by data from other levels of experience
(fighting is naughty, not because one finds out by trial and error that it hurts,
but because God in Heaven, daddy or Santa Claus and the Christ child have for-
bidden it).

We are right in the middle of our subject. I advance the following theory. When
meanings and values which do not appear plausible or self-evident from the
functional or experiential context are introduced into the pragmatic relationship between sign-user and sign (in plural and in a syntactical context as well),
when, therefore, unverifiable values which affect meanings (i.e. sanction or
stigmatize them) are introduced into the processes of symbolic interaction (which
take place with the help of signs), then we have a case of manipulation, possibly even of the need for manipulation.

2   THE NEW MEDIA

I use this term in the double sense of
- the media which have been developed from the old communication media with the
  help of micro-electronics and cable improvements and which operate for the
  most part with the audio-visual medium of the screen, and
- the new forms of communication made possible by communications technology
  which, increasing in quality and quantity, operate with communication subjects
  other than human beings, face-to-screen instead of face-to-face. The authority
of the screen as a, so to speak, infallible communication partner, is entering
more and more into competition with the fallible one. And the face-carriers are
losing the race for their attractiveness hands down (Mc Luhan).

Signs and their combinations are manufactured in the media, and produced and
disseminated on a massive scale. They are also stored - one asks another screen
at the "man-machine intersecting point" (as the computer people call it) and
one uses an "interface" to a large computer store, a giant technical brain.

The increased presence of these media in the form of appliances is altering the
structure of the environment at home, at work and in leisure-time. The "inner
world" (in the neuro-psychological/physiological sense) adapts itself in order
to cope with this changed (media) environment. This has produced occasional
triumphs for achievement psychology: sudden increases of IQ, training with
micro-computers in schools, etc.

Manipulation by accommodation? To simulate, and also partially to bring about, a
common community of signs among the individuals working on and with these communication techniques, general messages are increasing at the expense of concrete
information. And that means that the communication partner at the screen is being increasingly hypnotized. The communication partner,   faceless and no longer
tangible, is represented by the screen (Bandler).

3 THE MEDIA SYSTEM AND STOCKS OF SIGNS

The human beings at the "intersecting points" are connected - at least in the
so-called active communications media - with one another via a network system
(e.g. video-phone). However, they are generally played on by central institutions, i.e. they are provided with sign parcels which have been manufactured in
form and content. In the terminology of Symbolic Interactionism, this is called
starting learning processes which repeat continually the same signs and sign
combinations to improve understanding semantically and syntactically and which

transmit decoding patterns and strategies via these sign combinations. This process entails the simultaneous learning of values and evaluations in order to understand meanings and thus be "in". Such processes of communication and understanding are then extended in face-to-face contact, according to how communication takes place in the "presentation of reality by the media". The media give rise to over half the topics of conversation in West-Germany families (Bonfadelli, Mayer).

The authority of the stocks of signs of the so-called new media, as network appliances and as qualitatively altered transmission intersecting-points (face-to-screen), is continually on the increase just because their growing quantity sets off generalising processes which, threatening with the sanction of exclusion from the communication community, constitute this very community. This is achieved by transmitting sign parcels and by reference to, and consideration of, the parcels contents in groups.

Our "symbol environment" (Gerbner – here, too, synonymous with sign environment) is thus designed in the central offices of media organisations and "realised" by communication partners (receivers). The attraction of these "second realities" is sometimes so great that they no longer allow the awakening of interest in discovering primary (i.e. direct) reality and occasionally replace it voluntarily. In simplified, neuro-psychological terms this means that the brain makes no distinction between primary and secondary reality unless expressly told to do so by a, so to speak, meta-coding. But that is just what those people do not want who wish to take "as it were" for "it is" (Guttmann, Bergler).

4 COMMUNICATING AND ACTING

It is characteristic of media communication that the medium's communication partner (receiver) is not under direct social compulsion to act. The question of identification, with others and with oneself, none the less gains in importance in the sense of an alteration to the receiver's role: he is a part of media events as long as he does not interpose the above-mentioned meta-coding between them and himself. This integration of the communication partner in media events is termed "para-social interaction" (Horton). Symbolic Interactionism's concept of role is thus applied to the role of the media consumer. In the final analysis it therefore depends on how the receiver adopts the roles he has perceived - imaginatively or actively (Teichert).

The model of the "active viewer", as a person who can control intensity of reception, is caught up in the net of a paradox: "understanding" the media's message presupposes identification with the structure of the media's "world of symbols", yet independence from the products of manufactured reality requires distancing from identification. This explains why integrated receivers are unable to find a level on which to communicate with those who distance themselves analytically: the decoding keys used for evaluation are fundamentally different.

The paradox just described has given rise to a compromise which several authors - especially those involved in media education - have come out in favour of (Teichert). It allows the receiver (in consciousness of para-social interaction) to choose from, and interpret, the realities offered by the media.

It must be objected that this compromise implicitly, or unconsciously, assumes that the receiver has so much experience of the real world that he is able "to choose from the realities on offer". If this were always the case, the media would play the part of stimulating agencies for symbolic interaction, i.e. they would stimulate new combinations of symbols (= signs) and thereby give rise to new processes of understanding reality (the world). In comparison, media reality is "the other way round". One becomes acquainted with "symbol environments" in childhood and the experience thus acquired is projected on to the real

world. What can the real world hope to offer when judged according to reduced
likenesses produced by signs?

5 CONCLUSION

The present thoughts have been guided by the assumption that, in the real world
of existence, the media are increasing in quantity and quality and gaining in
significance. This is occuring situationally and ecologically at home, at work
and in leisure-time, but, in a broader sense, is also affecting the life-histo-
ries of each individual member of the "information and communication community".
That which is called "media behaviour" and which to a considerable degree reveals the preferences prevailing with regard to face-to-face or face-to-screen
communication, makes it easy to see this media behaviour as a key behavioural
factor, one practised in childhood and later used as a basis for behavioural
dispositions in front of screens in various life-situations (Prokop).

Behaviour is learnt through socialization, including those ecological contexts
in which media are present. Today, stocks of signs and their syntactic models
as well as coding and decoding strategies are by and large no longer generated
by social interaction but by "para-social interaction", i.e. by media consumption. Even if the sign material were to remain identical, then at least the
evaluations constituted by various levels of reality would differ. On the other
hand, we know that the mixing of various levels and the inability to differen-
tiate between levels themselves create new meanings and, in particular, new
evaluations.

If manipulation is everything which leads away from a primal understanding of
the self, then conventional socialization already constitutes manipulation. Yet
there is a qualitative difference between face-to-face or face-to-screen communication and manipulation: the medium does not permit the control and reversi-
bility possible in an interpersonal context. Seen thus, sign-manipulation by
the media is in itself final at every stage in the process.

I assume that we are concerned here solely with diagnosing and interpreting. The
question as to what consequences for socialization and media policies should be
drawn from the present considerations and insights must therefore remain unasked.

REFERENCES

H. Bandler/J. Grinder, Metasprache und Psychotherapie. Struktur der Magie I
                        (Paderborn 1981)

R. Bergler/U. Six, Psychologie des Fernsehens (Berne - Stuttgart - Vienna 1979)

H. Bonfadelli, Die Sozialisationsperspektive in der Massenkommunikationsfor-
               schung (Berlin 1981)

M. Brumlik, Der symbolische Interaktionismus und seine pädagogische Bedeutung
            (Frankfurt/Main 1973)

U. Eco, Einführung in die Semiotik (Munich 1972)

H. von Foerster, "Das Konstruieren einer Wirklichkeit", in P. Watzlawick (ed.),
                 Die erfundene Wirklichkeit (Munich 1981)

G. Gerbner (ed.), The Analysis of Communication Content (New York 1969)

G. Guttmann, Lehrbuch der Neuropsychologie, 3rd ed. (Berne - Stuttgart - Vienna 1982)

O. Horton, "Mass Communication and Para-Social Interaction", Psychiatry XIX (1956, 3)

G. Klaus, Wörterbuch der Kybernetik, II (Frankfurt/Main 1969)

R.A.M.Mayer, Medienumwelt im Wandel (Munich 1984)

M. Mc Luhan, Understanding Media: The Extensions of Man (New York 1964)

G.H. Mead, Geist, Identität und Gesellschaft (Frankfurt/Main 1968)

C.W. Morris, Grundlagen der Zeichentheorie (Munich 1972)

R. Posner, "Die Zahlen und ihre Zeichen. Geschichte und ökonomie der Zahlendarstellung", in K. Oehler (ed.), Zeichen und Realität (Tübingen 1984)

D. Prokop, Medien-Wirkung (Frankfurt/Main 1981)

A.M. Rose, "Systematische Zusammenfassung der Theorie der Symbolischen Interaktion", in Moderne Amerikanische Soziologie (Stuttgart 1967)

B.M. Scherer, "Peirces Analyse der Referenz im Rahmen seiner pragmatisch begründeten Semiotik", in K. Oehler (ed.), Zeichen und Realität (Tübingen 1984)

W. Teichert, "Fernsehen als soziales Handeln", Rundfunk und Fernsehen, XX (1972), XXI (1973)

P. Watzlawick (ed.), Die erfundene Wirklichkeit (Munich 1981)

Remote Education and Informatics: Teleteaching
F. Lovis (Editor)
Elsevier Science Publishers B.V. (North-Holland)
© IFIP, 1988

The Results of the Budai Language Studio in
the Remote Teaching of Foreign Languages

Zs. Pelle - A. Sobieski
Budai Language Studio
Hungary

Nowadays, more and more articles and studies deal with the increasing
requirements of language teaching. Learning languages is especially important
in Hungary, since it has a dominant role in our economic life, foreign trade,
and so on.

Most of the studies point out that the traditional form of language teaching
is not effective enough and that the introduction of the audio-visual method
couldn't solve the problems of language teaching.

Comparisons between Hungarian and foreign results were not very flattering to
us. However, we must not forget that the linguistic relationship between and
English and a Danish, Swedish or Dutch person is a great advantage, let alone
that all the means of communication are at the service of their language
teaching. The students can see or listen to films and radio programmes in
English and if they decide to do so, they can travel to England for practice.

So we must take into consideration all the circumstances and try to find the
most effective method, by which we can reduce the difference between the above
mentioned countries and Hungary.

I want to write about a teaching method which has proved successful during the
past 20 years. It is remote teaching. It shouldn't be a mystery, it doesn't
solve everything right away, but it can help a lot.

Remote teaching is a study which is carried out without the presence of the
teacher, but is stimulated by means of impersonal media, regular instructions
being given to the students. Remote teaching is a combination of other
teaching forms combined with special communicative media. This method of
language teaching is especially effective in the field of adult education.

The main advantages of this method are the control and regulation of the
rhythm of studying. The instructions, step by step, inform the students about
the significance of the given grammatical structures and give practical advice
about their application. This method is up-to-date, because one of its basic
elements is pedagogical control. It means that the students work
independently, controlled by the teacher from a certain distance. That's why
the organization of feed-back and ·the evaluation of the students' work are
more important than in traditional teaching methods. The experiments have
proved that continuous evaluation helps not only in the students'
self-evaluation, but either success or failure inspires them to make new
efforts. It is essential that the teaching package includes the possibility
of feed-back to help students in measuring their activity. The grammatical
exercises and tests provide this. The advantage of the method is the schedule
of studying. It is fundamental for a busy, working adult.

Nevertheless, remote teaching can't be used in its original form, it must be
modified according to the educational system of a country, and we must not

forget that economical conditions and levels of development differ. Even if the American or English remote teaching systems are very attractive, they are too expensive to permit establishing such a multimedia system in Hungary. What is the solution? It is the Spanish model. This can be used in Hungary because it is cheap, economic and suitable for teaching masses.

The sociological researches also prove that this form of teaching takes into account the adults' labour and living conditions. It can solve the problem of those who live far from a city: they would like to study languages but the personal and objective conditions are not satisfied.

Dear colleagues! You know very well how difficult it is to learn English, even in a traditional way. We must face the same problems in the field of remote teaching. However, in this method the teacher can't correct the students' mistakes on the spot. That's why a great experience acquited in traditional teaching must be reflected in the material, and the authors have to take into account the places where the students will presumably make mistakes. So the "invisible" teacher must call the students' attention to these grammatical traps. They can modify the structure of the material according to the students' needs.

On the basis of the Spanish remote teaching method, I and my colleague Mr Artur Sobieski, head of the Budai Language Studio, make an English teaching package for Hungarian students, especially for adults and those in higher education, in 1983. Our material consists of 12 units - 6 books - for beginners and another 12 units - 6 books - for the inttermediate level. The package also includes cassettes which contain all the vocabulary and the texts of the books. The cassettes were made with the assistance of native speakers. In addition, every teaching package contains tests relating to the grammatical material. Permanent telephone consultation is available. After Finishing the material the students take part in an intensive conversational course of 40 hours. The expense of the courses is included in the price of the educational package.

And our results so far: the Budai Language Studio has educational centres all over Hungary. It means that the students from the country needn't travel to Budapest for the conversational course and they can discuss their problems with the consultants at these centres.

At the ELTE University, at the faculty of Natural Sciences, there is an experimental group of beginners. The students began to study English with the help of this method in 1985.

At the Agricultural University in Godollo, 30 students lean English in the same way.

We have three experimental groups at the Institute of Forest Engineering. One of these groups will sit for the state examination for the intermediate level in January.

There have been several investigations into remote teaching in Hungary, sponsored by the Ministry of Industry. It should be evident that these investigations include language teaching as well, but up to now there has been place in the project of the Remote Teaching Office, Budapest, only for computer language, political and ideological education.

Dear colleagues! I teach future electrical engineers at the Technical University, Budapest, so I have no doubt about the importance oof computer language. But there should be no doubt that computer technology can be acquired only with the help of English. This language is indispensable in the field of industry, foreign trade, tourism, etc. With the help of remote teaching, several hundreds of thousands of students can learn languages, including higher education. This is a considerable number and it might solve the problem of the increasing shortage of language teachers. I want to illustrate the last sentence with two number: at ELTE University, 55 teachers are needed to teach 2000 students, while the Budai Language Studio has 6000 students and <u>two</u> teachers are enough to do all the duties - I mean telephone consultation, correcting the tests, etc. I don't think I have to coment on this.

Some of the official opinions deny the effectiveness of this method, but even so, we have won the confidence of the book distributing company "Muvelt Nep" and "Skala Metro" supermarket. We are grateful for their trust.

We have partners in the USA, the Soviet Union, Spain and West Germany, so we are permanently informed about the new results in the field of remote teaching.

The German teaching material is on the way to be published. It will be issued at the end of November. We intend to complete the Russian and Spanish versions as well.

We can't expect miracles from this new method. Only practice will prove if the method has brought revolutionary changes in the field of language teaching. This method doesn't mean that the traditional forms of teraching are not necessary. On the contrary, all individuals differ and they need varying forms of language teaching.

I'd like to finish my paper with an English proverb: "the proof of the pudding is in the eating".

Remote Education and Informatics: Teleteaching
F. Lovis (Editor)
Elsevier Science Publishers B.V. (North-Holland)
© IFIP, 1988

ROLE OF EDUCATIONAL INDUSTRY IN TELETEACHING
- A CASE STUDY IN JAPAN: KUMON

*Shoji Shiba
(University of Tsukuba, Sakura, Ibaraki, Japan 305)

*Takumi Matsuda
(Kumon Institute for Educational Research, 3-1 Gobancho,
Chiyoda-ku, Tokyo, Japan 102)

*Haruo Takano
(Kumon Institute for Educational Research)

1. EXPECTATION FOR INFORMATION EQUIPMENT - AN ILLUSION

In the past ten years, communication equipment has shown a remarkable development. Television has spread throughout the
country and the price of video camera and recorder has become re-
markably low. With the commercialization of digital and optical-
-fiber communcation systems, high-volume and high-quality information can now be easily sent. A series of new communication
methods - often termed new media in Japan - have also appeared
on the stage. Together with the development of computers, a totally new information environment is now being created in Japan.
Here, not only voice or numerical data but also figure and image
can be transmitted through systems like LAN (local area network),
VAN (value added network) or INS (information network system).

There is no doubt that such a new environment, though its formation is particularly noticeable in Japan, will sooner or later
develop in other countries. Since the transferring of technology
is not hampered by barriers of culture or economic systems, new
technology, so long as it pays off, can easily spread to countries all over the world.

On the occasion of this Teleteaching '86 Conference, we should
first bear in mind that it is held at a transitional period
when a new information environment is being formed. Based on this
recognition, we should be able to specify which direction future
teleteaching is heading for.

In doing so, we may be tempted to talk about an innovative information technology and its application to education. This
cannot be helped on one hand, but let us recall the lessons of
CAI (computer aided instruction) in the 1970s. People then held an
illusion that new computer technology can be immediately
applied to education and contribute greatly to its improvement.

What was the result then? It is true that its introduction was
successful in some particular fields or at an experimental level.
But if we are asked whether CAI was introduced and came to be
widely utilized in schools, the answer is obviously NO.

Despite the fact that computers were quickly introduced into
many schools for clerical work processing, they have not come
to be used for instruction. Most of us are now aware, whether it
is true or not, that it will take longer than we expected to
introduce computers to this field.

The same holds true for the innovation of information environment, centering on new media. It is needless to say that instruction is the key factor in education and its process is different
from that of factory production, educational data or office work
processing. Nevertheless, new information equipment is designed
for company uses and not for educational purposes.

It is obviously nonsense, therefore, to think about its application to the present instruction process. If we are to do that,
the process of instruction itself should first be changed. Until
such innovation be embodied, support from advanced information
equipment will give more fruitful results. In other words, what
we now need is the new system for instruction.

In this report, we will try to illustrate such innovative education systems for new methods of instruction by referring to one
successful example in Japan.

2. KUMON EDUCATION THROUGHOUT THE COUNTRY - REMOTE EDUCATION WITHOUT HARDWARE

There is a popular education system called KUMON in Japan. It
was started by Toru Kumon in 1958, based on his experience of
teaching mathematics to his second-grade son at home. At the
beginning, KUMON had only 13 classes with 300 students. After 28
years, however, it has developed into a nationwide education
system with 31,000 classes and 1,396,000 students.

See Chart 1 for the diffusion rate of KUMON classes in the official elementary school districts (districts with over 300 students, or the minimum-size district in the six-years elementary
school system with 50 students per grade or, in other words, most
of the districts in cities and towns). The average is 75.7% and
as for larger districts with over 900 students, it reaches over
90%. This means that official public schools and KUMON classes
coexist in many places of Japan.

Diffusion rate of KUMON class

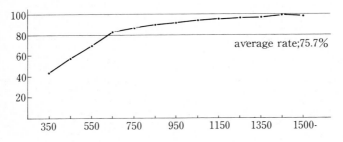

Number of students per elementary school district

Chart 1

It should be emphasized here that KUMON is a completely private
educational institution without any support from the national or

local governments. It has developed through its own efforts, supported by what may be called social needs.

What then, is the secret of KUMON's success? Why has it spread all over the country as widely as the official compulsory education system?

Moreover, KUMON's remarkable popularity was achieved through a seemingly conventional method having teaching material, classroom, instructor, headquarters and management system, without using any 'hardware' like computers. This is the reason why we think it appropriate to seek its secret here which may give up hints about future remote education.

3. WHAT IS KUMON? - TWO INNOVATIONS SUPPORTING ITS POPULARITY

KUMON is a self-study education method of particular subjects (mathematics, Japanese language and English) using material designed specially for this purpose.

When a child first comes to the KUMON class, he takes a placement test. The instructor scores it and finds out the level of subject matter that child can "easily" answer. Then, from that level, the child starts his everyday study at home and class attendance twice a week.

At home, he spends 10-20 minutes a day on 3-5 KUMON worksheets and after 3 days of self-study, he goes to the class. The class opens after school and the child can come into the class room at his convenience. Each lesson lasts 20-30 minutes.

When he comes to the class, he hands in the homework to the instructor and receives 3-10 KUMON worksheets in turn. He finishes them in the class and the instructor checks them. If there is any mistake, the child should correct them himself until he gets full marks. Then he receives homework sheets from the instructor and the lesson is over.

In this way, the child continues the cycle of self-study at home and classroom study/check under the guidance of the instructor.

This KUMON process looks no different from any other traditional education methods. We cannot find here the secret of its popularity with 1. 4 million children studying under this system.

As a matter of fact, the secret can be attributed to two innovations hidden behind the above-mentioned process: First, introducing quality improvement technology, which is widely used in industrial production, into the field of education; and second, introducing the Holonic way of management into the educational system management.

4. INTRODUCTION OF QUALITY IMPROVEMENT TECHNOLOGY IN EDUCATION

It is now widely accepted that Japanese industrial products are
superior in quality. This was achieved through quality improvement
technology called in many ways, such as "quality control", "total
control", "quality circle activities" or "company-wide quality
improvement". All of them have two fundamental tasks in common;
identifying variances of final result and processing toward result
respectively, and diminishing continuously those variances through
quality improvement activities. In fact, Japan's success was
brought by systematically repeating these two seemingly matter-of-
-fact factors.

4.1 KUMON Method of Controlling Variance

KUMON has skillfully introduced these two fundamental principles
in its educational method.

First of all, reducing variance is based on the following equation:

Variance in the outcome of education =

(a) variance in the knowledge to be conveyed

+ (b) variance in the study process
+ (c) variance in the satisfaction of the child studying

Thus, each of these three factors must be reduced in order to reduce the total.

As to reducing variance in the knowledge to be conveyed (a), subjects to be taught should first be specified. In mathematics, for
example, the final goal should be set up (differential and integral calculus in this case) and topics to be taught should be
chosen and given priority to. Then the course of study is designed from top to bottom (from the goal). The process here is linear,
divided into small steps. Through such careful planning of the
material, variance in the knowledge to be taught can be reduced
to a minimum.

Secondly, in order to reduce variance in the study process (b),
the childrens' study process should be controlled and
administered. In this regard, KUMON has a long-range standard
progress model and an average study completion time for each
small step. Instructors constantly check and compare the difference
between the standard and the actual progress of each child. If
there is a significant difference, it means that either the
teaching method or the material is inappropriate and some modification should be made. This is the type of control given at each
class and by KUMON system as a whole.

Third point, reduction of variance in satisfaction of the child
studying (c), is most important for the continuation of study. To
continue self-study, children must take interest in the work, or
in other words, feel the satisfaction of studying on their own.
Otherwise, self-study would not last long.

The index here is again the standard completion time for each small step. If the child can finish the step much faster than the average, he will get "bored". If he takes much longer, then he "may find it too difficult to continue". Between them exists a "just right" level for the child. As such, instructors constantly check the "just right" level of each child and prepare suitable material.

4.2 System of Constant Improvement for Better Education

The three systems of reducing variance described so far should not be fixed ones. They should be constantly revised and improved according to changes in the society and of children. Without it, the educational system loses its power and vitality.

KUMON's progress model and standard completion time are revised once every year. The reasons of dropping out of KUMON system or children's answering patterns (i.e. how often children repeat one question until reaching the correct answer) is analyzed in detail to evaluate the "just right" level. Furthermore, from 1.4 million examples, the conditions for speeding up the study process are extracted and then reflected in the teaching material.

It is indeed such constant revision that maintains the power and vitality of KUMON education system.

5. INTRODUCTION OF HOLONIC WAY OF MANAGEMENT TO EDUCATION

Holon is a new concept introduced by Arthur Koestler in 1968. Biological system (organism), in which the part has characters of the whole and the whole has those of the part, cannot be explained by conventional theories of atomism or wholism. Thus, the new word 'Holon' was created to go beyond the limit of constrasting the part and the whole.

This Holon concept has two elements: fluctuation and entrainment. It has recently drawn attention in the field of management as it is very useful in understanding new ways of management in recent innovative enterprises which cannot be explained by the conventional management concepts or theories.

KUMON is one of the typical examples of innovative enterprises. In its education system (and KUMON is a nationwide system!!), we can find various innovative attempts which do not exist in the ordinary management.

First is the existence of fluctuation, mentioned before. The conventional organization is structured in a hierarchal order like a pyramid where the role of each element is rigidly determined (Chart 2-A). The KUMON system has a flat and horizontal structure (Chart 2-B) with the headquarters (in charge of nationwide administration) and district offices (Chart 3). Under district offices are number of classes. For example, Sapporo Office in northern Japan with 9 staff administers 604 classes and Tokyo Office with 28 staff, 2,006 classes.

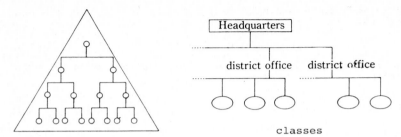

A:traditional pyramid structure   B:KUMON network-type structure

Chart 2

Chart 3

As shown in this structure, there is a great flexibility in the
activities of individual classes. Each class, as an independent
organization, is responsible for revealing the KUMON concept to
the local society, recruiting students, giving follow-up services
for parents, or expanding the class. It is not just a subordinate
element within the system under rigid control and regulation.
Each class is a part of the entire KUMON system and at the same
time, the class itself represents the KUMON education as a whole.
This is the very reason why freedom of fluctuation is necessary.

On the other hand, however, there exists no organization if each
KUMON element, scattered all over the country, only freely
"fluctuates". There should be some type of binding force in or-

der to maintain the KUMON identity as a whole. This is entrainment, the second concept of Holon.

In the traditional pyramid structure authority was the force which held the parts together. Authority, however, does not allow free fluctuation of each element and an alternative method should be adopted in new systems.

Entrainment means that each element itself recognizes its condition and position within the whole. Through this recognition, it is connected to the whole. In other words, this is to develop the ability of self discovery within the organization which may be called an ideal education.

For this purpose, KUMON offers a thorough training system. All instructors must attend a minimum 15 hours of training courses annually. Training is administered by each district office where courses are offered regularly. On an average, each instructor receives 36 hours of courses a year.

In addition to this formal entrainment system, there is also an informal type of entrainment such as classroom visits and voluntary study groups. Both are good examples of networking among the instructors. They come from different regions and offices to share their experience of teaching and to study teaching method and material.

The climax of such activities is the annual Instructors' Convention. During the two-day convention, reports on classroom management, successful teaching examples and on other topics are given. Last year in 1985, 2,700 people, or 17% of all KUMON instructors, attended this convention. In this way, close personal networking among instructors becomes the major force for effective entrainment.

The training and networking explained so far are what characterizes the KUMON entrainment method. More important, however, is that the core of KUMON entrainment is its corporate culture formed by its founder Toru Kumon.

Kumon's ideal is "to discover the possibilities given to an individual and develop them as much as possible". More concretely, "Even an elementary school child can solve equations or factorization by himself. Our mission is to publicize such real abilities of children."

This firm belief in the limitless ability of children (and also of the human being as a whole), is precisely what characterizes the KUMON corporate culture.

The belief then leads to strong motivation for better education. The KUMON system was started the year when the Soviet satellite Sputnik was launched. Toru Kumon then thought: "Launching a satellite is indeed a great project. But if we can shorten the scientific education course in Japan by one year, that may be even greater."

His strong commitment to education as shown in his words, has permeated   the whole KUMON organization. That is, commitment to social improvement through educational improvement, or in

other words, commitment to bringing the limitless ability of the
human being into full play for the betterment of the society.

Through this belief, KUMON could gain support from 1,4 million
children and expand nationwide so as to have classes in 76 % of major
school districts. Otherwise, it would only have ended in creating
new teaching material.

6. CONCLUSION - THREE PROPOSALS FOR EDUCATIONAL INNOVATION

We have so far seen an example of innovative remote education,
the KUMON system, which was born and developed in Japan. The
purpose of this report, however, is not to introduce KUMON activities but to focus on why one private educational institution
could grow so quickly into a nationwide network and to analyze
the driving force behind it. We are convinced that this would
contribute to the improvement of remote education, and education
in general.

There are three lessons we can learn from KUMON's success. First,
the driving force of innovating remote education (and education
in general) is not 'hardware' or 'software (or courseware meaning
teaching material)' but 'heartware'. This is demonstrated in
KUMON's corporate culture and strong commitment to education.
Without its corporate culture, which lies deep in our heart, KUMON
could not have attracted so many people. Thus, if we are to contribute to the innovation of education, whether at private educational institutions or at official public schools, we should bear
in mind that education is not a business but a social duty.

A plate is hung in our offices and our classrooms with our philosophy: "We will discover the potential with which each individual
is endowed, and, by expanding that gift to its utmost limit, will
develop mentally sound, responsible adults, and thus contribute
to society".

On the basis of our philosophy, we have been doing the best in
order to contribute to society, and we see with confidence the
fact that the philosphy becomes real.

The second lesson is that present-day education is no longer a
cottage industry and there should be a new style of management
that matches the new era. Not only preparing good instructors and
material, the KUMON education system developed such management
based on the concept of Holon.

The time has gone when education simply meant teacher, student
and classroom. As such, the necessity of new management suitable
for our diversified society should again be emphasized here. This
is particularly so with remote educaiton if it is to involve the
whole society.

The third lesson is to learn from other fields. The KUMON system
has applied quality improvement technology which was proved to be
effective in industrial production. It has then successfully resulted in the creation of new 'courseware' which might not have
been possible if KUMON was locked up in the traditional educational field.

The time has come to turn our eyes to other fields and utilize new ideas for teaching and designing of material.

In this sense, Teleteaching '86 Conference is meaningful, having many experts from different fields. It is our hope, and also our conviction,that this conference be the starting point for the creation and development of new education.

Reference:

Shoji Shiba, "The Excellent Education System for One and a Half Million Children," Programmed Learning and Educational Technology, vol.23-4, 1986.

Remote Education and Informatics: Teleteaching
F. Lovis (Editor)
Elsevier Science Publishers B.V. (North-Holland)
© IFIP, 1988

PRODUCTION RULE-BASED AUTHORING SYSTEM

Maria TOMANOVA

Sofia University, Laboratory of Informatics with Computer Center,
Bul.A. Ivanov 5, 1126, Sofia, Bulgaria

The recent research in Artifical Intelligence (AI) made a great
impact on the development of computer aided instruction (CAI)
programs, which play a major role in teleteaching. One approach in
creating intelligent tutoring systems (ITS) is applying the
principles of production rule systems.
The aim of the paper is to present a conceptual design of an
authoring system, called Production Rule-based Authoring System
(PROSYS) which can be a useful tool in teleteaching. The system
has AI diagnostic qualities. PROSYS can be easily used by
educational designers without substantial programming skills.

1. INTRODUCTION

The need for mass and flexible education is increasing, along with the
rapid development of technology. How shall these needs be satisfied?
Obviously, the old traditional forms of education cannot solve the problem
and it's natural that the new technology is to be involved. Remote
education with the aid of computers and telecommunications provides new
opportunities for learning. Computer aided instruction plays a major role
in the innovation of education and, in particular, in distance learning.
The first computer tutoring system appeared twenty years ago. Already
popular is the abbreviation CAI - computer aided instruction. There exist
CAI courses for special educational domains.

A higher level of automation is possessed by the authoring systems. They
propose a collection of software tools for the author to create his own CAI
course. An authoring system must possess at least the following
properties:
  1) ease in usage;
  2) it must support a wide variety of software tools - a simple authoring
     language, programming environment for the author;
  3) abilities to include colour graphics, sound affects and animation,
     for making the lessons more effective;
  4) response sensitivity and diagnostics;

Observations of the existing authoring systems and their authoring
languages shows the following: there exist systems with authoring languages
which are rather simple but allow restricted forms of lessons to be made.
On the contrary, there also exist authoring languages, which allow better
lessons to be made but are rather complicated for the educational designers
and teachers.   In the latter case, the author has to express his lesson-
scenario and tutoring strategy explicity, by writing a program in a special
authoring language. He must explicitly predict all possible situations
that can occur during the process of interaction between the student and
computer and program the possible paths through the lesson.

So the problem that rises here is to find a form of expressing the scenario
of a lesson which is both simple and allows effective response-sensitive
and adaptive CAI to be made. Recent research in artificial intelligence
has made a great impact on the development of CAI programs. Examples of
intelligent tutoring systems (ITS) are: SCOLAR (1970, [1]), SOPHIE (1974,
[2]), WUSOR (1982, [3]), WEST (1982, [4]).

One achievement in ITS is the production rule-based tutoring systems.
Production rule-based systems were proposed by Post (1943). There is a
simple underlying idea in them. Such systems express their decision-making
criteria as sets of production rules, which are declarative statements,
relating various system states to program actions.

Examples are: The system of Hartley and Sleeman (1973, [5]), Quadratic
tutor - the system of T. O'Shea (1982, [6]), GUIDON (1982, [7]), ReGIS -
the system of J.M.Heines and T.O'Shea (1984, [8]).

All these systems are created for a specific education subject. J.M.Heines
and T.O'Shea (8) suggest as a topic for further investigation the design
and implementation of production rule-based authoring system. The
production rule approach towards authoring systems seems rather promising,
because through it the following advantages are achieved:
  1) response-sensitivity and flexibility;
  2) ease in usage by non-programmers.

2. THE COMPONENTS OF A PRODUCTION RULE-BASED AUTHORING SYSTEM

We shall use the abbreviation P R O S Y S for Production Rule-based
Authoring system.

(1) SUBJECT-KNOWLEDGE REPRESENTATION

The knowledge about the subject to be taught is represented by a production
rule-based scheme. The subject-material is divided into small
instructional components - concepts or skills that the student must learn.
There exists a prerequisite relationship between the instructional
components, showing, for a given component, which components must be known
before starting to study it. This relation defines a partial ordering of
the components. it can be represented by a directed acyclic graph.

(2) THE TEACHING OPERATIONS

In the proposed PROSYS, for every component there are:
  1) on-line expositions of the subject-material, demonstrations with
     graphics and sound effects, related to a given component;
  2) set of on-line exercises over the subject-material, related to a
     given component;

(3) THE STUDENT MODEL

The student model represents the state of the student's knowledge. It uses
the subject-knowledge representation. For every component, that the
student studies, he receives a valuation. Moreover, the valuation for a
given component affects the valuations for its prerequisite and
postrequisite components.

The student model includes two additional characteristics - learning style and learning rate.

(4) THE PLANNER

The planner controls the global teaching strategy. For a given student with his student model and instructional goal, the planner makes an individual teaching plan.

(5) THE EXECUTOR

The individual teaching plan, constructed by the planner, is performed by the Executor. It uses a local teaching strategy, which is described in terms of production rules.

In their work, D.Peachey and G.McCalla (9) discuss the problems of planning techniques for intelligent tutoring systems and introduce the concepts Planner and Plan-executor.

3. THE SUBJECT-KNOWLEDGE REPRESENTATION

The proposed authoring system (PROSYS) has a production rule-based representation scheme of the subject-knowledge. That is why the system, using the diagnostic-information from the student model, automatically identifies the components of knowledge which the student lacks and routes him to the teaching operations related to those components.

What is required from the author is to divide the subject-material into the smallest possible components. The author has also to describe the prerequisite relationships between the components. PROSYS must have a simple authoring language and an intelligent interface with the author, so that he can enter the needed information about the lesson. The author has to enter information about the prerequisite relationships between the components and the sets of teaching operations about each component. The system will then process this information and create the specific subject knowledge production rule base. It is remarkable that the scenario of the lesson is then generated automatically by the system. The author has no need to predict explicitly all possible paths through the lesson, as in the traditional authoring languages. This makes the production rule-based approach very attractive.

In the left two columns, in Table 1 below, are listed the components of a course in PASCAL. In the right column are given the direct prerequisites for each component. We call direct prerequisites those that bring new information and don't follow from the previous prerequisites relationships. For example, all prerequisite components of component 7 are 2, 3 ,4, 6, but from them, only 6 carries new information and doesn't follow from the previous listed relationships.

The prerequisite relationships in the proposed course can be represented both by a directed acyclic graph and by a set of production rules. For a given instructional subject, the subject-knowledge representation is the set of production rules, expressing all direct prerequisite relationships between the components in which the subject material is divided.

Table 1

Number	Description of the component	Direct prerequisites
1	Algorithms	NIL
2	Symbols in Pascal	NIL
3	Identifiers	2
4	Numbers in Pascal	2
5	Comments	2
6	Constants and variables	3, 4
7	Definition of constants and types	6
8	Integers and real types	7
9	Boolean type	7
10	Character type	7
11	Enumeration type	7
12	Subrange type	7
13	Arithmetic expressions and arithmetic statement for assignment	8
14	Boolean expressions and boolean statement for assignment	9
15	Conditional statements	13, 14
16	FOR – Statement	13
17	WHILE – Statement	13, 14
18	REPEAT – Statement	13, 14
19	Compound Statement	13, 14
20	Comparison between the statements for cycle	16, 17, 18,19
21	Main rules of the structured programming	20
22	Arrays	7, 13
23	Sets	7, 13
24	Records and variants	7, 13
25	Files	7, 13
26	Pointers	7, 13
27	Statements for input and output	7
28	Characters, Input, manipulation and output	10
29	Labels. GOTO – statement	21
30	Program in Pascal	1,7,10,20,21
31	Functions	30
32	Procedures	30
33	Formal and actual parameters	31, 32
34	Recursion	32, 33
35	Scope of action of parameters	33
36	The top-down approach in programming	35

The production rule approach enables us to make both downward and forward inferences about the subject-components. If the student has studied some set of components, using the production rules, we can answer which components the student is ready to study next.   We can answer also the opposite question: for a given instructional goal, i.e. for a given set of components that a student must know, which he study before that.

4. THE TEACHING OPERATIONS

For every component of the subject material, there are related teaching operations. Let S denote the subject material, (Q(S), or simply Q - the set of components. For every q from Q there is a set of teaching operations A(q,i), i=1,2,...,n, which are expositions of new material and demonstrations and a set B(q,j),j=1,2,...m, which are exercises. It is more complicated to include teaching operations of laboratory type. They must be oriented towards the specific subject-material. All teaching operations are ordered by their level of complexity. The author has to enter them in the system.

The teaching operations perform a dialogue with the student. PROSYS analyses the student responses and updates the student model. In particular, the system gets information about the learning style and learning rate of the student. The learning style is defined by the proportion between the quantity of teaching operations from type A and type B that the student prefers.

The learning rate is defined by the speed with which the student is advancing with the material. This information is used by the system to act in the most adequate way with each student. Students who do well receive more complicated teaching operations quite quickly. The opposite is undertaken with the weaker students. This contributes to the response-sensitivity of the system.

5. THE STUDENT MODEL

The proposed student model is a list of valuations, related to every component of the subject-knowledge representation. Let Q be the set of components for a given subject material and x a component from Q. We shall denote by Val(x) the valuation related to the component x. The possible valuations are the following:

We use two positive values for mastery, zero - for lack of information, and two negative values for non-mastery of the given component.

Val(x)=2 shows that the student has demonstrated mastery by passing the given exercises for the component x.

Val(x)=1 when the student receives valuation 2 on some component V,PROSYS automatically inserts valuation max (Val(x), 1) if Val(x)>=0 and Val(x)+1 if Val(x)<0, for every component x from Q, which is a direct prerequisite of y.

Val(x)=0 shows that there is no information about the student's mastery of the component x.

Val(x)= -2 shows that the student has demonstrated non-mastery of the component x.

Val(x)= 1 when the student receives valuation -2 on some component y, PROSYS automatically inserts valuation min (Val(x), -1) if Val(x)<=0 and Val(x)-1 if Val(x)>0, for every component x from Q, which is a direct postrequisite of y.

Learning rate and learning style are also included in the student model.

6. THE PLANNER

In production systems, two directions of inference are possible - forward chaining and backward chaining. In the case of PROSYS, forward chaining means that if the student has studied a given set of components, PROSYS, using current information from the student model, automatically routes him to the next postrequisite component. Backward chaining means that for a given instructional goal, for example, to master component 20, PROSYS, using current information from the student model, automatically finds the partially directed subset of prerequisite components which the student has to study, so that he can be ready to study component 20.

This ability of PROSYS is used for the automatic constructing of an individual teaching plan for each student. The component of PROSYS which does the planning is called Planner.

7. THE EXECUTOR

The executing of the individual student's teaching plan is performed by the Executor. It uses local teaching strategy, represented by means-ends guidance rules.

Means-ends guidance rules relate different states, defined by the student model, to specific teaching operations.

Once provided with the individual teaching plan of the student, the Executor begins to apply actions, trying to fulfil it. If the student is doing well, he is automatically led forward with higher rate. If he is doing poorly, he is given more expositions and demonstrations. The learning rate is slower.

If the student fails on some component, there are three variants:

1) If there isn't any prerequisite component of which the student has demonstrated non-mastery, he is given more expositions of the subject-material and remedial exercises.

2) If there is only one prerequisite component of which the student has demonstrated non-mastery, he is routed to study that prerequisite component

3) If there is more than one prerequisite component of which the student has demonstrated non-mastery, he is routed top study the prerequisite component on which he has lowest valuation.

So, the Planner cares for the global teaching strategy, while the Executor cares for the local teaching strategy.

8. RESULTS

The widespread use of computers and telecomunications, and the increasing need of quality and efficient distance education, raises the question of creating authoring systems which possess AI qualities and at the same time can be used by non-programmers to create their own CAI courses.

We present a conceptual model of a production rule-based authoring system (PROSYS).

PROSYS can be easily used by educational designers without substantial
programming skills.   From them is required: 1) to divide the subject-
material into small components and analyze the prerequisite relationships
between them; 2) using the authoring language of PROSYS, to create the sets
of teaching operations for each component.

The system automatically generates an individual teaching plan for each
student, by his student model and instructional goal. The Executor, using
local strategy, represented by means-ends guidance rules, guides the
process of education.

9. CONCLUSIONS

PROSYS, as described here, is in an early stage of implementation in PROLOG
on IBM PC/XT.

During the process of implementation of the system, we are intending to
develop it in the following aspects: to create a simple authoring language;
to include laboratory environments for specific subject-materials; to
provide a friendly and intelligent interface with the author and with the
student; to develop the authoring system for computer network.

REFERENCES

[1] Carbonell, J. R., AI in CAI: an artificial intelligence approach to
    computer-assisted instruction. IEEE Transactions on Man-Machine
    Systems, 11 (1970), 190-202.
[2] Brown, J. S., Burton, R. R. & Bell, A. G., SOPHIE; a sophisticated
    instructional environment for teaching electronic troubleshooting.
    Report No. 2790 (1974). Bolt Beranek and Newman Inc.
[3] Goldstein, I. P., The genetic graph: a representation for the evolution
    of procedural knowledge, in Sleeman, D. & Brown, J. S., (eds.),
    Intelligent Tutoring Systems (London: Academic press, 1982).
[4] Burton, R. R. & Brown, J. S., An investigation of computer coaching for
    informal learning activities, in Sleeman, D. & Brown, J. S., (eds.),
    intelligent Tutoring Systems, (London: Academic Press, 1982).

[5] Hartley, J. R. & Sleeman, D. H., Towards more intelligent teaching
    systems. International Journal of Man-Machine Studies, 5, (1973), 215-
    236.
[6] O'Shea, T., A self-improving quadratic tutor, in Sleeman, D & Brown, J.
    S., (eds.), Intelligent Tutoring Systems, (London: Academic Press,
    1982).
[7] Clancy, W. J., Tutoring rules for guiding a case method dialogue, in
    Sleeman, D. & Brown, J. S., (eds.), Intelligent Tutoring Systems,
    (London: Academic Press, 1982, 1982).
[8] Heines, J. M. & O'Shea, T., The design of a rule-based CAI tutorial,
    International Journal of Man-Machine Studies (1985), 23,1-25.
[9] Peachey, D. R. & McCalla, G. I., Using planning techniques in
    intelligent tutoring systems, International Journal of Man-Machine
    Studies (1986), 24, 77-98.

Section 3
Remote Education of Informatics

Remote Education and Informatics: Teleteaching
F. Lovis (Editor)
Elsevier Science Publishers B.V. (North-Holland)
© IFIP, 1988

NEW FIELDS IN INFORMATICS TEACHING

Michel Bottero
Foundation X 2000
France

I.   BASES AND CONTENTS

I.1   FUNDAMENTAL VERIFIED IDEAS

The X 2000 Foundation has the responsibility of running and managing the network of X 2000 Resource Centres.

Today, X 2000 counts 140 Centres spread nationwide, thus forming a unique network for training in computers and experimentation in their latest applications.

The underlying thinking behind X 2000 has thus been proved valid: favouring local initiatives and bringing together multiple partners to create Resource Centres in microcomputing and telematics, linked into a single network, thanks to the structuring effect of a "foundation".

The X 2000 Resource Centres today fulfil a role in the computer field that in certain ways has been compared to that played by municipal conservatories in the area of music: acquisition of a cultural experience, initiation into applications, training in a technique.

The X 2000 Centres however are very distinct from purely municipal services, in that they are based on the central notion of multi-partnership, upon the blending of various yet converging desires of key figures in local development. Furthermore, the X 2000 Centres are dedicated to outofinancing and are thus securely anchored in the reality of economic life.

One could sum up the nature of the X 2000 Centres by listing the following specific strengths:

- The creation of major Resource Centres with autonomous means (in terms of staff, equipment, premises) thus making them different from the structure of "micro-clubs" and allowing for training and experimentation in computer use.

- Multipartnership, not simply to gather together these means, but rather as a philosophy vital to the life of these newly created Centres (rooted in and participating in their local development) that can only spring from local initiative.

- The liaison between these Resource Centres that is the task of the X 200 Foundation, so as to build up a true network and full sharing of experience, know-how and knowledge.

- The objective of <u>promoting and broadening computer culture to a wide range of consumers</u> (well beyond that of computer fan clubs): an unusual objective which stands out both from that of professional training bodies and from that of various socio-cultural animation institutions: an objective which however presupposes a seeking out of synergies with these organisations and institutions.

- <u>An action programme</u> of the X 2000 Centres keyed to two basic poles:

    . training in computer use
    . experimentation in the new <u>applications</u> of computers.

Over the last few months, the spread, the strong basis and the involvement in local development of the X 2000 project has gone from strength to strength. The Regional Councils of six French regions have entered into agreements for the opening up of Centres. Three of these regional agreements were signed at the end of 1985: Provence-Alpes-Cote d'Azur, Picardie and Franche Comte. Three further agreements were signed in 1986 with Languedoc-Roussillon, Aquitaine and the Herault department; several further agreements are currently under negotiation with other local authorities. These agreements provide that such authorities give significant support to the Centres with appropriate equipment and to aid the creation of the new Resource Centres.

I.2   <u>THE CONTENT OF THE X 2000 Centres</u>

It is clear to any outside observer that one of the key characteristics of the X 2000 project is the promotion of computer knowledge and practice. Being neither training Centres not "Maisons des Jeunes et de la Culture" (Youth Cultural Centres), the X 2000 Centres can proclaim even more their ultimate aim. Then, if this aim were based above all on the cultural appropriation of computer science, what is to be understood, what content is to be given to the objective?

The answer to this question seems to be moulded around the concept of innovation. For the X 2000 Centres, the diffusion of computer knowledge could be above all:

- an initiation into new products and applications using computers (social or technological innovations);

- research and use for this initiation of innovative educational methods (self-teaching, C.A.L.);

- experimentation and when required, production and promotion of software and teaching software that innovate or meet specific local needs.

Today, the services of X 2000 Centres are called upon both by:

- company workers' committees which wish to go beyond the simple framework of socio-cultural animation and offer their members proper taining for semi-professional semi-personal ends;

  - by companies themselves who feel the need to train all
    their staff in computer knowledge and no longer just
    train the accounts department in "accountancy
    applications" or the personnel department in "pay-
    personnel management applications", etc.

It is well worth pointing out this convergence of requirements, not only
because it is unusual (in France, perhaps it has never existed) but because it
bears evidence to the usefulness and targeting of the X 2000 Centres. Today,
they are virtually alone in providing the twin expressed desires. The ability
to satisfy a need is vital to the current development of the X 2000 Centres.

The number of requests sent to the X 2000 Centres can be explained by the vast
range of areas covered. The X 2000 Centres make their services available to
everyone - but with order and method.

Their area covers four key points:

  . initiation, training,
  . awareness, animation
  . experimentation, creation, research
  . advice and service.

Initiation - training

As we have seen, the founding of X 2000 Centres is based on training and
initiation. The range covered by these activities is in itself vast - going
from the most basic initiation to advance, lengthy training leading to
qualification. The main axis is generally semi-personal/semi-professional.
However, there seems to be an increasing trend towards more professional
training. This is why it is best to keep up frequent contacts with the
various training/teaching institutions (engineers, architects, farmers,
municipal employees, trainers).

Awareness - animation

Awareness and animation often break into a training proposal by themselves.
This can mean multiple training and demonstration meetings, animations during
school hours or after school, operations in the most varied of contexts, all
with the aim of making computers more understandable and conveying their
magic. It means participating in numerous colloquia, day sessions, week
sessions, salons, shows, or even the organisation of "summer universities".
It means cultural exchanges with certain foreign countries. It also means
activivies largely drawn from those of the end-users clubs.

Experimentation - creation

In the area of experimentation and creation, the main axis of the X 2000
Centre"s activity is also keyed to the educational field: production of
educational products, C.A.L. software, teaching programmes, etc. However,
research and production of management programmes are present in certain X 2000
Centres, along with the creation of software programs and system maquettes run
by computer.

Advice and service

Advice and service are still unequally spread among the X 2000 Centres. Yet
this promising function takes many shapes:

- advice in the choice of programs, program adaptation
  and test programs
- telematics services
- light maintenance of hardware.

As in this area we are as yet unable to give a fully accurate count, it is
worth noting the creation of data-banks by numerous X 2000 Centres:

- banks
- software libraries, teaching libraries
- building up of product assets (rental of teaching
  software and educational material: robots, automata)
- building up of image banks.

II. DEVELOPMENTS

II.1 TOWARDS A REFOCUSSING OC ACTION:

The range of activity covered by the X 2000 Centres may seem, from what you
have read so far, to be vast.

Yet in most of the X 2000 Centres, there is a clear recentring of their
activity.

Two major axes emerge:

- training in well tried uses of the computer,
- experiments of new applications of computer technology.

This brief resume may of course seem over simplified. Its underlying
classification is currently being discussed within the X 2000 network.
Therefore it is well worthwhile explaining in the clearest of terms what is
meant by training and experimenting for computer users.

The X 2000 Centres' experimentations have been widely published. They are
technological (educational robotics, memory card, graphic and musical
creation, etc.), social (applications for the handicapped, the illiterate,
jobs for the young, reintegration of ex-prisoners, etc.), cultural (often
linked to animation activities) or local (use of telematics, micros, creation
of programs for farmers, shopkeepers, craftsmen, etc.).

The training proposal of the X 2000 Network was also recently featured by
"Centre Info" the French official organism for information about training.
The X 2000 Centres' aim is to reach every kind of target group. Some will be
playing a significant role in jobs for the young, in particular regarding
qualification for the 16-25 year olds. Keenly attentive to the requirements
of their environment, the X 2000 Centres frequently give their favourable
reply to requests for specific of "a la carte" training requests. The
proposed training programme thus ranges from introduction and general
initiation to lengthy "qualifying" professional training, corresponding to the
needs of specific professions or businesses. It includes an overall
initiation to computers (basic notions, languages, systems, programming) and

training in office automation (word processing, tabling, file control) and integrated software programs (Framework, Open Access, Excel, etc.). This training offer is also increasingly geared towards computer applications by sector (accounting, craftsmanship, agriculture), but also towards electronics and maintenance, educational robotics, computer assisted learning (C.A.L.), telematics, etc.

II.2 TOWARDS A RENEWAL IN TRAINING PROPOSAL

When X 2000 was created, the main concern was to broadcast as widely as possible basic information about computers. The tactic adopted was that of short sessions, proposals of hours of initiation based on general notions of programming, algorithics, language (BASIC).

Consumer demand seemed substantial: the general public crowded round the doors of the Centres then open, drawn by true curiosity, sometimes tinged with uneasiness.

The X 2000 Centres programmed their activities to meet this demand, organising initiation into computers as a leisure activity, drawing on the experience of socio-cultural animation.

The partners active in the creation of the X 2000 Centres, convinced of its social and cultural appeal, agreed, to finance a large part of the activities.

Today, demand has changed. There are no longer queues at the doors of the X 2))) Centres for initiation: it would seem that the media, computer equipment in schools, computerisation of offices, along with the Resource Centres, workshops and clubs, have played a vital role in this initiation.

The X 2000 Centres have reacted: they operate far less in initiation, but rather downstream from the workshops and clubs which continue to fulfill this need.

Prime social demand has moved towards a need for training, following the acceleration of computerisation in places of work.

In particular, a large majority of *X 2000 Centres organise training sessions aimed at helping the young to ease into the new social and professional context of inevitable technological development.

To adapt oneself better to the evolution of demand naturally calls for a new organisation, a broadening of abilities, a project that asserts fuller professionalism.

The X 2000 Centres are thus faced with the necessary professionalisation of their approach.

The initiation sessions are gradually phasing out in favour of true training sessions organised as such, sold as such to individuals (at their expense or our of the 1% company training tax) or to any other interested organisation or company.

The X 2000 Foundation seeks to conclude outline agreements with national institutions faced with initiation and training needs for professions or specific economic agents.

One significant example of the *X 2000 Foundation's approach is given by the agreement signed on December 4, 1985 with the Architecture Department of the French Ministry in charge of Town Planning. This ministerial department is confronted with the inevitable evolution of the architect's profession, which has to absorb major technological advances such as, in particular, computer-aided conception (CAC) and computer-aided design (CAD).   The Architecture Department has judged that the X 2000 network could be a precious aid for initiation into these new applications, based on the equipment owned by the Centres, their abilities and (not the least important factor) the possibilities of self-training they can offer, allowing the continuation and extension of training sessions by trainees using the computer equipment themselves. The X 200 *Centres furthermore mean such training can lead to "experimentation"so that former trainees, following on from their training, move towards the creation and production of experimental applications.

While the X 2000 Foundation thus intends to favour training for professional purposes, it does not neglect training for cultural and social purposes. In January 1986, it signed an agreement with the Delegation for Professional Training to set up a training scheme of computer animations. This agreement stipulated that the X 2000 Foundation confer the overseeing of this long training session to the IFACE (Institut de Formation de la Chambre de Commerce et d'Industrie de Paris) in collaboration with three X 2000 Centres.

The initial session has been running since April and terminates in October 1986. The X 2000Foundation offered to these apprentice computer animators, during eh summer of 1986, a practical training session in various municipal services in the Paris area.

In this way, the X 2000 network meets a major need, expressed in particular by numerous municipalities - that of specialisation of agents in computer animation.

In this context of municipal needs, it should be noted that the X 2000 network, in conjunction with the Centres for Municipal Staff Training (CMST) has initiated several hundreds of civil servants into computer use and office automation (as one example the X 2000 Centre in Aid-en-Provence along has trained, to date, over 300 municipal employees).

II.3 <u>TOWARDS A NEW INSTITUTIONAL POSITIONING</u>

There has been a clear evolution in the positioning of the X 2000 Centres.

The X 2000 Centres were initially created as centres of animation of computer skills. Hence the high socio-cultural orientation and priority given to animation in certain Centres today. Yet it must be noted that this orientation is not that of the majority of X 2000 Centres. The X 2000 Foundation itself is seeking to reinforce the professional and economic vocation of its Centres rather than encouraging them to position themselves in competition with the municipal socio-cultural services. The reasons for this orientation have nothing to do with ideology. After all, certain X 2000 Centres could pride themselves on having been named "computer culture cnetres" by their institutional environment. Before coming across the X 2000 idea, we ourselves, some years ago, had wished to propose the term "municipal computer conservatory" to denote the para-municipal bodies which, like the music or ballet conservatories, offered the cultural practice that cannot be drawn directly from the theoretical teaching afforded by the State.

However the X 2000 project goes beyond a purely municipal vision, as numerous proponents or opponents of local institutions have well understood. X 2000 is based on the central notion of multi-partnerships, on the meeting of wills, various yet convergent, of the key actors in local development. X 2000 makes it possible to have the local decision makers in the centre of a group. X 2000 projects could hardly be conceivable without the active participation of local authorities. They could not be the fruit of just one cultural, educational, association, municipal, trade unionist or consular partner. Thanks to the blend of all these various partners, many of the X 2000 Centres today are well entrenched in the economy. The majority today are essentially Centres for training and experimentation into the most recent computer applications.

Remote Education and Informatics: Teleteaching
F. Lovis (Editor)
Elsevier Science Publishers B.V. (North-Holland)
© IFIP, 1988

THE USE OF DISTANCE LEARNING
TO PROVIDE PROFESSIONAL RETRAINING
IN COMPUTING

G. Davies and J. Preece
Computer Science Department
Faculty of Mathematics
The Open University
Walton Hall
Milton Keynes, MK7 6AA   United Kingdom

The United Kingdom Open University has been teaching
Informatics to undergraduates using distance-learning methods
for some years. Experience gained with these courses is
now being used to provide post-graduate level courses for
the retraining of people in industry. This paper describes
the evolution of these courses and the structure and content
of the retraining programme.

1 INTRODUCTION

The United Kingdom Open University (UKOU) is the largest university in the
United Kingdom and has considerable experience in teaching undergraduates by
distance-learning methods. This experience is now being used to provide
professional training courses for people in industry.

Distance learning can be considered as covering "the various forms of study
at all levels which are not under the continuous, immediate supervision of
tutors present with their students in lecture rooms or on the same premises,
but which, nevertheless, benefit from the planning, guidance and tuition of
a tutorial organisation". (Holmberg, 1978).

The use of distance-learning techniques for professional retraining can
reduce the cost of providing such training and allow the employee to remain
in full-time employment. It is also believed that some topics, which can
use large scale case studies, can be more effectively taught by the
techniques available to distance-learning. Since 1973, no fewer than 20,000
students have taken Open University Courses on computing and 14,000 students
have taken courses on electronics.

In this paper, these courses are discussed with particular relevance to the
UKOU's Industrial Applications of Computers programme. However, in order to
appreciate the evolution of this programme, a brief introduction to the Open
University, its courses on computing and the media used in distance-learning
is first presented.

2 THE UNITED KINGDOM OPEN UNIVERSITY (UKOU)

The UKOU enrolled its first students in 1971. 50,000 students now hold BA
degrees from the UKOU and currently there are 100,000 students studying with
it. The courses offered include those which lead to a BA degree, short non-
degree courses and post-graduate level courses. A BA with honours may be
awarded to a student who has accumulated 8 credits, where a half credit
course is equivalent to approximately 160 hours of study. The University
has a policy of 'open' admission, which means that students do not need to

have any academic qualifications in order to study with the OU. Most of the
tuition is by distance teaching which requires students to study
correspondence texts and listen to TV and radio broadcasts in their own
homes. This form of tuition enables many students to study at home whilst
still retaining full time employment.

The UKOU is organised from a central campus situated at Milton Keynes, 60
miles North West of London. The academic facilities are situated on this
campus and it is here that course teams work to produce the courses. Most
of the administration is also organised from this campus. There are two
large main frame computer systems; one is used for recording students' data
and carrying much of the University's administration and the other is used
to provide a computing facility for staff and students. TV and radio
production facilities are also available on this site, housed in a purpose-
built BBC building. As well as the central campus, there are 13 regional
centres which administer local tutoring and counselling provision, organise
examinations and provide local liaison between the central campus, students
and tutors. Each regional centre directly controls a number of study
centres. There are 260 study centres in total, located throughout the
British Isles. Each study centre provides a venue for tutorials and
contains audio-visual equipment and a point of access to the Open University
computing facilities at Milton Keynes and Newcastle.

3 COMPUTING COURSES AT THE UKOU

These can be considered as falling into 2 categories: Undergraduate courses
and continuing Education courses, and examples of each will now be
considered.

3.1 Undergraduate Courses

These courses are part of the BA programme and students usually have a
positive interest in computing as a subject and hope to take further courses
in Computer Science. There is a foundation course which is a prerequisite
for later courses. The courses currently offered are as follows. (All
courses are half credit.)

Computing and Computers (Foundation course). This course assumes no
previous knowledge of computing. It combines a broad survey of most aspects
of computing with a sequence of units designed to

(a)   teach the basic concepts of computing, and
(b)   to train students to solve problems by using the top-down approach to
       produce programs.

This course, therefore, contains an introduction to most of the topics that
are taught during the first year of a traditional Computer Science
undergraduate programme. There are currently up to 3,000 students taking
this course.

Computer-based Information Systems. This course is concerned with Data
Analysis, Data Modelling and Data Base systems, both Network and Relational.
This course usually has about 800 students.

Programming and Programming Languages. This course teaches the principles
and concepts associated with the use and design of both procedural and

functional programming languages. This course was new in 1986 and has a quota of 300 students (restricted by the number of available specially designed PCs).

Work has already commenced on re-writing the foundation course and extending it to a full credit. The Information Systems course will also be re-written for presentation in 1990.

Further developments include undergraduate courses on Software Engineering (1989), Computer Architecture and Operating Systems and Fifth Generation Computing.

3.2 Continuing Education courses

There are three types of continuing education courses: in-service training for teachers, computer language packs and retraining courses for industry.

In-service Training Packs for Teachers

These packs are designed to be studied in their own time by teachers with little or no knowledge of microelectronics or microcomputers. There are five packs and each requires about 40 hours of study. The general aim of the packs is to enable teachers more effectively to use microcomputers and microelectronics in their classrooms. There is an emphasis on practical work but there is no assessment of the teachers' performances. The five packs are:

. Awareness: This provides an introduction for beginners who have little or no knowledge of microelectronics or microcomputers.
. Educational Software: This is designed for teachers who have studied the Awareness Pack and who wish to know more about the design of educational software, so that they can assess critically the potential of programs for their own teaching.
. Micros in Action in the Classroom: This is designed for teachers who wish to consider how different kinds of educational software can be used in the classroom. The Awareness pack is recommended as a prerequisite for studying this pack.
. Learning about Microelectronics: This teaches about basic microelectronics. The Awareness pack is recommended as a prerequisite for studying the pack.
. Inside Microcomputers: This is about the design of microcomputers and builds upon the concepts taught in "Learning about Microelectronics".

Language Packs

Language Packs are relatively inexpensive 'teach yourself' packages for PASCAL and COBOL. A student may purchase a pack with or without a practical computing element. The practical computing is done via a terminal to one of the UKOU mainframes (DEC 20 system).

Retraining courses for industry

The Open University's experience with the courses just described has led to its involvement in this new area: the programme is aimed primarily at engineers, scientists and technical managers who have been practising in

industry for some years and who are finding their work transformed by the
introduction of computers and computer-oriented techniques.

The courses are produced with the co-operation of industry and are
relatively expensive. Consequently it is expected that companies will
subsidise the students. The program is called the 'Industrial Application
of Computers Program' and has the following modular structure.

FOUNDATION COURSES

Software Engineering	Computer Architecture and Operating Systems

Real-time Monitoring

Systems Modelling

CORE COURSES

Real-time Control

Project Management

Robotics and Computing	Man/Machine Systems	Computer Aided Engineering

SPECIALIST COURSES

Each course is a 1/4 credit equivalent, taking about 100 hours of study.
Software Engineering and Computer Architecture and Operating Systems are
Foundation Courses which cover the main principles of computers and
computing. They provide an essential background to computer applications in
an industrial context. The four following courses, from Real Time
Monitoring to Project Management, are Core courses dealing with computer-
based monitoring and control of equipment and processes. Students choose
two out of the three Specialist courses.

The courses have examinations twice a year and students can aggregate course
credits (eight) to obtain a postgraduate diploma, or, with the inclusion of
a project, an MSc degree.

As with all Open University courses there are no formal entrance
requirements, although some previous experience and knowledge is essential
to study the courses satisfactorily.

4   TEACHING METHODS

In this section, the methods of teaching the undergraduate courses,
exemplified by Computing and Computers, are compared with the methods of
teaching the continuing education courses on microcomputers and
microelectronics.

Computing and computers

There are 4 components to the course: course text; practical text; TV
programs and audio-cassettes, which together comprise the 16 units of work.
Each of these units should take the average student 10 hours of study. The

course text explains various topics on computing and is taught in what has
become traditionally "Open University style". Practical computing presents
a problem, because of the difficulty in teaching programming, the problem of
providing computing facilities and the difficulties and expense of assessing
students' performance and providing feedback (the course currently has up to
3.000 students). The practical computing units are worked on in parallel
with the course text. The TV programmes are used to explain concepts in the
text or to give case study examples to reinforce the text.

To help the student plan his study a study guide provided, which describes
the content of each unit, and advises him on how much time to allocate to
studying different topics. In most cases practical work takes the bulk of
the time - it is easy to underestimate the time needed for students to
complete the practical computing component.

Programming is taught, using many examples and a test at the end of the
section for the student to complete. Many diagrams are essential for
students at this level.

On this course students do all their practical work using a terminal
attached to one of two DEC 20's by telephone lines. The terminals are
situated in the study centres and instructions for their use are included in
a separate booklet. Students may be familiar with the terminals through an
earlier Maths or Technology course, containing a very small computer
component. Study centres will also usually provide an 'induction session'
at which a group of students are shown how to use the terminal. However,
students will often have no previous experience of using a terminal and
there will be no-one immediately available to answer their questions should
any difficulties arise. It is essential that students plan their activities
carefully before going to the terminal so that the booked sessions are
utilised fully. In the units, a two-colour format is used to distinguish
between student input and the computer's response.

Audio-cassettes are used to help to explain the study centre terminal
sessions and to advise the student on the planning of these.
TV programmes are used in three ways:

.   A general introduction to the use of computers in everyday life to
     justify the course, to stimulate interest and to set the scene.
.   Graphics and magnetic boards are used to illustrate particular concepts
     or to explain algorithms; for example, binary search.
.   To present Case studies of large operational systems; for example,
     British Airways Booking Systems.

The course texts provide many examples for self-assessment. In addition,
the student has to complete four assignments of four questions each, which
are sent to their tutors for marking and extensive comments. Although tutor
marking requires an extensive network of knowledgeable tutors and is
expensive, it is essential in order to give students feedback on their
performance. In this way, the student can improve his final grade (his
continuous assessment is included in the final grade). Help is also given
to the student by regular tutorials in groups of 20-25 at the study centres
where the student can meet fellow students and also a tutor who is familiar
with the marking of the assignments.

In-service Training Packs for Teachers

Each of the five packs; Awareness, Educational software, Micros in Action in
the Classroom, Learning About Microelectronics and Inside Microcomputers,
contains items of text, software on cassette or a small microcomputer, an
optional video and an audio-cassette. The way that each of these media is
used will now be discussed in more detail, with specific reference to the
Educational Software pack.

Educational Software Pack

This teaches about the design and use of educational software. In order to
study this pack, a teacher needs to be able to set up a microcomputer and to
run educational programs. Three main topics are taught:

- Some basic programming concepts.
- The design and use of different makes of software (for example,
  simulations, drill and practice, information retrieval).
- Criteria for designing or selecting education software.

The general aim of the pack is to help teachers to become knowledgeable
about computer software.

The basic programming concepts are taught by providing programs, which are
distributed on cassette tapes for five different microcomputers. The
teachers are required to change the programs using an editor and to unite
their own short procedures. The approach involves very careful guidance, so
that the teacher's confidence is built up. A three column format is used
with boxed key presses so that the teacher knows exactly which keys to
press. The plan is to:

- Tell the teacher what to do, i.e. which keys to press
- show him/her what to expect on the screen
- explain the basic principles, with one column being used for each
  purpose.

A 'trouble-shooting' guide is also included, so that the teacher can look up
any unexpected responses which are made by the microcomputer.

Teaching about different styles of software is done by providing small
sample programs for the teacher to examine. This work is supported by
questions, discussions and articles which cover large tutorial systems (for
example, PLATO and artificial intelligence), which cannot be demonstrated on
a microcomputer.

The section which teaches about software selection, evaluation and design
brings together the various concepts that are taught in the earlier
sections. the teacher is supplied with three commercially produced
educational software packages which he is required to examine and evaluate
with the aid of a list of design criteria. Video is used to show case
studies of a software development team at work and also how education
software is used in the classroom. It is considered important to build up
the confidence of teachers by showing them that computers can be used
effectively in the classroom.

Audio-cassettes are also used in these courses and consist of interviews with teachers recounting their experiences of using computers in the classroom.

Two particular problems have arisen with the production of this and other software packs:

. Writing and maintaining versions of software to run on different machines. for example, during the production of one version the manufacturer changed the operating system. A solution to this problem is to develop one's own microcomputer, but this is obviously expensive, time consuming and requires specialist expertise.
. The three column format and boxed key presses are expensive but they are important for teaching novices.

5   INDUSTRIAL APPLICATIONS OF COMPUTER PROGRAM (IAC)

This programme is a natural development from the undergraduate programme and in-service training courses for teachers. It provides in-service training for technical and managerial staff. By passing eight modules, a student becomes eligible for a postgraduate diploma. On completion of a project, the student is then eligible for a M.Sc degree.

It is generally accepted that there is no substitute for direct practical experience in computing technology. consequently, the IAC programme has adopted this principle and a practical approach to the presentation of ideas and techniques has been taken.

5.1 A practical approach

the practical approach means that the individual courses each have several, if not all, of the following features, as an integral part:

. 'hands-on' practical work involving appropriate equipment
. case studies which show ideas in an industrial context
. regular self-assessment questions throughout the course texts
. video material, showing working equipment or processes, or using dynamic graphics to illustrate complex interactions.

The practical work in several of these courses centres around a multi-purpose educational workstation. This workstation, HEKTOR III, has been developed from earlier versions used on other UKOU courses, in order to support two main types of practical work in these programmes.

In one mode, it is used as a terminal to a large computer network, via a (supplied) modem and the telephone system. In this way, students can:

. access data bases and electronic mail
. execute large software packages
. develop, execute and file their own programs
. down-line load application software for local use.

The workstation can also be used stand-alone or as a controller of experimental apparatus (such as a robot arm). The courses Software Engineering, Robotics and Computing, Real-time Monitoring, Real-time Control and Computer Aided Engineering, all use the same basic system, and any add-on extras needed for experimental work are included in the curse materials.

The practical work in the Software Engineering course uses HEKTOR III in both modes. Using it as an on-line terminal, students work within a UCSD Pascal programming environment provided by the Open University's mainframe computers, with access to the system support and software tools that such an environment offers. Although students may have some experience of programming, it is still necessary to give detailed instructions for the practical sessions. Used stand-alone, HEKTOR III provides a flexible student workstation, for both on-line and off-line work.

The practical approach to the Robotic courses demands that experimental work with a real robot be an integral part of the course work. Accordingly, a scaled-down industrial robot arm, with six-axis movement and capable of lifting one kilogram at full reach, is available for the practical work. The robot also has a pneumatic gripper, wired for such sensors as a microswitch or a photosensor.

The robot is controlled by a dedicated microcomputer with direct position feed-back from each joint. The controller and power pack are housed in a separate unit, which also allows for communication with external devices, via two digital inputs and two isolated delay-contacted outputs. The controller connects by cable to the HEKTOR III system, thus enabling on-line programming of the robot.

Students use the robot to experiment with

. pick and place
. stacking
. drilling
. paint spraying
. component assembly

Accessories supplied with the robot include simple jigs, an electric drill, and an airbrush. By their use, students will gain direct experience of several of the more industrially relevant robot tasks.

5.2 Multi-media teaching

The IAC programme has benefited from the experience gained in multi-media teaching by the UKOU. However, these modules are developed in a different manner from the undergraduate courses. There is more consultation with industry to ensure that the modules are relevant and practical and they are produced (in two years) using industrial consultants and fewer UKOU staff.

Each module uses some or all of the following media:

Course texts: the content of which is chosen to meet relevant industry needs and to provide technical updating for the career development of individual students. The style is active, not passive, with the students becoming involved via the extensive use of case studies, self-monitoring questions and practical exercises. Complex subjects are explained with a minimum of jargon while the inclusion of many diagrams and photographs supplements and enhances the written word.

Video cassettes are used, in preference to television programmes. The latest equipment and processors can be seen working and complex interactions are displayed, using dynamic graphics. The Software Engineering module uses a 90-minute video to provide an intensive case study of the development of a large software system, observing the software team in discussion, as well as explaining the development and structure of the project. the Robotics course also has a video-component, again consisting of case studies and industrial situations, that here make use of robots. Both videos show the mistakes that can be made in large projects. The Real-time Monitoring module has a 30-minute video which describes the monitoring system at a large ICI chemical plant. In conjunction with the text the student is shown how the system was designed and how some of the techniques in the module where applied. Video is used in a similar fashion in the Real-time Control and computer Aided Engineering modules.

Audio-cassettes are used to guide students through complex diagrams. The student has the diagram in front of him, while listening to an explanation on the audio-cassette. The Computer Architecture and Operating System module uses this technique to advantage. Other modules use audio-cassettes to provide information, via interviews with experts in the particular field.

Personal tuition is provided as with other Open University courses, students being provided with a tutor for 12 months, from whom they will receive advice and guidance by telephone and by comments on their submitted written work.

6   CONCLUSIONS

Many people doubted the effectiveness of large-scale distance learning when the Open University first began fifteen years ago. It is now accepted, however, that distance learning as practised by the UKOU (and other institutions throughout the world) is successful. The problems of teaching science and technology without easy access to laboratories have been largely overcome and so have many of the problems concerned with computing.

The Industrial Applications of Computer Programme is a new venture of the Open University into the sphere of updating technical staff in the field of computing. It is believed that distance learning is effective for in-service training for the following reasons:

- It is cost-effective: large numbers of people can be trained at work or at home, while continuing to work for a company or organisation.
- The courses are relevant as they are specifically designed to meet the current up-dating and training needs identified by British Industry. They have been produced by UKOU staff in collaboration with Industrial consultants.
- The courses are of high quality; this is ensured through the expertise of the course team and the eminence of the industrial and academic assessors who assess the work.
- The courses have a practical approach provided by experimental work, using the workstation, video material, case studies and an experimental robot.
- The courses are flexible. Students enrol at any time during the year and work at home or work at a time and pace to suit their own needs or the needs of their company or organisation.
- The courses have tutorial support.

REFERENCES
(1)   Holmberg, Borje. Distance Education - a survey and bibliography. Kogan Page Ltd. 1978.

Remote Education and Informatics: Teleteaching
F. Lovis (Editor)
Elsevier Science Publishers B.V. (North-Holland)
© IFIP, 1988

A DISTANCE EDUCATION COURSE ON CUSTOM_DESIGN CIRCUITS

P.GONDA - A.NÁDASI

EDUSYSTEM Instructional Development Associates, H-1053, Budapest,
Fejér Gy. u. 10. National Centre for Educational Technology,
H-1502. Budapest, Pf. 260.

1. INTRODUCTION

One of the main objectives of the activities performed within the framework of
the Microelectronics Investment Programme is the home production of custom-
-design circuits. Naturally, the new production technologies require new
professional knowledge and skills to be learnt by the manufacturers and the
users as well. According to preliminary estimates, the number of engineers
in need of the knowledge of design and utilization of custom-design circuits
amounts to several thousand in the middle of the eighties in Hungary. The
Government Commissioner for Microelectronics entrusted an independent,
private company EDUSYSTEM Instructional Development Associates with planning,
elaborating and evaluating the instructional development programme. Experts
on higher education, industry, production of audiovisual materials and
educational technology equally participated in the work of planning and
elaboration. Among others, members of following institutions participated in the
activities directed by EDUSYSTEM: Technical University Budapest (BME),
Telecommunication Co-operative (HTSz), Central Physical Research Institute
(KFKI), Kossuth Lajos University (KLTE), Microelectronical Company (MEV).

The system plan of training was completed in 1983, the programme of further
training, the textbooks and the audiovisual materials, as well as the set of
tasks and test items were completed in 1984. Further training courses started
in the Further Training Institute of Engineers of the Technical University
Budapest in October 1984.

2. PLANNING OF THE COURSE

It has become a necessity not only for the experts of the companies
manufacturing electronic circuits to acquire the design methods of the home
produced custom-design circuits in harmony with the new technologies, but a
new type of design approach must be established in those companies too,
which wish to incorporate these chips of a large-scale of integration into
the appliances, instruments and other equipment to be developed by them.
This technical development is not an autotelic task, but   it is one of the
conditions of holding our ground in economic competition on the basis of the
development of microelectronics.

On the basis of the estimation of the government programme performed in
1982, the knowledge and skills necessary for planning custom-design circuits
must be acquired by approximately 3000 experts of high-level technical training
between 1984 and 1987; these experts work in companies manufacturing
appliances and equipment operated in a diversity of fields of the industry
and agriculture. This was one of the conditions of planning the further
training necessary for the acquisition of special knowledge, the satisfaction
of which could not be guaranteed by the traditional methods and forms used
generally in technical further training. Another condition that had to be taken
into account in planning was that the number of technical-theoretical and

industrial-practical experts on the planning of custom-design circuits was - very understandably - very limited in Hungary; estimated around 15-20 people, engaged in higher education and the industry. This meant that the possible number of lecturers for a traditional further training course would have made possible the training of the 3000 desired experts only in a much longer period of time.

Recognizing the above conditions and analyzing them from the point of view of instructional development, we recommended the establishment of a training system which applies flexible, carefully elaborated and verifiable training methods and forms of organization, by building the curriculum in accordance with the training objectives and the previous knowledge of the course partici- pants, which is based on individual learning and the use of printed and audiovisual media.

3.   ELABORATION OF THE DEVELOPMENT

On the basis of analyzing the requirements, objectives, tasks and the curriculum and taking into account the above mentioned conditions, we elaborated for "THE PLANNING OF CUSTOM-DESIGN CIRCUITS" course a further training system based on individual learning within the framework of distance education, including the following teaching and learning forms:

- individual learning from textbooks and training programmes,
- individual problem solving and checking by self-testing,
- individual problem solving and checking by central tests,
- consultation and joint problem solving in group work,
- lectures with demonstration, using overhead projector transparencies and video recording,
- individual learning, in the further-training centres or at home with the help of borrowed video cassettes,
- supervised computer-aided design exercises in small groups.

Training based on individual learning within the framework of distance education has several advantages over the intensive, residential, "conventional" form of courses:

- the training time is tailored to the level of initial knowledge of the students and it is advantageous from the point of view of the efficiency of training;
- organized meetings (lectures, compulsory consultation and computer-aided design exercises) are held only if they are inevitably necessary; thus the students do not need unnecessary leave of absence from production, which results in significant savings of expenses too;
- the curriculum and media necessary for the students can be elaborated by the best experts in the form of printed and audiovisual programmes, so it is possible to provide the best lecturers for years.

When planning the whole system, it had to be taken into account that STUDENTS' ACCOMPLISHMENT CHANGES in the case of traditional training planned for a fixed period of time, adjusted to the general level of the students, while in the case of individualized training THE TIME ALLOTTED BY THE STUDENTS TO LEARNING AND THE METHODS AND FORMS OF CONVEYING THE CURRICULUM CHANGE, and accomplishment may be the same, i.e. equally good. Thus the main requirement of educational technology was for the planners of the course to create the necessary conditions for the students to be able to meet all the requirements, even though not with the same "investment".

When developing the course "THE PLANNING OF CUSTOM-DESIGN CIRCUITS", audiovisual media played an important role because of the requirements of "Mass production", and the method based on teaching packages elaborated on a module system seemed to be almost the only possible solution. During development the following tasks had to be carried out in order to produce the concrete teaching-learning materials:

- a clearly outlined structure of training;
- a carefully worded system of objectives and requirements accessible to the students too;
- a systematically planned draft of the curriculum, adjusted to the accomplishment of the students and the requirements;
- the module-structure of the curriculum, the description of the activities and tasks of the students;
- self-checking systems, tests and tasks elaborated according to the modules and the topics;
- continuous feedback for the teachers about the accomplishment of the students;
- a diversity of interaction opportunities between the teachers and the students, free and fixed "consultations";
- the accessibility of media in harmony with the objectives and the curriculum (printed and audiovisual materials, electronic media);
- personal and objective conditions assuring the utilization of theoretical knowledge, opportunities of solving tasks under industrial circumstances;
- an evelution system suitable for estimating the knowledge of the students, demonstrating the degree of fulfilling the requirements.

During elaboration all the conditions were fulfilled, the system of objectives, the textbooks, the test items for self-checking and central evaluation, the set of tasks and the overhead projector transparencies assisting consultations, as well as the programme of computer-aided design exercises and the series of video recordings discussing the whole theoretical material, were made for each topic.

The time of the whole course is 150...250 hours - depending on the individual initial knowledge of the students - of which 50 hours are compulsory lectures, consultations and computer-aided design exercises. The course closes with the solution of a complex development task and its defence in front of an examination committee.

4.   TOPICS AND TEACHING MATERIALS

The topics (modules) of the course are the following:

1. Design and manufacturing of integrated circuits
2. The operation of transistors
3. Basic digital circuits I
4. Basic digital circuits II
5. Digital systems
6. Specification and measuring of digital integrated circuits
7. Technological principles
8. Layout design I
9. Layout design II
10. Computer-aided design exercises

In addition to self-checking tests and tasks, the students have at their disposal the material of the whole course in the form of a textbook (1) and a workbook (2) as well as a 5-part and a 15-part colour video series. The video recordings are 50 minutes long and they are available on VHS and U-matic cassettes, both in the consultations centre and for borrowing.

The parts, contents and lecturer-experts of the 15-part video series are the following:

1. INTRODUCTION AND GENERAL SURVEY (dr.Kálmán Tarnay, András Ribényi)
   - a description of the contents of the video series;
   - the role and significance of custom-design circuits
2. THE MOST TECHNOLOGY (dr.Győző Drózdy)
   - photolitography;
   - mask production;
   - the main steps of slice technology
3. THE MOST TRANSISTOR (dr.Győző Drózdy)
   - the MOS structure;
   - the characteristics of the MOS transistor;
   - the principle of the MOS inverter
4. THE INVERTER (Péter Keresztes)
   - the basic inverter;
   - the types of inverters;
   - the characteristics of transfer;
   - inverter design
5. MOS GATE CIRCUITS (Péter Keresztes)
   - NAND and NOR gates;
   - complex gates;
   - layout variants;
   - circuit simulation
6. COMPLEX COMBINATION NETWORKS, CELLULAR LAYOUT DESIGN (András Keresztes)
   - code transformers;
   - multiplex circuits;
   - comparators;
   - parity generator checking;
   - cellular design
7. FLIP-FLOPS (András Keresztes)
   - SR and F flip-flops;
   - master-slave flip-flops;
   - setting
8. INPUTS AND OUTPUTS (András Keresztes)
   - connecting NMOS, CMOS and TTL systems;
   - inputs;
   - outputs;
   - three-level output
9. THE CMOS INVERTER (Béla Dávid)
   - the significance of CMOS circuits;
   - metal gate CMOS gate networks;
   - CMOS basic cells
10. CMOS CIRCUITS (Béla Dávid)
    - CMOS basic cells (flip-flops);
    - the transfer gate;
    - inputs and outputs;
    - making manual master drawings
11. THE FUNCTIONAL UNITS OF LOGICAL NETWORKS (dr.Ottó Szittya)
    - registers;
    - counters;
    - a binary adder
12. SPECIFICATION AND SIMULATION OF DIGITAL SYSTEMS (dr.András Jávor, Gyula Csopaki)
    - the elements of functional specification;
    - hardware descriptive language;
    - logical simulation;
    - simulation examples
13. THE METHODS OF LAYOUT DESIGN (dr.Piroska Vályi)
    - cell design;
    - chip design;
    - laws of design;
    - "stick-drawing"

14. THE MEANS OF LAYOUT DESIGN (dr.András Hegedűs)
   - manual layout design;
   - digitalization;
   - graphic descriptive language;
   - drawing machines;
   - pattern generator;
   - step-and-repeat camera;
   - the "chartpack" technique
15. FROM THE FINISHED SLICE TO THE CASED CIRCUIT (dr.Péter Gartner)
   - slice testing;
   - bonding;
   - encapsulation;
   - final testing.

The individual video programmes contain one lecture each, during which the explanation is assisted by electronic and graphic animations and location shots. More than 600 graphic drawings and about 4 hours of location shots were made for the series. The programme package compiled for the teachers contains, in addition to the material for the students, a methodological guide, the keys to the central tests, as well as a series of overhead transparencies consisting of close to 400 pieces.

5.   MAJOR FINDINGS OF THE COURSE EVALUATION AND SUGGESTIONS

In the review the two main directions of investigation were efficiency and success. The findings are listed in an order that allows one to illustrate the whole issue from social economical needs to analysis of course methods regarding the Custom Design Circuits (CDC) course.

5.1.   As regards efficiency the importance of the course exceeds the given convertibility rate. After executing the government program, and in a close relation to that, its impacts can be examined in the following dimensions:
- has it been successful in introducing a new technical culture in Hungary?
- is the intellectual capital required for implementation available?
- has it been successful in increasing the development rate of the economy,
- has the productivity of the national income been increased?

On the social level, the total revenues of the course cannot and will never be objectively measured because of the extremely numerous components. However efficiency can be detected at company or personal levels.

5.2.   It can be stated that the companies realize the importance of spreading micro electronics, but do not yet feel the need of applying CDC and this fact limits the expectations of the development engineers, and also the material and moral honour to those who completed the CDC course.

5.3.   Our investigations prove that a course training may at most aim at forming the attitude of the students who completed the course, but not that of the delegating superiors and users. Thus in order to have 3000 qualified engineers available or capable of CDC development, waiting for the government program to end, it would have been necessary in advance that top and mid level managers of the manufacturing and user companies would welcome the issue with a modern attitude.

5.4.   It is a serious problem that official recognition could not be provided for completing the course. What is a grater concern is that completing the course does not give even an informal honour. Managers of the few companies concerned could not come to an uniform decision whether the motivation of their engineers should be through pay rise, moral or material rewards. The only achievement has been that the graduating student "receives a diploma that entitles him or her to work on an expensive design tool..."

5.5. There are no national antecedents to the remote instructional form based on individual learning-already well proved in industrial extension training all over the world. It is an unfortunate finding that as regards the development level of our companies and the current way of thinking of their managers, the whole course – including also its contents – in fact seems to be a little ahead of its time, although its objective is to keep up with the challenge of time.

5.6. At present the CDC course as implemented is ideal for engineers working for smaller companies: for big companies the individually placed arrangement is the route to the future.

5.7. As regards course structure and target population the objectives of the course to form attitudes and also to develop designing skills should be handled separately. At present the orientation of managers is not solved.

5.8. Based on the opinion of CDC course students it can, with a fair certainty, be stated that although students have a very characteristic sympathy and antipathy towards the contents and the persons or tools communicating them, they basically agree to the themes, and understand or accept the importance of teaching them. The text book covering the theoretical base material needs rewriting in a few chapters only.

5.9. According to criteria followed during the inner evaluation, that is when "awarding marks" to the knowledge of the students of the CDC course, it can definitely be considered as successful. Relatively few results can be found below the 80 % performance threshold considered critical by many, and even the limit of the lower scattering interval is only in a few cases below 60%.

5.10. Since the CDC course has set as an objective the development of high level designing skills, the tests used for inner evaluation should in any case be re-worked before the new courses; also for their realistic evaluation. That re-working can easily be made if the instructors have time and further experiences available to them for constructing the tests.

5.11. The students stated that they would need regular self education and extension training even after the course. That is also called for by the technical development. They feel the need for such a training, but deem a recognition of the education also important.

5.12. Some of the students have suggested that the CDC subject is worth a proportionally designed course covering longer theoretical and practical knowledge, on completion of which students would receive an extension engineer diploma.

5.13. A significant percentage of the students did not undertake the exam. It can be stated that they did not undertake to prepare for and take the difficulties of an exam mainly because they considered it only a formal one. Graduating and obtaining a course diploma has no moral or material advantages for them.

5.14. One of the methods of the CDC course deemed most important, – the individual learning – did not receive a suitable importance. The reasons identified are:
- Organisers and instructors of the course in fact did not take the educational measures required to introduce the individual learning; for example the learning objectives had not been emphasized for the students, the instructional tools (15 hour video) destined for supporting the individual learning had not been made an integral part of the course of training, and evaluation of the initial knowledge had not been made. Organising the inner evaluation

was made less systematically and the provisions for learning motivation may be called incomplete.
- The instructional tools, primarily the video recordings which the individual learning, had been based on, did not act in compliance with expectations in the actual educational process. For example possibility for access and replay at any time had not been provided. Conditions for videoing were not attractive for the students.
- It is rather evident that the interests of course instructors (due to financial reasons and tradition) were in giving the lectures rather than in consultations, although it is the consultations that are the very supports for individual learning.

5.15.   The individual learning tools, primarily the problem book and the series of video recordings, fulfilled their functions in part only. Based on instructional technology development considerations and evaluation findings and data, this functional error can be corrected by increasing flexibility and implementing modular construction. In addition more actual methodical aids are required both for the course organisers and the students to operate the individualized system.

5.16.   More findings verify that text books and lectures are required together. In general students agree that the text books and the lectures are not really understood and elaborated without consultations. That opinion also supports the fact that full individualization of the course in its present form would not be advisable in BME MTI. In fact, it is suggested that first the presently used system that is based on partly individual learning, should be improved. If the organising institute of the course, or a company provides all technical conditions, the level of individualization may be increased.

5.17.   Findings and data obtained to date emphasize the importance and determinative role of organizing the CDC course again (if the higher number of students is still reasonable in the future). They also underline the impact and prominent part played by demand survey, target training accuracy, and routinely implementing outer and inner evaluations.

REFERENCES

(1) The planning of microelectronic custom-design microelectronic circuits I. - ed. by K.Tarnay, EDUSYSTEM, 1984, Budapest, 984 pages, + 54 insets.
(2) The planning of microelectronic custom-design microelectronic circuits II. - ed. by K.Tarnay, EDUSYSTEM, 1985, Budapest, 354 pages.

Remote Education and Informatics: Teleteaching
F. Lovis (Editor)
Elsevier Science Publishers B.V. (North-Holland)
© IFIP, 1988

CLEAR: COMPUTER LEARNING RESOURCE CENTERS

Fillia MAKEDON
Computer Science Program
University of Texas at Dallas
Richardson, Texas
75083-0688 USA

Hermann MAURER
Institutes for Information Processing (IIG)
Technical University, Schiesstattgasse 4a
A-8010 Graz, Austria

ABSTRACT

Most universities are still relying for their main
business, i.e. education, on traditional teaching methods
and the use of standard computing services. However,
standard computing services are no longer a sufficient
teaching support for computer science and related fields.
Mainframe, microlabs and other computing services are not
specifically designed to improve the quality and
efficiency of university teaching, something which is
particularly needed in high-demand fields such as computer
science. Rather, they are designed for research use or as
isolated tools for homework execution. What is needed, is
an efficient mechanism to integrate computer technology
into the university curriculum that is universally
accessible.

1. INTRODUCTION

The word CLEAR (Computer LEArning Resources) stands more for an
educational approach, than a center, a system, a lab or an equipment
configuration. It stands for an approach which should try to make
things clear and thus easier and faster to understand, a way to
compact and transfer knowledge effectively. The philosophy of CLEAR
is systematically to incorporate educational ideals and high-
quality teaching and presentation standards into the university
curriculum. Since, however, this is not meant to be a paper on
educational philosophy, we provide the fundamental strategies and
necessary technical information for the establishment of such much-
needed computer learning resources. Based on experimental results,
especially in high-demand technical areas, eg. computer science, we
outline strategies and provide equipment configurations for such
centers. CLEAR, however, is not meant only to serve computer
science needs. It is an interdisciplinary approach which allows
university environments a cost-effective computer network for
teaching the university community, industry, and off-campus users in
general.

1.1. Computer Science and Its Changing Role

Computer Science began as a discipline about 30 years ago. It
established itself as a science by first developing within itself
and then by reaching out into many application areas (animation,
robotics, graphics, simulation and others [4]).. Computer science

will continue to play a major role in a wide variety of application
areas and, as a result, a uniquely diverse educational role within
universities. Universities need, therefore, seriously to   examine
the consequences of this changing nature, by looking into its effect
on the methods of computer science education.

Computer science is full of instances where the use of computers can
help in the teaching process by improving the presentation of
material, especially material which involves dynamic aspects of
computation, (e.g., how an algorithm develops, or how a graph
changes with the computation). There are many known ways in which
the computer can assist in the teaching of computer science [12],
amongst them, computer aided instruction (CAI). Due to the dramatic
spreading of inexpensive yet powerful microcomputers, the interest
in using CAI has recently surged on many levels world-wide. It is
our belief that the time is ripe for CAI to play a stronger role in
university-level computer science teaching, if a pragmatic and cost
effective method is chosen. One such method, CLEAR (for Computer
LEArning Resource centers), is described in this paper.

1.2. A First Look at Computer Aided Instruction (CAI)

Although CAI is almost 25 years old, it has not yet achieved wide
recognition among the university (and especially the computer
science) community, as an effective tool of instruction. Until very
recently, one main reason for this was the poor price/performance
ratio of hardware and software. However, both the performance and
the performance/price ratio have dramatically increased and new
interest in CAI has arisen as a presentation tool, as an intelligent
tutor, as driver of other media (e.g. optical discs), as a
simulation tool, as intelligent software explanation tool, and so
on.

Major universities such as MIT (project ATHENA) and Carnegie Mellon
University (ANDREW project) have invested millions of dollars in
the development of sophisticated university-wide networks, one of
whose purposes is to involve faculty and students in the generation
of courseware and computer tools using time-sharing and advanced
personal computing. In contrast to CMU's or MIT's huge
undertakings, which involve high-power workstations with fast
communication networks, we propose the establishment of modest
Computer LEArning Resource (CLEAR) centers which are feasible in
cost for any college or university, because they are easy to set up,
efficient, cost effective and allow access to users inside and
outside the university. This is done using fairly slow
communication networks such as switched telephone lines.

The creation of a database of computer science lessons was started
by COSTOC, a major international project for COmputer Supported
Teaching Of Computer science under the direction of Prof. Maurer,
the second author. The use of COSTOC lessons relies on a database
which is accessed by intelligent terminals (personal computers).
This central database (fileserver) is used for lesson storage and
communication purposes, yet the actual execution of the lessons is
done locally. This is critical for fast response time and for
reducing the burden on the central system. The COSTOC project and
how it works for computer science is briefly described in a later
section and in detail in [15]. In this paper, we give design
strategies for universities on how to set up such resource centers
and we describe why they are important to computer science
education. We also report on pilot efforts in US and European

universities and outline the benefits.

2. CAI and Applications in Computer Science Education

2.1. Computers and Instruction

One broad classification of how computers can be used in the instructional process can be made by considering the computer in the following ways:

    i) as a mere tool,
    ii) as an instructional tool for specialized applications, and
    iii) as frontline instructor for general instructional material.

As a "mere tool", computers can be used for presentation purposes (in place of other devices such as slide projectors or blackboards), thus allowing high-quality support of oral presentations (for example, by means of dynamically changing graphics). Computers can be used as a working tool (for example, as a calculator or word processor); as an examination tool (for example, grading and compiling statistics), and as a management tool (administration, counselling, testing, etc.) (for more details see [9]).

Computers can also be used for specialized instructional applications. For example, as an "instructional tool" for simulation purposes (be it for simulated physics experiments or for pilot training); for educational games (such as teaching arithmetic, management games, etc.); for self-explanation (particularly of software and hardware) and for providing automatic assistance when working through software packages.

Finally, and as a central point of this paper, computers can be used directly for "front-line instruction," that is, as addition, extension, or partial replacement of other modes of teaching. In this context, applications range from using the computer for "presentation-type CAI" (i.e., resembling a classroom lecture but being self-paced, supported by new presentational possibilities and laced with some question-answer dialogues), to using the computer in conjunction with and as driver of other media (such as CD ROMS [19] or optical discs), or even as an intelligent tutor (potentially allowing natural language intercourse with the system, and based on some expert system relating to the instructional material at hand).

In order to understand the role of each of these possibilities for realistic help with university-level computer science teaching for "today and tomorrow" (for the next five to ten years), let us first look at the history and developments of CAI in the following section.

2.2. History and Development of CAI

The early CAI systems such as PLATO, were developed in the sixties at the University of Illinois at Urbana. They consisted of a large central computer which was accessed by a large number of (dumb) terminals. All educational material would reside inside and be executed in the central computer, while no processing would take place in the terminals. The material presented usually consisted of portions of information (frames). The student would control when new frames would be shown, while the general flow of the material (which frames to be shown, which to be skipped,...) would be partially controlled by the student, and partially be based on decisions of the lesson author who took into account the student's answers to test questions presented by the system.

The earlier CAI systems of this type were successful in some
situations but had too many weak points really to achieve a big
breakthrough. Some of the critically weak points were:
(1) The quality of presentation was usually restricted to monochrome
    text and static displays.
(2) The question-answer dialogue was quite rudimentary (e.g.
    multiple-choice only).
(3) An expensive central computer was required to serve any
    reasonable number of terminals, causing hardware costs in the
    $10,000 range per student station.
4) Due to the cost and effort necessary to create and maintain
    high-quality lesson material, insufficient lesson material was
    available to justify the installation cost except in isolated
    circumstances.
(5) The operation of a CAI lab (scheduling of students, maintenance
    of software, etc.) would usually consume much of the time saved
    in the instructional process, (i.e., time saved by shifting some
    of the instruction from the class to the CAI lab).

As late as 1980, both in the US and Europe, many early proponents of
CAI, understandably disillusioned, claimed that there was no
economic justification for CAI possible and that the only
justification would have to come from the quality of instruction
produced, a quality not always impressive in the early stages of
CAI. We show in this paper that the above assessment does not hold
true anymore. While only good CAI makes sense, it is also true that
CAI has become an economically feasible reality, if effectively
incorporated with approaches like CLEAR's.

The first attempts to improve CAI concentrated on the incorporation
of better graphic facilities. Some examples were newer display
technology, the incorporation of other types of devices (such as
slide projectors, better question-answer dialogue) and the ability
to perform simulation by on-line experimentation. While all of
these opened new niches for CAI, they did not suffice for a
breakthrough in its becoming widely acceptable.

It is the advent of powerful workstations and sophisticated, yet
moderately priced PC's that changes the picture. As we will argue,
the number of situations where CAI makes sense in one form or
another is steadily increasing. As a matter of fact, few
universities will afford not to use CAI in the foreseeable future,
when a large volume of high-quality courseware (lessons) is
available for a broad spectrum of microcomputers, the latter
becoming omnipresent both on and off campus. ([8]).

"Modern" CAI comes in many varieties, the suitability of each
depending on the application. A loose classification in four
groups is useful:

(a) MODERN PRESENTATION TYPE CAI: This kind of CAI is a derivative
    of earlier PLATO-type instruction. Information is presented in
    small chunks and requires both text and colour graphics as well
    as dynamic changes and animation. The "navigation" through the
    lesson is controlled by the student. A flexible question-
    answer dialogue is provided mainly for self-test purposes and
    interactive simulation of simple situations is available where
    explanation alone does not suffice. Each lesson is supported by
    some written documentation to be used in parallel when working
    through the electronic version of the material.

(b) SIMULATION AND SOFTWARE-EXPLANATION-TYPE CAI LESSONS: Learning
by experiment, learning by game playing, and learning about
certain software packages interleaved with the actual usage of
the software packages at issue provides powerful help for the
educational process where applicable.

(c) INTELLIGENT TUTOR SYSTEMS: CAI systems of this type are the most
ambitious ones. They attempt to provide instruction in a
question-explanation dialogue where the student is the one
mainly asking the questions, the system trying to approach the
quality of human, individualized instruction. Such systems
ideally require a knowledge base and a natural language
interface. Of course such systems also come in a wide variety,
from simple ones still running on standard PC's (e.g. written in
Prolog and allowing only a limited domain and syntax of
questions), to systems approaching the state of the art in both
artificial intelligence and computer graphics, requiring high-
speed processors and high resolution colour monitors.

(d) MEDIA-BASED SYSTEMS: Even the most powerful workstations
available today allow neither full-colour animation approaching
TV-movie, nor audio-output of hi-fi quality. Hence, the
combination of CAI and new media such as optical disks, allowing
the random access presentation of movie clips and high-quality
audio, is rather tempting. Some of the problems involved in its
usage (see section 2.3) may be partially overcome by the
emerging storage technology of CD ROM, see e.g. [19].

The above (a-d) is a crude classification and many systems will be
combinations thereof. Typically, modern presentation type CAI
systems will include some facilities for both simulation and other
media, a "super" CAI system may well combine an intelligent tutor
with other media, and so on.

While early CAI systems had the tendency to be central computers
with many dumb terminals, today's approaches are often directed
towards stand alone microcomputers. We feel strongly that this is
not desirable. Rather, CAI systems should include a network
component for communication and feedback purposes and to provide a
central lesson database. Furthermore, the execution of the lessons
should be decentralized in a PC or workstation for efficiency and
privacy reasons. In the next section, we will briefly examine the
usefulness of the four types of CAI mentioned for university
environments. In Chapter 3 we give specific recommendations and
guidelines for the establishment of Computer LEArning Resource
Centers (CLEAR).

2.3. Front-Line CAI at College and University Level

The choice of CAI material to support teaching at college or
university level should not be clouded by ideologies. CAI is not
meant to replace ordinary classroom teaching, but to support, extend
and replace it to a limited degree, as explained in [15]; nor is CAI
material particularly good if it runs only on very fancy machinery,
nor bad if it can be used on fairly inexpensive equipment, nor
conversely, either. Rather, the choice of CAI material should be a
pragmatic decision, based on what high-quality educational material
can be made available at a reasonable cost. The time has arrived
that any university not starting to provide electronic teaching
support in the future will be as second-rate as a university not
providing a good library or not providing access to some of the

major network-services.

Intelligent tutor-type CAI requires fairly powerful workstations and
sophisticated lesson material. This fact makes its use, for large
groups of students, a non-justifiable proposition based on the
quality of teaching alone. It takes us to the problem of early CAI
days. On the other hand, media-based CAI systems are less
expensive, as far as student stations are concerned, since prices of
about $2,500 per PC-optical-disk combination are not inconveivable
anymore. However, the production costs of the video disks remain
high and the problem of how to update the material easily is hard to
solve. It is therefore reasonable to assume that media-based CAI
has to first establish itself in true mass markets (e.g. driving
schools, high school subjects) before availability of much
university material can be expected. Concerning computer science
teaching, presentation-type CAI is also becoming additionally
attractive because of COSTOC [15], a project whose aim is the
creation of hundreds of high quality CAI lessons in computer
science, the first one hundred available by end of 1986.

An important aspect of presentation-type CAI is that lessons can be
collected in a central database and downloaded into widely
distributed PC's using a network, such as switched telephone lines,
which works at low (e.g., 1200 baud) speed. The availability of a
central lesson database and the accessing of lessons from this
database is a critical attribute of the CAI system chosen, if
lessons are to be periodically serviced for error correction, and
continuously improved or updated. Thus, it is this downloading
aspect that allows the setting up of inexpensive yet powerful
Computer Learning Resource Centers, as described in the next
chapter.

3. COMPUTER LEARNING RESOURCE (CLEAR) CENTERS

3.1. Main Features of CLEAR Centers

CLEAR centers should provide a cost effective way to set up a
database of lessons and information in general for the use by
university administration, staff, students, companies, and
organizations cooperating with the university, and the public in
general. We have identified the following desirable features for
CLEAR centers:

(1) The software to run a CLEAR center should be compatible on a
    variety of machines and executed on equipment also used for
    other purposes. The decision to acquire a dedicated central
    computer for the CLEAR center can thus be postponed until a
    certain volume of activity is reached, so that CLEAR centers can
    be easily upgraded.

(2) Access to the CLEAR center should be possible through existing
    LAN's and a switched telephone network. Services are provided
    in such a manner so that communication speeds of as low as 1200
    baud are still tolerable.

(3) A CLEAR center should provide general information and tools
    supporting teaching process, e.g., self tests for students,
    counselling of students, and most important, a large library of
    high quality lessons accessible by authorized users on and off
    campus.

(4) A CLEAR center should provide tools for lesson maintenance and

distribution as well as a communication component for permitting feedback on lesson quality, allowing students to ask questions, answering electronically, etc.

CLEAR centers with the above criteria can (see section 3.2) have a broad spectrum of applicability. In sections 3.3 and 4, we show how to set up CLEAR at a fairly low cost, e.g. using a prototype system developed at Maurer's Institution in Austria.

3.2. Applications and Benefits of CLEAR Centers

In this section we list some of the applications and benefits of CLEAR centers and provide relevant instances. The library of courses which CLEAR centers provide can be used in a number of instructional applications [15]:

1) For support of regular curriculum courses for both full-time students (using the courses on campus) and part-time students potentially working through some courses on their PC at home or in their office after having loaded the course into their PC via a telephone line;

2) For exam preparation: (e.g. Ph.D. qualifying exams) CLEAR can provide an assortment of previous exam questions and their solutions, or drill and practice for a language exam;

3) To allow students a "sneak preview" of courses: both as a student counselling tool and as a "marketing tool," CLEAR can advertise courses to students, including potential part-time students employed by local industry;

4) For self-testing of re-entering students and self-evaluation purposes;

5) To provide remedial material for students entering the university, or entering from other disciplines; this is especially applicable for independent study or self-paced type of courses: CLEAR can provide a guided mode of study which, due to its interactive mode, disciplines and motivates the student.

6) To provide continuing education material for users outside the university or students from other disciplines; (mechanisms of distribution or courseware and evaluation will be provided in a later paper);

7) Curriculum description: To inform staff on what material is covered in what class, for better coordination;

8) To allow students and staff to learn about a subject, much like working through a book but in a more palatable form (e.g. retrain mathematics faculty in order to teach undergraduate computer science courses);

9) To provide a high standard of teaching due to the fact that the courses from, e.g. the COSTOC project [15], are authored by recognized scientists; thus, university teachers who are not particularly expert in some areas will be able to teach classes more effectively with the support of the courses;

10) Computer science is becoming more and more divided into different "scopes" for different areas. There is computer science for computer scientists, computer science for engineers,

computer science for business majors, computer science for
operations research, computer science for computer engineers,
computer science for education specialists, computer science
for professionals, even computer science for musicians and the
humanities. Computer science departments need help in carrying
out their multidisciplinary role, i.e., providing high quality
courses to other departments and groups within the university.
A CLEAR center will provide not only a library of lessons and
tutorials, but also self-examination mechanisms which respond to
the different educational goals of computer science.

11) An issue with most computer science departments is how to reduce
the teaching load. This can be partly achieved by the shifting
of some of the teaching for any given course to CLEAR's CAI.
This also allows one to cover more material with the same load
per staff;

12) To provide "electronic colloquia" lessons on topics of current
interest;

13) As a general information tool, CLEAR provides ways for the
university to inform local industry in a time-independent yet
easily updatable form about what kind of courses and what kind
of research projects are going on (e.g. by providing lessons or
fragments of lessons on CLEAR). Conversely, industry can use
this method to alert the university as to industrial activities
and needs (again, by supplying a lesson or other information
material into the CLEAR center).

14) The use of a CLEAR center is not restricted to providing a
large lesson database accessible on and off campus (although
this is one of the major roles), but also provides other
informational, communicational transactional facilities. These
may typically include:
   (a) textual and graphic orientation concerning a department's
   research interests, requirement for degrees, course
   descriptions, etc.;
   (b) university information in general, on admission, on
   registration, on interdisciplinary programs, on financial
   support, and so on (some of this data may also be
   retrievable on special public terminals located on key
   points on, or even off campus).
   (c) CLEAR as a "window" to university for outside users might
   well be implemented by providing a mixture of "ordinary
   information" (such as that offered by videotex networks
   [2],[14]) for the superficial user, and of "lesson type
   information" for the seriously interested one.
   (d) Finally, CLEAR, like any other distributed electronic
   information system, can allow the user access to a
   tremendous variety of other services (e.g. automatic
   mailing, in printed form, or an invitation to everyone in a
   certain address file; we will return to this in section 4
   when reporting on some specific experiments).

3.2.1. CLEAR and Lesson Creation

One example of how lesson creation could be integrated into the
usual university activities to advantage is the following: Certain
Masters Theses projects would have a more lasting effect on a
department's history and evolution (instead of the usual trash can
route), if they included some tutorial material which can be used
in courses or as aid to other projects. It is after all true that

the best proof for someone's grasp of notions comes about when she/he has to teach it. More emphasis should be given to producing computer science graduates who are not simply experienced in using computer science tools, but in explaining them as well and being able to teach it, produce course notes or simply to relate it to non-computer scientists. A recent emphasis on technical writing training can be partially solved by this method.

3.2.2. CLEAR as a Seminar Library

A university's image depends not only on the quality of research and teaching it accomplishes, but also on things like the visiting speakers it attracts and the seminars it conducts. A great deal of time and money are often invested into this activity. A CLEAR center could serve as a "seminar library" for storing certain key colloquia talks by distinguished speakers prepared as a special assignment or for extra credit by students. The speaker would provide his/her notes and graphics and would then obtain a copy of the CAI lesson prepared from his/her talk, possibly as a form of "payment" or honor.

3.3. Criteria for the Implementation of CLEAR Centers

Computer networks, as they are now installed in most universities, are accessible by terminals from on- and off-campus, and can thus be used as rudimentary CLEAR centers. However, to function properly and effectively, the following general criteria need to be met:

1) A large database of lessons and of some general information must be provided on a computer of the network. Lessons and information material need to contain dynamic and animated colour graphics of reasonable quality, say at least 320 x 200 pixel resolution with 16 colours.
2) Lessons are downloaded from the database but executed locally (i.e., in the user's PC) for efficiency (to free the network from the task) and for privacy reasons, to assure that "Big Brother" cannot watch while a lesson is studied. [16]. This implies that terminals must be "intelligent," or PC's with a reasonable colour graphic capability.
3) The system must provide some messaging facilities to allow an electronic dialogue, at least one concerning the lesson material.
4) The system must permit the use of slow speed communication lines (such as phone lines with 1200 baud modems). This is certainly important to allow wide access and to permit parallel loading and execution of lessons, thus avoiding unacceptable waiting times.
5) The system must support a large number (say up to 100) serial ports at a reasonable cost (not exceeding $40,000).
6) The retrieval of lessons and of information must be straightforward. One must be able to use the system without knowing the intricacies of any operating system.

Configurations meeting all of the above constraints are not readily available. CAI systems do not usually support parallel loading and execution of lessons and often do not include animatable colour graphics. A price of, say, $400 per port for a large database system is not achievable on most commonly available hardware, and so on. For this reason, a variety of hardware and software components is now being developed and ready for pilot installations which will allow the establishment of even large cost-effective CLEAR centers. We describe the 3 major components of such CAI systems:

3.3.1 The Course Component

The second author has been involved in the development of Autool
([3],[6],[5]), an authoring tool which allows program-free
development of lessons well suited for CLEAR centers. Maurer is
also supervising the creation of a large number of computer-science
courses as part of the COSTOC project [15].

3.3.2. The Course Execution Component

An inexpensive yet powerful colour graphic micro called MUPID ([11],
[13]) has been developed at IIG, under Maurer's direction.   MUPID
is well-suited for Autool-lesson execution. Since MUPID conforms
to all major videotex standards (the European standards Prestel,
Teletel, CEPT and the North American standard NAPLPS), it is also
particularly well-suited as a graphic information retrieval station.
In its basic model it comes without an external storage unit: such
a unit is not necessary within the CLEAR concept (since lessons are
downloaded). Rather than using MUPID itself as one's terminal,
using the MUPID-board is a powerful alternative, but unnecessarily
expensive for dedicated CAI stations.

Of course, neither a MUPID or a MUPID-board is necessary
equipment for either the CAI system described or for the CLEAR
center software we will describe below. Any PC compatible with an
enhanced graphic will do as well, and the adoption of the software
to other colour graphic micros is in progress. Thus, MUPID is just
one attractive alternative for dedicated CAI labs.

3.3.3. The Hardware and Software Component

In addition to the CAI lessons and the terminals, CLEAR requires
hardware and software for running its database computer, which
includes network access. The second author has been involved in
the development of a software package called CONNEX which is now
available to universities for pilot installations in a preliminary
version. CONNEX supports all the functions of a CLEAR center
mentioned in section 3.2, i.e. handling of a lesson database, of
information material, of simple communication, and of transaction.
CONNEX is written in C and easily installed on any system
supporting C in a multi-task environment. It has been ported to a
number of installations successfully (sec.4).

The CONNEX system offers the following key advantage to CLEAR
centers: Once the average CONNEX user retrieves one lesson, he does
not bother the network and database computer anymore. This places
an atypically small workload on the main processor of the database
computer. Basically, the database computer acts just as a simple
minded fileserver. It is for this reason that hardware
configurations cannot often support as many users as they could,
since they lack the necessary I/O processing capacity. Hence,
for CLEAR centers, used for CAI purposes predominantly, a dedicated
database computer with just a large hard-disk and many serial
ports with a separate processor for each group, will prove a more
cost effective solution than using multi-purpose mainframes.
However, for an initial period and until the viability of the CLEAR
approach is established, a non-dedicated solution might often be
preferable.

3.4. Setting up the CAI Lab in a CLEAR Center

Let us now elaborate on one approach of intergrating CAI within CLEAR centers. The strategy is to develop the CAI resources in a step-wise and cautious manner so that expansion of the center occurs as the usage of the system increases.

To begin with, since every author of the COSTOC project automatically obtains [15] one complete CAI station (MUPID-based), this can be the first step towards a CAI lab. Adding 3 MUPIDS (including colour monitors, all necessary software and 20 lessons of CAI material for $8,000-$10,000) gives already a small lab of four stations, which is sufficient for servicing two classes with about 40 students each. This stand-alone solution (some three lessons available in battery-buffered memory at any point in time) is quite nice for student use since it provides a certain discipline as to the date by which material has to be worked through by students.

An alternative is to hook the four stations to a PC (using the so called Vertex-package) and using the hard-disk of the PC for storage of the lesson database. (A ten M byte hard-disk will hold almost 200 lessons. Instead of an ordinary PC, a model AT PC compatible can be used to support 8 student stations simultaneously. It is important to provide a mechanism for lesson-use evaluation and improvement. MUPID stations, for example, can be equipped with a "monitor program" which records all the key presses of a student and their timing anonymously.

Once the CAI lab has grown beyond 4 or 8 stations, it is time to start a CLEAR center based on the CONNEX software. This software, together with a comprehensive demo database can be made available to universities interested in cooperation with IIG and in COSTOC courseware. The CONNEX software can be installed on most comon mainframes and under most common operating systems (see section 4 for examples). It allows access to its lesson database by both MUPID-type stations and by using any PC with a suitable colour-graphic card. At the time of writing, only ega (the enhanced graphic adaptor for the IBM PC compatibles) is supported, but other variations are in preparation. Such a CONNEX-based CLEAR system can be expanded as much as desired and the capacity of serial ports on the database computer permits. For large CAI labs the use of dedicated database computers is, however, recommended. In such an environment, CONNEX completely hides the operating system, thus providing ease of use and high effectiveness.

To give an idea of the costs involved, we provide the following upper bound estimates: A database computer with a 70 M byte hard-disk, sufficient for more than 1000 lessons, a streamer-tape and 48 fully equipped serial ports, has been installed at IIG, Austria, for less than $20,000. Thus, a substantial CAI lab with about 50 student stations can be installed (including hardware, software, and a reasonable number of lessons) for much below $100,000.

Such a CLEAR lab is capable of supporting 25 three-hour per week classes and simultaneously resulting in a saving of 10-20 instructor hours. We feel, therefore, that our earlier statement that CAI has crossed the threshold of now being economically . feasible, is, indeed, justified.

4. REPORT ON SOME EXPERIMENTS

CAI lessons of the type already described (i.e. Autool lessons) are currently being used in two network modes. (a) within nationwide networks based on the videotex idea (see [13]) and (b) within CAI labs and CLEAR centers at a number of pilot universities. Since we have reported on (a) elsewhere ([13],[15]) and the focus of this paper is on CLEAR centers, we will concentrate on aspect (b), Our experience with (a) has been within the Austrian videotex system where some 500 lessons are currently available nationwide (at a cost of about 25 US cents per lesson retrieved) to about 5,000 users. This, combined with the preparation of hundreds of computer science courses within the COSTOC project, is probably one of the most massive CAI efforts ever, giving further justification for our belief that the time has come for CAI labs and CLEAR centers.

The status of CAI labs and CLEAR centers as of October 1986 is this:

- Two major CLEAR centers have been installed at the Technical University of Graz. One of them is based on a dedicated database computer running under OS9 (a UNIX-variant) on the little-known BEL computer; it supports a student lab (currently with 20 stations, to be upgraded step-wise to 80). The second CONNEX system at Graz is running on VAX for general university use. (Indeed it is the second CONNEX system which is also going to be used for administrative jobs like electronic input of letters to be printed and distributed to all people on some address file, registration of students for classes, etc.)

- Lesson material has been used successfully in connection with a second-year class on "Data Structures" in which some material was covered only in class, some only in lessons, some both in class and in lessons: over 80% of all students liked this kind of teaching, only 6% disliked it.

- The first large CONNEX system was installed in Karlsruhe in early 1986 with some 15 terminals; it was used very successfully, for example, in a 250 student class by offering almost 50% of the material taught in the form of CAI lessons (see [18]). This CONNEX system is running on a HP-computer.

- Another CONNEX system (installed on one of the VAX's of the university's computer network) is available at the Univ. of Denver, with about 15 terminals on campus. The lessons, as in Graz, are accessible by phone lines from outside locations; it has been used with good results. (The evaluation questionnaire is in the appendix).

- Smaller CAI labs (hopefully to expand into full-fledged CLEAR centers later) have also been installed at the University of Texas at Dallas and the University of Vienna, Austria.

- A number of further CAI labs and CLEAR centers are in the planning stage in a number of countries.

Based on the positive experiences mentioned above and on the steady increase of high-quality lesson material, we are confident that our approach to CLEAR centers is indeed a reasonable and pragmatic one: for moderate investments, CLEAR centers can achieve a major contribution to the role of universities.

APPENDIX

Evaluation of questionnaire concerning the CAI-Lab for Data
Structures and algorithms, Denver, June 1986:

1. My overall opinion of the CAI-lessons used is:
        I liked them a lot: 22   I liked them: 7
        They were acceptable: 1   I did not like them: 0
2. The CAI-lessons were a valuable support of classroom teaching:
        Positively yes: 20   Probably yes: 9
        Probably no: 0   Positively no: 1
3. I wish that CAI lessons would be available for many more
    courses:
        Very much so: 16   Yes: 14 No: 0
        Don't know: 1
4. CAI lessons can be used to a limited degree (as was done in the
    case of quicksort and heapsort) actually to replace classroom
    teaching:
        Yes: 26   No: 5
5. The written documentation provided for the lessons was:
        Useful: 21   Not necessary: 6
6. The questions in the lessons were (you may check more than
    one box):
        Useful: 20   Too easy: 10
        A nuisance: 1   Too difficult: 0
7. The pace of the lessons is:
        Good: 26   Too fast: 0
                                    Too slow: 5
8. The quality of the lessons is:
        Good: 27   Acceptable: 3
        Bad: 0
9. Indicate the quality of the lesson by giving a grade A, B, C,
    D, or F. (A=excellent, F=miserable quality, don't use
    again):
        Quick: 22 A; 7 B
        Heap : 20 A: 9 B
        Merge: 13 A; 6 B; 1 C
        Radix: 13 A; 5 B; 1 C
10. Indicate which of the lessons you have seen and how often:
        Mandatory lessons: quick: 1x0, 17x1, 7x2, 3x3 times
                                heap: 1x0, 16x1, 9x2, 3x3 times
        Optional lessons: merge: 11x0, 15x1, 2x2, 2x3 times
                                radix: 11x0, 14x1, 2x2, 1x3 times

All 31 students in the class filled out the above questionnaire.
Three lessons (Quick, Heap1, Heap2) were mandatory, i.e., covered
material not covered in class. The other lessons just supported
material covered in class.

REFERENCES

[1] H. Cheng, P. Lipp, H. Maurer: GASC -a Low-Cost, No-Nonsense
    Graphic and Software Communication System; Electronic Publishing
    Review 5(1985) 141-155.
[2] J. Gecsei: The Architecture of Videotax Systems; Prentice Hall,
    Englewood Cliffs, N.H. (1983).
[3] J. Garrat, F. Huber, H. Huemer: Autool - a new authoring system;
    Report 219, IIG Graz (1986).
[4] J.E. Hopcroft: The Impact of Robotics on Computer Science; Comm.
.   ACM 29 (1986), 486-498.

[5] F. Huber: Autool - An Authoring System for Videotex; Proc. of Conference on Teleteaching '86, Budapest, North-Holland Publishing Co., Amsterdam (1987,).

[6] D. Kaiser, H. Maurer: Autool-A New System for Computer Aided Instruction; Report 218, IIG Graz (1986).

[7] G. Kearsley: Authoring Systems in Computer Based Education; Comm. of the ACM 25 (1982), 429-437.

[8] F. Makedon: Personal Computers in Higher Education; Report prepared for the Austrian Federal Ministry of Science and Research (1985).

[9] J.W. Marlin, J.F. Niss: Microcomputer Management of Instruction - the Advanced Learning System; Microprocessing and Microprogramming 11 (1983), 117-126.

[10] H.A. Maurer: New Developments in Videotex and Their Implications for Computer Aided Instruction; Information Services and Use 3 (1983), 319-324.

[11] H.A. Maurer: The Austrian Approach to Videotex; Proc. of the 7th European Meeting on Cybernetics and System Research, North-Holland Publishing Company, Amsterdam (1984).

[12] H.A. Maurer: Authoring System for Computer Assisted Instruction; Proceed. of the ACM National Conference 1985, Denver, (1985), 551-561.

[13] H.A. Maurer: Nationwide Teaching Through a Network of Microcomputers; Proc. of IFIP World Congress '86, Dublin, North-Holland Publ. Comp., Amsterdam (1986), 429-432.

[14] H. Maurer: The Austrian Approach to Videotex; Proc. 7th European Meeting on Cybernetics and Systems Research, North-Holland Publ. Co., Amsterdam (1984), 589-592.

[15] H. Maurer, F. Makedon: COSTOC -Computer Supported Teaching of Computer Science; Proc. of Conference on Teleteaching '86, Budapest, North Holland Publishing Company, Amsterdam (1987;).

[16] H. Maurer, N. Rozsenich, I. Sebestyen: Videotex without Big Brother; Electronic Publishing Review 4 (1984), 201-214.

[17] J. Nievergelt: A Pragmatic Introduction to Courseware Design: Computer 13 (1980), 7-21.

[18] Th. Ottman: Can Teaching by Computers Replace Teaching by Professors? Proc. of Conference on Teleteaching '86, Budapest, North-Holland Publishing Co., Amsterdam (1987).

[19] P. Sammer: CD ROM as Storage Medium for Computer Aided Instruction; Proc. of Conference on Teleteaching '86, Budapest, North-Holland Publ. Co., Amsterdam (1987;).

Remote Education and Informatics: Teleteaching
F. Lovis (Editor)
Elsevier Science Publishers B.V. (North-Holland)
© IFIP, 1988

COSTOC: COMPUTER SUPPORTED TEACHING OF COMPUTER SCIENCE

Hermann MAURER
Institutes for Information Processing (IIG)
Technical University,
Schiesstattgasse 4a, A-8010 Graz, Austria

Fillia MAKEDON
Computer Science Program
The University of Texas at Dallas
Richardson, Texas 75083-0688 USA

The need for quality education in computer science is
becoming critical world-wide. This can be attributed to
three major causes: (i) computer usage is continuing to
grow in a multitude of diverse areas that affect everyday
life, (ii) not enough of the quality graduates that are
turned out remain in a teaching environment, despite the
explosive growth of university programs in computer
science, and (iii) the evolution of computer science as a
field is too fast-paced to be met by orthodox education
techniques; it is estimated that the "half-decay rate" of
the computer science knowledge is about 6 years. It seems
clear, therefore, that an "education crisis" exists which
can only be mastered with the very devices that have caused
it: computers. In fact, computer aided instruction (CAI)-
after almost three decades of unfulfilled promises- is
starting to turn into a realistic hope for supporting
computer science education.

A major international project in this direction is COSTOC,
for COmputer Supported Teaching Of Computer science. Its
aim is eventually to produce some 2,000 CAI high-quality
computer science lessons. This corresponds to about 2,000
contact-hours or 50 computer science monographs. The
lessons are designed to support, not replace, the
university classroom teaching. Coupled with high quality
colour graphic animation and the techniques of
"presentation-type" CAI, COSTOC lessons are particularly
suitable for the graphic illustration of dynamic
computational concepts.

In this paper, we elaborate on the method of COSTOC lesson
creation and integration into a university environment,
particularly one involved in teleteaching. Furthermore, we
explain in detail the reasons for choosing "presentation-
type CAI" (abbreviated PT-CAI) for COSTOC which can be
summarized as follows:
  (a) PT-CAI courses are easy to create and maintain,
  (b) PT-CAI courses can be distributed over simple and
      affordable networks, (c) PT-CAI courses can be
      executed on a wide variety of inexpensive home/
      personal computers and
  (d) PT-CAI affords a pragmatic compromise to books or
      mass-lecture computer science education: by not going
      to the limits of technology, affordable tools are
      obtained which nevertheless provide a significant
      improvement in education.

The present paper also describes COSTOC's potentials and
contributions to university education and its sound
approach to incorporating technology into education.   We
conclude the paper with some results from the first
university COSTOC experiments.

1. INTRODUCTION

The importance of computer science and related areas for the
economy and for society on the whole still keeps increasing.   At
the same time, the pertinent body of knowledge also continues to
increase dramatically (doubling in less than ten years).   Put
together, this makes the teaching of computer science a task of
alarming proportions at all levels.

In this paper, we are mainly concerned with teaching computer
science at the college or university level. (Problems of at least
similar proportions can also be noted in high school or pre-high
school situations).   In this context, we have identified the
following main problem areas:

(1)   How can one assure that sufficiently many professors are
      qualified and available to teach up-to-date university
      courses?
(2)   How can one assure that the professors themselves will be
      able to acquire new knowledge throughout their career?
(3)   How can one assure that students will be able to continue to
      learn throughout their professional life, after they have
      left the university environment?

It is our belief that traditional teaching techniques do not
suffice to solve any of the above problems.   Rather, a number of
new initiatives are necessary, one of which is the use of
computers as a teaching tool, coupled with the use of computer
assisted instruction (CAI).   CAI comes in many varieties (as will
be discussed later), one of them being presentation-type CAI
(abbreviated PT-CAI).   COSTOC (for COmputer Supported Teaching Of
Computer science) is an effort to develop quality PT-CAI by the
second half of the 1980's and early 1990's.   We discuss in this
paper how the COSTOC project answers the questions posed in the
previous praragraph.   We also explain why the COSTOC project has
chosen PT-CAI, thus providing efficient support to computer
science teaching now, rather than somewhere in the future.

2. THE COSTOC PROJECT

2.1. Aim

The aim of the COSTOC (Computer Supported Teaching of Computer
science) project is to create a body of knowledge on computer
science in the form of hundreds of CAI "lessons," each lesson
corresponding roughly to one hour of university level teaching.
COSTOC lessons can be worked through using a variety of fairly
inexpensive colour-graphic microcomputers.   These microcomputers
should be, ideally, networked to a database of lessons so that
lesson distribution is easy and feedback from the user to the
lesson administrator is possible.

2.2. A Database of Lessons

Typically, a university's lesson database can be installed on a

fairly simple-minded "fileserver", a central computer with a
sufficiently large hard disk which supports dozens or even
hundreds of serial ports of medium speed. This lesson database is
accessible by communication lines (as slow as the telephone, say
1200/ 1200 baud) by users from within and from outside the
university and provides support and partial replacement of
university lectures. It is important to understand that despite
the fact that the lessons are loaded into the memory of a
microcomputer from a central database, they are executed locally
in the user's PC. This philosophy is quite different from the
"big main frame and many dumb user terminals" philosophy or from
the "stand-alone micro" philosophy, both of which have been
adopted (with limited success) in many other CAI systems. Indeed,
the notion of PC's networked as described, should be one of the
essential corner-stones in setting up large, versatile, powerful,
yet inexpensive CAI environments. We refer to paper [8] for more
details.

COSTOC lessons are quality-controlled lessons in that they are
authored and authorized by outstanding professionals, specialists
in the area (see Section 6). The principle used in their creation
is that certain aspects of most subjects are much easier to
explain using the facilities in a COSTOC lesson (see Section 3 and
Section 5) than by teaching in an "overhead projector mode" and
conversely. Hence, shifting part of the teaching, wherever
suitable, to COSTOC lessons and applying usual classroom teaching
techniques elsewhere, makes a great deal of sense. The quality of
teaching can be improved, the load on the teacher reduced, and
more time for classroom discussions will become available, since
appropriate rudimentary or tedious explanations have been
delegated to COSTOC lessons. As a result, a department can form
its own database of easily digestible information, "an electronic
library", available to students, faculty, staff, and continuing
education users.

2.3. Computer Learning Resource Centers and COSTOC

A database of such CAI lessons, together with effective mechanisms
of integration into the university curriculum, is called CLEAR
(for Computer LEArning Resource) center. CLEAR, together with
COSTOC, is the model of a university resource center designed to
help with computer science teaching problems and extensions to
teaching problems in other areas, (see ref. [8] for CLEAR).

2.4. How a COSTOC Database of Lessons Can Be Useful: A First Glimpse

With hundreds of colleges and universities understaffed in
computer science, a database of COSTOC lessons can ease the job of
teaching courses even by professors not in that particular
speciality. By COSTOC, a certain level of quality of instruction
is assured. For example, a student not satisfied with the quality
of a particular course might choose also to consult a sequence of
COSTOC lessons on that topic.

The existence of a database of courses also eases the problem of
continuing education, both for university teachers and for people
outside universities (for example, personnel from industry,
high school teachers, etc.). Concerning university teachers, a
COSTOC database helps in two ways: first, material available this

way is usually easier to digest than reading a book. Secondly,
the availability of high quality presentation material to students
more or less forces the university teacher also to know about it.
Concerning professionals outside the university, a database of
courses is a valuable way of backing up the knowledge they obtain
otherwise; for example, by allowing them to go over some material
presented in a class they have missed, due to pressing professional
reasons.

3. WHAT COSTOC LESSONS LOOK LIKE

From the user's point of view, a COSTOC lesson consists of 40 to
60 small logical units called frames, each of which either
contains information in the form of text and colour graphics
(including dynamic changes and animation), or contains questions
to be answered.

The quality of the presentation of information is somewhat
dependent on the user's equipment. The minimum requirements are:
a 320 x 200 pixel resolution in 16 colours, the provision of
special characters as potentially defined by the author of the
lesson, and the availability of animatable colour graphics which
include a number of geometric objects (lines, polygons, circles,
splines,...) and attributes (fill-styles, flashing,...) [4].
Typically, an IBM PC clone with the enhanced graphic card will do.

On the other hand, MUPID, a PC with better graphics facilities
than just described [12], and developed at Maurer's (IIG)
institute in Austria, is probably the lowest cost model of a
COSTOC-PC in German-speaking Europe. In its version C2D-Jumbo, it
is available for about $600 US dollars, and this includes a colour
monitor. Using MUPID, COSTOC lessons can be packaged in a
particularly tight ("compressed") form so that they fit into a
"parcel" of 32 K bytes. This is convenient for data-transmission
and allows, together with the feature "continue reading while
starting to execute lesson", the use of networks with
communication speeds as low as 1200 baud.

A typical COSTOC lesson will appear to the user as follows:
(1) It starts with a welcome frame, followed by a frame containing
    a table of contents (e.g. showing 6-9 chapters). The user
    then selects a starting point. Working through the chapters
    sequentially is usually recommended.
(2) As one works through a chapter, the material (shown
    graphically and with dynamic changes where appropriate) is
    presented in small chunks at a speed entirely up to the user.
(3) It is also possible to return to the table of contents at any
    time to mark the current frame for later reference, to
    continue at any other point in the lesson, or to terminate the
    lesson. The author of the lesson has provided "shortcuts" for
    those who are already advanced. Also, "help frames",
    "question frames" and other material are available for the less
    well-prepared users.

Each lesson is supported with a documentation. Also provided is a
listing of important program segments, formulae, pictures, etc.,
to reduce the need to take notes while working through the lesson.
It is encouraged, however, to jot down some individual remarks as
they arise. In addition, lessons often refer to books for certain
details such as a formal proof of a theorem whose intuitive idea
and examples were presented in the lesson but whose formal proof

was omitted as something one can little improve on by using COSTOC-type CAI.

The presentation of information is sometimes interrupted by questions and "answer frames" which have two purposes. On the one hand, they help to keep the user motivated and develop comprehension skills. On the other hand, they inform the user of how well the material has been "digested" and they recommend looking at additional sections of the lesson where applicable. Altogether, the process of working through a lesson with questions inter-spersed, is expected to be a pleasant process. A number of experiments involving groups of students in Austria, Germany, and USA, as presented in [8], has already shown this.

4. PRESENTATION-TYPE CAI FOR COSTOC

COSTOC lessons as described in Section 3 can be called "presentation-type CAI" to distinguish them from other types of CAI such as:

(a) "SIMULATION-TYPE" CAI where the user learns by experimenting. Examples of this are: drawing functions to learn about parts of calculus, simulating the throwing of objects to learn about the law of gravity, or using an aeroplane simulator as part of pilot training.

(b) "INTERACTIVE SOFTWARE EXPLANATION-TYPE" CAI where a software package is explained and the user is permitted to switch back and forth between explanation and using the package.

(c) "MEDIA SUPPORTED" CAI where the microcomputer is mainly used for a question-answer dialogue and the actual information is presented by, for example, an optical laser disk driven by the microcomputer.

(d) "KNOWLEDGE AND USER MODEL-BASED" CAI where the user works with an expert system which teaches the student using an "approximate intelligence and understanding", such as a human teacher might provide.

COSTOC lessons are "PRESENTATION-TYPE" CAI of modest complexity, requiring medium-scale resolution colour graphics with animation, but not requiring fancy graphic work stations of high resolution and ultra high speed. The choice of "presentation-type" CAI for COSTOC rests on the following facts:

(1) Lessons based only on "SIMULATION-TYPE CAI" are quite expensive to create, difficult to maintain (because they require program maintenance), and apply only to a limited number of subject areas. Segments of simulation can be incorporated into COSTOC lessons in the form of Basic or Pascal programs, but we try to discourage authors from doing so (see below).

(2) "INTERACTIVE SOFTWARE EXPLANATION-TYPE" CAI has certainly its place, but applies, clearly, only to limited areas; it is close to what software vendors do (or should) provide anyway, in addition to user manuals .

(3) "MEDIA SUPPORTED" CAI necessitates extra equipment, for example, laser disks; the production of good material, due to

its cost, requires a large user population having such
equipment. This kind of CAI may soon be viable for certain
forms of mass-education (e.g. in driving schools), but does
not seem to be ready for large scale use in university
environments.

(4)   "KNOWLEDGE – AND USER MODEL BASED" CAI involves massive
effort in the creation of lessons and reasonably
sophisticated equipment to run it. Furthermore, lessons have
a volume which makes them hard to distribute, particularly
over narrow-band communication lines.

(5)   "PRESENTATION-TYPE" CAI, such as COSTOC lessons, are
comparatively easy to create, maintain, and distribute. They
require unsophisticated user stations which are available (or
soon will be) on and off campus in large numbers. Hence,
presentation-type CAI is the pragmatic way to go. For
further details see [8] and [9].

There are a number of further points supporting the choice of
"presentation-type" CAI for COSTOC:

(6)   Most education is either obtained from classroom lectures or
from books. This is not about to change; thus, anything that
can improve the delivery of knowledge beyond lectures and
books and is economically feasible is of value. In Section
5, we explain how COSTOC lessons improve on lectures and
books for certain kinds of instructional material. That
COSTOC CAI is indeed economical, has been shown in [8] and
[9].

(7)   The creation, maintenance, and distribution of COSTOC
courses require an amount of funding which makes the
creation of COSTOC courses feasible for an electronic
publishing company, once at least one hundred universities
willing to participate are found. This may be initially
difficult but certainly a more realistic approach than
finding about 10 times that many universities to participate
in a knowledge-based CAI system which requires equipment 10
times as expensive.

(8)   A main issue and weak spot of CAI which favors COSTOC-type
lessons must not be overlooked. The best system will not
give good lessons unless experts are involved in lesson
creation. It is difficult to get good scientists to write
pedagogically nice books (since it involves a great deal of
time). It will become more difficult to involve faculty in
CAI lesson production the more work that this involves.
Presentation-type CAI, on the other hand, being the simplest
to use, allows the author to delegate much of the CAI
programming work to an assistant. Thus, only with PT-CAI is there
hope for the involvement of a reasonable number of top
scientists in the lesson-production process.

(9)   Although PT-CAI does not represent the top-most technology in
authoring systems, COSTOC lessons go quite a way in providing
advanced graphic capabilities. Thus, PT-CAI seems a
reasonable compromise for university computer science
teaching for the next 5 to 10 years.

Presentation type CAI, the oldest version of CAI around, is often
met with reservation and distrust. What is overlooked here is
that the emergence of inexpensive high quality colour graphics
PC's has changed the situation completely since 25 years ago, when
CAI started. . Not only is the quality of teaching achievable
quite different, but also the cost aspect has changed dramatically
so that it now makes economic sense to apply it wherever possible.
This was not the case even three years ago.

5. WHAT MAKES COSTOC LESSONS BETTER THAN BOOKS OR LECTURES?

To explain the title of this section, let us state a number of
important assumptions first which address the situations where
COSTOC teaching is better:

-   We talk only about good COSTOC lessons (we address the quality
    aspect in Section 6);

-   The notions of "COSTOC friendly" and "COSTOC hostile" were
    coined by the well-known Finnish computer scientist, Arto
    Salomaa :   Not all topics are equally suitable for COSTOC-type
    lessons (nor is every topic one can teach suitable for books:
    there are few people who have learnt how to ride a bike from a
    book!).   Though the aim of COSTOC is to cover most computer
    science areas, it is also intended to emphasize within each area
    the "COSTOC friendly" aspects, leaving the "COSTOC hostile"
    to the accompanying lesson documentation.   Typically, examples
    illustrating an idea or the intuitive description of it or some
    notion or result, are COSTOC friendly; a detailed formal
    description is often not.   Thus, examples and intuitive ideas
    are emphasized in COSTOC lessons.

-   COSTOC lessons cannot compete with small, interactive classes by
    university teachers who are experts in their field, and
    excellent lecturers.   In reality, however, the majority of
    university classes in computer science are not small, nor is the
    majority of university teachers as qualified as described.
    Thus, the title of this section only claims that a significant
    part of computer science knowledge can be taught by COSTOC
    lessons better than is possible in large lecture classes, where
    almost no student-teacher feedback is possible and better than
    from a book.

Let us now return to the issue of why COSTOC lessons can be better
in material presentation than a book or a lecture.   The main
features available to COSTOC and not to the same extent available
to a book are: (a) colour, (b) pointing, (c) dynamic changes, (d)
animation, (e) question/answer dialogue and (f) self-paced lesson
execution.   The main features available to COSTOC and not, to the
same extent, available to a lecture are: dynamic changes,
animation, question/answer dialogue, and individualized pace of
lesson absorption.   In what follows, we discuss the above features
one by one.

The use of colour (a) is clearly more limited in books due to
pricing. It is also limited in blackboard-lectures since writing
and erasing with colour chalk is cumbersome.   An important
feature available to COSTOC and to a lecturer, but not in a book,
is pointing(b).   Suppose a large table of figures is shown and the

correspondence of two pairs of numbers, is to be explained: first
in row 3/ column 4, and row 7/ column 3, then in row 8/ column 3
and row 6/ column 5. The lecturer can do so by just pointing to
the pairs. The COSTOC lesson can do so by highlighting first one
pair of numbers, then the other one. In a book, a lengthy
description is necessary and some searching on the part of the
reader.

Dynamic change (c) is one of the most powerful tools available in
COSTOC lessons. Some examples of its use are, showing the
stepwise transition from state to state in a finite state machine,
in an algorithm, or in a process; highlighting successive parts of
a program, while at each step showing the current status of
variables, stacks, output so far, and including a comment on the
current situation. There are many areas where dynamic change
makes a big difference, such as, in natural language analysis [18] or VLSI
Fabrication Methods [16].

Dynamic change is, of course, almost impossible in books (unless
endless repetition of the same basic situation with the changes
highlighted is used). Hence, it is a concept alien to many of us.
(This is one reason why using all available COSTOC features does
not come naturally even to seasoned authors.) On the other hand,
dynamic changes during a lecture are easier on a blackboard than
when using transparencies. This is one reason why some good
lecturers have reservations in the excessive use of pre-made
transparencies.

It is clear that animation (d) is a advantage of COSTOC lessons
over books and lectures. Some very rudimentary animation may be
possible in a lecture by pushing around objects on the
transparency. The question/answer dialogue (e) available in
COSTOC cannot be handled fully in books (programmed-learning type
books trying this kind of feature are only an approximation of
this) and cannot be handled at all in large lectures.

It is clear that that self-paced lesson absorption and execution
(f) is very helpful in many ways. Although self-paced lesson
execution is possible in COSTOC lessons and books as well, the
interactive element of CAI provides something further, and very
important: it provides the motivation to keep interested in the
subject, especially in the case of independent study courses.
Furthermore, the non-judgemental interaction with a terminal
(versus that in a lecture) and the play element of a graphical
interaction are both key inducive mechanisms to learning, and what
made CAI attractive 25 years ago.

We have described a number of features in which COSTOC lessons are
better than books and lectures and good COSTOC lessons must
indeed make use of these features. However, let us examine those
teaching and learning features which are available in books and
lectures but not in COSTOC lessons. Specifically, books provide
easier "navigation"; searching through a book for a specific
diagram is simpler than searching in a COSTOC lesson for it. This
is one reason why a written documentation exists for each lesson.
Books are also more "transportable" since we can read them
anywhere, and more "information compact" (a typical screen holds
some 1000 characters, a full-sized book page 5000). The main
features available in a lecture but missing in COSTOC lessons are
voice and gestures. It is interesting to note that the above
features (with one exception) could all be integrated eventually
into COSTOC-like courses, by using digitized voice (see [17]),

high-resolution super-fast screens, browsing mechanisms and
portable PC's. What would still be missing would be the gestures.
How important are they?

6. COSTOC LESSON CREATION

6.1. Authoring Contract

A COSTOC "course" consists of 10 COSTOC "lessons", lessons 1
through 10, a written documentation of 50 - 80 pages, and a
special "sneak preview" of the course which we call Lesson 0.
This arrangement forms the basic unit of an "authoring contract".

Each COSTOC lesson consists of about 40-60 "frames" of 25-32 K
bytes of memory. Lesson 0 explains the aims, prerequisites,
structure, contents, references, and all other items relevant to
the course. It also contains sample segments of some of the other
lessons in the course to illustrate the level, way, and quality of
presentation. Indeed, it is Lesson 0 and the written
documentation which will allow potential users to decide whether
the course is usable for their purposes or not. As the number and
selection of courses grow, the need of a reviewing process will
arise which consists of published reviews in widely available
journals, such as exists for books today.

Authors of COSTOC courses are university professors who are
experts in the field of the authoring contract. The material in a
COSTOC course corresponds to roughly 4 weeks of teaching at 3
hours per week, ie. one lesson is equivalent to about one student
contact hour.

6.2. Authoring System: AUTOOL

Lessons are prepared with a special authoring system called
"Autool," developed jointly by the CDC of Austria and Germany and
IIG (Maurer's institute). Lessons are coded in a simple
"intermediate language." It is conceivable that other authoring
systems will also map on the same intermediate language in the
future.

The authoring system Autool (described in [5] and [4]) is
programming free, i.e. the author does not have to write programs
or program-segments. He/she simply "edits" the lesson with an
editing system. This system allows the generation of text,
graphics (including animation), a question/answer dialogue, the
linkage between frames, etc. If needed, the author may also
insert program segments but is discouraged from this for reasons of
maintenance , portability and the extra effort required.
Consequently, this feature has been used in only 2% of the
lessons. Authors of COSTOC courses design their courses after
studying a number of sample lessons, and following a set of given
specifications explained in a special document [7].

6.3. A Programming-Free System

The pros and cons of programming-free systems vs. authoring
languages have been discussed in the literature [9]. A
programming-free authoring system creating context-independent
frames was chosen for COSTOC. There are two reasons for this
choice: First, creation of lessons with programming-free systems
is simpler and needs no programming experience. Secondly,

changing and maintaining lessons is much easier.

We believe that the last point is particularly crucial. Suppose
person X wants to use course A which has been authored by person Y
but dislikes some of the frames. Some references may be missing,
a favourite result may not be mentioned, an example may not be
explained   well, or one of the program segments is written in
language L instead of the locally preferred dialect L'. In such a
case, person X can easily change the contentious points, obtaining
an individualized version fitting all requirements. No CAI system,
except for COSTOC-like systems using programming-free authoring
systems, permits this type of lesson modification readily. In view
of the rapid obsolescence of certain computer science material and
the strong individualism of many computer scientists, this feature
is very important.

Editing and quality control of the lessons is currently taking
place at the first author's institute, IIG. However, by mid 87,
the establishment of an "editorial board" will be completed, each
editor being responsible for the acquisition, advising and quality
control of a group of authors.

6.4. Authoring Teams and Recommended Authoring Procedures

We conclude this section by describing some experiences concerning
the authoring process. To create a full course of 10 lessons
including documentation, etc., is a major job, despite the tools
available. It requires a minimum of about 12 full weeks of work.
As a consequence, it is unrealistic to expect an author to try to
do a full course alone, without any assistance. The experience
has been that, after about five lessons, energy is evaporated and
the danger of giving up arises.

To prevent this from happening, COSTOC recommends that "authoring
teams" be formed, a team being of one professor with one to three
students. Two modes of work are then possible: (a) The professor
discusses the topics with the students. The students work fairly
independently while the professor reviews the lesson fragments
produced regularly, to guarantee quality control. (b) The
professor writes a detailed "script" for each lesson, typically
one page per frame, showing all formulations, features, graphics,
animations, questions, linkage, etc. to be used. This script is
then converted into a lesson by a "CAI programmer", i.e., a
student using the authoring system.

Experience shows that mode (a) works well only when good students
are available and is likely to produce a somewhat non-homogeneous
course. Although some authors have successfully used method (a),
we strongly recommend method (b). Method (b) is not only likely
to produce a homogeneous course, but also one of high quality.
After an initial learning phase, writing a script takes about a
day per lesson for the professor involved. Converting the script
into a lesson takes another 3-5 days. Further improvements of the
authoring tools may eventually cut the time for converting the
script from 3-5 to about 1-2 days. However, a long line of
developments of authoring systems is still necessary to achieve
this goal. A group of authors has already started a research
project whose aim is to produce the basis of an intelligent
authoring system by 1988.

7. HOW TO USE COSTOC COURSES IN THE UNIVERSITY

COSTOC courses can be used to support or supplement teaching
computer science at the university level in two major ways:

(1) As "back-up material" for full-time students, staff, and part-
    time students, COSTOC lessons provide detailed information on
    a given topic. For example, persons from industry may wish to
    increase or refer their knowledge on a topic. As remedial
    material, COSTOC courses can be used to make up for a lesson
    missed or to review a topic not understood in class.

(2) As "partial replacement" of classroom lectures, COSTOC is an
    approach which has been tried out successfully. In a 3-hour
    per week class, 1 hour can be replaced by COSTOC lessons,
    choosing material particularly suitable to COSTOC presentation
    In fact, by this shifting of classroom materil to COSTOC
    lessons, time can be freed during the allotted lecture period
    for discussions, additional examples, etc.

Student evaluations show that an overwhelming majority of students
prefer this "lecture/COSTOC lesson mix" to just "plain lectures."
The percentage in favour of such a mix has been independent of the
country involved (i.e., Austria, Germany, USA) or the class-size
(ranging from 30 to 250). Evaluation questionnaires also show
that an acompanying written documentation of lessons is, indeed,
necessary (see [15] and [8] for details).

7.1. COSTOC Equipment

To use the lessons, the equipment required is either PC's with a
suitable colour graphic card (the "enhanced graphic card"), or,
else, dedicated micros called MUPID, developed at IIG. MUPID is a
low-cost yet high quality graphic system. Whatever the equipment
chosen, it is recommended that a "fileserver" is provided to hold
the database of lessons. The fileserver is not used for CAI
purposes, but only for lesson retrieval and, possibly, simple
messaging. This type of configuration is desirable because it
allows easy access to all lessons with the use of telephone lines, by
a multitude of users from within and outside the university.

Another important attribute of COSTOC equipment is that it should
provide the possibility for lesson fedback. Student comments on
the lessons assure continuous lesson improvement. This can be
achieved either via messaging in the fileserver environment or by
using an installed CAI-lab bulletin board and a systematic method
of comment investigation.

It is worth noting that the effectiveness of a COSTOC-type course
does not depend simply on on the quality of lessons and the system
employed. Other unexpected factors, such as how lessons are made
available to the students, do come in. Experience has shown that
it is a mistake to make all the lessons of a course available
throughout the term. Rather, a certain discipline must be
established into the scheduling of lesson execution so that the
student is forced to follow the COSTOC lessons within designated
time frames. One simple but effective way is to give the students
of a class a period of only 2-4 weeks access to each lesson.

7.2. Some Cost Figures

Finally, a few figures are in order to give an idea of the costs
involved. To set up a COSTOC-type "CAI-Lab" which includes a
fileserver, the necessary systems software, and PC's with colour
monitors, about US $2000 per student station will suffice. Costs
as low as US $1000 per station have been achieved in some cases.
Ten student stations can accommodate about 200 students (if a
student takes one COSTOC-supported course per term). Since a
COSTOC course of 10 lessons costs about $2000, a substantial CAI
lab for 300 students taking two COSTOC courses each per term will
amount to some $50,000 to $80,000 for all hardware, software, and
courseware required. For further details consult [8].

8. CURRENT STATUS OF THE COSTOC PROJECT

At the time of writing, authoring contracts for about 400 COSTOC
lessons (= 40 courses) have been signed. Both authors of this
paper have been involved in the creation of one of these 40 COSTOC
courses to obtain first-hand experiences. Both authors have been
experimenting with the use of lesson material at their respective
universities.

Lessons and courses under contract deal with a variety of topics
including items such as: Structured Programming; Concepts of High
Level Programming Languages; Pascal; Modula 2; Ada; Lisp; Prolog;
Modelling of Computer Systems; Organization of Computer Systems;
Computer Architecture; Architecture of Microcomputers;
Supercomputers; Peripheral Equipment; Logic Networks; Digital
Design; VLSI; Introduction to Software Concepts in VLSI; Sorting
Techniques; Data Structures and Searching; Hashing; Tree-like Data
Structures; Computational Geometry; Operating Systems; Special
kinds of Operating Systems; Database Modelling and Design; Data
Base Management; Expert Systems; Natural Language Analysis;
Cryptography; Syntax Analysis; Automata, Machines and
Applications; Computation and Automata; Petri Nets; Graph
Theoretic Algorithms in Computer Science; Selected Topics from
Computer Networks; Office Automation; Operation Research.

About 30-50% of the above lesson material will be ready by end of
'86, and some 250 lessons by July '87. Further contracts are
being negotiated. Authors from all over the world are involved in
this massive effort, with the aim of assuring high quality course
material and wide-spread usage. A number of pilot installations
have already started and the first results are quite encouraging
[8].

9. CONCLUSIONS

The COSTOC project is just now starting to be visible and will not
reach full speed before the end of '87. However, even now it is
probably fair to say that it is one of the largest CAI projects in
computer science ever carried out. COSTOC contributes
significantly to Teleteaching in that it relies on networks of
microcomputers to distribute high quality computer science lessons
widely. Fileservers holding an available lesson database can be
accessed by phone from off-campus locations, thus allowing the
integration of the lesson material in an open univerity or
Teleteaching kind of setting (see [8] and [10] for further
details).

The aim of COSTOC is quite ambitious: it aims   eventually to
provide thousands of lessons corresponding to dozens of books.
So that,   COSTOC will provide, for the first time in history, a
good part of university level computer science packaged in
quality-controlled CAI lessons.   The usefulness of the project
cannot be underestimated; it will indeed provide a formidable
amount of support.   Nor should it be overestimated either; it is
not intended to replace ordinary classroom teaching by more than a
reasonable number of percentage points, but quite likely to a
higher degree than videos, movies, and TV-transmitted lectures do
nowadays.

REFERENCES

[1]   F. Blakovich, S. Lerman, R.P. Parmelee: Computing in higher
       education:the Athena experience, Communications of the ACM 28
       (1985), 1214-1224.
[2]   H. Cheng, P. Lipp, H. Maurer: GASC -- A low cost, no-nonsense
       Graphic and Software Communication System, Electronic
       Publishing Review 5 (1985), 141-155.
[3]   H. Cheng, H. Maurer: Teleprograms - the right approach to
       videotex if you do it right, Proceedings of the IRE
       Conference on Telesoftware London (1984), 75-78.
[4]   J. Garratt, F. Huber, H. Huemer: Autool - a new authoring
       system, Report 219 IIG Graz (1986).
[5]   F. Huber: Autool - an Authoring System for Videotex; Proc. of
       IFIP Conference on Teleteaching '86, Budapest, North Holland
       Pub. Co., Amsterdam (1987).
[6]   G. Kearsley: Authoring Systems in Computer Based Education,
       Communications of the ACM 25 (1982), 429-437.
[7]   D. Kaiser, H. Maurer: Autool - a new system for computer
       aided instruction, Report 218 IIG Graz (1986).
[8]   F. Makedon, H. Maurer: CLEAR - Computer Learning Resource
       Centers; Proc. of IFIP Conference on Teleteaching '86,
       Budapest, North Holland Pub. Co., Amsterdam (1987.).
[9]   H. Maurer: Authoring system for computer assisted
       instruction, Proceedings of the ACM National Conference 1985
       Denver (1985), 551-561.
[10]   H. Maurer: Nationwide Teaching Through a Network of
       Microcomputers, Proc. of IFIP World Congress '86, Dublin,
       North Holland Pub. Co., Amsterdam (1986).
[11]   H. Maurer: The Austrian Approach to videotex, Proceedings of
       7th European Meeting on Cybernetics and System Research,
       North Holland Pub. Co., Amsterdam (1984).
[12]   H. Maurer: R. Posch: MUPID2- Durchbruch fuer Btx, Report B 43
       IIG Graz (1984).
[13]   H. Maurer: New developments in videotex and their
       implications for computer aided instruction, Information
       Services and Use 3, (1983), 319-324.
[14]   J. Nievergelt: A pragmatic introduction to courseware design,
       Computer 13 (1980), 7-21.
[15]   Th. Ottmann: Can Teaching by Computers Replace Teaching by
       Professors? Proc. of IFIP Conference on Teleteaching '86,
       Budapest, North Holland Pub. Co., Amsterdam (1987).
[16]   K. Ch. Posch, R. Posch: VLSI; COSTOC Course Graz IIG (1986).
[17]   P. Sammer: CD ROM as Storage Medium for Computer Aided
       Instruction; Proc. of IFIP Conference on Teleteaching '86,
       Budapest, North Holland Pub. Co., Amsterdam (1987).
[18]   I. Witten: Natural Language Analysis; COSTOC Lesson Graz IIG
       (1986).

Remote Education and Informatics: Teleteaching
F. Lovis (Editor)
Elsevier Science Publishers B.V. (North-Holland)
© IFIP, 1988

A UNIVERSITY LEVEL INTRODUCTORY TELE-COURSE ON INFORMATICS

F. Mulder
Dutch Open university
PO-box 2960
6401 DL Heerlen, The Netherlands

INTRODUCTION

At the Dutch Open University different fields of study are offered to students through courses or packages of courses. One of those fields is informatics, which not only is important in its own right but also for studies in other subjects such as engineering , natural sciences, economics or business administration as well as in social sciences, law or arts. Because of this broad base of importance, a course has been developed which gives a broad introduction into informatics for students with quite different backgrounds and interests.

'Introduction to Informatics' is a 'tele-course', a course which can be studied at a distance from the central university institute. The course requires approximately 200 hours of study and consists of extensive printed self-study material (+ 1200 pages), three video productions (in total + 2 hours) and four computer practicals (in total + 25 hours).

CONTENTS OF THE COURSE

The separate components which can be distinguished in informatics are linked in the course and elaborated coherently in five different blocks (A-E); see the figure below.

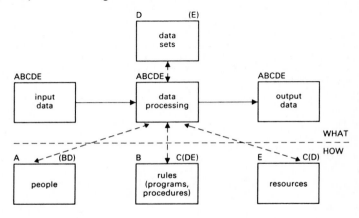

The starter is the **A-block** which, on the basis of rather simple cases, deals with the general concepts of data processing and information systems (with some attention to design aspects). Another important subject in this block is the role of information technology in society.

The **B-block** offers an elementary but fundamental approach to algorithm design as a first step towards program construction. Program Structure or Nassi-Shneiderman (NS)-Diagrams (using a simple pseudocode) serve as an important visualization tool in the process of learning the basics of structured programming. The so important role for data types in the design of algorithms, which NS-diagrams completely ignore, is covered by adding data type tables to these diagrams. By filling out what we call state tables, students can systematically trace algorithms, thereby learning to appreciate why algorithms do or don't work in the way you want them to.

After completing this (theoretical) block and having received a specific problem the student can implement the algorithm to be designed for the problem as a Pascal program on a computer, according to a simple set of transformation rules. This is done in the **C-block** in three computer practicals which can be done in the regional study centers on IBM-PC's. In a short practical the student can get acquainted, in part through Computer Assisted Learning (CAL), with the IBM-PC and its operating system (PC-DOS). A second short practical is concerned with the Pascal compiler (Turbo). In by far the longest practical, the student finally codes, tests and executes his or her own Pascal program.

In the **D-block** the structuring of large sets of data is the key issue. In a step-by-step picture-oriented approach the student discovers normalization as a powerful and elegant procedure for structuring data at the conceptual (or logical) level. Relations between objects (entities) are visualized by Data Structure Diagrams. The basic operations for manipulating data are introduced and exercised, first at the conceptual level and, derived from this, in a practical session with an IBM-PC. In this (fourth) computer practical each student performs predefined queries on a rather simple set of files using the query language of dBASE. This is preceded by a theoretical treatment of the database concept and a short explanation of the relational data model.

The last block, the **E-block**, is a technical one, dealing with distinguishable levels in computer architecture, software versus hardware, operating systems, data transmission and data communication networks. In this block the history of the technical development of computers is also handled.

STUDENT ACTIVITIES AND TUTORING

The video productions are well-suited for such an introductory course and are aimed at helping the student to appreciate such abstract concepts as algorithms and data structures or models in a compact but adequate way.

Throughout the course a considerable number of activity oriented questions and self tests with comprehensive feedback help the student to actively study the material and continually assess his or her achievements.

The course is a tele-course which however does not imply that (in its present state) students can completely confine themselves to working at home. The computer practicals and video productions must be done in nearby study centers. Students can also make use of personal tutoring in a study center in the case of specific questions or problems. This is primarily the case in the C-block where each student has to design his or her own algorithm and implement the corresponding Pascal program.

Furthermore, group meetings are quite often organized for examination training, while the final examination itself to date takes place three times a year in the study center places.

Of all these activities it is clearly the computer practicals which are a candidate for home-work as well. Actually an increasing number of students is already doing the practicals on their own homecomputers.

PERSPECTIVES

In a research project called 'Tele-education' the Open University is investigating the possibilities of a more extensive use of home-computers (not only for computer practicals!) along with network facilities (see the accompanying paper by Boon/De Wolf on 'Tele-education: an experiment in the Netherlands').

This may have far-reaching consequences, not only for the organization of the learning process (computer based tutoring, computer based self-assessments, computer based examinations, and so on), but also for the choice of the didactic concept for the course. For example, it is then possible to give serious consideration to an integration of theory and practice of programming (the B- and C-blocks of the course) instead of the rather strict separation of the two which has been explicitly chosen in the present course.

Time will tell........

Remote Education and Informatics: Teleteaching
F. Lovis (Editor)
Elsevier Science Publishers B.V. (North-Holland)
© IFIP, 1988

Distance Education
Through Multi-media

Wichit Srisa-an

Sukhothai Thammathirat Open University
Thailand

Introduction

A common educational problem of developing countries is the
inequality of educational opportunity. This means that only a
minority have the chance to study above the legally-required
minimum level. The higher up the educational ladder one goes, the
fewer the opportunities for further study. While the educational
needs of the people grow increasingly greater, the capability of
developing countries to meet these needs for higher education
remains limited. This is because resources are limited, and these
limited resources must be poured into other areas of the country's
development. This causes the quantitative and qualitative development of the people in general to be out of harmony with the country's
overall development even though, in fact, the quality of human
resources is the most important factor in a country's development.

In developing countries, human resource development is of crucial
importance. Such development not only increases the quantity of
trained manpower in response to national needs, but it also
improves the quality of life and work for people generally. As
human resources are developed, rising expectations are engendered
in the people for further education. But opportunities for education at the highest level are limited because resources are limited. Under these conditions of scarcity, inequality of educational
opportunities naturally arises. Such inequality can be erased only
by efforts to democratize education. Thus various models and
methods must be explored to make higher education truly education
for the masses. But it is essential that these approaches be
economical and efficient so as not to exceed limited resources.

In the past decade many countries in Asia have extended the range
of educational opportunities by adopting the open education
system and setting up, for this purpose, higher educational
institutions of distance teaching and learning. Pakistan's Allama
Iqbal Open University, Sri Lanka's Open University, China's
Central Broadcasting and TV University, Australia's Deakin
University, Japan's University of the Air, Korea's Correspondence
University, Indonesia's Terbuka Open University, India's Indira
Gandhi National Open University, and Thailand's Sukhothai
Thammathirat Open University - all these institutions of distance
teaching, despite their individual characteristics, do indeed have
one aim in common: to serve the needs of adults seeking to upgrade
professional qualifications and/or to acquire a real understanding
of the subjects chosen. At present, a large number of countries in
the developing world, especially those in Asia, have expressed a
great interest in providing higher education through distance
teaching systems. It is to be expected that other distance teaching
institutions will be established in many countries in the near
future.

In the past, whenever there were extensive educational reforms, the causes usually cited were social changes, academic and technological advances, or even political influences. It is true that the aforementioned items might well have been the stimulus or impetus for the educational changes. However, if a more profound analysis is made, it will be found that the factor having the greatest influence on the changes and serving as an important basis for the use of new methods in the field of education has been "the conceptual factor" which administrators and educational personnel have adopted as their guiding principle.

One of the concepts which has most influenced the provision in the present age is the concept of lifelong education, and education is, of course an important factor throughout one's life. It is a process and an activity which concerns people from birth to death. Education according to this concept must meet the needs of society and of individuals of all ages and categories. There must be models and methods of providing education which foster learning for both young people and adults – both formal and non-formal. The concept of lifelong education in the past decade has become a firm belief which has influenced education in various countries throughout the world.

If the concept of lifelong education is considered in its social aspect, it is generally accepted that today's society is a learning society. By this I mean that for a person to adjust successfully and contentedly to a rapidly changing society such as today's, he must ensure that his learning is constantly up-to-date. Continuous learning thus facilitates the leading of a successful life, and a member of society who wants to get ahead must make use of various types of education. Modern technology has become an important vehicle in providing lifelong educational activities. In the modern age there is thus a merging or coming together of the learning society and the technological society. Various social institutions, apart from educational institutions that impart knowledge to school-age children, have an important rôle to play in providing various types of education for young people and adults. The home, church, and many types of public and private agencies – including mass media insitutions – have been stimulated to play an ever-increasing role in improving the quality of life of the people.

Adopting the concept of lifelong education as a principle in providing education has resulted not only in the expansion of the scope and manner of such provision, but also in the development of many new educational methods. Of particular importance has been the establishment of open education using the distance teaching and learning system, which has been expanding rapidly in various countries throughout the world.

In general, the educational systems with which we are familiar usually can be characterized as "closed education", closed in three senses, namely:

1. Limited student enrolment – that is, the number of students admitted is limited to those who can be accommodated in terms of the number of desks, teachers, buildings, and supplies. This is because the students must come to study in a specifically designated place. Since there is a need to limit the number of students, this type of educational institution ordinarily

looks for a selection process which will ensure the number of quality students that it can accommodate. This in turn leads to the condition of limited opportunity, and perhaps has an effect on the equality of educational opportunities if the selection process is not correct and appropriate.

2. Structural limitations - that is, the process and structure of this type of educational system is ordinarily fixed fairly rigidly. It is difficult to provide learning activities which will satisfy individual needs and allow for individual expression, and there is very little flexibility and facility in the entire educational process.

3. Limitations concerning the learning environment - that is, teaching and learning are ordinarily limited to the classroom or lecture hall. Thus the learning environment is usually limited to the confines of the educational establishment itself, with the relationship between the teacher and students in the classroom being the most important consideration.

Open education featuring a distance teaching and learning system, on the other hand, could be considered "expanded education", in that it seeks to expand educational opportunities fairly and to the greatest extent possible. This alleviates the problem of limitations regarding the process, structure, and learning environment. Instead of using a conventional classroom with a teacher as the center of teaching and learning, open education emphasizes various types of educational media, which result from the application of advanced knowledge or technology to education. The intention is to have the students study to the fullest extent on their own without having to enter a conventional classroom. An important factor in open education at whatever level is instructional media, which is one component of educational technology.

In the past, there have been different experimental approaches to open education featuring various types of instructional media - both single media and mixed media. The first well-known approach was correspondence education, in which teaching materials were sent by mail directly to the student's home. It was believed that printed materials were the most efficient instructional medium. If the materials were written and organized and appropriate techniques were employed, the student could study by himself with very little or indeed no direct assistance from the teacher. Correspondence education has thus been an important medium for expanding educational circles, extending learning opportunities, and destroying barriers to learning, thereby making open education available to ever greater numbers of students.

With the advent of radio broadcasts, another medium was applied to the field of education. Radio broadcasts were used not only to supplement conventional classroom instruction, but also as a medium in open education as well. Schools or educational institutions of the air were established which broadcast radio lessons directly to the home. In some instances radio broadcasts were used in conjunction with correspondence education; in other cases the broadcasts were used as a single medium of instruction. An important development in the field of instructional media occurred when television was applied to education. Telecasts can be considered a highly effective instructional medium, for there are

pictures as well as sound. The subsequent introduction of color
TV has further enhanced the effectiveness of this medium in many
countries.

Research conducted both within and outside Thailand concerning
the effectiveness of different types of media has indicated that
each particular medium has its strong and weak points. The
exclusive use of one medium is not likely to be completely
effective. The use of the traditional classroom with regular
interaction between the teacher and students is highly effective
but can be used to only a limited degree, and it may not be
appropriate for certain age groups. Printed materials, while
obviously nothing new, can still be an effective core medium for
those who can read and write. Radio and television can effectively
spark student interest, but the student must pay very close
attention to the programs and tune in on time or the lesson will
simply pass him by. Of course, the programs can always be taped
for subsequent review at the learning speed of the particular
individual, but this can be fairly expensive. Open education at
present has thus turned to the use of mixed or multi-media,
instead of the exclusive use of one single medium. That is, printed
materials, electronic media such as cassette tapes and video-tapes,
and radio and television broadcasts have been combined in a mixed
media system, with one medium serving as the core medium and the
other media serving as supplementary media. This is done in order
to make teaching and learning more effective and interesting.
Thus we might say that the use of "multi-media" has been "multi-
beneficial" in terms of increasing the prospects and the
effectiveness of distance education.

DISTANCE TEACHING SYSTEM

Distance teaching means quite simply that the students and teacher
are at a distance from one another, with little opportunity for
face-to-face contact. They are, however, able to have joint educational activities through the use of various instructional media
geared to facilitate learning on the part of the students. The
bulk of this learning arises from self-study, at times and places
convenient to the students. Distance teaching thus involves the
communication of knowledge, attitudes, and skills to learners in
such ways as to enable them to acquire and extend them into the
conduct of their everyday lives. Since communicating the above-
mentioned items is the prime objective, this communication must
be as efficient and effective as possible within the constraints
of existing resources. In general, the criteria for determining
the efficiency and effectiveness of distance teaching involves
analyzing the extent to which learners have achieved the learning
objectives set by the curriculum or by themselves. Ideally, an
effective distance teaching system should ensure that the students
find the learning experiences stimulating, interesting, enjoyable,
and relevant to their aspirations and lifestyles. Thus the
effectiveness of distance education depends to a large extent on
the quality of the instructional media and delivery systems.

The selection and development of instructional media appropriate
to the conditions of individual societies is thus an important
problem. Factors to be considered in media selection include the
following:[1]

1. Availability

It is essential that the chosen instructional media and delivery
systems be technologically practicable; that is, the technology
to be used in the individual societies must have been adequately
developed, and there must be sufficient manpower to make continued
use of the technology.

2. Accessibility

The instructional media and the delivery systems to be used must
be accessible to both the distance teaching institution and the
learners. For example, if television is chosen as an instructional
medium, not only must there be appropriate and adequate air time;
but also the students must have TV sets capable of picking up the
programs.

3. Acceptability

The instructional media must be accepted both by the teachers and
the students. This concerns the aptitudes and attitudes of both
groups with respect to certain types of media. If the teachers or
students are not skilled in the use of a particular medium, it is
not likely to be very effective.

4. Validity

The instructional media must be appropriate for achieving the
objectives of the learning materials. Care must be taken to
choose media which are suitable for the content or subject matter
one wishes to convey.

5. Economics

The instructional media must not be over   expensive. This will
involve considerations of economies of scale and cost effectiveness.

Once development of distance teaching systems is undertaken in
various countries based on the criteria just mentioned, there are
two major approaches which can be followed, namely:

1. The Uni-Medium or Single Medium System - This is the distance
teaching system which has long been used in correspondence
education. Printed materials will generally be used as the core
medium, but this approach can involve the exclusive use of any
single medium, such as radio or telecision broadcasts. The extra-
mural studies programs of various universities in Australia which
use printed materials exclusively are a good example of the Single
Medium System.

2. The Multi-Media or Mixed Media System - This is the distance
teaching system developed later, most particularly in the period
when electronic media came to be used more widely in the field of
education. The multi-media system ordinarily employs one medium
as the main or core medium with other media playing a supplementary
role in order to bring about a more interactive format. Printed
materials or print media are generally used as the core medium,
with electronic media such as radio, TV, audiocassettes, video-
tapes, etc., serving as supplementary media. Most open universities
employ the multi-media system and feature printed materials as the
core medium. This is true of the Open University in the U. K.[4]
and Sukhothai Thammathirat Open University in Thailand.

In fact, the development of instructional media for self-study
in the form of mixing printed materials with other media actually
occurred on a widespread scale even before the advent of the open
universitites. One well-known example of the mixed media approach
is Linguaphone, which developed language lessons combining printed
materials with records and, subsequently, tapes to teach language
skills. Mixing of just these two media improved the effectiveness
of language teaching and enabled students to study on their own.
With advances in electronic technology, many different media could
be mixed together and used in the transfer of knowledge. This led
to an even more effective use of instructional media.

Regarding the media used for distance teaching and learning, a
survey conducted by the International Centre for Distance Learning
of the United Nations University[2] found that many institutions
used several different methods - correspondence, telephone, radio,
TV, audio, video, study center, and so on. As correspondence is
by far the cheapest method of communicating at a distance, only
27 out of 468 programs do not use correspondence as one of the
methods. Of all the distance-learning institutions, 29 per cent
use only correspondence, particularly in Western Europe and North
America.

The results show quite remarkable differences between regions.
The telephone is used as a teaching method by more than a quarter
of the programs in North America, Western Europe, and Australasia,
but is hardly used in Africa, Asia, or South and Central America.
Radio and television show a similar picture. Both are used world-
wide to roughly the same extent, but whereas the use of radio
greatly exceeds that of television in the developing world,
television is much more popular than radio in North America. This
almost certainly is due to the penetration of the media.

The cost of audio cassettes has fallen dramatically, and they now
offer a real alternative to the printed word. Australasia has been
quick to recognize this and to use it: no fewer than 70 per cent of
their programs use audio cassettes. Australasia is also leading
the way in the use of video cassettes.

Another striking fact is the very low use made of any technique
other than correspondence in Western Europe. This is probably
because much of the distance-learning activity is done by conventional institutions which only use the cheapest methods. Thus
radio and audio cassettes are the only other methods used widely.

Electronic media today have an increasingly important role in
distance teaching/learning systems, especially those media which
permit the development of interactive potentiality and allow
students convenient control over their use.

The media which have attracted special attention in this respect
are computers and, in particular, their application in Computer-
Assisted Instruction (CAI).

In distance teaching/learning systems employing a multi-media
approach, CAI is, therefore, one important medium that can
contribute significantly to enhancing the effectiveness of
distance education.

Since I myself have direct experience with the development of a
distance teaching system which uses the mixed media approach and

features printed materials as the core medium, I will emphasize
this approach in my paper. It could be viewed as one model of the
use of printed materials in distance education.

The distance teaching system which I will present as a case study
is the system developed at Sukhohai Thammathirat Open University
in Thailand. It is a case of the development of a distance
teaching system employing a mixed-media approach suitable for the
conditions of a developing country. The "STOU PLAN"[3] for Distance
Teaching System, which is composed of 5 stages, can be concisely
illustrated in the following chart.

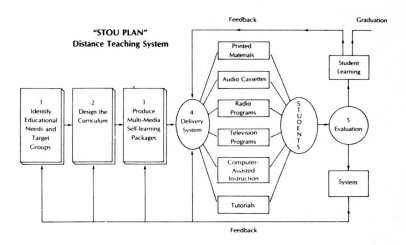

The first stage in the development of the distance teaching system
involves identifying the educational needs of the target groups
through preliminary surveys and research. This enables us to know
the needs of the general public as well as various individual
groups. This information can then be used as a basis for the
development of the following stage.

The second stage is curriculum development, and the structure of
the curriculum must be set up in such a way that it facilitates
the use of distance teaching techniques. The academic structure in
the "STOU PLAN" is based on the principle of course integration.
That is, an attempt is made to integrate different academic areas
into specific groupings or categories which will facilitate the
student's ability to synthesize and apply the knowledge acquired
and which will be easy to study on one's own. Course integration
is thus primarily of an interdisciplinary nature. The establishment
of the different schools has been carried out along the lines of
career and professional development rather than being discipline-
oriented in order to conform to the principle of course integration
just mentioned. The curriculum is thus divided into "course blocks,"
each of which carries 6 semester credits. Four-year bachelor's
degree programs are composed of 22-24 course blocks or 132 to 144
semester credits. The reason that the "STOU PLAN" has set up the
6-credit course block exclusively rather than subdivide into
smaller courses is based on two major principles, namely:

1. Academic principle - Setting up the course blocks in the manner just described facilitates course integration; that is, it makes it easier to integrate course content in an interdisciplinary fashion more completely than would be the case if smaller, less-encompassing courses were used. In terms of learning, this approach is appropriate for the distance education system since it enables the students to concentrate rather than diffuse their study efforts; for in any one semester, they will not have to study more than three blocks. The use of the course blocks allows us to oversee the standards and quality of the teaching/learning process to a fairly high degree. This is because the production and development of the course blocks is done by a course-production team. Academic standards are thus the responsibility of a group of academics rather than of individual instructors. Aside from this, the use of course blocks also facilitates the establishment of such supplementary media as radio, television, and special tutorial sessions. Particularly when there is a limited amount of time, it is easier to produce interesting programs related to the course blocks than would be the case if numerous smaller courses were used. When the curriculum structure featuring this block system is considered solely from the academic viewpoint, four positive aspects can be identified, namely:

(1) It facilitates academic integration;
(2) It facilitates self-study;
(3) It improves the oversight of academic quality and standards; and
(4) It facilitates the use of supplementary media in systems based primarily on printed materials.

2. Administrative principle - The use of the course-block system reduces the complexity of administration, making it more economical and efficient. Students are able easily to control their own study load, and the system is convenient with respect to registration, testing, and teaching. Students are able to register by mail, and examinations can be given in every province in the country on a single weekend. In addition, the course-block system helps avoid "academic monopoly" in which a single instructor is the sole authority on a particular subject. This is due to the fact that the course block has far more content and activities than could be produced by a single instructor on his own with a substantial teaching load. The course-block system also helps bring about an integrated approach to work, for the system demands that work be carried out as a team in the form of a course-production group. Each team has content specialists, an educational technologist, and an evaluation specialist who are jointly responsible for all phases of course production. This naturally results in integrated instructional materials and ensures that the educational system will be fully open, for it provides the opportunity for numerous specialists from outside institutions to participate in the development of the materials. The excellence which exists in society is thereby utilized to the fullest extent. An additional benefit is that this working together as an academic team helps bring about a spirit of teamwork in administrative work as well, a great advantage for the overall administration of the University.

The third stage involves selecting and producing the teaching media packages. The "STOU PLAN" was chosen to make use of a mixed-media approach based on the five following criteria: availability, accessibility, acceptability, validity, and economics. Printed

materials are the main or core medium, and tapes, radio and
television programs, and special tutorial sessions are the
supplementary media. For each course block, the student is
expected to spend approximately 180 hours per semester studying
the printed materials. (This amounts to roughly 12 hours per week
for 15 weeks). He also listens to at least one 60-minute tape
(for some course blocks, such as the English courses, the student
will listen to as many as 15 tapes), listens to fifteen 20-
minute radio programs, and views five 30-minute television programs.
He also has the opportunity to attend 10 hours of special tutorials
held in local study centers located in each province. In producing
teaching media packages according to the "STOU PLAN", the
first step is the production of the printed texts and workbooks. Then
selected portions of the text are used as the basis for tapes,
radio and TV shows, and tutorial-session workbooks. These latter
media are considered as supplements to the printed materials -
the core medium. The completed teaching package is thus in the
form of a multi-media self-learning package.

The fourth stage involves establishing delivery systems in order
to communicate knowledge to the students. The printed materials
and accompanying tapes are sent by mail to the student's home,
and radio and TV shows are broadcast at the same time throughout
the country. The tutorial sessions are held on weekends in local
study centers located in each province. CAI programs are provided
at selected study centers and function as "electronic tutors" for
such courses as science, mathematics, and statistics. The distance
education system established according to the "STOU PLAN" is thus
in the nature of home-based education.

The fifth stage is composed of evaluation and follow-up, which is
of two types. The first is evaluation of student learning by final
examinations held each semester in the local study centers.
A student must sit for the exam in the study center to which he has
been assigned, and the exams are held at the same time throughout
the country, ordinarily on weekends. The second type of evaluation
is system evaluation, which is conducted in order to obtain feed-
back that can be used to improve the effectiveness of the curriculum and the teaching/learning process.

THE PRODUCTION AND USE OF PRINTED MATERIALS

In distance teaching systems which use mixed media, with printed
materials as the core medium, such as in the "STOU PLAN", the
production of these materials is an important process and activity
of the Distance Media Production System. This system can be
graphically illustrated in the chart below.

The production of printed materials for use in distance teaching
can be carried out in various ways; for example, these materials
might be in the form of conventional textbooks or lecture notes.
The effectiveness of the printed materials in terms of helping the
student to study on his own depends largely on the format and the
way in which the content is presented. Special efforts were thus
made to develop a format suitable for printed materials which were
to be used specifically in distance teaching. One format in
widespread use in distance education. is the programmed textbook,
which is adapted from programmed instruction. The production of
this type of printed material aims at making the student an active
learner. Thus materials of an interactive nature must be produced,

and these include both a programmed text as well as an accompanying
workbook. Students who use this type of printed material will
master the content in small increments, in accord with their
study time. They must complete various activities or exercises as
part of learning the content of each unit, and they will receive
periodic feedback to indicate the extent of the progress in their
studies. Thus they experience a series of successes in their self-
study, and this encourages them to progress further in their
quest for knowledge.

In the block system of the "STOU PLAN" every block carries 6
semester credits. Each of these blocks has a programmed text and
a workbook, which are divided into 15 units, each of which
requires approximately 12 hours of study time per week. Each unit
begins with a unit lesson plan which spells out clearly the
topics, concepts, objectives, activities, and evaluation methods
for the unit. Then follows the presentation of the actual content,
which is broken down into sections. In each section there are
activities which the student must do in his workbook, and in each
unit there is a pre-test and a post-test, complete with answer
keys in order to give the student feedback.

From STOU's experience in developing these programmed texts for
use in the university's distance teaching system, it appears that
they have been quite successful and have accomplished their
purpose. The method of writing these texts is obviously more
complex than that used for writing ordinary texts. However, if
course writers are adequately trained before they commence their
work, these academics from various fields can accomplish their
task without undue difficulty.

CONCLUSION

In the development of distance teaching/learning systems employing
a multi-media approach, the most important consideration is the
blending or harmonizing of such media to permit distance education
to become even more effective.

From the author's experience, the harmonizing of the print medium
and the electronic media is of primary importance. The results
of experiments conducted at Sukhothai Thammathirat Open University
to date serve to confirm that the blending of printed materials
and computer-aided instruction is the most interesting development,
which promises to bring real benefits and, if this process were
to be extended and practised more widely, would enhance
considerably the effectiveness of distance education. Ultimately,
on the basis of such information, it is conceivable that distance
teaching will, more and more, come to rely on computers as the
main instructional medium in the emerging Computer-Based Education
(CBE).

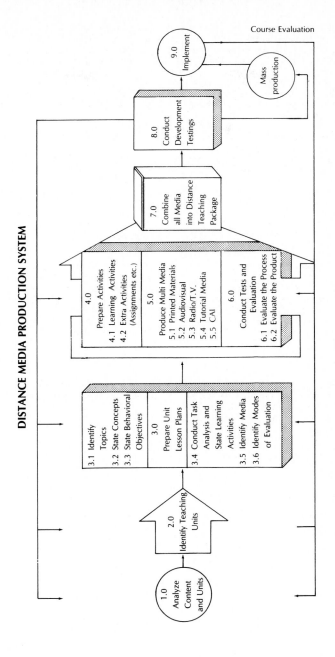

DISTANCE MEDIA PRODUCTION SYSTEM

References

[1]Michael J. Pentz and Michael W. Neil, Education for Adults at a Distance, Kogan Page, London, 1981, Chapter 4: pp. 97-125.

[2]Walter Perry, The State of Distance Learning Worldwide, International Center for Distance Learning of the United Nations University, 1984.

[3]Sukhothai Thammathirat Open University, Focus on STOU., Graphic Art Publishing, Bangkok, 1984.

[4]J.H. Horlock, "A University Without Walls," Media in Education and Development, Vol.17 No.2., June 1984, pp. 52-56.

Section 4
Courseware

Remote Education and Informatics: Teleteaching
F. Lovis (Editor)
Elsevier Science Publishers B.V. (North-Holland)
© IFIP, 1988

MEDIA SELECTION IN DISTANCE EDUCATION

F.H.D. Gastkemper

Dutch Open university
Department of Educational Media
PO-box 2960
6401 DL HEERLEN, The Netherlands

Decisions regarding media selection are to be placed in the broader framework of design, development and implementation of instruction and education as a whole. During this process, there will necessarily be made choices regarding the use of instructional media, implicitly or explicitly.
Instructional media can be defined as 'the physical means by which an instructional message is communicated' (Reiser & Gagné, 1983).
When one realizes that this implies the whole range from books and slides, via audiovisuals and computers to real objects and teachers, and many more in between, and that in many cases a number of these media are available at least in principle, then it is clear that some criteria or guidelines for choosing between them are very desirable indeed.
In fact, at least one empirical study has shown a systematic selection technique to yield better results in the choice of media than the intuitive approach (Romiszowski, 1974).
In this paper, two main questions on media selection will be discussed:
1. What does a systematic approach or a model for media selection look like?
2. Which specifics are to be considered for media selection with relation to distance education?
In addition to this, some attention will be given to media selection in the Dutch Open university.

What does a model for media selection look like?

Over the years a number of models for media selection have been developed. However different, these models also show important common features regarding fundamentals as well as components. Regarding common fundamentals, there are at least the following considerations:
1. Using a systematic approach or a model for media selection ensures completeness in the analysis and construction of the instructional situation. This may result in media-choices which are identical to those resulting from an intuitive approach, but this certainly is not always true and, e.g., financial differences can be very important.
2. Most models emphasize the instructional effectiveness of the educational system under construction. They do take into account practical and financial considerations also but never before the instructional aspects. In this way, the effectiveness of instructional systems will not be endangered or even nullified by strong practical or financial arguments only.

3. It is generally accepted that the instructional effectiveness of media varies with relation to (at least) different instructional tasks or functions, and different groups or types of learners. However, this is not a one-to-one relation: most instructional media can perform more than one function only, and a given function can often be performed by more than one medium.

Regarding the (common) features of media selection models in their structural components or dimensions, a comparative study on 9 models was included by Reiser and Gagné in their publication entitled Selecting Media for Instruction (Reiser and Gagné, 1983). They identify the following features:

1. Practical factors –	cost, availability and convenience factors. They speak for themselves and are generally considered to be very important but –as stated above– should not come first.
2. Physical attributes–	the characteristics or possibilities of the media. In some models these attributes are a dominant factor in the choice of media. Visuals, printed words, sound, motion, color and real objects as (aspects of) learning materials are in this view supposed to be differentially effective with regard to specific learning objectives.
3. Instructional setting–	as characterized by the answers to the following questions; Location of instruction? Instruction to individuals or in a group? If in a group, which size? It is not always clear in which way the answers to these questions are relevant to media selection, but nevertheless the instructional setting is generally put forward as a very important factor.
4. Learner characteristics–	reading ability and learner age are judged most important. The first is directly related to the suitability of specific media for study, like pictures and audio. Age, with relation to learning experience, could allow for more simple instructional aids. Sometimes the choice of media is related to age in combination with learning objectives.
5. Categories of learning outcomes–	grouping or classifications of learning objectives, mostly according to the model of Gagné; intellectual skills, verbal information, motor skills, attitudes, cognitive strategies. (Gagné, 1977) Sometimes categories of learning outcomes are a direct indication for the choice of specific media, but according to most models they are first to be complemented by a definition of instructional events.
6. Events of instruction–	can be defined as the external events which support or facilitate the internal learning processes (Gagné & Briggs, 1979). Those events in turn serve as a basis for the identification of needed 'stimuli', e.g. information or materials, and in accordance to these, then

media are chosen capable of presenting the intended 'stimuli'.
Instructional events can be categorized as follows:
- gaining attention
- informing the learner of the objectives
- stimulating recall of prerequisite learning
- presenting the stimulus material
- providing 'learning guidance'
- eliciting the performance of learners
- providing (corrective) feed-back
- assessing performance
- enhancing retention and recall
(Gagnè and Briggs, 1979)

In their comparison of (9) media selection models, originated between 1969 and 1981, Reiser and Gagnè conclude that both practical factors and physical attributes of media are important for all of the models, while learner- setting- and task-characteristics are not always. Nevertheless, in four (4) out of nine (9) models all factors are considered important.

After their overview of models Reiser and Gagnè propose a model of their own. As this model currently is one of the most widely accepted and used in practice it can serve as a point of reference for the following. Therefore a short description first.
The model takes the form of a series of (6) flow-charts. The authors prefer this format over other possible models like matrices or worksheets because of its ease of use.
From the format of their model, it can be derived that heavy emphasis is placed on the instructional setting (instruction versus self-instruction) and on an important learner-characteristic (readers versus non-readers). Four (4) of the six different flow-charts are based upon these distinctions. Of the remaining two (2), one is based upon the special case of the central broadcast situation, and one deals with the very special situation that job-competence should be (almost) perfect. From these broad categorizations one can arrive at the selection of media through answering a number of yes/no questions. These questions mostly refer to classification of the learning objectives under consideration, sometimes to events of instruction like 'motor practice' or 'adequate feedback' and sometimes to media-capabilities, namely in the area of visuals. The outcome frequently consists of a number of possible media-choices. A definite choice then can be made on the basis of practical, financial or other additional considerations.

The rationale behind the proposed choices and consequences thereof is given by Reiser and Gagnè in a discussion on the basis of learning theory and research, and cannot be dealt with in detail here. However, the relations between learning objectives, instructional events and media attributes can perhaps be illustrated by a few examples, starting from some of the media themselves.
The instructor, for instance, can provide the presentation of instruction in many ways, notably in the role of a manager of instruction with help of a variety of other media. In acting specifically as an instructor, he or she can be defined as a medium in the sense of 'personally delivered face-to-face oral speech'. This is a possible medium for the objective 'verbal information', and for the instructional event of 'guiding the learning of intellectual skills'. But for some audiences, say younger and/or less experienced learners, provisions for questioning and individualized feed-back should be available, that is; lecturing alone would not be enough.

As a second example, the computer is judged to be especially useful for instruction of intellectual skills, and certainly of the initial ones, where precise feed-back is very important. Moreover, computers can simply be seen as 'real equipment' where they are object of instruction.

Printed text, as a last example, is surely an efficient medium for 'verbal information' (the objective) to 'readers' (learner characteristic), and to competent readers also for skills like concepts and rules. Programmed texts even provide better conditions for this, eliciting responses and providing some feed-back.

With this, an outline of a generally applicable model for media selection and some of the rationale behind it are given. On to the second question;

Which specifics are to be considered for distance education?

Before an answer to this question is given, it should be mentioned that any model of media selction is designated for, and best applied at the most concrete level of education or instruction; courses, units, programs. On that level, e.g., learning outcomes and instructional events are clearly definable, which is much less exactly possible on the more abstract and generalized level of an instructional system like distance education. Consequently, medium choices on this level will necessarily also be of a more generalized nature.

Starting out from the (6) different features of selection models as discussed above, it is nevertheless possible to arrive at some a-priori characteristics which distinguish the selection approach for distance education from that for other types of instruction or education.

The most obvious differences are given in the 'instructional setting'. In general terms, distance education deals of course with dispersed locations, often to be operationalized as 'at home', and mostly with instruction to individuals. Instruction to groups is not impossible to achieve, but is frequently reduced to a minimum, inter alia for reasons of cost, organization, convenience etc.

This last type of considerations already refers to another characteristic distinction in the area of 'practical factors'. Cost may (implicitly) be important to any type of education or instruction, but availability of media and convenience of usage are evidently far more important in a situation of distance education than in a more traditional situation, where all chosen media are around, including the personal assistance for using them or acting as one of the media involved.

Regarding the (4) other aspects of media selection models no a-priori characteristic differences are given for different instructional situations, with a possible exception for one of the instructional events; 'providing (corrective) feed-back'. As far as learning objectives and learning tasks in relation to specific groups of learners ask for precise and individual feed-back, and as far as this is hard to accomplish by means of non-personal media, 'live' assistance can be needed. Such personal assistance is often difficult to provide for in distance education situations.

Other than that, learner characteristics, learning outcomes, events of instruction and physical attributes of media are all interdependent, but in themselves not related to specific instructional systems. However, an analysis of these 'entries' will sometimes lead to strong media choices which entail practical aspects which in turn are not feasible in distance education. In such cases, either another instructional situation should be chosen, or amends should be made with relation to target audience(s) or learning objective(s).

In the media selection model as proposed by Reiser and Gagnè, three of the (6) flow-charts bear some relevance to distance education. Two of these (3) deal with 'selfinstruction', the remaining one with the 'central broadcast' situation. The aspect of 'instructional setting' has clearly been judged to be of sufficient importance for setting these (3) flow-charts apart. The aspect of 'practical factors' has been taken into account as far as possible on this general level, by eliminating some of the 'candidate media' to choose from.

It is remarkable that in all (3) flow-charts the instructor is seen as one of the 'candidate media', and is proposed indeed as one of the possibly useful media in the broadcast-situation, but not for self-instruction. Evidently, a very strict interpretation of 'self-instruction' is intended. As an example for both the approach as such and the specific method involved, the flow-chart for 'self-instruction with readers' is given here. (Figure 1)

Chart C. Self-Instruction with Readers

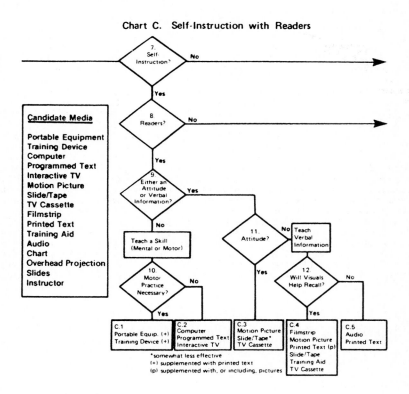

Figure 1. Flowchart panel applicable to the instructional situation "self-instruction with readers." Reiser & Gagné, 1983, p. 34)

Media selection in the Dutch Open university

In the Dutch Open university media selection is of course practised on
the level of individual courses, but was also needed on the institutional level to set up a policy for the planning of facilities, limiting the range of available media to a certain, somewhat standardized
extent, etc. As stated above, at this level no precise and definite
medium-choices can be made, but delineating the number of media to
choose from in practice appeared possible.
Although in the process of doing so no use could be made yet of the
selection model of Reiser and Gagné, the reasoning involved shows
striking resemblance to theirs. In fact, the same aspects of media
selection have been considered, in a comparable way. The outcome, a
number of possibly useful media, is not really contradictory to that of
Reiser and Gagné in their flow-chart regarding 'self-instruction with
readers'. It does however, include the 'instructor' as a medium but
also narrows down the number of useful media as compared to theirs.
This narrowing down is due to some additional information or expectations regarding learner characteristics and categories of learning
outcomes. As the Dutch Open univesity is an institute for adult education at post-secondary level, it was clear that all students would be
'readers' and a fair proportion also of a mature 'age', especially in
terms of study-habits viz., experience. Furthermore, the students could
be expected to be highly motivated. As to learning outcomes, it was
known from the beginning which areas of teaching would be dealt with.
From this, it was -tentatively- concluded that an overwhelming proportion of learning objectives would be of a cognitive nature. Not only
verbal information, but also intellectual skills and cognitive strategies would be intended.
Especially from the latter two it was derived that specific and sometimes highly flexible and/or individual (corrective) feed-back would
doubtlessly be needed. Considering the (differential) capacities of the
various media and taking into account that the Dutch Open university
allows students to start with their courses at any given moment and
work through them at their own pace, a self-study model and four (4)
basic media were chosen; printed text plus pictures, audiovisual media,
computer usage (including interactive video) and the 'instructor'. The
personal (or on request, group-)assistance which can be provided by the
latter as well as the electronic media which are as yet not generally
available for the student in the immediate study-situation (say, at
home), are made accessible through a number of study-centers all over
the country.
In the Dutch Open university an intermediate level of organisation/-
teaching is given in the (7) different academic areas. It will be clear
that in principle the selection of media as discussed above, is equally
applicable to all (7) areas. In practice however, some differentiation
of the 'media-profile' for these areas will evolve, mostly due to differences in the nature of learning outcomes, learning characteristics and
(perhaps) some practical factors.
The above order of media coincides with an increase in complexity, i.e.
the next medium always offers 'something more' -often at higher cost.
Very broadly stated and somewhat simplified, in terms of learning objectives, printed texts-plus-pictures and/or audiovisuals are a good
choice with relation to 'verbal information' and (some) 'cognitive
skills'. With relation to other (complex) 'skills' and 'cognitive strategies', computers and/or personal assistance are (additionally)
needed. Of course, this coarse distinction relates to events of instruction also; a critical function like 'providing (corrective) feed-
back' is only to a certain extent possible with help of printed texts
and audiovisuals, but significantly more so with (additional) help of

computers and/or personal assistance.
Here, it is not possible to go more precisely into the 'incremental steps' or 'add-on value' of the different media with respect to each other. But of course it is exactly these differences which are decisive for choosing and/or combining media in the process of concrete course-development. In general, the least complex and expensive, and best available and known media are chosen first when adequate. More complex (and expensive) media are only added if, and as far as they are really needed (Gastkemper & Van Enckevort, 1985).
The Dutch Open university officially started in the fall of 1984 and experience is still limited. So far however, there is little or no evidence to doubt the soundness of its media selection approach, in principle or in practice, as such.

References

Gagné, R.M.
The conditions of learning (3rd Ed.)
New York; Holt, Rinehart and Winston, 1977

Gagné, R.M. & Briggs, L.J.
Principles of Instructional Design (2nd Ed.)
New York; Holt, Rinehart and Winston, 1979.

Gastkemper, F.H.D. & Van Enckevort, G.
The use of Media in education at the Dutch Open university
Heerlen, Open university of the Netherlands, 1985

Reiser, R.A. & Gagné, R.M.
Selecting Media for Instruction
Englewood Cliffs; Educational Technology Publications, 1983

Romiszowski, A.J.
The Selection and Use of Instructional Media
London; Kogan Page, 1974

Remote Education and Informatics: Teleteaching
F. Lovis (Editor)
Elsevier Science Publishers B.V. (North-Holland)
 IFIP, 1988

TELESOFTWARE - THE SIMPLE WAY

Agoston TEMESI - Paul FERENCZY - Paul SÁRVÁRY

Institute of Telecommunications Electronics
Budapest Technical University
Muegyetem rkp. 1-3.
H-1111, Budapest, Hungary

1. INTRODUCTION

Telesoftware is a method of forwarding computer programs or data to home
computer owners via the broadcast television channels, without affecting in
any way either the tc programs or the teletext service. Originally the
vertical blanking interval was used for data signal transmission and to get
access to these data, the television receiver must have a dedicated interface
unit through which it is possible to download the programs or data to the
attached home computers. A somewhat less elegant, but much cheaper method has
been developed and tested at the Budapest Technical University. In this new
procedure the sound channel of the tv network is used to transmit the audio-
band data signals, while the vision channel and the teletext service is
unaffected. This method of telesoftwaring does not need any kind of special
equipment and could be used in tc programs directed for computer fans or
hobbyists, for whom a temporary fall-out of the sound channel makes no problem
at all.

2.   TELESOFTWARE THROUGH THE TELETEXT CHANNEL

The rocket speed growth of the home computer market is putting a world-wide
demand on software houses for all kinds of computer programs. The usual way of
distributing software is by no means of magnetic tapes (cassettes) and floppy
discs sold by retailers.

There are quite a lot of mainly educational, tutorial programs, however, which
are published in the literature practically free of charge. To make use of
such information the computer fan must key-in the data byte-by-byte, which
procedure can be very tiring and also time consuming. To help this situation
a new service, called telesoftware, was introduced in certain countries in
Europe, where an advanced teletext service had already been established.
Using the same techniques as the teletext data transmission, the computer data
are broadcast by the tc transmitters for those receivers, which are equipped
with dedicated hardware to extract the data from the television signal. This
extraced data thus becomes available for the home computer enthusiast in such
a way, that neither the tv programs, nor the teletext service is disturbed. In
fact, since a complete computer program can thus be downloaded within minutes,
the procedure can be cyclicly repeated over and over again, providing a long
time-slot (e.g. a whole afternoon or evening) for anybody to join in and pick
up the broadcast program at any desired time. To establish such a
telesoftware service involves sophisticated electronics at the transmitting
end and - as mentioned already - a specially designed interface in the tc
receivers, something similar to a teletext decoder.

3. TELESOFTWARE THROUGH THE SOUND CHANNEL

By sacrificing the television sound channel - only for the period of the downloading of a computer program - it is possible to achieve telesoftware without additional hardware in the receiver. Of course the fall-out of the sound channel rules out the possibility to transmit data at any time: this can be done exclusively during such tv programs as school-television or tv-teaching of computer programming, where the viewers will no doubt tolerate the non-standard use of the sound channel. It should be noted, however, that a similar method on a radio-sound-transmitter would not be feasible, because the average radio listener must never be disturbed by the irritating sound of the data signal.With television on the other hand it is possible to give a warning on the screen for viewers, and explain in writing the reason for the unusual sounds coming from the loudspeaker.Furthermore, the visual display can, obviously be used for detailed information of what is to be done by the computer owners, what is the title of the software just being transmitted?, etc.

To carry out a complete computer program downloading the following steps should be taken:

a/   At the transmitting end - preferably in the tv studio - the previously selected home computer should be loaded with the program (or data) to be broadcast.

b/   The audio output of the computer, which normally is connected to the recording input of a tape recorder, is to be connected through an appropriate voltage divider to the audio modulation input of the television transmitters. The voltage divider is chosen such that the data signal drives the sound transmitters with appr. 50% average modulation level (25 kHz peak frequency deviation).

c/   The viewers should be advised to connect their tape recorders to the audio output socket of their television receiver, and prepare for a program recording.

d/   An announcement is now to be made for the viewers asking them to mute their tv receivers, preferably the same text simultaneously being sent on the vision channel to be displayed on the tc screens

e/   The viewers who would like to take over the software should now be prompted visually to start their tape recorders for a complete recording.

f/   When the downloading of the software is finished, this should be indicated visually on the tv screens, prompting the viewers to stop their tape recorders.

g/   Finally, a visual indication should be given to the viewers advising them to disable the muting of the sound channels by setting the volume control back to normal.

4. PRACTICAL CONSIDERATIONS

By following each step as outlined above, at the end there will be a tape with the software recorded on it in exactly the same way as if it had been saved conventionally from a computer. The recording is ready for use, it can be loaded into the computer, may be edited, saved again, etc.

A few explanatory remarks seem to be appropriate at this point. First it may be questioned why a tape-recording was made instead of the direct loading of the home computers with the telesoftware? The reason is very simple: most home hobby computers need a relatively high signal level appr. 1~3 V for loading, which is not readily available at the audio output socket of the tv receiver. To avoid the use of an amplifier it is best to use the low signal level for tape-recording, not to speak of the inherent advantage of having the possibility of repetitions in case of subsequent "tape loading errors".

Another problem might be the non-standard type of tape-recorders used with some computers e.g. Commodore 64, ABC-80. Obviously if a specific software is downloaded, then it must be destined for a certain type of computer, different computers are usually not compatible at this level even if they are more or less software-compatible with each other. So if a specific type of computer uses a special type of tape recorder, as well as for the playback.

Finally some advice for those hobbyists, who prefer to file and archive their computer programs. The software arriving through the sound channel is more or less distorted, and it may be desirable to refresh this recording. This can be done easily by loading and then re-saving the program using the conventional computer routines.

5.   CONCLUSIONS

Several experiments have been carried out at the Budapest Technical University to test the feasibility of such a telesoftware method, which uses the sound channel of the television network for data transmission. Different home computers were tested and life-like situations were created and simulated. The results have shown that the temporary loss of the sound channel was not isturbing for the viewers taking part in the tests, and the sound channel proved to be quite adequate for data transmission. The resulting error-rate turned out to be negligiblylow, and even non-skilled persons could follow the steps to get new programs for their computers. All these advantages fully compensate for the temporary loss of the sound channel and the low cost of the realization makes the method very attractive.

Remote Education and Informatics: Teleteaching
F. Lovis (Editor)
Elsevier Science Publishers B.V. (North-Holland)
© IFIP, 1988

AUTOOL - AN AUTHORING SYSTEM FOR VIDEOTEX

Dipl.-Ing. Friedrich HUBER

Institutes for Information Processing
Technical University Graz
8020 Graz, Austria

1. INTRODUCTION

Among the many applications which are available for Personal Computers are systems for the creation of software for learning purposes, so-called authoring systems. The increasing capabilities of
PC's, such as high resolution colour graphics and fast processors
available at a moderate price, make these applications feasible. We
describe AUTOOL, an authoring system which has been developed for
MUPID, the Austrian Videotex Decoder. MUPID can also be used as a
home computer and hence can execute programs which are distributed
via Videotex (Telesoftware). AUTOOL enables a teacher to write
lessons on any topic without any programming knowledge, using
text, colour graphics and animation, as well as questions, to test
the student's understanding of the material. For special purposes
it is also possible to incorporate video and Basic programs.
AUTOOL is based on the famous PLATO system of Control Data and
uses a menu-driven editor for the writing and editing of lessons.
Lessons created in this way can be distributed either via discettes, Videotex, or local networks, such as CONNEX [3]. Not only does
this way of distribution offer cheap education to a large
audience, but it also guarantees an up-to-date standard of the
lessons. Chapter 2 describes the development of AUTOOL and chapter
3 how lessons are edited using AUTOOL. The student's view of a
lesson is presented in chapter 4. The following chapter deals with
the Videotex aspects of the authoring system. In chapter 6 some
conclusions are drawn and improvements that will be made are summarized.

2. COMPUTER AIDED INSTRUCTION

The age of computer aided instruction (CAI) started with Skinner's
work on "The Science of Learning and the Art of Teaching" [12].
There was one main reason for introducing computers into the field
of education: making education cheaper. Previously, there had been
several applications of computers where they had proved successful
in reducing costs. In the early sixties, various different
projects were started. Some of the projects only intended to
create courses on various topics such as physics, mathematics or
foreign languages. Other projects like TICCIT tried to investigate
whether it is possible to split teaching strategies and lesson
content. One of the biggest projects – PLATO – , which started at
the University of Urbana, Illinois, developed different models for
different purposes, such as drill & practice or simulation including graphics. Numerous other projects were started, some of
which survived, while others failed. A description of the major
projects and the different ways of using computers for teaching is
given in [6].

All in all, we can conclude that most of the expectations could not
be fulfilled for simple reasons. One of them was the high hardware costs. The PLATO system, e.g., was running on a mainframe

servicing several hundreds of terminals, and only big companies or the army could afford to buy such a system. And even if the hardware was only rented, a student contact hour cost about 13 dollars [11]. Another reason was the limited abilities of the terminals. Only a very few terminals could display graphics in various colours. Consequently, it was necessary to look for other techniques to facilitate the use of graphics. One of the successful approaches was an experiment using a flat plasma display. It guaranteed a flicker-free high resolution image and was able to superimpose slides and computer generated output [1].

Another important aspect of CAI is the way in which lessons are created. There are two quite different approaches: one is to use programming languages that may be dedicated to authoring purposes, the other is to use authoring systems [8]. Both have their advantages and disadvantages, but for most purposes programming-free systems seem to be better suited. First of all, the author of a lesson does not have to learn a programming language which is in most cases rather hard, but just how to work with an editor. In this way, a programmer becomes superfluous, and the person who knows all about the content of the lesson as well as the best teaching strategy can create the lesson. Secondly, the author can immediately see what he has created, without any translation, since all editing takes place onscreen and with easily manipulated objects. Furthermore, already existing lessons can be easily modified by others, not just by the author of the lesson, whereas changing a lesson written by means of a programming language can be a rather complicated process. Of course there will be some situations, where a programming-free authoring system lacks essential capabilities (e.g. in simulations), but a good authoring systems should allow the incorporation of programs.

Almost all of the drawbacks that prevented a wide acceptance of CAI in its early days have been overcome today. Hardware costs have been dramatically reduced, whereas the performance even of small systems has increased. There are high resolution colour displays available at a moderate price. Even personal computers offer some hundreds kBytes of memory, which is enough for storing a whole lesson. In conclusion, we believe that there is nothing to prevent an extensive use of computers for teaching purposes and we are, together with others, convinced that the computer will become an important delivery system for education within a few years [2].

In 1983, a project was started at the Institutes for Information Processing at the Technical University of Graz. Its aim was to adapt existing TLM lessons for the Austrian Videotex System. TLM is the Tutorial Lesson Model, one of several models of the PLATO system of Control Data. TLM is a frame-based lesson model which uses text and graphics with few colours, question/answer dialogues and learner controlled branches, to present tutorial knowledge on any topic. The institutes developed a software package for executing TLM lessons on MUPID, which is the Austrian Videotex decoder, built to the specifications of the CEPT standard with the ability of displaying text and graphics. With its 64K of user-RAM and a discette station it also can be used as a personal computer [5].

Because the original hardware for TLM lessons had fewer capabilities than MUPID, soon the idea was born to write an editor for generating lessons on MUPID. The first improvements that were achieved with AUTOOL, as the editor was named, were the availability of more colours and graphic objects than before. Furthermore, the answer analysis was improved, and it was made possible to incorporate Videotex pages into lessons and to call Basic programs. The structure of answers has been enriched, and there are

compound graphic objects available. The key ideas of the TLM
editor have been kept: it is a programming- free system based on a
menu-driven editor which is easy both to learn and use [4].

3. EDITING A LESSON

3.1. Frames

AUTOOL is a frame-oriented authoring system. There are several
different types of frames. The standard frame is called "normal
frame". Its purpose is to show tutorial facts using text and
graphics. There are 24 lines of text and 40 columns for text and a
separate line which is used by the system for displaying messages
to the student. The resolution of graphics is 320x240 pixels in 16
colours. Each normal frame has branches to two other frames, a
predecessor and a successor. These branches are set by the author
when the frame is edited. During execution of a lesson the learner
can choose which of these frames he wants to see next by pressing
a key.

Each frame containing at least one question is called a "question
frame". As soon as the author defines a question within a frame,
the editor automatically changes the type of the frame to a question frame. A question frame has one predecessor, which the
learner can reach if he wishes, and two successors (which may
coincide). The successors correspond to the correct and incorrect
answering of the last question in the frame, respectively. A question is either of type fill-in-the-blank or multiple choice and is
described in more detail later in this section.

For branching within a lesson there is an "index frame" available.
An index frame has one predecessor and up to nine successors,
which are reached during execution by typing a number between "1"
and "9". As with question frames, the type of an index frame is
automatically determined by defining an index object. Indexes and
questions in one frame are mutually exclusive.

The so-called "help frame" acts like a subroutine. It can be
reached from different frames, and after it has been displayed,
the learner is led back to the frame from which he had called it.
Except for its linkage, the help frame is built up like a normal
frame, i.e. without questions and branches.

If the author wishes to display a constant part of text or graphic
in more than one frame, he can use a "graphic frame". This frame
is displayed prior to the frame that calls it and the contents of
the call-frame are superimposed on the graphic frame. The graphic
frame has neither a predecessor nor a successor.

At least one frame within a lesson has to be a summary frame. The
summary frame serves as the end of a lesson and hence has no successor. Since there are no special objects within a summary frame,
such as a question or index object, the author has to change the
type explicitly.

3.2. Objects

Each frame is built up of objects. They are defined by typing a
single character which is either mnemonic (0 for circle, / for
line, u for circular arc) or an abbreviation (r for rectangle, a
for answers). During definition there is an "Undo" function available, which aborts the current definition.

The most common object is text. It can be displayed in 16 colours, four different sizes, seven blinking modes and a couple of other attributes. There are different character sets available, including one that can be defined by the author.

A great part of the objects are graphic objects. All objects of the C2-level are available (marker, line, arc, spline, circle, sector, segment, polygon, rectangle) including a special object (vector). Graphic objects can be drawn in 16 different colours, various linestyles and fillstyles. The thickness of lines can be chosen arbitrarily between 1 and 255 pixels. All graphic objects are drawn onscreen and can easily be manipulated (transformed, reshaped, modification of attributes). The author can group different graphic objects and store them on a discette with a specific name for later use. In this way he can build up his own graphic library containing the objects he needs most, thus reducing the amount of work considerably.

Answers can be defined in two ways: either as a multiple choice answer or as fill-in-the-blank. It is assumed that the question has already been defined as text. Regardless of the type, the learner has an author-definable number of tries to enter the correct answer. If all tries are incorrect, and if the answer was the last within the question frame, a branch is made according to the specifications of the author. A multiple choice question consists of up to 16 choices. The author can define whether a choice is correct or incorrect, as well as the feedback message for each choice. During learning, this message is displayed as soon as the learner types the corresponding key. In case of a fill-in-the-blank answer, the author can define three feedback messages: the first is displayed if the student's answer is correct, the others if it is incorrect. The author can force the student to repeat all wrong answers.

In case of a text answer, the author also has to define a model answer with which the student's answer is compared, in order to determine whether it is correct. Using special symbols the author can easily specify different model answers. He can for example define synonyms or a list of words, which can appear in any order within the answer. If not stated otherwise by the author, the student is allowed to enter "sloppy" answers, since typing or spelling errors do not necessarily lead to an incorrect answer. In case of a slight error, the student is shown the correct word as defined by the author and requested to repeat the answer. We believe that this is a better solution than using exact matching or just comparing part of each word with the model answer.

Text and graphics – including combined graphic objects – can be animated, i.e. moved across the screen. The author has to define the path, which is either a straight line divided into equal parts, a series of points, or a circular arc. The animated object is drawn at each point of the path, erased and drawn at the next point. The author can specify that no erasing should take place, leaving copies of the object along the path. Furthermore, it is possible to change the size or orientation of the object during animation. Animation has shown to be very useful for the explanation of dynamic processes or concepts like exchanging the values of two variables.

For simulation or demonstration purposes it is possible to incorporate Basic programs into a lesson. Programs enable the author to do things that are not possible with a programming-free editor, such as detailed interaction with the learner, or showing a specific sorting algorithm with numbers entered by the learner. The program itself can include graphics, so that the author can draw figures calculated from the student's input.

3.3. Editing Commands

After the author has created a frame he may wish to modify some objects. There are two ways of doing this: he can redraw the frame, stepping from one object to another or he can pick objects during frame creation. In the stepping mode, the screen is erased and built up again in the same sequence in which the author has defined the objects. After each object, the author may interrupt the display process and modify the object. Depending on the type of the object, the author is shown menus describing valid modifications. He can change the position of objects on the screen, or reshape graphic objects, or edit text. He can also insert new objects or delete old ones. The pick operation is used for changing only a few objects: a picked object is highlighted and the author can again apply all modification operations to it.

3.4. Preparing a lesson for distribution

After the lesson has been stored on a discette and tested, the author can make it available for distribution via Videotex. Using a special program, the lesson is optimized so that as few Videotex pages as possible are necessary for storing the lesson. The final pages also contain all programs and user defined character sets that are refered to in the lesson. To keep line costs low during learning, lessons have to require less than 32K of memory, which is equivalent to about one hour of student contact time. If a lesson is smaller than 32K then the telephone connection can be interrupted after loading the whole lesson, and the lesson can be worked through offline. Otherwise the connection has to be kept. Another result of the compression is that the student can start working through the lesson as soon as the first frames have been loaded; the rest of the lesson is loaded whenever the system waits for user input, reducing the time from selection of a lesson to its start.

4. EXECUTING A LESSON

There are several ways of executing a lesson: one is to use a discette station, the other is via Videotex or a local network and fileserver, such as CONNEX [3]. After conversion, lessons can also be worked through on an IBM PC with enhanced graphics adapter. Except for loading times there is no difference between them, and in what follows we describe how a lesson is executed via Videotex.

The editor generates a description of all objects in a lesson. This data is interpreted, i.e. displayed by a special program, called executor. The executor is also responsible for interaction with the learner in the case of answer and index objects. After the student has chosen one of the 50 currently available lessons, a check is made whether the executor has already been loaded into the memory. If necessary, the executor is loaded first, and starts then to load the description of the lesson. In this way, loading time for multiple access to lessons is reduced. After few frames have been loaded, the student may start looking at the lesson, while the rest of the lesson is loaded from Videotex whenever there is time for it, e.g. during waiting for learner input. After the whole lesson including programs and user defined character sets has been loaded, the telephone connection is automatically disconnected to keep line costs low.

The student is guided through a lesson by means of messages in the

last line of the screen. If the author has defined user controlled
pauses within a lesson, then the learner is requested to press any
key to continue, and at the end of a frame he can decide which
frame to see next. The messages in the last line are generated by
the executor. In the case of answers, author defined feedback messages
are merged with messages of the executor. If an index object is
encountered, the learner is asked to enter a number that corresponds to the defined branch. Any invalid input is ignored so that
the possibility of input mistakes is eliminated.

The student's activities are not monitored, for two reasons: first
we do not think that it is necessary after the lesson has been
tested, and secondly it simply would not be possible with the off-
line strategy of Videotex. In the Austrian Videotex system you do
not have to identify yourself as long as you just retrieve free
pages. All AUTOOL lessons are free of charge so that lesson execution is fully anonymous. However, since it might be of use to the
author to know which questions are too hard to answer or which
frames are hard to understand (this can be measured by the time
required to go through the frames), there is a special version of
the executor available, which monitors the student's activities
and stores the answers and other data into CMOS RAM. Because this
executor is only available when the lessons are executed locally
with a discette station, abuse of the traced data is avoided.

Additionally, a whole lesson can be copied from Videotex on to a
discette, which is mainly interesting for schools and other institutions.

5. WHY VIDEOTEX ?

There are some reasons why we think that Videotex is better suited
as a distribution medium than any other medium:

* All Videotex users have direct access to all lessons, which is
  not only advantageous to them, but also to those who offer
  lessons.
  As soon as a lesson is offered, it is available to all Videotex
  users without any delivery delay.
* No one is excluded from access to lessons at any time.
  A learner is not tied to any scheduling, as with other media like
  TV, and he is free to learn whenever it is most convenient for
  him. This is an especially user-friendly aspect of Videotex.
* All lessons are continuously up-to-date.
  Using electronic delivery, it is much easier to keep all lessons
  in an up-to-date standard than when discettes are mailed to
  the students. If an error is reported to the author of a lesson,
  the changed version can be made available immediately to all
  users. Using the communication facilities of Videotex, learners
  can make their suggestions in an easy and fast way.
* Videotex is cheaper than other media.
  The storage of a whole lesson costs about US $20 per month (for
  smaller lessons it is even less). To distribute the same lesson
  in a typed version, much larger costs would have to be calculated, not considering all the other advantages of the media.

6. SUMMARY

We have explained AUTOOL, the Austrian Videotex authoring system
which is, as far as we know, unique in its way. We believe that
using electronic media could be a solution to the problem of fast
and cheap distribution of high-quality teachware.

Nevertheless, AUTOOL will undergo two major revisions to make lesson creation even more comfortable: first, we want to use rubberbanding for the definition of graphic objects and secondly, the graphic input device will not be the keyboard but a mouse, which is easy to handle and cheaper than other comparable input devices.

REFERENCES

[1] Bitzer, D., The Wide World of Computer-Based Education, in: Rubinoff, M. and Yovits, M.C., (eds.), Advances in Computers, Vol. 15, (Academic Press, 1976) pp. 239-283.

[2] Bork, A., Personal Computers for Education (Harper & Row, New York, 1985)

[3] Cheng, H., Lipp, P., Maurer, H., GASC - A Low-Cost, No-Nonsense Graphic and Software Communication System, Electronic Publishing Review 5 (1985), pp. 141-155.

[4] Garratt, J., Huber, F. and Huemer, H., AUTOOL - A New Authoring System, IIG Report 219 (Technical University Graz, 1986).

[5] Fellner, W.D., Maurer, H., (eds.) MUPID2 - Überblick, IIG Report 182 (Technical University Graz, 1985).

[6] Hebenstreit, J., New Trends and Related Problems in Computer-Based Education, in: Gilchrist, B., (ed.), Information Processing 77, Proc. IFIP Congress 77 (North-Holland, Amsterdam, 1977), pp. 201-208.

[7] Kaiser, D., Maurer, H., AUTOOL - A New System for Computer Aided Instruction, IIG Report 218 (Technical University Graz, 1986).

[8] Kearsley, G., Authoring Systems in Computer Based Education, Comm. of the ACM, Vol. 25, No. 7 (1982), pp. 429-437.

[9] Maurer, H. A., New Developments in Videotex and Their Implication for Computer Aided Instruction, Information Services and Use 3 (1983), pp.319-324.

[10] Maurer, H.A., Nationwide Teaching through a Network of Microcomputers, to be presented at IFIP World Congress 1986, Dublin

[11] Pantages, A., Plato would have enjoyed PLATO, Datamation, May 1976, pp. 183-187.

[12] Skinner, B.F., The Science of Learning and the Art of Teaching, Harvard Educational Rev., Vol. 24 (1954), pp. 86-97.

Section 5
Technology

Remote Education and Informatics: Teleteaching
F. Lovis (Editor)
Elsevier Science Publishers B.V. (North-Holland)
© IFIP, 1988

TELECOMMUNICATIONS AS AN ASSET IN EDUCATION

Sylvia Charp, U.S.A.

With the increased emphasis on life-long learning and the greater demand for
education by those individuals who cannot avail themselves of the traditional
education provided at a specific educational institution, members of the education community are examining a variety of educational systems in order to
deliver education outside the regular school or college environment. Growing
uses of computers and communication devices have occurred on campus, off-campus
and in the home and we are providing opportunities for learning not previously
available. Many individuals require and desire educational opportunities, not
only those students who can attend regular school hours and can come to a residential campus. Provision must be made for those students who are handicapped,
have family responsibilities or who have any reason which prohibits the utilization of the normal or usual educational established patterns.

Adult learners are the most rapidly growing segment in education, especially in
American education. Demographers state that young people under the age of 25
will decrease by four million and those over the age of 25 will increase by 22
million. The increase in adult learners can be attributed to:

. need for new knowledge and skills as a result of automation
. new job opportunities available to women and minorities
. movement away from centers of learning and opening of job
   opportunities in remote places
. greater emphasis being placed on the value of access to information
   in order to function in a technological society.

Self-paced study has been in existence for many years. One estimate states
that over 3 million people in the U.S. study by correspondence each year.
Learning at a distance, through independent study, is provided to many individuals. Work is, therefore, done at the time and rate of speed most convenient
for the individual. However, certain disadvantages have been noticed. Participants readily lose interest and feel a sense of isolation from other students
and the institution providing the instruction.

The transition into the information age demands the development of innovative
educational delivery systems and the examination of technology as to its role
in providing the motivational and intellectual support lacking in traditional
correspondence courses.

"Distance learning" has become an integral part of at least two institutions in
the U.S. New York Institute of Technology, Westbury, NY, combines independent
study with on line communications. A student can obtain a baccalaureate degree
in a distance learning mode using the computer as a communication device
between the instructors and the student. The courses are still dependent on
printed material but students join classmates in conferences based on specific
courses, i.e. World History, Philosophy or any of the undergraduate courses
offered by the New York Institute of Technology distance learning program.
Communication technology permits interaction to occur between the instructor
and student and between students taking the same courses. The student engages
in the following learning activities:

. submitting homework assignments
. raising questions

. debating issues
. exchanging information

A specific course conference is organized by an instructor or mentor who guides
the student in various learning activities. Conference members receive, write
and send messages to the course conference center which, in turn, can be read
and reviewed by all participants. As members of the "electronic classroom",
students submit essay assignments and ask questions, or debate issues in a
collaborative network of shared information. These activities are just not
possible in a one student - one instructor correspondence or electronic mail
environment.

Messages are transmitted instantaneously and at any time of the day or evening.
All communications are numbered, stored and are immediately accessible when
required. The conferencing software maintains an on-going permanent record of
all messages so that a particular topic can be read or reviewed at any time.

In the preparation of homework assignments, students exchange ideas and look
forward to group-oriented communications and interactivity. Discussions are
usually organized around a specific topic. Users send private messages to
individuals participating in the discussion or communicate privately with the
instructor. Special student conferences permit interaction with one another
to discuss special issues or share a solution to particular topics. To become
a member of New York Institute of Technology's distance learning "electronic
classroom", a student needs the following equipment:

. .a personal computer
. a telephone and modem for sending digital information by telephone
  lines
. a communication software package at the user end
. access to a data communication network

The computer conferencing software is a VAX 11/785 located on campus. The
software is designed to organize the text based communication as it accepts,
stores and organizes messages and to provide users with access to these
messages.

The on-going ability to communicate with the instructor seems to be the most
favorably received aspect of the program. However, since the instructor plays
such an important role, proper training is essential. Willingness to participate must be established at the outset. Use of the computer conferencing system is quite simple and students are able to learn the fundamentals within the
first two weeks of the course. They spend, on the average, 1 - 1½ hours per
week on the system. Access to library data bases and other sources of information is enhancing the learner's ability to manipulate and share ideas.

It is important for students to verbalize about their activities and learning
accomplishments and to have the opportunity to interact directly with their
teachers and fellow students about material being studied. Computers effectively aid a student's communication process as well as **"individualizing"** instruction for that particular student. Students do learn from each other's
strategies, can work cooperatively to solve a common problem and do exchange
questions and comments electronically.

The University of Delaware, Newark, Delaware has been using terminals off-campus
since 1982 to provide lessons in mathematics, English and science to students,
12-18 years of age, who have been found to be deficient in those areas.

Plato terminals, which are networked to the central computers on the campus,
are placed in a residential facility for handicapped students. The project is
accomplishing the following objectives:

. Computer-based instruction is made available to the physically
  handicapped student
. Information is brought to students who have great difficulty in
  travelling to any school
. The skill level of the students involved is increased
. Cultural isolation of the students is diminished and learning of
  computing skills is made possible.

The Plato mainframe to which the terminals are networked has two processors,
two million words of extended memory and the capacity to serve 275 simultaneous
users.   At present, 336 terminal ports are connected to the system.   The
Delaware University Plato System is linked to a Plato network that permits
authors to exchange material and ideas with other Plato users in the U.S.

Many educational users of the computer exist and many institutions have implemented computer-based learning, computer assisted instruction, computer simulations and a number of other ways of integrating the course material into the
curriculum.   The convergence of computing and communication can satisfy the
growing dependence on information and the need for its accessibility. Educators can provide remote education and on-line communication for non-tradi-
tional learners.

1. Fundamental telecommunications concepts are not generally
    understood.

2. More needs to be known on the structure of conferencing systems,
    user behavior during remote sessions, technical aspects,
    accessibility to data bases and educational resources and
    societal effects of remote education.

3. Educators have had little contact with the transmission of voice
    and data and an aura of mystery prevails.

However, regardless of the numerous barriers that seem to surface, we must
continue to investigate the role of telecommunications, as an asset in the
learning process, and how to most effectively provide remote education to those
who can benefit from this type of educational environment.

Remote Education and Informatics: Teleteaching
F. Lovis (Editor)
Elsevier Science Publishers B.V. (North-Holland)
IFIP, 1988

THE VIDEOTEX TERMINAL, AS AN AUDIO-VISUAL TEACHING AID

Paul FERENCZY -   Elisabeth HORVÁTH

Institute of Telecommunications Electronics
Budapest Technical University
Műegyetem rkp. 1-3.
H-1111, Budapest, Hungary

1. INTRODUCTION

Videotex (viewdata) terminals originally provide means of communications with databases, using the conventional telephone lines
as the transmitting media. The data flow to and from the terminals
is thus confined to the voice frequency band. The terminals transform the received data into a visible image by displaying the
codes on a television screen.

By exploiting this feature of the videotex terminals it is possible to make an audio-visual setup together with a conventional
stereo tape recorder. On one of the sound tracks of the compact
stereo cassette a data signal is recorded, which is similar to
the one normally coming from a database. The other track carries
the recording of the accompanying sound (voice and/or music),
which is thereby inherently in synchronism with the data signal
producing the visual display. Although the performance of a video
cassette recorder (VCR) is obviously much higher than the displaying capability of a videotex terminal, the significant advantage
of this audio-visual system lies without doubt in the enormous
price difference between a VCR and an audio (stereo) cassette
tape recorder.

2. PREPARATION OF THE MASTER-TAPE

To prepare an audio cassette ready for direct use or for mass-
reproduction, first a suitable subject should be chosen. Typical
examples are: language lessons, music teaching, mathematics,
geometry, spelling exercises, etc. Next comes the task of out-
lining the basic content of the chosen lesson so that the lesson,
or lessons would each fit in into an approx. time-duration of
15-30 minutes. Next comes the task of writing the script book for
the whole program, including all the conversations, talks, music
inserts, etc., which should be audible during the replay. Parallel with the text, the script writer also has to plan carefully
the visual displays, which in turn may consist of written material
using the ASCII characters, and there is also the possibility of
inserting simple mosaic graphics illustrations conventionally
used in Prestel type teledata systems.

Having compiled the audio-visual script book, paying special
attention to the required synchronism between the audio and the
visual materials, the next phase of preparing the master tape is
to design and create all the necessary frames to be displayed on
a suitable teledata editing terminal. If the frames are designed
to be still pictures, then these should be recorded on floppy

disc, using the conventional teledata code-protocol. On the other
hand, if some of the frames are planned to show a certain amount
of animation, then this should be taken into consideration, before the floppy-disc prerecordings are made. Of course, to generate dynamic teledata pictures one must use an editing terminal
which is capable of producing such frames.

At this point all the preliminary work is done, so that the stereo
cassette tape recorder can be connected for the master recording
to be made. If the left channel is chosen for the sound track recording, then a good quality microphone should be attached to the
left input of the tape recorder. The right channel input then
must have an input signal exactly equivalent to the (Prestel)
teledata protocol: 1200 Baud data rate, the signalling frequencies
being 1300 Hz and 2100 Hz respectively. This signal is provided
by an interface unit connecting the tape recorder with the teledata editing terminal. This interface is essentially **provided** by
half of a modem used to connect a database to the telephone lines.
In this case, obviously the high data rate (1200 Baud) channel will
be used only, since the return channel (75 Baud) is of no use
during a data signal recording.

It is essential that during the whole recording procedure there
should be no breaks in the data-channel signal, since they would
lead to an automatic disconnection of the teledata display terminal. In other words, at any time between data-packet transmissions
the standby frequency of 1300 Hz (=logic high) must be held constant
at the right channel input terminal. The interface automatically
provides this signal, if its data input receives no coded data
to be forwarded to the teledata display terminal.

Having started tape recorder in the recording mode the speaker
should begin reading the text from the script book, while the
technician is operating the editing terminal in such a way that
the prerecorded frames - still, or moving - will arrive through
the interface at the data channel input at the desired time. If
musical inserts come up in the script book, then these should
suitably be mixed into the audio channel at the proper time.

3. REPLAYING THE MASTER TAPE

In contrast to the relative complexity of the recording procedure,
playing back the master tape is quite simple and needs no skilled
operator. Only two things are needed besides the master tape:
a teledata terminal and a stereo cassette tape recorder. One
simple connection should be made from the right audio channel
output of the recorder to the (telephone) line input of the terminal. Before starting the tape, the stereo balance setting should
be offset completely to the left so that only the left channel
would be audible in the loudspeakers. On certain tape recorders
it might be necessary to disconnect the right side loudspeakers,
e.g. by inserting a dummy plug into the right external loudspeaker
socket.

In order to enable the teledata terminal to receive and display
the data signal, the normal remote control should be used and
those keys should be pressed which are used to initiate a database call. Having done this, everything is set to start the
program flow. When the tape starts, the data channel immediately
begins to transmit the standby frequency of 1300 Hz, which in

turn informs the teledata terminal, that a "database" is answering the call on the telephone line. So the connection is built up in the normal way and as soon as the tape reaches a point, where teledata signals are recorded, the terminal will react to these as if they were coming from a true data base. The result is a display, or a series of displays, still or moving, and they automatically accompany the spoken words coming from the audio channel in perfect time synchronism.

It is possible to start the program from any intermediate point or to break the replay at any time, since the data and the audio signals are recorded on the same tape.

4. MULTIPLICATION OF THE MASTER TAPE

Once a master tape has been finalized, it can be replicated using the usual procedures for normal audio tape reproduction. It should be noted, however, that second, or higher generation copies of a master tape might develop display errors, due to the corruption of the data signal waveform on higher generation copies. Also it should be pointed out that out-of-tolerance tape recorder speed differences may result in erroneous picture/text reproduction.

5. CONCLUSIONS

It has been shown that a commercial stereo cassette tape recorder, together with a teledata terminal can be used to produce an audio-visual program, which otherwise would require a much higher priced video tape recorder and significantly more expensive video cassettes. Compact audio cassettes can be made and mass-reproduced with teaching programs covering all kinds of different subjects. To prove the feasibility of the outlined system, several demonstration cassettes have been produced at the Institute of Telecommunications Electronics, Budapest Technical University.

Remote Education and Informatics: Teleteaching
F. Lovis (Editor)
Elsevier Science Publishers B.V. (North-Holland)
© IFIP, 1988

USE IN CONTINUING EDUCATION OF TRAINING PACKAGES FOR
THE INTRODUCTION OF TECHNICAL EQUIPMENT AND APPLIANCES

G. Grósz Ph.D., L. Forgács Ph.D.
Institute for Continuing Education in Industry
Budapest, Hungary

1. Reasons for technical-professional extension training.

It has become clear to everyone by now that learning is not finished by
obtaining a qualification. Permanent and regular after-school training is
necessary for everyone. In the technical-professional practice this is
justified by the following:

a. There is insufficient time for the acquiring of the rapidly
   increasing amount of information during the traditional gradual
   school training. This is particularly true in the interdisciplinary faculties, for instance, biotechnology or
   bioengineering.

b. During the gradual training, insufficient time is available for
   the acquiring and training of the practical skills. In many
   cases, this hinders the efficient work of the engineers and
   technicians working in industry. Therefore, efforts must be made
   as early as possible to acquire the practical information or
   specialised professional knowledge.

c. The evolution of new professional fields and the restructuring of
   labour force require retraining, extension training and the
   continuous increase of knowledge.

d. There is a growing demand for the highly qualified experts in
   enterprises. For instance: in the fields of electronics,
   robotics, computer techniques, etc.

e. Individual interests: problems of existence, the possibility of
   progress, or spontaneous interest also motivate continuous and
   regular advanced training.

2. Continuing education - a new form of extension training.

It is well-known to everybody that in the competition for the domestic and
international markets only those economic organizations/enterprises and
institutions can be successful which are sufficiently sensitive and ready to
implement continuous innovation. Innovation is a non-stop development in
which the necessity of development of the human resources, i.e. the human
factor, constitutes the essential factor. Therefore, learning and training
have important roles in progress. However, it is not unimportant how much
time and what cost are involved in the process. Therefore, new and more
efficient forms of training and extension training, methods and means are
necessary, adjusting quickly to development. The new forms can bring about
results only through up-to-date information and with methods fully adjustiing
to the individual paces of learning.

A possible form of this solution is the application of continuing education as distance education, or remote education. Continuing education is a controlled teaching-learning process with feed back, in the course of which the tutor and the student are remote in space and time and the methodological acquisition of the information is assisted by the most modern materials, (software) and instruments (hardware) of educational technology.

The student is given a training package with all the information necessary for the learning of a given subject or material. The necessary information may be transmitted through various media, which aim at promoting the visual features and efficiency of education. The media may also include traditional instruments, such as overhead transparencies or slide-series with sound track, or textbooks, syllabi and test-sheets, etc, but the most modern media can also be used: video cassette recorders, video disk and personal computers as well.

With the help of continuing education, absence from work can be minimized, together with the losses of work time and the expenses of education. The application of continuing education can take place in the specific subject fields both in the field of complementary training and/or extension training.

In the following, we report on our effort of spreading the application of continuing education to a new field which promises wide use. This field is the training of correct operation, expertlike application and preventive maintenance of machinery and equipment, applied in the industry. To underline the importance of the question, an example is demonstrated and conclusions are drawn concerning eh significance of this form of education. The example is taken from an interdisciplinary field, introducing all the special features which may come to the surface in this area. Therefore, it is necessary to briefly define the concept and tasks of this interdisciplinary field: bioengineering and its applied field, i.e. clinical engineering, and also the ways in which the training packages can assist the application of medical appliances.

3.   Problems of application of the medico-technical equipment.

The efficiency of medical work is more and more influenced by the quality and technical state of the applied machines and equipment. Reliable results cannot be achieved with unqualified operating or absence of regular maintenance; since this greatly determines the right diagnosis and the suitable therapy. There is another problem that the clinical devices - some of them composed of the most complicated electronic circuitry and often attached to computers to perform controlling functions - are handled by medical staff, who are not trained as technicians. On the basis of all these, the education of the proper operating, handling and maintenance in the field of biomedical and clinical engineering play an even more important role.

The quick spreading of medica-technical insturmentations and devices calls continuously for, from all physicians, engineers and technicians, more and more additional knowledge. To acquire the fast increasing substance of knowledge, new educational systems and methods are necessary.

For this reason, a training package has been developed by the Institute for Continuing Education in Industry, for the proper handling and maintenance of the medico-technical equipment.

It was our principle that the teaching and understanding are made more effective by:

- schematic figures with short explanations and /or instructions,

- slides of circmstances of applicationor adjustment possibilities,
  video recordings of installation and practical use of equipment, and

- detailed instructions for students and/or speakers who introduce the
  equipment, according to subject and educational method, etc.

These media were put into a uniform system and the training package or
tutorial set was developed according to the aims of its use.

The training packages have different aims. They can be:

- informative materials for reference purposes, or

- teaching-learning materials comprising instructions for handling and
  preventive maintenance.

In the following we want to show as an example such a training package, about
operating tables with changeable table-tops.

4. Aim of application of training package for reference purposes.

To make people interested in, and the users, as well as the students,
participating in the individual and organized study, acquainted with clinical
operating tables with changeable table-tops, looking at the fields of
applications, technical characteristics, medical-professional, technical, as
well as economic advantages, and comparing them to other models.

Accordingly, this package is recommended for:

- hospital managers and executives, health-care administrators,
- hospital and health-care staff (doctors, nurses, assistants)
- traders of medical equipment,
- technical staff of hospitals (engineers, technicians),
- experts of service organizations and
- specialists in bioengineering.

The training package for reference purposes incorporates the following parts:

a. Videofilm on "Operating tables with changeable table-tops" to show the
   features and field of application of operating tables type MAC.

b. Series of slides to show the features of operating tables type MAC to
   illustrate the introductory presentation - adjusting to the skills of the
   audience (medical, technical or economic experts).

c. Illustrated technical syllabus for inquirers and lecturers. (It can also
   be used as a "brochure".)

d. General instructions for the experts making the introductory
   presentation.

e. Subjects and methodological guideline for the speaker making the
   introductory presentation.

f. Discussion questions/answers for the speakers with detailed explanations,
   data and comparisons.

g.   Scenario of the videofield for the information of the speaker in the
     preparatory stage.

The items a-c contain the professional material to be described; while items
d-g offer methodological assistance for the speakers, to make sure that the
contents of the presentations and the standard are equivalent in each case.

The training package can be applied during oral presentation or for practical
demonstration, for example, at exhibitions or in the form of individual
training.

The process and programme of the presentation (or demonstration), as well as
the steps of individual training are included in the subjects. Accordingly,
it is first preferable to have the oral presentation illustrated with slides.
The explanation absolutely necessary for the individual slide/pictures is
included in the illustrated technical syllabus or the sound cassette.   The
explanation can be eventually extended with the answers detailed in the
discussion questions/answers.

Subsequently the videofilm "Operating tables with changeable table-top" should
be shown and this would be preferably followed by answering the questions of
the audience. The most important problems, data and experience have been
collected in the discussion questions which have presented themselves most
often so far. This can best be used by the expert making the presentation for
giving correct and detailed answers to the questions. The subject and the
methodological guidlines provide assistance for the speaker in making his
introductory presentation (or demonstration) and for the use of the training
package in the course of this. This guideline is not obligatory, it can be
adjusted any time, in relation to the composition, the training of the
audience, the scene and the technical-economic possibilities.   Individual
items of the subjects can be changed, extended or reduced. However, it is
preferable to follow the guidelines, as in this way information of identical
standard and precision can be provided in different locations for different
audiences.

5.   Conclusions.

The training package mentioned is primarily of informative character, its task
is to introduce the equipment of a given type to the potential customers and
users.   Another training package promotes the correct operation and regular
preventive maintenance of the appliance, encouraging in this way the use of
the device, the maintenance of operating capability and the extension of
servicelife.   It is a general experience that the users - mainly the
technically unskilled staff - will either not read large operating manuals of
frequently 50 to 100 pages, or that the technical instructions will not be
understood. As a result, improper operation may take place, with damage to
the equipment.

Therefore, our training package demonstrates the operation with many and
detailed illustrations and technical drawings, with brief explanations or
instructions. At the same time, the correct operation and regular daily
maintenance are also demonstrated on videofilm. Methodological instructions
are also given for the use of the training package.

These points stand for a special and new type of continuing education, as in
the given case the aim is not to learn a whole subject, but to acquire
knowledge about a device or family of appliances and their expert application.

The learning guide and test sheets also belong to the essence of continuing education.   However, in our case the most perfect feedback is if the device operates normally and reliably.

With the help of such training packages, the learning of the features and operation of the appliance will be much shorter in time and more powerful through illustrations.   This training package can also be made an accessory of the device and in this way there will be no need for the operators to travel for a long time and over long distances to attend operating courses.   This is the way in which the modern teaching-learning methods and forms can actually become integral parts of innovation.

Remote Education and Informatics: Teleteaching
F. Lovis (Editor)
Elsevier Science Publishers B.V. (North-Holland)
  IFIP, 1988

UPGRADING HOME COMPUTERS INTO AUDIOVISUAL TEACHING MACHINES

Ferenc KIS-SZÖLGYÉMI,   Antal PÁLINSZKI,   Pál FERENCZY,
   Imre KOVÁCS

Institute of Telecommunications Electronics
Budapest Technical University
Műegyetem rkp. 1-3.
H-1111, Budapest, Hungary

1. INTRODUCTION

The significant spread of home computers has underlined their
possible usage as audiovisual teaching aids. In certain cases
(e.g. language teaching) the quality of the voice synthetizers
built into home computers is far from being satisfactory. This
problem can be solved by using a conventional stereo tape recorder
in combination with the computer and a colour display equipment.
One of the sound tracks can carry the synchronising signals to
control the computer, while the other track provides the audio
program in good listening quality, meant to accompany the displayed visual information. This latter one is produced by the computer
itself having been loaded with the properly written software.
Different kinds of tutorial materials can be made and multiplicat-
ed on prerecorded compact cassettes.

2. THE OUTLINE OF THE SYSTEM

The computerised audiovisual teaching set up, designed and developed at the Budapest Technical University consists of a home
(hobby) computer, a colour tv receiver and a stereo tape recorder.
The demonstration programs produced were made for the ZX-Spectrum
and the Commodore 64 hobby computers; other types of computers
may obviously be used too, provided they have facility to be
connected to tape recorders. Having been loaded with the proper
program the computer displays all the texts and figures comprising
the visual part of the teaching material. These displayed figures
and texts are synchronised firmly with the sound coming from the
loudspeaker of the tape recorder, since the data track, controlling
the computer triggers the program flow with short-duration sinewave bursts. These bursts must suitably be recorded together
with the audio-material, on separate tracks, so that even if
for some reason the tape is halted - for instance to provide
time for additional explanations - this will not upset   the
synchronism between picture and sound.

3. USING THE AUDIOVISUAL SYSTEM

Having assembled and interconnected the equipment   it should be
switched on. Next the computer must be loaded with the teaching
program. This can preferably be done by using the same tape
recorder and cassette which can easily carry not only the

combined audio program and the data bursts, but also the complete
software. The computer is then prompted every time a sinewave
burst comes up on the data track. It is advisable to make
 experiments to find the optimum settings of the tone, volume and
balance controls of the tape recorder. In the event of correct
settings the triggering of the computer will be faultless, while
the synchronising sine-bursts will practically be inaudible.

4. MAKING AUDIOVISUAL PROGRAMS

Besides the equipment mentioned so far, the only things needed
for making a cassette recording are an audio frequency (AF)
generator and a microphone. First the computer program should
be written, together with carefully located breaks in it, these
serving to stop the running of the program, waiting for a key
to be pressed. The script book of the complete audiovisual
program should be compiled, including the speeches, music, etc.
The microphone is connected to one of the stereo input channels,
while the other input should receive the suitable gated or keyed
AF generator signal. The AF generator output level is to be
adjusted to drive the recorder to appr. 0 dB recording level.
The frequency to be used is, e.g., 200 Hz. Starting both the
recorder and the computer program, the speaker should read the
text from the script book into the microphone. Every time it
contains a break (for a visual display to be changed), the AF
generator should be keyed in for appr. 3 seconds and also a
computer key should be pressed. This latter one will let the
program continue in the computer, while the AF generator signal
marks the point on the tape where a change in the display is
expected.

After the whole script book has been recorded on tape, the computer program should be **re-edited** so that the breakpoints, which
have so far waited for a key to be pressed, should become a
properly designed waiting routine. This latter one will wait
for the sound-bursts to come in, which in turn will let the
program continue. With this procedure the audiovisual program
is ready for use, or for mass-reproduction.

5. CONCLUSIONS

The research team at the Budapest Technical University has made
several demonstration cassettes to prove the feasibility of
the above outlined new audiovisual system. The home computers
involved were the ZX Spectrum and the Commodore 64. The demonstrations showed that a commercial stereo tape recorder can
significantly boost the computer's ability to serve as very
attractive audiovisual teaching machines.

Section 6
CD-ROM Video Discs

Remote Education and Informatics: Teleteaching
F. Lovis (Editor)
Elsevier Science Publishers B.V. (North-Holland)
© IFIP, 1988

THE VIDEO DISK AS A TEACHING AID

Dr. Franz Netta and Dr. Ulrich Staub
TELEMEDIA GmbH
D-4830 Gütersloh
P.O.B. 5555
Tel. 05241/ 80-2872
Tx: 933 822 sono

The need for teaching is rising.

A problem increasingly encountered in personnel recruitment is the lack of suitably qualified staff. And even for the most highly qualified employee, it is difficult nowadays to keep his level of information up to date with the shorter product life cycles. So the need for training is constantly increasing.

However, since the costs of instructors and lost manhours on attendance at courses are permanently rising too, the result is a conflict between the need for more training and an inability to bear the costs of conventional training methods.

Demands made of a high quality training medium

Positive changes in training methods can involve either the training content or the training media employed. High quality training media must be sufficiently flexible to adapt to different training contents or different training routines. In this respect, the laser video disk has the following features:

1. It is easy to use

2. The disk will not wear; it is robust and reliable

3. Each item of information is clearly identified via frame and section numbers

4. It can be cross-referenced to written material via unambiguous addresses

5. Each item of information can be accessed directly

6. Search times are extremely short

7. It allows high speed perusal ("scanning")

8. Frames can be frozen at any time and for any length of time /"scene freezing")

9. Reproduction is extremely flexible

10. It allows mass storage of individual frames/mixtures with films

11. Moving sequences can be presented in compressed form by series of frames

12. It has two separate sound channels

13. It can be linked to external computers (e.g. via VTX)

14. It can be used interactively as an instructor's aid, or for
    self-teaching workstations

The typical applications that follow reveal just how important
these features are for individual training applications.

Video disk applications in education and in-service training

The advantages of the video disk as a teaching medium become
evident from the applications that follow, and from comparison
with the other "visual" media - slides,films, video-cassettes
and computer graphics.

The use of video disks in schools

Klett Verlag have put five programs on to video disk to tie in
with the secondary grade I biology curriculum. Section and frame
number details on the video disk sleeve assist the teacher to
access the individual parts of the program. In some cases,
accompanying written material is provided.

Two of Klett's programs have been put to the test in 30 schools
in North Rhine-Westphalia, in trials organized jointly by Klett,
Philips and the "FEoLL".

From a provisional report on the trials by the "FEoLL", I quote:

> "... over 90% agreed:
> The advantage of the video disk is that I can interrupt a
> presentation at any time to add my own explanations.
> (Only 7 teachers out of 100 answered 'No' to this question).
>
> The statement with the second highest proportion of agreement
> was:
> The video disk is the sensible, logical progression from
> existing teaching media.
> (Yes: 89, No: 10)."
>
> "The teaching version of the video disk, the most user-friendly
> teaching and learning medium to date for educational media use,
> represents a qualitative leap, an extension of the possibili-
> ties offered by films, videos, slides and transparencies alone.
>
> With this medium, one no longer needs to concern oneself with
> technical and organization details, but can concentrate
> exclusively on the content and on getting it over in the best
> way for the students".

Given its frame-freezing capability and high memory capacity
(with 54,000 individual frames per side), the laser video disk
- unlike the VHD video disk which has only a limited frame-
freezing capability due to the wear on the video caused by
mechanical scanning - can easily replace the slides archive
still common in schools organizations. Hence the cost of handling
and transporting FWU slides via local picture libraries could be
greatly reduced, since all 40,000 or so FWU slides would fit on
a single video disk.

The use of video disks for in-house training

The Bundesinstitut für Berufsbildung (BIBE) [the Federal Institute

of Professional Training], a central media institution under the
Federal Ministry of Education, on the basis of its trials,
considers the laser video disk to be the most suitable AV medium
for educational and training purposes. It brings to fulfilment the
years of endeavour to make use in education of good quality still
and motion pictures, combined at will. Every section of film and
every individual frame, irrespective of whether it is an individual
frame of a film or a slide, can be accurately pinpointed and
projected for whatever length of time is required. Given the
possibilities of repeating, stopping and slow motion, over and
above the earlier "playback", this AV medium can thus be fully
integrated in education and/or training. Teachers and students gain
a universally usable tool with which they themselves can define
their own tuition."

The BIBB has already produced a series of its training films on
video disk, and is intending to expand its range continuously.

There follows a number of applications for the video disk in
occupational training and in-service training, arranged by sector:

The motor trade

In the USA, the major motor manufacturers use video disk players
(GM: 11,000 units; Ford: 5,000 units) for training dealers and
mechanics and for sales promotion purposes. Sales staff training
and customer information are cleverly linked on one and the same
disk, simply modified by different computer programs.

Before Ford decided to use the video disk, the company had a video
cassette system that proved unusable, due to the impossibility of
locating individual parts of films, excessive access times and the
high level of material wear.

Fiat in Germany has introduced video disk systems for just under
900 dealers: once again they are also being used both for training
sales staff and mechanics, and for customer information. These
systems have been extremely well received, and the network is
therefore continually being expanded.

Medicine

In addition to Essen University's video disk discussed in detail in
the paper "Special purpose data banks: the video disk and VTX in
medicine", by Dr. Anders and Mr. Philippi, pharmaceuticals
companies Pfizer and Boehringer of Mannheim - like Miles, Pfizer,
Merck and others in the U.S.A. - are using the video disk for in-
service training of doctors. Suffice it to say here that the doctors
are delighted with the video disk, due to the possibility of interactive working as opposed to the passive "cinema" consumption of
16 mm linear films (still the conventional method of in-service
training for doctors in many places). There are also major handling
advantages to a video disk system when compared with 16 mm
equipment.

The military

The USA Army, in trials carried out among American soldiers, found
that interactive video disk systems maintain a high level of
concentration for 54 minutes, as compared with just under 20 minutes

with other learning methods. On the strength of its findings, it
has now gone out to tender for 40,000 video disk players for use
in soldier training, particularly in the operation of technical
equipment. The introduction of video disks into NATO is already
being discussed.

Computer manufacturers

Major computer manufacturers such as IBM, DEC, CDC, NCR, Wang and
Apple, most of whom a few years ago were maintaining that all
teaching problems could be solved by the use of VTX or computer
graphics, have since introduced video disk systems both for
training their own staff and for external computer users.

VTX and computer graphics are no real alternative for training
purposes. They cannot transmit sound or photographs, let alone
films. And text alone is unable to provide sufficient motivation
for learning or to explain complicated visually recorded facts.

So, in America, IBM has set up "Guided Learning Centers" in 144
towns and cities, in each of which a series of self-tuition
workstations has been installed, with an integrated video disk
player/PC configuration. Based on their initial experience, IBM
have calculated a saving of 30% on training costs in comparison
with previous expenditure.

In England, too, 11 IBM Guided Learning Centers have already been
set up, and a similar project is scheduled for the near future in
Germany.

IBM are also seeking to train their PC customers by video disk
units installed with dealers, and in Europe alone, 1,500 players
have already been installed for this purpose.

Another highly interesting application is the training of technicians responsible for maintenance at nuclear power stations.

The advantages of video disk self-tuition systems

When using a video disk self-tuition system, the student himself
becomes active. He determines his own learning path and learning
rate, and receives a continuous feedback on his progress.

The only method surpassing the use of interactive video disk
tuition in terms of effectiveness is one-to-one personal tuition,
although here the cost would be prohibitive.

The advantages of the video disk self-tuition systems are,
specifically:

- . elimination of travelling and accommodation costs
- . limited loss of time/use of free time
- . learning is unobserved, hence no embarrassment
- . the rate of learning is individually set
- . the learning program is individual
- . learning sucess is constantly monitored

The interactive video disk self tuition unit consequently provides
optimum training quality for a maximum number of students, at
minimum cost.

Possible configurations:

A number of alternative hardware configurations is available for
video disk training units, specifically designed to suit different
applications.

Even the standard video disk player designed for the general
consumer will offer the first four of the video disk self tuition
system advantages mentioned above. However, operation via normal
remote control is non user-friendly and cumbersome for professional
use.

In view of these operating difficulties, the TELESELECT 1000 video
disk information system has been developed, easily operated by
anyone, even without being accustomed to the system. To work in
interactive mode with the video disk player, the user needs only
to enter a figure taken from a screen menu, via a ten-key keyboard.
Apart from an "index" key which returns him to the main menu,
there are no other operating keys. The TELESELECT 1000 system is,
for example, being used with great success by Pfizer and
Boehringer, in the in-service training of doctors mentioned
earlier.

Non computer-linked video disk systems already have a high
interaction capability naturally offering substantial cost and
reliability advantages, but if, in addition to this, individual
learning success monitoring and automatic teaching program adaptation in line with the user's progress are required, a computer
has to be incorporated in the video disk system.

One way in which this can be achieved is by combining the player
and the computer within a single housing. As a rule, the computer
program is then loaded either by the video disk as computer dump,
or via a plug-in EPROM. The advantage of an extremely compact
system has to be weighed against the disadvantage of limited
applications flexibility: the permanently installed computer is,
for example, difficult to use for other AV functions.

The second possible configuration involves linking a standard
personal computer, possibly with an integrated VTX decoder, with
a video disk player controlled via a standardized computer
interface. This configuration offers maximum applications flexibility and the maximum number of design variants in didactical/
method terms.

It is available, for example, in TELESELECT 2000 system, which
in addition to the system's full computer back-up, also offers:

-   maximum ease of handling (as with the TELESELECT 1000),

-   VTX page overlay with video information from the video disk
    and

-   (if the system is used in a network of several self-tuition
    work stations) country-wide program updating from a central
    computer, with no additional handling of hardware or data
    media at the place of use

As with all other training systems, however, the most important
design parameter in video disk self-tuition systems is not the

hardware, but the didactic/method conceptual design. However, the new hardware recently introduced - and in particular TELESELECT 2000 - opens up some new and extremely interesting possibilities in this field.

Remote Education and Informatics: Teleteaching
F. Lovis (Editor)
Elsevier Science Publishers B.V. (North-Holland)
© IFIP, 1988

CD-ROM AS STORAGE MEDIUM FOR COMPUTER AIDED INSTRUCTION

Peter SAMMER

Institutes for Information Processing
Technical University Graz
8010 Graz, Austria

1. INTRODUCTION

Although until recently the extent of usage of computer aided instruction (CAI) had failed to match past predictions, CAI [2], [4], [7] has nevertheless been firmly established in some areas of application [9]. Numerous experiments and projects at elementary, secondary and university levels, as well as those in industrial training programs, have shown that the importance of CAI is steadily growing. Until now, courseware has been distributed mostly via local area networks of large computer systems or disks or, as in some cases, via videotex systems [1], [3], [5], [6], [8], [10]. However, because of the rapidly growing amount of courseware and the amount of data involved it has become increasingly necessary to look out for other suitable storage media.

In this connection, optical storage media immediately suggest themselves because of their high capacity as well as their speed of data transfer. With its enormously large storage capacity (up to about 300,000 printed pages can be stored on one disk), a CD-ROM (Compact Disk Read Only Memory) opens up completely new ways of creating instructional material.

In our research, we have looked into the possibilities of applying CD-ROM to increase the use of computer graphics and audio-supported lessons. For example, digitized pictures, as well as digitized language, have until now hardly been used, because of their large storage requirements. Also, with a more systematized application of CAI courseware, the need for an extensive and easily accessible documentation arises. A CD-ROM makes it thus possible to store not only the entire educational software, consisting of text, graphics, pictures and audio information, but also a complete lesson documentation which can naturally also be printed.

Furthermore, the use of optical disks also guarantees a certain degree of copy protection. The simple way of distribution, the unproblematic handling and the durability of the disks are additional reasons which speak in favour of an application of CD-ROMs.

Following the introduction, the second section provides some basic information about the storage medium CD-ROM. In the third section we discuss some of the different possibilities CD-ROM offers for the use of graphics. The fourth section deals with the exploitation of CD-ROM's storage capacity for the integration of audio sequences into CAI. In the fifth section, we look into some aspects of cost and copy protection. Finally, the sixth part contains a few concluding remarks about CD-ROM.

2.   CD-ROM, A NEW MEDIUM

CD-ROM is a new and versatile medium for the distribution of information. For educational purposes, its unique ability of integrating text, complex graphics, voice and images at relatively low costs, turns CD-ROM into a flexible, future-oriented medium.

Although the idea of using CD-ROM as a storage medium is relatively new, the development of CD-ROM has nevertheless been based on internationally recognized standards. Originally set for Compact Audio Discs, these standards are today likewise applied to data processing.

Clearly, one of the most impressive aspects about CD-ROM is the relation between capacity and cost. Using an optical laser technique, a single-sided 120mm diameter disc can be used to store about 600 MBytes of data. Additionally, the inexpensive replication technique further reduces the cost/byte ratio considerably. As an illustration, a single Compact Disc can contain what corresponds to 300,000 pages of written text, several thousand optical images or hours of audio material – this in any chosen combination.

Because data stored on a Compact Disk is sealed under a protective coating and is read by means of a contact-free laser-optic system, the probability of data damage or simple wear is drastically reduced – an important aspect easily appreciated in school environment where educational software is often exposed to rough treatment.

A CD-ROM disk is built up in the following way: the spiral track is divided into sectors, each containing 2 Kbytes. Since the data is written with a constant linear density, each sector is addressable with an absolute sequence number from the start of the track. In connection with CD-ROM, absolute time is used to ensure compatibility with CD digital audio format. Consequently, sector addresses consist of number of minutes (0-60), number of seconds (0-60), and 75ths of a second (0-74). Using a time/position algorithm, fast access under microprocessor control is achieved.

The transfer of data from the CD-ROM drive is conducted via a bit-serial interface. The transmission rate for data is 1.41 Mbits/sec. [11].

The field of application of CD-ROMs is manifold. With its enormous storage capacity and fast access time, CD-ROM can be used in any area where immediate access to a vast amount of structured information is required, as for example in business, public administration, legal and medical professions, science and engineering. However, because of its singular ability to combine text, graphics, pictures and voice, CD-ROM stands out as a natural and highly effective medium especially suited for educational purposes. For this reason, we have made the educational application of CD-ROM the object of our study.

3.   GRAPHICS AND CD-ROM

Normally, computer graphics (e.g. vector graphics) are stored in coded form and must consequently first be decoded after being read into the computer from an external medium. The reasons for this are among others a demand for limited memory requirements and short transfer times. The importance of this demand is easily recognized when we consider the relatively small storage capacity of the floppy disks and the slow transmission rate of data via

telephone (as is the case with, for example, videotex or other
narrow-band communication lines). On the other hand, this method
implies that we must accept a relatively slow re-draw rate
(because of the necessary decoding). Despite this fact, this
method is, due to the slow transfer speed, still faster than using
digitized pictures.

By employing CD-ROMs, an optimal application of graphics stored on
pixel basis is made possible. If we calculate a storage
requirement amounting to 40KBytes for one pixel-wise stored
picture (sufficient for a resolution of 320 x 240 pixels if 16
colours are used), then it is still possible to store 15,000
pictures on one disk side. Since the data can be read directly
into the graphics memory of the computer from the CD-ROM (no
decoding is required), it is possible to build up complicated
graphics in a split second.

Graphics of this kind could be drawn with a paint editor which
enables direct painting on the screen. However, pictures stored on
pixel-basis could also first be drawn by means of a draw-editor.
This has the advantage that pictures or parts thereof can be
easily manipulated (change of colour, reduction of size, rotation,
etc.). Not until the graphics have been finished is the screen
memory read out, by means of an auxiliary function of the editor
and the information required for the pixel-wise storage is filed
on an external storage medium. In order to achieve a large variety
of creation possibilities, it seems in this connection that a
combination of draw and paint editor systems is the best solution.

Also, the use of digitized pictures could be greatly intensified
if used in connection with CD-ROMs. A video-picture recorded by
a camera, or a section of a picture can be coded via an
analog/digital converter in digitized form. After digitalization,
a graphic modification such as, e.g., point correction or line
correction is possible.

If the picture is stored pixel-wise, the storage requirements are
admittedly large, but we have the advantage, when the graphics are
re-displayed, of being able to read the data directly into the
graphics memory, which significantly reduces the time needed to re-
draw the picture. Consequently, because of their large storage
capacity and high rate of transmission, CD-ROMs make an
uncomplicated integration of digitized photographs into CAI
lessons possible.

Also, as far as animated graphics are concerned, additional
interesting aspects present themselves, compared to the present
possibilities, such as for example the use of sprites in a program.
In the following considerations we assume a suitable organization
of the data stored on the CD-ROM, in order to keep the access time
optimally short.

If a number of pixel-wise stored pictures is shown immediately
succeeding each other, a simulation of a film projected in slow-
motion (a few pictures per second), is achieved. If we do not
require the whole screen for the animated graphics, we can limit
the pictures to a smaller rectangular section where the film
simulation can be run with correspondingly shorter time between
picture sequences.

In order to create animated graphics it is not always necessary to
draw screen-size pictures anew. Sometimes we can reduce the
sections where the animation takes place to rectangles which can
vary in numbers, position and size. Since the changes do not take
place all the time, it can be advantageous to store the time

interval until the next picture, and, for each of the rectangles,
the co-ordinates of the starting point, their length and height,
and only then the graphics data on a pixel basis. Using suitable
software and the high speed of transfer of the CD-ROMs, we can thus
achieve animation on background graphics which can cover the whole
screen.

The application of CD-ROMs as storage medium for CAI lessons
offers the author of courseware not only entirely new approaches
to the creation of graphics, but it also opens up new ways of
integrating audio into CAI lessons.

4.   AUDIO-SUPPORTED LESSONS AND CD-ROM

In our opinion, the possibility of incorporating audio sequences
into CAI courseware is of high importance for the future success
of CAI. Especially, the teaching of languages could be in many ways
facilitated, so that, for example, in vocabulary lessons the words
would not only be displayed on screen, but also spoken at the same
time. Another obvious possibility is the use of audio information
in music courses (e.g., a guitar course). An equally important
aspect is the integration of audio sequences into lessons which
aim at the teaching of the handicapped.

A further advantage of audio-supported lessons is the fact that
the amount of text displayed on screen can be reduced at the same
time as exhaustive information can be transmitted acoustically.
The visual display of the instructional material can thus be fully
concentrated on graphics (animated or static) supported by the
most important key words.

However, it is necessary to take the large requirements for the
digital storage of music into account. A compact disc can contain
only slightly more than one hour of stereo music.

It is thus advisable to provide for a possibility of using an
audio-supported lesson without the accompanying sound. This means
on the other hand that it would be necessary to produce two versions
of each course, namely one with audio-support and another which
had been extended by corresponding information which would then be
displayed on the screen (see above).

At first sight, it seems as if the use of tapes as storage medium
for the pure acoustic information is simpler, since the production
of such tapes is relatively easy. Especially, demonstration and
test lessons could be quickly produced. The sound could then be
reproduced via a cassette recorder which had been integrated into
the CAI system. Unfortunately, such devices normally allow only a
"start/stop" control which means, of course, that a systematic
search of specific tape positions is not possible, and would
require a fairly long time, anyway. This has the disadvantage of
forcing authors to structure their lessons sequentially, hereby
highly limiting the desired degree of student inter-action.

CD-ROMs make it possible to create high-quality audio-supported
lessons where the users can define their own paths through the
material and where the audio lessons can be adapted to the
individual skills and needs of the users.

If we can do without hifi stereo sound, which requires extremely
large storage capacity (1.41 Mbits for one second), other kinds of
acoustic additions to CAI lessons become available, which are well
worth looking into.

One variant is a simple digitization of speech. Using this method, only the zero crossings of the frequency spectrum are analyzed and digitally stored. Hence the storage requirement for a sampling rate of 8,000 Hertz is less than 1 KByte per second of commentary, respectively about 3 MByte per hour. Because of its large storage capacity, a CD-ROM can thus contain data for about 200 hours of speech.

The playback of commentary which has been stored in this way can be carried out by means of an add-on device which consists in essence of a D/A converter and a loudspeaker on the monitor. As far as the acoustic quality is concerned, digitized speech can be placed between a tape and a speech synthesizer, i.e. is easily suited for mere lecture-style lessons.

A further variant is synthetically produced speech. A speech synthesizer (hardware and software) which is connected to a microcomputer, produces sound by means of a phoneme generator which converts written texts into artificial speech. Since the input data required for speech synthesis consists of the usual characters, we can calculate the storage requirements as one byte per character. If we calculate 2 minutes to read the contents of a standard A4 page (with about 2 KBytes), we arrive at only 60 KBytes memory requirement for one hour of synthetized speech.

To be sure, the quality of speech synthesizers leaves some improvements to be desired and necessitates, in the presently available form, a certain degree of tolerance.

5.   COSTS AND COPY PROTECTION

If we now consider the costs of the storage of courseware, CD-ROMs immediately suggest themselves because of their phenomenal cost/byte ratio.

It is recommendable to produce CD-ROMs in large numbers (several hundred discs), since mass production drastically reduces the cost of production (down to about 10 US$ per CD-ROM).

In a sense, optical storage discs guarantee in themselves a certain form of copy protection. Since it is only possible to write data on a CD-ROM when it is produced, pirate copies cannot be made. Also, fabrication of CD-ROMs is in itself a rather complicated and costly affair, which further contributes to indirect copy protection. A possible transmission of data to another storage medium can be easily prevented by the software producers, if they fully exploit the specific features of CD-ROMs and CD-ROM drives. It would, for example, be impossible to use floppy discs as storage medium, if a lesson contained digitized pictures, audio sequences or complicated animation requiring large storage capacity and high rate of transfer.

6. SUMMARY

With a reasonable relation between graphics, animated graphics, digitized pictures, simulation programs, audio sequences and documentation, an optical storage disc offers sufficient storage space for the entire software of a generously created lesson. Short access times, protection against damage and wear, high degree of reliability, easy and convenient handling, and finally also, the low costs of this new medium make CD-ROMs an ideal and obvious storage medium for the distribution of CAI lessons.

REFERENCES

[1]   Cheng, H., Lipp, P., Maurer, H., GASC – A Low-Cost, No-
      Nonsense Graphic and Software Communication System,
      Electronic Publishing Review 5 (1985), pp. 141–155.

[2]   Garratt, J., Huber, F. and Huemer, H., AUTOOL – A New Author-
      ing System, IIG Report 219 (Technical University Graz, 1986).

[3]   Huemer, H.; Maurer, H.; Sammer, P., Btx für die Ausbildung im
      universitären Bereich, Die Neuen Medien an den Hochschulen,
      Veröffentlichung des Bundesministeriums für Wissenschaft und
      Forschung, (Wien, 1986).

[4]   Kaiser, D., Maurer, H., AUTOOL – A New System for Computer
      Aided Instruction, IIG Report 218 (Technical University Graz,
      1986).

[5]   Maurer, H. A., New Developments in Videotex and Their
      Implication for Computer Aided Instruction, Information
      Services and Use 3 (1983), pp.319–324.

[6]   Maurer, H., Videotex als Mittel im Ausbildungsbereich,
      Tagungsband Videotex Europa, (Basel, 1985), IV/1–IV/7.

[7]   Maurer, H., Authoring Systems for Computer Assisted
      Instruction, Proceedings of ACM Annual Conference, (Denver,
      1985), 551–561.

[8]   Maurer, H., Nationwide Teaching through a Network of
      Microcomputers, IIG Report 223, (Graz, 1986).

[9]   Maurer, H., COSTOC – an Experiment in Computer Supported
      Teaching of Computer-Science, IIG Report, (Graz, 1986).

[10] Maurer, H.; Sammer, P., Btx und MUPID – erläutert durch Btx
      und MUPID, COSTOC Course Documentation 2, IIG Graz, (Graz,
      1985).

[11] Philips Export B.V., Philips Compact Disc ROM, Philips
      International B.V. Subsystems and Peripherals (Eindhoven,
      Holland, 1984).

Section 7
National Case Studies

Remote Education and Informatics: Teleteaching
F. Lovis (Editor)
Elsevier Science Publishers B.V. (North-Holland)
© IFIP, 1988

TELE-EDUCATION: AN EXPERIMENT IN THE NETHERLANDS

K.L. Boon and H. C. de Wolf

Dutch Open University
PO-Box 2960
6401 DL HEERLEN, The Netherlands

INTRODUCTION

The Open university is the only institute for distance education in the Netherlands that offers the possibility to obtain academic degrees. Most courses are based on printed texts but in some cases other media, viz. video, audio cassette, have to be used. From the start (1984) many discussions have taken place in order to evaluate the position of the computer in our system of education. At the start a decision was made to use PCs in the 18 study centres that are scattered throughout the country. In this way the student could do his practical computer work in one of those centres. Of course the capacity of each study centre had to be scheduled in order to avoid all kinds of organisational problems.
Although this approach seems quite appropriate one can easily mention a number of drawbacks:
- a student can only work for a fixed time (max 2 hours) with a computer.
  It is hardly possible to do some 'thinking' or 'studying' at the terminal.
- if a student wants to experiment, if for instance, he or she would like to build a simulation model in order to examine the behaviour of a dynamic system, he or she has to leave when time is up even if the experiment is not finished; the same holds for a student who has 'almost' finished his practical work.
- in the way indicated, computers can never be used as a continuous help. On the contrary, each course in which a computer has to be used is constructed in such a way that a student only has to go to a study centre a few times (max 3 times).
Because the prices of home-computers and PCs have dramatically decreased we can now consider whether other computer configurations are possible. Of especial interest is a construction in which a student can use a computer at home.

The start of the project
In 1984 the Open university together with Philips (manufacturer of electronic devices), Kluwer (publishing house) and PTT (national telephone services) started a group in order to find out in what way a computer could be used as a home educative terminal. It is worthwhile mentioning that at the start the most challenging plans were formulated. As an example: of course(!) the system should offer the possibility for online viewing of student activity. In this way the tutor could trace, for instance, errors in programing in almost 'real time mode'. It is not very difficult to discover the implications of these possibilities for the system from a technical and economic point of view...

Finally, it turned out that:
- the terminal should be attached to a modem. Other possibilities, e.g. broadcasting, turned out not to be very practical, at least for our situation (the Netherlands is a rather small country and many students have a telephone at home)
- the network should, at least at the start, make use of an already existing PTT-network (Viditel)
- two standards had to be adapted: MSX2 and MS-DOS.

The network should offer the following features:
- downloading of programs,
- tele-tutoring: personal help by means of a computer mailbox function,
- interactive selftesting: consisting of a set of tests to be used by the students themselves, providing results as well as feedback,
- tele-tasks: tasks which the students have to perform for obtaining cognitive skills, especially by using simulation techniques.

Finally, the system should give access to other networks, as it was considered to be of importance that a student should also become familiar with modern trends of working with a terminal at home.

The redesign of an already existing course

In order to have a first evaluation of this set-up, it was decided to redesign an already existing course. In this way we could compare the results of students using tele-education and students working with the conventional material. The course selected (title: Systems and their control) seems to be of special interest, because it has a number of components in which the computers have to be used.
viz:
- an introduction on how to work with a computer;
- a computer practical in which the student has to work with a simulation program.

In the figure the schematic set-up of both the conventional course and the redesigned course, is shown.

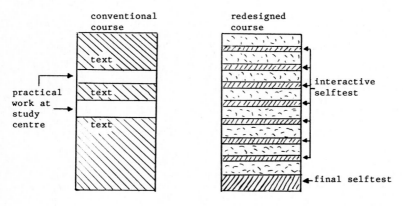

means text mixed with tasks, CAI and experiments that have to be done with the computer

It can be seen that a totally different media mix is chosen for the redesigned course. Now the text is mixed with:
- tasks to be done with the computer;
- subjects that are presented to the student by means of computer aided instruction (CAI);
- computer selftests: each selftest has a maximum of 2 levels, meaning that if a student does not know the answer to a question, a second easier question or a hint for the solution of the problem can be given;
- experiments that have to be done with the computer, e.g. to examine the behaviour of a given dynamic system.

As this form of teaching is not based only on CAI but rather on a mixture of written text and computer tasks we prefer to speak of "computer integrated textbooks" (CIT).

Some final remarks

In January 1987 a small group of students (ca. 60) will receive their homecomputer (MSX2 or IBM PC) and the rewritten course. In July these students will complete their course at the same examination as the students who worked with the conventional material.

Tele-education has a number of advantages. One of them is apparently to minimize the number of tutors. The most important question is: 'do we need any form of human tutoring?' Of course it is hardly possible to give a final answer to this question. We decided that the student should still have a tutor, even with CIT. The main reasons are that from a psychological point of view, it seems of importance to have a human tutor and sometimes situations are met in which only a human tutor can act.
...... after all we are teaching humans!

Remote Education and Informatics: Teleteaching
F. Lovis (Editor)
Elsevier Science Publishers B.V. (North-Holland)
© IFIP, 1988

TEACHING PRACTICAL ASPECTS OF COMPUTER SCIENCE AT A
LONG-ESTABLISHED DISTANCE-TEACHING UNIVERSITY

P.M. Fallick[*] and C. de Villiers [+]

Department of Computer Science and Information Systems, University
of South Africa, P.O. Box 392, Pretoria, South Africa

ABSTRACT

Computer Science and Information Systems have been taught at the
University of South Africa, a distance-teaching university, for the
past sixteen years. This paper gives a brief introduction to the
University and to the Department of Computer Science and Information
Systems, and then describes and discusses our approach to teaching
the practical components of the course.

1. INTRODUCTION - THE UNIVERSITY OF SOUTH AFRICA

South Africa's first university, the University of the Cape of Good Hope, was
established in 1873 and in 1916 became the University of South Africa - a
purely examining body. In 1946, however, it was decided to change the function
of the University to one catering for students who could not, for whatever
reason, study at a residential university. In 1951, therefore, the University
of South Africa, now popularly referred to as Unisa, became a fully fledged
distance-teaching university, and the very first such university in the world
to offer distance teaching right up to doctoral level.

The main campus for the university is in Pretoria and it is a prominent
landmark in that city. There are also regional offices in four centres which
provide students with library and study facilities as well as lecture halls,
and where registration of local students as well as other administrative
matters are dealt with.

The variety of subjects taught is ever-increasing. Six faculties (Arts,
Science, Economic and Management Sciences, Law, Education and Theology),
comprising 56 departments, offer tuition in more than 150 different subjects.
There are more than 1 300 lecturers at Unisa.

----

* Mrs. P. M. Fallick is a senior lecturer in the Department of Computer
Science and Information Systems at the University of South Africa.

+ Mrs. C. de Villiers is a lecturer in the Department of Computer Science
and Information Systems at the University of South Africa.

Unisa experiences a remarkable growth in the student numbers each year.   In
1974 there were 34 159 registered students.   By 1984 the number had doubled
and in 1986 the student enrolment exceeded 86 000. One out of every three
South African university students studies through Unisa.   As is probably the
case in all distance-teaching universities, Unisa's students are on average
somewhat older than the students at residential universities. The average age
of our students is 29.

As South Africa has two official languages, English and Afrikaans, all tuition
is offered in both these languages, with students having a choice as to the
language in which they receive their study material.

Students at a distance-teaching university usually have to study in a more
concentrated fashion than do those studying full-time at a residential
university. The maximum amount of information must be concentrated into study
material, student assignments that are set, feedback to the student on the
work submitted and the infrequent live lectures. As students are isolated from
other students studying the same subjects, the lecturer and study material are
frequently the only source of information, encouragement and stimulation with
regard to his studies.

Unisa has the same admission requirements as any other South African
university and its degrees are held in high esteem.

2. METHOD OF TUITION

As is the case throughout Unisa, the modules in Computer Science and
Information Systems are taught largely by means of the written word. On
registering, students receive study guides for each module for which they are
registered, in which the subject matter is explained and examples are given.
The lecturers communicate with students by means of tutorial letters; these
provide information of an administrative nature, assignments and other
information and are sent out periodically throughout the year. Occasionally
tape cassettes containing recorded lectures are also provided.   Facilities
exist at Unisa for staff to create video tapes and slide programmes. Our
department has made use of these to show students examples of different
computer facilities and to illustrate the history of computers. The student is
required to buy a prescribed book for each module and the library offers the
student a wide variety of additional reference material and periodicals.

Discussion classes, which can take the form of lectures or workshops, are held
at the regional offices from time to time.   These classes are arranged at the
discretion of the department, and the lecturers concerned travel to the
various centres to present the lectures.   Student attendance of discussion
classes is not compulsory, but if a student can attend them, he is advised to
do so since they offer valuable opportunities to make personal contact and to
discuss problems with his lecturers and fellow students.   It is found that
many students travel long distances to attend these lectures.   Students are
also encouraged to consult their lecturers either by letter or during personal
visits.

3. THE DEPARTMENT OF COMPUTER SCIENCE AND INFORMATION SYSTEMS

At the beginning of 1970 a department of Computer Science was instituted at Unisa and a total of 707 undergraduate students registered for this subject. The first postgraduate students, a total of 55, registered in 1972. The number of students registered has grown at an average rate of 26% per year. In 1986, 15 141 undergraduate and 768 postgraduate students were registered. The department has a staff of 24 lecturers, of whom 6 are professors or associate professors, and 8 administrative assistants as well as numerous part-time staff members who only mark assignments. At present we have vacancies for 6 lecturers.

4. TEACHING PRACTICAL ASPECTS OF COMPUTER SCIENCE

4.1. General

Naturally there are important differences between circumstances at a residential university and those at a distance-teaching university and these influence the way in which any subject is taught. These differences are accentuated in the case of subjects with a practical component.

4.3. Programming Languages

The policy in the Department of Computer Science and Information Systems has always been to teach basic programming principles such as sound design and structured programming and not to teach programming languages per se. Originally we decided to use PL/I as this is a powerful language which could be used to illustrate the concepts we wished to teach. First-year students were taught a subset of the language which was extended in later courses. COBOL was used at second-year level as it was used extensively in commercial applications.

As more students bought their own microcomputers we found it necessary to allow them to use a language which was more commonly available on a variety of microcomputers. Hence, for the past three years, first-year students have been given a thorough grounding in basic programming and data structures using a form of pseudocode, SPES, developed in co-operation with the departments of Computer Science at two of the other large universities in South Africa. Thereafter students are given the option of programming in PL/I, BASIC or Pascal. Schemes are provided showing the mapping from SPES to each of these languages.

At second-year level, students are expected to write more difficult programs using more advanced data structures. Again a choice between languages is given, this time PL/I, COBOL or Pascal. Assembler language programming forms part of another module on Computer Organization at second-year level. Practical programming involving still more advanced data structures continues in third year with FORTRAN, LISP, Pascal, and PL/I being used.

We have found that the introduction of choices of programming language at first and second-year level has created a number of problems for the lecturers concerned. This system necessitates setting and marking assignments and examination questions in all the languages. Staff who are experts in the languages should ideally be available to answer students' queries at all times. A considerable amount of co-ordination is required to ensure that such a system works equitably. It is for these reasons that it has been decided to allow students to use only Pascal in first-year programming as from 1987, and in second year as from 1988. Pascal has been chosen as it is a high-level, block-structured, strongly typed language which is readily available for a variety of microcomputers and facilitates the application of sound structured programming concepts.

4.4. Computer Facilities

THe provision of facilities for students to do practical work is always something of a problem at a distance-teaching university. Some departments require students to attend compulsory practical sessions, whilst others attempt to make arrangements with outside organizations to allow the students access to their facilities.

The Department of Computer Science and Information Systems at Unisa has had a variety of systems over the years which have been amended and improved largely as a result of better and cheaper technology becoming available.

Initially use was made of batch-processing facilities. Students submitted programs by post, either as code written on coding sheets or on mark sense cards to be run at Unisa. These programs were then marked and commented on by the lecturer, and posted back to the student. The student then had the opportunity to code amendments to his program and the whole process was repeated. The number of marks awarded was amended as further improvements to the task were received. The major problem in these systems was the long turnaround time (particularly when the program had first to be punched), exacerbated by the length of time it took before the program was satisfactorily executed.

Students having access to outside computers have always been permitted to develop their programs independently and just submit a final version. Over the years, more and more students have begun to use outside computers. Hence far fewer students make use of the postal systems than was originally the case.

More recently, Unisa made terminals connected to their Burroughs mainframe available at the branch offices for students to develop their programming assignments, and in 1986 microcomputer laboratories equipped with IBM micro-computers were established at the four branch offices to provide students with additional computer facilities.

A major change in policy in this department has recently been approved by the University. Students registering for Computer Science for the first time will only be admitted if they have access to a suitable computer (either their own, a friend's, employer's, or the terminals and microcomputers at the branch offices). This has been done firstly in order to ensure that students do gain some experience in working directly with a computer, and secondly to cut out the postal systems which were unsatisfactory because they were so time-consuming.

4.5. Programming Tasks

The number of programming tasks which the students are expected to complete and the level of difficulty of these tasks vary according to the academic level. Typically there are four programming assignments in the practical programming module at first-year level. These start off at a fairly elementary level and increase in difficulty to a program which requires the writing and use of functions, subroutines and an internal sort.

At second-year level the high-level language, practical programming module has two programming assignments requiring programs of approximately 250 lines of Pascal code or 350 lines of COBOL code. These tasks make use of data files and matrices. Students are expected to document their programs fully and test them thoroughly. In the Computer Organization module two very simple assembly language programs are required. In third year two fairly complex programming tasks are set, using tree structures, for example.

The level of assistance given to students in developing their programs varies according to the year of study and the individual needs of the student. Students are expected to attempt the programs on their own at first. In the first year, all attempts submitted are scrutinized and assistance in the form of written comments is given by the lecturer as thought necessary. This help is not very detailed but is more in the line of "check your logic" or possibly a reference. In second year the intention is that students develop their programs unaided. When a student requests help, however, this is provided.

4.6. Examination admission

The marks awarded for programming tasks and written assignments are used to determine whether or not the student should be admitted to the end-of-year examination. It is not possible to obtain sufficient examination admission credits without completing some of the programming tasks satisfactorily. It is also not possible to pass either first or second-year Computer Science without passing the practical programming modules. We can, therefore, be reasonably sure that our Computer Science graduates have completed a certain amount of programming.

4.7. Examinations

It has been found over the years that it is impractical to ask students to code programs in examinations, particularly since they write a single two-hour paper for each module. It is not fair to incorporate the marks obtained for programming during the year in the final results as we have no proof as to whether the programming was actually done by the student himself. The final evaluation of students practical programming ability is, therefore, difficult.

The approach at present in second year is to include a single program repeated in each of the programming languages and ask questions about it, hence testing the student's ability to read a program. We also ask the student to design, but not to code, a simple program to determine their ability in this regard. In addition, essay-type questions on theoretical aspects of programming are asked on, for example, testing, documentation techniques.

4.8. Systems Analysis and Design and Database Design

Modules are offered at third-year level on systems analysis and design and on database design. In the database module, practical exercises are limited to small examples. No real Database Management System is used to run these examples, however. Instead students learn about various approaches to database design such as networks, hierarchical databases and relational databases and normalization. In assignments they are asked to design and possibly code small sections of systems which are then checked manually by the lecturer.

In the systems analysis module students are required to complete a variety of practical assignments, applying one or more of the methodologies learnt, and a small practical project which is based on real-life systems, frequently in their own work environment.

4.9. Problem areas

Problems are experienced by both lecturers and students in teaching and learning practical aspects of Computer Science via distance teaching.

Lecturers find that the practical component of the students' work creates an enormous volume of work for the staff. Almost all assistance with practical work has to be given in writing to the student and is usually given individually. As the student numbers are so large, this necessitates a team of lecturing assistants. We envisage having three or four lecturers and an equal number of markers who work on a part-time basis from home, involved with the first-year programming modules. Care has to be taken in administering the work of such a team to ensure that efforts are co-ordinated and an even standard is maintained.

The fact that our students are permitted to submit programs developed on a wide variety of computers adds to the lecturers' problems. Not only do these programs have to be marked, but the lecturer is also expected to be able to answer questions about how a variety of computers and compilers work. This becomes very difficult when students are programming in assembly code, since there are significant differences between the various processors and assembly languages used by the students, and students frequently require detailed replies to their queries.

Another cause for concern is that it is virtually impossible for lecturers to ensure that work submitted by students is really their own work. On the other hand, there is a lot to be said for students forming study groups. On occasion it is obvious that two or more students have prepared only one program which is then submitted by each of them. Our response to this is simply to indicate that we are aware that this has been done and to warn the students not to rely too heavily on one another, but no penalties are given.

Another major problem recognised by the lecturers is the setting of a fair examination that tests the knowledge and problem-solving ability of the students.

There is a very high drop-out rate, particularly amongst our first-year Computer Science students. A thorough investigation into the reasons for this has been proposed but has not yet begun. We can, however, surmise why students drop out at the rate they do. Possibly the combined burden of a career and demanding studies is too much for some of them. It is also possible that some students take Computer Science for the wrong reasons. Some may be attracted to Computer Science by the highly paid jobs reputedly available in this field, whilst others are aware that this is an important and expanding area and that they should equip themselves for the future, but do not really need a degree course in Computer Science to fulfil their requirements. A short computer literacy or programming course would be sufficient. Unfortunately, many of the students are either not really interested in the subject itself or else are not capable intellectually of mastering it and hence quickly fall by the wayside.

The following are undoubtedly some of the major problems encountered by students:

a)   Difficulty in gaining access to a computer. It is unfortunate that there will probably inevitably be cases in the future where this problem will be insuperable and we forecast a drop in our student numbers as a result of this.

b)   The problems of isolation and the accompanying frustration are probably intensified in Computer Science by students' initial nervousness of the computer and the fact that a small problem may result in an inability to progress at all. We have had reports of students sitting in front of a microcomputer in the microcomputer laboratory for an hour without even getting started and eventually leaving, never to return. Unisa does help students to make contact with other students taking the same courses who live in the same area, in the hope that the students will be able to form study groups and help and encourage each other. We hope that by insisting that students have direct access to a computer or terminal we will be able to ensure that, by the time they graduate, our students have overcome any such fears they might have had.

5.   HOW MUCH PRACTICAL WORK IS IN FACT NECESSARY AS PART OF A DEGREE COURSE IN COMPUTER SCIENCE?

It has been suggested that far too much emphasis is placed on programming in our Computer Science course. Firstly, as a distance-teaching university we are not really in a position to be practically oriented and might thus be better advised to concentrate on the more theoretical aspects of Computer Science. Secondly, it is believed by many that Computer Science is an abstract science and that it is not really necessary to ensure that students have mastered the practical skills associated with it. Thirdly, students tend to lose sight of the most important issues in Computer Science when they write programs and tend to pay undue attention to syntax instead of program design and problem solving in more general terms. It is possible to test a student's understanding of the principles of Computer Science and his problem-solving abilities without requiring him actually to write working programs. However, it is easier for us to mark programs than algorithms which have not been subjected to the strict rules of a programming language.

A different point of view is that it would be wrong to allow students to graduate with a degree in Computer Science if they do not have basic programming skills, experience in using a computer first hand and may actually still be very unsure of their ability to function in a computer environment.

We at Unisa believe that steering a middle course is best. Practical programming is a necessary part of a Computer Science course but is not the over-riding consideration and should not be over-emphasised.

6. The Future

Just as the technological advances of the past fifteen years have influenced the ways in which we have handled the teaching of aspects of Computer Science, so we expect new developments will have a large impact on this area. Electronic mail, national networks and the advances made in Computer-Assisted Instruction are all being investigated to see how they can be used in the future. Research into aspects of Computer-Assisted Instruction, in particular, is under way. Mrs. Fallick, one of the authors, has developed a COBOL preprocessor as a teaching tool which assists students in learning COBOL by identifying syntax errors as each line of code is entered.

7. CONCLUSION

The Computer Science and Information Systems courses at Unisa are very popular, rather too popular, we sometimes feel, as our student numbers increase at a rate surpassing even that of the University of South Africa as a whole. While this puts pressure on the department, we are proud that we can help so many people improve their qualifications and hence equip themselves to find rewarding jobs in the fast-expanding data processing world. At the same time, we are helping to provide the data processing world with much-needed staff, albeit generally at a junior level. A large number of our students are already employed in data processing and improve their qualifications by studying our courses. Finally, many teachers make use of our courses to study Computer Science, thus enabling them to teach computer literacy and computer study courses at schools. The need for such courses at school level has been widely recognised and the shortage of teachers able to teach these courses is a severe problem.

In the 16 years in which Computer Science has been offered as a subject at the University of South Africa we feel we have learnt a great deal about what should be taught and how this can best be done. Frequently this has been learnt by trial and error. However, we have a policy of periodically revising our courses to adapt to changing requirements so that courses do not simply evolve, nor are they subject to endless ad hoc adjustments, but are planned to meet the challenges of the times.

Remote Education and Informatics: Teleteaching
F. Lovis (Editor)
Elsevier Science Publishers B.V. (North-Holland)
© IFIP, 1988

TELEMATICS SERVICES, EDUCATION AND CULTURE:
ASPASIE and its Role in France

Gerard LOISEAU
CNRS /National Scientific Research Centre/
Aspasie, Marne-La-Vallée X2000 Centre

Open learning with the aid of audio-visual methods often makes
use of CAI, or Computer Assisted Instruction. In France, however,
forms of open learning are increasingly being developed which take
advantage of on-line electronic information services (Telematics)
operating to TELETEL standards. The advantage of these standards
lies in their ability to make both text and graphics widely
available.

Yet open learning was not a prime objective of the French
telematics system. Such educational applications are newcomers
to this phenomenon of universal communication, and although
increasingly numerous, educational users still seem relatively
hesitant about adopting telematics services, not only for wide
distribution of information but also for creative teaching and
technical training. This view is borne out by the achievements
which Aspasie has had at its X2000 Centre in Marne-La-Vallée,
as will be seen in the second part of this article.

I. Telematics and Education in France

A. An Outline of French Telematics Services

In 1975 the French Government decided to back a distributed videotex service called ANTIOPE with four main objectives:

a/ To modernise the telecommunications network;

b/ To develop the telephone industry both nationally and for
purposes of export promotion;

c/ To set up national data banks and export technical expertise;

d/ To promote wider use of the telephone.

This early sense of direction was confirmed in 1978 with the
appearance of a report by Nora and Minc entitled "The Computerization of Society". This report brought a new term into current use
by describing a system combining the use of computers and telecommunications as "telematics". From then on the emphasis was on
Teletel, a French interactive videotex service which incorporates
user/machine dialogue, unlike the ANTIOPE system, which allows
videotex information to be received only. The term "telematics"
currently refers to Teletel standards, no matter whether the
information is conveyed on the national packet-switched data
network (Transpac) or on the traditional commuted telephone
network (RTC).

Following publication of this report the Minister for the PTT
(Postal and Telecommunications Administration) proposed a plan of
action for the development of telematics services, based on the
following points:

a/ Developing technical standards and networks;

b/ Collaborating with manufacturers in the development of input terminals and system servers;

c/ Seeking out potential suppliers of information content;

d/ Testing the market for future users of the medium in the light of experiments such as the one for the electronic telephone directory which was carried out in the Department of Ile et Vilaine in Brittany beginning in 1980, and in the new town of Velizy to the West of Paris in July 1981.

B.   Educational Applications for Telematics Services

1.   Elimination of Illiteracy

DIDAO is one of the earliest providers of telematics services, and specialises in education. In conjunction with the Immigration Office it provides "refresher courses" in arithmetic and French. As an experiment, thirty Moroccan motor industry graduates successfully made use of this educational facility.

2.   Courses

More and more courses are being produced in mathematics, computing and foreign languages. They are being provided by such institutions as the La Villette Science and Industry Campus in Paris or the University of Provence, which offer working students conventionally printed courses as well as courses via telematics, leading to such national diplomas as a mathematics degree. There are also private companies, such as CPLE for languages (via their Linguatel service) or Atlantel Sud-Ouest (via their Etud service).

Sometimes there is an educational aspect to a service which is not presented as such, for example an English-language messaging service for English-speaking users via the "Leon" service on Teletel 3.

3.   Knowledge Testing

There are many such services on offer, either independently or as an adjunct to course modules followed via telematics, as for example the Telesup service provided by the University of Provence. They generally teke the form of Multiple Choice Questions with a scoring system which makes it possible to test the level of knowledge in some particular subject area.

4.   Educational Games

There are many of these to be found, either under the heading of games services, or among the items provided by those producers of information who specialise more particularly in education.

5.   Tutoring Systems

a/ Services provided for pupils out of school hours by certain teachers such as J.Y.Garnery of the Ecole des Buttes in Creteil. Class books are available for remote inquiry. In addition, school children kept at home because of illness, for example, can carry on working by using the information which their instructor has entered into the system server.

b/ Advisory systems provided by service companies such as CRAC, with their SOS Homework service. Telematics services make it possible to bring together schoolchildren who are having difficulty doing their homework and educators who are paid for helping them out. Teletel 3 allows questions to be put to specialists either directly, with a reply being given at once, or via their electronic mailbox, with an off-line reply being given generally within about 24 hours.

6. STI/The Initial Telematics System/

As part of the "Computing for All" plan agreed by Government in January 1985, which aims to equip each school with at least one micro-computer, a telematics phase was added in Autumn 1985. Some 317 schools have been provided with micro-servers, which are usually IBM-PC compatible. Each computer has been supplied with an Initial Telematics Service comprising items of administrative information, games, graphics, specialised sections and newspaper facilities, so as to encourage the equipped sites to develop and set up the initial service sections. From the viewpoint of both the design and the technical development of the telematics service this STI was created by Aspasie by order of the Prime Minister and the Minister for State Education.

II. Aspasie, from Education to Culture

A. The Background

The Aspasie company has the task of designing and producing a system of communication based on telematics at Marne-La-Vallée. The company was established on the 14th January 1983, at Torcy, 25 kilometres east of Paris. Sector 2 of Marne-La-Vallée is known as Le Val Maubuee. It is here that Aspasie is developing its plans, and the area comprises six towns: Champs-sur-Marne, Croissy-Beaubourg, Emerainville, Lognes, Torcy and Noisiel, involving a total population of 70,000 people. Le Val Maubuee is a new and recently populated town which displays a markedly pyramid-like structure among its age groups, insofar as the number of young people under the age of 20 is twice the national average. In addition, the predominant social classifications are lower-salaried and clerical staff grades.

Aspasie is distinguished from other telematics systems by the fact that its partners in the scheme (some 65 at present, not counting individual participants) have total freedom to decide the form and contents of the 15,000 pages of information which they themselves produce. There are five categories of participant involved in setting up the data bank on the Aspasie system server. These are:

1. Individuals
2. Associations
3. Local authorities
4. Companies
5. The Education System

At this point it is appropriate to consider the use of telematics at local level for educational purposes, as used by education officials of Le Val Maubuee long before 14th January 1986, the day on which the Prime Minister inaugurated the first of the 317 telematics servers for the Ministry of State Education.

B.   Educational Information

People from Le Val Maubuee can call the Aspasie system server over
the switched telephone network by dialling (1) 60 17 20 00.   By
selecting the Education section on their Minitel they can first of
all find out about the school environment in which their children
are educated.   In accordance with the Aspasie philosophy, each
item of information is produced by the participants resident in
the data bank.   The following types of information can be found:

1.   General Information

a/ Of National Importance.   Aspasie has installed the SID data
bank of rights and procedures, and this service includes a
substantial section on education and training from which it is
possible to obtain details about free education, moving up from
primary to secondary education, university registration procedures
university for mature students, or open learning university
courses.

b/ Of Local Importance.   Here are two examples:

- The Department of Seine et Marne has installed a service giving
progress reports on the Computing for All scheme.   As a
consequence, the Aspasie server is used by all the staff concerned
within a much larger geographical area than the six townships of
Le Val Maubuee.

- In October 1985 the SAN (New Town Corporation) responsible for
the administration of Le Val Maubuee new town began providing the
first service giving details of school transport facilities. Each
child with access to one of the 2,500 Minitels distributed free of
charge in Le Val Maubuee can now find out at any time full details
of the school bus timetable for the journey from home to school or
college.   Similarly, each town hall puts out a certain amount of
data such as registration details, a list of schools, the menu for
the school meals service, rest centres, and so on.

2.   Life in School

In addition to the institutions, each school can use the server to
keep its local area informed of the school's activities.   Although
each group or educational establishment is completely free to
present the information in any way it pleases, the details are
generally organised as follows:

a/ The school's identification record, such as the Dragonfly
Primary School at Lognes.

b/ General information specific to the school, such as procedures
for returning to school after the summer holidays, or the education methods followed by the school, such as non-streaming and
the organisation of activities into ability groups at the
Children's Centre in Torcy.

c/ Educational activities at the school, such as the types of
group training carried out with the children. This might include
such things as micro-computing, DIY, silk dyeing, and so on, at
the Ecole Georges Brassens in Torcy.

3. Parent Associations

Whether representing opinions at the national level, such as the FCPE(Federation of Parent Associations) or created to meet a local need, such as the Torcy AAPEM (Le Mail Independent Association of Parents) all Parent Associations for schools in the Le Val Maubuee conurbation use the system server for displaying their objectives and their means of achieving them.

4. Information on Education and Full-Time Training

In Marne-La-Vallée such details are mainly supplied by the MEP (Mission for Full-Time Education). In addition to supplying the public with information on training courses, conditions for passing them, and the opportunities available in the Ile-de-France Region, this body provides a legal advisory service on training matters, lists of job vacancies, an information bulletin, a specialised messaging service, and a list of specialised organisations. This service totals just over 500 screens of information.

5. Field Mailbox

In April 1985 a primary school class from the Lions School at Croissy Beaubourg went away on a field visit to study bird behaviour. Aspasie provided the class with an electronic mailbox for the group to use. And so for a week parents, children, teachers and school administrators kept in touch by sending around a hundred messages between the site of the study tour at Pougy, and Croissy-Beaubourg. Since at that time the Minitels had not yet been distributed free of charge throughout Le Val Maubuee, each message from Pougy was printed out at Croissy school so that parents could read letters from their children on the spot and even send replies using the school's Minitel.

C. Creative Teaching

To speak of creative teaching in connection with telematics services would certainly have brought a charge of heresy only three years ago. Since it was well known that telematics provided information services, it was difficult to think of it as an instrument of creative teaching. The term creative does not refer here to remote supervision of open learning for consumption by the user, but a use of telematics which makes it possible to produce and communicate teaching material within a strictly localised area. Two examples produced in this way by Aspasie through its "Full-Time Education and Training Commission" have made it possible to measure the attraction of this new form of creativity in teaching, fully involved as it is in aspects of communications, since the children are increasingly aware that their work can be referred to by their friends, parents and acquaintances, or simply by anyone with a Minitel.

1. Creative Writing: Telematic Novels

a/ "The Story of a Very Funny School"

Even before Minitels had been given out free of charge throughout Le Val Maubuee during the second half of 1985, some schools had been given a telephone line and a Minitel for exchanging educational ideas. In addition to using group electronic mailboxes as in the situation at Pougy, the Ecole Georges Brassens at Torcy

used the mailbox concept to start a school telematic novel which
was to be the first of the genre. The theory was as follows:

From the technical point of view Aspasie suggested a single mailbox entitled "Novel" and a password to be shared by the schools
wishing to take part in the experiment. There were two:

- the Georges Brassens Primary School at Torcy;

- and the Lions Primary School at Croissy-Beaubourg.

From the educational point of view, the pupils, aided by their
teachers, called up the Aspasie server and then used one or more
screens for drafting contributions on a jointly chosen theme "The
Story of a Very Funny School". Every pupil involved was allowed
complete editorial freedom, and wrote when he or she wanted to and
in no fixed order.

b/ "Pere Noel"

The early lessons learned from this educational innovation, the
schools telematic novel, led executives of Aspasie's "Full-Time
Education and Training Commission" to ask the technical support
team for a number of software changes.

-   The Sequence of Messages

In the system as previously conceived, messages appeared on screen
in chronological order. This meant having to scan through every
message already sent in order to get to the last bit of text
entered. In terms of a conventional work of fiction, that would
be like having to start again at page one every time the book was
re-opened. It was impossible to go directly to screen 20, which
meant starting at the very beginning again, and this rapidly
became tiresome.

-   Ease of Access

By definition access to an electronic mailbox is protected. It
meant a password was needed not merely to write, but also in order
to read what the children had produced. There were therefore
limits to the size of audience which could access the screens.
Aspasie's technical team offered the Full-Time Education and
Training Commission another system of messaging which would
correct these defects. After further discussion the new technical
system, provided in direct response to a cultural and educational
demand, made the following things possible:
- Direct access to required information by date;
- Coordination of text input by a teacher acting as editor-in-chief.

This teacher assigns colleagues the password they need for
writing the schools telematic novel or novels;

- An unrestricted look-up facility for the 2,500 Minitel holders
in Le Val Maubuee at very low cost (Fr 2.25 per hour).

Beginning on 9th January 1986, three schools put this new messaging system to the test on the common theme of Pere Noel. The
experiment went on until 4th February during which time the
children input 19 screens of text.

c/ Taking Stock

Jean-Louis Bray, who is Director of the Georges Brassens School Group in Torcy, and the prime-mover behind these first two schools telematic novels, states that the average age of the children who worked on them was ten. This type of production has a number of advantages:

- It makes it possible to have a different approach to reading, almost like looking at a newspaper. Pupils learn to skip from page to page. There is no more painstaking, line-by-line reading as with school text books.

- Children learn to express themselves in writing more easily. The text of the novel is first of all prepared on a sheet of paper or on the board, and then transcribed in Minitel.

For "Pere Noel" the children had no constraints at all. They were allowed total freedom of expression. This independence in their writing, combined with the novelty value of the device and the ability to communicate their own work to other people, led to some unexpected results. Quite apart from the general air of excitement and interest which it generated, thanks to the "Pere Noel" novel two children who had been two years behind in their writing skills, and thus making no progress, actually contributed compositions of their own.

- It becomes an exercise in original and logical thinking. Jean-Louis Bray takes advantage of the way in which the screens for the telematic novel and the Aspasie data bank in general are organised to encourage his pupils to carry out their own research into tree-like information structures.

- It throws the school wide open. Telematic novels make it possible to exchange ideas between school groups which differ even though they are relatively close in the geographical sense. This makes it easy to set up face-to-face meetings to discuss the work which has been done. In addition to the school-to-school contact, communication now also exists between school and the home, even though there are still too few homes equipped with a Minitel. (The figure for Le Val Maubuee is about 10%).

For the future, Jean-Louis Bray suggests two further innovations:

- From the technical standpoint, to use Praxitele, a videotex graphics software package installed on schools nano-networks (see below). This would then allow novels to be illustrated, since it is very easy for children to produce graphic designs by composing directly on to the television screen with a light pencil. The software also makes text editing more flexible than is possible on the Minitel, as the cursor can be moved to any part of the page for correcting errors. Screens of text produced in this way can be amended at will. They are loaded on to the server and can be recalled, reworked, and then returned to the data bank.

- From the educational standpoint, perhaps a rather more tutor-led approach to future novels (at least in certain cases), with a more precise choice of theme while keeping the exercise to an appropriate time-scale. For instance it is much less fun to be writing about "Pere Noel" in February than in December.

2. Creating videotex graphic designs

Aspasie obtained a graphic design terminal in September 1983 with the assistance of the Ministry for Post and Telecommunications. Straight away some children began composing graphic designs. But training had to be done with care, and trainees had to go to company head office.

As part of the Computing for All programme, a number of schools were equipped with nano-networks, which are systems comprising a personal micro-computer of a type compatible with the IBM-PC, driving six or more home computers which were usually Thomson T07/70 or M05 devices. 14 schools or colleges in Le Val Maubuee have been so equipped.

From the standpoint of the telematics services, nothing officially existed until Autumn 1985. But then, at the Georges Brassens School in Torcy, various interested industrial parties transferred the Praxitele software on to the nano-network and produced the necessary utilities for graphic designs to be held on the "B" type (IBM-PC compatible) servers belonging to the State Education service, and if need be on any other server. As a result, ever since the second quarter of 1986 it has been theoretically possible for all schoolchildren in Le Val Maubuee to use either the nanonetwork at their own school or at a neighbouring school if their own does not have one, to take part in the fully decentralised production of videotex graphic design, without having to travel to some special place such as the company offices. There are two types of application which have been produced in this way:

a/ Illustrations of poems

Schoolchildren often produce and sometimes illustrate poetry collections which are shown to their parents at the end of the scholastic year. In June 1985, at the George Brassens school, two poems were illustrated on a videotex composing screen, "Lune" (moon) and "Definitions". The first screen is divided into two parts: one graphic showing a crescent moon plus a few words "the moon is a harp of roses".
On the second screen, the graphic does not change, just the text continuing the poem. The principle is similar to that of "Definitions". Here we have a dictionary giving the pupil's Christian names. Each name corresponds to a definition given by the pupil in question as his or her fancy dictates. For example, "Laure is a sunflower tied up to a panda eating a white strawberry in a flowerpot !"
The installation of the Praxitele software programme in the nano-networks, end of 1985, meant this kind of animation could be continued more easily, as the children could henceforth both compose in their schools, and as long on the Aspasie Composition terminals, and do so in an easier way thanks to the flexibilities of the software and to the use of the optical pencil. In this way the children produced another poem called "The Witches" with a similar functionary to the other two, unchanging graphics in the form of a logo, text differing screen by screen.
This kind of exercise is now open to all the children in Val Maubuee. Over and above the pedagogical impact already stressed by the telematic novels where are blended the various aspects of communications, written expression, reading, logic and the use of a new tool, the videotext graphic is enriching as:

+ it brings an extra dimension, that of graphics design. It thus aids imagination to flourish, adding to traditional graphic expression but without supplanting it in any way.

+ it adds a further dimension to traditional graphics. It is not simply recopying, often rather crudely, drawings on paper. The use of telematics holds the dynamism that attracts all children.

+ it allows for synergetic work. It adds to the traditional poetry writing, which already involves the children, the teachers and sometimes professionals, the Aspasie graphic designers who teach how to use the telematic tool for videotex illustrations. Subtly, in between the make-up of a drawing and that of the text, slip in the first outlines of a telematic culture.

b/ The Graphics competition

Up until April 1986, only four or five schools and their pupils had taken part in the use of telematics in its pedagogic creation-communication form, as experimented in Val Maubuee. In order to make known these new avenues of remote education, Aspasie organised a videotex graphics competition with the following bases: each schoolchild in Val Maubuee could offer a drawing made on the nano-network. Aspasie encouraged teachers to learn how to use Praxitele on nano-network so as to pass on their knowledge to the children. Whenever someone was missing, the Aspasie team travelled around the schools to give the necessary demonstrations. The children gave free rein to their imagination as no paper work was involved. Once installed in front of the screen, most of them were learning for the first how to compose whilst producing their drawing. The success of this competition was shattering. From the infant schools up to secondary level, 430 children from 25 different schools produced a drawing which was then stored on the Aspasie system server.
Now virtually all the schools in Val Maubuee are alive to this new possibility of pedagogic creation thanks to telematics. The drawings can be called up via Aspasie system server and are available either via the child's name or that of his school.
Many parents thus discover telematics through looking for the graphics designed by their child.

c/ In the future, it is likely that animators and teachers will fix more precise themes. In the north of France, for example, at Fontaine-Notre-Dame, M. Desobry, the school director, has chosen to prepare with his pupils a data bank on the theme of "eat better to live better". Called "Nutritional" this data bank includes 75 pages of information about a well balanced diet.
In Val Maubuee the themes may concern both scholastic activities and the local environment.
One such case is a project whose feasibility goes well beyond the capacity of the school both in terms of production and of the audience concerned. It is a telematic history of Val Maubuee in which would take part, in both the conception and the production, teachers, pupils, graphic designers, historians, institutions, associations and other interested individuals.
The gamble is major, as we are living in a recently inhabited geographical area. The residents know rather little about the past of their town. We are often made aware of this when demonstrating the Aspasie data bank. When we key in the code word "chocolate", we see the address of the town hall of Noisiel, one of the six communes in the Val Maubuee. This is on the "Place Emile Menier",

thus recalling that Noisiel is one of France's high spots for
chocolate - Menier installed his factories there last century.
The Aspasie data bank is gradually tending to become a privileged
repository to build a cultural identity for the inhabitants of Val
Maubuee, based both on storing a collective local memory and on
the collection of elements of daily life of social groups and
individuals who find a means of expression in Aspasie. But here,
we change gear. We slide in specifically pedagogical questions,
keyed to the acquisition of a telematic culture proposed by
Aspasie, leading ever more people to the acquirement of this new
means of communication, individually or as a collectivity.

D.   Telematics and paideia.

1.   The objectives of Aspasie.

The Greeks bequeathed us the notion of "paideia", taken up by the
Romans in the closely linked idea of "Humanitas". Henri-Irenee
Marou defines it as being "the state of a fully developed spirit,
having brought out all its potentialities". This action magnifies
that of education, at least on two points: quality and scope. It
is not limited to just scholastic institutions and its scope is
unlimited. This scope furthermore has varied over the ages. The
paideia of the V century B.C. clearly excluded any technical know-
how. Today "a well-tempered mind" can hardly exist without a
minimum of technical knowledge. Indeed we must avoid any further
cleavage between current social segments, between those who know
and those who do not. Here we are referring to the notion of
"computer illiteracy" which looms over more and more people in
every walk of life with the recent massive upsurge of micro-
technology. Without any technical culture, even the simplest, can
help towards a greater participation in our world. The control of
these micro-technologies which is virtually accessible to everyone
increases our ability to act in the world of education, in work,
in socio-economic and political life, in culture and leisure
activities. Naturally possessing this technical culture, enabling
us to master these new tools, neither translates ipso facto by
communication waves, nor does it spirit away other systems of
logic - state or ideological superstructures, social, economic or
political conflicts.
Participation in and control of the world today - and even more
tomorrow - can hardly be envisaged (at least in those countries
where the techniques of creation and communication have reached a
certain level) without individual and collective appropriation of
these technologies,   not merely to understand the uses proposed,
but also to act on the tools to fit them to a dynamic social
demand.

2.   The means deployed by Aspasie.

Here we are going to give a very succinct summary of the means
that Aspasie has used to encourage concretely a wide upsurge in
the image of telematic communication.

a/ Approach. Ever since its creation, Aspasie has assembled its
five categories of partners (individuals, association, collect-
ivities and local administrations, companies, teaching infra-
structure)into different groups. These commissions, education and
adult training, technical, sport, research environment, artistic
creation, administrative and social information, animation and
culture, have all drawn a maximum of people to participate in the

definition of a telematic system suited to the desires of a given
group of people wishing to acquire it.

b/ <u>Editorial independence</u>. Aspasie rejects the usual gulf between
the users of telematics and the suppliers of information.   Each
individual or group in Val Maubuee is a potential source of data.
Whilst being a media, source of proposals, central dispenser of
computer and telematics culture, Aspasie has no editorial role.
It produces no information other than that which concerns its own
activities, and it gives full freedom to its partners concerning
content and form.   Some partners only compose a few screens:
other, like the Maison des Jeunes et de la Culture Victor Jara of
Champs-sur-Marne, go to over 300.

c/ <u>Cost</u>. Minimal, especially when compared to that of Teletel 3.
For producers not belonging to the production sector, an annual
subscription fee of 300 francs.   For users, the information is
free, and the communication represents 2.25 francs per hour, at
peak time.   The data is transmitted via the traditional commuted
telephone network (RTC) which is very cheap for local calls.   In
a limited geographical area, it is thus perfectly possible to
offer a moderately priced telematic service.   This is indispensable to bring telematic culture fully through to a broad
audience.

d/ <u>The right technical network</u>.   The Aspasie telematic system is
based on the use of micro-technology.   It uses the telematic
communication (Teletel standards) of microcomputers, both for
graphic composition and for handling data.   The use of specific
tools (ease of use: omnipresence and multi-purpose: the possibility of creating its own programmes) has made it possible to
create a telematic system which, as its first goal, allows the
decentralised, broken out, production of data given by the
partners of Aspasie.   Instead of a classical configuration with a
serving system and consumers of data, we have a network designed
as follows:

*one common serving system, handling all the data;
*scattered sites of production in the areas, places of
activity, schools, institutions, administration, companies, household.   These are basically professional micro-computers equipped
with composing software programmes and nano-networks with the
Praxitele programme.
*terminals, Minitel or micro-computers

e/ <u>Training</u>. Aspasie proposes training courses that gradually set
its partners in control of the telematic tool, as it takes into
account two aspects:
*the apprenticeship of using software and equipment such as
proposed by service companies and manufacturers.   At this stage
the results start to be positive as the 65 partners (not including
individuals) have already learnt how to use a micro-computer to
compose some 2,500 to 3,000 information screens.
*the intervention of the partners in the offer.   This consists
of sending out requests to modify (perhaps oneself) the tools to
render them more suited to the cultural needs of Aspasie's members.
We have already quoted the case of the corrections concerning the
telematic novels with the change from "Story of a funny sort of
school" to "Pere Noel".
In the same way, the creation of the right technical network
illustrates the modification of the technical offer according to

cultural demands, since it is partly due to Aspasie that the
Praxitele programme was put on nano-network and that the screens
thus created could be retrieved on a server system.

With these means, Aspasie, in the Val Maubuee, is trying to meet
its goals of encouraging a fuller expression of citizens and hence
a finer participation in the day to day environment. Here it
reflects its symbol from ancient Greece, Aspasie, the concubine of
Pericles, whose influence it is said was often decisive in the
running of political life in Athens.

This swift overview of the French experience in telematics leads
us to think that this tool opens fresh horizons in the areas of
education and culture. It seems proper to add to the publication
of information and teaching material, the potential of textual and
graphic production which immediately take a dimension of communication. It would perhaps be most useful to start on in-depth
reflection on the intrinsic links between this production and its
communication capacity. In certain cases, managing to handle the
telematic tool may lead a wide public to express itself and to
participate more fully in its daily environment.

However, we have to measure our words. These phenomena are very
recent and the in-depth studies on their nature affects the
problems encountered (cost; relative unsuitability of programmes
and equipment), the resistance met (the burden of habit and
structures) is not that great. We can only hope that the elements
set forth here will encourage us to delve further into those few
tracks.

BIBLIOGRAPHY

I.   General Works

- Habermas, J;, La technique et la science comme ideologie
  (Denoel Paris, 1984)

- De la Haye, Y., Dissonances. Critique de la communication
  (La pensee sauvage, 1984)

- Laulan, A.M., La resistance aux systemes d'information (Retz,
  Paris, 1984)

- Marrou, H.I., Histoire de l'education dans l'Antiquite (Seuil,
  Paris, 1965)

- Roqueplo, P., Penser la technique. Pour une democratie concrete
  (Seuil, Paris, 1983)

II.   Telematics and Education.

- Ancelin, C. et Marchand, M., Le videotex. Contribution aux
  debats sur la telematique (Masson, Paris, 1984)

- Ancelin, C. et Marchand, M., Telematique. Promenade   dans les
  usages (Documentation franaise, Paris, 1984)

- Nora, S. et Minc, A., L'informatisation de la societe (Seuil,
  Paris, 1978)

- Stone-Iwassa, R., 10 ans deja: le videotex francais est-il
  majeur? (Institut National de la Communication Audiovisuelle,
  Paris, 1985)

- La telematique grand public. Aspects juridiques, economiques
  et sociaux (Documentation francaise, Paris, 1986)

- La lettre de Teletel. Numero 8, ler trimestre 1986

- De Linares, J., Minitel: un jouet de six milliards (Le Nouvel
  Economiste, 18 avril 1986)

- Liaisons, Academie de Creteil. Numero 10, avril 1986

- EAO et Telecommunications (Revue francaise des Telecommunications. Numero 57, decembre 1985)

- Bernard, P., La telematique fait exploser l'ecole. (Le Monde,
  17 avril 1986)

- Communique "Volet Telematique" - Plan Informatique Pour Tous
  (Services du Premier Ministre, 29 janvier 1986)

III. Concerning Aspasie

- Charon, J.M., Reflexion sur un projet de communication locale:
  ASPASIE (Bulletin de l'Idate. Numero 15, avril 1984)

- Clavaud, R., Allo, ici l'informatique. A Marne-la-Vallee, les
  associations s'adresseront en direct a leurs "clients" (Le Monde
  4-5 mars 1984)

- Corbineau, B., Aspasiennement votre: l'outil ne fait pas le
  moine (Bulletin de l'Idate. Numero 17, octobre 1984)

- Loiseau, G., Micro-technologies et strategies d'appropriation:
  le cas d'Aspasie (Bulletin de l'Idate. Numero 15, avril 1984)

Remote Education and Informatics: Teleteaching
F. Lovis (Editor)
Elsevier Science Publishers B.V. (North-Holland)
© IFIP, 1988

Can Teaching by Computer Replace Teaching by Professors?

- Results of an Experimental Study at the
  University of Karlsruhe

Thomas Ottmann

Universitat Karlsruhe
Postfach 6980
D-7500 Karlsruhe

1. Introduction

Computer-assisted instruction CAI projects started as early as the late
1950's. Initial hopes of saving labour, manpower and capital by automating
education at the university level by means of computers were not fulfilled.
Currently, however, one can observe a fresh impetus on CAI. There are serious
indications which allow us to predict an ultimate breakthrough of the computer
as the only two-way mass communication system used in the educational process
cf.[3]. Among the main reasons for this phenomenon we mention the following
ones:

. cheaper and better hardware colour and graphic displays,
   instant response time
. networks local area networks, interactive videotex and
   packet switching networks
. a better understanding of the specific advantages of the
   computer as a medium used for educational purposes good for
   algorithmically tractable topics, less appropriate for
   "philosophical" fields of knowledge
. easy-to-learn author languages
. a growing library of courseware.

In co-operation with the IIG of the Technical University of Graz, we started
in Karlsruhe a major CAI project, in summer 1985. The aims of the project are

. to develop courseware for a one-year course on algorithms
   and data structures, which is a mandatory subject for our
   students,
. to establish a CAI lab in the university, where the students can
   execute CAI lessons,
. to replace a considerable fraction of a course on algorithms and
   data structures by courseware,
. to evaluate both the used courseware and the acceptance of
   this way of teaching and learning by our students.

The project is based on the CAI system AUTOOL, developed at the Techinical
University of Graz, Austria, by Prof. Dr.H. Maurer and his group, [cf.2].
This system is a further extension of the PLATO system, developed at the
University of Illinois in the 1970's, later marketed by Control Data
Corporation.   In Graz the system was adapted to the videotex system and the
international CEPT standard.   AUTOOL allows one to write courseware by
editing using a graphic-editor, not programming a linked set of frames.

Frames may contain graphic and/or text, different colours, animation motion
and blinking.   It is further possible to include questions on both the
multiple choice and the free-text-answer types.   The CAI user, i.e. the
student working through an AUTOOL lesson, conducts a tutorial dialogue with
the computer lwhich is mainly user driven.   AUTOOL lessons can be read into a
micro-computer from a file-server which may be a simple disk drive, a
dedicated Unix-based system, or even the central computer of the interactive
videotex system.   After loading the interpreter, as telesoftware perhaps, and
loading a lesson into local store no further connection to the server is
required.   One of the most interesting aspects of the current project is that
it is even possible to work through an AUTOOL lesson at a home TV-set - once
the lesson and the AUTOOL executor are stored in the videotex- database and
the TV-set is provided with an intelligent terminal.

The ongoing project in Karlsruhe can be divided into the following 4 stages:
courseware writing, establishing a CAI lab, teaching students, and the
evaluation phase.   This sequence of stages only partially describes the
progress of the project in time.   For example, the results of the evaluation
phase are used to rewrite parts of the courseware.   In the next 4 sections
2,3,4,5 we shall describe the 4 stages in turn in some detail.   In Section 6
we shall summarize our experiences obtained so far and make some final
comments.

2. Courseware writing

Courses on algorithms and data structures belong to the core of every computer
science curriculum in the world.   Many different courses, both at the
undergraduate and at the graduate level, are mandatory for all students with
computer science either as a major or minor subject.   The field is not only a
standard topic for teaching, but is, also a very active research area.   Thus,
it is not surprising that the body of knowledge has grown considerably during
the last years.   Beyond classical topics like linked lists, trees, sorting
and searching, new ones have become important because of new hardware and new
applications.   Geometrical algorithms and data structures and parallel and
distributed algorithms belong among these new topics.   The whole field of
algorithms and data structures is ideally suited to CAI, because it is
algorithmically tractable by definition.   Using specific advantages of the
computer colour, graphics, animation, the ability of conducting a dialogue the
dynamic maniupulation of data structures and the intrinsic properties of
algorithms can much better be explained than by using one of the classical
media-book, blackboard, overhead projector.   However, one has to know how to
use the computer in the right way.

In Karlsruhe we began in May 1985 with a group of about 25 students who had
computer science as a minor subject in their third or fourth year at the
university, in order to write topics and topics arising from the research
pursued at our institute, in order to prepare courseware both for our own and
for widespread use.   Altogether about 30 lessons have been written so far,
using the AUTOOL/PLATO editor, basically by students but under permanent
control of the professor and an assistant.   The following topics are treated
in these CAI lessons:

Hashing:

. open addressing with linear and quadratic probing, double hashing, Brent's method,
. hashing with direct and separate chaining, coalesced hashing,
. extendable hashing,
. virtual hashing inclusive of linear hashing.

Search-tree structures:

. natural random trees,
. different classes of balanced binary trees like brother trees, AVL trees, weight balanced trees,
. B-trees as a structure for external storage of data,
. k-dim. trees.

Geometric algorithms and data structures:

. the scanline paradigm,
. geometric divide and conquer,
. recuction of the rectangle-intersection problem,
. segment- and interval-trees,
. priority search trees,
. Voronoi diagrams for points and line segments with various metrics, inclusive algorithms for nearest-neighbour search, minimum-spanning-tree construction, point location   problems.

Selected topics:

. data structures for the union-find problem and for priority queue implemenetation,
. graph algorithms for computing mst's,
. parallel sorting algorithms,
. backtracking as an algorithmic paradigm.

Many of these lessons consist of more than one package; one package roughly corresponds to a 1-hour lecture. The list of topics shows that we tried to cover both powerful algorithmic techniques like, e.g., backtracking and difficult algorithms like, e.g., virtural hashing, by courseware. Analytical results on algorithms and data structures are generally only mentioned and not derived in the respective CAI lessons. In parallel with writing courseware on the above topics we started to write a textbook covering the same material; thus we could provide both the students writing a lesson and the students working through a finished lesson with detailed written material. We were quite surprised how much the perspective to produce a CAI lesson for widespread use by the AUTOOL/PLATO system can motivate a student, though - on the average - it takes about 100 hours to prepare a 1-hour lesson, if one has to get to learn both the system and the material to be covered by the lesson.

What constitutes a **good** lesson? The results of the evaluation phase show that the right structure, precise and lucid text, appropriate, moderate, and not excessive use of colour, graphics and animation and a

sufficient number of good questions are characteristic properties of good lessons. As in all computer dialogues, Nievergelt's <u>Sites, Modes, and Trails</u> paradigm [5] should be observed. For more details, see Section 5. Of course, it it not surprising that not all students were able to make optimal use of the abilities offered by the AUTOOL system, though we always discussed a detailed plan of each lesson quite carefully before the student started the

editing process.   Our experience shows that one obtains the best results if
one chooses a fairly small portion of material to be presented in one lesson,
discusses the CAI lesson with the student at an early stage after he has
edited the firist five or ten frames, assures a transfer of knowledge from
system experts to novice users, and sharpens the student's eyes for precise
formulations which cannot be musunderstood.   On the average we, instructor
and student, went through each CAI lesson between 5 and 8 times.

Based on our experience during the last year we are convinced that a new type
of seminar at universities will emerge: Topics of current interest will be
worked out jointly by students and professors; however, the student does not
deliver a speech or a written elaboration but a CAI lesson.   Of course, this
is much more effort than a traditional seminar, both for the students and the
professor.   In many cases, however, the additional effort will pay off because
the "results" of such a seminar can be used to teach other students and to
speed up the transfer of knowledge.

3. Establishing a CAI lab

AUTOOL was designed to write CAI lessons which can be accessed in the
interactive videotex system, using a home TV-set.   However, at least in
Germany, it is currently still illusive to base a CAI project on the
assumption that each student has access to the national videotex the Btx-
system or has his privately owned computer.   Therefore, we established a CAI
lab as a computer classroom with currently 13 graphics terminals.   More than
250 students participated in the course where CAI lessons were offered.   The
students had access to the terminal daily from 9.00a.m to 7.00p.m..   We
reserved individually for each student one terminal for two hours per week;
however, after some time the students used the system fairly freely.   As one
result of the evaluation phase, we learned that two hours per student per week
is somewhat too short, if one course is accompanied or partially replaced by
CAI lessons.   About 80% of our students asked for time of betweeen 2 and 3
hours per week, preferably offered as two separate sessions.

Our CAI lab is equipped with microcomputers MUPID-C2D2 with Z80-CPU, 128 KByte
RAM, 64, of which are used for the bitmap display; in the remaining 64 KByte
the CAI lesson and the software to execute a lesson are stored. Each computer
is equipped with a colour display with a resolution of 320 x 240 points.

The 13 microcomputers are connected with a file-server which simulates the
videotex Btex central computer. As file-server we used a HP9000, series 300,
model 310, with 68010-VPU, 1 MByte RAM, 44 MByte disk and 13 serial interfaces; the communication rate is 4800 baud.   The file-server runs under
HP-UX, a UNIX V-like operating system.   We used the CONNEX software, cf. [1],
also developed in Graz, which allows a communication with the 13 MUPID
computers and the HP-computer in both directions.   Thus not only the lessons
and the software for executing the lessons can be distributed to the 13 CAI
stations; data generated at these stations can also be transmitted to and
stored at the file-server. We used this possibility in order to evaluate CAI
lessons by presenting students an electronic questionnaire and collecting the
answers at the file-server. Though we already obtained a number of
interesting results in this way, the method of "on-line evaluation" of CAI
courses can certainly be improved considerably.

Two of the 13 MUPID computers are also connected with a disk drive by a fast
19200 baud serial interface.   These are necessary in order to load CAI
lessons into the system.   The whole configuration is shown by Picture 1.

Configuration: CAI –Laboratory

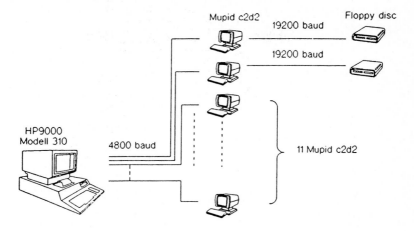

Picture 1

During the summer term of 1986, not only the CAI lessons developed in the
first stage at our university were available in our CAI lab. We
included a series of lessons on sorting which were written in Graz.
These lessons were also mandatory for the course on algorithms and data
structures in summer 1986. Beyond that, CAI lessons on other topics
which were not mandatory could be accessed by our students.

A considerable number of students made use of this possibility:

.   25% of the students worked through other CAI lessons on
     algorithms and data structures covering non-compulsory
     topics,
.   10% accessed lessons which introduce the AUTOOL system for
     potential authors of courseware,
.   12% accessed lessons on expert systems and natural language
     analysis,
.   10% played games chess.

Though these topics were not mandatory, altogether 52% of our students
worked through one or more of these lessons. This indicates that beyond
those lessons which are part of a specific course one could and should
always offer further topics to allow browsing by students.

4. Teaching a course on algorithms and data structures

Nievergelt [4] points out that CAI will fail to achieve its goals if the
system is not integrated into the whole organisation and administration
of learning established at the university. We integrated CAI lessons as
follows into a standard course on algorithms and data structures, in
summer 1986. Before we started using CAI lessons, the course consisted
of 3 lectures per week, 10 weeks per term. We decided to cover exactly
the same material as before, but to replace 5 of the 10 3-hour lectures
by CAI lessons. Analytical material was presented only by using
blackboard and oral presentation; the material covered by CAI lessons was
not presented again by the professor in class. However, detailed

written material was delivered to the students, closely related to the
CAI lessons.   The whole course was accompanied by exercises where
students were supposed to solve problems.   Their solutions were then
discussed by the professor and his assistants jointly with the students
in small groups.   In these exercises, of course, the material presented
only by CAI lessons was also presupposed.

Not all CAI lessons covering compulsory material of the course were
accessible from the very beginning of the term.   Instead we tried to make
the progress of learning of our students more continuous by keeping the
respective relevant CAI lessons in the system only for a limited time
between four and six weeks.   Comments by the students show that this form
of organisation had indeed the desired effect. It was more difficult than
in a traditional course for a student to be passive until the end of the
term and to start actively learning just a few days before the written
examination.

At the beginning of the experiment the system was still quite unstable:
Hard- and software errors were quite frequent and the user interface had
several serious deficiences 17% of the astudents complained about
technical problems when working through a CAI lesson.   Fortunately, the
system and its implementation were improved considerably during the
summer.   However, it may very well be that the initial difficulties had
some negative effect on the evaluation of this experiment by our
students.   Therefore, their overall very positive impression is even
more surprising.

The following topics were covered by CAI lessons only:

.   5 lessons on sorting which were written in Graz: Shellsort,
    Quicksort, Radixsort, Heapsort 2 packages
.   Hashing with open addressing,
.   Hashing with direct and separate chaining 2 packages,
.   natural random trees 4 packages,
.   brother trees 2 packages,
.   backtracking 2 packages.

CAI lessons covering the latter 5 topics were developed in Karlsruhe.
We knew already that the lessons were of different quality, among them
even lessons of non-acceptable quality which should be replaced by better
ones. This holds true for the lesson on hashing with direct and separate
chaining.   On the other hand, we had the intuitive feeling that the first
lesson on hashing with open addressing and the two packages on backtracking were really good lessons!   In order to derive criteria to
distinguish between good and bad CAI lessons, we intentionally left a few
lessons in the experiment which we considered as bad ones and asked the
students to evaluate all lessons.

5. Evaluation

As already mentioned, the experiment of teaching a course on algorithms
and data structures to a large audience by replacing 1/2 of the usual
material by CAI lessons has been evaluated by the students themselves.

In order to obtain a reasonable questionnaire, a pretest with a sample of
48 students was carried out, after the series of CAI lessons on sorting.
Some of the results of this pretest are reported in [6].   As a result of

this pretest, an electronic questionnaire with 40 questions, to evaluate single lessons, was made accessible to the students in the system. Instead of asking questions we presented statements on which the student could express his opinion by choosing between 5 possibilities, ranging from full agreement to full rejection. The statements referred to the quality of the respective CAI lessons in comparison also with traditional ways of learning in lectures and by books.

Among the 294 participants in the experiment, 191 answered the electronic questionnaire at least once; and 29% of the 191 even answered it 5 times and thus evaluated all lessons relevant for the experiment. Each of the 5 lessons has been evaluated by roughly 100 students. Therefore we believe that the obtained results are indeed significant.

Beyond this evaluation of 5 single lessons by an electronic questionnaire, 107 students answered an additional written questionnaire at the end of the term, by which we wanted to obtain an overall impression from our students about this way of teaching a course. Here students were also encouraged to make verbal comments of any kind. We shall sketch the main results of the evaluation phase and refer to [7] for the many interesting details.

Many of the 40 statements of the electronic questionnaire obtained quite different votes for the 5 different CAI lessons. This may indicate what constitutes a good lesson. The statements which were almost uniformly evaluated can lead to general recommendations for course authors. We start with a report of the evaluations of single lessons.

a) Dialogue structure. Independent of the quality of the quality of a CAI lesson, the student generally follows the recommended path. However, he wants to have more and other possibilities to branch than the authors implemented in the 5 lessons. In order to help the student always to know where he is in a lesson, it is good to place a key-word on each frame always at the same position. This is one way of implementing Nievergelt's Sites, Modes, and Trails - principle, because the AUTOOL system already tells the user what he can do, where he can go and how he can go there.

b) Presentation of the content. Bad lessons contain, that is the impression of the student, too much material and make him tired. This is not correlated with the real amount of material and the real time which the student spent at the terminal to work through the lesson. We also asked for the time. Students want to have more examples and fewer general statements; this is independent of the quality of the lesson. However, the quality of a lesson is very much dependent on its structure.

c) Text and formulations. This is one of the most important criteria to distinguish between good and bad lessons: clear statements which cannot be misunderstood are an absolute necessity in CAI lessons. If a lesson is bad the student has the impression that too many new concepts have been introduced and not sufficiently explained. This subjective impression may be wrong, however; there may be only a very few new notions that have been introduced, but, unfortunately, not by clear, easy to understand and consistent definitions.

d) Graphics and Colour. Independently of the quality of the lesson, students complained about a too frequent change of colours. Furthermore, fewer different colours, both in text and graphics, were wanted. On the other hand, a majority agreed that the use of colour and graphics has facilitated the understanding of the content of a lesson.

However, slowly displaying just for fun "nice" graphics which do not

contribute very much to the content of a lesson is generally felt to be
boring.   The right design of graphics, with a reasonable layout of the
screen, utilizing spatial analogies and analogies in colours on the
screen, can make good lessons better, but cannot make bad lessons good.

e) Questions and Answers.   Students want to have many questions.   They
hardly ever feel that a question is too difficult to answer.   Though
they have always the possibility to skip a question, they rarely do so.
Many, not too simple and clearly stated questions should be included in a
CAI lesson in order to obtain a good lesson; whether the questions are of
the multiple choice or free-text-answer types does not matter.

The students generally agreed that they have understood those lessons
which they and we considered to be good ones; it is surprising that they
believed that they learned at least something from those lessons which
were considered to be bad ones.

Even after they had seen between 7 and 10 CAI lessons, a large majority
of the students still had fun when working with a good lesson.
Comparing the computer with other media book or lecture, it turns out
that a CAI lesson is preferred to a lecture rather more than it is
preferred to a book.   A good CAI lesson is preferred both to a book and
to a lecture.   The same does not hold for a bad one.

As regards the overall impression of our students about this way of
teaching a course, we asked them about their opinions before and after
the experiment: From the sample of 107 students, 22 had no idea, 18 were
positive, 53 ambiguous and 14 negative about CAI before the experiment;
after the experiment, 78 were positive, 22 ambiguous and 7 negative.   We
consider this as an overwhelming vote in favour of CAI.

6.   Conclusion

Can teaching by computers replace teaching by professors? Based on the
experiences of the CAI project in Karlsruhe so far, the answer must be at
least partially affirmative.   Certainly, students can understand a new
topic easier and faster by a good book, or a good lecture delivered by a
competent professor, than by a bad CAI lesson.   However, our experiment
shows that a good CAI lesson beats both a book and a lecture.   However,
the right topic has to be chosen!   Writing good CAI lessons requires a
considerable amount of pedagogical talent.   However, our experiment also
proved that even students are able to become authors of good lessons when
using the AUTOOL system and guided by a professor.

Students appreciate a mixture between different ways of teaching.   CAI
lessons constitute a welcome variation.   At least in the area of
algorithms and data structures, there are a number of topics ideally
suited for CAI which can be explained by a CAI lesson much better than by
any of the traditional media using blackboard, or slides, or book.   Thus
CAI can at least improve the teaching of a professor if he knows how to
use this new medium in the right way.

In Karlsruhe we have run an "in-house" experiement by setting up a
computer classroom where students could work with CAI lessons.   The
AUTOOL system on which we based our project has, of course, other very

attractive and promising aspects.   Sometimes the student can use a CAI
lesson at home, like a book, when studying a certain topic.   If he had

access to interactive videotex he need not even leave his study room. Whether or not this will ever happen depends not only on the selection of courseware, but also on the development of the interactive videotex system, or some other data network, for private use, The latter point is, of course, a political issue.

Acknowledgement:

I should like to thank Ch. Icking, H. Maurer, P. Lipp, M. Simonis, P. Widmayer, and all the students participating in the project for their help and readiness to cooperate. The Stiftung Volkswagenwork supported the project by grant I/62-452 and Hewlett Packard Company by a hardware donation.

References

1   H.Cheng, P. Lipp, H. Maurer and R. Posch: GASC - ein Graphik - und Software Kommunikationssystem, in: Proceedings GI Jahrestagung 1985, Wien, IFB, 679-690

2   J. Garrat, F. Huber and H. Huermer: AUTOOL - ein BTX-orientiertes Autorensystem, Berichte des IIG der TU GRAZ, Nr. 206, 1985

3   R. Gunzenhauser and G. Knopik: Neuere Entwicklung des rechnerunterstutzten Lernens, in: Uberlicke Informations-verarbeitung 1985, Hrsg. H.A. Maurer, BI, 1985, 99-118

4   J. Nievergelt: A pragmatic introduction to courseware design, IEEE Computer, 1980, 7-21

5   J. Nievergelt: Errors in dialog design and how to avoid them, in: Document preparation systems, Hrsg, J. Nievergelt et al., North-Holland, 1982, 7-21

6   Th. Ottmann and P. Widmayer: Modellversuch computergestutzter Informatikunterricht: Algorithmen und Datenstrukturen, Tagung Informatik Grundbuildung in Schule und Beruf, Kaiserslautern, 29.9. -1.10.1986, IFB, Springer Verlag

7   M. Simonis: Computerunterstutzte Informatikausbildung an der Hochschule - eine Begleituntersuchung zum Karlsruher Modell-versuch im Sommersemester 1986, Diplomarbeit, Karlsruhe, 1986

Remote Education and Informatics: Teleteaching
F. Lovis (Editor)
Elsevier Science Publishers B.V. (North-Holland)
© IFIP, 1988

INFORMATION TECHNOLOGY IN HUNGARIAN EDUCATION

György PARIS

Institute for Science Management and Informatics.
H-1372. Budapest, P.O. Box 454. Hungary

THE PRESENT SITUATION

The rapid development of science and technology, the appearance
of micro electronics, and the penetration of computer technology
into various fields of the social division of labour have all
called attention to the importance of teaching computer technology. It has become clear that the tasks facing society can be
solved with the necessary efficiency required in our age only
with the help of computers and information technology.

Acknowledging the given structure and nature of Hungarian schools
and education - when determining the tasks of education - the
first thing to consider is that it takes at least 5-8 years to
put a decision into practice. This means that when setting the
tasks of education, one has to think 10-15 years ahead.

Accordingly, the teaching of computer technology in Hungarian
higher education started in 1969. In the first period this was
limited to the training of experts, then from 1975 on it began to
include training in the application of computer technology. At
technical universities and universities of the natural sciences
the training of future teachers started. In 1980 a decision was
made to teach information technology in the whole of the education system.

THE SCHOOL-COMPUTER PROGRAM IN OUR EDUCATION SYSTEM

The 1980 educational program made the following requirements:

- to make the advantages of computer technology and its efficient
use widely known. In the following 10-15 years the teaching of
computer technology has to be organized throughout public education, and in higher education it has to be developed further.
Adult education has to be organized for those who need information technology, and evening schools and correspondence courses
- in connection with this structural change, a retraining of
teachers may be necessary;

- to provide for the training of teachers and staff who are not
familiar with the field;

- the same applies to teachers in higher education;

- in public as well as higher education, teaching materials,
collections of problems and exercises, and experiments have to be
revised or rewritten;

- software in the necessary amount and quality should be prepared, made available and spread;

- it is imperative that in the whole of the educational system, from elementary school to postgraduate level, there should be a sufficient amount of hardware - from pocket calculators and programmable small computers to professional PCs, and in higher education, also small, medium and large computers.

This means that the program bore a relation to <u>public</u> and <u>higher education</u> and had <u>cultural</u> aspects as well.

ELEMENTARY SCHOOL EDUCATION

In the 1985/86 school year, according to the school computer program, in about one tenth of the 3700 elementary schools experimental computer courses started with several computers, either in optional classes or in the form of extra-curricular courses. The optional classes had started already in the 1984/85 school year following a decree of the Ministry of Education. At the beginning of the 1986/87 school year, about one third of the elementary schools, about 1000 schools, had one or more computers.

The number of educational programs is growing as a result of a secondary school program writing competition, and there is a choice of programs now to meet the requirements of elementary education.

SECONDARY SCHOOL EDUCATION

In secondary technical schools, the teaching of information technology started with the training of computer technicians, programmers and process organizers and with information processing and the application of computers. In secondary grammar schools, with operator training and the optional computer classes. This was followed by the wide-spread introduction of the basics of information technology in extra-curricular courses as part of the <u>school-computer program</u> in all secondary schools except adult, evening and correspondence courses and health and typists' schools.

The first Hungarian PC model manufactured in relatively large series was ordered for the program and the PCs reached the schools in March 1983.

Following the guidelines of the Ministry of Education, extra--curricular courses started <u>in all types of secondary schools (Grammar, comprehensive, vocational)</u>. In the 1983/84 school year, 1537 beginner's and 318 advanced courses were run. The experiences of these courses prove the hypothesis that with the development of micro electronics and information technology, teachers and students alike take part in the development of teaching materials. The so far more or less passive participants of education have become active participants in the educational process.

To help the introduction of computer technology in education the Institute for Science Management and Informatics conducted a <u>secondary school educational program competition</u>. By June 30th 1986, 20,000 programs were distributed in the schools.

By the end of the 1985/86 school year, secondary schools got as many as 1930 computers as part of the program and had altogether 2765 PCs. So by the end of the 1985/86 school year, in 56 % of the schools there were 2 PCs, in 34 % of them 3-5, and in the remaining 10 % 6-22 PCs. At the end of the 1985/86 school year, a computer served an average of 130 students.

The distribution of computers went parallel with the basic training of abut 1,000 teachers.

The National Pedagogical Institute deals with the pedagogical and methodological aspects of the widespread introduction of computer technology, prepares for it and for its application in other subjects. They have examined the necessary changes required by appearance of computers in pedagogy, the management of public education and their application in various fields. These changes affect the relationship between school and its social environment.

Since, as a result of the rapid introduction of this technology, the search for new methods takes place at the same time as practical work, there has been a need for an exchange of experiences, to organize exhibitions and conferences. Several exhibitions were organized in the counties and in Budapest where schools could present the results they achieved. Secondary school computer technology competitions have been organized annually since 1983. 3200 students from 340 schools entered the 1985/86 competition, though a year before only 500 did so.

In the summer holidays, camps were organized by various institutions and social organizations with excellent possibilities to learn computer technology.

TEACHER TRAINING

At the natural sciences faculties of universities, students can become familiar with the possibilities of bigger computers, with the use of various programs for their application, and how to make use of their bigger capacities. Programs made to solve scientific, statistical and techno-scientific problems and calculations are also widespread.

At the arts and humanities faculties of universities, and at art schools, the spreading of computer technology has fallen behind, and the lag here is the greatest. At present there is only one university where computer technology is taught to future teachers (of the humanities) with two subjects: the basics of computer technology, and computer methodology.

For teacher training at universities and colleges, the computers required by the school computer program are available. At present, in all institutions with teacher training a school-computer room operates. We should mention here the subject "technical knowledge" which is a very computer oriented supplementary course.

In spite of all the efforts so far, the goal that every student should be near an accessible computer to a sufficient degree has not yet been reached.

ADULT EDUCATION

Some estimate 100,000 as the number of personal computers owned
by the population. Most of them are believed to be used for
games. Therefore,there is still a lot to be done to extend the
use of PCs by programs designed for educational, cultural and
household purposes.

The general training of the public is to be undertaken by public
education. Courses on computer technology have been launched by
a great number of community centres and cultural institutions.
An outstanding part is being taken in the dissemination of knowledge on computer technology by TIT (Society for the Dissemination of Scientific Knowledge) and NJSZT (János Neumann Computer
Science Society). The latter has started a micro-club movement
on its way, for acquiring practice in computer technology, which
serves as a framework to mobilize the available computer capacity
of institutes, factories and private enterprises.

The efficient cooperation with Hungarian Television was further
strengthened by negotiations between the Ministry of Education
and the Chairman of Hungarian Television in 1983, which helped
to launch programmes for computer technology training on School
Television.

The press also has a significant role in supporting computer
technology training, and we therefore contributed to the
establishment of a computer column in the weekly magazine
"ÖTLET" (IDEA) and a new monthly "MIKROMAGAZIN".

In cooperation with a film-making company we prepared a training
package of 16 units (including film, video, slides and a book),
which introduces its user into the rudimentaries of computer
technology.

DEVELOPMENT PROGRAMME FOR THE COMING FIVE YEARS

This programme should embrace various areas of training and education extensively, in accordance with the long-term development
programme and developments already realized, so that it can live
up to demands expected to be posed by the whole of society. The
training of information technology therefore should not fail to
be extended to the whole of education in order that

- the whole society should get acquainted with the rudimentaries
  of information technology:

- those who actively use it should be prepared for the employment of information-electronics;

- experts should be trained in the field of information technology and electronics.

THE SCOPE OF THE PROGRAMME

In the elementary schools, the principal aim is to have the rudimentaries of electronics and information technology acquired,
along with cultural elements of information technology and to

extend this knowledge to the whole of society, thereby ensuring that at further stages practical knowledge and expert training can be put into practice. During the period 1986 to 1990, the conditions for achieving these aims should be established in elementary education. It follows then that in the period mentioned above:

- in all elementary schools, the necessary materials in methodology, reference boosk, thesauruses, software-products for training and other aids should be available;

- there should be at least 2 teachers per school who are well versed in electronics and information technology, and annually about 1400 teachers should be trained at courses on the subject;

- annually, about 700 schools should be given computers;

- 3-10 school computers should be available per school;

- up-to-date interfaces and peripherals should be available for use to the school computers.

In secondary education, the aim is to acquire the rudimentaries and user's knowledge, as well as to train experts in the field of electronics and information technology. In the secondary schools, all pupils should participate in information-electronics training. A great emphasis should be laid on expert training as well. During the coming five-year period the basic knowledge of electronics and information technology should be acquired by all taking part in the system of secondary education.

In order to reach the aims of the development programme in secondary education the following principles should be fulfilled:

- all the necessary methodological materials, thesauruses, teaching aid softwares, films, books, video-tapes, etc., should be available in the required quantity and to adequate standards;

- there should be at least 4 teachers on the average per school who are trained properly to teach information-electronics;

- an average of 18 computers should be available per school, giving priority to technician training schools and to those which have achieved results above the average;

- the computers should be equipped with up-to-date interfaces and accessories for use;

- in accordance with special training purposes, word processing, simplified automatized planning systems and equipment for mechanical and other purposes should be bought.

In higher education, a high level practical knowledge of information-electronics should be acquired and experts, instructors and teachers should be trained.

In order to attain the afore-mentioned aims, the teaching of the knowledge of use should be made general at the technical colleges and universities, the science faculties, as well as the schools of economics and colleges. The teaching of practical knowledge should be more extensive at agricultural colleges and the faculties of humanities and teacher training colleges. This discipline should be introduced into law faculties, medical colleges and art academies.

Some principal ideas to be considered as to aims related to teacher training:

- the modernization of information-electronics teaching materials should be speeded up, with a stronger emphasis on system aspects;

- along with modernization of teaching materials, improved and updated materials, books and software should be worked out;

- the improvement of methods and syllabuses designed for in-service training of teachers and instructors should be developed;

- the major organizational units of universities and colleges should be given personal computers;

- all higher educational institutions should be given professional personal computers with interfaces and other accessories based in modern laboratories.

An overall modernization of teaching information-electronics at courses is necessary for those participating in re-training and in-service training programs.

Special efforts should be made to put into practice the program aiming at the training of the general public, which is being carried out by various social organizations, headed by NJSZT. The ultimate objective is to create a training programme which will make it possible in the long run for everyone to learn the rudimentaries of this new discipline.

The realization of this programme requires a lot of input on behalf of both the whole society and those involved in the programme. The impression gained so far encourages us to trust that the programme will end on a winning note.

Remote Education and Informatics: Teleteaching
F. Lovis (Editor)
Elsevier Science Publishers B.V. (North-Holland)
© IFIP, 1988

ONE YEAR EXPERIENCE IN TELETEACHING
AND CBT (COMPUTER BASED TRAINING):

RESULTS, ACHIEVEMENTS AND DRAWBACKS

Wolfgang PREE

FIM, University of Linz
A-4040 Linz/Austria

Contents:

1. General Remarks

    1.1 BASIC-Programming-Course
    1.2 TOP JOB - A Computer-Game to Learn the Basic Concepts of
    Data Processing
    1.3 The "Operating System Concepts"-Course

2. Organisation

    2.1 BASIC-Course
    2.2 TOP-JOB

3. Statistics (Concerning the BASIC-Course)

4. Conclusions and Experience with the Design and Development of
    Teachware

    4.1 Consequences Resulting from the Established Form of
    Organisation
    4.2 Less Efficiency of the Course-Organisation because of
    Technical Restrictions
    4.3 Comparision of Developing Teachware by Programming and by
    Using an Authoring-System
    4.4 Characteristics for High-Quality Teachware

5. Summary

1. General Remarks

The FIM (Research Institute for Microprocessor-Technology) offers
two courses on data processing and computer-science in the
Austrian viewdata-system (called "BTX"). We regard BTX as very
suitable for teleteaching because of the following characteristics, in particular:

a) Electronic-Mailing (which is the minimum requirement of a
    teleteaching-system) covers:

    -- Asynchrony: The receiver of a message does not have to
        be available at the moment of sending.

    -- Two way information-flow.

b) Viewdata offers the means to store and service the teachware
    centrally.

The Courses offered via BTX are the following:

1.1 BASIC-Programming Course (since October 1st, 1985)

This course consists of 7 lessons, 6 exercise-blocks and a
communications-program.

It covers a general introduction to programming and is designed
for beginners. The question "What is a program?" is answered by
showing up analogies from daily life, e.g. a (cooking) recipe,
the several activities in building a house, and so on.

The emphasis however is on the explanation of the most important
BASIC-commands. Simple programming-problems are solved.

The communications-module serves for the build-up of a "class-
community" (see "2. Organization"), which is an essential part of
how the course is organized and run.

It is worthwhile to mention that the lessons, exercises and the
communications-module are programmed in BASIC. This was done
because at the very beginning of BTX in Austria BASIC was the
only available programming language.

1.2 TOP-JOB -
    A Computer-Game to Learn the Basic Concepts of Data
    Processing

In this course the player can "work" in three hierarchical levels
according to his/her knowledge: GREENHORN, JUNIOR or MASTER.
During the game the player can "collect" bonus scores for expert-
and general-knowledge based upon correct answers to corresponding
questions.

As far as the basic knowledge on dataprocessing is concerned,
various lessons are offered and it is assumed that the player,
i.e. student, works them through carefully. All questions put by
TOP-JOB are based on knowledge contained in the lessons.

The goal of the game is to maximize the product of expert- and
general-knowledge-points. This guarantees that there is an
optimal balance between expert and general knowledge.

On the MASTER-Level one can collect the most points, but it is difficult to stay on this level throughout the whole game, because there are many expert-questions. If two expert-questions cannot be answered at this level, as a penalty the player is moved to the level below. On the other hand the player is not forced to start with the lowest level if he already has enough expert-knowlegde to "survive" a higher-level or if he thinks he has. If the player overestimates his knowledge, the lessons on the lower levels have to be studied in order to ascend again. So the regular way is to "work one's way up" from the GREENHORN to the MASTER-level.

The purpose of connecting computer-games with teachware is to enlarge the group of potential users:

Viewdata-users who play computer-games
Viewdata-users who use teachware

Users who "play" TOP-JOB

1.3 Course "Operating System Concepts"

This course was developed within the scope of the COSTOC-project in cooperation with the IIG (Institutes for Information-processing Graz) using the AUTOOL-authoring-system. The course consists of 12 lessons each comprising up to fifty frames.

2. Organisation

2.1 BASIC-Course

a) The communications-module:

This module enables the simulation of a class-community: interested viewdata-users enrol by the means of a dedicated answer-page, (which also is used to charge the registration-fee (AUS 20.000)). Then the student is added to the table of current-students. This list itself is stored in a viewdata-page. It is ensured by the communications program that only authorized persons (=members of this list) can use the communications - module. Consequently every student is entitled to find out who else is taking the same course currently for communication purposes.

The communications-module is used to send messages from the students to the teacher and viceversa. It also may be used for mailing among the students themselves. These messages may be questions, solved exercise-problems or just "normal" mail.

b) Exercises, additional information:

After the admission of a viewdata-user to the course, additional information material is sent to the student by postal mail.

This information consists of:

- Additional exercises whose solutions are to be sent to the teacher using the communications-module.

- A brief description of the BASIC-program-development-system which enables the user to test his exercise programs without assistance.

  The postal service to convey these textbooks was given preference over electronic mailing for the following reasons:

- Only a few viewdata-users have a printer connected to their decoder and it would be an unreasonable demand to force users to write down extensive information from the screen.

- The viewdata-electronic-mail concept is suitable for short messages. One message-page can take up to 500 characters.

- The transmission of graphics (e.g. flow-charts) within the electronic mailing system is not yet possible.

c) Diagram of the information flow:

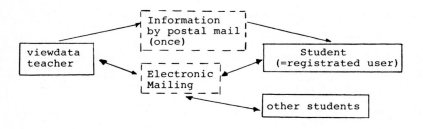

2.2 TOP-JOB

A modification of TOP-JOB to a course with the same structure as the BASIC-course can be made without problems. Because of lack of free capacity at the FIM, this modification hasn't been undertaken yet.

It is worthwhile mentioning that the TOP-JOB software also is used for seminars we present outside the university. In such cases that part of data which represents what we have called "general knowledge" is replaced by other information according to the wishes or needs of the audience or the contractor.

3. Statistics (concerning the BASIC-course)

a) Number of course members registered during the period from 1. 10. 85 to 31. 7. 86 (10 months): 70

b) "Drop-Out" Statistics:
The course-members can be divided into two groups:
Group 1: (36 students) Users, who are not interested in the course but in its organisation (form of the information-material, graphic viewdata-pages,...).

Group 2: (34 students): Users, who are interested in learning.

The members of group 1 only very seldom used the communi-cations-module to send questions or solved exercise-problems to the teacher. These course-members therefore should not be counted as "drop-outs".

The number of "drop-outs" in the second group is very small. Most of these students work through the whole course completely. Sometimes however the more difficult or rather cumbersome problems are skipped (see also: "4.1 Consequences Resulting from the Established Form of Organisation").

c) Knowledge of the really interested course-members:

The course-members are not asked about their preknowledge, but many of them make some remarks about their know-how when sending their solutions of the exercise-problems. Generally subscribers of the course have no preknowledge in data-processing or BASIC-programming. This is in accordance to the potential profile the course has been designed for.

d) Age of the course-members: from 10 years up. (= wide range!)

e) Statements about the organisation:

72 % of the coursemembers are content with the organisation of the course (this includes the sending of exercises and information material by postal mail and the possibilities of the communications module).

f) Frequency of calls for the lessons and exercises of the BASIC-course:

viewdata page   number of calls within 10 months

Lesson 1   118
Lesson 2   102
Lesson 3   98
Lesson 4   127*)
Lesson 5   86
Lesson 6   77
Lesson 7   94

*) Explanation for this statistical anomaly:
In this lesson the most important BASIC-commands are featured.

These statistics are interesting, because the BASIC-lessons can be called not only by the course-members, but by all viewdata users. We also remind you that each lesson can be downloaded to the decoder.

4. Conclusions and Experience with the Design and Development of Teachware

4.1 Consequences Resulting from the Established Form of Organization

-- Drawbacks of this "loose" course-organisation:
Because of lack of deadlines it is very difficult for the course-members to solve their exercise problems conse-
-cutively.Particularly large-scale-exercises are skipped.

-- Advantage of this "loose" course-organisation:
A high grade of flexibility is guaranteed which in particular is essential for working people.

4.2 Less efficiency of the Course-Organisation because of Technical Restrictions

The maximum baud-rate of 1200 in the Austrian viewdata-system causes a load time of 2 minutes for the communications-module. Therefore a student waits with his questions until he has enough messages to use the communications-module efficiently. This results in a loss of information: often the answer to such a question is essential for the understanding of the following lessons.

4.3 Comparision of Developing Teachware by Programming and by Using an Authoring-System

-- Using a programming language:

Directly programmed   subject-matter can bring very good results for the students. For all those people who have to design, develop or service teachware, the limits of this kind of teachware-development become evident: It is the most expensive way to develop teachware because it is very inflexible when being forced to update the produced teachware. Nevertheless this method has its advantages in certain fields, e.g. simulation, within which the student can set parameters and watch the resulting effects; and testing of sorting algorithms.

When the FIM-BASIC-course was developed, no authoring-system was available, so it was programmed in BASIC.

TOP-JOB was programmed in BASIC, too, because the game-environment could only be generated by using a programming language.

-- CBT (= Computer Based Training) with authoring-systems:

These systems enable the author to develop teachware without any programming knowledge. Without doubt, all authoring-systems have one advantage in common: Because the author is not forced to learn how to write a program in a high-level-language, the group of authors is extended to those experts, who, from the methodical and didactical viewpoint, are best qualified to develop teachware.

4.4 Characteristics for High-Quality Teachware

-- There is only a minimum of full-text-pages.

-- Facts can be better and faster understood by the means of an alternating build-up of text- and graphic components. In books, these facts can only be shown by static diagrams.

-- Facts, which can be explained with moving graphics, can fully use the advantages of CBT.

Examples for such fields of learning:

- Algorithms applied on data-structures, which can be visually represented.

- Even slow-motion, computer-animated films can bring new understandings of (certain) phenomena.

Example from physics:

Emission of electromagnetic waves of charges in motion. In books often diagrams are shown, which cover only a small part of this phenomenon.

-- The quality of teachware declines if it is not possible to present useful graphics or symbolic visualities.

5. Summary

Computer Based Training (=CBT) will become a major instrument in our "retraining society". Without CBT it will not be possible to fulfil the demands and requirements of training, education and further education.

The development-costs of teachware are the motor or the brake in using CBT.

The "programmed classes" in the late 60s failed by the technical limits of data-processing.

CBT of the 80s should not fail by commercial limits set to the development costs of teachware of nowadays.

The positive feedback from the two courses offered by the FIM (BASIC-programming-course, TOP-JOB-game/course) furnishes evidence that a sensibly-conceived system can be applied efficiently, particularly in the field of adult education.

Remote Education and Informatics: Teleteaching
F. Lovis (Editor)
Elsevier Science Publishers B.V. (North-Holland)
© IFIP, 1988

THE SOCIAL AND CULTURAL ORIGINS OF THE NETWORK X 2000
A CENTRAL SUPPORT OF THE POLICY
OF COMPUTERIZATION OF FRENCH SOCIETY

Jean A. Vergnes
l'Universite d'AIX-MARSEILLE III

Up until the beginning of the 1980's, the progressive introduction
of computers has enabled the optimization of the functioning of
the Civil Services, the improvement of the management of companies,
the controlling of industrial processes, the acceleration of
development in all the fields of scientific and technical research.

These thousands of electronic machines devoted to the processing
of information, this raw material which our civilization greatly
uses, have been introduced with a great number of the working
population not really fully aware of their number, the importance
and the depth of the transformation of our civilization which
could or is going to be the outcome, their vital economic role
(Imagine for a moment the social economic effects resulting from
a massive break-down of all the computers in the world due to a
gigantic and terrible electromagnetic atmospheric disturbance!).

Indeed, the opinion polls and the surveys show that an important
percentage of the working population still is not aware of the
unavoidable process of mutation of our society, and that an
important number of the executives and managers still avoids all
realistic and objective reflection on the inherent problems in
the introduction of the technologies (*) of data processing in
professional daily life.

Today, few suspect that the next twenty years are going to be
characterized by an acceleration of the transformations of our
society, due to the performances of new electronic components and
the developments in the applications of artificial intelligence.

The reasons for this ignorance, this denial are multiple:
historical, psychological, conjunctural,.....

Historical? For example:

- To have, historically, in France, defined " Informatique" as
Computer Science, favouring the confusion between "informatics"
and "electronics".

- To have harboured for data processing this connotation of
"scientific", maintaining the confusion between "informatics" and
"mathematics".

Psychological? For example:

- The impression of an alienation of power resulting from the non-
mastering of information (or a partition of information) by the
manager on behalf of other people.

(*) The adjective "NEW" has not been used: It has a short lived
and relative meaning. What is new for some is not necessarily so
for others.

Conjunctural?

The "informatics crisis of 1986" is due to:

- The publicity concerning the failures of the computerization
  of companies

- The absence of a coherent policy for computerization, taking
  into account in particular the rapid evolution of the technologies of the processing of information

- At the same time, the even more rapid evolution of costs, of
  reliability and of power

- The absence of normalisation

- Information which is insufficient, sometimes obsolete, and
  other times too idyllic

- The inadequacies in the syllabuses of training programmes.

This reveals a fundamental need of objective and realistic
information, but also of awareness, of initiation and obviously
of training programmes for adults.
Information, awareness, initiation and training of which the
contents must be continually kept up to date, and training which
must be accessible to everybody.

This enhances a policy of the computerization of society concerning the scholastic population and above all, the people
involved in working life.

We are essentially interested in the problems connected with the
computerization of the business world.

What training programme syllabuses must be proposed in 1986?
Computerize yes! but what for?
Computer-tool or Computer-science?
Rapid or progressive computerization of society?
Are there existing means to achieve these objectives?

Here are several questions which demand undivided attention and
reflection.

Firstly, with regards to the training programmes, it must be
remembered that the concepts of an "ultimate cultural experience"
must be abandoned: Working life must follow its course in
parallel with "continuous" training periods, which implies the
setting up of adapted educational structures for adults.

This being specified, it must be considered that since 1981, data
processing has developed two different orientations:

The first concerns data processing for computer experts; data
processing which necessitates many years of studying, and which
concerns the handling of major computer systems, the conception
of elaborate programmes, and fundamental or applied research.

The second is more recent, little known to executives and to the
general public, (it is a problem of information and of awareness),

seldom or not taught at all in the traditional syllabuses (it is a problem of training).

The aspects of difficulty in the handling of data processing are becoming relatively transparent: one can speak of data processing for users, of a computer-tool, of an economically essential data processing.

To understand this second aspect, it must be understood that since 1981 the concept of micro data processing has passed from being that of "home enthusiasts" to that of professional usage. 1981 was the year where the first PC IBM appeared on the market.

The success of this micro data processing is due to the accumulation of discoveries and of new concepts and of their systematic use on a very large scale in micro data processing: microprocessors, operating systems, widespread professional software...

A MICRO-PROCESSOR is an electronic component of several millimetres squared, including today more than 25,000 elementary and automatically interconnected components, destined to reproduce the functions of the central processor of a computer (the essential part of a computer) which, in 1945, weighed 35 tons, and used as much electricity as a factory, and for an extra peculiarity, spent more time broken down than in working order, in spite of a stupendously high cost.

The micro-processors are produced in millions of models at a unitary cost in the order of ten dollars.

Next, the OPERATING SYSTEM of a computer whose essential characteristic is to take charge of the communications between MAN AND MACHINE, abolishing at the same time a great number of technical constraints, imposed in the past on the user, the disappearance of which renders the machine more convivial and easier to handle.

Finally and above all, WIDE SPREAD PROFESSIONAL SOFTWARE, programmes of great distribution, of a relatively small cost (when compared to the cost of original software), of a relatively rapid apprenticeship which doesn't necessitate an extensive knowledge of the concepts of computer science. 5,000 software programmes have been drawn up in FRANCE, 100,000 in the world.

The different types:

The HORIZONTAL SOFTWARE PROGRAMS such as the software programs for word processing, the management of files, the lists of numbers (the tables, which originate from the micro-data processing "explosion" of the 1980's), communication (transforming a micro-computer into a terminal, into a data bank,.....), graphics,.....

The HORIZONTAL SOFTWARE PROGRAMS which develop today in a systematic manner and on a large scale, sector by sector, profession by profession. For example, the software programs for medical surgeries, for artisans,.....

These software programs associated with an operating system (The SOFTWARE) and with a micro-computer (The HARDWARE) form a unit, a professional tool: A DATA PROCESSING SYSTEM, whose essential part is not always the most visible (*).

The growth of the software market (50%) is approximately twice as fast as that of hardware: which gives an idea of the importance of the "Software" phenomenon.

Today the use of a micro data processing system no longer presents any great difficulties, it doesn't require any profound theoretical knowledge.

It implies an apprenticeship in the use of data processing machines including determined applications and an introduction to the principal concepts, becoming indispensable for economic survival.

It is on this basis that, since 1982, Summer Universities and certain training centres of data processing have been developed.

The NETWORK X2000 which was set up in 1984 is based on a similar idea. This network is directed by the FOUNDATION X2000 whose president is also the president of the AGENCE DE L'INFORMATIQUE, which clearly signifies that this network is placed under the trusteeship of the MINISTRY of INDUSTRY.

Consisting in 1986 of just under 200 centres on a national plan, the objective of this network is, on the one hand, to participate in the diffusion of the "informatics' culture" (minimum vocabulary, principal concepts, basic principles which do not need any particular scientific or technical knowledge), and, on the other hand, to train in the professional usage of data processing machinery.

In other words, it is a question of participating in the progressive introduction of the applications of data processing technologies in all the economic sectors of society.

How can the network be defined?

It is an assembly of computer centres interconnected by physical (Telematics) and intellectual (Human relations) connections. These connections assure the exchange, the sharing and the communal use of human and cultural resources.

These centres are selected according to their dynamism, their ability, the specificity of the services they provide, and their pedagogic project. Their activity is essentially based on:

- Training programmes: companies, tradesmen, artisans, self employing professions,   educational systems, country services....

- Experimental actions: training in prison environments, pedagogic and automation projects, telematics, training in agrarian environments, training in the educational system, help given to the handicapped, musical or graphical creation, first level maintenance in micro processing, memory cards for students, the exporting of know-how to foreign countries,.....;

    (*) The quality, the efficiency and the price of a data processing system depends more and more on the SOFTWARE.

This recital of activities, widely varied, shows the multiplicity
of the public concerned: executives, farmers,the self employed,
students, teachers, craftsmen, the handicapped, artists,...;

In certain cases, with the agreement of the Ministry of Education,
computer activities are arranged during school time for the pupils
of primary or secondary education: this only happens occasionally.

The origin of these centres is very variable; likewise their
importance, their status and their means of finance. The future
is based on their innovative ability in the context of their
proposed training programmes, in their promoting actions of data
processing systems in response to specific needs.

The span of activities is represented by four categories:

- 1 - Initiation and Training: starting from the most elementary
  initiation to high level training. The most frequent is the
  apprenticeship of traditional software programmes (word processing, manipulating files, tables, vertical professional
  software programmes).

- 2 - Awareness and Animation: carried out within the educational
  framework.

- 3 - Production and Creation: essentially pedagogic software.

- 4 - Advice and Services: a future activity.

To give an idea of the activity of an X2000 centre, take for
example the "CENTRE D'INFORMATIQUE SOCIALE" in Salon de Provence:
In 1985, 1,000 people followed different training programmes.
Also, 3 missions abroad were accomplished in 1985 and 4 in 1986.

There are 3 permanent computer experts (or nearly), 2 young
computer experts who are completing their military service as
civilians, 2 part-time secretaries and numerous other experts who
help with the teaching of the training programmes when their work
allows them.

The centre has 70 micro computers including 2 "nanoréseaux".

And finance? The basic principle is that it is self-financing.

The centres have numerous backers (private, sector, country
organisations, ministries), the credits of operation essentially
originate from the selling of the completed training programmes.

Also, the centre receives subsidies provided by the local county
organisations and direct help with data processing equipment from
the FOUNDATION X2000, once the application to join the NETWORK
X2000 of the centre concerned has been accepted. The centre exists
therefore before its request to join the network X2000.

This network, launched by a State agency, has a sufficiently
flexible structure to allow each centre to remain autonomous, to
adapt itself to local demand and to be innovative.

This network most often uses specialists outside their
professional activities, which benefits the acquired skills in an
ever growing field.

This network allows everybody, whether they work or not, to have access to this "informatics culture", to satisfy their curiousity, to teach themselves, to initiate themselves to the use of data processing machinery in their daily working life.

This network replies to a need: it allows each citizen to inform and prepare himself for this new civilisation of information and communication, the XXI century, as commonly referred to by the media.

This network forms an integral part of the policy of the computer-isation of society, its perpetuity depends on its ability to innovate and to adapt itself continually to the evolution of the technologies of information.

List of Participants

Avolio, L C
Viale civilitá del Lavoro
P O B 10253
00144 Rome
Italy

Avrault, J P
IIASA
Laxenburg
Austria

Boon K L
Open Universitiet
Valkenburgerweg 167
6419 A Heerlen
Netherlands

Bottero, M
Centre X2000
7 Place de la Défense
92090 Paris - La Défense
Cedex 26
France

Bruggemans, K
BRT-Schoolvitzendingen 3 N14
Reyerslaan 52
B 1040 Brussels
Belgium

Charp, S
39 Maple Avenue
Upper Darby
PA 19082
USA

Davies, G
Faculty of Mathematics
The Open University
Walton Hall
Milton Keynes
MK7 6AA
England

Fallick, P M
University of South Africa
P O B 392
Pretoria
South Africa

Faragó, G
International House Language School
Bajcsy Zsilinszky út 62
1053 Budapest
Hungary

Ferenczy, P
Institute of Telecommunication Electronics
Budapest Technical University
Müegyetem rakpart 1-3
1111 Budapest
Hungary

Forgács, L
Ipari Távoktatási Leányvállalat
Arany János u 10
1051 Budapest
Hungary

Foucault, J
Centre X2000 d'Amiens
4 Rue de Prague
80000 Amiens
France

Gáspár, F
Coordination Centre
Csajkovszkij u 11
Moszkva 121314
USSR

Gastkemper, F H
Dutch Open University
P O B 2960
6401 DL Heerlen
Netherlands

Grósz, G
Ipari Távoktatási Leányvállalat
Arany János u 10
1051 Budapest
Hungary

Horváth, E
Institute of Telecommunication Electronics
Budapest Technical University
Müegyetem rakpart 1-3
1111 Budapest
Hungary

Huber, F
Institut für Informationsverarbeitung
Technische University Graz
Schiesstattgasse 4A
8010 Graz
Austria

Kiss-Szölgyémi F
Institute of Telecommunication Electronics
Budapest Technical University
Müegyetem rakpart 1-3
1111 Budapest
Hungary

Kovács, Gy
John von Nuemann Computer Society
Báthori u 16
1054 Budapest
Hungary

Kovács, I
Institute of Telecommunication Electronics
Budapest Technical University
Müegyetem rakpart 1-3
1111 Budapest
Hungary

Loiseau, G
CNRS
Centre X2000
Marne-La-Vallée
France

Lovis, F
8 Little Reeve's Avenue
Amersham
Buckinghamshire HP7 9JA
England

Makedon, F
Computer Science Program
The University of Texas at Dallas
Richardson
Texas 75083-0688
USA

Martinez, V
Facultdad de Informatica
Universidad Politecnica de Madrid
Carretera de Valencia km 7
28031 Madrid
Spain

Maté, L
Facultdad de Informatica
Universidad Politecnica de Madrid
Carretera de Valencia km 7
28031 Madrid
Spain

Matsuda, T
Kumon Institute of Education
Gobancho Grand-Building 3-1
Chiyoda-ku
Tokyo
Japan 102

Maurer, H
Institut für Informationsverarbeitung
Technische University Graz
Schiesstattgasse 4A
8010 Graz
Austria

Mayer, R A M
Deutsches Jugendinstitut
Saarstrasse 7
8000 München 40
FRG

Meistrup, E
Arhus Amts Informatikcenter
Halmstadsgade 6
DK-8200 Arhus N
Denmark

Mühlbacher, J R
Forschunginstitut für Mikroprozessorttechnik
Johannes Kepler Universität Linz
4040 Linz
Austria

Mulder, F
Open Universitiet
Valkenburgerweg 167
P O B 2960
6401 DL Heerlen
Netherlands

Netta, F
Telemedia GmbH
P O B 5555
4830 Gütersloh
FRG

Ottmann, T
Informatik Universität Karlsruhe
P O B 6980
7500 Karlsruhe
FRG

Pálinszki, A
Institute of Telecommunication Electronics
Budapest Technical University
Müegyetem rakpart 1-3
1111 Budapest
Hungary

Páris, Gy
Institute for Science Management and Informatics
P O B 454
1372 Budapest
Hungary

Paulsen, M F
Norsk Data-Institut
P O B 10
1321 Stabekk
Norway

Pazos, J
Facultdad de Informatica
Universidad Politecnica de Madrid
Carretera de Valencia km 7
28031 Madrid
Spain

Pelle, Zs
Budapesti Müszaki Egyetem
BME Nyelvi Intézet
Honvéd u 24
1055 Budapest
Hungary

Philokypru, G
University of Athens
Panepistimiopolis
Athens 15771
Greece

Polák, J
Charles University Computing Centre
Malostranské nám 25
11800 Praha 1
Czechoslovakia

Pree, W
Forschunginstitut für Mikroprozessorttechnik
Johannes Kepler Universität Linz
4040 Linz
Austria

Quale, A C
Norsk Data-Institut
P O B 10
1321 Stabekk
Norway

Sammer, P
Institut für Informationsverarbeitung
Technische University Graz
Schiesstattgasse 4A
8010 Graz
Austria

Sárváry, P
Institute of Telecommunication Electronics
Budapest Technical University
Müegyetem rakpart 1-3
1111 Budapest
Hungary

Schlageter, G
Fernuniversität
P O B 940
5800 Hagen
FRG

Schmidt, E
Dask-Aalborg Skolenaesen
Hasserisvej 174
9000 Aalborg
Denmark

Sechovcov, V
Czec Techical University Prague - Elektrofaculty
Suchbátorovó 2
Praha 6
Czechoslovakia

Six, H W
Fernuniversität
P O B 940
5800 Hagen
FRG

Sobieski, A
ELTE TTK
Zsolna u 11
1125 Budapest
Hungary

Spoonley, N
International Management Institute
4 Chemin de Chonhes
1213 Geneva
Switzerland

Srisa-an, W
Sukhothai Thammathirat Open University
Pakkred Nonthaburi 11120
Bangpood
Thailand

Staub, U
Telemedia GmbH
P O B 5555
4830 Gütersloh
FRG

Stern, W
Fernuniversität
P O B 940
5800 Hagen
FRG

Swetter, R
QBIT Interactiv Media
Hengelveldstraat 29
P O B 9550
3506 GN Utrecht
Netherlands

Sykora, R
Czech Technical University
VVIS
Husova 5
11000 Praha 1
Czechoslovakia

Takano, H
Kumon Institute of Education
Gobancho Grand-Building 3-1
Chiyoda-ku
Tokyo
Japan 102

Temesi, A
Institute of Telecommunication Electronics
Budapest Technical University
Müegyetem rakpart 1-3
1111 Budapest
Hungary

Tissot, J L
7 Place de la Défense Immeuble PCBl
92090 Paris La Défense
Cedex 26
France

Tomanova, M
Sofia University
Laboratory of Informatics
Bul A Ivanov 5
1126 Sofia
Bulgaria

Unger, C
Fernuniversität
P O B 940
5800 Hagen
FRG

Vergnes, J A
Université d'Aix-Marseille
Centre d'Informatique Sociale
89 Bd A Briand
13300 Salon-de- Provence
France

Villiers, C de
University of South Africa
P O B 392
Pretoria
South Africa

Warren P
University of Denver
Colorado
CO 80525
USA

KV-025-746

A MANUAL OF
CROP EXPERIMENTATION

A Manual of Crop Experimentation

S. C. PEARCE B.Sc., Ph.D., D.Sc.(Lond.)
Honorary Professor of Biometry, Applied Statistics Research Unit
University of Kent at Canterbury

G. M. CLARKE M.A., Dip.Stats.(Oxford), F.I.S.
Consultant in Applied Statistics, Applied Statistics Research Unit
University of Kent at Canterbury

G. V. DYKE M.A. (Oxford)
Consultant in Field Experimentation, Applied Statistics Research Unit
University of Kent at Canterbury

R. E. KEMPSON B.Sc. (Lond.), M.Sc., Ph.D
(Kent)
Lecturer in Applied Statistics, Wye College, University of London

CHARLES GRIFFIN & COMPANY LTD
London
OXFORD UNIVERSITY PRESS
New York

CHARLES GRIFFIN & COMPANY LIMITED
16 Pembridge Road, London W11 3HL, U.K.

Copyright © Applied Statistics Research Unit of the University of Kent at Canterbury

All rights reserved. No part of this publication may be reproduced or transmitted in any form or by any means, electronic or mechanical, including photocopying, recording, or by any information storage and retrieval system, without permission in writing from Charles Griffin & Company Limited.

First published 1988

Published in the USA by Oxford
University Press, 200 Madison Avenue,
New York, N.Y. 10016

ISBN 0–19–520631–2

British Library Cataloguing in Publication Data
A Manual of crop experimentation.
  1. Crops—Experiments
  I. Pearce, S. C.
  631'.0724   SB51

ISBN 0–85264–289–X

Typeset in Great Britain by
Latimer Trend & Company Ltd, Plymouth

Printed and bound in Great Britain by
Redwood Burn Limited, Trowbridge, Wilts

Preface

For some time the Applied Statistics Research Unit of the University of Kent at Canterbury has been arranging courses in statistics for scientists engaged in agricultural research. The first of these was a three-week course run on-site for the staff of the Bangladesh Agricultural Research Council twice in 1984. After further development this course was next given at the International Institute of Tropical Agriculture, Nigeria, in 1985. The course was then developed again and expanded, resulting in a three-month course, given in Canterbury in 1985 and 1986, and hopefully to be repeated on an annual basis from now on. This manual now makes the material covered in these courses generally available. The four authors are the lecturers who participated in the earlier courses overseas and who form part of the larger lecturing team for the Canterbury-based course.

A central feature of these courses has been their thoroughly practical nature, and there has been a deliberate policy of mixing agronomists and biometricians together. The philosophy here has been that it is instructive for each group to be aware of the problems that the other faces, and this interaction has been found to work well in practice. The text reflects the content of the courses: it can either be used as a manual to complement such courses, or can be used as a text in its own right. All stages of the manual are regarded as parts which go together to make up a whole.

The sections of the manual have been developed out of the handouts used to complement the course lectures. Each section is therefore fairly complete in itself, though some have been expanded for this text to emphasize the inter-sectional relationships as much as possible. The sections have been placed in a natural order so that the reader may go through the material in logical sequence, from start to finish, if the intention is to do this rather than use the manual as a work of reference.

A number of people, in addition to the authors, have contributed in one way or another to this manual. In particular thanks go to Dennis Cooke and Michael Kenward for helpful comments from reading earlier versions of the text, and also, in the case of Michael Kenward, for help with the production of solutions to exercises. Byron Jones, Byron Morgan and Andrew Rutherford are also to be thanked for their advice and comments. Thanks go as well to the secretarial staff of the Applied Statistics Research Unit for their patient and painstaking typing of the text throughout its various versions, and especially to Margaret Wells for her organizational work in addition in connection with the courses.

It is hoped that this will be the first of a series of texts arising from courses in Applied Statistics developed at the University of Kent. Further information on these and on the Applied Statistics Research Unit can be supplied on request.

PHILIP M. NORTH
Director, Applied Statistics Research Unit
University of Kent at Canterbury

1988

Contents

Chapter 1

How experiments are conducted

'... and a most curious country it was.... The ground ... was divided up into squares....'

Lewis Carroll, *The Adventures of Alice Through the Looking Glass*, Chapter 2

1.1   Introduction

Anyone who visits a crop research institute—and even more, anyone who flies over one—will see, like Alice, that the ground is divided into squares or, at least, into rectangles. That is because the comparison of different treatments (whether they are different forms of fertilization or anything else) requires that they be grown as close together as possible. It is true that an experimenter could apply each treatment in a different field. He could then reasonably claim that they were being applied as a farmer would apply them, but if there were only one field for each treatment there would be a major difficulty in interpretation. Fields differ for many reasons. There would be no way of knowing whether the differences observed between the fields of an experiment would have been there anyway or were due in part to the various treatments applied.

To avoid that fault another experimenter might go to the opposite extreme. He could take a small area that appeared to be uniform and then divide it into smaller areas, the basic units known as 'plots'. Then each of his treatments could be applied to a selection of plots, chosen so as to be a fair sample of the whole of the experimental area. He might reasonably claim to have made a sound comparison of the various treatments. Nevertheless, he would be open to another criticism, namely, that his plots were so small that his treatments were not realistically applied. Deep ploughing, for example, could have become double digging and the knapsack sprayer could have replaced the spraying machine. A good experimenter should avoid both extremes. In principle there is no objection to using complete fields as plots, but it does lead to an experiment of immense size with plots that are basically very different one from another. If the plots are too small, on the other hand, they may indeed be comparable but it is not possible to apply treatments to them in the same way that a farmer would apply them in practice. Also, data collected from very small plots cannot properly be used to represent performance in a larger area. (It is not enough to multiply by the ratio of the areas because there will be edge-effects, which may be important in a small plot but negligible in a large one.) Some compromise between the extremes is called for.

In Chapter 2 we shall examine practicalities in the field, how to choose plot size, for example, how to apply treatments and how to record data. Then in Chapter 3 we shall look at the statistical ideas needed to deal with the sort of data that will result. Thereafter we shall look at some of the special problems that will arise. Most of the ideas and problems arise from the need to specify precisely the objectives of a study before an experiment is started in the field. We shall consider that in Chapter 5.

1.2   Replication, randomization and local control

Replication

There are several characteristics that are regarded as essentials of good experimentation. One has already been mentioned, namely, the use of plots of reasonable size. Another is 'replication', i.e. the use of several plots for each treatment. If there is only one for each, there will be no way of deciding how accurately the experiment has been conducted. If there are several, the differences between them will show how much uncontrolled natural variation there is in the measurements. In an agricultural context that is important. The chemist in his laboratory can forecast with some certainty how accurate his determinations will be, but in the field nothing is certain until it has happened. In a dry year some plots will suffer worse than others. That will introduce differences between plots, quite apart from those brought about by the treatments. In a wet year, or a windy one, the pattern of good or bad land could be very different. Also in some years, damage from birds, insects, fungi, etc. will be an additional source of variation, the extent of which could not have been estimated and whose pattern could not have been foreseen. For such reasons the precision of each new experiment has to be assessed separately. An experienced person learns to make rough forecasts of precision, but whether those forecasts will be right or not must depend upon the weather and other disturbing influences.

Randomization

That leads to another important characteristic of a good experiment, namely 'randomization'. It is in any case needed for reasons of objectivity.

If the experimenter can declare that plots were allocated to treatments by the use of random numbers or by the shuffling of cards, we shall be reassured that the best plots were not deliberately selected for some favoured treatment. There is however a more important reason for randomizing, namely, the determination of precision. Where there is replication, i.e. there are several plots for each treatment, a comparison of those plots will show how much variation has been introduced by differences in the soil, differences in the plant material, inaccuracies of measurement, etc. At this point care is needed. Confronted with the task of allocating four treatments to twelve plots, most people would disperse those for each treatment, i.e. they would opt for something like this:

$$
\begin{array}{cccc}
A & B & C & D \\
B & C & D & A \\
D & A & B & C
\end{array}
$$

However, that will not do. It is true that dispersal leads to the four samples of plots, three for A, three for B, etc., being on average as similar as possible, but it maximizes the differences between them. In fact, although dispersal leads to the area being sampled better for the comparison of treatments, by a paradox it leads to a high estimate of the sampling error. The contrary fault arises when plots for a treatment are kept together, e.g.

$$
\begin{array}{cccc}
A & B & C & D \\
A & B & C & D \\
A & B & C & D
\end{array}
$$

Here each treatment samples the total area in a most ineffective manner, but because the plots of any one treatment are close together, they will give more uniform results than plots in general. The paradox is resolved when plots are allocated to treatments at random. (It is true that each of the systematic allocations just considered has a a small chance of turning up by a chance randomization, but that possibility can be accepted.) Ways of randomizing will be discussed in Section 2.6.

Local control

One last point concerns the control of local variation. If the area allotted to the experiment shows marked systematic differences, e.g. it slopes or there is a water-course down one side of it, most people would rightly be suspicious of any scheme in which those differences were ignored. (The matter will be examined further in Section 1.8.) The favoured device is to divide the land into 'blocks', not necessarily all of the same size, each block uniform within itself, or, at least, as uniform as can be contrived. That is called a 'block design'. If no systematic differences are apparent and if none are known from past experience with the land, the plots can be allocated at random within the total area. There is then only one block, not several. In that case the design is said to be 'completely randomized'.

The analysis of data

We shall now direct our thoughts to one topic that underlies many others. Having allocated our plots to the treatments and having measured yield or some other important quantity on each plot, what are we going to do with the data? Our answer is going to determine much else. We shall have to record data bearing in mind what is to be done with them, and we shall have to interpret data bearing in mind what was recorded in the field. The method we shall describe is called the 'analysis of variance'.

It should be emphasized that what follows in the next two sections concerns arithmetic and nothing more. The real skill lies not in the calculation of the analysis of variance, a task that is essentially mechanical and best left to computers, but in the interpretation, which requires careful thought. The approach to data based on the analysis of variance is one of great flexibility and subtlety and one that illuminates a wide range of problems. We cannot begin to use it until we can perform the calculations, but that is only a step on the way. The arithmetic is not an end in itself, necessary though it is.

1.3 The analysis of variance for an orthogonal block design using sweeping

The measurement of variability

Before illustrating the approach it may be helpful if we explain how statisticians measure variability. Always there must be a 'hypothesis' to say what is expected. We will take a very simple case. Someone has declared that if we were to weigh a lot of similar objects we should find that they all weighed 30 grams. Now that we have a clear-cut statement of what to expect we can set to work and see if it is true. We will suppose that we start and get values of 30, 30, 30 (excellent) and then we get 31 (no need to bother much) then 30, 30 and then 29 (again, no need to worry) followed by 30, 29, 30 but then we get 33. At that point we do begin to wonder whether the hypothesis really holds, or perhaps needs to be more complicated. Let us examine our reactions and see if they were justified. First of all, we regarded 29 and 31 in much the same light; we disregarded the signs. Then, we took a deviation of 3 as being much more serious than three deviations of 1. How far was that reasonable? At this point the mathematicians come to our aid by telling us that we should really be looking at the squares of our deviations. We were therefore quite right to equate deviations of $+1$ and -1 and to regard a single value of 3 as much more important than three of 1. The position will be examined further in Chapter 3, beginning at (3.3.1).

In most statistical work experimenters are continually setting up hypotheses, taking some data and then asking how far the data deviate from what the hypothesis says they should be. The next step is to aggregate those deviations by squaring each one and adding the squares. In the analysis of variance we first work out deviations assuming that there is no effect of treatments. Then we allow for the treatments and get a new set of deviations. They are of special importance, both in practice and in the theory of the subject, so they have a special name. They are called the 'residuals'—but they are deviations just the same. Finally we ask if the sum of squared deviations ignoring the treatments is so very different from the sum of squared deviations when we do take treatments into account i.e., the sum of squares of the residuals.

Orthogonality

A block design is said to be orthogonal if all the blocks are made up in the same way with respect to treatments. (Treatments do not have to be equally replicated.) To take an example, the following design is orthogonal:

Block	I	A	A	B	C	D	E	(Note that the plots
	II	A	A	B	C	D	E	would of course have to
	III	A	A	B	C	D	E	be allocated at random
								within each block and
								not disposed systemati-
								cally as here.)

A completely randomized design has only one block. Its data can be dealt with as if the design were orthogonal.

The method of sweeping

A body of data is 'swept' when each value is reduced by an appropriate mean. For example, in the following data

I	A 22	B 17	C 21	
II	C 26	A 17	B 23	(1.3.1)
III	C 20	B 15	A 22	

there are three causes of variation to be considered: two of these are blocks and treatments. The third comes from a lot of small sources, such as, for example, the effects of variable land, variable plant material, the inevitable inaccuracies of measurement and much else. Those combined sources are often described collectively as the 'error' of the experiment, but the term is rather harsh, implying as it does that someone has been at fault. Some prefer to call the last component the 'residual variation', i.e. what is left when block and treatment differences have been allowed for, and that name has its critics also. Here we shall use 'error', the quotation marks implying an inexact use of the word. Such a design as that at (1.3.1), in which each treatment occurs once in each block, is said to be in 'randomized blocks', or more correctly 'randomized complete blocks'.

Additivity

To amplify what has been said, the data of a block design are thought of as made up of three components. First, there is the inherent fertility of the block in which the plot occurs. (It will be recalled that blocks were chosen to be as uniform as possible in that respect.) We shall write that component, b_i, where i is the number of the block. Then there is the effect, t_j, brought about by the plot receiving Treatment j. (That is really what we want to know about.) Finally, there is the residual, e, which sums up the various sources of variation comprised in 'error'. Each plot has its own e and it should not be much affected by the treatment applied to the plot, which is a matter of chance. (That assumption will have to be examined later, especially in Chapter 9, but for the moment we merely state it.) In the analysis of variance we assume that the three components can just be added, i.e., a datum equals

$$b_i + t_j + e \quad \text{for the plot}$$

The assumption of 'additivity', as it is called, serves well enough in most cases, any deviations from it being absorbed in e. Provided those deviations are small, little harm results.

First we will note the block means, i.e., I, 20; II, 22; III, 19. Sweeping by them gives:

I	A, $+2$	B, -3	C, $+1$
II	C, $+4$	A, -5	B, $+1$
III	C, $+1$	B, -4	A, $+3$

These quantities are called 'deviations'. It will be seen that in any block they sum to zero. The effect of blocks has now been removed, so they represent the action of treatments and 'error'. Squaring the deviations and adding gives 82, which will be called the 'stratum total sum of squares'. (Stratum in this instance means the variation of plots within blocks. The term will be explained further in Section 1.9.) In all this it is necessary to carry enough decimal places, though not so many as to become a burden. The best number will be considered in Section 1.10.

Treatment means are now A, 0; B, -2; C, $+2$. Sweeping by them gives:

$$
\begin{array}{llll}
\text{I} & \text{A,} +2 & \text{B,} -1 & \text{C,} -1 \\
\text{II} & \text{C,} +2 & \text{A,} -5 & \text{B,} +3 \\
\text{III} & \text{C,} -1 & \text{B,} -2 & \text{A,} +3
\end{array}
\qquad (1.3.2)
$$

These quantities are called 'residuals'. They sum to zero over any block or any treatment and represent only the action of 'error'. The sum of their squares is 58, called the 'error sum of squares'.

Degrees of freedom

We have now found two sums of squares, one for the stratum total and one for the 'error', but how would we expect them to be related? Since the residuals were derived using a more adaptable hypothesis than that which led to the deviations (i.e., allowance was made for a possible effect of treatments), we should expect them to give a better fit, but better by how much? Here a note on degrees of freedom may be helpful. Originally there were nine data with no constraints upon them. They were then swept by three quantities (the block means), also unconstrained, leaving six degrees of freedom for treatments and 'error' combined. When they were swept the second time, however, the three treatment means necessarily summed to zero. Consequently only two of them can be regarded as independent; once two are known, the third follows. That reduced the degrees of freedom for 'error' alone to four.

The position is this: if p quantities are under study and there are no constraints upon them, there are p degrees of freedom. If however there are h constraints, there are only $(p - h)$ degrees of freedom because only that number of values can be assigned at will. The other h have to be chosen to satisfy the constraints. If Tom, Dick and Harry are each asked to give a number, those numbers collectively have three degrees of freedom, provided there is no collusion between them and provided they are free to choose whatever number they like. Suppose though that their choice of numbers is part of a trick by an entertainer and Harry, who comes last, is an accomplice told always to choose a number that will make the total come to 21. Tom says 6, Dick says 9 so Harry says 6.

Despite appearances there are only two degrees of freedom. So it is with the treatment means. That for A is 0 and that for B is -2. Since all three must sum to zero that for C must be $+2$, but that is a forced move and contributes nothing to the degrees of freedom.

In a block design with b blocks, v treatments and n plots, the stratum total, derived as it is from sweeping n data by b block means, will have $(n - b)$ degrees of freedom because the block means are unconstrained. Sweeping by treatments takes out another $(v - 1)$, leaving $(n - b - v + 1)$ for the 'error'. If $n = bv$, which corresponds to the case of randomized blocks, there are $(b - 1)(v - 1)$ degrees of freedom for 'error'.

The analysis of variance table

The analysis of variance is presented below. The treatment line was found as the difference between that for the stratum total, in which treatments have been ignored, and that for the 'error', in which they have been allowed for.

Source	d.f.	s.s.	m.s.	F	
Treatments	2	24	12.0	0.83	
'Error'	4	58	14.5		(1.3.3)
Stratum total	6	82			

In each line the mean square (m.s.) is found by dividing the sum of squares (s.s.) by the degrees of freedom (d.f.). The F-value is the ratio of the treatments and 'error' mean squares. It is sometimes called the 'variance ratio' or VR.

To clarify nomenclature, the 'error' mean square is more usually called the 'error' variance and will be written as s^2. Its square root is called 'the standard error of an observation'. The standard error expressed as a percentage of the grand mean is called 'the coefficient of variation'.

1.4 The analysis of variance for an orthogonal design using summation terms

An alternative method is to use 'summation terms'. First the data are written out, together with the block totals, treatment totals and the grand total, i.e.

	A	B	C	
I	22	17	21	60
II	17	23	26	66
III	22	15	20	57
	61	55	67	183

Four summation terms, S, S_b, S_t and S_o, are formed thus:

S, the total term, equals the sum of squares of the data, i.e.
$22^2 + 17^2 + \ldots + 20^2 = 3817$

S_b, the block term, equals the sum of squares of the block totals, divided by the block size, i.e.
$(60^2 + 66^2 + 57^2)/3 = 3735$

S_t, the treatment term, equals the sum of squares of the treatment totals, divided by the treatment replications, i.e.
$(61^2 + 55^2 + 67^2)/3 = 3745$

S_o, the grand total squared, divided by the number of plots, i.e.
$183^2/9 = 3721$ (the 'correction term').

Then the treatment sum of squares equals $S_t - S_o = 24$, the 'error' sum of squares equals $S - S_b - S_t + S_o = 58$ and the stratum sum of squares equals $S - S_b = 82$.

In the example the calculations are simplified because all blocks contain the same number of plots and all treatments are equally replicated. If those conditions do not hold, each total on being squared should be divided by the number of data it contains. Strictly speaking,

$$\begin{aligned}
S_b &= 60^2/3 + 66^2/3 + 57^2/3 = 3735 \\
S_t &= 61^2/3 + 55^2/3 + 61^2/3 = 3745
\end{aligned} \tag{1.4.1}$$

1.5 Residuals

The method of sweeping has two main advantages. It is essentially simple and therefore adapted to computers. Also, it isolates the residuals and therefore enables an experimenter to see which plots are making large contributions to 'error'. It also has a serious disadvantage in requiring a lot of arithmetic for what it achieves. For that reason it is not generally used except for special reasons. With a computer, simplicity of arithmetic is more important than brevity, so many computer packages proceed by sweeping, and an understanding of the method will sometimes help in reading the output.

Residuals are very important. They represent that part of the variation between plots that cannot otherwise be explained. If the 'error' mean square of an experiment has been unusually large, it is helpful to go over the experiment plot by plot and see where the large residuals lie. Clearly something has happened that requires consideration. Large residuals can result from poor technique, untried and little-understood equipment, inexperienced observers, source of material and much else. Also, things can go wrong. If the large residuals are all in a group, that suggests a good or bad patch in the field that was not allowed for in the choice of blocks. Another possibility is that they all occur in one treatment, perhaps one with a large mean. In that case, it might be better to use some other scale of measurement (see Chapter 9). Various other possibilities exist. In general an experimenter just wants to know about the 'error' mean square, but the figures in (1.3.2) are more informative because they show where it came from.

As has been said, an advantage of the sweeping method is that it gives estimates of the residuals. If residuals are required when summation terms have been used, they can still be obtained, though by a laborious method. The analysis of variance may have been calculated more easily but the whole will have been more difficult.

In an orthogonal block design, the error sum of squares is given by $S - S_b - S_t + S_o$. That will serve as a mnemonic of a residual, which equals

datum − block mean − treatment mean + grand mean.

Thus, for the plot in Block II with Treatment C, the residual is

$$26 - 66/3 - 67/3 + 183/9 = +2$$

which is the value found at (1.3.2).

1.6 Row-and-column designs

There are occasions when it is not possible to associate all the differences in the field with a single system of blocks. For example, there could be a slope and that would call for blocks along the contours to allow for the many effects associated with altitude, e.g. depth of soil, exposure, and much else. In addition, there might be a stream down one side of the experimental area and that would call for blocks across the contours, i.e. at right angles to those already used, to allow for water effects. In that case, it might be best to have two sets of blocks crossing one another, known as 'rows' and 'columns'.

The commonest row-and-column design is the Latin square, in which each treatment occurs once and once only in each row and each column, e.g.

$$
\begin{array}{cccc}
A & B & C & D \\
C & A & D & B \\
B & D & A & C \\
D & C & B & A
\end{array}
$$

A row-and-column design is said to be orthogonal if each row is made up in the same way with respect to treatments and each column likewise. An obvious example is a Latin square, but the definition includes a design like this one:

$$
\begin{array}{cccccccc}
D & A & C & A & B & D & C & B \\
C & C & D & B & A & A & B & D \\
A & D & B & C & D & B & A & C \\
B & B & A & D & C & C & D & A
\end{array}
$$

or one like this:

$$
\begin{array}{cccc}
A & B & B & A \\
B & A & B & A \\
A & B & A & B \\
B & A & A & B
\end{array}
$$

Whatever row-and-column design is chosen, before use the rows should be permuted at random and then the columns likewise.

In an orthogonal row-and-column design much the same procedure applies as for an orthogonal block design in sweeping. The steps are as follows:

(1) Sweep by rows.
(2) Sweep the resulting values by columns to obtain deviations.
(3) Sum the squares of the deviations to give the stratum total. (We recall that the stratum is that of plots within both rows and columns.)
(4) Sweep by treatments to obtain residuals.
(5) Sum the squares of the residuals to give the 'error' sum of squares.

Applying the method of summation terms to a row-and-column design, five are required, i.e.

$S,$ the total term derived from the data

$S_r,$ the row term derived from row totals

$S_c,$ the column term derived from column totals

$S_t,$ the treatment term

and $S_o,$ the correction term.

The treatment sum of squares equals $S_t - S_o$, as before. The stratum total sum of squares is $S - S_r - S_c + S_o$, i.e. $(S - S_o) - (S_r - S_o) - (S_c - S_o)$. That leaves $S - S_r - S_c - S_t + 2S_o$ for 'error'.

If there are r rows, c columns and v treatments, there will be rc plots. Sweeping by rows leaves $(rc - r)$ degrees of freedom. Sweeping further by columns leaves $rc - r - (c - 1) = (r - 1)(c - 1)$ for the stratum total. Since there will be $(v - 1)$ degrees of freedom for treatments, there will be $(rc - r - c - v + 2)$ for 'error'. If, as in a Latin square, $r = c = v = k$, that equals $(k - 1)(k - 2)$.

For a row-and-column design a residual equals

Datum − row mean − column mean − treatment mean + 2(grand mean)

(1.6.1)

If only a few residuals are needed, perhaps after the analysis has been worked out, (1.6.1) is convenient. If all are needed, it would have been easier to have swept in the first place.

1.7   An examination of assumptions

The method of sweeping shows clearly some of the assumptions being made in the analysis of variance. First, it implies that the effect of a treatment is much the same wherever it is applied. That can scarcely be strictly true. For example, if a range of new strains is being tested, the hope being to find some that are drought-resistant, and if the land is of varying moisture, it is not to be expected that the assumption will hold precisely. In fact, small departures are absorbed into 'error'. Nevertheless, fields vary in different ways and it would be better to allocate them so that the variability any one exhibits is not of the same kind as the treatments to be applied. Thus one with variable water would be a particularly bad site for a trial of drought-resistant strains.

To take the matter further, it is assumed that the effects of treatments are much the same whatever the block. That is the assumption of additivity already mentioned in Section 1.3. If blocks have been formed with the intention of keeping dry and wet plots together, the difficulty of the last paragraph has merely been transferred. Also important is the assumption that the effect of rows is the same whatever the column. Given a diagonal streak of good or bad land across the area, the assumption fails disastrously and a large 'error' will arise for no apparent reason.

Another assumption, though a much less obvious one, concerns the residuals, which are combined to give a common 'error' mean square as if all were subject to the same sources of variation. Clearly, that would not be so if the area contained a very variable patch. (It is a good practice to avoid hazards of that kind, even if it does mean leaving gaps between blocks so that the patch is not used. It may be sown and harvested, though not as part of the experiment.) The assumption also implies that the residuals are normally distributed (see Section 3.1). That can be important. For example, only with normally distributed quantities is the estimate of the 'error' mean square independent of the mean. For many of the tests that will be described in Chapter 3, the assumption is essential for complete validity.

One way of dealing with all these difficulties is to use 'transformations' (see Chapter 9). For example, the total weight of plants commonly fails the assumptions, but not if it is transformed to its logarithm.

1.8 Blocks, rows and columns

The traditional way of controlling local variation in a site is to divide the land into blocks such that the main differences lie between them. Then each block is fairly uniform within itself. Sometimes that is easier said than done, though there are times when it can be accomplished without difficulty. To use examples already given, the site may slope, or there may be a stream down one side. More often there is no particular reason to form blocks one way rather than the other and that can be awkward. If there are marked differences in the land but it is not clear where they lie, blocks could even do harm, because their boundaries could cut across contours of fertility and encapsulate in each block a wide range of good and bad areas. General experience suggests that in most cases square blocks are beneficial, but even that cannot always be relied upon either. Another difficulty is that some sources of local variation, e.g. bird damage, wind damage, areas of impeded drainage, may appear in a certain season but not in others, so they cannot readily be allowed for in the design of the experiment.

With a small experiment, i.e. one with about 16 plots or fewer, it is usually not a good idea to use blocks at all unless there are obvious sources of local variation that need to be controlled. Using blocks diminishes the number of degrees of freedom for 'error'. (There should be at the very least six or eight, though 20 are desirable.) In a small area there is probably not much local variation to control and the loss of error degrees of freedom could be serious.

In a large experiment the situation is different, even if only because blocks are needed for purposes of administration. Where operations like the application of treatments, harvesting and data recording are likely to take more than one day, block boundaries are needed to provide a stopping place. If the district is one subject to unpredictable rain, even more block boundaries are needed in case someone should start an operation in the morning and be driven off by rain later in the day. With a large experiment there is not the same need for conserving 'error' degrees of freedom. Also, there is likely to be more local variation to control. There is therefore greater advantage in having blocks, but it is still desirable to know the fertility patterns before deciding how they should be formed.

It should be emphasized that blocks have to fit the local variation or they are no good. For that reason they may have to be of different shapes. Also, they do not have to be of the right size to take each treatment once. Sometimes the site is such that that is not possible. In that case it may be that a non-orthogonal design should be preferred (see Chapter 4). Its data will be less easy to analyse, but the important consideration is to have blocks that will control the local variation. If blocks are ineffective the experiment may be of little value anyway. If such is the case, simplicity or complexity of statistical analysis are scarcely a relevant issue.

As has been said, it is sometimes necessary to use two sets of blocks at right angles, as in a Latin square. Although row-and-column designs have their place, they should not be used unless there is a good reason for doing so. In general row-and-column designs do control local variation better than block designs, but when they fail the result can be disastrous. Also, just as block designs leave fewer degrees of freedom than those that are completely randomized, two blocking systems leave even fewer. That could be serious.

Row-and-column designs have one advantage that can be relied upon. Sometimes there is fear that the outside plots will be different from the rest. Those on one side catch the wind while those on the other are sheltered. All outside plots may do rather better than inside ones on account of having more space. In such circumstances the first and last row and the first and last column can pick up a lot of variation that in a block design would become part of the 'error'. Even so, a better solution would be to provide an adequate discard area round the experimental area.

1.9   Strata

When we have got our plant material ready and we look at the land, we have to make plots that can be compared one with another. We shall not get a good experiment if we compare two treatments, one on good land and the other on bad, or if we plant well-growing bushes for one and stunted bushes for the other. We have to find groups within which comparisons can fairly be made with the added requirement of randomization to avoid favouritism. In statistical parlance, we are seeing our material in 'strata' within which we can work. So far we have looked at one approach. We assumed that our plants (or seeds or cuttings) were fairly similar and the chief lack of uniformity lay in the land. We therefore divided it into blocks and we were proposing to make our comparisons between plots within blocks. That is in fact a good way of going to work; we can show what we are doing by writing

$$\text{Total area} \rightarrow \text{Blocks} \rightarrow \text{Plots}$$

That means that there are two 'strata':

$$\text{Blocks/Total area} \qquad \text{Plots/Blocks}$$

Usually the treatments would be applied to plots, and comparisons would be made within blocks; that is, to work in the second stratum, but there would be nothing wrong in applying some treatments to complete blocks and comparing them within the area as a whole. To do that would be to work in the first stratum.

In the first stratum, i.e. Blocks/Total area, a deviation equals

$$\text{Block mean} - \text{Grand mean}$$

In the second, i.e. Plots/Blocks, it equals

$$\text{Plot value} - \text{Block mean}$$

If there had been only one block, i.e. if the design had been completely randomized, the second of these would have been

$$\text{Plot value} - \text{Grand mean}$$

and the first would not exist.

Nevertheless there are other strata possible, as the rest of this section will show. The need is to find a unit to which the treatments can be applied at random but in a practical way, and to group those units so that good comparisons can be made between them. For example, each plot could be divided further into sub-plots, giving this scheme:

$$\text{Total area} \rightarrow \text{Blocks} \rightarrow \text{Plots} \rightarrow \text{Sub-plots}$$

In the third of the strata so formed, i.e. Sub-plots/Plots, a deviation equals

Sub-plot value − Plot mean.

In the second, i.e. Plots/Blocks, it equals

Plot mean − Block mean

and in the first, i.e. Blocks/Total area, it equals

Block mean − Grand mean.   (1.9.1)

Note that it is now the sub-plots that are being measured, the value for a plot being the mean of its sub-plot values. What we have done is to add an additional stratum, namely, Sub-plots/Plots, to the two of a block design.

It would be permissible to apply some treatments to sub-plots and to make comparisons within plots. Other treatments could be applied to plots within blocks. That might be a useful device. For example, if it were a matter of studying different depths of ploughing in conjunction with different levels of fertilization, the ploughing treatments could only be applied in long narrow plots that ran across the field, but it would be possible to divide those strips into sub-plots, which could receive the fertilization treatments. Such a design is said to be in 'split-plots'. That possibility will be examined in Sections 7.1 to 7.5. With a row-and-column design there are basically three strata:

Rows/Total area
Columns/Total area
Plots/(Rows and columns)

Usually only the last is used, but it is permissible to apply treatments to, say, the rows and to make comparisons within the total area. It is not usually done because there are not enough rows, but occasionally there are enough for them to be treated differently. Such a design can be written

Total area → (Rows × columns)

The deviations for the three strata are respectively

Row mean − Grand mean
Column mean − Grand mean
Plot value − Row mean − Column mean + Grand mean.

The matter can be taken further. For example it would be possible to divide the plots into sub-plots, as was done with the block design. That gives

$$\text{Total area} \to (\text{Rows} \times \text{columns}) \to \text{Sub-plots}$$

and again an additional stratum has been added at the end, namely Sub-plots/Plots, with deviations equal to

$$\text{Sub-plot value} - \text{Plot mean.} \qquad (1.9.2)$$

Also, it would be possible to have a number of row-and-column designs, say, Latin squares, all with the same treatments but at different sites, the whole being regarded as a single experiment. In that case it would be possible to apply different treatments to the squares and to make comparisons within the whole, always assuming that there were enough sites to make that useful. Such a scheme could be written:

$$\text{The whole} \to \text{Sites} \to (\text{Rows} \times \text{columns}).$$

The strata are now: Sites/The Whole, Rows/Sites, Columns/Sites, Plots/(Rows × columns), with deviations respectively.

$$\text{Site mean} - \text{Grand mean}$$
$$\text{Row mean} - \text{Site mean}$$
$$\text{Column mean} - \text{Site mean}$$
$$\text{Plot value} - \text{Row mean} - \text{Column mean} + \text{Site mean.}$$

The point being made is simply this: so long as local control is effected either by 'nesting' areas of different size, e.g.

$$\text{Plots/Blocks}$$

or by crossing them, e.g.

$$(\text{Rows} \times \text{Columns})/\text{Total area}$$

it is always possible to break down the total deviations, i.e.

$$\text{Plot value/Total area}$$

into component deviations that add up to that total. It is then possible to intervene with treatments in any stratum. Hence, the choice of design is not restricted to those in blocks or to those in rows and columns, but extends to any stratum. A fuller description will be given in Section 7.5. In all cases, however, the general procedure is the same. First the deviations are calculated for each plot (or sub-plot if that is the smallest area). The deviations are squared and added to give the stratum total. They are then swept by treatments to give the residuals, which are themselves squared and added to give the 'Error'.

Change of strata

Once made, strata should not be altered. Here a distinction should be made between the analysis that is to be used for the interpretation of the data and other alternative analyses calculated as a guide to future blocking. As far as the first is concerned it is important to use the blocks of the original design. There is an old adage, 'As the randomization is, so should the analysis be'. The randomization was appropriate to the blocks originally chosen and the true analysis is determined by that. When the experiment has been completed the residuals may suggest that the blocks had been formed in an unfortunate manner. It is quite legitimate to insert alternative blocks and analyse again to see if that would have given a smaller 'error' mean square. (That may well require the computational method set out in Section 4.2 because the design with modified blocks is unlikely to be orthogonal.) If a reduced error is indeed found that could be a guide for the future; the fact must not alter the interpretation of the data as they will be presented in a report. The reason, as has been said, lies in the randomization. It was made so that the 'error' mean square for the original design should be estimated correctly, i.e., without bias. The same randomization will not do the same for some other blocking system. Consequently the determination of error for the alternative design will not be strictly correct, though it should be good enough to show if there is indeed a marked superiority in the second way of blocking.

A distinction is here being made between the interpretation of data for the purposes of the experiment, i.e., to clarify the doubts that led to its inception, and studies to see if it could have been designed better, i.e., a 'post-mortem'. As to the latter, we strongly recommend that past data should be used to provide information for future designs. At the least the 'error' mean square should be noted to help decide the size of later experiments of the same kind. Also, if there was argument at the design stage as to how the experiment should have been designed, it is wise to look at the data using the rejected blocking system to see if it would have made any difference. All that is desirable and sound practice. What is wrong is trying this and trying that until pleasing results are obtained. In any case, the alternative analyses are not strictly correct, so it would not be right to present conclusions based upon them.

The matter chiefly arises when blocks have proved to be very similar and someone wants to omit them. The randomization was within blocks and the analysis should allow for them. A similar question arises when the columns of a row-and-column design prove ineffective and someone wants to use only one blocking system, that of rows. Again the analysis must follow the randomization. That is not to say that hints for future designs should be ignored; a lot can be learnt by looking at past analyses in a constructive way, but that is a different matter.

1.10 Precision in calculations

In writing down the calculations needed in an analysis of variance, it is important to strike a balance between giving too many decimal places, which is wasteful, and not giving enough, which leads to rounding error.

It is also advisable to write everything down neatly with the decimal points one below the other and successive digits all on the same spacing. Sometimes one sees two quantities to be added written like this:

$$14.88888889$$
$$1\ 2\ .\ 3\ 7\ \ 5$$

That is to invite mistakes. First a decision should be made as to the number of decimal places and then everything should be written consistently. If four places are needed, the figures should be written like this:

$$14.8889$$
$$12.3750$$

Then everyone can see what is intended.

Also, in a statistical context one should beware of the bias introduced by rounding all final digits of 5 in the same direction. If the figures are:

$$13.25 \qquad 14.50 \qquad 12.75 \qquad 12.25 \qquad 13.00$$

their true sum is 65.75. If only one decimal place is needed, they should not become

$$13.3 \qquad 14.5 \qquad 12.8 \qquad 12.3 \qquad 13.0$$

or

$$13.2 \qquad 14.5 \qquad 12.7 \qquad 12.2 \qquad 13.0$$

because those sets sum respectively to 65.9 and 65.6. It is better always to round to a number that ends in an even digit, i.e.

$$13.2 \qquad 14.5 \qquad 12.8 \qquad 12.2 \qquad 13.0$$

The total is now 65.7, which is nearer the true value. (Some people always conclude with an odd digit. One way is as good as the other; it is just a matter of convention.)

We can now pass to the number of decimal places needed in the calculations. The first task is to decide the number of decimal places really needed in the data. That will be written as e and rules for finding it appear below. Once that is decided, everything else follows. Deviations and residuals should be worked out to $(e + 2)$ places, sums of squares, mean squares and summation terms to $(2e + 2)$, treatment means in a report to either e or $(e + 1)$, and standard errors to $(e + 1)$ or $(e + 2)$ respectively [(1.10.1)]. In the case of the 'error' mean square it is desirable to have at least four significant digits. The value of F should be given to two decimal places unless the value is very large.

The rule works well but it depends upon the correct determination of e, i.e. the number of decimal places required in the data themselves. (Note that e is the number of places needed, not the number available. Sometimes recorders give too many or too few, but that does not affect the argument.)

In general the data should be given to a precision that allows for at least 20 possible values or preferably 30. For example, if we are given data to one decimal place that lie between 7.2 and 9.6 they allow for 25 possible values, which is rather low but acceptable, so we can put e equal to 1. (It would have been the same if the range had been 107.2 to 109.6 or, for that matter, 1797.2 to 1799.6.)

If the data had in fact been given only to the nearest unit, all would have been 7, 8, 9 or 10, and we should have to point out that that is not good enough. (With visual scores we might have to accept such coarse grading, but we should avoid it when we can.) If, on the other hand, they had been given more precisely—if, for example, they had ranged from 7.21 to 9.58, giving 238 possible values—we would still have e equal to 1 for the calculated figures, but we could retain the additional decimal place in the data themselves. (The same comment applies when we get data presented to the nearest half or quarter, e.g. data that range from $47\frac{1}{2}$ to 74. Here it would have been good enough to have measured to the nearest unit, so we put $e = 0$, but we do not have to discard the fractions if they are there.)

It is possible for e to be negative. If the range went from 7932 to 8316, it would have been good enough if they had been measured to the nearest ten, so we put $e = -1$.

A difficult case arises when we seem to be part way between two values of e; for example, if we are confronted with data that lie between 49.2 and 65.1. If we take e to be 1. i.e. if we accept the decimal place, we are allowing for 160 possible values, which is more than enough. If we take $e = 0$ that allows for only 16, which is too few. When the higher value of e gives more than 75 possible values, it is permissible, though not essential, to give e a value half-way between the two values. It should however be understood that doubtful cases will be decided in favour of the higher precision. In the above case e could be taken as $\frac{1}{2}$. That makes $e + 2 = 3$, $2e + 3$, $e + 1 = 2$, and so on.

To take an example, if the data of a randomized block design are correctly written with $e = 1$, as here

Block	I	II	III	IV
Treatment A	14.6	15.3	14.0	16.6
B	15.3	16.4	15.4	17.1
C	13.9	14.0	14.6	15.2

the deviations should be written with three decimal places ($e + 2 = 3$)

0.000	+ 0.067	− 0.667	+ 0.300
− 0.700	+ 1.167	+ 0.733	+ 0.800
+ 0.700	− 1.233	− 0.067	− 1.100

which gives a sum of the squared deviations of 6.7933 with four places ($2e + 2 = 4$).

The residuals, also to three places, are

+ 0.075	+ 0.142	− 0.592	+ 0.375
− 0.150	+ 0.317	− 0.117	− 0.050
+ 0.075	− 0.458	+ 0.708	− 0.325

The sum of their squared values is 1.4783, also with four places; that is the 'error' sum of squares. Those values give a treatment sum of squares of 5.3150. The mean squares are 2.6575 for treatments and 0.2464 for 'error'. Since the 'error' mean square has four significant places (i.e. 2, 4, 6 and 4) it can be left as it is. If the number of significant places falls below four, an extra decimal place is called for. The value of F should be written 10.79.

Using summation terms, they should be written with four decimal places, ($2e + 4$), i.e.

Total	2784.8400
Block	2778.0467

Treatment   2777.7950
Correction   2772.4800

Adding and subtracting them will be easier and less liable to error if the corresponding figures range neatly one above the other. Also long summation terms are better written in groups of three or four digits on either side of the decimal point to make them easier to read, like this:

149 7412.3907
or   1 497 412.390 7

and not as an unbroken line, like this

1497412.3907

The treatment means should be written as 15.1, 16.0, 14.4 ($e = 1$), or perhaps 15.12, 16.05, 14.42 ($e + 1 = 2$) if they are needed with special precision. The standard error of a treatment mean should have two decimal places, i.e. as 0.25.

1.11   The role of the statistician in crop experimentation

A field experiment involves a number of stages. At each there are statistical considerations.

Stage 1   Inception   Any good experiment has clearly defined objectives. They must be specified right at the start in the form of 'contrasts of interest', which will be explained in Sections 5.1 and 5.2. Thereafter everything must be subordinated to obtaining good estimates of those contrasts. (At this stage the treatments are chosen and the relationships between them clarified.)

Stage 2   Resources   Once objectives have been decided, it is necessary to examine the resources available. First there is the land, whether it is variable or not, and whether it is suitable for the task in hand. If it is variable, is there any system of local control (blocks, etc.) that will make it more uniform? Other enquiries should concern plant material (seed quality, etc.) including plant variability, the skill of the workers involved, and the adequacy of the equipment available to them.

Stage 3   Design   The design adopted should pay respect to what has been learnt in Stages 1 and 2, so that the experiment shall be both relevant and practicable. The design should find expression in a plan which makes everything clear to those who will have to work on the experiment, whatever their capacity. The scheme should lead to no difficulty in applying the treatments, obtaining the data and carrying out ordinary farm operations. Also, the design must be such that the statistician can see his way to analysing the data.

Stage 4   Implementation   The plan having been handed over, there could well be other preliminary documents, such as the results of soil samples, notes on the source and quality of the plant material and on the weather at sowing or transplanting. Now is the time to start a diary of the experiment in which such matters will be noted in the future. Other operations are the surveying and laying out of the experiment in the field, the application of differential treatments, the recording of what can be measured and the scoring or grading of other features, like leaf colour, which can be observed but do not lend themselves to measurement. It is essential that the statisticians know about all these operations. If they do not, they may design experiments that no one can implement, or analyse data with no idea of what they really represent.

Stage 5   Data analysis   The calculation of analyses of variance can be a highly technical process, but the statistician's skills must not stop there. Above all it is necessary to assess well those contrasts that were defined at Stage 1 and were written into the design at Stage 3. Further, it is often useful to look back at Stage 2 and enquire how well the design has allowed for the sources of variation expected and how far other more important sources have been ignored. Not least, the data can be examined to pick up any faults of implementation at Stage 4.

Exercise 1A

Four cultivars, A, B, C, D of dwarf beans were arranged in a completely randomized design with four replicates each. The layout of the design was as indicated below and the leaf areas (cm²) were recorded, as shown, three days after germination.

Five of the plots suffered damage from a windborne insectide spray from a neighbouring field and these plants are indicated as missing (m).

D 7	A17	B10	C17	A17	D 6	B14	A15
C15	D 8	B14	D10	C16	A19	B13	D 5
A18	D 7	D 6	B12	B10	A10	C m	D m
C15	B 9	A16	C12	B 6	C m	A m	C m

Work out the analysis of variance and write out the residuals on the field plan. Do the residuals suggest anything to you?

Exercise 1B

An experiment on six bean varieties, A to F, was carried out in four randomized blocks. Yields were as follows:

I	F	9.0	D	14.6	C	18.3	E	14.2	F	14.1	C	17.4	II
	E	14.1	B	21.9	A	22.4	B	25.6	A	23.9	D	19.2	
III	C	12.7	D	15.8	E	11.5	E	12.1	D	16.1	C	15.9	IV
	A	21.1	B	23.7	F	6.4	A	19.6	F	12.3	B	18.3	

Data represent fresh weight of crop in kilograms per plot of 36 m^2 and are presented according to the field plan. Write the residuals on a copy of the plan and work out the analysis of variance both from the deviations and the residuals and by the use of summation terms.

[Data from P. Dagnelie, *Principes d'Expérimentation* (1981), p. 94. Sub-plots have been ignored.]

Exercise 1C

An experiment was conducted on ten strains of carrot, here called A–J. It had four randomized blocks, each consisting of a line of plots. The four lines were side by side. Yields were as follows:

Block I		Block II		Block III		Block IV	
J	27.7	I	35.5	G	30.2	A	31.8
I	36.7	E	33.0	C	31.2	F	31.8
G	32.6	D	25.2	B	31.9	D	22.3
F	30.6	A	28.0	E	30.1	I	32.4
B	33.4	J	34.3	I	35.7	B	29.8
D	22.2	F	30.0	D	24.4	H	29.5
E	30.2	B	29.5	A	28.3	C	25.8
A	30.0	C	29.0	H	27.6	E	27.8
H	30.1	G	31.7	J	31.7	G	30.8
C	32.9	H	29.7	F	28.5	J	27.7

Work out residuals and the analysis of variance using two methods.

Note: The residuals are of interest because the blocks are very long and narrow, so trends along them are to be expected. The position will be examined in more detail in the Exercises of Chapter 8.

[Data from A. A. Rayner, *Biometry for Agriculture Students* (1969), pp. 267–8.]

Exercise 1D

One early example of a design in randomized blocks compared sixteen fertilizer treatments, A–Q (I omitted), in four blocks. The data from Blocks III and IV are given below. Work out residuals and consider whether the block boundaries had been formed to best advantage

		Block III						Block IV			
A	351.5	L	495.5	J	443.0	C	383.5	P	559.0	Q	550.0	B	359.0	E	395.5
K	472.5	B	367.5	G	455.5	O	502.5	C	328.5	H	390.5	J	483.0	O	512.0
E	357.5	F	381.5	Q	531.0	D	316.0	N	522.0	M	444.0	A	325.O	D	259.0
N	385.5	H	354.0	P	496.5	M	474.5	F	410.5	G	351.5	K	430.0	L	394.5

Data represent the yields of potatoes in pounds per plot of unstated area (1 pound = 454 grams).

[Data from T. Eden and R. A. Fisher, *J. of Agricultural Science*, **19** (1929), p. 207.]

Exercise 1E

An experimenter had three promising new varieties of maize, which we will call X, Y and Z. He wished to compare them with his existing recommended variety, which we will call R. To discover how the new varieties compared, he tested all four in a Latin square. The following figures give yields in cavans per hectare. (A cavan is a measure of volume used in the Philippines: 1 cavan = 77.5 litres.)

Y	32.8	Z	24.2	R	28.5	X	26.9
R	29.5	X	23.7	Z	28.0	Y	25.8
X	33.4	R	14.2	Y	33.3	Z	23.6
Z	31.3	Y	25.8	X	33.1	R	13.2

Work out the analysis of variance using two methods.

[Data from K. A. Gomez and A. A. Gomez, *Statistical Procedures for Agricultural Research with Emphasis on Rice* (1976), p. 27.]

Exercise 1F

An experiment was conducted on six strains (A–F) of maize using a Latin square. The following data represent bushels per acre. (In general, it is better to record crops by weight, but it is admittedly easier on occasion to measure by volume.)

B	20.3	C	14.9	A	13.7	D	14.7	E	16.7	F	18.6
E	18.2	A	15.3	C	10.1	F	15.3	B	10.8	D	11.3
A	12.2	E	16.7	F	12.2	C	11.2	D	11.4	B	10.5
D	18.9	F	17.9	E	16.8	B	16.0	A	14.3	C	16.4
F	17.7	B	20.1	D	17.0	A	15.3	C	15.5	E	17.0
C	18.7	D	17.9	B	19.9	E	17.7	F	18.4	A	12.1

Work out the analysis of variance using both methods.
1 bushel = 36.4 litres   1 acre = 0.405 hectare

[Data from C. I. Bliss, *Statistics in Biology*, Vol. I (1967), p. 309.]

Exercise 1G

An experiment was conducted to compare the cropping of four new raspberry varieties, B, C, D and E, with a standard variety. A. The following data came from the row-and-column design used:

B	88	A	246	E	174	A	236	C	61	D	83
C	122	A	165	A	194	B	97	D	118	E	145
D	132	E	124	A	221	A	127	B	105	C	100
A	149	C	76	D	96	E	122	A	145	B	68
A	253	D	106	B	94	C	98	E	151	A	145
E	195	B	106	C	130	D	93	A	180	A	128

The data represent ounces of fruit per plot. The area of each plot is not stated. (One ounce = 28.4 grams)
Calculate the analysis of variance.

Note: If the treatment summation term is needed, it should be calculated using the method of (1.4.1).

[Data from S. C. Pearce, *Field Experimentation with Fruit Trees and Other Perennial Plants*, p. 92 of first edition (1953).]

Chapter 2

Practical matters of experimentation

Note: Many of the topics of this chapter are dealt with more fully in the book by Dyke (1987).

2.1 Introduction

If an agricultural field experiment is to be successful, careful attention must be given to all stages of its existence, from the choice of the site and the drawing of the plan to the harvesting of the crop and the recording of the yields of the plots. In this chapter we discuss some of the points that commonly arise in settling the correct procedure at all these stages.

Agricultural crops, like most biological material, have an intrinsic variability which, at least with present knowledge, cannot be eliminated. If, at some particular stage of the conduct of an experiment, there is a choice between an easy, slightly inaccurate procedure and a more arduous or more lengthy but more accurate procedure, it may be tempting to choose the easier option. For example, if a fertilizer is measured by volume instead of by weight, the variation of quantity from plot to plot will be slightly increased. In many circumstances, the effect on variability of the crop yields will be very small in comparison with the irreducible variability likely in the experiment. The experimenter should, however, think twice (at least) before settling for the second best; any noticeable departure from the maximum accuracy that can reasonably be achieved tends to encourage a careless attitude to the experiment at all stages. Most agronomists visiting a research station for the first time have confidence in the experimentation in proportion to the tidiness of the plot-work. They take that as showing the keenness and discipline of the field workers and scientists; it is difficult to put much trust in an experiment that has unnecessary defects, even small ones. If a less good method is adopted, it should be for a considered reason that can be argued convincingly. In general the pursuit of excellence should dominate all else.

2.2   Choice of site

Assuming that a particular field or plantation has been allocated for an experiment, the exact site should be chosen so as to minimize likely variation, at least within blocks. Such variation may be caused by changes of soil, for example between the top and bottom of a slope, by past farming operations—for example, ploughing on different dates—by different degrees of shelter, or perhaps by nearby trees. Edges of fields are conspicuously different from the interior parts, sometimes because of cross-ploughing, spraying overlaps, sometimes because of incursions by trespassers. It may be wise to modify the design to allow for features of the site, for example, to change from randomized blocks to a row-and-column design, or to change the direction of the blocks.

In the analysis of variance it is assumed that the differential effects of treatments will be the same anywhere. For that reason it is wrong to accept a site for which that assumption will not hold. For example, the effect of fertilizers will be different on poor soil from what it would have been on rich. It would therefore be foolish to allocate a field with a wide fertility range to a study of level of fertilization, though it would be less objectionable for a trial of insecticides.

2.3   Size and shape of plots

Anyone who proclaims the optimum plot size for a particular crop, regardless of circumstances and treatments, should be disbelieved; no such optimum can exist. He is oversimplifying a problem that has many aspects. For a given crop on a given site there will be an optimum size for plots testing fertilizers, another for comparisons of cultivations, another for tests of sprayed fungicides. On another site the pattern of variability of the soil will indicate, at least for some of these types of experiment, different plot sizes. A season of heavy storms may cause patchy lodging or local waterlogging and indicate, perhaps too late, that unusually large plots should have been used. For those reasons calculations of optimum size based on analyses of uniformity trials are of little value in the determination of plot size for experiments, except for those of a single type in closely similar conditions. The analysis of a uniformity trial ignores the fact that, at least on some sites, treatment-effects in real experiments will vary with changes of conditions within the site. It is true that the assumption of additivity (Section 1.3) requires that such variation should be minimal, but it does sometimes arise with block designs and similarly with row-and-column designs, which differ only in having two sets of blocks. That casts doubt on calculations of optimum plot-size from uniformity data. We urge rather that practical considerations are most important in settling plot-size and we list below some of the commoner ones.

(1) The nature of the treatments may necessitate discard areas (which receive the respective plot-treatments) or guard areas (treated uniformly throughout the experiment).

(2) Crop-sampling may be best done in 'sacrifice' areas adjacent to the areas taken for yield. (See Section 2.8).

(3) Machinery used for sowing, spraying, harvesting, etc., may influence one or both of the dimensions of the plot.

(4) Will the produce be weighed at the site or carted to a central station for weighing? Either way careful planning is needed and the plot size may have to be chosen to fit in.

(5) The area available for the experiment, leaving out any obviously anomalous parts for the land allocated, may place restrictions on the individual plots, both as to size and shape. (It may be wise to extend the area excluded beyond the minimum if the remaining plots are to be comparable. This could call for a change of site.)

In short, the plots must be thoroughly practical in both size and shape. Once a tractor has started to cross the land, unless special arrangements have been made it must continue to the other side, but long, narrow plots could be most suitable for the application of fertilizer. Treatments have to be applied properly; also, crops have to be harvested and measurements made. All that has to be considered in a choice of plots.

2.4 Marking out

Marking out the plots of an experiment usually involves setting out right angles and distances, most of the latter determined in advance by the dimensions of each plot, and of paths or guard areas or headlands between plots. Some of the distances may depend on hazards of the chosen site; for example a gap may be left in a row of plots to avoid soil contaminated by the ashes of a bonfire.

Occasionally a field of a particular shape may suggest plots of parallelogram shape, with angles not equal to 90°, in order to make best use of the available area. If wide machines are to be used, that causes complications. In some experimentation (for example on curved contour strips) other layouts of a more flexible type will be needed. In the remainder of this section we consider only a conventional experiment with rectangular or square plots, all of equal size.

The first step is to mark out the rectangle (rarely a square) that will contain the whole experiment, including any gaps left to avoid dubious patches. Lengths are usually set out by use of measuring tapes—though the surveyors' chains used in the past were also suitable—and right angles by means of optical square, crosshead, or a Pythagorean triangle with sides in the ratio 3:4:5. In general the rectangle will not close; that is, if we mark out the four sides successively the final point will not coincide with the starting-point. Mostly that is on account of the angles not being exactly 90°. For that reason, corrections must be made to angles, not to lengths. That also ensures that all plots will be of equal dimensions as well as of the same shape. Once the sides have been measured, it is necessary to divide them equally to determine the corners of individual plots. Here again, discrepancies can arise. If so, it is important to adjust all plots equally or some will be wider than others.

Although for most purposes the metric system is best, there are circumstances which suggest the use of feet and inches, for example, the availability of a seed-drill of many spouts with unit spacing of 7 inches. A mixture of units (e.g. plot-lengths in metres, width in feet and inches) presents no great difficulty, provided a doubly-marked tape is available. The only task made more difficult is the calculation of plot-area, and that has only to be done once and in conditions of comfort indoors. Excessive accuracy, e.g. measuring to the nearest millimetre, is absurd in connection with crop-plant experimentation; the width of a plot, however, should be written down with enough significant figures to reconcile the width of many plots with the total width across the experiment. Measuring tapes have been known to stretch with much use and should be checked from time to time.

2.5 The plan

The plan of an experiment is the chief means of conveying information between the various people involved in the field work. Often those performing the analysis and interpretation of the results will need it too. (All these jobs may be done by the same person, but even so people can forget details so a record is needed.) In most experimentation the plan should be in such a form as to make the field worker's task as easy as possible; he (or she) may be tired, cold, wet or hot or may be hurrying to finish a job. Perhaps a difficult task is involved like sowing different batches of seed on the plots of a variety trial, before dark, before a thunderstorm, or before the farmer wants his seed-drill back. A mistake made by the field worker at such a stage, even if it is detected and recorded, may seriously damage the experiment. Other users of the plan are almost always able to study it in better conditions and with less urgency. The guiding principle, then, is to produce a plan that serves the field worker as well as possible. Sometimes, e.g. if the experiment involves the application of treatments at different dates, like the sowing of different varieties in autumn and the application of different rates of fertilizer in the following spring, it may be helpful to provide, in addition to the full plan, simplified 'overlays'. They will include only symbols needed at a certain stage, for example one overlay might show varieties but not rates of fertilizer. A plan or overlay should be carefully checked, preferably not by the person who drew it.

One great help is a generally agreed system of plot numbering. It should be decided in the first place with the interests of the field workers in mind. Thereafter, everyone else should use it, up to those responsible for data input to the computer. If that is done, two important sources of error are minimized. (1) Direct copying, which is a potent source of error, because it appears to be so simple; everyone supposes him or herself able to do it, but minds wander. (2) Indirect copying, in which figures are de-randomized in the process of copying. For a preview of the conclusions, people will work out treatment means from the field sheets, and that is all right provided nothing final is built on them. They should be only interim indications.

We conclude this section by listing some of the things that are required on the plans of most experiments:

(1) Alignments of plots should be correctly indicated, in one or two directions as appropriate.
(2) Dimensions of each plot, and of the whole experiment, together with clear indications of the positions and widths of all paths, gaps, etc.
(3) Orientation. Usually a North point is shown.
(4) Plot-numbers, treatment-symbols.
(5) Block-boundaries.
(6) Name, location and date of experiment. Also its reference number if it had one.
(7) Crop, variety, seed-rate or plant spacing.
(8) Full description of treatments under test, and of 'basal' ('blanket') applications.
(9) Any normal farming operations that must be omitted.

The exact location should also be made clear by reference to nearby features that can be relied upon not to alter.

Field labels

Related to the plan is the system of plot labels. The one should complement the other. If abbreviations are used on the plan, they can be used on the labels also. At no point should there be any conflict between the two.

Sometimes there are conflicting ideas about what to put on the labels. Put too much and they look confusing; put too little and an opportunity will have been missed. One particularly difficult matter concerns the treatments. If they are not shown, there could be difficulties when they come to be applied; if they are, the information could prejudice the taking of some records, especially if plots are to be scored. (Field recorders can be told not to read labels except to check the plot number, but they can hardly fail to see what is clearly displayed. Further, if they are also the people who had to apply the treatments and they remember how the plan went, they can scarcely be expected to put the information out of their minds.) To take another consideration, sometimes the treatments will have been applied before the labels were set up. In that case there is little point in displaying them. (The argument that visitors will be interested need carry no weight; they should be conducted round by someone with a plan, not left to wander.)

Whatever else the labels show, the plot number is essential. Ideally plots should have a standard order that is used for all purposes, the application of treatments, the recording of data and the presentation of data to the computer. Further it should be decided with the interests of the field staff in mind. Even then, there may be occasions when they will want to deal with plots in a different order. If that does happen, it is a courtesy on their part to write boldly on the sheets 'Plots in non-standard order' to help people further down the line, who otherwise might not notice the change. How is the standard order to be chosen? Most people when they have finished one row will want to work back along the next, like this:

1	2	3	4	5	6	7	8
16	15	14	13	12	11	10	9
17	18	etc.					

There is in fact a word to describe such a progression; it is *boustrophedon*, meaning the way in which an ox would plough. Field workers do it in the same way and for much the same reason as the ox.

The alternative is to work along each row in the same direction, like this:

1	2	3	4	5	6	7	8
9	10	11	12	13	14	15	16
17	18	etc.					

Its chief feature is that all plots are approached from the same direction. This is perhaps not much of an advantage except in scoring, because the sunny side of a plot can look very different from the shady side. In any case good field recorders know that, and they avoid letting it interfere with their scoring. Whatever method is chosen it should ensure that all plots of a block are kept together. Further, it is good practice to distinguish the last plot of a block with a label of a different colour or a different shape. In that way the field staff know where they can safely stop if they have to do so. In the above example, if there were blocks, four plots wide and two plots deep, the following might be a good system of plot numbering:

4	3	2	1	16	15	14	13
5	6	7	8	9	10	11	12
		18	17				

If it is found that the field staff do not follow the standard order once it has been decided, that suggests that it was badly chosen in the first place.

Once a suitable system of numbering has been agreed, try to use it always. The numbering of plots should never be changed during the life of an experiment. If necessary in a long-term experiment if plots are subsequently split, plot 1 may become sub-plots 11, 12, . . ., or 1a, 1b, . . .

2.6   Methods of randomizing

We list below some of the many methods of allocating treatments at random to plots within blocks, or sub-plots within whole plots, together with notes on necessary precautions. Much of this applies to the randomization of row-and-column designs, but we do not deal with these in detail.

(1)   By use of published tables of 'random numbers'. (They are really tables of numbers, generated in some complicated but systematic way, that have passed various tests. They are therefore known to be free from undesirable sequences likely to lead to bias.) For 2–10 treatments, it is possible to use digits one at a time provided all treatments are to be equally replicated. For 11–100 there is another method which can well be adopted as standard and used even when the treatments are few enough to be represented by single digits. If the number of treatments exceeds 100, it is readily extended. The method is this: If the next plot can have A treatments, a two-digit number is taken at random and divided by A. The remainder indicates the treatment to be chosen. Thus, if $A = 12$ and the random number is 87 ($= 12 \times 7 + 3$), the third treatment should be chosen for that plot. There are three points to be noted. (a) The double zero, 00, should be read as 100. (b) If the random number is an exact multiple of A, that indicates the last treatment on the list. (c) If 100 is not a multiple of A there are some two-digit numbers that should be avoided. For example, if $A = 12$, no use should be made of 97, 98, 99 or 00; to do so would be to give Treatments 1, 2, 3 and 4 nine chances of being selected as compared with eight for the rest. That is to say, the range of random numbers must

terminate at the highest multiple of A less than 100 in the case where 100 is not itself a multiple.

The method can be illustrated by supposing that a block with six plots is to contain treatments A, A, B, C, D and E. It will further be supposed that the first two-digit random numbers given by tables are 22, 81, 68, 00, 53, 16, 45, 51, 34. The stages are:

(i)   The first random number is 22. Since $A = 6$ and $22 = 6 \times 3 + 4$, the fourth treatment is indicated. That leaves AABDE.

(ii)   The second number is 81. Since $A = 5$, that indicates A for the second plot, which leaves ABDE.

(iii) The next number 68, is an exact multiple of A ($= 4$). Accordingly E should be chosen. That leaves ABD.

(iv)   The next number is 100, which is not itself a multiple of A, so it must be ignored, though all numbers from 01 to 99 would have been acceptable.

(v)   The next number is 53, which indicates the second out of the three treatments still available, i.e., B. The choice now lies between A and D.

(vi)   The final number is 16. It is even, so D is chosen for the next plot and A for the last. The result of the process has been to assign the treatments in the order CAEBDA. The other random numbers can be disregarded or used to start another block.

(2)   By use of a computer to generate random numbers. Some machines, however, have quite crude generators, so, if many experiments are being designed, there may be a risk of repeating similar patterns.

(3)   By shuffling packs of cards, either made up specially for the purpose, or normal playing cards.

(4)   By dice, for example, a 10-sided die (a treasured possession of one of the authors).

(5)   By tossing a coin (which we hope is unbiased). Add imaginary treatments to make the total number a power of 2 (e.g. 32) and use each toss to decide whether to discard the first or second half of the treatments remaining at each stage; some runs of tosses indicate imaginary treatments and are ignored.

In the case of a row-and-column design it is necessary to find a design that has the right allocation of treatments to rows and columns and then to permute both rows and columns at random.

2.7   The application of treatments

Once the treatments that are to be compared have been settled it is necessary to plan how they should be applied. If they are varieties or rates of fertilizer the matter is fairly simple, but even then problems can arise. Should varieties be sown at the same seed-rate measured by weight or by number of seeds per unit area? Should allowance be made if the seed of one variety is of poor germination? Surely fertilizers should be applied evenly? But, in experiments designed to be the basis of recommendations to farmers, who are likely to apply them unevenly, perhaps they should be applied about as they would be on farms.

Often the treatments to be compared are really different systems of farming. An exceptionally early-ripening variety may require harvesting before the others in the experiment—with some awkward consequences. A new system of cultivation may permit earlier sowing than is traditional, but that raises a difficult question. Should plots be sown at different dates, or should the new system be penalized by delay until all plots can be sown on the same day?

Machines used to apply treatments often need to be calibrated to assess their performance; for example a seed-drill may need adjustment if it is to deliver the same amounts of seed of different varieties per unit area. Calibration should be done in conditions similar to those on the experiment. Nevertheless, the measurement of amounts used on the plots of an experiment is not necessarily satisfactory because machines must start and stop work beyond plot boundaries. Finally, experiments should not be used only to test cultural practices, varieties, etc.; sometimes they are needed to test experimental techniques. For example, there might be different opinions on how to record the crop, and some plots might be recorded using both methods to see if they led to different results.

It need hardly be said that treatments should as far as possible be applied to plots following the plot order described in Section 2.5. Sometimes, indeed often, that is difficult and cannot be insisted upon, but some bad practices should be avoided. For example, in a spraying experiment it is decidedly wrong to make up Spray X today and to apply it; then, on the next fine day to make up Spray Y and so on until all treatments have been applied but over a period of time. Good experimenters do better than that.

2.8 Sampling in a field experiment

Sampling of a field experiment may be needed before the plots are marked out, after the crop has been harvested, or at any stage between those extremes. Soil may be sampled for determination of nutrients, pH, organic matter, salinity, soil-borne pests or diseases. The crop may be sampled during growth for chemical analysis, for estimation of leaf-area, for diseases or pests; it may be sampled just before or during harvest for measures of quality, for dry matter or for nutrient content. The plots may be sampled after harvest to assess losses incurred before or during harvest. This tiresome list by no means exhausts the possibilities.

Sampling a field experiment is different from sampling a field crop for the purpose of a survey; the remainder of this section is not a guide to the conduct of sample surveys but of experiments. Once treatments have been applied, all sampling should be done by plots. Occasionally, e.g. when deciding what 'basal' (or 'blanket') operation to use before the crop is grown, other methods may be used. (That might be done when deciding whether or not to lime a possibly acid site.)

The two main objectives are:

(1)   to assess differences between treatments so that the knowledge of their effects on yield can be supplemented by understanding of their probable mode of action;
(2)   to provide calibration data which can be used to make more accurate estimates of the effects of treatments on yield (or other primary observation), typically by use of analysis of covariance (see Sections 8.5, 8.6 and 8.7).

For both these objectives the great need is to establish differences between plots, not absolute values. Here experiments differ from surveys. If two sampling schemes are practicable and if one gives more accurate estimates of plot-differences than the other, even though it may have a degree of bias, it is the more accurate that should be adopted.

There are three main ways of planning the sampling of plots (we are thinking mainly of sampling the growing crop):

(1)   Random sampling
(2)   Stratified random sampling
(3)   Fixed-pattern sampling

Random sampling implies a separate pair of random numbers (chosen from suitable ranges) to define the position of each sample within each plot.

Stratified sampling is appropriate when there is important variation within each plot of a known pattern, for example, between land marked by tractor wheels and the remainder, or between rows sown by different spouts of a seed-drill. The variation of plot-means is lessened if the same proportion of samples is taken from each type of land within each plot. Also, plots may be divided into strata in some purely geometric manner, e.g. by subdividing the plot into four sub-plots.

Fixed-pattern sampling implies the location of samples in the same positions relative to the boundaries of all plots. It minimizes the effects of patterned variation, known or unknown, related in any way or at any stage to operations on the plots. It provides no estimate of within-plot sampling 'error', whereas random sampling of whole plots or of strata within plots does provide estimates of sampling error, provided there are at least two samples in each plot or stratum. Such estimates are needed if alternative sampling schemes, e.g. taking more or less samples per plot, are under consideration for future work. For all other purposes the relevant estimate of error is the one based on differences between plot-means. This is equally true whether sampling is done for either, or both, of the purposes indicated previously.

If substantial destructive sampling is planned it may be advisable to increase the plot-size so that a part of each plot, after excluding discard areas near edges, may be given over entirely to sampling, leaving a separate area for estimation of yield. Sometimes sampling may be confined to discard areas, provided they are not unduly unrepresentative. Samples may be taken solely from yield areas, or partly from discard, partly yield areas. Sampling from yield areas gives the best chance of detecting a relationship between yield and the sample observation; if sampling is from 'sacrifice' or discard areas the relationship is blurred by an unknown degree of within-plot variation.

Sampling part of an experiment, e.g. from certain treatments only, may be necessary occasionally, some treatments being of no interest to the sampler. If sampling affects yield areas, that will bias the estimate of some treatment contrasts. Sometimes, on the other hand, a lower degree of replication will suffice. Sampling all plots on a selection of blocks is less objectionable. Nevertheless it may increase 'error' variance if treatments behave differently in different blocks. As explained in Section 2.3, that usually does happen to some extent, though not to such a degree as to call for a change of site (Section 2.2).

Adjusting recorded yields to allow for the effect of crop-sampling is arbitrary unless the sampling can be done just before harvest and without damage to the adjacent crop. Some thickly-sown crops may make good almost all the 'lost' yield by more vigorous growth of plants adjacent to small sample areas. On the other hand, sampling apple shoots, to measure growth soon after planting, will almost certainly leave permanent effects. Hence sampling all plots equally is much preferable to sampling some only.

Samples are sometimes bulked before examination; bulking samples taken from one plot at one time is usually acceptable. Bulking samples from different plots is a more risky practice and usually better avoided. For example, if fresh yield and percentage dry matter are positively correlated between plots, bulking equal weights of produce from replicates will cause underestimation of the mean yield of dry matter.

2.9 Scoring the plots of an experiment

A perceptive, conscientious agronomist who regularly examines the plots of an experiment can estimate colour, growth, population of plants, weeds, some diseases, some pests, and no doubt many other things that may be important. The estimates may not be quantitative, but they should put the treatments into their correct order and distinguish between large and small effects of treatments. Many of the characters he or she can estimate would be difficult or impossible to measure by use of instruments, at least without doing substantial damage to the crop. An industrious person can record scores for one or two characters on each of 100 plots in less than an hour without setting a foot in a plot. So, within its limitations, scoring is an efficient means of gathering subsidiary information.

Regular scoring can reveal mistakes in the application of treatments and isolated mishaps, such as failures of a seed-drill. If the experimenter pays some attention to nearby non-experimental crops during a scoring visit, indications may be found that explain a trend in fertility on the site. General notes about the state of the crop in relation to other areas of the same crop at the same time can be useful when an experiment is reviewed perhaps months later.

When setting out to make scores the experimenter should first look quickly at all the plots and establish the appearances of extreme conditions; the palest and the darkest, the least weedy and the most weedy, or whatever is appropriate. Scores can then be allotted to these extremes; perhaps 0 and 4, or 0 and 6. The plots are then studied in order, one block or row or column at a time. As far as possible, even numbers should be used for scores 0, 2, 4, 6 (say) but the intervening odd numbers can be used when necessary. (This procedure is a little simpler than starting with 0, 1, 2, 3 and then finding it necessary to resort to 0.5, 1.5 etc.; the actual numbers used make no difference to the final result.) The experimenter should score without knowledge of the plot-treatments and, if possible, should look at all plots from the same direction. Anything exceptional about any individual plot should be noted. Finally, a description of the scale of scoring should be written on the record sheet ('0 = 5 cm tall, 6 = 15 cm', for example) together with a note of the general state of the crop.

Most people can usefully distinguish about 2 to 10 different grades; an example of the simplest grading is to score plots '0' for light-green leaves and dark ones '1' in an experiment testing nitrogen fertilizer on a cereal crop. In the same experiment, some weeks later, one might score for lodging, using grades 0, 1, 2 ... 10 corresponding to 0, 10, 20 ... 100 percent of area lodged. The difference lies in the second having a numerical base which the first lacks.

In principle, scores may be analysed statistically like any other quantity. In practice they can cause problems on account of discontinuity. As was explained in Section 1.10, it is desirable that a variate should be able to take at least 20 values, but it would be unwise to attempt so many grades, even in the best case when they have a quantitative basis. (Without one, no observer can hope to keep so many standards clearly in mind.) One possibility is to use more than one observer and to add their scores. If more than one practised person is available that is a good plan, but it would be a mistake to supplement the team with an inexperienced novice, whose scores might be little better than a sequence of random numbers. If only one good observer is available and discontinuity is a problem, the analysis of variance will only be an approximation.

The fact is that some people are not good at scoring. Partly it is a matter of temperament. The injudicious put down extreme values with little reason. At the other extreme are the timorous who will not put them down at all. In between are the judicious who make wise use of them. Further, in a team the injudicious will outweigh the more cautious when scores come to be added. People reveal a lot about themselves in the way they score. The person in charge should now and again look at the grades returned by his staff to detect both those who think everything either superb or terrible and those who will never commit themselves even when faced by the remarkable.

There are also differences in training. People have positively to be taught to look at all plots from the same direction and to take precautions of that kind. They also have to be taught to distinguish between related phenomena. For example, large blossoms are not the same as numerous blossoms, but at first glance they create much the same impression. Again, no one can score the incidence of a disease without knowing where to find it. Two varieties of different habit may be equally infected, but the damage may be more obvious on one than on the other.

Finally, the best way to learn is to have one's scores checked, either by a more experienced observer or by a proper weighing. Too many scientists think that their scoring must be good because they understand the underlying botany, but that is often a distraction rather than a help. If it is a matter of observing leaf colour, for example, the first requirement is that the observer shall not be colour-blind. Botany has nothing to do with it. One of the writers was impressed by the confidence with which a group of horticulturists scored the crops of apple trees. When they had departed he noticed that the pickers, who claimed no scientific skills but whose ease of working depended upon their putting the right number of boxes under each tree, were much better. No one will learn to score well without the feed-back that comes from checking their figures against other people's or, even better, against objective data.

2.10   Harvesting and recording

Yields are usually the most important observations made on an experiment. Other quantities are often calculated from them, for example uptakes of nutrients. The area taken for yield should be the same for every plot, except where an accident has reduced the good area of a plot and in some spacing experiments. If there is any doubt about including plants near the edges of the harvested area, for example in wheat sown broadcast, the same person must make the decision on all plots of a block (or row, or column). Harvest should be done by blocks (or rows or columns) to equalize conditions (weather, fatigue or workers) as much as possible. If there are several workers or gangs, each one should be given a block or group of blocks and told to harvest all the plots so defined. The object is to confound all 'extraneous' variation with block-differences.

Harvest produce should be labelled with plot-number, not treatment; partly to lessen the risk of bias, conscious or unconscious, partly to deal with designs in which there are duplicated treatments within a block. Write down the area harvested exactly as it is measured; do not calculate in the field. '100 feet by 15 rows at 10 cm' is fine. It can be worked out and checked at leisure later. Do not record yields to an unnecessary degree of accuracy; that increases the risk of gross error in recording, or in later manual copying of results. As a guide: guess the smallest likely standard error per plot, halve it, round yields to the next convenient unit smaller than or equal to this. Avoid manual copying like the plague; if it has to be done, it must be checked. But yield records should be copied, perhaps by xerography, or the use of carbon-backed paper, and the two copies separated as soon as possible. At all costs avoid losing both copies!

Produce may be weighed on the site, or 'at home'. For weighing on the site a spring balance or steelyard on a tripod, or better, a 'tipping jib', may be used. Spring balances should be checked occasionally. At base a fixed balance will probably be used; direct links to a microcomputer, or to a mainframe, are sometimes available. Avoid parallax errors in reading balance-dials; have a second worker to verify the readings. Tare weights may be constant. If so, some balances can be set to read net weights directly. If tares are variable, they must be recorded as a separate variate; working out the net weight in the field is too risky. If samples are needed for the determination of the percentage of dry matter, they should be taken from well-mixed produce at the time of weighing.

Procedures for recording need to be carefully worked out and not left to improvisation when the time comes. It is important to have a good system of labelling containers as well as plots. If someone can go round before harvest and note the numbers of the containers assigned to each plot, there will be less difficulty later in deciding the plot to which a lost

container belongs. It is also important to have well-established procedures, understood by all, so that the yield of a plot is put in the right
place until collected and so that no one harvests across plot boundaries.
Where experimenters appreciate the difficulties, such matters are attended
to and clear procedures are laid down. Sometimes, unfortunately, no one
realizes that there are problems to be resolved and that can lead to
disaster.

Exercise 2A

You are asked to lay out a block in the freshly ploughed field. It is to be
30 metres long and 16 metres wide so as to contain five plots, each 6 metres
by 16 metres.

Start by setting up a base-line AB 30 metres long. At B set up a line at
right-angles to AB and mark a point C 16 metres from B. (Turn left at
each corner). Set up a right angle at C and mark D at 30 metres from C. At
D set up another right angle and mark point E at 16 metres.

What is the distance between A and E? If they do not coincide adjust the
angles at C and D to bring them together.

Now mark P, Q, R, S in AB so that AP, PQ, QR, RS and SB are all 6
metres; if there is any discrepancy move P, Q, R, S until the 5 distances are
equal. Similarly locate W, X, Y and Z in CD. How long is it since your
tape (or chain) was checked?

Exercise 2B

An experiment is to be designed in four randomized blocks with six
treatments, A, B, C, D, E and F. Reference to tables of random numbers
gives the following four sequences of two-digit numbers:

71	46	30	49
52	85	01	50
27	99	41	28
61	62	42	29
96	83	23	56
83	07	55	07
52	83	51	14
62	80	03	42

Using the four columns respectively for Blocks I, II, III and IV, allot the treatments at random within each block.

Exercise 2C

Before an experiment is harvested, score its plots for crop weight. When the data are available, check your scores against them. We suggest that you do it more than once.

Exercise 2D

Find an experiment on cereals (or some similar crop) in which the treatments are affecting the growth of plants. Score each plot for height of plants with some quantitative base in mind, i.e., one grade equals 5 cm, or something like that. Then go round again with a measuring scale and see how good your scores were. (How do you determine the height of a plot anyway? The plants in it will vary.) Again the exercise can be done more than once.

Exercise 2E

The 96 plots of an experiment fall into eight blocks as follows:

```
1  1  1  1  2  2  2  2  3  3  3  3  4  4  4  4
1  1  1  1  2  2  2  2  3  3  3  3  4  4  4  4
1  1  1  1  2  2  2  2  3  3  3  3  4  4  4  4
5  5  5  5  6  6  6  6  7  7  7  7  8  8  8  8
5  5  5  5  6  6  6  6  7  7  7  7  8  8  8  8
5  5  5  5  6  6  6  6  7  7  7  7  8  8  8  8
```

Suggest a scheme for numbering the plots.

Exercise 2F

Draw the plan of an experiment that you might have to deal with in your normal work; put in all necessary details. To save time we suggest a limit of 16 plots.

Exercise 2G

The crop growing on the experiment of Exercise 2F is to be sampled during growth for some secondary character (e.g. total dry matter, or plant population, or an insect pest). Decide which character is to be studied and write full instructions to the field worker for the sampling of the plots.

Exercise 2H

Working as in Exercise 2A, mark out all the points needed to define the plan below, which is not to scale.

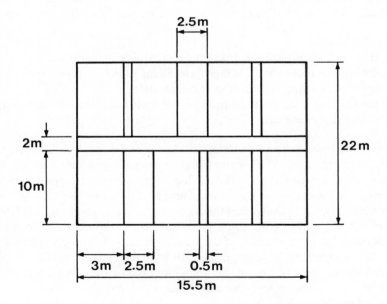

Chapter 3

Basic statistics

Note: Sections 3.1 to 3.6 set out the basic statistical knowledge assumed in the rest of this manual. A reader who finds the material completely unfamiliar is advised to do some preliminary reading first. We suggest the book by Clarke (1980), but there are others.

3.1 The Normal distribution

In order to carry out statistical inferences from experimental data, we need to assume that data follow some particular known distribution. Most analyses commonly used in agricultural statistics assume that data are normally distributed. The conditions for a normal distribution to apply are

(i)   there is a strong tendency to take a central 'average' value;
(ii) deviations from this 'average' are equally likely to be positive or negative, i.e. the distribution is symmetrical;
(iii) the frequency distribution drops off quickly from the 'average', large deviations being very unlikely.

There is a mathematical definition that is more precise, but those are the main characteristics. The normal distribution is sometimes called the 'Gaussian' and sometimes the 'Laplacian', but we have preferred 'normal' as being the most usual term, at least among English-speaking workers.

We can sometimes argue that these conditions (i), (ii) and (iii), are likely to hold theoretically. With a new crop, uniformity data are useful; plot a histogram of a large amount of data under standard growing conditions and see whether it is symmetrical. If it appears to conform to the conditions, the normal distribution may not hold exactly, but it should be close enough to the truth to be acceptable.

Specifying the mean, μ, and the variance, σ^2, fixes completely which member of the normal family of distributions is used: larger σ indicates a more scattered, or spread-out, set of measurements. We commonly assume that two different treatments applied to a crop will alter only its

44

mean value of yield, growth, etc., not its scatter or variability; often this appears satisfactory, but it may not always be so.

If a measurement X is normally distributed with mean μ and variance σ^2, then $Z = (X - \mu)/\sigma$ follows the *standard normal* with mean 0 and variance 1. Tables give us those values of Z *outside* which p percent of this distribution lies ($\frac{1}{2}p$ percent at the top and $\frac{1}{2}p$ percent at the bottom). A few useful values are:

$p\%$	10	5	2	1	0.2	0.1
Value of Z	± 1.645	± 1.960	± 2.326	± 2.576	± 3.090	± 3.291

When a random sample of r observations is drawn from a normally distributed population, their mean $\overline{X}$ will also follow a normal distribution (in repeated samplings), with theoretical mean μ and variance σ^2/r. Hence $Z = \dfrac{\overline{X} - \mu}{\sigma/\sqrt{r}}$ is again standard normal.

We should note here a certain inconsistency in nomenclature. Although people commonly talk about 'the 5 percent level', they more usually write it as '$P = 0.05$'. So long as it is understood that both expressions mean the same thing, no harm is done. In what follows we shall use either terminology as may be convenient.

Much statistical theory is built on the assumption that quantities are distributed normally. In fact, if we had enough data to detect divergences every time, we should probably find that most measurements do *not* follow the distribution exactly, though for most of them the assumption holds closely enough. After a while the observant practitioner comes to notice occasions when one or other of the characteristics (i), (ii), and (iii) above, is lacking. That is the time to consider the position and think about possible transformations (see Chapter 9).

Note: The 'shorthand' expression $N(\mu,\sigma^2)$ is often used to stand for a normally distributed variable whose mean is μ and variance σ^2.

3.2   Use of samples for estimation and hypothesis testing

At the outset of a programme of research, an estimate of μ will be needed. The sample mean, $\bar{x}$, is a good estimator of μ, but it is much more informative to have a 'confidence interval' which will cover the true (but unknown) value of μ in the population with a stated probability. This gives an idea of how precisely μ has been estimated: a very wide interval gives very little information about μ.

If σ^2 is known, the variance of $\bar{x}$ is known also, i.e., σ^2/r, so

$$Z = \frac{\bar{x} - \mu}{\sigma \sqrt{r}}$$

will be standard normal and will lie within the range ± 1.96 with probability 0.95. Hence

$$Prob \left(-1.96 < \frac{\bar{x} - \mu}{\sigma/\sqrt{r}} < +1.96 \right) = 0.95, \quad \text{so that}$$

$$Prob \left(\bar{x} - 1.96\sigma/\sqrt{r} < \mu < \bar{x} + 1.96\sigma/\sqrt{r} \right) = 0.95 \qquad (3.2.1)$$

which is a 95 percent confidence interval for μ based on the known σ^2 and the sample size. Increasing r leads to a narrower interval.

If an interval with higher probability of covering μ is required, it will be wider: a 99 percent confidence interval uses 2.576 instead of 1.96 in (3.2.1).

Later in a research programme, with enough knowledge or experience of a crop to propose a specific value μ_o for its mean, we shall wish to test this 'hypothesis' (see Section 1.3).

Using a sample of r observations, and assuming it is drawn from a normal distribution with known variance σ^2, test the hypothesis 'true mean $= \mu_o$' by calculating $Z = \dfrac{\bar{x} - \mu_o}{\sigma/\sqrt{r}}$ in which $\bar{x}$ is the mean of the sample of r. If Z lies between -1.96 and $+1.96$, within the central 95 percent of the standard normal distribution, then μ_o is an acceptable value for the true mean; otherwise reject this hypothesis. A value of Z outside ± 1.96 is called 'significant at the level $P = 0.05$', meaning that it gives significant evidence against the hypothesis being tested, which is usually called the 'null hypothesis'.

Although P is usually taken to be 0.05, other values may be used, for example 0.01 or 0.001 if we want stronger evidence. If the null hypothesis is true, there is a probability of only P that the data would have fallen out as they actually did. As P becomes smaller there will be a growing suspicion that the null hypothesis must be false, but the point at which this suspicion turns into conviction will depend upon the reasonableness of the null hypothesis itself. It may be so speculative and come at so early a stage in the research programme that we reject it at quite a high value of P, say, 0.20. On the other hand, it may be so well established that a low value of P will lead first to questions whether the experiment itself has been properly conducted rather than to doubts about the hypothesis. The value $P = 0.05$ has generally been felt to be convenient as a working level by applied statisticians but it has no greater status than that. It is not derived from any law of Nature.

Sometimes the experimenter may declare that, if a treatment is going to have an effect, it will be in a certain direction. For example, he may be applying a spray in the belief that it can only reduce the infestation of an insect pest. There are some questions to be asked here. Is he quite sure? Could the spray not kill some important predators and so bring about the opposite effect from what is intended? (Also, if he is really going to declare that the spray can have an effect in only one direction, which sounds rather dogmatic, he had better say so right at the beginning. If he says it later, he may find himself accused of changing the rules in the middle of the game.) However, he is quite certain. The spray may possibly decrease the level of infestation; it cannot increase it. That firm belief will change the nature of the test to be used.

It follows from the declaration that any increase in infestation is to be disregarded; it must have arisen from chance. If limits like those at (3.2.1) are set at ± 1.96 times the standard error, there is a $2\frac{1}{2}$ percent chance of Z falling below the lower limit and so discrediting the null hypothesis. There is also a $2\frac{1}{2}$ percent chance of its lying above the upper limit, but that will be ignored if it occurs. In fact, we are really working to $2\frac{1}{2}$ percent when we wanted 5 percent. The correct approach is to use ± 1.645 times the standard error. That is the usual value for a 10 percent level of chance, but if only half the extreme deviations are to be regarded as meaningful, it gives the desired 5 percent level.

In saying that the treatment could not possibly increase the infestation the experimenter was setting up an 'alternative hypothesis' that, in this example, the true value may be less than μ_o but cannot be more. In that case positive values of Z support the null hypothesis rather than the alternative and should be seen as doing so.

The process just described is called a 'one-tail' test. Where there is no good reason to say which way a change will go, the 'two-tail' test, rejecting both extremes (large and small) of Z, should be carried out.

3.3 Estimating and testing μ when σ^2 is not known

In practice, if μ is not known in a population then neither is σ^2 known. The estimate of σ^2 from the sample is

$$s^2 = \frac{1}{(r-1)} \sum_{i=1}^{r} (x_i - \bar{x})^2. \tag{3.3.1}$$

This estimate has to be used instead of σ^2; but $\dfrac{\bar{X} - \mu}{s/\sqrt{-r}}$ is not normally distributed and (3.2.1) needs modification. The necessary distribution is that studied by 'Student' (W. S. Gosset), the t-distribution. Its shape is similar to the standard normal, but its spread depends on the sample size, being broader the smaller r is; tables therefore have to give percentage points of t (as in Section 3.1) for each separate value of degrees of freedom. Degrees of freedom (abbreviated d.f.) number $(r - 1)$ when a sample of r values is available to estimate σ^2 (see Section 1.3). For many purposes the variance is taken as the 'error' mean square from the analysis of variance and has the 'error' degrees of freedom.

Confidence intervals follow from the result that, when a sample is drawn from a normal distribution of unknown variance, $t = \dfrac{\overline{X} - \mu}{s/\sqrt{-r}}$ is distributed as t with $(r - 1)$ d.f. If $\pm t_{(5\%)}$ denotes those values of t with $(r - 1)$ d.f. between which the central 95 percent of the distribution lies, then

$$Prob\ (- t_{(5\%)} < \frac{\bar{x} - \mu}{s/\sqrt{r}} < + t_{(5\%)}) = 0.95.$$

That is perhaps more conveniently written as:

$$Prob\ (\bar{x} - t_{(5\%)}s/\sqrt{r} < \mu < \bar{x} + t_{(5\%)}s/\sqrt{r}) = 0.95 \qquad (3.3.2)$$

which is a 95 percent confidence interval for the true value of the mean, based on a sample whose mean is $\bar{x}$ with estimated variance s^2.

For example, $t_{(5\%)}$ with 15 d.f. is ± 2.131 (instead of ± 1.96). For samples larger than 30, the $t_{(5\%)}$ values become very close to standard normal, so t need only be used in 'small' samples even if the population variance σ^2 is not known.

Also, for testing a hypothesis that the true mean is μ_o, using a sample of n observations whose mean is $\bar{x}$ and from which the variance has been estimated as s^2, $t = \dfrac{\bar{x} - \mu_o}{s/\sqrt{r}}$ is tested against the tables of t with $(r - 1)$ d.f. (instead of the standard normal tables). Otherwise the procedure exactly follows that described in Section 3.2.

It is a weakness of much statistical practice that so much attention is given to testing and so little to estimation, although latterly the balance has perhaps moved a little more towards estimation. Mostly an experimenter has quite a good idea of the sort of response he can expect from his treatments, but he may have doubts how large it will be. For example, there may be little doubt that a fertilizer application will increase yield, but there could be serious reservations whether the gain in crop will pay for the cost. Again, in a trial of varieties known to be different, a test is absurd; the only sensible thing is to estimate the differences known to exist.

3.4 Difference between two means

In the case where independent random samples are drawn from two normal distributions, r_1 observations from the first whose variance is σ_1^2, and r_2 from the second whose variance is σ_2^2, the difference between the two sample means $\bar{x}_1 - \bar{x}_2$ is again normally distributed. The mean of this distribution of differences is $\mu_1 - \mu_2$, these being the true means in the two distributions, and its variance is

$$\frac{\sigma_1^2}{r_1} + \frac{\sigma_2^2}{r_2}$$

We shall write that as V, the variance of the difference. Therefore the quantity

$$Z = \frac{(\bar{x}_1 - \bar{x}_2) - (\mu_1 - \mu_2)}{\sqrt{V}}$$

once again follows a standard normal distribution.

A 95 percent confidence interval for the true value of $(\mu_1 - \mu_2)$ based on the sample and using the known σ_1^2, σ_2^2 is found by exactly the same argument as (3.2.1):

$$Prob\{(\bar{x}_1 - \bar{x}_2) - 1.96\sqrt{V} < (\mu_1 - \mu_2) < (\bar{x}_1 - \bar{x}_2) + 1.96\sqrt{V}\} = 0.95.$$
$$(3.4.1)$$

Often in agricultural trials we require a test of the hypothesis that the true difference $(\mu_1 - \mu_2)$ is equal to D; frequently D is 0 but it does not have to be so. This is carried out by examining the value of

$$Z = \frac{(\bar{x}_1 - \bar{x}_2) - D}{\sqrt{V}}$$
$$(3.4.2)$$

which follows a standard normal distribution if the hypothesis is true; with probability 0.95, we therefore expect it to lie between -1.96 and $+1.96$. The hypothesis is rejected only if Z lies outside this range.

In the common practical situation where σ_1^2 and σ_2^2 are not known, calculations can best proceed if they are assumed to be equal, i.e. $\sigma_1^2 = \sigma_2^2 = \sigma^2$. Therefore the first step is always to test whether the sample variances s_1^2 and s_2^2 calculated separately, in the usual way, for each sample differ significantly (section 3.5). If they do, and the sample sizes r_1, r_2 are less than about 15 each, no further calculations should be attempted. For r_1, r_2 between 15 and 30, provided one sample is not very much larger than the other, results obtained from the following calculations will be reasonably reliable even if s_1^2 and s_2^2 do differ, while samples larger than 30 can be treated as 'large' and the values of s_1^2, s_2^2 can be used instead of σ_1^2, σ_2^2 in the formulae already given above, i.e. (3.4.1) and (3.4.2).

Provided s_1^2 and s_2^2 are not significantly different, a 'pooled' estimate, s^2, of the common σ^2 is found as

$$s^2 = \frac{(r_1 - 1)s_1^2 + (r_2 - 1)s_2^2}{(r_1 + r_2 - 2)}$$

Then the quantity

$$t = \frac{(\bar{x}_1 - \bar{x}_2) - (\mu_1 - \mu_2)}{\sqrt{s^2\left(\frac{1}{r_1} + \frac{1}{r_2}\right)}}$$

follows Student's t-distribution with $(r_1 + r_2 - 2)$ d.f. for any values of r_1 and r_2. Just as we wrote V for the known variance of the difference of means, i.e.

$$V = (1/r_1 + 1/r_2)\sigma^2$$

so we will write

$$\hat{V} = (1/r_1 + 1r_2)s^2.$$

Here $\hat{V}$ is an estimate of V found from using s^2 as an estimate of σ^2. In using it we shall have to depart from the normal distribution and go to the t-distribution instead. Hence a 95 percent confidence interval for the true value of the difference $(\mu_1 - \mu_2)$ is given by

$$(\bar{x}_1 - \bar{x}_2) - t_{(5\%)}s\sqrt{V} < (\mu_1 - \mu_2) < (\bar{x}_1 - \bar{x}_2) + t_{(5\%)}s\sqrt{V} \qquad (3.4.3)$$

instead of (3.4.1). Here s^2 is the pooled estimate of variance and $t_{(5\%)}$ is the 5 percent point of t (i.e. $P = 0.05$) with $(r_1 + r_2 - 2)$ d.f. In the same way the test of the hypothesis that $(\mu_1 - \mu_2)$ equals D is to compare

$$t = \frac{(\bar{x}_1 - \bar{x}_2) - D}{\sqrt{\hat{V}}} \qquad (3.4.4)$$

with table values of Student's t with $(r_1 + r_2 - 2)$ d.f. Two-tail or one-tail tests, depending on the alternative hypothesis, are carried out as described in Section 3.2.

With the appearance of (3.4.3) and (3.4.4) we enter the realm of comparative experiments. Means are not being compared with constants but with one another. That is especially relevant in an agricultural context, where no one expects the yield of a crop to be the same in all locations and at all times, but there is nevertheless a reasonable expectation that differences will be reliable. In other words, if we compare two treatments and observe an advantage for one of them at one place, we shall expect to find a similar advantage elsewhere and in different seasons, provided that conditions are broadly similar.

3.5 Variance in samples from normal distributions

The unbiased estimate of σ^2 is found from a sample $\{x_1, x_2, \ldots, x_r\}$ of r observations as

$$s^2 = \frac{1}{(r-1)} \sum_{i=1}^{r} (x_i - \bar{x})^2.$$

For use in estimation and testing, the result needed is that $(r-1)s^2/\sigma^2$ follows the chi-squared distribution with $(r-1)$ d.f., $\chi^2(r-1)$. [In the unusual case where the population mean is known, the best estimator of the variance is

$$s_o^2 = \frac{1}{r} \sum_{i=1}^{r} (x_i - \mu)^2, \quad \text{and} \quad \frac{rs_o^2}{\sigma^2} \quad \text{follows } \chi^2_{(r)}.]$$

Tables of χ^2 contain a row for each number of degrees of freedom, and they give the values above which p percent of the distribution lies, for a selection of P-values such as 99 percent, $97\frac{1}{2}$ percent, 95 percent, 5 percent, $2\frac{1}{2}$ percent, 1 percent. To find a 95 percent confidence interval for σ^2, when μ is not known, use

$$Prob \left(\chi^2_{(L)} < \frac{(r-1)s^2}{\sigma^2} < \chi^2_{(U)} \right) = 0.95$$

in which $\chi^2_{(L)}$ and $\chi^2_{(U)}$ are the $97\frac{1}{2}$ percent and $2\frac{1}{2}$ percent points in the tables for $(r-1)$ d.f. This gives

$$Prob \left(\frac{(r-1)s^2}{\chi^2_{(U)}} < \sigma^2 < \frac{(r-1)s^2}{\chi^2_{(L)}} \right) = 0.95 \qquad (3.5.1)$$

as the 95 percent interval for σ^2 based on the sample.

In order to test a hypothesis that the true value of the variance in a population is σ^2, when we have a random sample of r observations from it whose estimated variance is s^2, the value $\dfrac{(r-1)s^2}{\sigma^2}$ is calculated. If this lies between $\chi^2_{(L)}$ and $\chi^2_{(U)}$ (as defined above) we can accept that σ^2 is a reasonable value for the true variance.

When comparing two estimated variances, to test the hypothesis that the samples giving them were drawn from populations with the same true value of variance, it is their ratio that is required. If the estimates are s_1^2 and s_2^2, from samples of r_1 and r_2 observations respectively, s_1^2/s_2^2 follows the F-distribution with $(r_1 - 1)$ and $(r_2 - 1)$ d.f. It is important to keep d.f. in the right order. Because of the way in which F tables are usually printed it is also necessary to write the ratio so that s_1^2 is the larger estimate, and the ratio is greater than 1. When the calculated ratio is significantly greater than 1, i.e. greater than the value in the table at the chosen probability level ($P = 5$ percent, 1 percent, etc.), we should not accept a hypothesis that says the two population variances were equal.

We have here reached a test that has special relevance to the analysis of variance. In Chapter 1 we obtained some simple examples of such analyses. Their common feature is the obtaining of two variances, one for treatments and the other for 'error', and we did in fact work out F as their ratio. We are now in a position to say whether these F-values are significant or not. If there were no differences due to treatments, the two mean squares would be measuring the same σ^2 and F would, within statistical limits, be 1.00. If F so far exceeds that value that the probability of its doing so by chance is small ($P < 0.05$, say, or some other low value) then we are forced to consider whether there may indeed be effects of treatments. If there are, they will inflate the treatment mean-square but not that for 'error'. (Note by the way, that the F-test uses only one tail. No provision is made for the case where the mean square for treatments is less than that for 'error'.)

At this point someone may be surprised that we raise the question at all. Of course, he may say, there are treatment differences. Why, do we suppose, is the experiment being done at all if none are expected? The question is a fair one; in many instances an F-test is quite unnecessary. The treatments have been included in the full knowledge that they must have an effect. Sometimes, however, there can be doubts, e.g. a strange scorch has appeared on the leaves and someone suggests that it indicates a deficiency of magnesium. In that case, a test is called for to see if there is a difference between plots that have received a dressing of magnesium sulphate and those that have not. As with all these questions, the important thing is to see clearly what the experiment is intended to do. If the general effects of the treatments can be foreseen and the enquiry concerns only the magnitudes of those effects, no test is needed (least of all an F-test), only estimates. If, on the other hand, a 'Yes or No' answer is required to the question whether there are any treatment differences, a test is in order. Even then there may be no place for an F-test but rather for a series of t-tests of the kind considered in (3.4.3), mostly with $D = 0$.

3.6 More general contrasts among means assuming orthogonality

In Chapter 5 we shall examine in some detail contrasts between the treatments, that are more complicated than simple ones like $\bar{x}_1 - \bar{x}_2$, but we will make a start now. Suppose that one treatment, A, is a standard method of cultivating a crop, while two other methods, B and C, both involve using additional fertilizer but in different ways. An interesting comparison, or contrast, among the means is to look at the difference between A and the average of B and C: i.e. to consider $\bar{x}_A - \frac{1}{2}(\bar{x}_B + \bar{x}_C)$. We shall now examine the position for orthogonal designs.

This is an example of a general contrast

$$l\bar{x}_A + m\bar{x}_B + p\bar{x}_C,$$

where l, m, p are numbers ('constants'), here 1, $-\frac{1}{2}$, $-\frac{1}{2}$, respectively. They must sum to zero. Provided the samples of experimental plots used for each treatment were chosen independently (in a properly randomized experiment) the variance of the contrast will be

$$l^2\text{var}(\bar{x}_A) + m^2\text{var}(\bar{x}_B) + p^2\text{var}(\bar{x}_C).$$

Also this contrast will follow a normal distribution, so long as the distribution of each x is normal. Often each treatment will have the same replication, but provided a design is orthogonal, the treatment means will still be estimated independently of each other (as for example in Section 5.2) without having to be equally replicated. If A, B, C are replicated r_A, r_B, r_C times respectively, then the variance of $l\bar{x}_A + m\bar{x}_B + p\bar{x}_C$ is

$$l^2\frac{\sigma_A^2}{r_A} + m^2\frac{\sigma_B^2}{r_B} + p^2\frac{\sigma_C^2}{r_C}. \qquad (3.6.1)$$

In experimental work we can usually assume $\sigma_A^2 = \sigma_B^2 = \sigma_C^2 = \sigma^2$ say, and an estimate of σ^2 is found from the residual 'error' mean square in analysis of variance. This estimate has the same degrees of freedom as the 'error' mean square, i.e. f. The estimated variance of the contrast is then

$$s^2 \left(\frac{l^2}{r_A} + \frac{m^2}{r_B} + \frac{p^2}{r_C} \right) \tag{3.6.2}$$

and it has f d.f.

In the example above, $\bar{x}_A - \frac{1}{2}(\bar{x}_B + \bar{x}_C)$ $(= d)$ is an estimate of $\mu_A - \frac{1}{2}(\mu_B + \mu_C)$, and it has variance

$$s^2 \left(\frac{1}{r_A} + \frac{1}{4r_B} + \frac{1}{4r_C} \right) = V, \text{ say,}$$

with f d.f. Then a 95 percent confidence interval ($P = 0.05$) for the true value $\mu_A - \frac{1}{2}(\mu_B + \mu_C)$ $(= \delta)$ is

$$d - t\sqrt{V} < \delta < d + t\sqrt{V} \tag{3.6.3}$$

in which t stands for the upper and lower 5 percent points of Student's t with f d.f.

Although significance tests for contrasts are usually done in an analysis of variance as F-tests, there is an equivalent t-test of the hypothesis that the true value of the contrast is zero. In the example above, if

$$\mu_A = \frac{1}{2}(\mu_B + \mu_C) \tag{3.6.4}$$

then

$$t = \frac{\bar{x}_A - \frac{1}{2}(\bar{x}_B + \bar{x}_C)}{\sqrt{V}}$$

follows the t-distribution with f d.f. and can be tested in the same way as any other t-variable.

3.7 The Binomial distribution and proportions

When counting the number of items of a special type among a random sample of n members from a population, let us denote the number of the special type found in the sample by r. Suppose the following conditions hold:

(i) the sample size n is fixed before selection begins;
(ii) the proportion of special type in the whole population is p, and this remains unchanged throughout the sampling, as each fresh member is selected: the population being sampled must therefore be large, or at least capable of regenerating according to the same rules, as in genetic inheritance.

Then r follows the biomial distribution, given by

$$Prob\ (r) = \frac{n!}{r!(n-r)!}p^r(1-p)^{n-r} \quad \text{for } r = 0, 1, 2, \ldots, n$$

where $n!$ stands for n-factorial, i.e.

$$n! = n \times (n-1) \times (n-2) \times \ldots \times 3 \times 2 \times 1.$$

After repeated sampling, each sample being of size n, the distribution of r has mean np and variance $np(1-p)$.

Often the sample proportion $\hat{p} = r/n$ is of interest; this has a distribution whose mean is p and variance $p(1-p)/n$. It follows that the distribution is not going to be exactly normal. For one thing there is no constant variance, σ^2; for another, the distribution is not symmetrical unless $p = 0.5$. However, when n is large (in practice, greater than 100 is usually satisfactory) and p is not too near 0 or 1 (say in the range 0.1 to 0.9) the distribution of a sample proportion can be taken as approximately normal, with mean p and variance $p(1-p)/n$. Confidence intervals and significance tests can therefore be calculated as though we were dealing with a normal distribution, though the results obtained are approximate rather than exact theoretically.

A 95 percent confidence interval for the true value of p, based on a sample of n giving a sample proportion $\hat{p}$, is given by

$$\hat{p} - 1.96\sqrt{\frac{\hat{p}(1-\hat{p})}{n}} < p < \hat{p} + 1.96\sqrt{\frac{\hat{p}(1-\hat{p})}{n}} \qquad (3.7.1)$$

The hypothesis that p is the true proportion is tested by calculating

$$Z = \frac{\hat{p} - p}{\sqrt{p(1-p)/n}}$$

and testing it as a standard normal variable. We note that (3.7.1) is an analogue of (3.4.1) with $V = p(1-p)/n$.

If two samples of sizes n_1 and n_2 are available, giving sample proportions $\hat{p}_1 = r_1/n_1$ and $\hat{p}_2 = r_2/n_2$ of the same special type of member, it is often required to test the hypothesis that the true proportions are the same, i.e. $p_1 = p_2 = p$. If this is true then $\hat{p}_1$ has variance $p(1-p)/n_1$ and $\hat{p}_2$ has variance $p(1-p)/n_2$; the best estimate of p using all the data from both samples is $\hat{p} = (r_1 + r_2)/(n_1 + n_2)$ and this is what must be used in the test. The variance of $(\hat{p}_1 - \hat{p}_2)$ is

$$\left[\frac{\hat{p}(1 - \hat{p})}{n_1} + \frac{\hat{p}(1 - \hat{p})}{n_2} \right]$$

which we write S^2 for short. If $p_1 = p_2$ then $Z = (\hat{p}_1 - \hat{p}_2)/S$ is approximately a standard normal variable and can be treated as in Section 3.2.

An approximate 95 percent confidence interval for the true difference $p_1 - p_2$ does not of course make the assumption that they have common value p, and therefore the expression for variance is different from S^2: it is instead

$$\left(\frac{\hat{p}_1(1 - \hat{p}_1)}{n_1} + \frac{\hat{p}_2(1 - \hat{p}_2)}{n_2} \right) = V, \text{ say.}$$

Then a 95 per cent confidence interval for $(p_1 - p_2)$ follows from

$$Prob \left((\hat{p}_1 - \hat{p}_2) - 1.96\sqrt{V} < (p_1 - p_2) < (\hat{p}_1 - \hat{p}_2) + 1.96\sqrt{V} \right) = 0.95$$
(3.7.2)

This is a further analogue of (3.4.1).

The methods described above are satisfactory for simple tests and inferences about binomially distributed variables and proportions. But observations of $\hat{p}$ can only be subjected to analysis of variance after transformation (see Chapter 9).

3.8 Measurements following the Poisson distribution

When counting items that arise independently of one another, at random in space (or time), the Poisson distribution may be appropriate. If the items (for example, insects, lesions on a leaf, or weeds) occur at a constant average rate of m per unit area, and if a large number of unit areas are counted, the actual number of items in each unit being c, then the distribution of c follows the Poisson. If the rate per unit area, m, does not remain constant over a complete population of units being studied then the Poisson distribution will not be a suitable model. Another case where it does not work is when the items being counted are not fully independent of one another but tend to arise in groups.

The mean and the variance are both equal to m in a Poisson distribution, and if m is greater than about 5, the Poisson variable c can be well approximated by a normal distribution whose mean and variance are both m. These results lead to approximate confidence intervals and to methods of testing which are similar to those already described. If a single Poisson variable c has variance m, then the mean of n observations $\bar{c}$ will have variance m/n. Hence an approximate 95% confidence interval for the true value of m, using its sample estimate $\bar{c}$, is given by

$$Prob \left(\bar{c} - 1.96 \sqrt{\frac{\bar{c}}{n}} < m < \bar{c} + 1.96 \sqrt{\frac{\bar{c}}{n}} \right) = 0.95. \qquad (3.8.1)$$

Also, the sample may be used to test a hypothesis that the true mean is M, by calculating $Z = (c - M)/\sqrt{M/n}$ and treating Z as a standard normal variable (as described in Section 3.2).

Poisson distributions often form suitable models also for counts taken over time, such as numbers of radioactive particles emitted per minute from a source, and for counts per unit volume such as the number of organisms per ml of liquid. The same conditions must hold, namely that items arise individually (not in groups) at random at a constant average rate (per minute or per ml).

As in the binomial case, a transformation (see Chapter 9) is needed if data following Poisson distributions are to be used in an analysis of variance.

3.9 Uses of tests and estimates

As was remarked in Section 3.3, skill in data analyses lies largely in knowing what to test and what to estimate. Several methods for doing what may be appropriate have been set out in this chapter, but when should each be used?

The answer in any instance must depend upon the questions asked of an experiment. Unless they are clearly understood, the answers may well be irrelevant to the experimenter's needs. The quality chiefly needed in planning an experiment is clear-headedness. Once the experimental problem is perceived with sufficient clarity, it is to be hoped that someone has the statistical skill to solve it. If no one has the skill, it can perhaps be acquired by reading, whether in this book or another. There is nothing to be said for by-passing the whole consideration and using some test because it looks impressive or because the computer package makes it available.

As long as there are only two treatments, all tests come to the same conclusion. As will be explained in the next Section, the t-test at (3.4.4) with $D = 0$ is the same as the F-test in Section 3.5. The difficulties come when there are more than two treatments, because then there are several contrasts that could be examined. Which are the important ones and how are they related?

We will suppose that there are four treatments, A, B, C, D, and we will suppose that they give means of 25, 29, 28 and 32 units respectively. If we are going to rely upon t-tests, we have to look at all six differences, i.e.

$$(A - B), - 4 \qquad (B - C), + 1$$

$$(A - C), - 3 \qquad (B - D), - 3$$
$$(A - D), - 7 \qquad (C - D), - 4$$

We might find that only $(A - D)$ was significant at $P = 0.05$. We can scarcely declare in general that there are treatment differences when only one out of six has shown up at the level of one-in-twenty. On the other hand, an F-test, which averages the six contrasts, may declare them collectively not to be significant. A procedure that allows a genuine effect to be missed by diluting it with a lot of others is equally unsatisfactory. What then is to be done?

One much-used technique is that of multiple comparisons based on one of the various multiple range tests. We strongly urge you not to use them. What they do is to search out the largest difference, in this example $(A - D)$, and to examine its significance, bearing in mind that it has been selected from six possible candidates. As a piece of probability theory that is all right, but it does not relate to practicalities. The treatments are not nameless, their characters being of no importance, but a set, carefully selected to answer the questions under study, and we must know what those questions are. A procedure that ignores purpose and would give the same answer whatever the nature of A, B, C and D is clearly inadequate, if not downright wrong. The correct procedure is that presented in Chapter 5, i.e. the purpose of the experiment should be expressed as contrasts of interest, which are then tested or estimated. When we can write down the questions in a form that relates to the analysis of variance, we can try to use our analysis to find the answers.

Is there then no need for the F-test, which is really a test of a composite hypothesis? It can in fact be useful in answering general questions, especially in conditional situations. To return to the example with four treatments, A, B, C and D, we might learn that the treatments represented increasing applications of fertilizer. Further enquiry to elucidate the questions might reveal that there were two, the second conditional upon the first:

(i)   Do the figures suggest a departure from a straight-line relationship of yield on fertilizer application?
(ii) *If so*, what is the shape of the response curve?
      If not, what is the ratio of increased yield to increased fertilizer?

The general question at (i) calls for a test to decide what to do at (ii).

However, as has been said, estimation is more usually appropriate than testing, because mostly people know more or less what will happen and they want it quantified. That in no way diminishes the need to find out exactly the purpose of the investigation. When we give a figure for the quantity being estimated, we must append a variance or a standard error so that a judgement can be made as to the precision of our estimate. We have mentioned this in Section 3.6 and we shall return to it in Section 5.2.

3.10 Computational procedures

Before leaving the subject some words are needed on computation. From what has been said it will be clear that the difference between estimation and testing is one of logic. The aim is to provide answers relevant to the questions being asked. When it comes to the calculations, however, there is little difference. For most of the procedures already presented and for most of those that will come later, the main arithmetical operations are the same.

(i)   Data are collected and it is believed that they are all subject to the same sources of variance, the effect of which is represented by σ^2. (Note that the Binomial and Poisson distributions negate that assumption from the start.)

(ii)   Methods are sought of finding a quantity, s^2, that will provide an estimate of σ^2. Once s^2 is found, we call s 'the standard error of an observation'. Sometimes the variance is found as in (3.3.1), but in the analysis of variance, s^2 is taken to be the 'error' mean-square as at (1.3.3). Sometimes other methods are used.

(iii)   Each standard error, s, when found is associated with a certain number of degrees of freedom, which measure the amount of information used in its estimation. If there were an infinite number of degrees of freedom, Section 3.3 would reduce to Section 3.2, i.e. σ would be known. At the other extreme, with few data, the number of degrees of freedom may be barely sufficient.

(iv)   Attention is then concentrated on some quantity A, chosen because it gives the required information. Thus, in Section 3.3 A was the mean of a sample of n data. The mathematicians are now called in to find the standard error of A in terms of s. In the case of the sample mean they reply that it is $s/\sqrt{n}$. In other cases they may give expressions that are more complicated.

At this point estimation and testing diverge though not in arithmetic. In estimation, confidence limits are put round the estimate of A with limits $A \pm t \times$ (the standard error of A), where t is looked up in tables using the appropriate significance level and the number of degrees of freedom. That was done at (3.6.3). If, on the other hand, someone wants to test whether A has its expected value, a, the procedure is to take $(A - a)$, divide by the standard error of A and ask whether the result is less than t, the same value being used as before. That was done at (3.6.4), a being zero. In a sense this comes down to asking whether a lies within the confidence limits of A. The difference lies not in the arithmetic but in the motivation for doing it.

The F-test may appear to be different and it is so because it tests a composite hypothesis. It does not ask if A differs from B, but whether A, B, C, ..., etc. differ among themselves. That is both its strength and its weakness. It asks a general question, which can also be a confused one. If, however, there are only two quantities, A and B, to be compared, it becomes in effect a t-test. That can be seen easily by looking at tables. If there is only one contrast under study, the F-test has one and f degrees of freedom. Then at any significance level, $F = t^2$ where t has f degrees of freedom. To take an example, for $P = 0.01$ and twelve degrees of freedom, $t = 3.055$. For the same P and $(1, 12)$ degrees of freedom. $F = 9.33 = t^2$. In fact, whenever the two tests are both available, they will always give the same answer.

Note: The general practice in this text will be to cite F-values in the analyses of variance as a matter of course, despite the reserve expressed in Section 3.9 as to their not always being appropriate. We shall do so because an F-value gives a general indication how far there are treatment differences to be sought, though it will be understood that there could be important effects of treatments when the overall F is not significant. Further, we shall adopt the convention of using one asterisk, *, to indicate a significance level of $P = 0.05$, two, **, for $P = 0.01$ and three, ***, for $P = 0.001$.

Exercise 3A

64 observations are selected at random from a normal distribution whose variance is 25. Their mean is calculated and found to be 11.1. Test the hypothesis that the true value of the population mean is 10.

Exercise 3B

200 observations are selected at random from a distribution whose mean is thought to be 5 and variance known to be 8. The mean of the 200 observations is 4.77. Test the hypothesis that the population mean is 5.

Repeat this for a sample size of 20 with the same mean instead of 200.

Exercise 3C

A group of 10 strawberry plants is grown in ground treated with a chemical soil-conditioner, and the mean yield per plant is 114 g. Experience has shown that when the same variety of strawberry is grown under similar conditions, but with no soil-conditioner, the mean has been 110 g and the variance 84. Test whether it can reasonably be claimed that the soil-conditioner had a beneficial effect on yield.

Exercise 3D

The weights of a large number of plants taken at random in a region have been measured, and the mean and variance in this population are respectively 102 lb and 49 lb^2. If 100 plants from an adjacent region are weighed in bulk, and their mean weight is 99 lb, is there any evidence that the plants in the second region are of a different size from that in the first? If only five plants had been available, how would you examine their weight records?

Exercise 3E

8 observations from a normal distribution were 1.6, − 0.8, 0.1, − 0.4, 1.2, 0.7, 0.3, 0.5. Test the null hypothesis that the distribution has mean 0.1. Also set 95 percent and 99 percent confidence limits to the true value of this mean.

Exercise 3F

A random sample of 25 seeds of a given variety is planted in pots. The mean time from planting to opening of the first leaflet is 5.8 days. The variance estimated from the data was 4.84. Assuming that this time is normally distributed, test the hypothesis that its mean is 4. Also set 99 percent confidence limits to its true value.

Exercise 3G

Two samples of observations on the diameters of fungal mycelium colonies gave these results: Sample A of 11 observations had mean 6.65

and variance 15.2824, while Sample B of 16 observations had mean 4.28 and variance 8.0275. (Both variances were estimated from the data.) Assume the diameter to be normally distributed. Find a pooled estimate of variance (check that it is valid to 'pool'). Test the null hypothesis that the samples came from distributions with the same mean. Also set, separately for Samples A and B, 95 percent confidence intervals for the true values of their means. Comment on the results.

Exercise 3H

Soya bean seedlings were grown in pairs of adjacent pots, one pot of each pair being watered twice as often as the other (with half the volume each time). The differences in height at the end of a given period of time (expressed as more regular *minus* less regular in each pair) were + 6.0, + 1.3, + 3.1, + 6.8, − 1.5, + 4.2, − 3.3, + 2.7, + 10.2, + 0.1, − 0.4 mm. Test whether regularity of watering made a significant difference to height.

Also set 95 percent confidence limits to the true difference in height due to regularity of watering.

Exercise 3I

Seedlings from a specially bred population have in the past shown normally distributed weight increases, with variance 15 units, when grown in standard conditions for a fixed period. Six new seedlings are selected at random, and grown for the same fixed time at a higher temperature. Their weight increases are 18, 21, 12, 16, 25, 20 units. Are they more variable in growth than those fed on the standard diet?

Exercise 3J

Repeat Exercise 3I, assuming that any change in variability due to a higher temperature will be an increase and cannot be a decrease.

Exercise 3K

The height to which seedlings of two apple varieties (A and B) grow in standard conditions in a greenhouse is assumed to be normally distributed. From A, 10 seedlings grow 44, 26, 1, 79, 53, 38, 62, 80, 33, 13 cm and from B, 12 seedlings grow 33, 47, 55, 39, 24, 61, 38, 12, 26, 64, 52, 51 cm. Test the null hypothesis that the variance of height is the same in both varieties. Also set 95 percent confidence limits to the true value of variance for each variety.

Exercise 3L

A large normal population has mean 100 and variance 10. Find 95 percent confidence limits to

(a) the value of one single observation drawn from this population.
(b) the mean value of 10 randomly selected observations from this population,
(c) the mean of 100 randomly selected observations from this population.

If the variance had not been known, how could limits be found?

Exercise 3M

A sample of 9 plants of the same variety were grown in one type of soil in a greenhouse and after a fixed time they were removed and dried. Their dry weights were 25.5, 22.3, 24.7, 28.1, 26.5, 19.0, 31.0, 25.3, 29.6 g. A further sample of 11 similar plants were grown in identical conditions but in another type of soil. Their dry weights were 31.8, 30.3, 26.4, 24.2, 27.8, 29.1, 25.5, 28.9, 30.0, 26.9, 29.7 g. Do the two soil types have different effects on the plants?

Exercise 3N

Two formulations of an insecticide are tried out by a number of farmers. Preparation A is given to 250 farmers, of whom 172 claim it is effective; B is given to 200, of whom 158 say it is effective. Is there evidence of a difference between A and B? (It may be assumed that the 450 farmers were fairly chosen at random.) Also find the approximate confidence limits (95 percent) for the proportion of satisfied farmers who had used each of A, B. For preparation A, how many farmers would be needed in order to estimate the proportion of successes to within ± 3% (with 95 percent confidence)?

Exericse 30

50 samples, each of unit volume, were drawn at random from a liquid suspension containing cells. Each sample was examined under a microscope, on a slide, and the average number of cells per unit volume for these 50 samples was 4. Set approximate 95 percent confidence limits to the mean number of cells per unit volume in the whole suspension.

Chapter 4

Analysis of variance from non-orthogonal designs

4.1 Why use non-orthogonal designs?

Although there are considerable simplifications resulting from the use of orthogonal designs as defined in Sections 1.3 and 1.5, there are times when the experimenter has to resort to non-orthogonality. For example, the land may be a narrow strip running downhill and only wide enough to take at most three plots across itself. Clearly, blocks should be formed on the basis of altitude, which means that each must contain three plots of minimum size or perhaps two larger ones. If the number of treatments exceeds three, a non-orthogonal design is unavoidable. If there were four, to take the example further, it would be possible to leave out each treatment in turn, like this:

Block					
I	B	A	D	leaving out	C
II	C	B	A	leaving out	D
III	B	D	C	leaving out	A
IV	C	A	D	leaving out	B

Sometimes too the design was originally orthogonal, but someone made a mistake in executing it and the experimenter is left to analyse the data that have in fact been obtained, though the design is not what was intended. The situation may be quite complicated.

There is no need to be afraid of non-orthogonality. It is better avoided because of the complications it causes, but if no orthogonal design will fit the site or if mistakes have been made, the data can be analysed in a completely valid manner. In Sections 4.2 and 4.5 a method will be given that can be used with any block design, provided it has been randomized. (That is not quite true because the method of finding variances, given in Section 4.3, can cause difficulties with some of the 'confounded' designs to be presented in Chapter 7, but those difficulties can be overcome.) Simpler methods will be described (Sections 4.7 to 4.12) for some of the commoner forms of non-orthogonality that might be introduced deliberately. (Where it was not intended but arose as the result of an accident, mostly the general method has to be used.)

In these days of computers it may be asked why analytical difficulties should stand in the way of using desirable designs. The question is a good one, but non-orthogonal designs have a further disadvantage. It relates to the variances of contrasts. If the 'error' mean square is written as s^2,

$$\text{the variance of a contrast} = Ks^2, \qquad (4.1.1)$$

where the constant, K, depends upon the contrast seen in relation to the design. The expressions (3.6.1) and (3.6.2) give K for orthogonal designs. For non-orthogonal designs K can never be less than the values so obtained and usually it will be more; that is to say, the variances of contrasts may be inflated. (In choosing a non-orthogonal design a large part of the skill lies in arranging that the contrasts of least interest shall be the ones to suffer most.) To understand exactly where the inflation occurs it is necessary to work out an array of figures called the 'covariance matrix'. Its full use will become apparent in Chapter 5; here it will be used only in a limited way.

The mention of matrices may alarm some readers, but there is no need for that. For purposes of reading the present text it is necessary only to know what a matrix is. It is an array of numbers, written in rows and columns, such that meaning can be attached both to the rows and to the columns. It is in fact what most people call a 'table of figures'. It is true that mathematicians have developed an advanced system of algebra to deal with matrices and true also that nowadays the theory of experiment designs depends upon that system. Nevertheless no knowledge of matrix algebra is required for an understanding of this book. To continue with nomenclature, the numbers entered in a matrix are called its 'elements'. There will be one concession to the mathematicians. Where a symbol represents a group of values, not a single value, following the practice in matrix algebra it will be printed in bold face type.

In this chapter the analysis of variance for a non-orthogonal design will be treated in the same way that Sections 1.3 and 1.4 dealt with the analysis for orthogonal designs. That is to say, only arithmetic will be considered. Interpretation can come later.

4.2 The analysis of variance for any block design

The following method ('the Kuiper–Corsten iteration') applies whether the design is orthogonal or not. (If it is orthogonal, simpler methods are available.)

Consider the following data from a non-orthogonal design:

Block   I   A, 14   C, 16   D, 14   E, 17
       II   B, 12   A, 11   D, 13   C, 16
      III   E, 16   C, 17   B, 17   A, 14   (4.2.1)
      IV   D, 19   B, 15   E, 16   A,   9

The block means are I, 15.25; II, 13.00; III, 16.00; IV, 14.75. Sweeping by them gives

Block   I   A, -1.25 C, $+0.75$ D, -1.25 E, $+1.75$
       II   B, -1.00 A, -2.00 D,   0.00   C, $+3.00$
      III   E,   0.00   C, $+1.00$ B, $+1.00$ A, -2.00 (4.2.2)
      IV   D, $+4.25$ B, $+0.25$ E, $+1.25$ A, -5.75

The deviations correctly add to zero in each block. The treatment means are now A, -2.75; B, $+0.08$; C, $+1.58$; D, $+1.00$; E, $+1.00$. They will be called collectively, v_1. Sweeping by them gives

Block   I   A, $+1.50$ C, -0.83 D, -2.25 E, $+0.75$
       II   B, -1.08 A, $+0.75$ D, -1.00 C, $+1.42$
      III   E, -1.00 C, -0.58 B, $+0.92$ A, $+0.75$ (4.2.3)
      IV   D, $+3.25$ B, $+0.17$ E, $+0.25$ A, -3.00

Although these quantities sum to zero over treatments they do not do so over blocks, as residuals should. (If the design had been orthogonal they would have done so.) As it is, they give block means of

$$I, -0.21; \ II, +0.02; \ III, +0.02; \ IV, +0.17,$$

which quantities will be called u_1. Sweeping by u_1 gives

Block   I   A, $+1.71$ C, -0.62 D, -2.04 E, $+0.96$
       II   B, -1.10 A, $+0.73$ D, -1.02 C, $+1.40$
      III   E, -1.02 C, -0.60 B, $+0.90$ A, $+0.73$ (4.2.4)
      IV   D, $+3.08$ B,   0.00   E, $+0.08$ A, -3.17

In turn (4.2.4) gives rise to treatment means, v_2, namely

$$A, 0.00; \quad B, -0.07; \quad C, +0.06; \quad .D, +0.01; \quad E, +0.01.$$

Clearly this process can continue, v_2 forming u_2, u_2 forming v_3 and so on until a set of zeros is obtained. The deviations obtained at that stage can fairly be regarded as residuals, since they will sum to zero over both blocks and treatments. In effect the original data at (4.2.1) will have been swept first by blocks and then by $V = \Sigma v_j$ and $U = \Sigma u_i$.

These calculations are best set out in the form of the Kuiper–Corsten iteration. There is one further point of nomenclature: the symbol Q is used to represent the treatment totals in (4.2.2). Here Q equals $(-11.00 + 0.25 + 4.75 + 3.00 + 3.00)$ for the treatments A to E in order.

The first step is to write down the 'incidence matrix'. It has a row for each treatment and a column for each block. The values in it show the number of times that treatment occurs in that block. To the right of it is written v_1, but space has to be left for v_2, v_3, etc., which will be derived later.

$$
\begin{array}{cccc@{\qquad}r@{\qquad}l}
 & & & & v_1 & \\
1 & 1 & 1 & 1 & -2.75 & \\
0 & 1 & 1 & 1 & +0.08 & \\
1 & 1 & 1 & 0 & +1{,}58 & (4.2.5) \\
1 & 1 & 0 & 1 & +1.00 & \\
1 & 0 & 1 & 1 & +1.00 &
\end{array}
$$

The next step is to work out u_1. It is formed by multiplying out successive columns of the incidence matrix and v_1; the result is then divided by the respective block size, i.e.,

$$
\begin{aligned}
u_1 &= (-2.75 + 1.58 + 1.00 + 1.00)/4 &&= +0.21 \\
& (-2.75 + 0.08 + 1.58 + 1.00)/4 &&= -0.02 \\
& (-2.75 + 0.08 + 1.58 + 1.00)/4 &&= -0.02 \\
& (-2.75 + 0.08 + 1.00 + 1.00)/4 &&= -0.17
\end{aligned}
$$

It should be written horizontally below the incidence matrix. Then each row of the incidence matrix is successively multiplied out by the values of u_1 and then the sum divided by the appropriate treatment replication, to form v_2, i.e.

$$
\begin{aligned}
v_2 &= (\;\;0.21 - 0.02 - 0.02 - 0.17)/4 &&= \;\;\;0.00 \\
& (-0.02 - 0.02 - 0.17)/3 &&= -0.07 \\
& (\;\;0.21 - 0.02 - 0.02)/3 &&= +0.06 \\
& (\;\;0.21 - 0.02 - 0.17)/3 &&= +0.01 \\
& (\;\;0.21 - 0.02 - 0.17)/3 &&= +0.01
\end{aligned}
$$

Those values are then written to the right of v_1. Next u_2 is formed from v_2 in the same way that u_1 was formed from v_1, i.e.

$$
\begin{aligned}
u_2 &= (\;\;0.00 + 0.06 + 0.01 + 0.01)/4 &&= +0.02 \\
& (\;\;0.00 - 0.07 + 0.06 + 0.01)/4 &&= \;\;\;0.00
\end{aligned}
$$

$$(0.00 - 0.07 + 0.06 + 0.01)/4 \quad = \quad 0.00 \qquad (4.2.6)$$
$$(0.00 - 0.07 + 0.01 + 0.01)/4 \quad = -0.01$$

The values of $\mathbf{u}_2$ are written horizontally below $\mathbf{u}_1$ and they give rise to $\mathbf{v}_3$. There is no need to go on because all the values are now less than 3% of the precision to which the data were measured, which was to the nearest unit. All values in $\mathbf{v}_3$ lie between ± 0.03 so the iteration can be discontinued. The treatment effects, $\mathbf{V}$, can be found by summing $\mathbf{v}_1$, $\mathbf{v}_2$, $\mathbf{v}_3$, etc., i.e.

$$-2.75 \quad +0.01 \quad +1.65 \quad +1.01 \quad +1.01 \qquad (4.2.7)$$

for the five treatments, A to E in that order. However, these changes in the estimates of treatment effects need consequent changes in the estimates of block effects. They are found by calculating $\mathbf{U}$, which is the sum of $\mathbf{u}_1$, $\mathbf{u}_2$, etc., i.e. I, $+0.23$; II, -0.02; III, -0.02; IV, -0.18.

With these revised figures it becomes possible to calculate the residuals again. Thus, to take the first plot (Treatment A in Block I) its residual is obtained from its deviation (-1.25) by adding the element of $\mathbf{U}$ $(+0.23)$ and subtracting the treatment effect, i.e. the element of $\mathbf{V}$ (-2.75). That gives 1.73. The residuals are therefore:

Block					
	I	A, $+1.73$	C, -0.67	D, -2.03	E, $+0.97$
	II	B, -1.03	A, $+0.73$	D, -1.03	C, $+1.33$
	III	E, -1.03	C, -0.67	B, $+0.97$	A, $+0.73$
	IV	D, $+3.05$	B, $+0.05$	E, $+0.05$	A, -3.19

It will be seen that they now correctly sum to zero in all blocks and in all treatments, at least within the limits set by rounding.

The stratum total sum of squares is found in the usual way by summing the squares of the deviations set out in (4.2.2) i.e. $(-1.25)^2 + (0.75)^2 + \ldots + (-5.75)^2 = 79.5000$. It has the usual degrees of freedom, namely 12. (It may be noted that deviations should be calculated ignoring treatments; consequently, the procedure just adopted is correct despite the later adjustment of block means using $\mathbf{U}$.) The 'error' sum of squares is likewise found by summing the squares of the residuals set out in (4.2.7) i.e. $(+1.73)^2 + (-0.67)^2 + \ldots + (-3.19)^2 = 35.394\,44$. There is, however, an independent way of obtaining the treatment sum of squares by multiplying out the values of $\mathbf{Q}$ with the treatment effects, $\mathbf{V}$, namely

$$(-11.00 \times -2.75) + (0.25 \times 0.01) + (4.75 \times 1.65) + (3.00 \times 1.01)$$
$$+ (3.00 \times 1.01) = 44.1500 \qquad (4.2.8)$$

with 4 degrees of freedom. It will be seen that rounding errors have prevented exact agreement, but the analysis of variance can be taken to be

Source	d.f.	s.s.	m.s.	F
Treatments	4	44.10	11.03	2.49
'Error'	8	35.39	4.424	
Stratum total	12	79.50		

$$(4.2.9)$$

The discrepancy has been resolved by taking the larger of the two estimates of 'error'.

The treatment means need adjustment because some treatments do not occur in all blocks and so receive an advantage or disadvantage according as they occur in blocks that are good or bad. The adjusted means are found by adding the values of **V** to the grand mean, which in this instance is $236/16 = 14.75$, i.e.

$$
\begin{aligned}
&\text{Adjusted mean of } A = 14.75 - 2.75 = 12.0\\
&\text{Adjusted mean of } B = 14.75 + 0.01 = 14.8\\
&\text{Adjusted mean of } C = 14.75 + 1.65 = 16.4\\
&\text{Adjusted mean of } D = 14.75 + 1.01 = 15.8\\
&\text{Adjusted mean of } E = 14.75 + 1.01 = 15.8
\end{aligned}
\qquad (4.2.10)
$$

4.3   Variances, etc.

A covariance matrix (see Section 4.1) for the adjusted treatment means can be found by the use of the iteration. To take Treatment A first, it has 4 plots, there being 16 in all. Accordingly, we take $\mathbf{v}_1$ as

$$(1/4 - 1/16, - 1/16, - 1/16, - 1/16, - 1/16)$$

$$= (+ 0.1875, - 0.0625, - 0.0625, - 0.0625, - 0.0625)$$

and enter the iteration with it at (4.2.5). The calculation makes **V** equal to $\mathbf{v}_1$, because $\mathbf{u}_1$ proves to be a series of zeros. That provides the first row of the covariance matrix.

Turning now to Treatment B, it has 3 plots, so $\mathbf{v}_1$ is now

$$(- 1/16, 1/3 - 1/16, - 1/16, - 1/16, - 1/16)$$

$$(0.0625, + 0.2708, - 0.0625, 0.0625, - 0.0625).$$

Using that as the v_1 at (4.2.5) leads to V as

$$(0.0625, +0.2936, -0.0701, -0.0701, -0.0701)$$

which gives the second row of the covariance matrix, and so on. Actually, there is no need to do more, because subsequent rows will be permutations of the second. The matrix is in fact:

$$\begin{pmatrix} +0.1875 & -0.0625 & -0.0625 & -0.0625 & -0.0625 \\ -0.0625 & +0.2936 & -0.0701 & -0.0701 & -0.0701 \\ -0.0625 & -0.0701 & +0.2936 & -0.0701 & -0.0701 \\ -0.0625 & -0.0701 & -0.0701 & +0.2936 & -0.0701 \\ -0.0625 & -0.0701 & -0.0701 & -0.0701 & +0.2936 \end{pmatrix} \quad (4.3.1)$$

As will appear in Section 5.4, it should really be multiplied throughout by the 'error' mean square i.e. 4.424. The uses of this matrix will be explained in more detail in Section 5.2. Here it suffices to show how it gives the value, K, introduced at (4.1.1). For an orthogonal design it is $(1/r_1 + 1/r_2)$, where r_1 and r_2 are the replications of the two treatments. Thus, here, if the design had been orthogonal, K for the contrast of treatments A and B would have been $(1/4 + 1/3) = 0.5833$. As it is, we must use the covariance matrix at (4.3.1). We add the diagonal elements that relate to the two treatments, namely, 0.1875 and 0.2936. From the total we subtract the two off-diagonal elements that relate to them, i.e., -0.0625 (twice). That gives

$$K = 0.1875 + 0.2936 - 2(-0.0625) = 0.6061 \quad (4.3.2)$$

which is more than 0.5833. The 'information loss', as it is called, is measured by the 'efficiency factor', which is the ratio of the two values of K, i.e. $0.5833/0.6061 = 0.962$. (We may note that the off-diagonal elements are necessarily equal because a covariance matrix is always symmetric, so their equality in this instance is no coincidence.)

Turning to the contrast between treatments B and C, if the design had been orthogonal K would have been $(1/3 + 1/3) = 0.6667$, but for the design actually used it is

$$0.2936 + 0.2936 - 2(-0.0701) = 0.7274$$

giving an efficiency factor of $0.6667/0.7274 = 0.917$. It will be noticed that the efficiency factor is not necessarily the same whatever the contrast.

The difference between the adjusted means of treatments A and B can be found from the values at (4.2.10). It is -2.8 ($= 12.0 - 14.8$). Its variance found from (4.1.1) is (0.6061×4.424), the error mean square in the analysis of variance being used as the value of s^2. Hence the variance is $2.681 = 1.64^2$, so the standard error is 1.64 and the difference equals 1.71 times its own standard error. That of course is the value of t as defined at (3.4.4), D being zero. Similarly the difference between treatments B and C is -1.6 and its standard error is 1.79, t being therefore 0.89.

4.4 A warning

The whole method depends upon two relationships:

(1) If each value of **u** is multiplied by the corresponding block size, products sum to zero.

(2) If each value of **v** is multiplied by the corresponding treatment replication, the products sum to zero.

Thus, in the first iteration, i.e. for $\mathbf{u}_1$ above (4.2.4),

$$4(+0.21 - 0.02 - 0.02 + 0.17) = 0.00$$

and for $\mathbf{v}_2$ below (4.2.4),

$$4(0.00) + 3(-0.07 + 0.06 + 0.01 + 0.01) = 0.03$$

which is near enough, but such rounding errors can build up. If the check fails badly it is wise to make it work by adding or subtracting a constant from all values. Suppose, for example, that a **v** had read

$$(-1.05 + 1.06 - 0.21 + 0.62 - 0.12)$$

which gives

$$4(-1.05) + 3(1.06 - 0.21 + 0.62 - 0.12) = -0.15.$$

It would be better to amend the **v** to:

$$(-1.04 + 1.07 - 0.20 + 0.63 - 0.11).$$

Then

$$4(-1.04) + 3(1.07 - 0.20 + 0.63 - 0.11) = +0.01,$$

which is much better.

Since differences are preserved, comparisons between treatments are unaltered.

4.5 Two simplifications

There are two main simplifications that should be noted and looked out for. One always arises when the design is orthogonal and sometimes in other instances. It is the case when $\mathbf{u}_1 = \mathbf{O}$. As a result, $\mathbf{V} = \mathbf{V}_1$ and there is no need to continue the iteration. (That occurred in Section 4.3 when finding the first row of the covariance matrix.) The other arises quite often in cases of intended non-orthogonality and occasionally when the design has become non-orthogonal on account of an accident or mistake. It will sometimes be noted that one set of values of $\mathbf{u}$ bear a constant ratio, p, to the one before. In fact, it happened at (4.2.6) with $p = 1/12$, though more decimal places are needed to see it.

$$\mathbf{u}_1 = (+\,0.2083,\ -\,0.0208,\ -\,0.0208,\ -\,0.1667)$$
$$\mathbf{u}_2 = (+\,0.0174,\ -\,0.0017,\ -\,0.0017,\ -\,0.0139)$$

If $\mathbf{u}_2 = \mathbf{u}_1/12$ then $\mathbf{v}_3 = \mathbf{v}_2/12$, $\mathbf{u}_3 = \mathbf{u}_3 = \mathbf{u}_1/12^2$, $\mathbf{v}_4 = \mathbf{v}_2/12^2$ and so on. It is known that

$$a + ap + ap^2 + ap^3 + \ldots = a/(1 - p)$$

provided $p^2 < 1$ and the summation continues without end. (Such a series is known as a geometric progression.) It follows, with $p = 1/12$ and $1/(1 - p) = 12/11$, that

$$\mathbf{V} = \mathbf{v}_1 + 12/11\ \mathbf{v}_2$$

Here $a =$ an element of $\mathbf{v}_2$ and $1/(1 - p) = 12/11$. Working out $\mathbf{V}$ by this alternative method, the results agree with (4.2.7). In fact, it gives a better answer because the summation has been taken further, not stopping at $\mathbf{v}_3$, but in this instance the $\mathbf{v}$'s are diminishing so rapidly that the advantage is small. Also

$$\mathbf{U} = 12/11\ \mathbf{u}_1.$$

In carrying out the iteration on a desk computer it is worthwhile looking out to see whether a geometric progression appears. This can save a lot of work.

4.6 Concurrences

Whenever two treatments come together in the same block, they are said to 'concur'. More generally, if treatment A occurs a times in a block and treatment B occurs b times in that block, they are said to make ab

concurrences. If such figures are summed over all blocks, the result is the number of concurrences of those two treatments in the whole experiment.

In what follows it will be assumed that all blocks are the same size, each containing k plots. The number of treatments will be written v and the number of plots, n.

4.7   Designs with total balance

If all pairs of treatments have the same number of concurrences, λ, in the experiment, the design is said to be in 'total balance'.

Block	I	A B C	Block	III	A F G	Block	VI	B E F
	II	A D E		IV	B D G		VII	C D F
				V	C E G			

Here $k = 3$, $v = 7$, $n = 21$ and $\lambda = 1$.

The above design is in 'balanced incomplete blocks', which is a particular form of total balance. The additional requirements are that all treatments are applied to the same number of plots, r, and that a treatment occurs either once in a block or not at all, never twice or more. Also $k < v$. Here $r = 3$.

Whether the design is in balanced incomplete blocks or not, if it is in total balance the following gives a general method of analysis:

(1)   Sweep the data by block means to give deviations.
(2)   Sum the deviations over treatments to give the 'adjusted treatment totals', $Q_1, Q_2, \ldots, Q_v$.   (4.7.1)
(3)   Work out the 'effective replication', R, such that $R = v\lambda/k$. In the example, $R = 7/3$.   (4.7.2)
(4)   The treatment sum of squares will equal
$$(Q_1^2 + Q_2^2 + \ldots + Q_v^2)/R. \qquad (4.7.3)$$
(5)   The quantities, Q_A/R, $Q_B/R, \ldots$, etc. are estimates of the so-called 'treatment parameters' which show the relative effects of the various treatments. They have a number of uses. For present purposes it is enough to note that the 'adjusted treatment means'—adjusted, that is to say, for the differences between blocks—are found by adding the grand mean to each treatment parameter, i.e. the adjusted mean for Treatment j is estimated by
$$\text{Grand mean} + Q_j/R. \qquad (4.7.4)$$
(6)   The variance of the difference between two adjusted treatment means is
$$2(\text{'Error' mean-square})/R. \qquad (4.7.5)$$

If an analysis of variance is attempted by use of the Kuiper–Corsten iteration, it will be found that the geometric progression starts at once with a constant ratio of $p = (v - k)/\{k(v - 1)\}$.

4.8 Designs in supplemented balance

Sometimes it is not possible for all the treatments to be equally replicated. In that case it is often possible to designate one of them 'the supplementing treatment' and allow it to be different from the rest. Sometimes that is positively advantageous, as for example in Exercise 1G, where one treatment holds a position of special importance in the scheme of the experiment. Sometimes, on the other hand, a few plots of an untreated control may be introduced into an experiment on insecticides, only to establish the existence of the pest in the area. For a design to be in 'supplemented balance', the following conditions must obtain:

(1) The supplementing treatment has r_o plots: each of the others has r.
(2) The supplementing treatment concurs λ_o times with each of the others, which concur λ times with one another.

The following is an example:

Block	I	O	B	C	D
	II	O	A	C	D
	III	O	A	B	D
	IV	O	A	B	C

Here $v = 5$, O being the supplementing treatment, $k = 4$, $r_o = 4$, $r = 3$, $\lambda_o = 3$, $\lambda = 2$.

For all such designs the Kuiper–Corsten iteration can be used, but a simpler method is available, as follows:

(1) Sweep by block means to give deviations.
(2) Sum the deviations by treatments to give adjusted treatment totals
$$Q_o, Q_1, Q_2, \ldots, Q_{v-1}. \tag{4.8.1}$$
(3) Find the two effective replications
$$R = [\lambda_o + (v - 1)\lambda]/k \tag{4.8.2}$$
and
$$R_o = R\lambda_o/\lambda.$$
(4) The treatment sum of squares is
$$Q_o^2/R_o + (Q_1^2 + Q_2^2 + \ldots + Q_{v-1}^2)/R. \tag{4.8.3}$$
(5) The treatment parameters are now estimated by
$$Q_o/R_o, Q_A/R, Q_B/R, \ldots \text{ etc.}, \tag{4.8.4}$$
each value of Q being divided by the appropriate effective replication. For most purposes it is enough to find the adjusted treatment means by adding the grand mean to each of the parameters. That is

not quite correct because no allowance is being made for the unequal replication, but the bias is usually so small as not to matter. To be precise, the quantity

$$\frac{r}{R} - \frac{r_o}{R_o} \frac{Q_o}{n} \qquad (4.8.5)$$

should be added to each value. (Here n stands for the total number of plots in the experiment.) Clearly differences between means have not been affected.

(6) The variance of the difference between two adjusted treatment means is

$$(1/R + 1/R_o)s^2 \qquad (4.8.6)$$

if the supplementing treatment is involved or $2s^2/R$ if it is not, where s^2 is the error mean square.

In the two cases $K = 1/R + 1/R_o$ and $1/R + 1/R$ respectively. This means that R and R_o have taken the places of r and r_o. In the example $R = 11/4$, $R_o = 33/8$.

4.9 Simple lattices

If there are a lot of new varieties to be tested it may not be possible to manage more than two replicates. If the number of variates is a perfect square, $v = p^2$, it is possible to use a 'simple lattice'. With such a low degree of replication it would be unreasonable to expect a high degree of precision. Nevertheless, using a simple lattice is a great improvement on having only one plot of each variety. In any case it may give the highest degree of replication possible.

The treatments are written in a square in any convenient order, e.g. for $v = 16$,

$$
\begin{array}{cccc}
A & B & C & D \\
E & F & G & H \\
I & J & K & L \\
M & N & O & P
\end{array} \qquad (4.9.1)
$$

Then eight (or $2p$) blocks are needed. The first p are made up of the rows of the square, i.e.,

Block				
I	A	B	C	D
II	E	F	G	H
III	I	J	K	L
IV	M	N	O	P

A further p are needed for the columns, i.e.

Block	V	A	E	I	M
	VI	B	F	J	N
	VII	C	G	K	O
	VIII	D	H	L	P

It will be seen that each treatment concurs once with $2(p-1)$ others and not at all with the other $(p-1)^2$.

Again the Kuiper–Corsten iteration is available, but it is usually easier to use the following:

(1) Sweep by block means to find deviations.
(2) Sum the deviations over treatments to give adjusted treatment totals, $Q_A, Q_B, \ldots, Q_P$ and assign them to a table based on the original format at (4.9.1)

				Row totals
Q_A	Q_B	Q_C	Q_D	R_1
Q_E	Q_F	Q_G	Q_H	R_2
Q_I	Q_J	Q_K	Q_L	R_3
Q_M	Q_N	Q_O	Q_P	R_4
C_1	C_2	C_3	C_4	$0 =$ the grand total
	Column totals			

From this point it will be convenient to designate each treatment by two suffixes, the first to indicate the row in the format in which it occurs and the second for the column. Thus, Q_G will become Q_{23} and so on.

(3) The values of Q are then summed over rows and columns to give row totals of $R_1, R_2, \ldots, R_p$ and column totals of $C_1, C_2, \ldots, C_p$ as above.
(4) The treatment sum of squares equals

$$\tfrac{1}{2}[\Sigma \Sigma_{i\ j} Q_{ij}^2 + (\Sigma_i R_i^2 + \Sigma_j C_j^2)/p] \tag{4.9.2}$$

(5) The parameter for Treatment ij is estimated by

$$\tfrac{1}{2}[Q_{ij} + (R_i + C_j)/p] \tag{4.9.3}$$

The adjusted treatment means are found by adding the grand mean.
(6) The variance of the difference between two adjusted treatment means is

$$\left[\frac{p+1}{p}\right]s^2 \tag{4.9.4}$$

if the treatments concur and

$$\left[\frac{p+2}{p}\right]s^2$$

if they do not. As ever, s^2 is the error mean square.

It is usually desirable to include some standard varieties for comparison with the new ones. Further, in order to obtain good comparisons with the standards, each of them can be entered into the lattice more than once. That helps to overcome the difficulty that the total number of treatments, including duplicates, must be a perfect square. Also, there should be no difficulty about obtaining more seed for the standard whereas it is likely to be in short supply for the new ones. Where the same variety is duplicated it is sensible to allot it to two treatments that otherwise would not concur. For example, given the format used at (4.9.1), if there were 14 new strains it would be sensible to allot the standard to A and G or some other non-concurring pair. If that were done, the simpler method of analysis would not be available, but it is always possible to use the Kuiper–Corsten iteration.

There are other designs for comparing numbers of varieties and some of them do not require a restriction to perfect squares. There are, for example, those of Patterson and Williams (1976) and those of Patterson and Hunter (1983). In the absence of special computer programs, it will be recalled that the Kuiper–Corsten iteration is of general application.

4.10 Triple lattices

Occasionally it is possible to find enough material for a third replicate. If that is so, a 'triple lattice' may well provide the best design.

As with a simple lattice, p^2 treatments are assigned to a square format like the one at (4.9.1). The first p blocks are derived from the rows of the format and another p blocks from the columns. Then a Latin square is applied and another p blocks derived from its letters. Thus, if the square were

$$
\begin{array}{cccc}
\alpha & \beta & \gamma & \delta \\
\delta & \gamma & \alpha & \beta \\
\gamma & \delta & \beta & \alpha \\
\beta & \alpha & \delta & \gamma
\end{array} \;,
$$

the Greek letters give four additional blocks, namely

IX	A	G	L	N	(α)
X	B	H	K	M	(β)
XI	C	F	I	P	(γ)
XII	D	E	J	O	(δ)

The method of analysis is very like that for a simple lattice. The data are first swept by block means to give deviations, which are summed according to treatments to give Q_A, Q_B, ... etc. Now comes the first change. With a simple lattice it is enough to find row totals, R_1, R_2, etc. and column totals, C_1, C_2, etc. Here it is necessary to add L_1, L_2, etc., being the Q-totals for the letters of the Latin square. From this point the general method is the same, though the algebraic expressions need modification.

The treatment sum of squares equals

$$\frac{1}{3}\left[\sum_i \sum_j Q_{ij}^2 + (\sum_i R_i^2 + \sum_j C_j^2 + \sum_h L_h^2)/(2p) \right].$$

(4.10.1)

The parameter for treatment ij is

$$\frac{1}{3}\left[Q_{ij} + (R_i + C_j + L_h)/(2p) \right].$$

(4.10.2)

and adjusted treatment means are found in the usual way by adding the grand mean to all the parameters.

The variance of the difference of two adjusted treatment means is

$$\left(\frac{2(p+1)}{3p}\right) s^2$$

(4.10.3)

if the treatments concur and

$$\left(\frac{2(p+3)}{3p}\right) s^2$$

(4.10.4)

if they do not. Again, s^2 is the error mean square in the analysis of variance.

4.11 Non-orthogonal row-and-column designs

With row-and-column designs, which have two blocking systems, there can be as much difficulty in fitting everything into the given area as with block designs, perhaps more. For example, with seven treatments, it might be possible to arrange for seven columns so that the treatments can be orthogonal to rows, but it might not be feasible to divide the area the other way to obtain seven rows. In that case, one possibility is to take the design in balanced incomplete blocks that begins Section 4.7 and rearrange it thus:

```
F   B   D   A   G   E   C
A   E   G   B   C   D   F
G   F   B   C   E   A   D
```

It will be seen that the treatments are disposed orthogonally with regard to the rows (the first blocking system) and in total balance to the columns (the second). Such a design is said to be of Type O:OT. The letter before the colon shows how the columns are disposed relative to the rows. (It is a requirement of a row-and-column design that they shall be orthogonal.) The two letters after the colon show respectively how the treatments are disposed relative to rows (here orthogonal) and to columns (here in total balance). (More specifically where, as here, the orthogonal component contains only one plot of each treatment and the non-orthogonal is in balanced incomplete blocks, the design is said to be a 'Youden square').

It will be understood here and throughout that a row-and-column design, once written down, must be randomized before it is used. First a specimen design, like that at (4.11.1), must be written down with the treatments allocated both to rows and columns in the required manner. Then the rows must be permuted at random and lastly the columns.

The analysis of data from such a design presents little difficulty. First, as for any row-and-column design, the data are swept first by row means and then by column means to give deviations. Then the deviations are summed by treatments to give the Q-values. From this point there is no need to bother further with the blocking system, whether rows or columns, to which the treatments are orthogonal. It has been dealt with completely by the sweeping. It is necessary to consider only the non-orthogonal component and that is analysed in whatever way is usual, whether by the Kuiper–Corsten iteration or by one of the special methods set out in Sections 4.7 and 4.8. An example will illustrate how all that is done. We will take a design of Type O:TO with field plan and data like this:

A 16	D 15	B 20	A 15	C 14
B 19	A 15	D 16	C 17	D 18
C 14	B 19	A 19	D 16	B 22
D 16	C 16	C 15	B 17	A 16

(4.11.1)

For the non-orthogonal component $v = 4$, $k = 5$, $r = 5$, $n = 20$, $\lambda = 6$, $R = 4.8$.

The first step is to find the deviations. Sweeping by rows gives:

A	0	D	-1	B	$+4$	A	-1	C	-2
B	$+2$	A	-2	D	-1	C	0	D	$+1$
C	-4	B	$+1$	A	$+1$	D	-2	B	$+4$
D	0	C	0	C	-1	B	$+1$	A	0

A further sweep by columns gives the deviations, namely:

A	$+0.50$	D	-0.50	B	$+3.25$	A	-0.50	C	-2.75	
B	$+2.50$	A	-1.50	D	-1.75	C	$+0.50$	D	$+0.25$	(4.11.2)
C	-3.50	B	$+1.50$	A	$+0.25$	D	-1.50	B	$+3.25$	
D	$+0.50$	C	$+0.50$	C	-1.75	B	$+1.50$	A	-0.75	

The sum of their squares gives the stratum total sum of squares, which is 64.50 with 12 degrees of freedom.

The columns are orthogonal to both rows and treatments. Their effect has therefore been completely allowed for in the sweeping; it remains to adjust the treatment effects by the rows, to which treatments are non-orthogonal.

Treatment totals of deviations, Q, can be found from (4.11.2), namely,

$$
\begin{array}{cccc}
A & B & C & D \\
-2.00 & +12.00 & -7.00 & -3.00
\end{array}
\qquad (4.11.3)
$$

The treatment sum of squares is

$$[(-2.00)^2 + (+12.00)^2 + (-7.00)^2 + (-3.00)^2]/R$$

where R was found below (4.11.1). That value is appropriate because the only non-orthogonality is that of treatments relative to rows. The columns are orthogonal both to rows and treatments, so their effect was sufficiently allowed for when sweeping by their means. Once that had been done, it was as if the design were one of treatments in the blocking system given by rows. Hence R is the effective replication both for that design and for the full design in rows and columns.

If the non-orthogonality in rows had taken some less usual form it might have been necessary to have taken treatment means at (4.11.3) to obtain the starting vector, v_1, for the Kuiper–Corsten iteration. The incidence matrix required would have been that of treatments and rows, namely,

2	1	1	1	$v_1 = -0.40$
1	1	2	1	$+2.40$
1	1	1	2	-1.40
1	2	1	1	-0.60

However, none of that is necessary here, where the non-orthogonality has a defined form. We note that R has already been worked out from (4.7.2) and equals 4.8, so the treatment sum of squares from (4.11.3) is 42.92. It has three degrees of freedom, so the analysis of variance reads:

Source	d.f.	s.s.	m.s.	F
Treatments	3	42.92	14.307	5.97
'Error'	9	21.58	2.398	
Stratum total	12	64.50		

As to treatment means, no adjustment is needed on account of the columns, which are orthogonal with respect to the treatments, but it is required for the rows, which are non-orthogonal. In this instance (4.7.4) applies. The grand mean is 16.75 so the adjusted means are:

A	B	C	D
16.33	19.25	15.29	16.12

The variance of the difference of two adjusted means is shown by (4.7.5) to be $0.9992 = (0.9996)^2$.

Other non-orthogonal components may be used. The following design arose when the statisticians were asked for a plan to add treatments, O, A, B, C, and D to an experiment in which there were four blocks of ten rootstocks, each plot containing a single cherry tree. The treatments were (A, B, C, D), the injection of four different viruses, or (O), not injecting anything. The design was like this:

Rootstocks

Blocks	a	b	c	d	e	f	g	h	i	j	
I	B	C	B	A	C	D	A	O	O	D	
II	O	D	C	B	O	C	B	A	D	A	(4.11.4)
III	A	A	O	D	B	B	O	D	C	C	
IV	C	O	D	C	A	A	D	B	B	O	

The treatments are orthogonal to rows and in total balance relative to columns, i.e. the design is of Type O:OT.

In general, it is better to avoid designs in which the treatments are non-orthogonal to both rows and columns. For one thing, they are usually very complex; for another, any non-orthogonality loses information. It is bad enough to have the information loss from one blocking system without having it from two.

The last point needs a little explanation. A completely randomized design, i.e. one without blocks, is said to be 'of full efficiency'. If two treatments have replications of r_1 and r_2 plots, the variance of the difference between their means (see Section 3.4) is

$$Ks^2, \quad \text{where } K = 1/r_1 + 1/r_2. \tag{4.11.5}$$

We will first consider block designs. When they are orthogonal, there is no 'information loss', and the expression at (4.11.5) still applies, but not if there is non-orthogonality. With a non-orthogonal row-and-column design the position is worse because there could then be two information losses, one due to the rows and the other to the columns. For that reason, doubly non-orthogonal designs are better avoided as being inefficient, though there are occasions when practical considerations leave no alternative. Also, the better local control and the consequent reduction in s^2 could outweigh the loss of efficiency. One simple form will be described in the next section.

4.12 Supplemented balance in both rows and columns

When the designer of an experiment is in real difficulties with the land and is not able to contrive rows and columns that will permit orthogonality, he is in a most awkward situation. There is, however, one class of doubly non-orthogonal row-and-column design that is quite feasible and not too difficult to evolve. It is the class in which the treatments are in supplemented balance with regard to both rows and columns, i.e. those Type O:SS.

Examples are easily given. First, there is the Latin square in which one row and one column are omitted, the two intersecting in a plot with the supplementing treatment, e.g.

A	B	C*	D	O						
C	O	B*	A	D	giving	A	B	D	O	(4.12.1)
B*	D*	O*	C*	A*		C	O	A	D	
O	A	D*	B	C		O	A	B	C	
D	C	A*	O	B		D	C	O	B	

Plots marked with an asterisk are to be omitted

Then there is the Latin square with a row and column added, the additional plot at their intersection being assigned the supplementing treatment, e.g.

$$
\begin{array}{ccc|c}
\text{A} & \text{O} & \text{B} & \text{B} \\
\text{B} & \text{A} & \text{O} & \text{A} \\
\text{O} & \text{B} & \text{A} & \text{O} \\
\hline
\text{O} & \text{A} & \text{B} & \text{O}
\end{array}
\quad \text{giving} \quad
\begin{array}{cccc}
\text{A} & \text{O} & \text{B} & \text{B} \\
\text{B} & \text{A} & \text{O} & \text{A} \\
\text{O} & \text{B} & \text{A} & \text{O} \\
\text{O} & \text{A} & \text{B} & \text{O}
\end{array}
\tag{4.12.2}
$$

Also, there is the Latin square with a column added and a row omitted, the supplementing treatment being at the intersection, e.g.

$$
\begin{array}{ccccc|c}
\text{B} & \text{D} & \text{O} & \text{A} & \text{C} & \text{B} \\
\text{O} & \text{C} & \text{D} & \text{B} & \text{A} & \text{C} \\
\text{C} & \text{A} & \text{B} & \text{O} & \text{D} & \text{A} \\
\text{D*} & \text{O*} & \text{A*} & \text{C*} & \text{B*} & \text{O*} \\
\text{A} & \text{B} & \text{C} & \text{D} & \text{O} & \text{D}
\end{array}
\quad \text{giving} \quad
\begin{array}{cccccc}
\text{B} & \text{D} & \text{O} & \text{A} & \text{C} & \text{B} \\
\text{O} & \text{C} & \text{D} & \text{B} & \text{A} & \text{C} \\
\text{C} & \text{A} & \text{B} & \text{O} & \text{D} & \text{A} \\
\text{A} & \text{B} & \text{C} & \text{D} & \text{O} & \text{D}
\end{array}
\tag{4.12.3}
$$

Again plots marked with an asterisk are to be omitted.

There are many other possibilities. For example, if at (4.11.4) there had been only nine rootstocks, the omission of the last column would have given a design of Type O:SS. Such designs need to be validated in the usual way by a random permutation of rows followed by a random permutation of columns. Also, they are best suited to problems in which one treatment does have a different status from the rest. If that is not so, a difficult choice has to be made. Nevertheless, it will usually be better to proceed with a design that is statistically less than perfect if the alternative is to use a system of rows and columns that makes difficulties in the field. (Another occasion for using such designs will appear in Section 10.8.)

The method of analysis is not difficult. First, as for any other row-and-column design, it is necessary to sweep by rows and then by columns to find the deviations. The treatment totals of deviations will be written **Q**, as before.

It is now necessary to find R and R_o for the row-and-column design. Both follow easily from the 'components', i.e. the designs given by rows and columns separately. To take R first and using the suffixes r and c to indicate, respectively, the designs in which only the rows are considered or only the columns, r being the actual replication,

$$
R = R_r + R_c - r. \tag{4.12.4}
$$

Thus, for the design at (4.12.3), ignoring columns and using only the blocking system given by rows, $k_r = 6$, $\lambda_r = 6$, $\lambda_{or} = 5$, $v = 5$, $R_r = 29/6$. Turning now to the design in which only columns are considered, $k_c = 4$, $\lambda_c = 4$, $\lambda_{oc} = 3$, $v = 5$, $R_c = 19/4$. Hence

$$R = 29/6 + 19/4 - 5 = 55/12 = 4.58.$$

The expression for R_o is more complicated:

$$R_0 = \frac{b\lambda_{or} + c\lambda_{oc} - rr_o}{b\lambda_r + c\lambda_c - r^2} R \tag{4.12.5}$$

where $b \ (= k_c)$ is the number of rows and $c \ (= k_r)$ is the number of columns. Hence, in this instance,

$$R_o = \frac{20 + 18 - 20}{24 + 24 - 25} \times \frac{55}{12} = 3.59.$$

From this point, with Q, R and R_o known, everything proceeds as in steps (4), (5) and (6) of Section 4.8. Also, the adjustment at (4.8.5) is available if needed.

4.13   Residuals with non-orthogonal designs

When data are analysed using the Kuiper–Corsten iteration, as described in Section 4.2, the residuals are calculated explicitly as at (4.2.7) and there are no difficulties. Nor are there any problems when shorter methods are used for special designs, because the residuals can be estimated from the treatment parameters. In several cases expressions have been given to enable those quantities to be found, i.e. at (4.7.4), (4.8.4), (4.9.3) and (4.10.2). The method is as follows. The deviations are already known. From each one the appropriate treatment parameter is subtracted. Finally, the resulting figures are swept by block means to give the residuals. Row-and-column designs will be considered later.

At this point it may be helpful to return to the data at (4.2.1), the deviations being at (4.2.2). The values for Q are

A, -11.00;   B, $+0.25$;   C, $+4.75$;   D, $+3.00$;   E, $+3.00$.

The values of R and R_o are respectively $11/4$ and $33/8$. Hence the parameters are

A, -2.67;   B, $+0.09$;   C, $+1.73$;   D, $+.09$;   E, $+1.09$.

Sweeping the deviations by the parameters gives:

Block	I	A,	+ 1.42	C,	− 0.98	D,	− 2.34	E,	+ 0.66
	II	B,	− 1.09	A,	+ 0.67	D,	− 1.09	C,	+ 1.27
	III	E,	− 1.09	C,	− 0.73	B,	+ 0.91	A,	+ 0.67
	IV	D,	+ 3.16	B,	+ 0.16	E,	+ 0.16	A,	− 3.08

A further sweep by block means gives the residuals already found at (4.2.7). (Actually the figures just found are rather better, the block and treatment totals in the main lying closer to zero.)

The adjustment for non-equality of replication at (4.8.5) equals − 0.08. It will be seen that the adjusted treatment mean for A is

$$\text{Grand mean} + \text{parameter for A} + \text{adjustment}$$

$$= 14.75 - 2.67 - 0.08 = 12.0,$$

which is the value at (4.2.9), and so for the other treatments also.

With a simple lattice there is usually little point in finding residuals because there are only two replications. Since residuals necessarily sum to zero over each treatment, each large residual must be balanced by another—of the same magnitude but of opposite sign—on the second plot of the same treatment. There is usually no way of knowing whether the first plot had given an abnormally high value or the second an abnormally low one. For some other purposes, however, e.g. those set out in Chapter 12, residuals need to be known.

With the row-and-column designs described in Sections 4.11 and 4.12 much the same method applies. The singly non-orthogonal designs in Section 4.11 need one final sweep, by either rows or columns, according to which one carries the non-orthogonality. The doubly non-orthogonal designs in Section 4.12 must be swept twice before finishing, once by rows and once by columns, because the treatments are non-orthogonal to both blocking systems.

Exercise 4A

The following data have been made up to illustrate what happens when two plots in a randomized block design are interchanged as the result of an error.

Block	I	A	14.7	A	13.9	C	12.5	D	14.2
	II	B	16.4	B	17.1	C	13.3	D	15.0
	III	A	15.4	B	17.6	C	15.0	D	16.7
	IV	A	16.3	B	18.2	C	16.6	D	17.4
	V	A	16.8	B	19.1	C	17.8	D	18.9

The letters A–D indicate treatments. Note that plots have not been given in field order but rearranged so as to show what has happened.

Analyse the data. Find the standard error of the contrast between the adjusted means of (i) A and B, (ii) A and C, (iii) C and D, both for the achieved design and for the one intended.

[Data from S. C. Pearce, 'Randomized blocks with interchanged and substituted plots', *J. Royal Statist. Soc.* **B10** (1948), pp. 252–6.]

Exercise 4B

The following data have been made up to illustrate the case in which one treatment has been substituted for another in certain blocks of a randomized block design. (In this instance Treatment B has been substituted for A in Blocks I and II).

Block	I	B	1.74	B	1.69	C	1.81	D	1.86
	II	B	1.85	B	1.97	C	1.96	D	1.94
	III	A	2.01	B	1.90	C	2.00	D	1.91
	IV	A	2.14	B	1.99	C	2.11	D	2.06
	V	A	1.96	B	1.96	C	1.95	D	1.90
	VI	A	2.08	B	1.94	C	2.02	D	2.06

The letters A–D indicate treatments. Again plots are not in field order. Analyse the data. Find the standard error of the contrast between the adjusted means of (i) A and B, (ii) A and C, (iii) B and C, (iv) C and D, both for the achieved design and for one in randomized blocks.

[Data from S. C. Pearce, 'Randomized blocks with interchanged and substituted plots', *J. Royal Statist. Soc.*, **B10** (1948), pp. 252–6.]

Exercise 4C

The following data have been made up to illustrate a design in Balanced Incomplete Blocks. In this instance, $b = 10$, $v = 5$, $k = 3$, $r = 6$, $\lambda = 3$. The letters A–E indicate treatments.

Block						
I	D	34	E	30	A	26
II	D	34	B	33	E	26
III	B	30	A	27	D	30
IV	E	31	C	27	A	26
V	C	22	D	30	E	26
VI	B	33	C	22	A	23
VII	A	27	C	23	D	28
VIII	C	21	E	25	B	26
IX	D	29	B	29	C	23
X	E	27	A	25	B	26

Analyse the data in such a way as to obtain residuals. Having found them, can you suggest a better way in which the experiment could have been designed?

Exercise 4D

An investigator had ten new varieties of maize (A–J) and three standard varieties (X, Y and Z). He compared them using balanced incomplete blocks. The data, which represent crop weight in pounds per plot, were as follows:

Block								
I	C	25.3	F	19.9	I	29.0	X	24.6
II	C	23.0	D	19.8	H	33.3	Y	22.7
III	J	16.2	X	19.3	Y	31.7	Z	26.6
IV	B	27.3	E	27.0	H	35.6	X	17.4
V	G	23.4	H	30.5	I	30.8	J	32.4
VI	D	30.6	E	32.4	F	27.2	J	32.8
VII	A	34.7	E	31.1	I	25.7	Y	30.5
VIII	C	34.4	E	32.4	G	33.3	Z	36.9
IX	A	38.2	B	32.9	C	37.3	J	31.3
X	B	28.7	D	30.7	I	26.9	Z	35.3
XI	A	36.6	D	31.1	G	31.1	X	28.4
XII	A	31.8	F	33.7	H	27.8	Z	41.1
XIII	B	30.3	F	31.5	G	39.3	Y	26.7

Analyse the data and note any of the new varieties that appears to be significantly better than each of the standards.

[Data from W. G. Cochran and G. M. Cox, *Experimental Designs*, 2nd edn (1957), p. 448. It is not stated in the original presentation which of the thirteen varieties were the standards, so the last three have been assigned that status, as is implied by the text. For purposes of an exercise the doubt does not matter, though it would be very important if anything depended upon the decision.]

Exercise 4E

A study was made of the control of the *Venturia* fungus on apples, using the design presented at (4.8.1). On a scale that measured the size of the lesions, the data were:

Block								
I	A	2.5	B	1.5	C	1.4	O	2.5
II	B	4.7	C	4.3	D	10.4	O	6.6
III	A	3.3	C	1.2	D	7.3	O	4.0
IV	A	6.4	B	4.9	D	8.8	O	4.8

Is there evidence that any of the spray treatments, A, B, C and D, reduced the incidence of the fungus as compared with doing nothing, i.e. treatment O?

[Data from S. C. Pearce, *Biological Statistics: an Introduction*, (1965), p. 94.

Exercise 4F

An experiment was conducted on apples to see the effect of 'thinning', i.e. of removing fruitlets at an early stage of development so that the ones left would be able to grow larger. There were 60 trees. In the absence of any obvious environmental differences they were divided into five blocks each of twelve trees for purposes of administration. There were four treatments:

A Control—no thinning.
B Hand thinning of 'king fruit', i.e. of those from the first bud of each blossom cluster.
C Hand thinning of fruit on laterals.
D Thinning by a chemical spray, which would of course not discriminate between different kinds of fruitlets.

In four of the blocks (not IV) three trees were allocated at random to each treatment, but in Block IV four trees were allocated to each of B, C and D. In that way less emphasis was given to the control, which was considered to be of less importance. In Block III some trees died, so examination of the full data will be left till Chapter 12.

The following data give the crop in pounds (1 pound = 454 grams) per tree. Note that crop, though important, is subsidiary to the main purpose of the study, which concerned size and colour of fruit. With respect to crop, A is as important as B, C or D, but the design does not allow for that.

Block I	D	122	D	125	C	112
	A	76	B	189	B	119
	D	154	C	125	B	117
	C	121	A	170	A	148
Block II	D	105	B	142	D	143
	C	129	A	180	A	139
	C	130	C	134	D	181
	A	263	B	171	B	184
Block III	Omitted					
Block IV	D	143	D	187	D	181
	B	235	B	202	C	121
	C	148	C	124	D	143
	B	200	B	219	C	190
Block V	D	187	A	259	C	149
	B	217	B	215	A	83
	B	169	D	181	D	194
	C	178	A	190	C	162

Write down concurrences for all pairs of treatments and decide what class of design was used. Analyse the data to find adjusted treatment means and standard errors of contrasts between pairs of treatments.

[Data presented by permission of the Director of the East Malling Research Station, where the experiment was carried out.]

Exercise 4G

The following figures come from an experiment designed in a simple lattice. They represent the number of tillers per square metre of rice.

First replicate

Block								
	I	A	147	B	152	C	167	D	150
	II	E	127	F	155	G	162	H	172
	III	I	147	J	100	K	192	L	177
	IV	M	155	N	195	O	192	P	205

Second replicate

Block								
V	A	140	I	182	E	165	M	152
VI	J	97	B	155	N	192	F	142
VII	G	155	O	182	C	192	K	192
VIII	P	182	H	207	L	232	D	162

In the first replicate blocks correspond to rows of the format

A	B	C	D
E	F	G	H
I	J	K	L
M	N	O	P

In the second they correspond to the columns. Analyse the data.

[*Note*:   In the next exercise a third replicate from the same experiment is added.]

[Data from K. A. Gomez and A. A. Gomez, *Statistical Procedures for Agricultural Research with Emphasis on Rice* (1976), p. 36.]

Exercise 4H

There was a third replicate to the last example, which makes the design a triple lattice. The additional data were:

Third replicate

Block								
IX	A	155	F	162	K	177	P	152
X	E	182	B	130	O	177	L	165
XI	I	137	N	185	C	152	H	152
XII	M	185	J	122	G	182	D	192

In the first replicate blocks correspond to rows of the format

A	B	C	D
E	F	G	H
I	J	K	L
M	N	O	P

In the second they correspond to the columns and in the third to the letters of the Latin square

a	β	γ	δ
β	a	δ	γ
γ	δ	a	β
δ	γ	β	a

Analyse all the data available using the short method.

[Data from K. A. Gomez and A. A. Gomez, *Statistical Procedures for Agricultural Research with Emphasis on Rice* (1976), p. 36. There were in all five replicates, the full design being in total balance.]

Exercise 4I

What are the values of R and R_o for the designs at (4.12.1) and (4.12.2)?

Chapter 5

Contrasts as a means of specifying purpose

5.1 The need to specify objectives

No experiment will be conducted to best advantage unless everyone is agreed about what needs to be done. Some method is required for writing down the sort of information that is to be obtained. More than that, it may be necessary to set out what is being assumed.

The statistical approach is to specify 'contrasts'. For example, there could be four treatments, A, B, C and D. There must have been good reasons for choosing them, but what were those reasons? We can suggest a few of the more likely answers to that question, but any experiment may provide unexpected and unusual cases. We will just indicate some of the more common ones.

(1) It may be that A is the standard method, while B, C and D are new ideas advanced as possible improvements. In that case the immediate need is not to compare B, C and D among themselves but to compare each of them with A. That defines three contrasts, which will be written:

$$
\begin{array}{cccc}
A & B & C & D \\
(-1 & +1 & 0 & 0) \\
(-1 & 0 & +1 & 0) \\
(-1 & 0 & 0 & +1)
\end{array} \tag{5.1.1}
$$

The first contrast represents the mean of B less that of A; the means of C and D do not come into it. The others are similar.

The expressions at (5.1.1) are really a sort of shorthand. The experimenter has values, Y_A, Y_B, Y_C and Y_D, one for each treatment. In the case of an orthogonal design or one that is completely randomized they are the treatment means; in the case of a non-orthogonal design the method has been given at (4.2.10), with simpler expressions for special designs at (4.7.4) and (4.8.4). The contrasts at (5.1.1) indicate that we want to know about

$$(-Y_A + Y_B), \quad (-Y_A + Y_C), \quad (-Y_A + Y_D).$$

93

(2) It could be that A, B, C and D represent increasing applications of something, e.g. increasing concentrations of a spray substance or increasing dressings of a fertilizer. In that case the need is to establish the shape of the response curve, whether it is straight or not, and perhaps whether it has a maximum within the range under study. Suitable contrasts will be sought in Sections 5.7 and 5.8.

(3) It sometimes happens that the effect of a treatment depends upon the presence or absence of another. For example, Variety A may yield better than Variety B on unfertilized soil, but B may be better where fertilizer is supplied. Similarly, a spray may control fungal infection in ordinary conditions but not where sprinkler irrigation is used. Conditional effects like that are called 'interactions'.

When an interaction is suspected it is better to study the two factors in conjunction; that is to say, each needs to be investigated along with the other. Thus in the example of the two varieties with and without added fertilizer, the four treatments are needed, namely:

AO	Variety A	No fertilization
AF	Variety A	Fertilized
BO	Variety B	No fertilization
BF	Variety B	Fertilized.

There are three degrees of freedom between those four treatments. The first contrast compares plots of Variety A with those of Variety B, i.e.

$$
\begin{array}{cccc}
\text{AO} & \text{AF} & \text{BO} & \text{BF} \\
(+1 & +1 & -1 & -1).
\end{array}
\qquad (5.1.2a)
$$

The second picks up the effect of fertilization, i.e.

$$
(-1 \quad +1 \quad -1 \quad +1) \qquad (5.1.2b)
$$

There are three ways in which four things can be divided into two pairs, and (5.1.2) gives only two of them.

There is a third:
$$
(-1 \quad +1 \quad +1 \quad -1)
$$

What does it mean?

It is in fact the 'interaction'. Suppose that fertilization had had the same effect on both varieties, i.e. the contrasts

$$
\begin{array}{r}
(\ 0 \quad\ \ 0 \quad +1 \quad -1) \\
\text{and} \quad (+1 \quad -1 \quad\ \ 0 \quad\ \ 0) \qquad (5.1.3)
\end{array}
$$

gave the same result. Then their difference would be zero, i.e. the contrast

$$(-1 \quad +1 \quad +1 \quad -1) \tag{5.1.4}$$

would be zero—just as the first two would be zero if there were respectively no effect of varieties or of fertilization. If it is not zero, then the fertilizer is having different effects on the two varieties and the contrast at (5.1.2b) represents the sum of those effects. More meaning attaches to the 'particular effects' at (5.1.3).

In general, the contrast for an interaction is found by multiplying out those for the two 'main effects' from which it is derived. Thus, here

Treatment	Variety (V)	Fertilization (F)	Interaction (V × F)
AO	+ 1	− 1	$(+1) \times (-1) = -1$
AF	+ 1	+ 1	$(+1) \times (+1) = +1$
BO	− 1	− 1	$(-1) \times (-1) = +1$
BF	− 1	+ 1	$(-1) \times (+1) = -1.$

It should be noted that there is a logical order for examining the contrasts. The first thing is to look at the interaction at (5.1.4). If it is small, it is reasonable to conclude that the effect of fertilization is much the same for the two varieties or, to put the same thing in another way, the difference between the two varieties is much the same at both levels of fertilization. It is therefore reasonable to look at the 'main effects' at (5.1.2), but if there is an interaction the next step is to look at the 'particular effects'. Those for fertilization are given at (5.1.3); those for variety are

$$\begin{array}{llll} (+1 & 0 & -1 & 0) \quad \text{with no fertilization} \\ (\ 0 & +1 & 0 & -1) \quad \text{with fertilization} \end{array} \tag{5.1.5}$$

It should be noted that if X interacts with Y then Y interacts with X. Thus, the contrast at (5.1.4) can be derived either as a difference of those at (5.1.3) or of those at (5.1.5). Factorial design will be considered in more detail in Chapter 6.

5.2 A look at fundamentals

Before proceeding further it may be helpful to go to fundamentals. The following approach is too long to be used in practice, but it does show what will be happening in the sections that follow. They will set out the methods used in practice, but they are really short cuts of the full procedure.

The point is this. Any contrast, however expressed, whether as a function of means or in any other way, is really a contrast of data. For example, let there be three randomized blocks, each of four treatments, A, B, C and D, then the data may be represented thus:

$$
\begin{array}{cccc}
y_{1A} & y_{1B} & y_{1C} & y_{1D} \\
y_{2A} & y_{2B} & y_{2C} & y_{2D} \\
y_{3A} & y_{3B} & y_{3C} & y_{3D}
\end{array}
\qquad (5.2.1)
$$

The first particular effect at (5.1.3), i.e. the difference between the means of treatments A and B, equals

$$(y_{1A} + y_{2A} + y_{3A})/3 - (y_{1B} + y_{2B} + y_{3B})/3.$$

Taking the data in order of rows at (5.2.1), this may be written

$$(+1 \quad -1 \quad 0 \quad 0 \quad +1 \quad -1 \quad 0 \quad 0 \quad +1 \quad -1 \quad 0 \quad 0).$$

Clearly it has a variance of

$$[(+1)^2 + (-1)^2 + 0^2 + \ldots + (-1)^2 + 0^2 + 0^2]\sigma^2/9 = 2\sigma^2/3.$$

Considering now the main effect of varieties at (5.1.2a), it may be written thus in terms of the data:

$$(+1 \quad +1 \quad -1 \quad -1 \quad +1 \quad +1 \quad -1 \quad -1 \quad +1 \quad +1 \quad -1 \quad -1)/3$$

and its variance is $4\sigma^2/3$. Further the covariance of the two is

$$[(+1)(+1) + (-1)(+1) + 0(-1) + \ldots + (-1)(+1) + 0(-1) + 0(-1)]\sigma^2/9$$

which is zero. In that case they are said, using a technical term already encountered in the context of blocks and treatments, to be 'orthogonal' to one another.

The above method is short enough in the simple case just considered, but it would be impossibly prolix in many instances. It would, for example, be a very lengthy process to work a Kuiper–Corsten iteration algebraically on the data. That is why simpler methods are needed, though they can obscure what is really going on.

5.3   Contrasts of interest written in matrix form

We have seen two ways of expressing a contrast, but we will now show a third in which it is written as a matrix. (In Section 4.1 we explained that a matrix is only an array of numbers written in rows and columns, both rows and columns having meaning.) In the 'matrix of the contrast' there is a row for each treatment and a column also. We will illustrate how it is formed by using the contrast $(+4 -1 -1 -1 -1)$.

The first row of the matrix is found by multiplying the contrast by its own first coefficient, thus;

$$+16 \quad -4 \quad -4 \quad -4 \quad -4.$$

The second is found similarly by multiplying the contrast by its second coefficient, which gives:

$$-4 \quad +1 \quad +1 \quad +1 \quad +1.$$

The other rows are the same as the second, so the full matrix is:

$$\begin{pmatrix} +16 & -4 & -4 & -4 & -4 \\ -4 & +1 & +1 & +1 & +1 \\ -4 & +1 & +1 & +1 & +1 \\ -4 & +1 & +1 & +1 & +1 \\ -4 & +1 & +1 & +1 & +1 \end{pmatrix} \tag{5.3.1}$$

It is necessarily square and symmetrical. Any contrast can be written as a matrix in this manner.

There are times when we want to express not a single contrast but the relationship between two different ones. This also can be done by way of a matrix and we will illustrate the method by considering the first two contrasts at (5.1.1), namely,

$$(-1 \quad +1 \quad 0 \quad 0) \quad \text{and} \quad (-1 \quad 0 \quad +1 \quad 0).$$

We take the first contrast and multiply it by the first coefficient of the other. This gives

$$+1 \quad -1 \quad 0 \quad 0.$$

That is the first row of the matrix to be generated. Then we multiply the first contrast by the second coefficient of the other. Since that coefficient is zero, we shall get a second row consisting entirely of zero elements. Proceeding in that way, we form the entire matrix like this:

$$\begin{pmatrix} +1 & -1 & 0 & 0 \\ 0 & 0 & 0 & 0 \\ -1 & +1 & 0 & 0 \\ 0 & 0 & 0 & 0 \end{pmatrix} \qquad (5.3.2)$$

It is square but no longer symmetrical. Its usefulness will be explained in Section 5.6.

5.4 Covariance matrices

To complement the matrices that express the contrasts of interest and the relationships between them, we need others to show the attributes of possible designs. The two, purpose and capability, have to be seen in relation one to the other. Designs are not good or bad in themselves; they are good only in so far as they provide precise estimates of the contrasts declared to be of interest.

The attributes of a design can be expressed by giving its 'covariance matrix'. The matter was touched on in Sections 4.1 and 4.3; we shall now look at it more fully. First of all, a covariance matrix, like the matrix of a contrast, has a row and a column for each treatment. For any design that is orthogonal, whether in blocks or in rows and columns (including those that are completely randomized), an element on the diagonal is equal to the variance of an observation, σ^2, divided by the replication, r, of the treatment to which the element refers, i.e., σ^2/r. Off-diagonal elements equal zero. Hence, if we have five treatments in six randomized blocks, the covariance matrix will be

$$\begin{pmatrix} 1/6 & 0 & 0 & 0 & 0 \\ 0 & 1/6 & 0 & 0 & 0 \\ 0 & 0 & 1/6 & 0 & 0 \\ 0 & 0 & 0 & 1/6 & 0 \\ 0 & 0 & 0 & 0 & 1/6 \end{pmatrix} s^2 \qquad (5.4.1)$$

It will be noticed that we have used s^2 instead of σ^2. If the true variance, σ^2, were known, we would use it, but we are writing in the context of the analysis of variance where σ^2 has to be estimated by s^2, the 'error' mean square with a stated number of degrees of freedom. The matrix at (5.4.1) is therefore not the covariance matrix itself but an estimate of it. It is as near the true matrix as we can get, and for most purposes it serves very well.

That is the way by which to find the covariance matrix of an orthogonal design. The more difficult case, when the design is non-orthogonal, has already been considered in Section 4.3, where it was found by using the Kuiper–Corsten iteration. Sometimes the task can be performed more easily. Thus, the methods used in Sections 4.7 and 4.8 show that covariance matrices for designs in total and supplemented balance can be found using R or R_o, as may be appropriate, instead of r in generating matrices like the one at (5.4.1).

5.5 The variance of a contrast

To find the variance of a contrast if a certain design is used, it is necessary to know both the matrix of the contrast and the covariance matrix of the design. They will be of the same size, their elements corresponding each to each. It is necessary only to multiply corresponding elements and to add the products to obtain the variance, Ks^2, defined at (4.1.1).

We will suppose that someone is interested in the contrast

$$(+4 \quad -1 \quad -1 \quad -1 \quad -1).$$

Its matrix has been presented at (5.3.1). One possibility is to use six randomized blocks. In that case, the covariance matrix is at (5.4.1), so we can begin. We have

1	product of $+16$ and $s^2/6$	$= 16s^2/6$
4	products of $+1$ and $s^2/6$	$= 4s^2/6$
8	products of -4 and 0	$= 0$
12	products of $+1$ and 0	$= 0$
25	products with a total of	$3.333s^2$

Hence, the variance of the contrast is 3.333 times the 'error' mean square in the analysis of variance. The square root of that quantity will be the standard error of the contrast.

We can take another example by supposing that someone wanted to study the same contrast using the design that gave rise to the covariance matrix at (4.3.1). It was non-orthogonal, but the method is the same. We now have:

1	product of $+16$ and $0.1875s^2$	$= 3.000s^2$
4	products of $+1$ and $0.2936s^2$	$= 1.174s^2$
8	products of -4 and $-0.0625s^2$	$= 2.000s^2$
12	products of $+1$ and $-0.0701s^2$	$= -0.841s^2$
25	products giving a total of	$5.333s^2$

In this instance K equals 5.333. We know from (4.2.9) that s^2 is 4.424, so we can go further and say that the variance of the contrast is 23.593 and its standard error is 4.86, the square root of 23.593. From (4.2.10) it appears that the contrast itself equals

$$4(12.0) - 14.8 - 16.4 - 15.8 - 15.8 = - 14.8,$$

which is 3.05 times its standard error. Contrasts like

$$(+1 \quad -1 \quad 0 \quad 0 \quad 0) \quad \text{and} \quad (0 \quad +1 \quad -1 \quad 0 \quad 0)$$

give the results already obtained at (4.3.2) and (4.3.3).

This is perhaps the place to mention that there is no need to strive for equality of replication as if it were an end in itself. Indeed, Sections 4.8 and 4.12 have already shown that there are occasions when it can well be abandoned. It is not necessary with orthogonal designs either. For example, in the situation that gave rise to the contrasts at (5.1.1) there is a lot to be said for giving the standard enhanced replication. If the intention is solely to compare each new variety with the standard, the ideal is to give the standard a replication a times that of the others, where a is the square root of the number of new treatments. Thus, if A is the standard and B, C, D and E are new treatments, five blocks of AABCDE would be better than six of ABCDE, always assuming that the increased 'error' mean square, s^2, that may result from using larger blocks will not annul the advantage given by a lower value of K. To examine the position further, the design with unequal replication will give the covariance matrix

$$\begin{pmatrix} 0.1 & 0 & 0 & 0 & 0 \\ 0 & 0.2 & 0 & 0 & 0 \\ 0 & 0 & 0.2 & 0 & 0 \\ 0 & 0 & 0 & 0.2 & 0 \\ 0 & 0 & 0 & 0 & 0.2 \end{pmatrix} s^2$$

In that case the variance of a contrast like $(-1 +1 0 0 0)$ will be $0.300s^2$. If the matrix at (5.4.1) had been used, the variance would have been $0.333s^2$. The gain is not great but, if it can be achieved at no cost, it is worth having.

5.6 Contrasts in the analysis of variance

If the value of a contrast is squared and divided by the value of K, the result gives the sum of squares corresponding to that contrast in the 'error' line of the analysis of variance. It will have one degree of freedom. For example, to return to Example (3) of Section 5.1, we will suppose that the four treatments were studied in five randomized blocks. The diagonal elements of the covariance matrix will all equal 0.2. Further, the three contrasts at (5.1.2) and (5.1.4) give respectively the following matrices:

$$\begin{pmatrix} +1 & +1 & -1 & -1 \\ +1 & +1 & -1 & -1 \\ -1 & -1 & +1 & +1 \\ -1 & -1 & +1 & +1 \end{pmatrix} , \begin{pmatrix} +1 & -1 & +1 & -1 \\ -1 & +1 & -1 & +1 \\ +1 & -1 & +1 & -1 \\ -1 & +1 & -1 & +1 \end{pmatrix} \text{ and } \begin{pmatrix} +1 & -1 & -1 & +1 \\ -1 & +1 & +1 & -1 \\ -1 & +1 & +1 & -1 \\ +1 & -1 & -1 & +1 \end{pmatrix} \quad (5.6.1)$$

It emerges that for each of the contrasts relative to the given covariance matrix, $K = 0.8$.

We will now suppose further that the treatment totals were:

$$AO, 50; \quad AF, 60; \quad BO, 44; \quad BF, 48.$$

That being so, the treatment sum of squares can be found as a difference between the two summation terms, i.e.,

$$(50^2 + 60^2 + 44^2 + 48^2)/5 - 202^2/20 = 27.80.$$

The next step is to estimate the contrasts:

Main effect of varieties	$(+50 + 60 - 44 - 48)/5 = +3.60$	
Main effect of fertilizer	$(-50 + 60 - 44 + 48)/5 = +2.80$	(5.6.2)
Interaction	$(-50 + 60 + 44 - 48)/5 = +1.20.$	

Consequently the three sums of squares are:

Main effect of varieties	$(3.60)^2/0.8 = 16.20$
Main effect of fertilizer	$(2.80)^2/0.8 = 9.80$
Interaction	$(1.20)^2/0.8 = 1.80.$

It will be seen that the three sums of squares, each with one degree of freedom, sum to 27.80, which has three; that is the total found from the summation terms.

However, this property does not always hold. To take a different example, the contrasts at (5.1.1) give components that do not add up correctly. First, to evaluate the contrasts themselves, they are:

A v. B	$(-50 + 60)/5 = +2.00$	
A v. C	$(-50 + 44)/5 = -1.20$	(5.6.3)
A v. D	$(-50 + 48)/5 = -0.40.$	

Since K is now 0.4, the sums of squares are:

A v. B	$(2.00)^2/0.4 =$	10.00
A v. C	$(1.20)^2/0.4 =$	3.60
A v. D	$(0.40)^2/0.4 =$	0.40.

The sum is now 14.00, not 27.80 as before.

There is clearly some important difference between the two sets of contrasts and it lies in the orthogonality already noted in Section 5.2. The word was used of blocks and treatments in Section 1.3 to indicate that their two effects can be estimated independently of one another. It is used in the same sense here. A knowledge of the value of the contrast $(+1 +1 -1 -1)$ tells us nothing about the value of $(+1 -1 +1 -1)$, but a knowledge of $(-1 +1 \ 0 \ 0)$ does affect our expectation of the value of $(-1 \ 0 +1 \ 0)$. The contrasts at (5.6.2) have been estimated independently of one another, but that is not true of those at (5.6.3).

Orthogonality is readily tested. To find out if $(+1 +1 -1 -1)$ and $(-1 +1 -1 +1)$ are orthogonal, it is necessary to write down a matrix like that at (5.3.1), except that the rows are governed by one contrast and the columns by another. This has already been done at (5.3.2) though for a different pair of contrasts. The result here is

$$\begin{pmatrix} -1 & +1 & -1 & +1 \\ -1 & +1 & -1 & +1 \\ +1 & -1 & +1 & -1 \\ +1 & -1 & +1 & -1 \end{pmatrix} \tag{5.6.4}$$

The matrix so found is then multiplied out by the covariance matrix of the design in the same way that the matrix at (5.3.6) was multiplied out by those at (5.2.1) and (4.3.1), the products being added. If the result is zero, the two contrasts are estimated orthogonally by that design. Here the covariance matrix is

$$\begin{pmatrix} 0.2 & 0 & 0 & 0 \\ 0 & 0.2 & 0 & 0 \\ 0 & 0 & 0.2 & 0 \\ 0 & 0 & 0 & 0.2 \end{pmatrix} s^2 \tag{5.6.5}$$

which gives:

2	products of -1 and $0.2s^2$	$= -0.4s^2$
2	products of $+1$ and $0.2s^2$	$= +0.4s^2$
6	products of -1 and 0	$= 0.0$
6	products of $+1$ and 0	$= 0.0$
16	products with a total of	0.0

The total being zero, the two contrasts are orthogonal, at least for this design. Turning to the other contrasts, i.e., those at (5.6.4), the total is $+0.2s^2$, which is not zero, so the two contrasts are not orthogonal. (They would be so only if the mean of treatment A could be determined perfectly and that is, of course, quite impossible. Any discrepancy in its determination will affect both contrasts equally; for that reason they cannot be estimated independently.)

Where the covariance matrix has the simple form of (5.6.5) considerable simplification becomes possible. In general, if all diagonal elements of the covariance matrix have the same value, a, and all off-diagonal elements similarly equal β, then each treatment can be ascribed an effective replication of

$$R = 1/(a - \beta) \tag{5.6.6}$$

which will apply whatever the contrast. It leads to the conclusion that, for any contrast,

$$K = U/R \tag{5.6.7}$$

where U is the sum of squares of the coefficients of the contrast. Thus, for the contrasts at (5.1.2) and (5.1.4), $U = 4$ and $R = r = 5$, so $K = 0.8$, the figure already found. Another example is afforded by the balanced incomplete block design at the beginning of Section 4.7. Here the Kuiper–Corsten iteration shows all a to be $18/49$ and all β to be $-3/49$. From (5.6.6) R should be $7/3$, the figure that was found at (4.7.2).

Further, in this simple but common case, i.e., that of constant a and constant β, orthogonality between two contrasts is established by multiplying out the coefficients, each to each, and adding the products. If they sum to zero the two contrasts are orthogonal for that design; if they do not, the contrasts are mutually dependent. Thus, for the case studied at (5.6.4),

$$(+1)(-1) + (+1)(+1) + (-1)(-1) + (-1)(+1) = 0, \tag{5.6.8}$$

but for that at (5.3.2), where two contrasts from (5.1.1) were considered,

$$(-1)(-1) + (+1)(0) + (0)(+1) + (0)(0) = +1$$

and the contrasts are not orthogonal.

The matrix at (5.6.5) exemplifies also another special case—and a very common one—that of an orthogonal (or completely randomized) design with all treatments equally replicated. In that case $R = r$ and the rule given in the first paragraph of this section can be expressed in an improved form. To take the calculations at (5.6.2) as an example, the method is to work out the contrast in terms of the treatment totals instead of the means and to use the divisor, rU, instead of K. In that way the sum of squares for the main effect of varieties is found as

$$(50 + 60 - 44 - 48)^2/(5 \times 4) = 16.20. \tag{5.6.9}$$

The advantage lies in the minimization of rounding errors.

The rest of this chapter will be taken up by a study of a particular sort of contrast, namely, that mentioned in Example (2) of Section 5.1. The treatments now have a clear structure, being increasing quantities of some substance applied to the soil or the plants.

5.7   Quantitative levels of factors

It often happens that the levels of a factor depend upon some quantity like the concentration of an insecticide or the number of times it is applied. Qualitative factors like varieties or the form of nitrogenous fertilizer also give useful information, but it is of a different kind. The most important distinction is that quantitative factors have an in-built structure that needs to be respected. We shall examine them now.

Three levels only

We will first consider the case in which a factor, X, is used at three equally spaced levels, which we will call x_0, x_1 and x_2. Their responses will be called respectively y_0, y_1 and y_2. If the responses lie on a straight line when plotted against the levels of X, i.e., if

$$y_j = a + bx_j \quad \text{for } j = 0, 1, 2,$$

then

$$y_0 = a, \quad y_1 = a + b, \quad y_2 = a + 2b. \tag{5.7.1}$$

Hence b can be estimated from both $(y_1 - y_0)$ and $(y_2 - y_1)$. Consequently, their difference,

$$y_0 - 2y_1 + y_2,$$

should be zero. We therefore examine the contrast $(1 - 2\ 1)$. If it is not significant at an acceptable level, there is no need to regard the graph of the responses against the levels as departing from a straight line. This contrast is called the 'quadratic effect'.

However, we still have not isolated the effect of b, though we have obtained two estimates of it, both of the same precision, namely

$$(y_1 - y_0) \quad \text{and} \quad (y_2 - y_1).$$

Their average, the so-called linear effect, provides a better estimate of b than either of the quantities given above. It is $\frac{1}{2}(y_2 - y_0)$. The sum of y_0, y_1 and y_2 is clearly $3(a + b)$, so now that b is known we know a also. The sum of squares between the three levels can thus be broken into two contrasts,

$$L, \quad \text{the linear effect, measured by} \qquad (-1 \quad 0 + 1)$$
$$\text{and} \quad Q, \quad \text{the quadratic effect, measured by} \quad (+1 - 2 + 1). \qquad (5.7.2)$$

Where (5.6.6) holds, they are orthogonal, each with one degree of freedom. To take matters a little further, if the response is indeed quadratic, i.e., if

$$y_j = a + bx + cx_j^2, \qquad (5.7.3)$$

then the three treatments give means estimated by

$$a, \quad a + b + c \quad \text{and} \quad a + 2b + 4c.$$

Hence the contrast, L, estimates $2b + 4c$, Q estimates $2c$, while the general mean of data is $(3a + 3b + 5c)/3$, so a, b and c can all be estimated if need arises.

More than three levels

If there are more levels, more contrasts arise. If there are four, a 'cubic' term, C, has to be added to those already considered, the contrasts being

$$L, \quad \text{the linear effect, measured by} \qquad (-3 \quad -1 \quad +1 \quad +3)$$
$$Q, \quad \text{the quadratic effect, measured by} \quad (+1 \quad -1 \quad -1 \quad +1) \quad (5.7.4)$$
$$\text{and} \quad C, \quad \text{the cubic effect, measured by} \qquad (-1 \quad +3 \quad -3 \quad +1)$$

Those contrasts repay study. If the response is really linear, as at (5.7.1), it will be found that Q and C will be zero. (On account of 'error' they will not be exactly so, but they should not depart much from it.) If the response is really quadratic, as at (5.7.2), C will be zero, but not L or Q. Only if there is a cubic term in the response curve, i.e., only if the curve is given by

$$y_j = a + bx_j + cx_j^2 + dx_j^3 \qquad (5.7.5)$$

will C depart from zero. Any pair of L, Q and C will be orthogonal if (5.6.6) holds.

Response curves do not usually follow polynomial expressions of the kind we have been using, so there is little point in going further. The three we have found are useful, because L indicates a general rise or fall as x increases, Q indicates a general curvature, and C picks up an inflexion, e.g. the case when a curve starts off rising at an increasing rate but ceases to rise so quickly as it nears a maximum. If the only reason for having more levels is to obtain a better fit of the response curve, restraint is called for.

Sometimes five equally spaced levels are used. In that case a 'quartic effect' can be found in addition to the others, the contrasts being

L,	the linear effect, measured by	$(-2$	-1	0	$+1$	$+2)$	
Q,	the quadratic effect, measured by	$(+2$	-1	-2	-1	$+2)$	(5.7.6)
C,	the cubic effect, measured by	$(-1$	$+2$	0	-2	$+1)$	
Qu,	the quartic effect, measured by	$(+1$	-4	$+6$	-4	$+1)$	

The cubic and quartic effects cannot do much more than indicate a departure from the simple curvature measured by Q. There are, however, occasions when many levels are needed, the purpose usually being to fit some other sort of response curve or to detect the point at which a discontinuity occurs. (For example, if the growth of a plant is measured at regular intervals, there may come a time when the setting of blossoms or some similar phenomenon will inaugurate a new phase in which the growth rate will be different. Such matters, however, lie outside the scope of the present text.)

It should be noted that the contrasts at (5.7.2), (5.7.4) and (5.7.6) have a logical order of testing. If there is an effect of C or Qu, then the response curve is not quadratic in form, so it would be a mistake to discuss a and b as if it were. Likewise, if there is an effect of Q, C or Qu, the response is not a straight line, so it would be wrong to cite b as the slope, except as an average, because there is no constant slope. The matter will be exemplified at the end of this section.

An example

To take an example, Campbell (*Statistics in Biology*, 1967) has presented some fictitious data from an experiment with five randomized blocks of five treatments, namely, maize at relative densities of 20, 25, 30, 35 and 40 plants per unit area. The data represent yield of dry matter per plot in kilograms. The 'error' sum of squares with 16 degrees of freedom was 42.170. Treatment totals were:

$$20, 87.9; \quad 25, 118.2; \quad 30, 135.9; \quad 35, 141.0; \quad 40, 135.7$$

so the sum of squares for treatments was 380.802 with four degrees of freedom. It will be convenient to set out the means also, i.e.,

$$20, 17.582; \quad 25, 23.64; \quad 30, 27.18; \quad 35, 28.20; \quad 40, 27.14.$$

From (5.7.6) the value of the linear effect is

$$[-2(87.9) - 1(118.2) + 0(135.9) + 1(141.0) + 2(135.7)]/5 = +23.68.$$

From (5.6.6) the K-value is

$$[(-2)^2 + (-1)^2 + (0)^2 + (+1)^2 + (+2)^2]/5 = 2,$$

so the contribution of the linear effect to the treatment sum of squares is $(23.68)^2/2 = 280.371$. Similarly the value of the quadratic effect, Q, is -16.76 with K equal to 2.8, so its contribution is 100.321. For the cubic effect, C, and the quartic, Qu, the contributions are respectively 0.097 and 0.014, a total of 0.111 with two degrees of freedom. They will be taken together as indicating deviations from the quadratic form. The analysis of variance therefore reads:

Source	d.f.	s.s.	m.s.	F
Linear effect, L	1	280.371	280.371	106.36***
Quadratic effect, Q	1	100.321	100.321	38.06***
Deviations, C and Qu	2	0.111	0.056	0.02
'Error'	16	42.170	2.636	
Stratum total	20	422.973		

The very low value of F for the deviations from the quadratic is rather remarkable. (It is perhaps the result of the data having been simulated on a computer. They are not genuine.) At least it dispels any suspicion that the cubic and quartic effects may be important. From the mean squares for L and Q it is clear that density had a marked effect which was not linear. Indeed the curvature is such that there is a maximum at a density of 30 or so. Since the relationship appears to be quadratic in form, the successive values for the five densities can be written in the form of (5.7.3) as

$$a, a + b + c, a + 2b + 4c, a + 3b + 9c, a + 4b + 16c$$

The situation can be summarized thus:

(1) The mean of those quantities is
   $(a + 2b + 6c) = (17.58 + 23.64 + 27.18 + 28.20 + 27.14)/5 = 24.75.$
(2) The contrast, L, has the value of $(10b + 40c) = 23.68$.
(3) The contrast, Q, which equals -16.76, may be represented as $14c$.

This makes the response curve, corresponding to (5.7.3), to be

$$y = 17.62 + 7.16x - 1.197x^2.$$

It has a maximum at $x = 2.99$, corresponding to a density of 34.9. At that point the yield is 28.33.

A warning has already been given about assuming a quadratic relationship when there is evidence of a cubic or a quartic effect, but that does not apply here.

5.8 General method of deriving contrasts for quantitative levels

The levels, $x_1, x_2, x_3, \ldots$ that specify the treatments need not be equally spaced, though it is more convenient if they are. If they are not, the linear, quadratic effects, etc. can still be found. The method is more easily illustrated than described.

We shall suppose that the levels are 0, 2, 3, 4 and 6. For the linear effect we need a contrast with coefficients, p_0, p_2, p_3, etc. that themselves exhibit linearity, i.e.,

$$p_j = a + bx_j. \tag{5.8.1}$$

That is to say,

$$p_0 = a, \quad p_2 = a + 2b, \quad p_3 = a + 3b,$$
$$p_4 = a + 4b, \quad p_6 = a + 6b.$$

Since those values are the coefficients of a contrast they must sum to zero, i.e., $5a + 15b = 0$. Only the ratio of a and b matters, so we will write $a = -3b = +1$. Using (5.8.1), this makes the contrast of the linear effect, L, to be $(-3 \ -1 \ 0 \ +1 \ +3)$.

The quadratic effect, Q, similarly needs a contrast with coefficients that exhibit a quadratic relationship. That is to say, a coefficient q_j should have the form,

$$q_j = f + gx_j + hx_j^2. \tag{5.8.2}$$

The required coefficients are accordingly

$$f, \quad f + 2g + 4h, \quad f + 3g + 9h, \quad f + 4g + 16h, \quad f + 6g + 36h.$$

It is required that L and Q shall be mutually orthogonal. In the case of some more complicated designs that could be difficult to achieve, but if the conditions are such that (5.6.6) holds, it is required only that

$$-3f - (f + 2g + 4h) + (f + 4g + 16h) + 3(f + 6g + 36h)$$

shall equal zero, i.e., $20g + 120h = 0$. That suggests making g equal to -6 and h equal to $+1$.

It is also required that the coefficients shall indicate a contrast, i.e., they must sum to zero. Hence,

$$5f + 15g + 65h = 0.$$

With the values of g and h already adopted, this makes f equal to $+5$. The contrast of the quadratic effect, Q, is thus shown by (5.8.2) to be
$$(+5 \ -3 \ -4 \ -3 \ +5).$$
If a cubic component is required, it should have coefficients of the form,

$$c_j = s + tx_j + ux_j^2 + vx_j^3.$$

The values of c_j should sum to zero. They should also do so when multiplied by the respective values of p_j and by those of q_j. In the example the contrast of the cubic effect is $(-1 \ +3 \ \ 0 \ -3 \ +1)$.

Exercise 5A

The following data represent a design that has been completely randomized. There are four treatments

A   is the untreated control;

B and D   involve treatment by a substance,
           X, obtained from two different
           manufacturers;

C   involves treatment by substance Y.

The data are:

A	34	37	40	29	29
B	38	44	36	40	47
C	48	51	48	56	52
D	31	35	36	36	32.

Work out an analysis of variance, the treatment sum of squares being partitioned thus:

(1)   Control *v.* treatments
(2)   Substance X *v.* substance Y
(3)   One manufacturer of X *v.* the 'other'.

Check that the three contrasts you use are orthogonal.

Exercise 5B

In Exercise 1C the ten strains are not all of one variety. Strains A–E come from one variety and F–J from another. Modify the analysis accordingly and interpret the result.

Exercise 5C

The data given below, which come from a Latin square, show yields in pounds of wheat from plots, each with an area of 0.025 acre. Treatment O is lack of fertilization. In Treatment S sulphate of ammonia was applied as a single dressing in March, whereas in M the same amount was applied in regular monthly dressings over a six-month period. In Treatment C an equivalent amount of nitrogen was applied as cyanamide in a single dressing in October, whereas in D half was applied as cyanamide and half as dicyanadiomide, also in one dressing in October.

D 72.2	M 55.4	O 36.6	C 67.9	S 73.0
O 36.4	C 46.9	M 46.8	S 54.9	D 68.5
M 71.5	S 55.6	D 71.6	O 67.5	C 78.4
S 68.9	O 53.2	C 69.8	D 79.6	M 77.2
C 82.0	D 81.0	S 76.0	M 87.9	O 70.9

Suggest a set of contrasts that appears to you to do justice to the treatment structure and analyse the data accordingly.

1 acre = 4047 m^2 1 pound = 454 grams.

[Data from A. A. Rayner, *Biometry for Agriculture Students* (1969), p. 273.]

Exercise 5D

An experiment was carried out on the fertilization of potatoes. Treatment A represents lack of fertilization, while B–F represent different fertilization schedules. The experiment was laid out in four randomized blocks, the plots each having an area of 1/85 acre. The following table shows both the field plan and the yields in pounds per plot.

	F 331	B 286	E 312	D 292	F 323	A 185	
I	C 311	D 280	A 177	C 294	B 278	E 322	II

	F 313	C 266	A 182	C 291	B 253	E 328	
III	E 319	D 284	B 258	A 193	D 233	F 319	IV

The treatments were as follows:

A   No fertilization
B   Nitrogen alone
C   Nitrogen + phosphorus
D   Nitrogen + lime
E   Nitrogen + phosphorus + potassium
F   Special mixture of the three elements (nitrogen, phosphorus and potassium)

Consider what treatment contrasts are of greatest interest and find the sum of squares for each. Complete the analysis of variance and present results in kg/ha.

1 acre = 4047 m^2 1 pound = 454 grams

[Data from A. A. Rayner, *Biometry for Agriculture Students* (1969), p. 247.]

Exercise 5E

The following figures represent yields of sugar beet from an experiment intended to compare five substances containing nitrogen.

$$A = (NH_4)_2SO_4; \quad B = NH_4NO_3; \quad C = CO(NH_4)_2; \quad D = Ca(NO_3)_2;$$
$$E = NaNO_3$$

All were applied so as to give 100 units of nitrogen per acre. In the sixth treatment (O) no nitrogen was applied. The design was a Latin square:

O	D	A	B	E	C
28.2	29.1	32.1	33.1	31.1	32.4
E	B	C	O	D	A
31.0	29.5	29.4	24.8	33.0	30.6
D	E	O	C	A	B
30.6	28.8	21.7	30.8	31.9	30.1
C	A	B	D	O	E
33.1	30.4	28.8	31.4	26.7	31.9
B	O	E	A	C	D
29.9	25.8	30.3	30.3	33.5	32.3
A	C	D	E	B	O
30.8	29.7	27.4	29.1	30.7	21.4

Data are in tons per acre (1 acre = 4047 m^2, 1 ton = 1.016 tonnes)

Consider what contrasts between the treatments are of greatest interest to yourself and find the sum of squares for each. Complete the analysis of variance.

[Data from T. M. Little and F. J. Hills, *Agricultural Experimentation: Design and Analysis* (1978), p. 79, John Wiley & Sons, New York.]

Exercise 5F

In Exercise 1E write down the contrasts of interest. Confirm that for each contrast the *t*-test gives the same result as the *F*-test. (*Note*: in a variety trial there is no need of a test to show that differences exist, but it would be unwise for a research institute to recommend a new variety as giving a higher crop, if it might well be no better, or even worse, than the standard.)

Exercise 5G

An experiment was carried out to find the best rate of seeding for a given variety of rice, using six rates set out in four randomized blocks. Grain yields in kg/ha were:

Seeding rate	I	II	Block III	IV	Total
25	5113	5398	5307	4678	20 496
50	5346	5952	4719	4264	20 281
75	5272	5713	5483	4749	21 217
100	5164	4831	4986	4410	19 391
125	4804	4848	4432	4748	18 832
150	5254	4542	4919	4098	18 813

They gave an analysis of variance, as follows:

Source	d.f.	s.s.	m.s.	F
Treatments	5	119 8330	23 9666	2.17
'Error'	15	165 8375	11 0558	
Stratum total	20	285 7705		

Satisfy yourself that the coefficients for the linear and quadratic contrasts are

L, $(-5 \quad -3 \quad -1 \quad +1 \quad +3 \quad +5)$;
Q, $(+5 \quad -1 \quad -4 \quad -4 \quad -1 \quad +5)$.

Partition the sum of squares for treatments, separating out the linear and quadratic effects. If the departure from a parabola looks interesting, further contrasts are:

Cubic, $(-5 \quad +7 \quad +4 \quad -4 \quad -7 \quad +5)$

Quartic, $(+1 \quad -3 \quad +2 \quad +2 \quad -3 \quad +1)$

Quintic, $(-1 \quad +5 \quad -10 \quad +10 \quad -5 \quad +1)$.

Write a short report on what you conclude about the yield response to different seeding rates, together with any recommendation you think should be made.

[Data from K. A. Gomez and A. A. Gomez, *Statistical Procedures for Agricultural Research with Emphasis on Rice* (1976), page 20.]

Exercise 5H

Experimenters sometimes use the sequence, 0, 1, 2, 4, for applications of fertilizer or sprays. (It annoys the statisticians because the progression is neither arithmetic nor geometric.) Find the contrasts that correspond to the linear, quadratic and cubic effects.

Exercise 5I

In Exercise 6C it will be necessary to deal with nitrogen at levels, 0, 40, 70, 100, 130. Anticipate that problem by working out the linear and quadratic effects now.

Chapter 6

Factorial designs

6.1 Summation terms in a factorial design

The main effects and interaction introduced at (5.1.2) and (5.1.4) can be approached in another way using summation terms (see Section 1.4). For the moment a method will be given for use with designs that are orthogonal and such that all treatments have r plots, i.e. for the case considered at (5.6.8). Let the treatments described in Example (3) of Section 5.1 have totals T_{AO}, T_{AF}, T_{BO}, and T_{BF}; then the treatment sum of squares is

$$\frac{(T_{AO}^2 + T_{AF}^2 + T_{BO}^2 + T_{BF}^2)}{r} - \frac{(T_{AO} + T_{AF} + T_{BO} + T_{BF})^2}{4r}$$

The two summation terms will be called

$$S_{VF} = (T_{AO}^2 + T_{AF}^2 + T_{BO}^2 + T_{BF}^2)/r$$
and $$S_O = (T_{AO} + T_{AF} + T_{BO} + T_{BF})^2/4r$$

because in the first the data have been classified by both variety (V) and fertilization (F), whereas in S_O they have not been classified at all. (Previously S_{VF} has been called S_t.)

If now the main effects are studied separately, two more summation terms will be needed, namely

$$S_V = [(T_{AO} + T_{AF})^2 + (T_{BO} + T_{BF})^2]/2r$$
and $$S_F = [(T_{AO} + T_{BO})^2 + (T_{AF} + T_{BF})^2]/2r$$

to give sums of squares of respectively $(S_V - S_O)$ and $(S_F - S_O)$, the first for varieties and the second for fertilizations.

It appears then that the treatment sum of squares amounts to $(S_{VF} - S_O)$, of which $(S_V - S_O)$ is due to varieties acting alone and

115

$(S_F - S_O)$ is due to fertilizer acting alone. That leaves $(S_{VF} - S_V - S_F + S_O)$ for the interaction in which the two work together.

As to degrees of freedom, there are three between four treatments; of those one is for the difference between the varieties and one for the difference between the two levels of fertilization. That leaves one for the interaction.

6.2   The $m \times n$ factorial design

In the examples examined so far, each factor has had two levels, but there is no need to accept that restriction. There could be many varieties and many fertilizer programs. It would still be sensible to test them together in all combinations to see how far the choice of fertilizer should depend upon the variety, or the choice of variety depend upon the level of fertilization that it is proposed to use. The same goes for any other two factors that need to be studied together.

An example is afforded by the data in Table 6a, where there were five varieties (A–E) with three methods of cultivation. Using the methods set out in Section 1.4, the following summation terms arise:

$$S \ \ = 61^2 + 56^2 + \ldots + 50^2 = 198\,184.00$$
$$S_b \ = (929^2 + 869^2 + 807^2 + 815^2)/15 = 195\,578.40$$
$$S_t \ = (190^2 + 223^3 + \ldots + 257^2)/4 = 197\,013.50 = S_{vc}$$
$$S_O \ = 3420^2/60 = 194\,940.00$$

The basis for these figures is the fact that the block totals are respectively 929, 869, 807 and 815 and that the treatment totals are those set out in Table 6β.

Accordingly the analysis of variance reads:

Source	d.f.	s.s.	m.s.	F
Treatments	14	2073.50	148.11	11.69***
'Error'	42	532.10	12.67	
Stratum total	56	2605.60		

Clearly there are large effects of treatments, but it is not yet clear where they lie. That will become more apparent when the treatment line is partitioned according to the factorial structure. Two more summation terms are required:

The data in the following table were recorded on a cowpea experiment in which there were four randomized blocks. The fifteen treatments were derived from all combinations of five varieties (A–E) with three methods of cultivation (1, 2, 3). The figures represent yields per plot in pounds. Each plot had an area of 0.01 morgen.

I	$B_1$61	$A_1$56	$E_3$62	$C_1$63	$A_2$66
	$D_2$53	$B_2$59	$D_1$65	$D_3$60	$B_3$60
	$E_1$60	$A_3$60	$C_3$65	$C_2$66	$E_2$73
II	$A_3$50	$C_1$53	$E_2$77	$A_2$57	$B_1$58
	$D_1$61	$D_2$53	$C_2$58	$E_3$68	$D_3$58
	$C_3$56	$B_2$55	$E_1$61	$B_3$59	$1_1$45
III	$E_3$67	$C_3$50	$C_1$49	$A_2$50	$A_3$45
	$B_2$51	$B_3$54	$E_2$77	$D_3$56	$B_1$55
	$E_1$50	$C_2$52	$D_2$48	$A_1$43	$D_1$60
IV	$E_1$53	$D_3$60	$E_3$60	$B_2$52	$B_1$56
	$E_2$65	$D_1$63	$D_2$55	$A_3$48	$A_1$46
	$B_3$54	$C_2$55	$C_1$48	$C_3$50	$A_2$50

1 morgen = 8565 m^2 1 pound = 454 grams
Note that $e = 0$ (see Section 1.10)

[Data from A. A. Rayner, *Biometry for Agricultural Students* (1969), pp. 439–40.]

Table 6β   Treatment totals for the data set out in Table 6a (Each total is based on four data)

		Varieties					
		A	B	C	D	E	Cultivation totals
Methods	1	190	230	213	249	224	1106
of	2	223	217	231	209	292	1172
cultivation	3	203	227	221	234	257	1142
Variety totals		616	674	665	692	773	3420

$$S_V = (616^2 + 674^2 + \ldots + 773^2)/12 = 196\,029.17$$
$$S_C = (1106^2 + 1172^2 + 1142^2)/20 \quad = 196\,049.20$$

(In both cases the divisor is the number of data in the totals that have been squared.)

From this point it will be better to think of S_t as S_{VC}, because it arose from classifying the data by both factors V and C. The main effect of Varieties clearly has a sum of squares of $(S_V - S_O)$ with $(v - 1)$ degrees of freedom, where v is the number of varieties. (Here $v = 5$). The main effect of cultivations has a sum of squares of $(S_C - S_O)$ with $(c - 1)$ degrees of freedom. (Here $c = 3$). That leaves

$$(S_{VC} - S_O) - (S_V - S_O) - (S_C - S_O)$$
$$= S_{VC} - S_V - S_C + S_O$$

with

$$(vc - 1) - (v - 1) - (c - 1) = (v - 1)(c - 1)$$

degrees of freedom for the interaction. Hence the full analysis is

Source	d.f.	s.s.	m.s.	F
Varieties (V)	4	1089.17	272.29	21.49***
Cultivations (C)	2	109.20	54.60	4.31*
Interaction (V × C)	8	875.13	109.39	8.63***
'Error'	42	532.10	12.67	
Stratum total	56	2605.60		

The important feature here is the large interaction, and we need to see where it comes from. At this point it will be easier if we convert the values in Table 6β to means, namely:

	A	B	C	D	E
1	47.5	57.5	53.2	62.2	56.0
2	55.8	54.2	57.8	52.2	73.0
3	50.8	56.8	55.2	58.5	64.2

Each of those values is the mean of four data, each of which has a variance of 12.67 ($= s^2$). Accordingly, a difference between any two of them has a variance of $(\frac{1}{4} + \frac{1}{4})$ 12.67 = 6.335 = 2.52^2, so the standard error of a difference is 2.52.

What happens now should depend upon the questions being asked. It could be that someone wants to know if it matters much what cultivation is used. The main effect of cultivations is significant ($P = 0.05$), but the large interaction warns us that the effect of cultivation depends on the variety. Hence we should ask the question of each variety separately. The following sums of squares, each with two degrees of freedom, will enable us to do so. Each is the difference of two summation terms derived from the data for a single variety (see Table 6β).

$$A \quad (190^2 + 223^2 + 203^2)/4 - 616^2/12 = 138.17$$
$$B \quad (230^2 + 217^2 + 227^2)/4 - 674^2/12 = 23.17$$
$$C \quad (213^2 + 231^2 + 221^2)/4 - 665^2/12 = 40.67$$
$$D \quad (249^2 + 209^2 + 234^2)/4 - 692^2/12 = 204.17$$
$$E \quad (224^2 + 292^2 + 257^2)/4 - 773^2/12 = 578.17$$

The five sums of squares represent the combination of the main effect of cultivations and the interaction of cultivations and varieties (i.e. 984.33 with 10 d.f.). The individual values of F are A, 5.45**; B, 0.91; C, 1.60; D, 8.06**; E, 22.82**, each with two and 42 d.f. It certainly appears that the varieties have very different responses to a change in cultivation method. Without knowing more about the exact nature of those methods and those varieties, it is not possible to pursue that line of enquiry much further.

There is no one way of interpreting an analysis of variance. Everything depends upon the questions being asked, but we do emphasize that the first thing to look at in an $m \times n$ factorial design is the interaction. If it is appreciable there is no point in looking at the main effects.

6.3 The $m \times n \times p$ factorial design

It sometimes happens that there are several factors and not just two. An obvious example is afforded by the classical NPK fertilizer trial in which all three elements, nitrogen, phosphorus and potassium, are applied at a range of levels. There could be more factors than that. For example, with some species large dressings of potassium may lead to a scorch on the leaves that can be cured by magnesium, so someone might want a fourth factor. That would make the scheme NPKMg. There could be even more.

However, the immediate object of study is the experiment with three factors, called the $m \times n \times p$ factorial. That means that there are m levels of the first factor M, n levels of the second factor N, and p levels of the third factor P.

That gives mnp treatment totals. The sum of their squares divided by the number of data in each will be called S_{MNP}, the suffixes indicating that the data have been formed into totals using all three factors. The correction term, S_0, is found by squaring the grand total of data and dividing by the total number of plots. Then the treatment sum of squares equals

$$S_{MNP} - S_0 \text{ with } (mnp - 1) \text{ degrees of freedom.}$$

There are three main effects, each with its own sum of squares, i.e.,

$$M \quad \text{s.s.} = S_M - S_0 \text{ with } (m - 1)\text{df}$$
$$N \quad \text{s.s.} = S_N - S_0 \text{ with } (n - 1)\text{df}$$
$$P \quad \text{s.s.} = S_P - S_0 \text{ with } (p - 1)\text{df}$$

There are also three interactions

$$N \times P \quad \text{s.s.} = S_{NP} - S_N - S_P + S_0 \text{ with } (n - 1)(p - 1)\text{df}$$
$$M \times P \quad \text{s.s.} = S_{MP} - S_M - S_P + S_0 \text{ with } (m - 1)(p - 1)\text{df}$$
$$M \times N \quad \text{s.s.} = S_{MN} - S_M - S_N + S_0 \text{ with } (m - 1)(n - 1)\text{df}$$

There is still something left over, namely

$$S_{MNP} - S_{NP} - S_{MP} - S_{MN} + S_M + S_N + S_P - S_0$$

It has the remaining degrees of freedom, i.e.

$$(mnp - 1) - (m - 1) - (n - 1) - (p - 1) - (mp - n - p + 1)$$
$$- (mp - m - p + 1) - (mn - m - n + 1) = (m - 1)(n - 1)(p - 1)$$

This 'three-factor interaction', as it is called, can be looked at in three ways. It can be taken to indicate:

(1) that the interaction, $N \times P$, depends upon the level of M.
(2) that the interaction, $M \times P$, depends upon the level of N.
(3) that the interaction, $M \times N$, depends upon the level of P.

In fact, all three interpretations mean the same thing, though biologically one may be the easiest to explain.

The method can be illustrated thus: Let $m = 3$, the levels being M_1, M_2 and M_3. Let $n = 2$, the levels being N_1 and N_2. Let $p = 4$, the levels being P_1, P_2, P_3 and P_4. Suppose that the 24 treatment totals, each based on four data, were

	P_1	P_2	P_3	P_4	Total
M_1N_1	20	24	25	27	96
M_1N_2	18	21	22	23	84
M_2N_1	26	28	28	30	112
M_2N_2	22	28	27	27	104
M_3N_1	24	29	31	32	116
M_3N_2	22	26	29	35	112
Total	132	156	162	174	624

The vertical margin to the right gives the MN-totals and the horizontal margin below gives the P-totals. Before calculating summation terms, however, these values will need to be checked: it can be done like this.

The first step is to form M × P and N × P totals, and then to form further margins, i.e.

	P_1	P_2	P_3	P_4	Totals
M_1	38	45	47	50	180
M_2	48	56	55	57	216
M_3	46	55	60	67	228
N_1	70	81	84	89	324
N_2	62	75	78	85	300
Total	132	156	162	174	624

The vertical margin gives the M– and N– totals, and they should be checked from the vertical margin of the table above ($96 + 84 = 180$, $112 + 104 = 216$, $116 + 112 = 228$, $96 + 112 + 116 = 324$, $84 + 104 + 112 = 300$).

Similarly the horizontal margin should be obtained from both parts of the table ($38 + 48 + 46 = 132 = 70 + 62$, $45 + 56 + 55 = 156 = 81 + 75$, etc.). Finally, the grand total should be obtained from the three main classifications:

$(132 + 156 + 162 + 174 = 624 = 180 + 216 + 228 = 324 + 300)$.

If everything agrees it is time to calculate the summation terms. They are:

$$
\begin{aligned}
S_{MNP} &= (20^2 + 24^2 + \ldots + 35^2)/4 & &= 4151.50 \\
S_{NP} &= (70^2 + 81^2 + \ldots + 85^2)/12 & &= 4101.33 \\
S_{MP} &= (38^2 + 45^2 + \ldots + 67^2)/8 & &= 4140.25 \\
S_{MN} &= (96^2 + 84^2 + \ldots + 112^2)/16 & &= 4102.00 \\
S_M &= (180^2 + 216^2 + 228^2)/32 & &= 4095.00
\end{aligned}
$$

$$S_N = (324^2 + 300^2)/48 \qquad\qquad = 4062.00$$
$$S_P = (132^2 + 156^2 + \ldots + 174^2)/24 = 4095.00$$
$$S_0 = 624^2/96 \qquad\qquad\qquad = 4056.00$$

It will be recalled that each of the MNP-totals contains four data and this explains the divisors. It follows that the treatment sum of squares $(S_{MNP} - S_0 = 95.50)$ with $23[= (3 \times 2 \times 4) - 1]$ degrees of freedom is partitioned thus:

Source	d.f.	s.s.	m.s.
M	2	39.00	19.500
N	1	6.00	6.000
P	3	39.00	13.000
N × P	3	0.33	0.111
M × P	6	6.25	1.042
M × N	2	1.00	0.500
M × N × P	6	3.92	0.653
Treatments	23	95.50	

As with any other factorial design, it is best to start with the highest-order interaction. Here it is M × N × P. If that is significant there is little point in looking further because the operation of any factor depends upon the levels of the other two, so the most reasonable course is to set out the 24 treatment means without attempting to generalize about them.

If M × N × P appears not to exist, the next step is to look at the two-factor interactions—here they are N × P, M × P and M × N. If any of them are significant, a two-way table is indicated. If none of them shows up, it is all right to proceed to the main effects, which can then be presented without any conditions implied by the interactions.

6.4   Higher factorials

Experiments can contain many factors. There is no need to stop at three. If there are more, there will be higher-order interactions. However, it can sometimes be quite difficult to interpret a three-factor interaction; with four or more, the task can be virtually impossible. Nevertheless, in an exploratory situation at the beginning of a research project, it is not unusual to include a lot of factors for the sake of their two-factor interactions. That gives an indication of what factors should go together in a series of subsequent experiments, i.e. if they interact they should not be separated, at least not until the interaction is better understood. This will be discussed in more detail in Sections 7.7, 7.8, 7.9 and 7.10.

All interactions can be found from summation terms by a simple regular rule. A term like S_{MNP} is said to be of the third order; one like S_{MN} of the second, and so on. Then any interaction sum of squares is found by taking the corresponding summation term, i.e. S_{MNP} for $M \times N \times P$ or S_{MN} for $M \times N$, subtracting all relevant terms of one order less, adding all relevant terms of two orders less and so on, altering the signs each time until the correction term, S_0 is reached. Thus the sum of squares for the five-factor interaction, $A \times B \times C \times D \times E$, is

$$S_{ABCDE} - (S_{BCDE} + S_{ACDE} + S_{ABDE} + S_{ABCE} + S_{ABCD})$$
$$+ (S_{ABC} + S_{ABD} + S_{ABE} + S_{ACD} + S_{ACE} + S_{ADE} + S_{BCD} + S_{BCE}$$
$$+ S_{BDE} + S_{CDE})$$
$$- (S_{AB} + S_{AC} + S_{AD} + S_{AE} + S_{BC} + S_{BD} + S_{BE} + S_{CD} + S_{CE} + S_{DE})$$
$$+ (S_A + S_B + S_C + S_D + S_E) - S_0.$$

It will have $(a - 1)(b - 1)(c - 1)(d - 1)(e - 1)$ degrees of freedom. Thus it will be seen that the rule gives the familiar expressions for interactions with two or three factors.

6.5 Contrasts of factorial designs

Any main effect can be described as a set of contrasts. If it has p levels, $(p - 1)$ contrasts are needed. For example, if $p = 4$, the following three will sum up the main effect:

$$
\begin{array}{cccc}
(+1 & -1 & 0 & 0) \\
(+1 & +1 & -2 & 0) \\
(+1 & +1 & +1 & -3)
\end{array}
\qquad (6.5.1)
$$

If the treatment totals were T_A, T_B, T_C, T_D, each based on r plots, the three sums of squares would be

$$\frac{(T_A - T_B)^2}{2r}, \quad \frac{(T_A + T_B - 2T_C)^2}{6r} \quad \text{and} \quad \frac{(T_A + T_B + T_C - 3T_D)^2}{12r}$$

They sum to

$$\frac{T_A^2 + T_B^2 + T_C^2 + T_D^2}{r} - \frac{(T_A + T_B + T_C + T_D)^2}{4r}$$

That is the familiar expression for a main effect, i.e. the difference between two summation terms, one for treatments and the other the correction term.

The method can be extended to any number of levels. Thus, if there were six, five contrasts would be needed, as follows:

$$
\begin{array}{rrrrrr}
(+1 & -1 & 0 & 0 & 0 & 0) \\
(+1 & +1 & -2 & 0 & 0 & 0) \\
(+1 & +1 & +1 & -3 & 0 & 0) \\
(+1 & +1 & +1 & +1 & -4 & 0) \\
(+1 & +1 & +1 & +1 & +1 & -5)
\end{array}
$$

There is no need to use these particular contrasts if some other set would be appropriate, e.g. if there was need of linear, quadratic and other effects, etc. It is only that the contrasts just described are always available.

With an interaction the contrasts are found by multiplying out contrasts of two main effects. For example, with an $m \times n$ design, if $m = 3$ and $n = 2$, the contrasts (1) and (2) in Table 6 γ represent the first main effect as a linear and a quadratic effect. Contrast (3) represents the main effect of the second factor. Contrasts (4) and (5) which are derived respectively from (1) and (3) and from (2) and (3), represent the components of the interaction.

TABLE 6γ   Contrasts in a 3 × 2 design

	(1)	(2)	(3)	(4)	(5)
M_1N_1	-1	$+1$	-1	$+1(= -1 \times -1)$	$-1(= +1 \times -1)$
N_2	-1	$+1$	$+1$	$-1(= -1 \times +1)$	$+1(= +1 \times +1)$
M_2N_1	0	-2	-1	$0(= 0 \times -1)$	$+2(= -2 \times -1)$
N_2	0	-2	$+1$	$0(= 0 \times +1)$	$-2(= -2 \times +1)$
N_3N_1	$+1$	$+1$	-1	$-1(= +1 \times -1)$	$-1(= +1 \times -1)$
N_2	$+1$	$+1$	$+1$	$+1(= +1 \times +1)$	$+1(= +1 \times +1)$

(6.5.2)

That explains why the number of degrees of freedom for an interaction always equals the product of those for the two main effects, i.e. each contrast of one set is multiplied out by each contrast of the other set.

6.6   Yates's algorithm

If all factors are at two levels, the values of the various contrasts can be found by a method that is appealing in its simplicity. The steps are as follows:

In the extreme left-hand column we will make a list of all the treatments. In the case of a quantitative factor we shall represent the higher level by a small letter, corresponding to the capital letter that indicates the factor. The absence of the letter means that the treatment has the factor at its lower level. If all factors are at the lower level we shall designate the treatment by (1). For a qualitative factor it is immaterial which level is regarded as the higher and which as the lower, so long as consistency is maintained. Further, we shall list the treatments in 'standard order'. That is to say, we shall start with treatment (1) and m and then we shall add factor N to expand the list to (1) m n mn. Then we shall introduce factor P to make it

$$(1) \quad m \quad n \quad mn \quad p \quad mp \quad np \quad mnp.$$

Obviously the process can be continued indefinitely until the last factor has been included. Against each treatment we give the total of its data. We shall call this 'Column 0'. We illustrate the entire algorithm in Table 6δ, where each total represents the sum of four data.

Having formed Column 0 we calculate Column 1 from it. First we write down the total (302) of the first and second entries in Column 0; the next value is the sum of the next two entries in Column 0, i.e., $104 + 257 = 361$, and we continue in that way to the bottom of the column, which gives $129 + 274 = 403$. Next in Column 1 we write down the corresponding differences, beginning with the second minus the first ($181 - 121 = 60$). It is important to take them in proper order and to put in the sign, whether positive or negative. Thus the next entry is $+ 153$, namely $257 - 104$. We continue to the bottom of the column, the last entry being $+ 145$ ($= 274 - 129$). Column 2 is calculated from Column 1 in exactly the same way, and we continue until the number of the last column is that of the number of factors, which here equals 3.

TABLE 6δ   An example of the application of Yates's algorithm

Column	0	1	2	3	
(1)	121	302	663	1362	Grand total
m	181	361	699	+ 408	M
n	104	296	+ 213	+ 166	N
mn	257	403	+ 195	+ 188	M × N
p	123	+ 60	+ 59	+ 36	P
mp	173	+ 153	+ 107	− 18	M × P
np	129	+ 50	+ 93	+ 48	N × P
mnp	274	+ 145	+ 95	+ 2	M × N × P
Odds	477	708	1028		
Evens	885	1062	1096		
First half		1362	1770	2124	
Second half		+ 408	+ 354	+ 68	

In the last column we have the contrasts expressed in terms of the treatment totals, so we can use the method at (5.6.8). Further, a simplification is possible because in the contrasts for the various effects each treatment has a coefficient of ± 1. Accordingly U equals the number of treatments and rU equals the number of plots.

In the example of Table 6δ, where there are 32 plots in all, the sum of squares for the main effect of M is $(+ 408)^2/32$, i.e., 5202.00, while that for the main effect of N is $(+ 166)^2/32 = 861.125$ and so on. The full partition of the treatment sum of squares is:

Source	d.f.	s.s.
M	1	5202.000
N	1	861.125
P	1	40.500
M × N	1	1104.500
M × P	1	10.125
N × P	1	72.000
M × N × P	1	0.125
Total treatments	7	7290.375

The other components in the analysis of variance ('Error', Stratum total, etc.) are calculated in the usual way.

There are certain checks that should be made, as follows.

We calculate the sub-totals entered below the columns as in the example. Here 'Odds' column $0 = 121 + 104 + 123 + 129 = 477$ and 'Evens' column $0 = 181 + 257 + 173 + 274 = 885$.

In column 1 'First half' $= 302 + 361 + 296 + 403 = 1362$
'Second half' $= + 60 + (+ 153) + (+ 50) + (+ 145) = + 408$.

'First half' column 1 should be the sum of 'Odds' + 'Evens' in column 0, i.e. $302 + 351 + 296 + 403 = 477 + 885$. The 'Second half' column 1 should sum to 'Evens' − 'Odds' in column 0, i.e. $+ 60 + 153 + 50 + 145 = 885 − 477$. We repeat these two checks with columns 1 and 2, and again with columns 2 and 3.

A simple rule for writing the contrasts

The contrasts of the various effects can be read downwards in the following table, all coefficients being either $+1$ or -1. They were obtained by the method at (6.5.2).

The Yates table for the example is:

	G	M	N	M × N	P	M × P	N × P	M × N × P	
(1)	+	−	−	+	−	+	+	−	
m	+	+	−	−	−	−	+	+	
n	+	−	+	−	−	+	−	+	
mn	+	+	+	+	−	−	−	−	(6.6.1)
p	+	−	−	+	+	−	−	+	
mp	+	+	−	−	+	+	−	−	
np	+	−	+	−	+	−	+	−	
mnp	+	+	+	+	+	+	+	+	

The columns of this table give a ready means of calculating the value of any effect. Suppose, for example, that the interaction of M and N is required. Its value can be derived from the appropriate column, i.e. it comes from the contrast

$$(+1 \quad -1 \quad -1 \quad +1 \quad +1 \quad -1 \quad -1 \quad +1) \qquad (6.6.2)$$

The table can be derived very simply. In any main effect a treatment has $+1$ for its coefficient if it has the factor at its higher level and -1 if it has the lower. In an interaction its coefficient will depend upon the number of factors represented at their upper level. If that number is even, the coefficient will be $+1$; if it is odd the coefficient will be -1. Thus, for M × N when there are three factors, M, N and P, the working goes like this:

(1) has no higher level	0 is regarded as even,	hence $+1$;
m has one higher level, M,	1 is odd	hence -1;
n has one higher level, N,	1 is odd	hence -1;
mn has two higher levels,	2 is even	hence $+1$.

We are dealing with the interaction, M × N, P not coming into it. Consequently, it is immaterial whether P has its higher or its lower level. For that reason p, mp, np, and mnp will have the same coefficients as (1), m, n and mn respectively. The rule provides an easy way of writing down the contrasts for a 2^k design. (With an interaction of odd order it will reverse all signs, but that is of no importance where the value of the contrast is to be squared, though it is vital to note what has happened when interpreting the meaning.)

6.7 Quantity–quality interactions

Suppose that an experiment has been conducted to compare two forms of nitrogen (A and B) at three levels (0, 1, 2). In the ordinary way, given a 2×3 factorial set of treatments (A0, A1, A2, B0, B1, B2), the contrasts of interest would be:

Main effect of form of fertilizer.

$$(+1 \quad +1 \quad +1 \quad -1 \quad -1 \quad -1)$$

Linear effect of increasing applications

$$(-1 \quad 0 \quad +1 \quad -1 \quad 0 \quad +1) \qquad (6.7.1)$$

Quadratic effect

$$(+1 \quad -2 \quad +1 \quad +1 \quad -2 \quad +1)$$

Interaction

$$(-1 \quad 0 \quad +1 \quad +1 \quad 0 \quad -1) \quad \text{and} \qquad (6.7.2)$$
$$(+1 \quad -2 \quad +1 \quad -1 \quad +2 \quad -1)$$

They would all be mutually orthogonal, giving a simple covariance matrix like that considered at (5.6.8). However, in this instance A0 is the same as B0, and such contrasts are unsatisfactory. A0 and B0 cannot be used to compare the effect of form of fertilizer, which is better measured by

$$(0 \quad +1 \quad +1 \quad 0 \quad -1 \quad -1) \qquad (6.7.3)$$

Its interaction with increasing level of application is

$$(0 \quad +1 \quad -1 \quad 0 \quad -1 \quad +1).$$

This leaves one contrast still not identified. It must be orthogonal to all those already found and turns out to be

$$(-1 \quad 0 \quad 0 \quad +1 \quad 0 \quad 0)$$

That is to say, it is the contrast between the two identical treatments. Really that belongs to 'error'; it is not a treatment effect at all. When it has been transferred, only four degrees of freedom are left for treatments. On reflection it will be seen that this is correct because there are in fact only five, not six treatments.

More complicated cases arise, e.g. there could be several forms of nitrogen; but the general principle remains, i.e. to isolate the contrasts that really belong to 'error', and to form meaningful contrasts from what remains.

Exercise 6A

An experiment was conducted on sugar cane in five randomized blocks. There were two fertilizer factors, phosphorus at two levels and potassium at four equally spaced levels. Treatment totals in tons per acre were:

	K_0	K_1	K_2	K_3
P_0	180	248	277	285
P_1	251	307	342	346

First of all, work out the treatment sum of squares and partition it thus, using summation terms as in Section 6.2:

P	1
K	3
P × K	3
Treatments	7

Then use orthogonal contrasts to partition further, as in Section 6.5:

P	1
Linear K	1
Quadratic K	1
Cubic K	1
P × Linear K	1
P × Quadratic K	1
P × Cubic K	1
Treatments	7

1 acre = 4047 m^2 1 ton = 1016 kg

[Data from W. G. Cochran and G. M. Cox, *Experimental Design*, 2nd edn, 1950, p. 161.]

Exercise 6B

An experiment was conducted to study the control of blight on potatoes. The field plan and the plot yields in pounds are given below. Each plot consisted of four rows, three feet apart, and 16.5 feet long.

	$v_2 f_1$	$v_2 f_3$	$v_2 f_2$	$v_1 f_2$	$v_3 f_1$
	34.1	41.7	36.0	55.9	35.9
Block I	$v_3 f_4$	$v_2 f_4$	$v_2 f_0$	$v_3 f_0$	$v_3 f_2$
	76.3	63.9	21.3	36.6	54.2
	$v_3 f_3$	$v_1 f_4$	$v_1 f_1$	$v_1 f_3$	$v_1 f_0$
	72.2	100.9	55.8	72.7	39.0
	$v_1 f_1$	$v_1 f_4$	$v_3 f_0$	$v_3 f_4$	$v_2 f_1$
	51.9	88.3	35.7	88.2	21.0
Block II	$v_3 f_2$	$v_1 f_3$	$v_1 f_0$	$v_2 f_2$	$v_2 f_3$
	42.9	64.7	42.2	24.5	41.0
	$v_2 f_4$	$v_3 f_1$	$v_1 f_2$	$v_3 f_3$	$v_2 f_0$
	62.1	33.1	65.6	66.5	11.4
	$v_3 f_4$	$v_2 f_2$	$v_1 f_2$	$v_3 f_3$	$v_3 f_0$
	66.3	26.4	60.1	52.7	35.9
Block III	$v_3 f_2$	$v_2 f_3$	$v_1 f_0$	$v_2 f_0$	$v_2 f_4$
	39.1	59.8	45.2	11.8	69.0
	$v_1 f_3$	$v_2 f_1$	$v_1 f_1$	$v_3 f_1$	$v_1 f_4$
	75.1	28.3	47.2	53.1	102.1

[1 foot = 0.305 m   1 pound = 454 grams]

Calculate the analysis of variance, partitioning fertilizer effects into a linear and quadratic component and another for departure from the quadratic form.

[Data from A. A. Rayner, *A First Course in Biometry for Agriculture Students* (1969), p. 466.]

Exercise 6C

An experiment was conducted to find the best level of nitrogen fertilization of rice. Because that might depend upon the variety, a factorial experiment was decided upon with four randomized blocks. The data, which give grain yields in kilograms per hectare, were as follows:

Variety	Nitrogen in kg/ha	Block I	II	III	IV
A	0	3852	2606	3144	2894
	40	4788	4936	4562	4608
	70	4576	4454	4884	3924
	100	6034	5276	5906	5652
	130	5874	5916	5984	5518
B	0	2846	3794	4108	3444
	40	4956	5128	4150	4990
	70	5928	5698	5810	4308
	100	5664	5362	6458	5474
	130	5458	5546	5786	5932
C	0	4192	3754	3738	3428
	40	5250	4582	4896	4286
	70	5822	4848	5678	4932
	100	5888	5524	6042	4756
	130	5864	5264	6056	5362

Analyse the data, separating the linear and quadratic effects in the treatment sum of squares and the interaction. The form of the linear and quadratic effects can be derived from Section 5.8. (See Exercise 5I.)

[Data from K. A. Gomez and A. A. Gomez, *Statistical Procedures for Agricultural Research with Emphasis on Rice* (1976), p. 58.]

Exercise 6D

An experiment was conducted on maize using two randomized blocks, each of 16 plots. There were three factors:

A, B   Two varieties
I, U   Plots infested or uninfested with witchweed
F_1–F_4 Four fertilizer treatments, namely
     F_1 No added fertilizer
     F_2 Superphosphate alone added
     F_3 Superphosphate and manure added
     F_4 Superphosphate, nitrogen and potassium added.

Data were as follows. They represent yield of grain in pounds per plot of 0.01 morgen.

	BIF_3	BUF_1	AIF_3	BIF_4
	13.5	12.8	15.8	11.6
	AIF_1	BUF_4	AIF_2	AUF_1
I	10.4	17.1	12.5	14.8
	BIF_2	BUF_2	BIF_1	AIF_4
	11.8	16.9	9.5	11.3
	BUF_3	AUF_3	AUF_4	AUF_2
	22.3	24.9	19.9	19.7
	BUF_2	AIF_1	BIF_2	AUF_4
	16.0	10.0	9.5	19.2
	AUF_2	BUF_1	BIF_1	AUF_3
II	18.0	13.0	9.6	22.0
	BIF_3	AIF_4	BUF_4	BUF_3
	13.4	11.4	16.6	20.0
	AIF_2	BIF_4	AUF_1	AIF_3
	10.1	9.2	14.0	13.6

1 morgen = 8565 m^2 1 pound = 454 grams

Calculate a complete analysis of variance.

[Data from A. A. Rayner, *A First Course in Biometry for Agricultural Students* (1969), p. 456.]

Exercise 6E

There are four factors, each at two levels, namely, the presence or absence of

> *m*   manure
> *n*   nitrogen
> *p*   phosphorus
> *k*   potassium.

The crop is grass and figures represent the total yield of six cuts. The $2^4 = 16$ treatment totals, each representing four plots, are:

(1)	121	k	168	
m	181	mk	217	
n	104	nk	290	
mn	257	mnk	321	
p	123	pk	173	
mp	173	mpk	250	
np	129	npk	351	
mnp	274	$mnpk$	362	Grand total 3494

The analysis of variance so far reads:

Source	d.f.	s.s
Treatments	15	26 791.9
'Error'	45	4 074.2
Stratum total	60	30 866.1

Calculate the full analysis of variance, giving a complete partition of the treatment effects into components, each with one degree of freedom. Starting with the highest-order interaction, attempt an interpretation.

[Data from W. G. Cochran and G. M. Cox, *Experimental Designs* (1950), p. 158.]

Chapter 7

Split plots and confounding

7.1 Split-plot experiments

In certain experiments it is necessary or advisable to use two different types of plot, a feature which leads to the split-plot design. In factorial experiments it may be essential for practical reasons to apply the same level of one treatment to several adjacent plots. In that case complete randomization is not possible. Certain treatments such as chemical sprays or fertilizers can be applied over small areas, whereas ploughing methods may require much larger plots. As a result one factor, comprising the 'main treatments', is applied to plots, sometimes called 'main plots' to distinguish them. The other factor, comprising the 'sub-treatments', is applied to 'sub-plots', which are divisions of the main plots. In effect the main plots serve as blocks for the sub-plots. The position is that described in Section 1.9. Another use of split-plot designs comes when it is required to place emphasis, the intention from the beginning being to study one factor more precisely than the other (see Section 7.4).

The procedure for arranging a split-plot design is first to devise a basic experiment which uses the main-plot treatments. The basic experiment is usually arranged in randomized blocks, although it is possible to use a completely randomized design or a Latin square or some non-orthogonal design instead. Each of the main plots is then divided into an equal number of similar units (sub-plots) and the sub-plot treatments are randomly allocated to them in some orthogonal manner. This allocation requires a separate randomization for each main plot.

As a result of the randomization process there are three strata of error variation:

(a) between blocks, if they are present, within the whole;
(b) between plots within blocks if there are any, and otherwise within the whole;
(c) between sub-plots within plots.

The main-plot error is used for comparisons of main-plot treatments, but

134

both the sub-treatments and the interaction between the two sets of treatments are tested against the sub-plot error.

In a three-factor experiment it is possible to extend the process through the division of the sub-plots into sub^2-plots (or sub-sub-plots), if that seems appropriate. Such an experiment has a further stratum.

7.2 Example of an experiment in split plots

An example from *Statistical Methods* by G. W. Snedecor and W. G. Cochran (1967, p. 370) used three varieties of alfalfa (lucerne) on the main-plots in six randomized blocks. Each of the main plots was divided into four sub-plots, the sub-plot treatments being four cutting schemes. All sub-plots were cut twice: the second cut took place on 27th July. (The data of the first are not given.) Some of the plots received a further cut as follows: B, 1st September; C, 20th September; D, 7th October, but A was not cut further. The yields in tons per acre for the following year are set out in Table 7*a*.

Table 7*a* Yields in tons per acre for an alfalfa (lucerne) experiment with three varieties and four cutting treatments

		Block					
Variety	Cutting	I	II	III	IV	V	VI
Ladak	A	2.17	1.88	1.62	2.34	1.58	1.66
	B	1.58	1.26	1.22	1.59	1.25	0.94
	C	2.29	1.60	1.67	1.91	1.39	1.12
	D	2.23	2.01	1.82	2.10	1.66	1.10
Cossack	A	2.33	2.01	1.70	1.78	1.42	1.35
	B	1.38	1.30	1.85	1.09	1.13	1.06
	C	1.86	1.70	1.81	1.54	1.67	0.88
	D	2.27	1.81	2.01	1.40	1.31	1.06
Ranger	A	1.75	1.95	2.13	1.78	1.31	1.30
	B	1.52	1.47	1.80	1.37	1.01	1.31
	C	1.55	1.61	1.82	1.56	1.23	1.13
	D	1.56	1.72	1.99	1.55	1.51	1.33

Two further tables are required for the analysis. They are formed from the data as two-way tables, the first for blocks and varieties, the second for cutting dates and varieties.

					Block			
		I	II	III	IV	V	VI	Total
Variety	Ladak	8.27	6.75	6.33	7.94	5.88	4.82	39.99
	Cossack	7.84	6.82	7.37	5.81	5.53	4.35	37.72
	Ranger	6.38	6.75	7.74	6.26	5.06	5.07	37.26
	Total	22.49	20.32	21.44	20.01	16.47	14.24	114.97

(7.2.1)

			Cutting date			
		A	B	C	D	Total
Variety	Ladak	11.25	7.84	9.98	10.92	39.99
	Cossack	10.59	7.81	9.46	9.86	37.72
	Ranger	10.22	8.48	8.90	9.66	37.26
	Total	32.06	24.13	28.34	30.44	114.97

The sums of squares can be found from the summation terms as usual, but there are important differences from the general method for factorial experiments. As always with randomized blocks, the main-plot error is the interaction between blocks and main-plot treatments, while the sub-plot error is formed from the interaction of blocks with all other effects.

7.3   The analysis of variance for a split-plot design

If there are b blocks and a factor, M, with m levels is applied to main plots, while another factor, N, with n levels is applied to sub-plots, the analyses of variance are as follows. Note that there are three strata: (a) blocks/total area, to which no treatments have been applied; (b) main plots/blocks which carries M; and (c) sub-plots/plots which carries N and also M $\times$ N. However, no treatments have been applied in (a), so it can be ignored.

	Source	d.f.	s.s.
(a)	Blocks	$b - 1$	$S_b - S_0$
(b)	M	$m - 1$	$S_m - S_0$
	'Error i'	$(b - 1)(m - 1)$	$S_i - S_b - S_m + S_0$
	Stratum total i	$b(m - 1)$	$S_i - S_b$

(c)	N	$n - 1$	$S_n - S_0$
	M × N	$(m - 1)(m - 1)$	$S_{mn} - S_m - S_n + S_0$
	'Error ii'	$m(b - 1)(n - 1)$	$S_{ii} - S_i - S_{mn} + S_m$
Stratum total ii		$bm(n - 1)$	$S_{ii} - S_i$

There are two total terms, S_i and S_{ii}, based respectively on the main plots and the sub-plots. This feature will be illustrated below in a worked example. It will be seen from the degrees of freedom for 'Error ii' that effectively a number (m) of experiments in randomized blocks, each with $(b - 1)(n - 1)$ degrees of freedom for 'error', have been carried out on the plots of each of the main treatments. The form of the sum of squares shows the same. This can be a useful way of looking at a design in split-plots, especially if something goes wrong. Any damage will then extend only to the component for the main treatment involved. The rest should be all right.

If the main treatments had been disposed in some other way, say in a Latin square, the main plot analysis would be altered accordingly, but the sub-plot analysis would have remained the same.

To take the example at (7.2.1), $b = 6$, $m = 3$ and $n = 4$. The analysis of variance requires calculation of the following summation terms:

$$
\begin{aligned}
S_i &= (8.27^2 + 6.75^2 + \ldots + 5.07^2)/4 &&= 189.2749 \\
S_{ii} &= (2.17^2 + 1.88^2 + \ldots + 1.33^2) &&= 192.7065 \\
S_b &= (22.49^2 + 20.32^2 + \ldots + 14.24^2)/12 &&= 187.7346 \\
S_m &= (39.99^2 + 33.72^2 + 37.26^2)/24 &&= 183.7628 \\
S_n &= (32.06^2 + 24.13^2 + \ldots + 30.44^2)/18 &&= 185.5472 \\
S_{mn} &= (11.25^2 + 7.84^2 + \ldots + 9.66^2)/6 &&= 185.9358 \\
S_o &= 114.97^2/72 &&= 183.5847
\end{aligned}
\tag{7.3.1}
$$

In the sense of Section 1.10, e has been taken as 2.

The analysis of variance is therefore:

	Source	d.f.	s.s.	m.s.	F
(a)	Blocks	5	4.1499	0.8300	
(b)	Varieties (V)	2	0.1781	0.0890	0.65
	'Error i'	10	1.3622	0.1362	
Stratum total i		12	1.5403		

(7.3.2)

(c)	Cuttings (C)	3	1.9625	0.6542	23.36
	V × C	6	0.2105	0.0351	1.26
	'Error ii'	45	1.2586	0.0280	
Stratum total ii		54	3.4316		

Leaving aside for the moment the error variances, the first line to look at is the one for interaction. Clearly there is no reason here to believe that the effect of cuttings depends upon the variety, so it is correct to proceed to the main effect for cuttings and work with means taken over all varieties, namely

$$
\begin{array}{cccc}
A & B & C & S \\
1.78 & 1.34 & 1.57 & 1.69
\end{array}
\qquad \text{S.E.} = 0.039 \qquad (7.3.3)
$$

The standard error is obtained from 'Error ii'. Since each mean contains 18 data, S.E. $= \sqrt{0.0280/18} = 0.039$.

From these data, i.e. those at (7.2.1), there is no statistical evidence that the varieties differ, but since they are genetically different it is not to be expected that they will in fact be giving the same yields.

We note that the split-plot design has been very effective in reducing the error of the experiment, at least for the effect of cuttings and the interaction, which appear in the last part of the analysis. The sub-plot 'error' variance of 0.0280 is only 21 percent of that for the main plots. The consequent loss of information in the main plot analysis would be of little importance if, as seems likely, varieties were introduced only to see if they would provoke an interaction.

Some computer packages give the variance ratio between Error i and Error ii. It is useful as showing how far any advantage was gained by splitting the plots.

7.4   Strata in relation to split plots

This is perhaps the moment to relate an analysis of variance like that at (7.3.2) more closely to the consideration of strata in Section 1.9. There are in fact three strata involved, namely:

Blocks/Total area   Plots/Blocks   and   Sub-plots/Plots.

The first is null because no differential treatments have been applied to blocks. Nonetheless the block line was given largely as a matter of convention, though it does have its uses. It must be assumed that blocks have been chosen to pick up differences in the site and that other differences have become associated with them as part of the administration of the experiment. It is therefore reassuring that quite a lot of variation has been removed by them. Action would be required only if blocks had been ineffective.

The second (Plots/Blocks) carries the varieties. It also is not of great importance if, as appears likely, the varieties were introduced only to provoke an interaction. (If that was the intention things have worked out badly because the varieties are in fact very similar. Of course, they may differ in habit or season and that could be useful.) Finally, the important results are those in the third stratum. It carries cuttings, which had been applied within that stratum, and the interaction, which appears where it does because both factors are involved in its calculation. It is therefore satisfactory that its 'error' variance is so low.

It is sometimes assumed that when a succession of classifications are nested one within another, as here (i.e. Sub-plots $\rightarrow$ Plots $\rightarrow$ Blocks $\rightarrow$ Total Area), the 'error' variances in the strata will decrease as the units become smaller. At (7.3.2) that expectation has been fulfilled, the successive variances being

Blocks/Total Area	0.8300
Plots/Blocks	0.1362
Sub-plots/Plots	0.0280

The first was found as $(S_b - S_0)/5$.

However, this does not necessarily happen and a simple example will show why. Suppose that a block has a pronounced fertility gradient. In particular we will suppose that the north end has better soil than the south. Accordingly, plots are made long in the north–south direction and narrow east–west, so that each shall have its fair share of good and bad soil. Now someone wants to divide plots into sub-plots. If the plots are divided by north–south boundaries so that sub-plots are as long as the plots but narrower, it is to be expected that the 'error' for sub-plots/plots will be less than that for plots/blocks. However, that division may not be possible; it could give sub-plots so narrow that edge-effects were serious. If instead the plots were divided by east–west boundaries, the fertility pattern, which was so carefully eliminated in the plots/blocks stratum, will now appear in that of sub-plots/plots. In each plot one sub-plot will be on the good land in the north, another on the poor land at the south, with others in between. Consequently, the 'error' variance for sub-plots/plots will be appreciably greater than that for plots/blocks, the opposite of what was hoped for.

Much the same problem arises when blocks are chosen wrongly and cross the fertility contours instead of lying along them. (This was discussed in Section 1.8.)

In Section 1.9 a number of other suggestions were made how plots of different sizes might arise, and there is no need to look at them all because they have much the same characteristics. Perhaps the chief problems occur when it is necessary to work out standard errors of treatment differences. They will be considered in the next section.

One special case does deserve notice. It was mentioned in Section 1.6 that a row-and-column design allows for edge-effects. That is true, but difficulties arise if the plots are split. Necessarily some sub-plots will be more subject to those edge-effects than others. This is not a general argument against splitting plots with row-and-column designs. It applies only when there are marked edge-effects that are meant to be removed by the rows and columns. If there are, a discard area round the edges is essential.

Strip-plot or criss-cross designs

Before proceeding to details about split-plot designs we should mention another possibility, namely, the 'strip-plot design' or, as it is often called, the 'criss-cross' design. In a split-plot design plots with the same level of one factor are kept together. A strip-plot design on the other hand contains rows and columns; one factor is applied at random to the rows and the other to the columns. (Naturally there is a fresh randomization in each block.) The result might be like this:

	Ab	Cb	Bb	Db			Cc	Bc	Ac	Dc
Block I	Aa	Ca	Ba	Da		Block II	Cb	Bb	Ab	Db
	Ac	Cc	Bc	Dc			Ca	Ba	Aa	Da

and the other blocks likewise. The strata may be written

$$\text{Total area} \rightarrow \text{blocks} \rightarrow (\text{rows} \times \text{columns}).$$

The design is especially useful when there are difficulties about applying either factor on a small area. So long as there is no interaction of rows and columns it gives a particularly good estimate of the interaction of the two factors.

As to analysis, in principle the design is quite straightforward. If there are m row-treatments and n column-treatments, it is easiest to think of the blocks as providing a third factor, B, with b levels. At (7.3.2) the analysis could then have been regarded in these terms:

	Source		d.f.	Composition
(b)	Main effect of M		$(m-1)$	M
	'Error i'		$(b-1)(m-1)$	$B \times M$
(c)	Main effect of N		$(n-1)$	N
	Interaction		$(m-1)(n-1)$	$M \times N$
	'Error ii'		$(b-1)(n-1)$	$B \times N$
		with	$(b-)(m-1)(n-1)$	$B \times M \times N$

In the case of a strip-plot design the second analysis is divided to read:

Main effect of N	$(n-1)$	N
'Error' for N	$(b-1)(n-1)$	$B \times N$
Interaction	$(m-1)(n-1)$	$M \times N$
'Error' for $M \times N$	$(b-1)(m-1)(n-1)$	$B \times M \times N$

$$(7.4.1)$$

Hence each effect, M, N and $M \times N$, has an 'error' variance appropriate to itself. Although the F-test for the interaction is usually sensitive, there are problems when seeking particular effects within the interaction. As the next section shows, there can be difficulties even with a split-plot design. They are much more serious with the designs considered here.

7.5 Standard errors in a split-plot experiment

Before proceeding to work out standard errors of differences there is a point to be cleared up. It relates to the scaling of the main-plot analysis, which at (7.3.2) was actually calculated on a sub-plot basis. This in fact is usual practice but perhaps a little explanation is required. At (7.3.2) everything depends upon S_i, S_b, S_m and S_o, all of which were found at (7.3.1) using divisors derived from the number of sub-plots in each total, not the number of main plots. For example, the divisor for S_m was 24, not six, as might be thought appropriate for a main-plot analysis. In fact it does not matter which basis is adopted so long as everything is consistent. To achieve this, the first part should be worked in sub-plot units. (It is clearly not possible to do the opposite and calculate the second part in main-plot units, so there is not really any alternative.) This was done at (7.3.1). To take an example, the divisor for S_b was 12 not 3. Except possibly for the interaction, the standard errors in a split-plot design do not raise any problems, provided everything be done within a single stratum. The main treatments, for example, lie entirely within the stratum of plots within blocks, being applied to plots and randomized within blocks. If anyone enquires about varieties in (7.3.1) their means are:

Ladak, 1.67   Cossack, 1.57   Ranger, 1.55.

A difference between such means has a variance of

$$(1/24 + 1/24)\ 0.1362 = 0.0135 = (0.106)^2.$$

Note that everything is being worked on a sub-plot basis, as recommended above, even though main-plot comparisons are involved.

For the main effect of sub-treatments everything lies in the stratum of sub-plots within plots, and the only relevant line is that for 'error ii'. The calculations have already been given at (7.3.3).

The interaction is a little more complicated. In most instances only the sub-plot analysis is involved. Thus the F-value at (7.3.2) is 1.26 ($= 0.0351/0.0280$) with 6 and 45 degrees of freedom. Again if someone should ask about the means of the various cutting treatments for the variety Ladak, they are:

A 1.88   B 1.31   C 1.66   D 1.82.

Differences between them represent comparisons of sub-plots within the same main plots, so 'Error ii' is appropriate and the difference of two such means has a variance of $(1/6 + 1/6)\ 0.0280 = 0.00933 = (0.097)^2$ with 45 degrees of freedom.

The complication comes when someone wants to compare main treatments for a specified sub-treatment, e.g. varieties for cutting method A. The means are:

Ladak 1.88   Cossack 1.76   Ranger 1.70   (7.5.1)

The standard error of such a difference involves both parts of the analysis. (It is no longer true that all comparisons are made between sub-plots within the same main plots). What is needed is a combined variance, found in the following way.

Let the two 'error' variances be V_i and V_{ii} with f_i and f_{ii} degrees of freedom respectively; then the combined variance is

$$[V_i + (s - 1)V_{ii}]/s = V_c.$$

where s is the number of sub-plots to a main plot. Thus in the example at (7.3.2)

$$V_c = [0.1362 + (3 \times 0.0280)]/4 = 0.2202/4 = 0.0550.$$

The next step is to find L, where

$$L = \frac{V_i}{V_i + (s-1)V_{ii}} = \frac{0.1362}{0.2202} = 0.6185.$$

Then f_c, the degrees of freedom for V_c, are found thus:

$$\frac{1}{f_c} = \frac{L^2}{f_1} + \frac{(1-L)^2}{f_2}$$

$$= \frac{0.3825}{10} + \frac{0.1455}{45} = 0.0415$$

so $f_c = 24.2$. (Note that degrees of freedom in this context do not have to a whole number.) Hence the standard error of a difference between two of the means at (7.5.1) is $2 \times 0.0550/6 = 0.135$ with 24.1 degrees of freedom. It will be necessary to interpolate in F-tables to find the values required, but that need not be too difficult.

7.6 Split-plot analysis by sweeping

Mostly data from split-plots are analysed using summation terms. Each analysis will contribute its own residual, one component in each stratum, which together will make up the 'total residual' in Section 7.11. In general this will be more useful than their components in detecting where unexpected variation came from, but sometimes the problem is to find which plot within a block is different, or which sub-plot within a plot. It is then that sweeping may be called for. In any case, the operation repays study because it illuminates what goes on in the analysis of split-plot designs and so helps understanding of the way in which many computer programs tackle the problem.

To take the main-plot analysis first, the deviations as given in Section 1.9 equal

Plot mean − Block mean.

As a result each value will occur s times, where s is the number of sub-treatments. Thus, to take the data at (7.2.1), the deviations for Ladak are found in this way. The plot means for the six blocks are respectively:

$$2.068 \quad 1.688 \quad 1.582 \quad 1.985 \quad 1.470 \quad 1.205 \qquad (7.6.1)$$

These figures come from the first line of the table at (7.2.1). The block means come from the horizontal margin, i.e.

$$1.874 \quad 1.693 \quad 1.787 \quad 1.668 \quad 1.372 \quad 1.187.$$

Hence, taking the sub-plots of Ladak, the deviations are

+ 0.194	− 0.007	− 0.205	+ 0.317	+ 0.098	+ 0.018
+ 0.194	− 0.007	− 0.205	+ 0.317	+ 0.098	+ 0.018
+ 0.194	− 0.007	− 0.205	+ 0.317	+ 0.098	+ 0.018
+ 0.194	− 0.007	− 0.205	+ 0.317	+ 0.098	+ 0.018

For the two varieties there are likewise six values, each repeated four times, i.e.

Cossack
+ 0.086	+ 0.012	+ 0.056	− 0.216	+ 0.010	− 0.100

Ranger
− 0.279	− 0.006	+ 0.148	− 0.103	− 0.107	+ 0.080.

The sum of squares for 'Error i' and varieties is therefore

$$4[(+ 0.194)^2 + (− 0.007)^2 + \ldots + (+ 0.080)^2] = 1.5432.$$

This figure does not quite agree with those for the stratum total at (7.3.2) though it is near enough. Where there is a discrepancy the method of summation terms is usually more accurate. The next step is to take variety means of the deviations and to sweep by them. Means are

Ladak + 0.069,   Cossack − 0.025,   Ranger − 0.045.

That makes the main plot residuals (each arising four times):

Ladak	+ 0.125	− 0.076	− 0.274	+ 0.248	+ 0.029	− 0.051
Cossack	+ 0.111	+ 0.019	+ 0.081	− 0.191	+ 0.035	− 0.075
Ranger	− 0.234	+ 0.039	+ 0.193	− 0.058	− 0.062	+ 0.125

and hence the sum of squares for 'Error i' is

$$4[(+ 0.125^2) + (− 0.076)^2 + \ldots + (+ 0.125)^2] = 1.3614.$$

Again the figure is near that in (7.3.2). The discrepancies arise from rounding errors, which are made worse because everything has to be multiplied by four. (An additional decimal place in the deviations and residuals would most likely have cleared matters up.)

For the sub-plot analysis the deviations equal

Sub-plot datum – Plot mean.

That is to say, for Ladak, using the plot means found earlier, the sub-plot deviations are:

A $+ 0.102$ $+ 0.192$ $+ 0.038$ $+ 0.355$ $+ 0.110$ $+ 0.455$
B $- 0.488$ $- 0.428$ $- 0.362$ $+ 0.395$ $- 0.220$ $- 0.265$ (7.6.1)
C $+ 0.222$ $- 0.088$ $+ 0.085$ $- 0.075$ $- 0.080$ $- 0.085$
D $+ 0.162$ $+ 0.322$ $+ 0.238$ $+ 0.115$ $+ 0.190$ $- 0.105$

Similar figures can be found for the other two varieties, making 72 in all. The sum of their squares, 3.4318, is that for the combination of treatments (main effect of cuttings + interaction) and 'Error ii' in the sub-plot analysis at (7.3.2). Note that the main effect of varieties belongs to a different stratum and was removed along with the plot means to which it contributed.

The rest of the detailed calculation is left to the reader. In outline it goes like this. The next step is to sweep for the cutting means, which must of course be based on the deviations, like those at (7.6.1). Taken over all three varieties they are:

$$A + 0.184 \quad B - 0.256 \quad C - 0.022 \quad D + 0.094.$$

The values so found have squares that sum to 1.4688. The reduction $(3.4318 - 1.4688 = 1.9630)$ is the cuttings sum of squares at (7.3.2).

The last step is to sweep the figures last found by their means for all combinations, i.e.

Ladak	$+ 0.025$	$- 0.104$	$+ 0.019$	$+ 0.060$	
Cossack	$+ 0.009$	$- 0.014$	$+ 0.027$	$- 0.022$	(7.6.2)
Ranger	$- 0.033$	$+ 0.117$	$- 0.047$	$- 0.037$	

Sweeping by these means might appear to allow for all the treatment effects, not just the interaction, but this is to miss the point that the data have already been swept by the main effects. (That of varieties was removed in the formation of the deviations for the second stratum. It will be noted that the values at (7.6.2) sum to zero over both margins, so that main effects do not enter further into the calculation.) Sweeping further gives the sub-plot residuals. It will be found that the sum of the squares is 1.2581 which is effectively the value for 'Error ii' at (7.3.2).

A perusal of the above calculations will do much to explain what happens in a series of sweeps—how a sweep once made thereafter gives zero margins for its effect, so that the same sum of squares is not removed twice, and how each sweep reduces the sum of squares by an amount appropriate to the new effect introduced. (The word 'effect' is used here in the sense of a main effect or a block effect or an interaction.)

7.7 The idea of confounding

In a split-plot design one of the contrasts, the main plot effect of varieties in the example in Section 7.2, is transferred to another stratum. Since comparisons in that stratum are expected to be less good, the effect is to some extent being sacrificed to obtain better comparison of the others. Nevertheless, information about it can commonly be recovered if this is thought to be important. Indeed, that was done in the main-plot analysis at (7.3.2). This was not a very precise analysis, its 'error' variance being 0.1362 with 10 degrees of freedom as compared with 0.0280 with 45 in the sub-plot analysis. In some circumstances one might not want to be bothered with this analysis, but it is there. Such information as it has to impart can always be 'recovered' by working it out.

In many instances it is not a main effect but an interaction that is sacrificed. Given a lot of factors, the two-factor interactions are usually very important. If anyone questions that, he can ask himself why both factors have been introduced into the same experiment if there is no thought that they might interact. It would be simpler to have two experiments. Three-factor interactions are also useful, though not to the same extent, but interactions with four or more factors usually defy interpretation even if they are shown to exist. There is therefore no great objection to sacrificing them if this would help the precision of estimation of other contrasts that are of greater interest. Further, if they are sacrificed for that reason, there is little point in 'recovering' them by a split-plot design; no-one would be interested.

When a contrast is sacrificed in this way, it is said to have been 'confounded'. In a split-plot design, a main effect is confounded and it is usual to recover such information as is available about it. If an interaction is confounded, recovery is not usual.

The relationship between split plots and confounding may be illustrated thus: Let there be two factors A and B giving rise to the treatments

$$(1) \qquad A \quad B \quad AB.$$

If now some blocks contain only (1) and A, while the rest contain only B and AB, the result is a design in split-plots. Factor B is on main plots, which are here identical to the blocks, while A is on sub-plot. (It is true that the nomenclature has changed somewhat, but the relationship is clear.) If instead some blocks contain only (1) and AB, while the rest contain only A and B, it is now the interaction that has been confounded, i.e.,

$$(+1 \quad -1 \quad -1 \quad +1)$$

instead of the main effect

$$(+1 \quad +1 \quad -1 \quad -1)$$

but the idea is the same

The idea can be taken further, as the following will show.

Confounding with a 2^k design

In exploratory experiments it can be helpful to investigate the effect of several factors simultaneously to identify those that show promise and are therefore of special interest. When the most important ones have been found, more detailed experiments may be conducted in which these factors are tested at more levels. Less important factors can be omitted. Factorial experiments can become very large as the number of factors increases, and the size of the experiment can induce unwanted problems. In particular it may not be possible to find enough similar units so that each block shall contain each treatment. In that case only some treatments can occur in any one block. That situation arose in various forms in Chapter 4. Here we will consider another solution. Instead of estimating all contrasts, though allowing some of them to have a reduced efficiency factor, we shall eliminate some altogether in order to obtain better estimates of the rest. In general the least important interaction is the one of highest order, though that is not necessarily so. Mostly a two-factor interaction should be retained. (If it is unimportant, why were the two factors put in the same experiment?) The confounding of a main effect gives a design in split plots.

To take a simple example, we will suppose that an experiment is to have three factors, A, B and C, each at two levels. We shall suppose further that the design is either orthogonal or completely randomized and that all treatments have r replicates, consequently it will be possible to use the methods given at (5.6.7) and (5.6.8). So long as blocks of eight plots are seen as a reasonable solution, there is no great difficulty about design, but what can be done if someone objects that smaller blocks are essential?

If we may sacrifice an interaction, we can design the experiment in blocks of four plots. The obvious one to sacrifice is $A \times B \times C$, since the two-factor interactions are probably precious. We know from (6.6.1) that the coefficients of the contrast that we propose to sacrifice are

$$(-1 \quad +1 \quad +1 \quad -1 \quad +1 \quad -1 \quad -1 \quad +1),$$

the treatments being taken in standard order, i.e. (1), *a*, *b*, *ab*, *c*, *ac*, *bc*, *abc*. (As in Section 6.6 we are avoiding confusion between treatments and effects by using small letters for one and capitals for the other.) When we confound, we assign the treatments with a positive coefficient, i.e.,

$$a, \quad b, \quad c, \quad abc$$

to half the blocks, which should be chosen at random, and

$$(1), \quad ab, \quad ac, \quad bc$$

to the other half. The interaction of A × B × C has now become a contrast between blocks instead of within them. If anyone wants to recover it, he or she will have to compare those blocks that contain [*a b c abc*] with those that contain [(1) *ab ac bc*]. This is what was done to recover the main effect confounded in the example of a split-plot design, but here, where an unimportant interaction has been confounded, it is unlikely that anyone will bother. (The situation is a little confused on account of the nomenclature. What are called *blocks* here were *main plots* when we were in a context of split plots, and *plots* here were *sub-plots* then.)

However, all contrasts orthogonal to the one confounded are as they were before. We can now compare the form of the analyses as they would have been without confounding and with it. We shall assume that there are 32 plots.

Degrees of freedom with and without confounding

	Without	With
A	1	1
B	1	1
C	1	1
B × C	1	1
A × C	1	1
A × B	1	1
A × B × C	1	—
'Error'	21	18
Stratum total	28	24

To find the degrees of freedom for the stratum totals, we note that there are four blocks without confounding but eight with. Confounding has given rise to two disadvantages; there are fewer degrees of freedom for 'error' and the three-factor interaction has been lost. The great gain comes from the use of blocks of more acceptable size.

There are other ways in which the two sets of treatments could have been obtained. For example, we could have taken the first set,

$$a \quad b \quad c \quad abc$$

and have 'multiplied' each treatment in it by another treatment that was not contained in it. This operation of multiplying factors and treatments is one to which we shall have to become accustomed. As we saw in Section 6.6, the effect of including a factor in an interaction is to reverse signs if it occurs in the treatment. The effect then of including a factor twice is to restore the original position. Consequently, $A^2 = B^2 = C^2 = 1$. The same rule will apply to treatments. Here, if we multiply each treatment in the first set by ab, a treatment that does not occur in it, we get

$$a \times ab = b, \quad b \times ab = a, \quad c \times ab = abc, \quad abc \times ab = c.$$

That is to say, we have generated the second set from the first.

Another way is to expand the polynomial,

$$(1 - a)(1 - b)(1 - c) = (1) - a - b - c + ab + ac + bc - abc$$

which gives the two sets from the positive and negative coefficients in the expansion.

With these methods available, we can ask how we would have confounded, say, the interaction, $B \times C$. (In general we would not want to do so, but we are considering only technique.) To take the first method, from Section 6.6 we see that it is represented by the contrast, $(+1 + 1 - 1 - 1 - 1 - 1 + 1 + 1)$, so the two sets of treatments are

$$(1) \quad a \quad bc \quad abc \quad \text{and} \quad b \quad ab \quad c \quad ac.$$

When there are only two sets the second method seems superfluous, but we will illustrate it nonetheless. We will take the first set and multiply throughout by b. That gives

$$(1) \times b = b, \quad a \times b = ab, \quad bc \times b = c, \quad abc \times b = ac.$$

Finally, we can expand

$$(1 + a)(1 - b)(1 - c) = (1) + a - b - c - ab - ac + bc + abc.$$

The change here, where A does not enter into the interaction, is to use $(1 + a)$ instead of $(1 - a)$. All methods have led to the same result.

The method applies to all cases where all factors are at two levels. If, for example, there were four factors, A, B, C and D, the four factor interaction would be confounded if half the blocks contained

$$(1) \quad ab \quad ac \quad ad \quad bc \quad bd \quad cd \quad abcd \qquad (7.7.1)$$

and the rest contained

$$a \quad b \quad c \quad d \quad abc \quad abd \quad acd \quad bcd. \qquad (7.7.2)$$

With the unconfounded contrasts there is a simple way of finding the sum of squares for each; it was given in Section 6.6.

7.8   Confounding more than one contrast

The method given in the last section makes it possible to design an experiment with blocks only half the usual size, but that may not be enough. If someone wishes to have block size reduced to a quarter, it is possible to confound further interactions.

We shall take the example at the end of the last section in which the interaction, $A \times B \times C \times D$, was confounded between two sets of blocks, each block containing eight plots. We shall attempt to divide further into new blocks, each of four plots. To do that we shall confound the three-factor interaction, $A \times B \times C$. This involves having

$$(1) \quad d \quad ab \quad ac \quad bc \quad abd \quad acd \quad bcd \qquad (7.8.1)$$

in one set and

$$a \quad b \quad c \quad ad \quad bd \quad cd \quad abc \quad abcd \qquad (7.8.2)$$

in the other. That enables us to draw up four lists of treatments, a, β, γ and δ, such that $A \times B \times C \times D$ is confounded between lists a and β on the one hand compared with lists γ and δ one the other, and $A \times B \times C$ is confounded between a and γ on the one hand and β and δ on the other, i.e.

a (1)	ab	ac	bc
β ad	bd	cd	$abcd$
γ d	abd	acd	bcd
δ a	b	c	abc

We did that by putting into

α all those treatments common to (7.7.1) and 7.8.1),
β all those treatments common to (7.7.1) and (7.8.2),
γ all those treatments common to (7.7.2) and (7.8.1),
δ all those treatments common to (7.7.2) and (7.8.2).

We shall assign the treatments in α to one-quarter of our blocks, which we shall choose at random, β to another quarter, also chosen at random, and so on. (We need scarcely add that the treatments should be assigned at random within the blocks also.)

We have now achieved a design in blocks of four plots such that our two designated contrasts are confounded, but we have done more. Four things can be put into pairs in three ways. We have paired α and β to leave γ and δ and we have paired α and γ to leave β and δ. What happens if we pair α and δ to leave β and γ? That gives us the contrast between

and

$$(1) \quad a \quad b \quad c \quad ab \quad ac \quad bc \quad abc$$
$$d \quad ad \quad bd \quad cd \quad abd \quad acd \quad bcd \quad abcd,$$

It appears that we have also confounded the main effect of D. This is not necessarily a bad thing—we confounded main effects without comment in Section 7.6—but, if we are going to do it, we should act of set purpose and not inadvertently.

In general, if we confound two contrasts, we confound also their 'generalized interaction', i.e., the result of multiplying them following the rule given in the last section that $A^2 = B^2 = \ldots = 1$. That is what happened in the example above, because

$$(A \times B \times C \times D) \times (A \times B \times C) = D.$$

Before leaving this example we may note that the various groups of treatments could have been obtained from one another using the method of multiplication given in the last section. Thus, if α is multiplied throughout by some treatment not contained within itself, say b, the result is [b a abc c], which is δ. If this is now multiplied by some treatment that is in neither α nor δ, say ad, the result is [abd d bcd acd], which is γ. That leaves [ad bd cd $abcd$] for the last list. The method does not help much in forming lists in the first place but it provides a convenient means of checking them.

Usually multiple confounding is not called for with only four factors, because blocks of eight plots can usually be found. Its chief use comes with five factors or more. (If there are five factors, that calls for 32 treatments.

A single confounding will reduce the number of plots needed in a block to 16, but even this may be too many.)

To take an example, we confound $A \times C \times D$, $B \times C \times D \times E$ and $A \times D \times E$ in a 2^5 design. The first, $A \times C \times D$, requires division into

a ab ae abe c bc ce bce d bd de bde acd abcd acde abcde

and

(1) *b e be ac abc ace abce ad abd ade abde cd bcd cde bcde.*

What we have done was really very simple. We decided what would be involved in confounding the interaction $A \times C \times D$ in a 2^3 design, namely, division into

$$[a \quad c \quad d \quad acd] \quad \text{and} \quad [(1) \quad ac \quad ad \quad cd]. \tag{7.8.3}$$

Then each of those treatments was multiplied by the treatments, (1), *b*, *e* and *be*, to give the solution, the additional factors being B and E.

The next contrast to be confounded is $B \times C \times D \times E$, which calls for the division of the treatments into sets,

b ab c ac d ad e ae bcd abcd bce abce bde abde cde acde

and

(1) *a bc abc bd abd be abe cd acd ce ace de ade bcde abcde.*

The additional factor is now A. We have taken the grouping of a 2^4 design with the four-factor interaction confounded, and we have then multiplied each of the treatments so obtained by both (1) and *a*.

We can now form our four lists:

a	c	d	ab	ae	bce	bde	$abcd$	$acde$
β	a	bc	bd	ce	de	abe	acd	$abcde$
γ	b	e	ac	ad	bcd	cde	$abce$	$abde$
δ	(1)	be	cd	abc	abd	ace	ade	$bcde$

As before, the first confounded interaction, $A \times C \times D$, is given by the difference between lists a and β as compared with γ and δ; the second, $B \times C \times D \times E$, by the difference between a and γ as compared with β and δ. This leaves the difference between a and δ as compared with β and γ.

Examination shows that it gives the third contrast to be confounded, namely, $A \times B \times E$.

If a fourth contrast is added, not only will it be confounded itself but its generalized interaction with the first three will be confounded as well. The following example may be of interest. It represents a 2^5 design in which seven contrasts are confounded, viz. $A \times C \times D$, $B \times C \times D \times E$, $A \times D \times E$, $A \times B \times E$, $C \times E$, $A \times B \times C$, $B \times D$. (The fact that some of the confounded contrasts are two-factor interactions explains why such confounding is not really desirable with fewer than six factors.) The lists are

a	(1)	abd	ace	$bcde$
β	a	bd	ce	$abcde$
γ	b	ad	$abce$	cde
δ	c	$abcd$	ae	bde
ε	ab	d	bce	$acde$
ς	ac	bcd	e	$abde$
τ	bc	acd	abe	de
θ	abc	cd	be	ade

We are not now seeking r blocks of 32 plots, where r is the degree of intended replication, but $8r$ blocks, each of four plots, one-eighth of the blocks to take each of the lists at random. Between 32 treatments there would ordinarily be 31 degrees of freedom, but here seven of the contrasts have been confounded so there are only 24. The outline analysis of variance will have the following form.

Source	d.f.
Unconfounded contrasts	24
'Error'	$24 (r - 1)$
Stratum total	$24r$

A sum of squares can be found for each of the unconfounded contrasts by the use of Yates's algorithm, as set out in Section 6.6, and the method given at (5.6.8).

7.9 Single replication designs

The factors in an exploratory experiment may be quite numerous. Initially there may be no intention of studying the whole subject in depth;

it is just that there are many ideas on how research should proceed, and the proposal is that the factors should be put into one experiment to see which look hopeful. It is true that the investigator could carry out an experiment on each, but that would be wasteful. If all the proposals are put into one 2^k design then, supposing that there are no high-order interactions, each factor will gain from the replication afforded by the others. To take an example, if a 2^5 experiment is conducted and there are no major interactions with more than two factors, then each combination of A and B, i.e., (1), a, b and ab, has its replication increased eight-fold by being studied at eight combinations of C, D and E, i.e., (1), c, d, e, cd, ce, de and cde, with which there is no interaction. (This is called 'hidden replication', but we must insist that it exists only if there are no important interactions. Nevertheless, even if three-factor interactions are likely, there is still a four-fold gain in replication if there are no likely four-factor interactions. That surely can safely be assumed.)

Given a large number of factors it is feasible to design a 2^k experiment with a single replication. (For the moment we will not try to introduce any blocks.) To resume the case of five factors, there are five main effects, namely, A, B, C, D and E; there are also ten two-factor interactions, namely, A × B, A × C, A × D, A × E, B × C, B × D, B × E, C × D, C × E and D × E. That leaves 16 degrees of freedom for higher order interactions. Most of them probably do not really exist; any that do are unlikely to be large. It is therefore reasonable to use them collectively as 'error'. The estimate so made may be a little inflated, but that is a fault on the right side. Sometimes there are three-factor interactions that are expected for prior reasons to be important. If that is so, they should be excluded from 'error' and dealt with separately, thereby reducing the degrees of freedom for 'error'; that is quite legitimate. What is wrong is the examination of each interaction with the intention that, if it appears to be having little effect, it can always be put into 'error'. The procedure is wrong because the 'error' is then being formed from interactions selected on account of their low sums of squares. To avoid such bias the components of 'error' should be fixed from the start, and changes made only rarely and for strong reasons.

There is no difficulty about introducing blocks; one of the discarded interactions can be confounded between two halves of the area. If need be, three could be confounded between quarters. Everything is as in Section 7.8 except that the various lists are no longer replicated and, consequently, information about confounded interactions can no longer be recovered by a comparison of blocks. However, it is so unusual for anyone to want to recover information about interactions, especially high-order ones, that the loss is small.

A singly replicated experiment need not have all factors at two levels, but in an exploratory situation this is usual. There are times, however, when doubts about the correct level of some quantitative factor require that there be three or even more levels. If that is so, there is no objection to using the number required, though it may increase considerably the total number of plots. Some such designs will be considered in Sections 7.11 and 7.12.

7.10   Fractional replication

With numerous factors, especially if all have two levels, it is possible to go even further and to use fractional replication. The problem of total size of the experiment may be serious. For example, if the total number of plots is not to exceed 500, a 2^k experiment with a single replicate must not have more than nine factors. (A 3^k experiment, if one is proposed, must not have more than six.) Some may find a solution by discarding factors, at least for the moment; others may try to minimize the number of levels of each. A third possibility is to use only some of the treatments. That will be done here. Naturally some information will be lost, but since 'error' will have to be estimated from the highest-order interactions this may not matter much.

To illustrate the approach we will suppose that someone wants a 2^6 design. A single replicate would require 64 plots, but this is considered to be too many. We will therefore see what can be done with 32. We shall start by choosing an interaction as the 'defining contrast'. Usually it will be best to take the one of highest order, in this instance

$$A \times B \times C \times D \times E \times F,$$

to separate the 64 treatments into two lists. It is immaterial which of the two we choose. We could make our selection at random or in any other way. Here we shall assume that we have chosen:

(1)	*ae*	*be*	*cf*	*abcd*	*abdf*	*acef*	*bcef*
ab	*af*	*bf*	*de*	*abce*	*abef*	*adef*	*bdef*
ac	*bc*	*cd*	*df*	*abcf*	*acde*	*bcde*	*cdef*
ad	*bd*	*ce*	*ef*	*abde*	*acdf*	*bcdf*	*abcdef*

$$(7.10.1)$$

We then allocate those 32 treatments to the plots at random.

We can see the consequences of this procedure better with a simpler example. We shall therefore consider only four factors and consider what interpretation could be made of only eight plots with the treatments

Plot	1	2	3	4	5	6	7	8	
Treatment	(1)	*ab*	*ac*	*ad*	*bc*	*bd*	*cd*	*abcd*	(7.10.2)

If we wanted the main effect of A we would have to compare plots 2, 3, 4 and 8 with plots 1, 5, 6 and 7. (We recall what was said in Section 5.2 about all contrasts ultimately being a comparison of data.) Suppose though that we wanted to know about B × C × D, then we would want to compare those plots on which b, c and d were represented an even number of times with those in which the number was odd. (That goes back to Section 6.6.) This being so, we want to compare plots 2, 3, 4 and 8 with plots 1, 5, 6 and 7. In fact, the two contrasts are estimated in exactly the same way. If the difference between the two sets of plots were large, we would not know whether we had a main effect of A or an interaction of B, C and D. Since a main effect is more likely to have a large effect than a three-factor interaction, we would opt for the former. The two effects, A and B × C × D, are said to be 'aliases'. It is like one person having two names, and we cannot be sure which is the right one, though we may make a guess. Any contrast has an alias in the generalized interaction of itself and the defining contrast. Thus,

$$A \times (A \times B \times C \times D) = B \times C \times D.$$

Hence B × C × D is an alias of A and vice versa.

To return to (7.9.1), there are six main effects, those of A, B, C, D, E and F, each with an alias that is a five-factor interaction, so it can be ignored. There are also 15 two-factor interactions, A × B, A × C,..., E × F, each with a four-factor interaction as its alias. Again, if there is a large effect, there will be little doubt which contrast is the cause. Finally there are 20 three-factor interactions that form ten pairs of aliases, namely,

A × B × C and its alias D × E × F
A × B × D and its alias C × E × F
···   ···   ···   ···
A × E × F and its alias B × C × D

Here interpretation is impossible. (Of the two interactions that form a pair there is no reason to prefer one to the other.) Nevertheless, the sums of squares of those ten contrasts can be combined to give an 'error' sum of squares with ten degrees of freedom. In fact, the outline analysis of variance looks like this:

Source	d.f.
Main effects	6
Two-factor interactions	15
'Error'	10
Stratum total	31

Computations required

The calculation of such an analysis is a little lengthy, not on account of any inherent complications but because there are 21 effects to be evaluated. First, the stratum total can be found either by sweeping, as in Section 1.3, or as a difference of two summation terms, one for the data and the other for the general mean (S and S_0 in Section 1.4). Evaluation of the sums of squares for the 21 contrasts of interest is not difficult because a modification of Yates's algorithm is available. (The algorithm is explained in Section 6.6.) We shall illustrate it by a simple example in which there are only three factors, giving rise to eight treatments. If a half-replicate is used, there will in fact be only four of them in the experiment, say a, b, c, abc. We shall ascribe data of a, β, and δ respectively to the those plots.

We have four plots, so we think first of four treatments, (1), a, b and ab, factor C being ignored. Of the four treatments thus formed, two, namely (1) and ab, do not occur in the experiment, so we shall introduce C by expanding them to c and abc. In the table of the algorithm, Column 0 can now be found and the rest of the calculations follow, i.e.,

	0	1	2
$(1) \to c$	γ	$a + \gamma$	$a + \beta + \gamma + \delta$
$a \to a$	a	$\beta + \delta$	$a - \beta - \gamma + \delta$
$b \to b$	β	$a - \gamma$	$-a + \beta - \gamma + \delta$
$ab \to abc$	δ	$-\beta + \delta$	$-a - \beta + \gamma + \delta$
Odds	$\beta + \gamma$	$2a$	
Evens	$a - \delta$	δ	
First half		$a + \beta + \gamma + \delta$	$2a + 2\delta$
Second half		$a - \beta - \gamma + \delta$	$-2a + 2\delta$

The three quantities needed to find the sums of squares by use of the method at (5.6.8) are:

Main effect of A (alias B × C) $a - \beta - \gamma + \delta$;
Main effect of B (alias A × C) $-a + \beta - \gamma + \delta$;
Main effect of C (alias A × B) $-a - \beta + \gamma + \delta$.

All can be derived from Column 2.

Of course, the example has concerned an experiment so small that it would never have arisen in practice. It does however illustrate how to deal with the data from any fractionally replicated design. If there are k factors, the method is to ignore one of them and to start Column 0 with a complete set of the rest. Then the last factor is introduced where necessary, to make each treatment into one of those in the actual design. After that, everything is as usual. One advantage is that the sum of squares is calculated for all contrasts. Consequently the 'error' can be found by the addition of sums of squares for all relevant interactions, i.e. those involving three factors or more, but ignoring those of the two highest orders, because they are aliases of the main effects and the two-factor interactions. Because the 'error' sum of squares can be found directly, a check is afforded by everything summing to the stratum total.

More elaborate cases

If there had been seven factors, A, B, ..., G, there would have been seven main effects, each with a six-factor interaction as its alias, and 21 two-factor interactions, each with a five-factor interaction as its alias. Since there would have been 63 degrees of freedom in all, that leaves 35 degrees of freedom for 'error', made up of 35 three-factor interactions, each having as its alias a four-factor interaction, namely,

$$A \times B \times C \quad \text{with its alias} \quad D \times E \times F \times G,$$
$$A \times B \times D \quad \text{with its alias} \quad C \times E \times F \times G,$$
$$\ldots \quad \ldots \quad \ldots \quad \ldots \quad \ldots \quad \ldots \quad \ldots$$
$$E \times F \times G \quad \text{with its alias} \quad A \times B \times C \times D.$$

If the experiment is too large for a single block, one of the contrasts used for 'error' can be confounded to divide the treatments into two lists, one for each block. Multiple confounding can be used, as in Section 7.8, if circumstances call for it. No new principle is introduced by the fractional replication.

If a half-replicate still gives too many plots, it is possible to declare a further defining contrast and to use only a quarter of the treatments. In that case the generalized interaction of the two declared defining contrasts has equal status with them and, in consequence, each contrast under investigation has three aliases, not one. Such a scheme is feasible only when there are many factors.

7.11 Confounding with a 3^k design

So far we have considered only the confounding of a 2^k design, but there are other possibilities. For example, if quadratic effects were of interest, someone might want a 3^k design.

We will first look at the 3^2 case, principally in order to show the approach. The treatments may be written:

$$00 \quad 01 \quad 02 \quad 10 \quad 11 \quad 12 \quad 20 \quad 21 \quad 22.$$

Here the first digit gives the level of factor A, whether 0, 1 or 2, and the second does the same for factor B. Clearly the two degrees of freedom for the main effect of A can be found by adding the totals of three triplets of treatments, i.e.

$$[00\ 01\ 02]\quad [10\ 11\ 12]\quad \text{and}\quad [20\ 21\ 22].$$

They will provide a summation term, S_A, which with S_o the correction term, will give the desired sum of squares. The same can be done for the main effect of B, the triplets then being

$$[00\ 10\ 20]\quad [01\ 11\ 21]\quad \text{and}\quad [02\ 12\ 22].$$

It is not so obvious that the interaction sum of squares can be calculated similarly. It has four degrees of freedom and it has to be evaluated in two parts. The first comes from the triplets:

$$[00\ 11\ 22],\quad [01\ 12\ 20]\quad \text{and}\quad [02\ 10\ 21].$$

Their three totals will give rise to a summation term, S_I. The second comes from

$$[00\ 12\ 21],\quad [11\ 20\ 02]\quad \text{and}\quad [22\ 01\ 10].$$

That gives a summation term, S_J. Each component will, of course, have two degrees of freedom. The sum of squares for the interaction will be $(S_I - S_J - 2S_0)$ with four.

The conventional way of confounding a 3^2 design is to have six blocks, each of three plots. Each of the triplets associated with the interaction will be assigned to one block, like this:

Block	I	00	11	22
Block	II	01	12	20
Block	III	02	10	21
Block	IV	00	12	21
Block	V	11	20	02
Block	VI	22	01	10

With such a design the main effects are completely unconfounded. Component I of the interaction is confounded between Blocks I, II and III, but may be found from Blocks IV, V and VI. Component J is similarly confounded between Blocks IV, V and VI, but may be found from Blocks I, II and III. (It need hardly be said that really the triplets should be allocated to blocks at random and the treatments should be assigned at random to the plots of that block. For purposes of explanation, however, it is easier if the underlying pattern can be retained.)

The design just given represents traditional wisdom, but it may be asked if anyone really wants an interaction with an efficiency factor of one-half. (See Section 4.1.) In any factorial design the interactions are rarely well enough determined to carry the weight they are required to bear. If a factor is large, no one should look at the main effects associated with it; only if it is small may one desert the particular effects. It needs to be estimated with considerable precision for such important decisions to depend upon its magnitude. It may be unconventional, but we do suggest that there are times when it would be better to have the main effects at half-efficiency and to estimate the interaction with full efficiency. If the object of the experiment is to find out whether the two factors interacted or operated independently of one another, there would be no doubt about the design to choose. One would assign to blocks the triplets associated with the two main effects. In that case the design would go like this:

Block	I	00	01	02
Block	II	10	11	12
Block	III	20	21	22
Block	IV	00	10	20
Block	V	01	11	21
Block	VI	02	12	22

It would then be necessary to base the calculation of the main effect of A on the data in blocks IV, V and VI and that of B on blocks I, II and III.

The situation is different if there are three factors. We could then be in the familiar situation of wanting the main effects and the two-factor interactions but of being willing to lose the interaction of all three factors. It has eight degrees of freedom, two for each of four components, W, X, Y and Z. In each component there are three sets of nine treatments, and each set will give a data total. The totals of a component will give a summation term from which can be found the sum of squares for the two degrees of freedom. The sets are

W

000	012	021	101	110	122	202	211	220
002	011	020	100	112	121	201	210	222
001	010	022	102	111	120	200	212	221

X

000	011	022	102	110	121	201	212	220
001	012	020	100	111	122	202	210	221
002	010	021	101	112	120	200	211	222

Y

000	*011*	*022*	*101*	*112*	*120*	*202*	*210*	*221*
001	*012*	*020*	*102*	*110*	*121*	*200*	*211*	*222*
002	*010*	*021*	*100*	*111*	*122*	*201*	*212*	*220*

Z

000	*012*	*021*	*102*	*111*	*120*	*201*	*210*	*222*
001	*010*	*022*	*100*	*112*	*121*	*202*	*211*	*220*
002	*011*	*020*	*101*	*110*	*122*	*200*	*212*	*221*

The experiment will need twelve blocks each of nine plots. The sets given above are each allocated one block and the treatments are allocated at random to its plots. Component W will be confounded between the three blocks to which its sets are applied, but its sum of squares can be found from the other nine blocks. It is the same with components X, Y and Z. Hence the whole interaction can be found, but with an efficiency factor of three-quarters.

If the three-factor interaction is indeed of little importance, there will be little occasion to investigate it. The stratum total could be found in the usual way. Then the summation terms could be worked out, as in Section 6.3, to find the sums of squares for the main effects and two-factor interactions. What is left could legitimately be attributed to 'error', the eight degrees of freedom for the three-factor interaction being merged with those that would be used for 'error' anyway. If the sum of squares for the confounded interaction is needed, the somewhat laborious method given above is always available.

Mixed confounding, in which some factors are at two levels and some at three, is decidedly awkward and is better avoided. It is, however, possible to use the method illustrated at (7.8.3). There the interaction of three of t two-level factors was confounded, and each resulting treatment was associated with all combinations from the other factors. There is no requirement that those other factors shall all be at two levels; the method applies however many levels they have.

7.12 Confounding a 4^k design

Given factors each at four levels, confounding is not difficult provided all factors are quantitative with levels equally spaced. The method is to associate each level with a treatment from a 2^2 factorial set. To take an example, we will suppose that factor A has levels 0, 1, 2 and 3. We will associate them thus with factors U and V:

0	1	2	3
(1)	V	UV	U

The contrasts that ordinarily arise from U and V are:

Main effect of U	$(-1$	-1	$+1$	$+1)$
Main effect of V	$(-1$	$+1$	$+1$	$-1)$
Interaction	$(+1$	-1	$+1$	$-1)$

The main effect of U is effectively a comparison of the two upper levels of A, namely, 2 and 3, compared with the lower levels, namely, 0 and 1. As such it does not pick up the linear effect as effectively as the more usual $(-3 - 1 + 1 + 3)$, but it will serve the same general purpose. The main effect of V is exactly the contrast used at (5.7.4) to show the quadratic effect, which leaves U × V. In so far as it represents an inflexion, it could serve much the same purpose as a cubic effect. In fact, it is more usually confounded. Even if there were only the one factor, confounding U × V would reduce block size from four to two. That is not usual, but if there were two factors, A and B, at four levels, they could be represented respectively by U and V, and by W and X. It could be convenient to confound U × V or W × X or U × V × W × X. Indeed, all three could be confounded at the same time to give blocks of four plots, since any one of them is the generalized interaction of the other two. Another scheme might be to confound only the four-factor interaction, thus using blocks of eight plots and leaving U × V and W × X to give warning of any cubic effects. Also, there is no limit to the number of four-level factors that can be dealt with in this way.

Mixed confounding with factors at three and four levels is particularly awkward, but with factors, some with two levels and some with four, it is quite easy. An experiment with h factors at two levels and k factors with four is readily transformed to one with $(h + 2k)$ factors, each at two levels. Further, as with the 4^k design, there are a number of interactions that can readily be dispensed with.

Given an interest in quadratic effects, which with a 4^k design are estimated without loss of efficiency, as are their interactions, it can be argued that four levels are better than three. An objection comes from the estimation of the linear effects being less than ideal (its efficiency is 0.8, equivalent to the loss of 1/5 of its replication) but that may not matter if, as is usually the case, the linear effects are large compared with the quadratic.

7.13   Total residuals

Whenever we work in several strata—and this happens consistently with split plots and designs in which an interaction is confounded—we need to think carefully about residuals. It follows from what was said in

Section 1.9 that each plot will have a residual in each stratum. To anyone who is trying to find out why a certain 'error' sum of squares was larger than expected, this is a convenience. He has to look at the residuals in that stratum to see if any are unduly large. The situation is different if the residuals are being examined to find any features of the land that should be allowed for on another occasion. For that purpose 'total residuals' are more useful, being simply

Datum − treatment mean.

It does not matter what contrasts are confounded, whether main effects or interactions. Neither does it matter how blocks were formed. What is required is a measure of the inherent fertility of the plot. The experiment that happens currently to be on the site and the design adopted to implement it are irrelevant for that purpose. Further, the treatment whose mean is required results perhaps from a combination of many factors, e.g. *abcde*.

Where replication is low, no residuals are going to be of much use because they are calculated under the constraint that they must sum to zero over each treatment. Hence, if there are only two replicates, each residual, p, must have a counterpart, $-p$, at the other plot with the same treatment. Clearly p measures local peculiarities at two locations and, if it is large, there is no way of saying which location brought that about. (This was one reason for not considering residuals in Sections 4.9 and 4.10. Even with three replications residuals are difficult to interpret.)

Where there is only one replication, as with the designs considered in Section 7.9, the calculation of residuals becomes very complicated.* (The 'error' is made up from a number of interactions.) The situation is no less complicated with fractional replication. Some computer packages find the residuals by a method that is completely sound but not of a kind to be attempted by anyone without suitable software. What they do is this: The program evaluates all the contrasts that do not belong to 'error'. Then it takes the deviations, which are found in the usual way, and adjusts each by the values of the relevant contrasts. As we have said, the method gives correct values for the residuals, but the calculations are not of a sort to be undertaken lightly, and they will not be described here.

Exercise 7A

Five varieties of spring wheat were sown in a randomized blocks design

---

*But for 2^k experiments the Yates table facilitates it.

in four blocks. The soil was treated with three different levels of nitrogen randomly allocated to equal areas within each plot. The design and yields in t/ha were as follows:

	V2			V5			V1			V4			V3		
	N1	N3	N2	N2	N3	N1	N1	N2	N3	N1	N3	N2	N2	N1	N3
Block I	4.6	5.5	5.3	5.0	5.4	4.7	5.5	6.1	6.4	5.0	6.0	5.7	5.5	4.9	5.8
	V1			V3			V2			V5			V4		
	N3	N1	N2	N1	N3	N2	N3	N2	N1	N2	N3	N1	N2	N1	N3
Block II	5.8	5.0	5.5	4.9	5.5	5.4	5.4	5.0	4.7	4.6	5.0	4.2	6.2	5.7	6.5
	V5			V1			V3			V2			V4		
	N2	N3	N1	N2	N3	N1	N3	N1	N2	N1	N3	N2	N1	N3	N2
Block III	4.8	5.0	4.6	5.4	5.9	5.0	5.5	4.8	4.7	5.0	5.8	5.1	5.3	6.7	5.8
	V2			V3			V4			V1			V5		
	N3	N1	N2	N3	N2	N1	N2	N1	N3	N1	N2	N3	N3	N2	N1
Block IV	5.9	5.0	5.6	4.8	4.6	4.0	5.1	4.7	5.4	5.2	5.5	5.8	5.2	4.8	4.4

Analyse and give in outline a report on the results.

Exercise 7B

An experiment was conducted on ways of protecting oats against a pest. On the main plots there were two treatments: seeds infected and not infected. On the sub-plots there were three seed protectants (C = Ceresan M, P = Panogen, A = Agrox) in comparison with an untreated control 0. The data, which represent yields in bushels per acre, were as follows:

Seed	Protectant	Blocks			
		I	II	III	IV
Infected	O	42.9	41.6	28.9	30.8
	C	53.8	58.5	43.9	46.3
	P	49.5	53.8	40.7	39.4
	A	44.4	41.8	28.3	34.7
		190.6	195.7	141.8	151.2

Not infected	O	53.3	69.6	45.4	35.1
	C	57.6	69.6	42.4	51.9
	P	59.8	65.8	41.4	45.4
	A	64.1	57.4	44.1	51.6
		234.8	262.4	173.3	184.0

Analyse and outline a report on the results.

1 bushel = 36.4 litres   1 pound = 454 grams.

[Data from R. G. D. Steel and J. H. Torrie, *Principles and Procedures of Statistics: a Biometrical Approach*, 2nd edn, p. 384.]

Exercise 7C

An experiment on the yield of grass was conducted with five cutting treatments A–E, arranged in a Latin square. With treatments A–C crops of hay were taken on 24th June, 15th July and 31st October. With A, crops had been taken on three previous occasions, with B on two and with C on one. With treatments D and E, crops were taken with relation to the emergence of ears; with D at emergence and 28 and 70 days afterwards; and with E at 28 and 84 days after emergence. Each plot was divided into four sub-plots and four grass mixtures W, X, Y and Z were assigned at random within each plot. Data, which represent weight of dry matter, were as follows:

CW 648	BW 453	EW1032	DW 562	AW 452
X 532	X 463	X 933	X 540	X 427
Y 323	Y 294	Y1215	Y 407	Y 439
Z 434	Z 309	Z 827	Z 511	Z 449
DW 392	EW 781	AW 739	CW 630	BW 624
X 528	X 759	X 826	X 568	X 490
Y 493	Y 588	Y 632	Y 567	Y 618
Z 299	Z 890	Z 550	Z 523	Z 508
AW 489	CW 499	DW 529	BW 456	EW1204
X 620	X 551	X 673	X 366	X 958
Y 400	Y 428	Y 422	Y 554	Y 967
Z 476	Z 294	Z 676	Z 510	Z 950

BW 610	AW 378	CW 759	EW 826	DW 432
X 976	X 436	X 734	X1104	X 677
Y 509	Y 354	Y 457	Y 866	Y 383
Z 457	Z 336	Z 602	Z1380	Z 449

EW1036	DW 289	BW 626	AW 911	CW 596
X 765	X 511	X 445	X 918	X1020
Y 474	Y 339	Y 601	Y 704	Y 438
Z 704	Z 256	Z 466	Z 551	Z 632

Work out an analysis of variance and give an outline of its interpretation.

[Data from S. C. Pearce, *Biological Statistics: an Introduction*, p. 134.]

Exercise 7D

An experiment was conducted on oats in six randomized blocks. Each plot of 1/80 acre was sown with one of three varieties X, Y or Z and then divided into quarters for levels of nitrogen. (It may be assumed that the four levels were equally spaced.) The data, which represent yields in quarter pounds, were as follows:

	Z	N3	156	N2	118	Z	N2	109	N3	99	
	Z	N1	140	N0	115	Z	N0	63	N1	70	
I	X	N0	111	N1	130	Y	N0	80	N2	94	II
	X	N3	174	N2	157	Y	N3	126	N1	82	
	Y	N0	117	N1	114	X	N1	90	N2	100	
	Y	N2	161	N3	141	X	N3	116	N0	62	
	Z	N2	104	N0	70	Y	N3	96	N0	60	
	Z	N1	89	N3	117	Y	N2	89	N1	102	
III	X	N3	122	N0	74	X	N2	112	N3	86	IV
	X	N1	89	N2	81	X	N0	68	N1	64	
	Y	N1	103	N0	64	Z	N2	132	N3	124	
	Y	N2	132	N3	133	Z	N1	129	N0	89	
	Y	N1	108	N2	126	X	N2	118	N0	53	
	Y	N3	149	N0	70	X	N3	113	N1	74	
V	Z	N3	144	N1	124	Y	N3	104	N2	86	VI
	Z	N2	121	N0	96	Y	N0	89	N1	82	
	X	N0	61	N3	100	Z	N0	97	N1	99	
	X	N1	91	N2	97	Z	N2	119	N3	121	

(one acre = 4047 m^2 one pound = 454 g)

Using summation terms, analyse the data, then partition the lines for the main effect of nitrogen and the interaction through the method of contrasts.

[Data from F. Yates, 'Complex experiments', *J. Royal Statist. Soc.*, (1937), Supplement **2**, p. 198.]

Exercise 7E

The following data come from an experiment on peas with eight treatments, formed by factorial combinations of presence or absence of nitrogen (N), phosphorus (P) and potassium (K). There were six blocks, each with four plots, and the data represent yields in pounds per plot. Each plot had an area of 1/70 acre.

I	pk	49.5	(1)	46.8		n	62.0	k	45.5	II
	np	62.8	nk	57.0		npk	48.8	p	44.2	
III	n	59.8	k	55.5		np	52.0	nk	49.8	IV
	npk	58.5	p	56.0		(1)	51.5	pk	48.8	
V	p	62.8	n	69.5		nk	57.2	pk	53.2	VI
	npk	55.8	k	55.0		np	59.0	(1)	56.0	

(1 acre = 4047 m^2 1 pound = 454 grams)

Obtain the appropriate analysis of variance and write notes on the interpretation.

[Data from F. Yates, 'Complex experiments', Supplement to *J. Roy. Statist. Soc.*, **2** (1935), p. 204.]

Exercise 7F

(a)   Divide a 2^4 experiment into 4 blocks so as to confound the ABD and BC contrasts.

(b)   Divide a 2^5 experiment into 4 blocks so as to confound the ABE and BCDE contrasts.

(c)   Divide a 2^5 experiment into 8 blocks so as to confound the ABE, BCDE and ACDE contrasts.

In each case write down the other contrasts which are confounded.

Chapter 8

Correlation, regression and the analysis of covariance

8.1 Correlation

Two measurements have been taken on a number of units. The question may arise whether they are associated or not: it is on such occasions that correlation coefficients can be useful.

To take an example, an experimenter surveys crops at a number of sites and records the yield per square metre at each. It also occurs to him that the differences in yield may be due to differences in soil pH, so he measures that as well. Calling the yields y and pH x, he has ten pairs of figures, like this:

x	6.7	6.6	5.9	7.2	5.7	7.0	7.1	6.9	6.5	6.8
y	13.1	14.6	11.8	16.4	10.9	19.6	17.3	15.5	12.3	18.9

If these are plotted in the usual way, the diagram is as at Fig. 8.1. The dotted lines mark the means of x and y, namely 6.64 and 15.04 respectively. They divide the diagram into four quadrants. It will be seen that nine of the ten pairs of observations lie either in the bottom left-hand quadrant, in which both x and y are below their means, or in the top right-hand one, in which both x and y exceed their means. That is strong evidence that the two are associated. If x and y were distributed independently of one another, the points could be expected to lie about equally in the four quadrants.

The argument is made more precise if actual positions on the diagram are taken into account, not just the quadrants. For example, the last point ($x = 6.8$, $y = 18.9$), where both x and y lie clear of the dotted lines, provides stronger evidence of an association than the first ($x = 6.7$, $y = 13.1$), where neither variable is far from its mean. We shall therefore

168

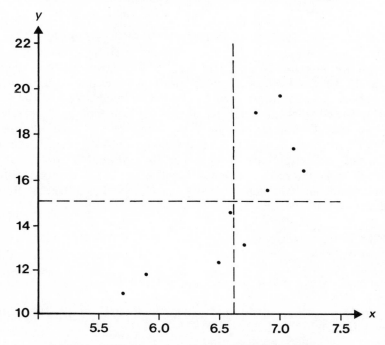

Fig. 8.1   **Yields (y) of survey sites plotted against soil pH (x)**

sweep both x and y by their means, i.e.,

x	+0.06	-0.04	-0.74	+0.56	-0.94	+0.36	+0.46	+0.26	-0.14	+0.16
y	-1.94	-0.44	-3.24	+1.36	-4.14	+4.56	+2.26	+0.46	-2.74	+3.86

The sum of squares for x and y are found in the usual way by squaring residuals—there are no treatments, so the deviations and the residuals are the same—and adding. Calling them E_{xx} and E_{yy},

$$E_{xx} = (+0.06)^2 + (-0.04)^2 + \ldots + (+0.16)^2 = 2.2040$$

$$E_{yy} = (-1.94)^2 + (-0.44)^2 + \ldots + (+3.86)^2 = 81.9640.$$

Both quantities could have been obtained using summation terms, as described in Section 1.4, namely,

$$E_{xx} = (6.7^2 + 6.6^2 + \ldots + 6.8^2) - (66.4)^2/10 = 2.2040$$

$$E_{yy} = (13.1^2 + 14.6^2 + \ldots 18.9^2 - (150.4)^2/10 = 81.9640.$$

So far we have looked at the variability of the two quantities taken separately. To examine how they vary together, we need to multiply them together instead of squaring each. For example, to take the first site, it is the only one where the residuals are of opposite sign. Consequently it will make a negative contribution to a sum of products, namely, $(+0.06) \times (-1.94) = (-0.1164)$. The rest, on the other hand, will all make positive contributions. Furthermore, those where both residuals are large will make a larger contribution than those where one residual (or both) is small. The next step is to work out E_{xy}, which is to be the sum of products of residuals, thus:

$$E_{xy} = (+0.06)(-1.94) + (-0.04)(-0.44) + \ldots + (0.16)(+3.86)$$
$$= +10.7540.$$

The same quantity could have been obtained from summation terms, thus:

$$E_{xy} = (6.7 \times 13.1) + (6.6 \times 14.6) + \ldots + (6.8 \times 18.9) - (66.4 \times 150.4)/10$$
$$= +10.7540.$$

It is important that E_{xy} and quantities derived from it should always be given their signs. Unlike E_{xx} and E_{yy}, which are necessarily positive, E_{xy} could be negative and that would be important.

However, the immediate problem is the measurement of correlation. The basic value is E_{xy}, but it needs to be scaled. As it stands, if y were measured in some other units, e.g. kilograms instead of pounds, it would be multiplied by a suitable constant. In that case E_{yy} would be multiplied by the same constant squared.

To avoid difficulties of scaling, the correlation coefficient, r, is taken to be

$$r = \frac{E_{xy}}{\sqrt{E_{xx}E_{yy}}} \tag{8.1.1}$$

In the example, $r = +0.800$, which is high. In general, r varies between -1 and $+1$. The extreme values, ± 1, indicate a strict straight-line relationship with no extraneous variation, the slope of the line being upwards or downwards depending on the sign of E_{xy}, whether positive or negative. If $r = 0$, this can imply that there is no association, though other interpretations are possible. Other values indicate some association, either positive or negative, but not as close as that implied by $r = \pm 1$.

Some care is needed in the interpretation of correlation coefficients. For example, they do not show causation. The data given above do indeed suggest that the species does not like acid soil, but in this particular area it could be that acid soils are mostly shallow. In that event the real interpretation might be that the species does not like shallow soil. (It might even prefer a site of low pH, other things being equal, but other things are not equal.)

It should also be noted that correlation coefficients are based on departures from a steady increase or decrease in y as x changes—in other words, on the idea of a straight-line ('linear') relationship. If however, the relationship is markedly curved, that will lead to a reduction in the value or r. The following is an extreme case:

x	10.9	12.0	13.7	14.8	13.2
y	24.1	20.9	21.1	24.4	19.8

The correlation coefficient, r, is virtually zero, but plotting the points shows that there is in fact a clear relationship between x and y, though it is not given by a straight line.

Many tables have been produced to show whether a given value of r does or does not differ from zero. They are entered with one degree of freedom fewer than those of E_{xx} and E_{yy}. Thus the value of $+ 0.800$ found above can be tested with eight degrees of freedom. It lies outside the limits of ± 0.765 given in the table for $P = 0.01$ and is therefore unlikely to have arisen by chance from a population in which x and y were in fact uncorrelated. Another method of assessing the relationship will be given in the next section.

8.2 Linear regression

The previous section dealt with correlation, which is the extent to which two quantities depend upon one another for their value. Nevertheless, to know, as in the example of the soil acidity and the crop yields, that there is a significant correlation coefficient is to have evidence only that there is a relationship of some sort with a component of linearity. It does not say exactly what that relationship is.

The simplest case is that in which it is assumed to be a straight line, i.e.

$$y = a + bx + e \tag{8.2.1}$$

where a and b are constants and e is a residual. This equation is said to give the 'linear regression of y on x', and b is called the 'regression coefficient'. The value of b indicates the increase (if positive) or the decrease (if negative) in y that goes with one unit increase in x. If (8.2.1) can be taken as a reasonable representation of the relationship, then $\hat{b}$, the best estimate of b, is E_{xy}/E_{xx}. In the example, where $E_{xx} = 2.2040$ and $E_{xy} = +10.7540$, $\hat{b}$ is $+4.88$. That tells us that if there is an increase of 1.0 in pH, we could expect on average an increase of 4.88 units in yield.

Several points need to be noted. As has already been said, causation should not be assumed. To follow up a suggestion already made, there could be a chance relationship, valid only for that locality, between, say, pH and soil depth. Nevertheless for that locality the relationship given at (8.2.1) with b estimated as $+4.88$ is genuine, though it might not hold elsewhere. That is the observed relationship of yield to pH for those sites.

Another point concerns the inverse relationship, which arises when x is estimated from y. The regression coefficient of x on y is E_{xy}/E_{yy} $= +0.1312$. Some would expect the inverse coefficient to be $1/4.88$ $= 0.2049$, but this would be a mistake. Supposing that there had been no relationship then both regression coefficients would have been zero. In general their product (E_{xy}/E_{xx} multiplied by E_{xy}/E_{yy}) equals r^2, not 1. In this instance $4.88 \times 0.1312 = 0.640 = (+0.800)^2$.

A caution concerns the form of (8.2.1), which implies that plotting y against x will give a straight line. If the line is in fact curved, the approximation will be a bad one. Further, a lot of variation will be ascribed to the random residuals, e, when it is really due to failure of the assumption of linearity.

Given a solution for b, it becomes possible to work out a revised variable, y', in which the disturbing effect of the variable x has been removed.

With a knowledge of the regression coefficient, b, we can estimate what the values of y would have been for any chosen value of x, but which value should we choose? The experimenter may resolve this question by saying that he wants to know y for that range of sites, and the mean value of x is 6.64, so that is what he wants. For the first site, where $x = 6.7$ and $y = 13.1$, y should be adjusted to $13.1 - 4.88(6.7 - 6.64) = 12.8 = y'$ say. For all the sites the y'-values are:

x	6.7	6.6	5.9	7.2	5.7	7.0	7.1	6.9	6.5	6.8
y	13.1	14.6	11.8	16.4	10.9	19.6	17.3	15.5	12.3	18.9
y'	12.8	14.8	15.4	13.7	15.5	17.8	15.1	14.2	13.0	18.1

It will be seen that the mean of the y' is the same as that of the y. (This is because x has been adjusted to its mean.) Also, the sum of squared deviations for y' equals

$$E_{yy}(1 - r^2) = E_{yy} - E_{xy}^2/E_{xx} \tag{8.2.2}$$

Here it is 81.9640 $(1 - 0.6400) = 29.5070$. That can readily be confirmed from the summation terms, because

$$(12.8^2 + 14.8^2 + \ldots + 18.1^2) - (150.4)^2/10 = 29.0640.$$

(The discrepancy arises from rounding errors. Actually, in this instance 29.5070 is to be preferred because it comes directly from the original data, whereas 29.0640 is derived from the data by a train of calculations, each subject to approximation.) As to degrees of freedom E_{yy} had nine. In passing to $E_{yy}(1 - r^2)$ another quantity had to be estimated and allowed for, namely b, so there remain only eight.

However, the experimenter might have made a different response to our query about the value of x that he wanted. He might have replied that he wanted a figure for neutral soil, i.e. $x = 7.0$. In that case y' gives values of

14.6   16.6   17.2   15.4   17.2   19.6   16.8   16.0   14.7   19.9.

The change in the standard value of x from 6.64 to 7.00 has led to a corresponding change in the mean value of y' amounting to $+1.76 = +4.88 (7.00 - 6.64)$, but the sum of squares is unchanged, being

$$(14.6^2 + 16.6^2 + \ldots + 19.9^2) - (168.0)^2/10 = 29.6600.$$

However, differences between sites will remain the same whatever value of x is adopted. Thus, to compare the first two sites, $14.6 - 16.6 = -2.00 = 12.8 - 14.8$.

Another important consideration is the precision with which b estimates the true value of b. The variance of b is in fact

$$\frac{\text{Variance of } y'}{E_{xx}} \tag{8.2.3}$$

In the present example, the variance of y' is $29.5070/8 = 3.6884$ and $E_{xx} = 2.2040$, so the variance of b is 1.6735 and its standard error is $1.294 = \sqrt{1.6735}$ with eight degrees of freedom. The estimated value (4.88) therefore differs from zero by 3.77 times its standard error (1.294).

Another matter is the significance of the departure of b from zero, which is the same as the significance of r. If the regression on x is not allowed for, the sum of squares for y is E_{yy}. In the present example, it is 81.9640 with nine degrees of freedom. If the regression is allowed for then the sum of squares is $E_{yy}(1 - r^2) = 29.5070$ with one degree of freedom fewer. That leads to an analysis of variance like this:

Source	d.f.	s.s.	m.s.	F
Regression	1	52.4570	52.4570	14.22***
'Error'	8	29.5070	3.6884	
Total	9	81.9640		

The significance lies rather beyond the level, $P = 0.001$. Actually, the test is readily thought of in algebraic terms. If the degrees of freedom for E_{yy} number f, then

$$F = \frac{(f-1)r^2}{1-r^2}$$

(8.2.4)

with 1 and $(f-1)$ degrees of freedom. Here, where $f = 9$ and $r = +0.800$, $F = 14.22$ as before. Further, $3.77^2 = 14.21$, so the test used below (8.2.2) has given the same result (see Section 3.10).

The simple relationship used at (8.2.1) does not necessarily hold, but in many cases a simple tranformation of the variables will justify it. For example, let

$$Y = pX^q$$

be the underlying rule. Transforming X and Y to their logarithms, x and y, gives

$$y = \log p + qx.$$

(8.2.5)

That is the same as (8.2.1) with $\log p$ for a and q for b. It could be asked what has happened to the residuals e. In fact, if a random quantity, e, is added to the right-hand side of (8.2.5) it will often be found that it has the properties expected of a residual. That is because a transformation will often change the quantity actually measured, chosen perhaps for practical convenience, into another quantity that is botanically more fundamental. However, this is a large subject and one that will be dealt with more fully in Chapter 9.

The assumptions underlying linear regression can usefully be examined. First of all, it is taken for granted that there is in fact a straight-line relationship between x and y. If the relationship is really curvilinear, the fact will appear from examination of the estimated residuals, e, which will no longer appear to be in random order as x increases. Instead, groups of positive and negative values will be found. It is also assumed that the residuals are distributed normally about zero. This also may be called into question if the line is not straight. Nevertheless, as a first approximation people do often fit straight lines where a curve would be better. Incidentally, no assumptions are required about the distribution of x. Sometimes it is convenient to use a variable that takes only a limited number of values, e.g. $x = 0$ for male, $x = 1$ for female, and there is no objection to that.

A final point concerns the interpretation of a regression coefficient. It should never be cited as if it represented a law of Nature. The reason is that two quantities, x and y, can often be related by several mechanisms. For example, if x is the height of a plant and y is its number of seed pods, what is the regression of y on x? It all depends on the reason for x being variable. If some plants are in shade and others in full sun, it is possible that the shaded ones will grow higher to find the light and, in consequence, have less resources for reproductive activities, i.e. the regression will be negative. On the other hand, if some plants grow more because they are better fertilized, they could well have more seed pods, i.e. the regression is positive. In many instances both effects will operate and the regression coefficient—and also the correlation coefficient—will be positive or negative according to which dominates. Hence a regression coefficient once found can be taken as summing up the situation for those particular conditions, but it will not necessarily apply in other conditions, where the relative importance of the two mechanisms could quite possibly be different.

8.3 Partial and multiple linear regression

By comparison with (8.2.1) y may depend upon two variable quantities, w and x, i.e.

$$y = a + bx + cw + e. \tag{8.3.1}$$

The determination of b and c is now more complicated than that of b in the last section, because each of x and w can affect y indirectly through the other as well as directly. For example, yield (y) could be affected by depth of topsoil (x) and the amount of fertilizer applied (w). If w is disregarded, then $b = E_{xy}/E_{xx}$ as before; if x were disregarded c would equal E_{wy}/E_{ww}. The same equations would hold if x and w were independent of one another, but suppose that someone has been compensating for shallowness of soil by applying more fertilizer, i.e. there is a negative correlation between x and w. Then if x has a high value, this will affect y directly, but it means that w will have to be low, and this also will affect y. (That is the indirect effect of x on y.)

To cope with these complications we will amend the notation. In (8.2.1) we shall in future write b as b_{yx}, i.e. the regression coefficient of y on x. In (8.3.1) we shall write b as $b_{yx.w}$, i.e. the regression coefficient of y on x, w being held constant. Similarly c will be written as $b_{yw.x}$. In that way x and w can be varied independently. In short (8.3.1) will become

$$y = a + b_{yw.x}w + b_{yx.w}x + e. \qquad (8.3.2)$$

Further it can be shown that

$$\hat{b}_{yw.x} = \frac{E_{wy}E_{xx} - E_{wx}E_{xy}}{E_{ww}E_{xx} - E_{wx}^2} \qquad (8.3.3)$$

$$\hat{b}_{yx.w} = \frac{E_{ww}E_{xy} - E_{wx}E_{wy}}{E_{ww}E_{xx} - E_{wx}^2}$$

It will be recalled that a circumflex accent above b shows that an estimate has been made of the true value, which is not known.

The sum of squares for the regression of y on both w and x takes up two degrees of freedom. It equals

$$\hat{b}_{yw.x}E_{wy} + \hat{b}_{yx.w}E_{xy}$$

leaving as 'error',

$$E_{yy} - \hat{b}_{yw.x}E_{wy} - \hat{b}_{yx.w}E_{xy} \qquad (8.3.4)$$

analogous to (8.2.2). This quantity is sometimes written

$$E_{yy}(1 - R^2) \qquad (8.3.5)$$

where R is called the 'multiple' correlation coefficient of y on both w and x. Again there is a parallel in (8.2.2).

The following example shows what may happen. Some bushes were planted fairly closely so that they had little opportunity to spread, though they were of course free to grow vertically. After a time their heights and spreads in metres and their crop yields in kilograms were:

		(1)	(2)	(3)	(4)	(5)	(6)	(7)	(8)
Height	(h)	2.4	2.6	2.3	2.4	2.6	2.3	2.1	2.0
Spread	(s)	1.6	1.7	1.4	1.5	1.6	1.5	1.4	1.5
Yield	(y)	41	47	39	42	44	40	38	36

As a guide to the future someone wants to know if it would be possible to use h and s as a means of crop forecasting. He points out that h is difficult to measure and is therefore to be avoided if possible, whereas s is readily found. The first task is to work out the sums of squares and products in the usual way.

$$E_{hh} = 0.319 \qquad E_{ss} = 0.075 \qquad E_{yy} = 84.88$$
$$E_{sy} = +2.02 \qquad E_{hy} = +4.94 \qquad E_{hs} = +0.112.$$

Hence from (8.3.2)

$$b_{yh.s} = +12.68 \qquad b_{ys.h} = +8.01.$$

Also, using (8.3.4), the sum of squares with two degrees of freedom, for the double regression, is

$$(+12.68)(+4.94) + (+8.01)(+2.02) = 78.82.$$

That leaves an 'error' sum of squares of 6.06 ($= 84.88 - 78.82$).

This does not end the matter because the enquiry concerns the possibility of using only one of h and s. If we had regressed y on h alone, this would have given a sum of squares of $E_{yh}^2/E_{hh} = 76.47$. That leaves 2.35 ($= 78.82 - 76.47$) for any added benefit from knowing s as well. The analysis of variance is therefore

Source	d.f.	s.s.	m.s.	F
Regression on h alone	1	76.47	76.47	63.09***
Gain from using s also	1	2.35	2.35	1.94
'Error'	5	6.06	1.212	
Stratum total	7	84.88		

It is clear that the variation in h has explained most of the variation in y, so h could be used to forecast y. Further, once h is known, there is little advantage in knowing s as well.

As a matter of nomenclature, the first line, corresponding to b_{yh}, is called the 'total regression' of y on h. The second, corresponding to $b_{ys.h}$, is called the 'partial regression' of y on s, h having been allowed for.

The enquirer hoped to be able to use s alone. If he had done so, it would have accounted for a sum of squares of 54.40 ($= E_{sy}^2/E_{ss}$) leaving 24.42

($= 78.82 - 54.40$) for the added effect of knowing h as well. The analysis of variance is

Source	d.f.	s.s.	m.s.	F
Regression on s alone	1	54.40	54.40	44.88***
Gain from using h also	1	24.42	24.42	20.15***
'Error'	5	6.06	1.212	
Stratum total	7	84.88		

It appears then that s does provide quite a lot of information about y, but clearly it benefits from supplementation by h, which completes the story. The enquirer must therefore be told that, reluctant though he may be to measure h, this really is required if he is to make a good forecast.

8.4   Curvilinear regression

An ability to use two regressor variables, w and x, instead of only one, x, makes possible the fitting of simple curves. For example, if w is put equal to x^2, (8.3.1) becomes

$$y = a + bx + cx^2 + e \tag{8.4.1}$$

Here a little caution is necessary. It is conceivable in biology that the relationship between x and y should effectively be a straight line, at least over a limited range, but parabolae like that at (8.4.1), though common enough in physics, are unusual in plant physiology. Going from (8.3.1) to (8.4.1) the most that can justifiably be said is that a significant value for c shows that the relationship is not straight. When that is so, the response curve is better left undecided unless some more thorough study can be undertaken.

If the sole intention is to detect any deviations from linearity, some have thought it better to replace (8.4.1) by

$$y = a + bx + \sqrt{x} + e \tag{8.4.2}$$

Some people have a reservation about (8.4.1), their reason being the shape of the curve when x^2 is graphed against x. It starts fairly flat, but begins to rise sharply as x increases; it is, in short, rather abrupt and not at all sinuous. For that reason they prefer (8.4.2) as being more likely to fit the facts. In the main (8.4.2) is quite successful, though (8.4.1) is more usual.

For purposes of illustration we shall use (8.4.1) to try to detect any deviations from the straight-line relationship given at (8.2.1). For that we use the data

$w = x^2$	44.89	43.56	34.81	51.84	32.49	49.00	50.41	47.61	42.25	46.24
x	6.7	6.6	5.9	7.2	5.7	7.0	7.1	6.9	6.5	6.8
y	13.1	14.6	11.8	16.4	10.9	19.6	17.3	15.5	12.3	18.9

Hence

$$E_{ww} = 365.63 \quad E_{xx} = 2.2040 \quad E_{yy} = 81.9640$$

$$E_{xy} = +10.7540 \quad E_{wy} = +138.945 \quad E_{wx} = +28.372$$

and

$$b_{yw.x} = \frac{+1.1223}{0.8781} = +1.278$$

$$b_{yx.w} = \frac{-10.1625}{0.8781} = -11.573$$

From (8.3.4) the sum of squares due to both w and x is equal to 53.1157. This compares with the figure for x alone of 52.4721, leaving only 0.6436 for the added effect of w, which is clearly not significant. The analysis of variance is

Source	d.f.	s.s.	m.s.	F
Regression on x alone	1	52.4721	52.4721	12.73**
Gain from using x^2 also	1	0.6436	0.6436	0.16
'Error'	7	28.8483	4.1212	
Stratum total	9	81.9640		

In fact, the curvilinear component has contributed so little that it has actually led to an increase in the 'error' mean square. Even that does not prove that the relationship of y and x is straight, though one can say without reservation that the present data show no evidence of curvature. However, over the range of x used, x^2 and x are so closely correlated ($r = +28.372/\sqrt{365.63 \times 2.2040} = +0.999$) that it would in any event be nearly impossible to distinguish their effects apart from one another. The calculations have nevertheless illustrated the method.

8.5   The analysis of covariance—principles

In the analysis of covariance there is a variate, y, that is to be subjected to the analysis of variance, but there are fears that it may be unduly variable on account of its association with x, another variate, which is not for the moment of interest on its own account but could be important as explaining part of the 'error' variance in y. The technique can best be explained by an example.

The following data were presented by Rayner (1969, p. 407). An experiment had been conducted on maize, using five randomized blocks with five treatments, A, B, C, D, and E. The y-variate was pounds per morgen, but it so happened that the same plots had been recorded in the previous year before the treatments had been applied. Those figures will constitute the x-variate. They can be expected to indicate good and bad patches of soil. It is important to note that x could not have been affected by the treatments. If it had been, the whole of the following procedure would be invalid.

The data were as follows, the upper value giving y and the lower x:

	I		II		III		IV		V	
				Block						
B	37.1	D	42.7	A	37.1	B	40.4	A	37.3	
	51.2		52.9		62.0		54.7		64.0	
A	33.7	A	36.5	C	51.0	A	37.1	B	46.2	
	53.0		62.8		62.8		63.5		69.5	
D	34.3	E	51.3	D	45.8	C	50.2	E	47.0	(8.5.1)
	48.0		59.4		61.5		66.2		54.1	
E	32.6	B	40.7	B	44.4	D	44.0	D	25.8	
	44.8		60.9		59.9		62.2		47.9	
C	33.7	C	42.7	E	56.5	E	50.4	C	49.0	
	47.9		56.7		59.2		56.2		61.2	

(1 pound $= 454\,\mathrm{g}$ 1 morgen $= 8565\,\mathrm{m}^2$

The following calculations would not ordinarily be used in practice, though they could be and they do show the argument.

First both variates, x and y, are swept by blocks to find their deviations, thus:

B	+ 2.82	D	− 0.08	A	− 9.86	B	− 4.02	A	− 3.76
	+ 2.22		− 5.64		+ 0.92		− 5.86		+ 4.66
A	− 0.58	A	− 6.28	C	+ 4.04	A	− 7.32	B	+ 5.14
	+ 4.02		+ 4.26		+ 1.72		+ 2.94		+ 10.16
D	+ 0.02	E	+ 8.52	D	− 1.16	C	+ 5.78	E	+ 5.94
	− 0.98		+ 0.86		+ 0.42		+ 5.64		− 5.24
E	− 1.68	B	− 2.08	B	− 2.56	D	− 0.42	D	− 15.26
	− 4.18		+ 2.36		− 1.18		+ 1.64		− 11.41
C	− 0.58	C	− 0.08	E	+ 9.54	E	+ 5.98	C	+ 7.94
	− 1.08		− 1.84		− 1.88		− 4.36		+ 1.86

$$(8.5.2)$$

These figures lead to the residuals in the usual way, i.e. sweeping by treatments, to give

B	+ 2.96	D	+ 3.30	A	− 4.30	B	− 3.88	A	+ 1.80
	+ 0.68		− 2.44		− 2.44		− 7.40		+ 1.30
A	+ 4.98	D	− 0.72	C	+ 0.62	A	− 1.76	B	+ 5.28
	+ 0.66		+ 0.90		+ 0.46		− 0.42		+ 8.62
D	+ 3.40	E	+ 2.86	D	+ 2.22	C	+ 2.36	E	+ 0.28
	+ 2.22		+ 3.82		+ 3.62		+ 4.38		− 2.28
E	− 7.34	B	− 1.94	B	− 2.42	D	− 2.96	D	− 11.88
	− 1.22		+ 0.82		− 2.72		+ 4.84		− 8.24
C	− 4.00	C	− 3.50	E	+ 3.88	E	+ 0.32	E	+ 4.52
	− 2.34		− 3.10		+ 1.08		− 1.40		+ 0.60

$$(8.5.3)$$

Of the 25 pairs of residuals, 19 have the same sign and only six are of opposite sign. That does imply that plots that were good or bad in one year behaved similarly in the year after.

We shall now assess the correlation between the two years' records. Summing squares and products of the residuals gives

$$E_{xx} = 321.22 \quad E_{xy} = + 273.72 \quad E_{yy} = 420.66.$$

Hence $r = + 0.745$ and $b_{yx} = + 0.852$. That is to say, for every one pound of crop above expectation in the preliminary year, a plot had an excess of 0.852 pounds in the experiment itself. This knowledge will now be used to improve precision. In an ordinary analysis of y the 'error' sum of squares is 420.66 with 16 degrees of freedom, which gives an error variance of 26.29. Using the adjustment, from (8.2.2) the 'error' sum of squares is $420.66 − (273.72)^2/321.22 = 187.42$ with 15 degrees of freedom, giving an error variance of 12.49, which is much better.

To complete the analysis using this long method, it is necessary to take sums of squares and products of the deviations at (8.5.2) to produce D_{xx},

D_{xy} and D_{yy}, analogous to E_{xx}, E_{xy} and E_{yy}, which came from (8.5.3). They are:

$$D_{xx} = 492.47 \quad D_{xy} = 171.09 \quad D_{yy} = 851.11$$

all with 20 degrees of freedom. Adjusting y by x gives

$851.11 - (+ 171.09)^2/492.47 = 791.67$ with 19 degrees of freedom.

In the adjusted analysis of variance the sum of squares for treatments can be found by subtracting 'error' from the stratum total.

Source	d.f.	s.s.	m.s.	F	
Treatments	4	604.25	151.06	12.09***	(8.5.4)
'Error'	15	187.42	12.49		
Stratum total	19	791.67			

If y had not been adjusted, the F-value would have been only 4.09 with 4 and 16 degrees of freedom.

We have given residuals for x and y at (8.5.3), but we might reasonably want to know what the residual is after y has been adjusted by x. There is no problem about that. For the first plot, x and y residuals are respectively $+ 0.68$ and $+ 2.96$. Hence the residual of y' is $+ 2.96 - (+ 0.852)$ $(+ 0.68) = + 2.381$. All the other plots can be dealt with in the same way. When that is done, it will be found that the sum of the squared residuals is 187.43. Apart from a small effect of rounding, this is the 'error' sum of squares at (8.5.4).

8.6 The analysis of covariance in practice

The method just given is too long for most purposes if everything has to be done by hand, though it would serve very well for a computer program. Also, it is completely general and could be used in conjunction with the Kuiper–Corsten iteration set out in Section 4.2 because that gives both the deviations, as at (8.5.2), and the residuals, as at (8.5.3). After this the calculations can proceed as shown.

Given an orthogonal design, however, the calculations can be done more simply by using summation terms. Those for x^2 and y^2 are the same as for an analysis of variance for those two variates: those for xy are found by multiplying together corresponding values for the two variates instead of squaring each.

To take the total term first, for x^2 it equals

$$51.2^2 + 52.9^2 + \ldots + 61.2^2 = 84\,219.91,$$

and for y^2 it equals

$$37.1^2 + 42.7^2 + \ldots + 49.0^2 = 45\,198.85;$$

so for xy it equals

$$(51.2 \times 37.1) + (52.9 \times 42.7) + \ldots + (61.2)(49.0) = 61\,062.43. \qquad (8.6.1)$$

Similarly for the treatment term, totals are

	A	B	C	D	E	
x	305.3	296.2	294.8	272.5	273.7	(8.6.2)
y	181.7	208.8	226.6	192.6	237.8	

Hence the treatment terms are

x^2: $[305.3^2 + 296.2^2 + \ldots + 273.7^2]/5 = 83\,403.50$
y^2: $[181.7^2 + 208.8^2 + \ldots + 237.8^2]/5 = 44\,320.70$
xy: $[(305.3 \times 181.7) + 296.2 \times 208.8) + \ldots + (273.7 \times 237.8)]/5$
$$= 60\,338.12$$

and so on for others.

	x^2	xy	y^2
Total	84 219.91	61 062.13	45 198.85
Blocks	83 727.44	60 891.34	44 347.74
Treatments	83 403.50	60 338.12	44 320.70
Corrections	83 232.25	60 440.75	43 890.25

Those terms lead to analyses of variance and covariance as follows:

Source	d.f.	x^2	xy	y^2	
Treatments	4	171.25	− 102.63	430.45	(8.6.3)
'Error'	16	321.22	+ 273.72	420.66	
Stratum total	20	492.47	+ 171.09	851.11	

From here it is but a step to (8.5.4). As usual when summation terms have been used, there is an 'error' line which gives an aggregated figure for the action of residuals, but they are nowhere seen as individuals.

From now on we shall be chiefly interested in y after it has been adjusted by x. Treatment totals have already been given at (8.6.2); the means are derived from them, as follows:

	A	B	C	D	E	
x	61.06	59.24	58.96	54.50	54.74	(8.6.4)
y	36.34	41.76	45.32	38.52	47.56	

The x-means differ only as a result of the sort of variation included in 'error'. Treatments can have had no effect because the x-data were recorded before they were applied. It is therefore correct to adjust y by x using a regression coefficient derived from the 'error' line, namely $b_{yx} = +273.72/321.22 = +0.852$.

There is an important point here. As was explained at the end of Section 8.2, a regression coefficient does not express some immutable law. The effect on y of a change in x depends upon the reason for x changing. If it is altering on account of 'error', there could be one regression coefficient; if on account of treatments, there could be another. That indeed is what has happened here. Calculated from the 'error' line the regression coefficient is $+0.852$, but from the treatment line it is -0.599 ($= -102.63/171.25$). We are justified in using the former figure only if we can be assured that the differences between treatments with respect to their x-means were brought about by the action of 'error'. In this instance there is no room for doubt in the matter. First of all, in the analysis of variance for x^2, given at (8.6.3), the F-value is 2.13, which is not large enough to suggest that there was any effect due to the treatments. There is, however, a more powerful reason. Since the x-values were all measured before the treatments were applied, any differences must be due to 'error', so we were quite right to adopt $+0.852$ as the relevant regression coefficient.

Examination of the x-means at (8.6.4) shows that the treatments had not had equal good fortune from the randomization. Treatment A had in the main been assigned to good plots, while D and E had been rather unlucky. It is now proposed to use the regression coefficient to adjust all y-values to a standard value of x equal to the grand mean, i.e. 57.70. In the case of Treatment A this gives

$$36.34 + (57.70 - 61.06)(+0.852) = 33.48.$$

Hence the adjusted treatment means for y are

$$
\begin{array}{ccccc}
\text{A} & \text{B} & \text{C} & \text{D} & \text{E} \\
33.48 & 40.45 & 44.25 & 41.25 & 50.08
\end{array}
\qquad (8.6.5)
$$

The mean of these figures is 41.90, the same as that for the unadjusted means at (8.6.4), but this is because the mean of the x-values is unchanged. If all the x-means had been standardized at some other value, the adjusted y-means would all have been raised or lowered by some constant. Consequently, they are not invariant, though differences between them will remain the same.

We shall now look at the standard error of some of those differences, taking as our example that between A and B. The difference is

$$
\begin{aligned}
&[36.34 + 0.852(57.70 - 61.06)] - [41.76 + 0.852(57.70 - 59.24)] \\
&= (36.34 - 41.76) + 0.852(-61.06 + 59.24).
\end{aligned}
\qquad (8.6.6)
$$

We shall look at the two terms separately.

The first $(36.34 - 41.76)$ is the difference of two unadjusted y-means, each based upon five data from an orthogonal design. Its variance is therefore

$$
(1/5 + 1/5)(\text{Error variance}) = 0.4\,(\text{Error variance}).
$$

Further, once we have allowed for the effect of x, the error variance in question is that at (8.5.4), namely 12.49. Its multiplier, here 0.4, is the constant, K, defined at (4.1.1) and considered further in Section 5.5.

The second term, $+0.852\,(-61.06 + 59.24)$, may be written $d\,\hat{b}_{yx}$, where d is the difference between the two x-means (in this instance $d = -1.82$). The variance of $\hat{b}_{yx}$ has been given at (8.2.3), so the variance of $d\,\hat{b}_{yx}$ is

$$
\left(\frac{d^2}{E_{xx}}\right) \times (\text{Error variance}).
$$

Taking the two terms together, the variance of the difference at (8.6.5) is

$$
\left(\frac{1}{5} + \frac{1}{5} + \frac{1.82^2}{321.22}\right) \times 12.49
$$

$$
= 5.125 = 2.26^2.
$$

The standard error is therefore 2.26. Since the difference in fact equals $-6.97\,(= 33.48 - 40.45)$, it is 3.08 times its own standard error.

Someone may point out that d also is estimated subject to error. That is true, but it does not affect the argument. We chose to adopt $d = -1.82$, and we could have chosen some other value if we had wished. The fact that the true difference may have been rather different from -1.82 does not affect the other fact that we opted for that figure.

A difficulty arises in practice because each treatment difference has its own d and therefore its own variance, namely

$$\left(K + \frac{d^2}{E_{xx}} \right) \times \text{(Error variance)} \tag{8.6.7}$$

where K is the multiplier of the error mean square in ordinary analysis of variance for that design. (In the example $K = 0.4$.) It is here useful to note that if all possible values of d are taken, i.e.

A − B	+ 1.82	B − D	+ 4.74
A − C	+ 2.10	B − E	+ 4.50
A − D	+ 6.56	C − D	+ 4.46
A − E	+ 6.32	C − E	+ 4.22
B − C	+ 0.24	D − E	− 0.24

the mean of the squares will always equal

$$\frac{2(D_{xx} - E_{xx})}{v(v - 1)}.$$

(It is assumed that the design is orthogonal with v treatments, all of which have the same replication.) Moreover, because F_x, the F-value for treatments in the analysis of variance for x, equals

$$\frac{f(D_{xx} - E_{xx})}{(v - 1)E_{xx}}$$

where f is the number of degrees of freedom for 'error' in that analysis, a mean of the values at (8.6.7) is given by

$$\left(K + \frac{2F_x}{fr} \right) \times \text{(Error variance)} \tag{8.6.8}$$

In this example $F_x = 2.13$, $f = 16$ and $r = 5$, so a mean variance from (8.6.8) is $0.4532 \times 12.49 = 5.661 = (2.38)^2$. The error variance was found from (8.5.4). Hence an average value for the standard error of differences at (8.6.5) is 2.38. That for the difference of A and B was only 2.06 because those treatments had much the same x-mean, as (8.6.4) shows.

Mostly it is enough to report the value given by (8.6.8), though the conscientious may like to add the maximum given by the largest value of d. (In the example this is 2.58, given by comparison of Treatments A and D). If for any particular contrast an exact figure is required, (8.6.7) is always available.

The above results can readily be generalized to other contrasts. Suppose, for example, that someone wanted to know about the extent to which Treatment A differed from the rest, i.e. he was interested in

$$(1 \quad -\tfrac{1}{4} \quad -\tfrac{1}{4} \quad -\tfrac{1}{4} \quad -\tfrac{1}{4}). \tag{8.6.9}$$

He should first evaluate the contrast for both x and y using the means at (8.6.4):

$$c_x = +4.2 \qquad c_y = -6.95$$

Then, after adjustment this becomes

$$-6.95 + 0.852(0 - 4.2) = -10.53.$$

The same result could have been obtained from the means at (8.6.5). It will be seen that x has been adjusted to zero, that being its value if all the x means are standardized to a constant value.

For the contrast at (8.6.9), if the design is orthogonal and all treatments have five plots, then (from Section 5.5) $K = 0.25$. The adjustment adds c_x^2/E_{xx}, so the variance of the adjusted contrast is

$$\left(K + \frac{c_x^2}{E_{xx}}\right) \times (\text{Error variance}) \tag{8.6.10}$$

That equals $3.808 = 1.95^2$. Hence the value of the contrast (10.53) is 5.40 times its standard error (1.95).

A similar conclusion could have been obtained from the analysis of variance at (8.6.3). The first task is to extract from the treatment line the component sum of squares or products for the contrast, i.e.

$$x^2, 70.56; \quad xy, -116.76; \quad y^2, 193.21.$$

Here K is taken to be 0.25, as found previously. (This leaves 100.69, +14.13 and 273.24 respectively for the other three degrees of freedom.)

We can now construct a shorter form of (8.6.3), discarding any components not needed for the moment.

Source	d.f.	x^2	xy	y^2
Contrast	1	70.56	− 116.76	193.21
'Error'	16	321.22	+ 273.72	420.66
Total	17	391.78	+ 156.96	613.87

Adjusting the total line gives

$$613.87 - (156.96)^2/391.78 = 550.99$$

with 16 degrees of freedom. The adjusted line for error is known from (8.5.4), so the new analysis reads

Source	d.f.	s.s.	m.s.	F
Contrast	1	363.57	363.57	29.11***
'Error'	15	187.42	12.49	
Total	16	550.99		

It leads to exactly the same conclusions as the calculations at (8.6.10). With all single-degree effects, F in an analysis equals t^2 when standard errors are used instead (Section 3.10). This is true here ($29.11 = 5.40^2$ as nearly as rounding errors allow).

8.7 Double covariance

Sometimes it would be useful to be able to adjust y by two quantities, w and x. Although more calculations are involved, they are not more difficult. The analyses of variance and covariance have columns for w^2, wx, x^2, wy, xy, and y^2, six in all, compared with the three at (8.6.3). The error line gives E_{ww}, E_{wx}, ..., E_{yy} and leads to $b_{yw.x}$ and $b_{yx.w}$ as at (8.3.3). From that point it is easy to find the 'error' sum of squares for y after adjustment by both w and x, the expression being that at (8.3.4).

Where a treatment contrast is to be tested, its line in the analyses of variance and covariance is merged with that for 'error' to give D_{ww}, D_{wx}, ..., D_{yy}, and a second use of (8.3.4) will give the adjusted sum of squares for the contrast and 'error' combined. Essentially the method is that described above (8.5.4), the adjusted sum of squares for the contrast being found by difference. Note that the error line has lost two degrees of freedom, not one as before.

The adjusted means for the treatments raise no problems because the partial regression coefficients of y on w and x are known ($\hat{b}_{yw.x}$ and $\hat{b}_{yx.w}$ above). If w needs to be adjusted by d_w and x by d_x, the mean value for y needs to be adjusted by

$$\hat{b}_{yw.x}d_w + \hat{b}_{yx.w}d_x \tag{8.7.1}$$

A mean so adjusted has a variance of

$$K + \frac{E_{xx}d_w^2 - 2E_{wx}d_wd_x + E_{ww}d_x^2}{E_{ww}E_{xx} - E_{wx}^2} \times \quad \text{Error variance} \tag{8.7.2}$$

analogous to (8.6.7). Where differences of means are under study, d_w and d_x are the differences between the w- and x-means of the two treatments. Contrasts can be dealt with as at (8.6.10) but using c_w and c_x, not c_x alone.

Just as it was possible to give a mean value for use at (8.6.8), a mean value can be found for (8.7.2). First, it is necessary to know F_w and F_x. A similar value, G, is required from the column for wx, i.e.

$$G = \frac{f(D_{wx} - E_{wx})}{(v - 1)E_{wx}}$$

The correlation coefficient ρ between w and x is also needed, i.e.

$$\rho^2 = \frac{E_{wx}^2}{E_{ww}E_{xx}}$$

A mean of possible values at (8.7.2) is given by

$$\left[K + \frac{2(F_w + F_x - 2\rho^2G)}{fv(1 - \rho^2)}\right] \times (\text{Error variance}) \tag{8.7.3}$$

Covariance efficiency

The use of covariance adjustments leads to a situation very like that at (4.1.1). The variance of a contrast is given by Ks^2. As a result of the adjustment, K is increased to K'. Appropriate expressions have been given at (8.6.7), (8.6.8), (8.6.10), (8.7.2) and (8.7.3). The increase in K is accepted in expectation of a decrease in s^2, and the ratio, K/K', is called the 'covariance efficiency factor' or COVEF. It must be matched by a decrease in s^2 or the covariance analysis will have done harm rather than good.

There is, however, an important difference from the case considered in Section 4.1. The usual efficiency factor (EF) can be calculated before the experiment is initiated, but the COVEF is known only when x has been determined and the randomization is known. It would be wrong to go on randomizing again and again until a high COVEF had been obtained, so anyone who embarks on a covariance analysis has to take a chance. From (8.6.8) it appears that if F equals one,

$$COVEF = Kfv/(Kfv + 2). \qquad (8.7.4)$$

It follows that the covariance efficiency factor is usually high in large experiments because then f will be large. Thus, for a difference of means in a Latin square, where K equals $2/v$,

$$COVEF = f/(f + 2) \qquad (8.7.5)$$

always assuming that F equals one.

This sheds light on the use of an inspired guess for a covariate, which might reduce s^2 but might not. The risks are less in a large experiment than in a small one. If f is large, the covariance efficiency factor will be higher and the loss of one degree of freedom from 'error' of little importance.

8.8 Choice of variables

In the data at (8.5.1) the x-values represent crop in the previous year and a good correlation was found with y, but this cannot be relied upon. As was explained in Section 1.8, the fertility pattern in a wet year can be quite different from that in a dry one or in an early season from a late one, so adjustment of one annual crop by another can often be disappointing, though it has worked very well here. (Perhaps the two seasons were very similar or perhaps there were permanent characteristics of the site.) The correlation between x and y depends quite a lot upon Treatment D in Block V doing badly in both years as is shown at (8.5.3). Was there perhaps something to be seen there? An examination of the site might prove revealing.

The method is usually more effective with perennials, but even then it can fail. One difficulty comes from biennial effects. Crop lost in one year is carried over to the next, so correlations between successive years can be poor, whereas the crops in successive two-year periods may be closely related.

The greatest uses come when something is discovered after an investigation has started. For example, one experiment proved to be very variable in crop and the residuals were examined. They showed a line of poor plots that cut across all the blocks. Local staff were asked to examine the site and they reported a streak of gravel where the low residuals were found. They were told to sample all plots for soil and to measure the gravel content. As a result a covariance adjustment using the gravel content data reduced the error variance to a quarter of its former value. Nevertheless, this was a rescue operation which should not have been necessary. The local staff were at fault for not having examined the site more carefully beforehand.

There are times when the site has been examined beforehand and has been found to vary in so many ways that no single blocking system is going to allow for everything. In such an event it is often best to block as well as possible and to measure characters not otherwise allowed for—soil texture could be one of them—for use as covariates. Deliberate action such as that is good, whereas the carelessness in the previous example was bad.

A common use of covariance is with x-values derived from location or some similar characteristic. For example, an experiment has blocks that form vertical strips on the plan, like those at (8.5.1). After the experiment has started, someone thinks of a reason why they should have gone horizontally. It is perfectly possible to adjust on to a 'pseudo-variate' that will at least remove the linear effect of the trend suspected. At (8.5.1) it would go like this

$$
\begin{array}{ccccc}
5 & 5 & 5 & 5 & 5 \\
4 & 4 & 4 & 4 & 4 \\
3 & 3 & 3 & 3 & 3 \\
2 & 2 & 2 & 2 & 2 \\
1 & 1 & 1 & 1 & 1
\end{array}
$$

That will be gone into more thoroughly in Section 8.9. Alternatively, covariance might be used to allow for edge-effects. That could be done using a pseudo-variate like this:

$$
\begin{array}{ccccc}
1 & 1 & 1 & 1 & 1 \\
1 & 0 & 0 & 0 & 1 \\
1 & 0 & 0 & 0 & 1 \\
1 & 0 & 0 & 0 & 1 \\
1 & 1 & 1 & 1 & 1
\end{array}
$$

(It would be better to leave a wider discard area round the experiment.

Although the pseudo-variate might well be effective, it is nonetheless second best.)

There will be more about pseudo-variates later, especially in the next section and in Chapter 12. It should be noted that with pseudo-variates it is not always best to adjust to the mean of x. In the first example above, it would be wise to adjust everything to $x = 3$ so as not to affect the grand mean of y, but in the second example most people would adjust to $x = 0$, that being the value intended.

8.9   Fertility trends and covariance

In some experiments with many treatments it may be difficult to use blocks because they would have to be so large. It is true that a block does not have to contain all the treatments. The designs in Section 4.7 to 4.10 show how this can be arranged, but there are other approaches that can be considered.

To take an example, a large factorial experiment (Lester, *Rothamsted Experimental Station, Report for 1979*, Part 2, pages 17–25) contained 134 plots, all differently treated, in a completely randomized design. Experiments of that sort, like the serially balanced ones to be described in Section 10.6, are especially vulnerable to variation in fertility arising from environmental differences. Many methods of analysis have been used to eliminate, at least in part, the effects of smooth variation, whether in one direction or in two. For example, some have used the total residuals (Section 7.13) to provide a measure of local fertility, and this method will be considered in Section 10.8. In this section we shall consider ways in which the analysis of covariance can be used to allow for trends across the experimental area by adjusting upon pseudo-variates, a method which is an extension of the approach in the last section.

If all the plots of an experiment lie in one line and are equally spaced, it may be convenient to number them 1, 2, 3, . . . from one end and to use the plot number as a pseudo-variate, x. In effect, this is to allow for a steady linear trend, so it may be better to include also $w = x^2$ (or perhaps $w = \sqrt{x}$), which can allow for curvature.

The same approach can be used with long, narrow blocks like those in Exercise 1C. Here the blocks are in effect columns. Clearly it was believed at the planning stage that the main sources of variation would be across the experiment, but there could be differences between the rows as well. Anyone who was bothered by the long blocks could assign an x-value of -9 to the four plots of the top row, of -7 to the plots of the next row and so on, those in the bottom row all being assigned a value of $+9$. If now the yield, y, were analysed with a covariance adjustment on x, allowance would have been made for any steady trend from top to bottom. A second pseudo-variate, w, could be used to allow for curvature.

There is an alternative. Whether there is a single line of plots or a number of narrow blocks, it may be better to use Fourier functions. The method is as follows. In Exercise 1C the top row could be assigned the angle 0° and the bottom one 180°. Intermediate rows would be assigned other angles going up by equal steps, i.e. 20°, 40°, etc. Then two pseudo-variates could be derived as the sine (x) and the cosine (w) of those angles. To take the example further, for the ten rows the values of x and w would be derived thus:

Row	1	2	3	4	5	6	7	8	9	10
Angle	0°	20°	40°	60°	80°	100°	120°	140°	160°	180°
x	0.00	0.34	0.64	0.87	0.98	0.98	0.87	0.64	0.34	0.00
w	1.00	0.94	0.77	0.50	0.17	− 0.17	− 0.50	− 0.77	− 0.94	− 1.00

It will be found that such pseudo-variates often provide a covariance adjustment that is both supple and effective. They are able to cope with a wide range of fertility patterns.

That is about as much as can be done using only two variates, x and w, for adjusting y. Those who have to work out all the arithmetic by hand may not wish for more, but those who have computers can be more ambitious. Using powers, x, x^2, x^3, etc., there is usually not much advantage in going beyond x^2 and almost certainly none in going beyond x^4. Fourier functions provide more scope. The use of sin θ and cos θ, where θ is the angle of the plot, can be extended by adding sin (2θ) and cos (2θ) and then sin (3θ) and cos (3θ) and so on. Again, matters should not be taken too far. In particular, when using covariance to allow for row effects, the number of pseudo-variates should not exceed the number of degrees of freedom between rows, supposing that they had been used. This, in effect, turns the original block design into one in rows and columns. If it was necessary, why was it not done in the first place? As it is, the resulting row-and-column design is unlikely to be much good. Although treatments will have been applied to columns in a considered manner, the allocation to rows will have been arbitrary, being the result of randomization. It is likely therefore that standard errors of contrasts will be much inflated to allow for the differential effect of pseudo-variates and a poor experiment will have resulted. (Of course, there are times when the original designer misjudged the fertility pattern and something has to be done to allow for the real one, but it is to be hoped that such occasions are rare.)

When all plots form a single line the situation is different. It is then sound to take as many pairs of Fourier functions as may be needed, but again with the proviso that there must be enough degrees of freedom left for 'error'.

This deals with the elimination of trends in one direction. Often that is enough. In Exercise 1C, for example, the blocks look after differences across the experiment from left to right. It has been suggested that if there are any differences up and down the experiment, pseudo-variates can be used to remove their effect, though a warning has been given not to be too ambitious. What happens in the genuine two-dimensional case, when there are effects to be removed in both directions?

If only two pseudo-variates can be managed, they obviously have to be x_1 (distance across) and x_2 (distance up or down) but that is unlikely to be effective if trends are not linear, so more are needed. One good plan is to use five:

$$x_1, \quad x_2, \quad x_1^2, \quad x_2^2 \quad \text{and} \quad x_1 x_2.$$

This fits a paraboloid and is often very successful. It avoids the difficulty that often besets row-and-column designs. As was explained in Section 1.8, when rows and columns are used, additivity is important and is partly a matter of orientation of the experiment on the land. So long as x_1 and x_2 and x_1^2 and x_2^2 alone are used, the difficulty remains, but it can be met by combining them in $x_1 x_2$. Similar considerations can apply when using Fourier functions. Here two approaches are possible:

$$\cos \theta_1 \cos \theta_2, \quad \cos \theta_1 \sin \theta_2, \quad \sin \theta_1 \cos \theta_2, \quad \sin \theta_1 \sin \theta_2$$

This helps when rows and columns may interact. (θ_1 and θ_2 are angles for rows and columns respectively.) The alternative is to use

$$\cos \theta_1, \quad \sin \theta_1, \quad \cos \theta_2, \quad \sin \theta_2, \quad \text{etc.}$$

This has the advantage that the number of covariates used for modelling rows need not be the same as the number for columns. Both sets of covariates can be extended by using 2θ, 3θ, etc., as well as θ.

Exercise 8A

In the following body of data, explore the relationship of y to x_1 and x_2:

x_1	x_2	y
9.1	5.4	30.9
10.7	8.0	58.8
11.4	7.3	56.7
13.8	7.9	67.5
14.1	3.9	32.4
14.5	4.1	46.7
8.3	3.7	13.2
12.6	6.4	55.2
7.3	6.3	33.6
7.9	6.4	36.4
9.2	7.2	47.2
15.8	5.9	64.5
12.9	6.4	51.3
5.1	5.3	17.5
10.1	5.5	34.8
10.3	2.6	19.4
10.0	7.8	55.2

How far does the result depend upon the relationship of x_1 and x_2?

[Data devised by D. A. Preece.]

Exercise 8B

Four bodies of data (I, II, III and IV) are given below. For each one calculate the sums of squares and products for x and y and work out the regression equation of y on x.

I		II		III		IV	
x	y	x	y	x	y	x	y
10	8.04	10	9.14	10	7.46	8	6.58
8	6.95	8	8.14	8	6.77	8	5.76
13	7.58	13	8.74	13	12.74	8	7.71
9	8.81	9	8.77	9	7.11	8	8.84
11	8.33	11	9.26	11	7.81	8	8.47
14	9.96	14	8.10	14	8.84	8	7.04
6	7.24	6	6.13	6	6.08	8	5.25
4	4.26	4	3.10	4	5.39	19	12.50
12	10.84	12	9.13	12	8.15	8	5.56
7	4.82	7	7.26	7	6.42	8	7.91
5	5.68	5	4.74	5	5.73	8	6.89

For each body of data, plot y against x.

[Data devised by F. J. Anscombe, Graphs in statistical analysis, *American Statistician*, **27**, pp. 17–21.]

Exercise 8C

An experiment on old apple trees was conducted to try to make them more fruitful again. The treatments, A–E, involved growing various grass mixtures, etc. under the trees to prevent the growth of weeds. In the sixth treatment, O, the local practice was followed by letting the weeds grow but turning them into the soil once a year.

There were two variates:

y, crop in pounds during a four-year period after starting treatments;
x, number of boxes of crop (to the nearest tenth of a box) during a four-year period before starting the treatments.

Data were as follows:

		Block						
	I		II		III		IV	
	X	Y	X	Y	X	Y	X	Y
A	8.2	287	9.4	290	7.7	254	8.5	307
B	8.2	271	6.0	209	9.1	243	10.1	348
C	6.8	234	7.0	210	9.7	286	9.9	371
D	5.7	189	5.5	205	10.2	312	10.3	375
E	6.1	210	7.0	276	8.7	279	8.1	344
O	7.6	222	10.1	301	9.0	238	10.5	357

The design was in randomized blocks.

Work out the analysis of variance for y. Then calculate it with a covariance adjustment on x. Note in what ways the assessment of treatment effects is modified.

1 pound = 454 grams　　　One box holds about 40 pounds

[Data from S. C. Pearce, *Field Experimentation with Fruit Trees and Other Perennial Plants*, 1st edn, 1953, p. 113.]

Exercise 8D

An experiment was carried out in New Zealand on grass with four treatments, LP, L, P and (1), where L represents addition of lime and P of phosphate. There were eight randomized blocks. (Only four are given here to ease the load of computation.) Further, each plot was divided into two sub-plots, one of which received a dressing of Ammonium molybdate (M) and the other did not.

The area was first burnt to remove the scrub. It was then sown with grass and clover and given a dressing of urea. Two crops of hay were taken and their combined yield is here called x. After application of treatments, a further crop was taken, here called y. All data represent yields in grams after air drying.

Block		LP		L		P		(1)	
		O	M	O	M	O	M	O	M
I	x	1035	1137	887	913	1280	1240	930	891
	y	950	1250	530	491	1140	1135	676	685
II	x	433	954	554	839	605	949	571	903
	y	488	800	618	694	925	1406	660	714
III	x	523	544	779	321	570	556	648	709
	y	1380	1280	824	566	1212	1043	718	728
IV	x	320	646	619	301	418	448	372	629
	y	538	958	492	501	737	863	246	592

Note that with a split-plot design each main effect and interaction is tested using the 'error' mean-square of the stratum to which it is applied. (As explained in Section 7.4, where an effect is partly in one stratum and partly in another, the situation is very complicated and better avoided if possible.)

Carry out an analysis of variance of y with a covariance adjustment on x.

[Data from C. I. Bliss, *Statistics in Biology*, 2 (1970), p. 484.]

Exercise 8E

Someone points out that in Exercise 1C the blocks are rather long and he suggests that it might be advantageous to take out the linear effect of the position in the field. Examine the data with that in mind and see if it helps.

(Hint: In effect this means adjusting on a pseudo-variate, x, that measures distance along the blocks. It will be easier if all values are whole numbers and the mean is zero. That suggests $+9$ for all plots in the top row, $+7$ for those in the next, and so on to -9 for those in the bottom row.)

Exercise 8F

After seeing the results from Exercise 8E, our critic is still not satisfied. He asserts that trends are rarely steady and he wants a curvature effect as well. Examine the data, adjusting on the Fourier functions, cos θ and sin θ, as pseudo-variates.

Note: As presented here the critic appears to have asked for one amendment after another in the hope of obtaining results more to his taste. If that was indeed his motivation, he was behaving in a reprehensible way. On the other hand, if he had been apprehensive from the start about those long narrow blocks and had wanted the fullest protection against trends along them, he would have shown a meticulousness that can only be commended. In general, the form of an analysis should be decided without reference to the data. If something objective, like a streak of gravel, is discovered at a late stage, there could justifiably be an attempt to allow for it, because it would certainly have led to modifications in design if it had been found in time. On the other hand, a data analyst who uses first this device and then another to find something that he can declare significant may well succeed, but the resulting analysis will probably be nonsense.

Exercise 8G

The following data come from one of the earlier published examples of the use of randomized blocks. There were four blocks for the comparison of 16 varieties of potato, A to Q with I omitted. The first two blocks raise no obvious queries, but to modern eyes it does look as if the other two blocks had been formed in an unfortunate manner. Data represent yield in pounds per plot (1 pound = 454 grams).

	A	L	J	C	P	Q	B	E
	351.5	495.5	443.0	383.5	559.0	550.0	359.0	395.5
	K	B	G	O	C	H	J	O
	472.5	367.5	455.5	502.5	328.5	390.5	483.0	512.0
—	E	F	Q	D	N	M	A	D
	357.5	381.5	531.0	316.0	522.0	444.0	325.0	259.0
	N	H	P	M	F	G	K	L
	385.5	354.0	496.5	474.5	410.5	351.5	430.0	394.5

The difficulty, as Exercise 1D showed, is that residuals in the lower part are mostly low and those in the upper part are mostly high, which suggests that the blocks would have been better if they had been two rows deep and eight columns wide.

Apply a covariance adjustment with $x = +3$ in the top row, $+1$ in the second, -1 in the third and -3 in the one at the bottom. Does it reduce the 'error' variance?

[Data from T. Eden and R. A. Fisher, *J Agricultural Science*, **19** (1929), page 207.]

Chapter 9

Transformations

9.1 Justifying assumptions

In Section 1.7 we looked at some of the assumptions made in calculating an analysis of variance and thereafter we have assumed that those assumptions hold. Mostly they do, but sometimes they fail. When they fail, the fault may be with the way in which the various quantities were measured.

To be specific: (1) it is assumed that the various parameters for blocks, treatments, etc. can just be added and do not need to be combined in some other way; (2) it is also assumed that the residuals are all subject to the same sources of variation and therefore all have the same variance of estimation, σ^2, their distribution being normal (see Section 3.1).

If a model is proposed in which parameters are multiplied, $y = ax^p w^q$, then taking logarithms gives $\log y = \log a + p \log x + q \log w$, the parameters $\log a$, p and q now appearing in an additive model that relates $\log y$ to $\log x$ and $\log w$. It may be that $\log y$ is a more basic measurement in a system than is y itself; for example, if y is the size of an organism that is growing exponentially then it is the ratio of final size to initial size that is fundamental biologically.

It may be asked what happens if a transformation is used that enables one assumption to be fulfilled while falsifying the other. The answer is that the difficulty arises only rarely. Transformations well used are more than a statistical expedient to satisfy the mathematicians. As in the example above, they may direct attention to a quantity that is more meaningful than the one actually measured. The point is illustrated by the true story of a botanist who was studying the spread of *Venturia* fungus on apple fruits. At first he was content to measure the diameter of lesions, but later he contrived a means of recording their areas instead. When he gave the data to the statisticians for analysis they found that both assumptions were falsified. The parameters did not combine by addition and the larger data were more variable, defects that could be corrected by using a square-root transformation. In fact, that restored the original basis of measurement. The intention was to measure the spread of *Venturia* from the spore that had been deposited by wind on the apple face, thus initiating a lesion. The measurement really needed was a mean radius from the site of the original spore and that was better measured by a diameter than by an area. (If the intention had been to measure damage to the fruit, a square-root transformation of areas would still have been correct on statistical grounds. The underlying biological phenomenon was the same in each case and that is what needed to be measured.)

9.2   Use of residuals

The assumptions can often be checked by plotting the residuals e against the data y. If the assumption of constant variance and normality is satisfied, the diagram will be as in Case 1 of Fig. 9.1; that is to say, the values will be grouped round the value $e = 0$, and will become increasingly sparse as one moves away from that value. Also the spread of the residuals will be the same for all values of the data, not as in Case 2, where higher values are subject to more variation. Patterns sometimes arise in which all the larger variances are all of one sign and are balanced by a lot of small ones of the opposite sign. That situation also can benefit from a transformation.

A more awkward situation is illustrated by Case 3. Here the residuals come not from one treatment but from two, one represented by crosses and the other by circles. The diagram casts serious doubt on the assumption that data are all equally variable, those from the crosses

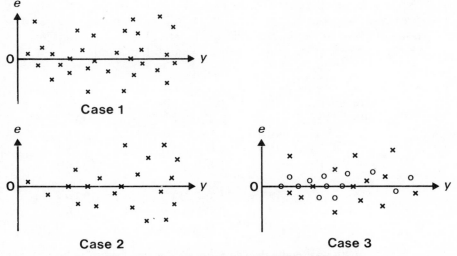

Fig. 9.1   Examples of residuals e, plotted against data values y

showing a wider spread than those from the circles. if there were a difference in means, the difference in variability could be another aspect of Case 2, but that is not so. It appears that the application of one treatment has itself been a source of 'error' when the other has not. (This is quite plausible if the first involved manipulation, like pruning and thinning, absent in the other.) The situation is difficult and will receive attention in Section 9.6. It will not be helped by a transformation because that will affect both treatments and the difficulty will remain.

There are many cases. In skilled hands the device of plotting residuals against data can reveal a lot.

Another useful device is to make a field plan of an experiment and place the value of the residual on each plot; any systematic pattern in those residuals could indicate a fertility trend which the design used has failed to take out. (For example, perhaps a Latin square ought to have been used instead of randomized blocks.) Damage to plots through exposure or accident can also be revealed by this method.

The more important assumption mentioned in Section 9.1 is the one that concerns constancy of variance. If we know how the variance of a set of observations is related to their size, it is possible to find a function of y that will have constant variance. If an analysis of variance is carried out using this function then the assumption (2) is satisfied. As we have said, often the other two assumptions, (1) and normality in distribution, will be satisfied better on this new scale of measurement than when using y itself.

9.3   The logarithmic transformation

When the standard deviation of an observation is proportional to its size (Case 2 above), the function $z = \log y$ will have constant variance. The range of a set of observations indicates the size of their standard deviation, and is used as a quick guide whether or not to transform.

Example:

Treatments		A	B	C	D	E
Block	I	14.6	20.2	12.2	25.2	30.1
	II	15.4	20.1	13.5	25.0	31.6
	III	16.8	23.4	14.0	28.7	32.5
	IV	15.8	21.4	13.2	28.0	34.0
Mean		15.6	21.3	13.2	26.7	32.0
Range		2.2	3.3	1.8	3.5	3.9

Plant growth is often analysed in this way, which is natural because the transformation directs attention from actual size to growth rate. That is what the treatments and the sources of 'error' actually affect.

Nevertheless, the transformation needs to be used with care. First of all, if zeros are possible, even though none may occur in the data set, the transformation needs to be used, if at all, with discretion, because log 0 is minus infinity. As a datum that would be absurd. (Where the transformation is used to convert sizes to growth rates the difficulty does not arise, because a plant cannot be of zero size.)

Another use for the transformation comes with insect colonies, which also can grow exponentially. Here, of course, zeros are possible because there may be no colony. That leads to the question of discontinuity.

As was explained in Section 1.10, data should be recorded to a sufficient degree of precision. If this means measuring to the nearest millimetre instead of the nearest centimetre the effort should be made. Sometimes, however, that will not be possible. Then zeros appear as an approximation, even though a genuine observation of zero is absurd. Also in counting insects, fruits, etc. only whole numbers will make sense. The data may look like this:

$$4 \quad 2 \quad 5 \quad 1 \quad 6;$$

where such serious discontinuity appears, it is advisable for mathematical reasons to analyse $\log (y + 3/8)$ instead of $\log y$. That also helps with the occasional instance when y appears to equal zero. (This can arise as a result of rounding a small but non-zero datum.)

9.4 The square-root transformation

If the variance, rather than the standard deviation, of an observation is proportional to its size, as when data follow a Poisson distribution (Section 3.8), $z = \sqrt{y}$ will have constant variance. Insect counts often (but not always) need this transformation, as do counts of the number of weeds per unit area of soil or the number of fungal lesions per unit area of leaf. The range of observations is roughly proportional to the square of the mean on these scales; it is only in the transformed units that the residuals have constant variance.

Again there is a limitation. Since z is defined only for zero or positive values of y, the square-root transformation must be wrong—or at least suspect—if there is any possibility of y being negative.

Again, discontinuity can cause difficulties. If any arise, it is better to use $z = \sqrt{y + 3/8}$ than $z = \sqrt{y}$.

9.5 The angular transformation

The third transformation to be considered here is different because it is no more than a statistical expedient without biological meaning. Data are often presented as a proportion or a percentage. For example, someone examines a sample of n leaves and reports that r of them exhibit a certain deficiency symptom. As a result there is a need for an analysis of $p = r/n$ or perhaps of $100r/n$.

Such a variate can be decidedly awkward. From Section 3.7 it appears that the variance of p is $p(1 - p)/n$, which is not constant. The value of n can be standardized. Indeed, it is wise to do so. Sometimes a recorder will examine all the leaves on each shoot, even though the latter vary in length. It would be better to devise a sampling method to obtain a constant number, n, from each plot. That removes one cause of unequal variances, but it does nothing about the other, namely the different values of p itself.

A formal solution of the problem is to analyse not p but an angle, θ, such that

$$\sin^2 \theta = p.$$

The case of highest variance of p comes in the middle of its range, where $p = 0.5$ and $\theta = 45°$. If $p = 0.25$ then $\theta = 30°$; if $p = 0$, $\theta = 0°$ and so on. The transformation cannot be used outside the range of p between 0 and 1.

Although the transformation can be useful, it does make results difficult to interpret because it has no real biological meaning. Fortunately, it can often be avoided. For example, when all data lie within the range $p = 0.15$ to $p = 0.85$, an analysis in terms of θ will give results little different from one in terms of p. Sometimes when there are values of p well below 0.15 or well above 0.85, there is little alternative to the use of θ.

The transformation can be especially awkward with factorial designs. The absence of an interaction usually means that two factors combine by ordinary addition. Thus if Treatment (1) gives a mean of μ, A gives a mean of $a = \mu + (a - \mu)$ and B one of $\beta = \mu + (\beta - \mu)$, then AB is expected to give

$$a + \beta - \mu = \mu + (a - \mu) + (\beta - \mu).$$

That is the interaction as usually understood. To look at the situation more closely, we will suppose that 75 percent of insects survive if nothing is done, but only 50 percent if spray A is applied, and only 25 percent if spray B is used instead. This means that $\frac{2}{3}$ survive when A is used alone and $\frac{1}{3}$ when B is used instead. When used together, it is to be expected that $75 \times \frac{2}{3} \times \frac{1}{3}$ percent will survive, i.e. $16\frac{2}{3}$ percent. Since their effects are expected to combine by multiplication, a logarithmic transformation is required, but that would lead to variances even more diverse than those found before it was used. On the other hand, an angular transformation will stabilize the variances while making nonsense of the interaction. The θ-values for (1), A and B are respectively 60°, 45° and 30°, so, in the absence of an interaction, AB is expected to give a θ-value of 15°, corresponding to a p-value of 0.07, which is not the same as the 0.17 required by the biological concept of independence of action. It will be found, however, that all transformations give trouble at times. Where difficulties become too great, a possible alternative is the method of the next section.

Given discontinuity, the best form of the angular tranformation is

$$\sin^2\theta = \frac{r + 3/8}{n + 3/4}$$

9.6 Single degree of freedom effects

It sometimes happens that no transformation can be suggested. It could be that the variate for analysis is some 'index' or 'coefficient' that biologists have found useful. It is perhaps calculated in some complex manner, and the statisticians can only guess how it will be distributed. Alternatively it could be that some of the treatments require a lot of manipulation of plants, e.g. tree forming, which leads to differential variability but not of a sort that is associated with high and low means. A third example arises with different modes of application of fungicides or insecticides. Some modes may lead to patches of poor pest control, and this will increase variability for those treatments. Whatever the reason, transformations do not always provide a solution.

In that case it is sometimes possible to take each contrast with its single degree of freedom and to find an estimate of its variance. That can be done if there are enough replications and if the design is in blocks. We shall explain the method using a body of data that raises no special difficulty but is nonetheless very suitable for our purpose. We shall take the data for Variety X in Exercise 7D. They give a six-fold replication of four treatments, i.e. nitrogen fertilizer applied at four equally spaced levels. The data are:

Treatment	I	II	III	IV	V	VI	Total	
			Blocks					
N_0	111	62	74	68	61	53	429	
N_1	130	90	89	64	91	74	538	(9.6.1)
N_2	157	100	81	112	97	118	665	
N_3	174	116	122	86	100	113	711	
	572	368	366	330	349	358	2343	

The corresponding analysis of variance reads:

Source	d.f.	s.s.	m.s.	F	
Nitrogen levels	3	8136.45	2712.15	16.65	
'Error'	15	2443.30	162.89		(9.6.2)
Stratum total	18	10579.75			

It remains to partition the treatment line into the linear, quadratic and cubic effects, each with a single degree of freedom, as shown at (5.7.4), namely

$$L, (-3 -1 +1 +3); \quad Q, (+1 -1 -1 +1); \quad C, (-1 +3 -3 +1).$$

We begin by evaluating each contrast for each block separately, i.e.,

	I	II	III	IV	V	VI	Total	
L	+ 216	+ 172	+ 136	+ 102	+ 123	+ 224	+ 973	
Q	− 2	− 12	+ 26	− 22	− 27	− 26	− 63	(9.6.3)
C	− 18	+ 24	+ 72	− 126	+ 21	− 72	− 99	

We will take L, the linear effect, first. Its value of U at (5.6.7) is 20 and the replication is six, so its sum of squares is $(+973)^2/(20 \times 6) = 7889.41$. The block values are now squared and added and the sum divided by U to give

$$[(+216)^2 + (+172)^2 + \ldots + (+224)^2]/20 = 8522.25.$$

The difference, $8522.25 - 7889.41 = 632.84$ with five degrees of freedom, is the component of 'error' that specifically relates to the linear effect.

For Q, the quadratic effect, U equals 4. That makes the sum of squares for Q in the treatment line 165.38 and the component of 'error' 512.87. For C, the cubic effect, where U again equals 20, the two figures are respectively 81.68 and 1297.57. We can now take the analysis of variance already found and partition two of its lines, the one for treatments and the one for 'error', as follows:

Source	d.f.	s.s.	m.s.	
Linear effect (L)	1	7889.41	7889.41	
Quadratic effect (Q)	1	165.38	165.38	
Cubic effect (C)	1	81.68	81.68	(9.6.4)
'Error' (L)	5	632.84	126.57	
'Error' (Q)	5	512.87	102.57	
'Error' (C)	5	1297.57	259.51	
Stratum total	18	10 579.75		

That is an extension of what was done at (7.4.1). Apart from rounding errors, everything at (9.6.4) adds correctly to its total at (9.6.2). However, no F-values have been given because there is an ambiguity. Is F for the linear effect 48.43 ($= 7889.41/162.89$) with 1 and 15 degrees of freedom, or is it 62.33 ($= 7889.41/126.57$) with 1 and 5 degrees of freedom? In the present instance, where there is no reason to doubt the 'homogeneity' of the 'error', the answer must be 48.43. In the ordinary way no one would have bothered to have calculated the analysis at (9.6.4). However, now that it has been worked out, some may be surprised that the three 'error' components, one for each of L, Q and C, are so different. We will therefore look into the matter formally.

The method is to use 'Bartlett's test', which depends upon the criterion known as χ^2. (That received previous mention in Section 3.5.) The question is: can the three components (126.57, 102.57 and 259.51) really be regarded as random variants of 162.89? We write down the logarithms of the four variances, thus:

$$\log 126.57 = 2.1023$$
$$\log 102.57 = 2.0108$$
$$\log 259.51 = 2.4142$$

$$\log 162.89 = 2.2119$$

Then we multiply each of the logarithms by the corresponding number of degrees of freedom and proceed to take a difference between the figure for the pooled variance and those for the separate ones, i.e., we find

$$A = 15(2.2119) - 5(2.1023) - 5(2.0108) - 5(2.4142) = 0.5420.$$

If the three separate variances had been exactly the same, A would have been zero. It is not so and its value tells us how different the variances are. To apply the test we need a further value, found from the reciprocals of the degrees of freedom, namely,

$$1/5 + 1/5 + 1/5 - 1/15 = 0.5333.$$

We divide that by $3(g - 1)$ to obtain W, where g is the number of component variances. Here $g = 3$. That makes $W = 0.08889$. Finally we calculate

$$\chi^2 = 2.3026A/(1 + W)$$
$$= 1.146.$$

The value of χ^2 is referred to tables with $(g - 1)$ degrees of freedom. As a result there is no suggestion that the component variances are significantly different, the value of P being rather more than 0.5, so the use of the pooled variance at (9.6.2) appears to be justified.

This approach has led to an expected conclusion. In other circumstances there might have been no reasonable basis for expecting either a homogeneous or a heterogeneous 'error'. In that case we might have been glad to have the evidence of the test. The approach by single degree-of-freedom effects has other uses because the data might have failed to satisfy some other essential assumption. For example, the data at (9.6.1) might have represented a variate that was not necessarily additive. To take another example, the treatments could have been such that the data were correlated within blocks. (That would have happened if the data were diameters taken at different distances along a shoot, each shoot forming one block.) The method is not perfect, but so long as a number of independent estimates can be made of each contrast of interest, it is required only that those estimates shall be distributed in an approximately normal manner. Each contrast can have its own 'error' variance. If it is suggested that the variances should be pooled, we may have to ask whether they are all estimates of some common value. If that question does arise, Bartlett's test is available.

We should note, by the way, that the table at (9.6.3) is not entirely typical. For that particular set of contrasts the column headed 'Total' could have been obtained directly from (9.6.1) or by adding the rows of (9.6.3). That is not always the case. Where the two methods differ, the values required are the row totals.

We may illustrate a different case by considering the well-known law advanced by Mitscherlich. It says that when fertilizer is applied at evenly spaced levels, as at (9.6.1), successive increments in yield bear a constant ratio to one another. Calling the yields for levels 0, 1, 2, 3 respectively a, b, c and d, the law declares that

$$(c - b)/(b - a) = (d - c)/(c - b) \qquad (9.6.5)$$

We shall use the data at (9.6.1) to examine whether that is so.

The first task is to find a variate that will measure the extent to which the two sides at (9.6.5) differ. The obvious solution is to take their difference, but that is not satisfactory because with real data it is quite possible that a will equal b, or c will equal b; in either event our variate will be infinite in value. One possibility is to use

$$H = (c - b)^2 - (b - a)(d - c).$$

If the law holds exactly, H will equal zero. This is not entirely satisfactory either, because H is made up of squares and products of the data; if they are distributed normally it is not to be expected that H will be distributed in the same way. The obvious device is to use a square-root transformation, but that is not feasible here where the variate, H, can take negative values. We shall therefore accept some measure of non-normality, recognizing that the longer tails of the distribution will diminish sensitivity, not increase it.

We proceed thus: for each block we work out the value of H and then we apply the method of Section 3.3 to see whether the mean of H differs significantly from zero, i.e.,

I	II	III	IV	V	VI	Total	
+ 406	− 348	− 551	+ 2200	− 54	+ 2041	+ 3694	(9.6.6)

The sum of squares attributable to the difference between the mean value of H ($+ 616$) and its expected value (0) is $(+ 3694)^2/6 = 2\,274\,273$ with one degree of freedom. The sum of squares for 'error' is

$$(+ 406)^2 + (- 348)^2 + \ldots + (+ 2041)^2 - 2\,274\,273 = 9\,370\,711$$

with five degrees of freedom. That makes F equal to 1.21. Hence the data could well have followed Mitscherlich's law. Nevertheless the outcome has not been entirely satisfactory because of the two large values of H, one for block IV and the other for block VI, both of which arise from a high value of c for those blocks. (There is in fact some evidence of an optimal application somewhere around level 2, in which case the law is not being followed strictly.) On the other hand, the analyses at (9.6.2) and (9.6.4) do not suggest much curvature. The fact is that we do not have enough data to determine the precise form of the response curve, though we have had enough to show the method.

Another example comes from Section 9.5, where Treatment (1) gave a mean kill of μ, A gave a and B gave β. In the absence of an interaction what should we expect from AB? If factor A in the absence of B kills a proportion a/μ, and if factor B in the absence of A kills a proportion β/μ, we would expect the two working independently to kill a proportion $\alpha\beta/\mu^2$. That would leave an infestation of $\alpha\beta/\mu$. It was pointed out in Section 9.5 that such an interaction can be studied only with a logarithmic transformation, whereas an angular is needed to stabilize the variance. Writing γ as the observed result from AB, one solution would be to use the method given above to see whether the mean of $(\gamma - \alpha\beta/\mu)$, when calculated over blocks, did in fact differ from zero.

The same approach could be useful with Case (3) in Section 9.2. As with all these examples, a difficulty could arise from a lack of degrees of freedom to give a satisfactory estimate of the 'error' variance. In Section 1.8 we emphasized that there should at the very least be six or eight, but 20 were desirable. With these partitioned 'errors' there can rarely be any reasonable hope of such standards being attained. The effect is not any loss of validity, but there could be serious loss of sensitivity.

It should be mentioned that the blocks do not have to be complete. For example, we may suppose that treatments A and B concur in b blocks; it would therefore be possible to compare them knowing the variance appropriate to their difference, there being $(b - 1)$ degrees of freedom for that purpose. Treatments A and C may also concur several times, though in a different set of blocks. Nevertheless that does not matter; we require only enough concurrences to provide the degrees of freedom for the calculation of the variance. (We should note however that difficulties might arise if someone wanted to know about a contrast that involved several treatments. We should then be limited to those blocks in which they all occurred.) We should explain that the neat summation of the component 'error' sums of squares at (9.6.4) to the combined value at (9.6.2) can be expected only if the same blocks are used throughout.

9.7   Presenting results after transformation

The results of an analysis of variance are valid only on the transformed scale of measurement, i.e. in terms of the logarithms, square roots or θ-values, as the case may be, and not on the original scale. Means can be compared only on the transformed scales because it is only in those units that they are all subject to the same error. It is often a good plan to transform back again to aid understanding of the results. For example, the mean of 1, 4, 9 and 16 is 7.5, but if their square roots 1, 2, 3 and 4 are used the mean is 2.5, which after back-transformation gives 6.25 $(= 2.5^2)$. People sometimes complain that the result looks arbitrary, but it is not. The original value of 7.5 was obtained giving equal weight to all data. If a square-root transformation is really required, the higher values have a higher standard error and should rightly be accorded less weight. That is why the transformed mean has drifted downwards, i.e. towards the better established data. Since all means will do the same, the effect on treatment differences may well be small, but there will be protection against attaching too much importance to a mean that was high on the original scale only because of one high but poorly determined value.

Nevertheless, that is not entirely satisfactory. It is true that an experiment does not estimate treatment means as such but only differences between them; but people do quote individual means, especially of crop weights, and they complain if they find a consistent negative bias. There is in fact a conflict and it needs to be recognized. What is clear is that tests need to be based upon the means of transformed variates and that confidence limits should be calculated in the same way, even if it does lead to the limits on the back-transformed variate being asymmetrical. For example, suppose that a treatment gives a mean of 10.0 on the transformed variate using square roots. The standard error is, say, 1.5. Then if the appropriate value of t is 2.20, the confidence limits are $10.0 \pm 3.3 = 6.7$ to 13.3. A back-transformation to restore the original scale of measurement gives limits of $(6.7)^2$ and $(13.3)^2$, i.e. 44.9 to 176.9, the mean itself being back-transformed to 100.0. That may look strange, but higher values have higher variability and the upper limit is correctly further from the mean than the lower. Such apparent discrepancies need to be dealt with sensitively in any report. In many instances the experimenter will have worked out treatment means from the untransformed data, and it may be difficult to convince him that the statistical analysis is correct when each back-transformed mean is lower than the correponding untransformed. Sometimes it is best to explain that the back-transformed values are adjusted for purposes of the analysis; sometimes they are better omitted. That need not be a serious loss, provided all conclusions can be justified from the analysis of transformed values.

9.8 Transformations in the analysis of covariance

The variable y may be transformed if necessary for the same reasons as in analysis of variance, but x is not subject to the same assumptions: it can follow any distribution, its variance need not be constant, and all that is required is a *straight-line* relationship of y on x. Transformation of x may be needed to achieve this, but that is a different problem.

9.9 Some ideal cases

Many years ago, Cochran gave expressions for the resulting error variance if all assumptions are completely justified. That is at once a challenge and a warning. It is a challenge because it sets standards; it is a warning because it reveals that people make assumptions about their data and do so as a matter of course. Whether those assumptions are justified is another matter. Mostly in calculating an analysis of variance it is taken for granted that the effect of treatments is the same in all blocks and that all residuals are distributed normally (see Section 3.1) with a standard error that is constant over the whole experiment. A transformation is introduced to make both those assumptions hold for that particular body of data. How well does it succeed?

Cochran showed that if the original data follow a Poisson distribution (see Section 3.8) and a square-root transformation is used to correct for the non-constant variance, the error mean-square will equal 0.25. (In fact, there are other distributions for which the square-root transformation is appropriate, so some other figure does not show that anything is seriously wrong, but it does contradict the idea of an underlying Poisson distribution.)

A similar result applies for the case where the data derive from a Binomial distribution. In each plot a sample is taken of n leaves (or fruits or bark samples, etc.) and an analysis is desired of the proportion of leaves, etc. with a certain characteristic. That is the occasion for using the angular transformation. If everything is correct, the error variance will be $821/n$.

Finally there is the case for which a logarithmic transformation is used, i.e. the standard error of any datum is assumed to be k times its value. If that is really so, the error variance will be $0.189/k^2$.

In fact, these ideal values are rarely attained. It is nonetheless useful to know about them. If a test is needed whether the observed variance accords with what was expected, one is given in Section 3.5, namely, if s^2 is the observed variance and σ^2 is its expected value, then fs^2/σ^2 is distributed as χ^2 with f degrees of freedom; f is the number of degrees of freedom used for the estimation of s^2.

Exercise 9A

Three different formulations, A, B, C, of a selective weedkiller were used in an experiment on the growth of soya beans. Eight replicates of each concentration were included in a completely randomized layout, and samples of the soya bean plants were taken from each of the 24 plots after a fixed period. The damage per plot was recorded for analysis as follows:

A:	12	8	15	10	17	19	11	16
B:	32	20	28	37	25	22	29	34
C:	49	60	59	44	40	52	46	48

Examine whether the data require transforming before analysis, and then complete an analysis.

Exercise 9B

An experiment was carried out using five treatments, A–E, in six randomized blocks to promote early germination of seeds, each plot being a pot in the greenhouse. After a fixed period the number of cotyledons to appear was as follows:

Block	A	B	C	D	E
I	8	6	6	5	17
II	18	15	12	10	30
III	10	8	5	2	10
IV	25	27	23	20	48
V	12	8	8	3	25
VI	10	11	6	4	15

Discuss what transformation, if any, to use.

Exercise 9C

The numbers of insects present on each of 8 samples of leaves (of fixed area) of the same crop taken from plants receiving four different spray treatments are as follows:

Variety								
A	3	0	0	6	8	1	12	10
B	21	3	65	8	4	38	11	48
C	25	44	14	18	2	31	0	0
D	15	27	4	0	10	12	0	1

Treatment C is the one currently being used. Do any of the others differ from it in their ability to limit insect damage?

Chapter 10

Some special topics

10.1 Series of experiments

Introduction

If similar experiments are done on several sites in the same season, it is commonly found that the variation of any chosen treatment-contrast between experiments is greater, often much greater, than is indicated by the variation between replicates within each site. In other words there is a treatment × site interaction. If the series of experiments extends over several seasons, there will probably be substantial variations that can be described as treatment × years and treatment × sites × year interactions. The essential problems of designing and reporting a series of similar experiments are the assessment and interpretation of such interactions and the estimation of average treatment-contrasts over all sites and seasons, or of certain sub-sets of sites and seasons, with appropriate measures of confidence, e.g. standard errors.

In a country like England, the weather in one season may be very different from the weather of another, but in any one season most sites will have fairly similar weather. In such conditions we may expect treatment × site interactions to reflect mainly variations between sites in soil or husbandry, whereas treatment × year interactions will be the consequences mainly of variations in weather. There can of course be exceptions; for example, in a generally dry season a few sites may be affected by isolated heavy falls of rain. In other conditions the weather may be less variable from one season to another, or it may be less consistent over the area to be studied. In either case different interactions are to be expected.

Design

The design of a series of experiments has two components, the choice of sites and the design of the experiment at each site. Those two aspects are not independent; they are discussed in the next two sections.

214

Two main strategies can be distinguished, though there may well be intermediate possibilities.

(a)   If the object of the series is to study a particular component (or a few components) of the treatment × environment interaction it is best to choose equal numbers of sites to represent each specified set of environmental conditions. Imaginary examples are:

(1)   the four combinations of hillside or valley floor in zones of high or low rainfall;

(2)   light or heavy soils after crops of legume or maize.

If the conditions are clearly defined and if each set of conditions can be assumed to represent fairly accurately the conditions in large areas of the country, it may not be necessary to select many sites in each combination of conditions—perhaps two in each will suffice.

(b)   Instead, the object may be to formulate recommendations for growers and to estimate the effects on regional or national average yield if the recommendations are widely applied. In this case it is necessary, first, to define precisely the population of fields to be studied, and, second, to choose a truly representative sample of these fields for the sites of experiments of the series. Examples of well-defined populations are:

(1)   all fields of maize larger than 0.1 hectare in District A,

(2)   all fields where wheat in 1986 follows barley in 1985 on the clay-with-flints soils in England.

Sites may be chosen strictly at random, by stratified sampling (e.g. one field per civil parish) or by other methods; often strictly random sampling is impracticable, but the biometrician must beware of any bias that may be introduced by non-random sampling.

The design (in particular, the number of replications) at each site is related to the number of sites. In general the more sites, the fewer replications are needed at each. The reason is that as the number of sites is increased, the interpretation of the results will depend more on the treatment × sites interaction than on the treatment × replicates interaction (that is, 'error') within sites.

There is a range of possible schemes; most research programmes could be allocated a point somewhere in this range.

(i)   The investigation is based on a single experiment at one site, the intention being to generalize over an area typified by that site. The treatments of this single experiment probably have a factorial structure, and it may well be that the 'error' will have to be estimated from high-order interactions. The design may be orthogonal or non-orthogonal, with or without confounding.

(ii)   Several rather simpler experiments are dispersed over the area, which is thereby sampled by more than one site. Such a scheme enables an assessment to be made of the treatments × site interaction in order to find out how far successful treatments depend upon having the correct environmental conditions.

(iii)   Many experiments are dispersed over the area. Although they will all be fairly simple, each will have enough degrees of freedom to determine its individual 'error' variance. In that way it would be possible, say, to find the response of rice to different levels of nitrogen fertilizer and to do so over the area as a whole.

(iv)   Some very simple trials, each consisting of perhaps two to six plots, are dispersed over many sites to estimate the effect of one or two simple changes in the husbandry of farmers' fields. For example, the investigation might concern the contrast between a new recommended variety of maize as compared with the traditional one. The investigation might well cover the whole country. Since there are no longer enough degrees of freedom to determine the 'error' variance at each site, some pooled figure will have to be used.

(v)   In the extreme the investigation becomes a survey and not an experiment at all. There would be very many sites. The intention would be either to estimate mean yield over the whole area or to detect localities in which the farming system under study might prove unsatisfactory.

In general, at all levels apart from the first, the sites should be chosen at random, or as nearly as possible at random, if the intention is to estimate some quantity over the area; but some selection is permissible if the intention is to compare different environments. At level (i) (the single experiment) the choice of site may reasonably be governed, at least partly, by the need to minimize 'error' variation. Moving down the range, especially at level (iii) or more, a rigorous system of selection of sites, with an element of random choice, becomes increasingly important to ensure that the chosen sites shall truly represent the relevant population of fields. It is not permissible at these levels to reject a sub-set of fields because experiments on them are expected to have large 'errors' as such rejection will entail a risk of bias. Ideally, every experiment of a series would have the same design and number of replicates. (There may be exceptions to this rule if complicated confounding is involved but that is beyond the scope of this manual.) If circumstances make it necessary, however, individual experiments may use different designs. (An example would be a series laid down in randomized blocks with a few 'difficult' sites requiring Latin squares.) Similarly, a site with a limited amount of near-uniform land can be included by using fewer replications than the standard, or by use of plots smaller than standard. More extreme cases of the use of different designs will be mentioned below.

The method of data analysis depends upon the level of the investigation. The single experiment at Level (i) should be analysed with care, the purpose always being borne in mind. In a survey at Level (v), however, it may suffice to find a figure for yield per unit area. (To say this is not to decry the considerable skills needed to interpret a survey; they are, however, different from those needed to interpret an experiment. The present text is concerned only with experiments.)

Assuming that there are enough degrees of freedom for 'error' in each experiment to provide a useful estimate of variance, mean squares should be tabulated in case any definable subset of sites (e.g. those on sandy soils) tend to give larger (or smaller) 'errors' than the remainder.

It is possible to test for non-homogeneity (see Sections 3.5 and 9.6), but there is usually no reason why different sites should give equal variances. Any site showing an outstandingly large variance may at this stage be re-examined for hitherto undetected mistakes, e.g. a mistake in recording of one or more yields of misapplied treatments. For any set (or sub-set) of sites believed to have approximately equal 'error' variances we can calculate a pooled estimate. If designs vary, it is probably best to add together the sums of squares (in terms of yield per unit area) and divide by the total degrees of freedom.

Next comes the combined analysis including all (or nearly all) sites. It is reasonable to reject the results of a site only if there is strong evidence of a serious mistake; it should not be omitted solely because its 'error' mean square is unduly large. It is possible to use a weighted analysis, giving each site a weight in inverse proportion to its 'error' mean square. (This rule is subject to modification if different sites have different numbers of replicates.) Nevertheless, this should usually be avoided, for two reasons, first because each 'error' mean square is a sample from a population of possible values, so that the weights usually have a substantial random component; secondly, because undue weight may be given, accidentally, to a particular type of site, perhaps the less weedy ones or those on deeper, less variable soils. Equal weighting avoids these dangers, besides being simpler.

The combined analysis uses as data the estimated treatment-means of all the sites. The simplest analysis takes the form

Sites	S	$(s - 1)$ d.f.
Treatments	T	$(v - 1)$ d.f.
Sites × Treatments	S × T	$(s - 1) \times (v - 1)$ d.f.

There are s sites and v treatments; for the moment we assume all the experiments were done in the same season.

Where the same treatments occur at several sites there is a formal resemblance to an experiment in randomized blocks, the sites taking the place of blocks. Consequently F-tests, t-tests, standard errors, etc., can all be found using familiar methods. Nevertheless the resemblance is a little superficial. In a randomized block experiment the 'error' sum of squares is usually that for the interaction of blocks and treatments, as was pointed out at (7.4.1). At Level (iii) the interaction of sites and treatments may itself be the subject of study. It is therefore helpful to have an 'error' for each site determined in the usual way. At this stage there are several possibilities. For example, Bartlett's test, described in Section 9.6, may suggest that they could well be pooled. Perhaps some other solution seems better. The point is that it is usually possible to find an 'error' variance with which to compare the interaction of sites and treatments.

Two examples may help to make this clear.

First, a series of variety trials may include some varieties resistant to a particular disease and some varieties susceptible to it. The incidence of the disease may vary widely from site to site. A contrast between a resistant and a susceptible variety will vary more between sites than a contrast between two resistant, or between two susceptible varieties. Second, in a series of factorial experiments testing N, P and K, the crop-response to N may well vary more between sites than the response to P. These considerations, which may rarely apply to variation between replicates on one site, make it necessary to examine the separate components of the sites × treatments sum of squares. In the second example given above we could calculate sums of squares for

$$N \times \text{sites}$$
$$P \times \text{sites}$$
$$K \times \text{sites}$$
$$N \times P \times \text{sites}$$
$$\text{etc.}$$

We can assume that the true (population) values of the corresponding variances are different. (The opposite assumption is usually dangerous.) Then each main effect and interaction needs a separate test of significance (and standard error) based on an appropriate mean square. (In this example we might expect that at least some of the mean squares involving interactions of sites with interactions N × P, etc. would show no clear signs of heterogeneity, and this would justify pooling the corresponding sums of squares.) If in this example N was applied at three or more rates, it would be necessary to examine separately the site-to-site variation of the linear, quadratic, etc. contrasts of the main effect of N. This relates to the methods given in Section 9.6.

Next the analyst should look for any relationship between treatment-contrasts (e.g. linear N) and the fertility of the site, measured by the general mean of all plots, or perhaps by the mean yield of plots without applied N; there are many possibilities. In a series of variety trials, it may be possible to distinguish between varieties that are more (or less) sensitive to differences in fertility between sites. If other data are available (e.g. soil pH, soil organic matter, incidence of disease), other useful relationships may be detected by appropriate regression analysis. An alternative approach to the assessment of 'sensitivity' is the comparison of the mean square for site differences calculated for each variety separately, but exact tests of significance are not easily derived by this method.

Finally, the tabulated contrasts should be carefully scanned, together with a table of characteristics of the sites, both permanent (e.g. altitude, soil type) and ephemeral (e.g. sowing date). Any relationship that is suggested should be reported, with the reservation that this is of the nature of a correlation and not necessarily a causal relationship.

Experiments over several seasons

If there are several experiments in each of several seasons the preliminary analysis of treatment-estimates of all experiments takes the form

Sites	S	$(s-1)$ d.f.
Years	Y	$(y-1)$
Sites × years	S × Y	$(s-1)(y-1)$
Treatments	T	$(v-1)$
Sites × treatments	S × T	$(s-1)(v-1)$
Years × treatments	Y × T	$(y-1)(v-1)$
Sites × years × treatments	S × Y × T	$(s-1)(y-1)(v-1)$

(s sites, y years, v treatments)

There is a strong resemblance to the analysis at (7.4.1).

Again this analysis can be repeated for any single treatment contrast, or sub-set of treatment contrasts. If the mean squares for T × S, T × Y, T × S × Y show strong evidence of heterogeneity the interpretation of the results is complicated; some relatively simple situations may, however, emerge. If, for example, T × Y is the largest mean square, it is likely that differences in weather are the most important factors determining treatment-effects, and prediction of effects in future seasons is correspondingly uncertain (unless weather can be predicted). If T × S × Y is the dominant source of variation this may be explained by variations in weather at different sites in any one season; again accurate prediction of further effects requires forecasts of weather—though which aspects of weather (e.g. rainfall early in the season, temperature at anthesis, etc.) are important is difficult to determine. If forecasting future treatment-effects is the object, a rough working rule is to base tests of significance, etc. on $T \times Y$ or $T \times S \times Y$ using the larger of the two mean squares, or, if they differ little, a pooled value.

Making the best of a bad job

If it is necessary to gather together information on, for example, the responses of a crop to N-fertilizer, and there are many experiments already done, each including a test of N but of varied design, some including other factors, an extension of the method described above may be used.

First, if different experiments test N at different rates, a response to a standard rate of N may be estimated for every experiment by use of a suitable fitted response-curve. Secondly, if some experiments include a factor (e.g. organic manure M) that is believed to have an interaction with N-fertilizer while other experiments do not, a response under standard conditions can be calculated and used in a combined analysis.

10.2   Rotation experiments

There are two main types of rotation experiment. They both involve one or more sequences of crops which can be repeated indefinitely; in the experiment the sequences—or perhaps there is only one—may be planned to run once, twice or many times. If the intention is to stop the experiment when the sequence(s) have run once, it is perhaps better to call the experiment a 'crop-sequence' experiment and keep the name 'rotation experiment' for experiments designed to run through the crop-sequence(s) at least twice.

The first type is designed to investigate treatments applied to one or more crops of a rotation, the same rotation being followed on all plots. For example, an organic manure and inorganic fertilizers could be compared in a rotation of wheat, potatoes and barley. The treatments might be applied cumulatively, year after year to each crop on the same plots, or they might be applied to the potatoes only, with residual effects measured in wheat and barley. Such an experiment may be in one phase, e.g.

> 1985   potatoes
> 1986   wheat
> 1987   barley

or it may have one or more replicates in each phase, thus:

Phase:	A	B	C
1985	barley	potatoes	wheat
1986	potatoes	wheat	barley
1987	wheat	barley	potatoes
1988	and so on.		

This more elaborate scheme needs more land and much more work, but it allows us to judge the 'reliability' of the results, i.e. how much the results of past seasons can be expected to hold true for future seasons, more quickly than the simpler scheme above.

The other type of rotation experiment is used to compare different crop rotations, often in conjunction with tests of other factors, for example organic manures and nitrogen fertilizer. An example is a test of the inclusion of a leguminous crop in place of non-legume, perhaps cowpea or groundnut in place of a cruciferous oilseed crop in rotation with cereals.

The range of types of rotation experiment is very great and we shall not attempt to deal with all of them, but almost all such experiments have features in common and here are some of them.

(1)   Rotation experiments involve changes in soil properties. (If an experiment does not do that, it does not need to be continued on the same plots year after year.) Movement of soil between plots, therefore, whether by cultivation or by erosion, is a hazard even if the rate is small enough to be unimportant in a one-year experiment. This may indicate large plots with wide discard areas at their edges, or special precautions, e.g. grass paths between plots.

(2)   The experimenter, together with the biometrician, must look ahead in time. Will it be possible to introduce a new variety of crop, or a deeper plough, during the experiment, if one becomes available and is favoured by growers? If so, when?

(3)   Should spare plots, e.g. duplicates of the simplest cultivation system, or of the growers' commonest crop rotation, be included from the start, to be used if later experience suggests one or more new treatments that were not thought of or did not exist initially?

(4)   Alternatively, should plots be made big enough to allow splitting them later for sub-plot tests of a factor or factors that may later be thought necessary, e.g. a test of nitrogen fertilizer in a legume versus graminaceous test, or a date-of-sowing test in a cultivation experiment?

(5)   Should all phases be included, or one only, or is a compromise possible, e.g. 3 of the 6 phases of a 6-year rotation? If different phases are included, how do they start: with different crops in the same calendar year, or with the same crop in successive years? (One of the most difficult problems arises when rotations of different lengths have to be compared.)

The analysis of the results of a rotation experiment can be complex. For example, if an experiment runs through several rotations the yield of crop A on Plot x in year 1 and the yield of crop A on the same plot in the next rotation will probably be correlated. Normally one would expect the correlation to be positive, but the opposite might happen. Meanwhile the yield of crop B on Plot x in year 2 may be correlated, positively or negatively, with the yield of crop A in year 1. Mean crop-yield may show a trend with time, positive or negative, either because the weather is changing with time, or because new crop-varieties are introduced or because of new methods of control of pests, diseases or weeds. (It may just be that the crops are being managed with increasing skill.) Such trends may affect all treatments equally, or they may not. For example, better weather may have more effect on well-fertilized plots than on badly-fertilized ones, and deep cultivation may have cumulative effects.

If an experiment has run through several rotations a preliminary analysis should include, at least:

(a)   mean of yields of treatments;
(b)   mean values of each useful contrast between treatments (or means of treatments), with standard errors based on the variation of that contrast between years. If all contrasts of a set (e.g. linear and quadratic contrasts for 3 rates of fertilizer) have variation not significantly different, they may perhaps be pooled;
(c)   for each contrast the trend, i.e. linear regression on year, with standard error calculated appropriately;
(d)   an examination of variation of treatment-contrasts in relation to major differences in weather between years.

The main type of long-term experiment not included under these headings involves long-continued monoculture with tests of fertilizers or varieties or cultivations, etc.

10.3   Experiments with trees and bushes

Sources of variation

Crops grown on trees and bushes are perennial; experiments on such crops last for more than one season, in some cases for very many seasons. During this time the units—the trees or the individual bushes—increase greatly in size. There are also different sources of variability that change in importance (Pearce, 1960b). Three basic sources of variability are:

(A)   that inherent in the material at planting;
(B)   the different extent of shock experienced by each tree at planting;
(C)   the effects of soil variation over the experimental area.

With tree crops, such as apples and pears in the United Kingdom, an experiment needs to be planned at least two seasons ahead, for the individual trees must first be raised in a nursery before they can be planted out into the land used for the permanent experiment. More trees are raised than will be needed; those that grow badly and seem weaker than average are discarded, but a random choice must then be made from the acceptable trees. Unless choice is random, any experimental results can be criticized as not being generally applicable. (In a botanical experiment intended to elucidate some point in physiology, closely standardized tree material may be required, but no-one should apply the result to practical agriculture, for which purpose representative plants are essential.) The initial variability (A) diminishes with the passage of time and can eventually be neglected.

It is also found that the variability described in (B) diminishes fairly quickly; if some trees are removed after a few years, leaving a more widely spaced experimental layout to form a second phase of the experiment, those trees that remain may again suffer something like (B) for a short time. The third source of variation (C) builds up steadily over time. Eventually it will dominate all other sources and can lead to higher variability than is usual with annual crops.

All this affects the selection of material in the nursery. In a short-term experiment, e.g. one to see if trees can be brought into bearing earlier, it is important to have trees closely graded as to initial size, though in that case it may be wise to regard the investigation as 'botanical' rather than 'agricultural'. When the first experiment is finished, the trees can perhaps be used for some other study using the methods to be described in Section 10.8. By that time (C) may have taken over and the initial selection of plants can be forgotten. In a long-term experiment, on the other hand, a wider range of initial size and growth may be completely acceptable, but trees with crooked stems and poor graft unions should be rejected because the cumulative effects of such defects build up over the years and lead to much the same results as (C).

The choice of design is likewise affected by the expected duration of the experiment. In a short-term study there is no need to go to great lengths to control local variation because (C) will not have the time to become important, but when the experiment is intended to go on for a long time a major aim should be to reduce (C) by careful choice of blocks, or, if necessary, the use of rows and columns, based on proper knowledge of the sources of soil variation (and climatic trends, etc.) through the experimental site.

Calibration

When a trial of a particular species is to last a long time, it is useful to be able to calibrate, i.e. to find a measurement that will predict how crops will vary from one plot to another. That is best done as early as possible in the life of experimental trees, as soon as they are planted into their permanent field positions. With fruit trees one or two seasons' growth is usually allowed before different treatments such as fertilizers are applied; during this time, regular measurements of the circumference of the trees at a standard height above ground (the 'girth') may give a very good way to show how vigorously they are growing. That gives a good indication of future cropping, at least in early years. In the ordinary way calibration is effected by means of the analysis of covariance (see Chapter 8).

With this in mind there is a lot to be said for planting areas to which no treatments are applied initially but the trees are calibrated for future use. Indeed, that can be done very effectively if foresight is exercised. Thus an area could be planted choosing some varieties that grow quickly and others that take longer. As an example, a single unit-plot may contain four varieties laid out A B C D, which after the first phase is thinned to A   C   ; but that will work only if A and C pollinate one another (or are self-fertile). Alternatively,

$$
\begin{array}{cccc}
A & B & C & D \\
A & B & C & D
\end{array}
$$

may be thinned to

$$
\begin{array}{cccc}
A & & C & \\
& B & & D
\end{array}
$$

which keeps all varieties and gives a second phase in which trees are spaced as evenly as possible. (That, however, may not be desirable if B and D are much larger trees than A and C.)

If trees are likely to develop at widely different rates, the experiment can be designed so that the slower-growing varieties are in alternate rows; when the trees have grown enough for the original layout to become crowded, quite a lot of information will already have been discovered about the faster-growing varieties and they can be removed. The remaining layout then contains the slower-growing varieties, which were in alternate rows originally but now form the second phase of the trial at double the previous spacing distance. When planning an experiment in this way, care must be taken that all through the life of the trial any varieties that are not self-fertile will have adequate pollinator varieties remaining in the layout.

At thinning, the trees that remain are likely to suffer different amounts of shock. As a result it may be that no suitable calibrating measurement can be found for the second phase of the experiment. Of course, if the contrasts sought are those between varieties, or if the treatments have to be applied before planting, calibration is difficult if not impossible, because the calibrating variate must not be subject to the effects of treatments. The reasons were given below (8.6.4).

When mature trees are taken over, perhaps on a commercial planting with no history of differential treatments, calibration by the total crop over the last few years can be very effective, but again a lot depends upon species. An example is given in Exercise 8C.

Guard rows

In a long-term experiment, roots can spread a long way, especially if some plots are given less fertilizer than is needed for healthy growth. Also, when different chemical sprays are used in an experiment, there will be drift through the air, and when trees are older that becomes a serious problem. So rows of 'guard' trees are needed to separate the experimental plots from one another. These are trees that are in neither plot, to left or to right, and they mark the edge of spraying application, the left side receiving a different pesticide from the right. Often they do not receive a spray, because of the danger of drift across into an experimental plot. If an experiment is to go into a second phase after thinning, careful design of the layout is needed to ensure adequate guarding during the second phase. Since guard rows are not in the experiment for measurement purposes, it is sometimes very useful to place in those rows any varieties needed for pollination of the experimental trees. The need for guard rows means that some of the land used is 'wasted' for experimental purposes, and the extent of this can be reduced by using unit plots that consist of several trees, perhaps a tree of each of three or four varieties; to use single trees as plots wastes more material in guarding.

Adding of treatments

Because tree experiments last a long time, and also because they take a while to establish before beginning experimental treatments in the first place, provision should be made wherever possible for using the material again for a second experiment with a new set of treatments, if the first experiment gives all its important information fairly quickly. (That topic will be considered in Section 10.8.) When a new problem is put to the research worker, it is useful to have some ready-made material available for an experiment immediately, because it avoids the delay while a site is prepared and material is set up. (This is also a reason for planting trees with no initial plan beyond their calibration.) Another reason for changing treatments can be that unexpected problems or effects occur in applying those chosen originally.

Residual effects on the land

When an experiment finally ends and the trees are uprooted, the effects on the soil last a very long time and will have to be taken into account in any future use of an experimental site. Such a site can sometimes be a useful asset to a research institute, but it can also impose annoying restrictions on its future use.

Experiments on bushes

Bush crops share similar problems to tree crops, though experiments on them will be of shorter duration and there will not be the same delay in getting them established. A useful calibration variate in the early seasons of an experiment is often the amount of wood growth made before cropping begins. However, variation in cropping can so disturb wood growth that it is no longer useful for calibration. In many bush crops, size will be regulated by pruning rather than thinning, so that experiments will not have more than one phase; but it may still be useful to change to a new set of treatments before the natural life of the bushes is over.

Recording of harvest

Harvesting usually needs to be done tree-by-tree, and it is essential to have individual trees labelled and numbered very firmly to avoid errors through loss of identity. Since the crop from each tree may be quite large, more than one day is often needed for harvesting the whole area; in case it spreads over several days—through weather delays or sheer volume of work—it is desirable to harvest a block at a time, and so tree experiments are nearly always designed to contain blocking in some form (randomized blocks, or row-and-column designs). When a crop ripens slowly, two harvesting periods may have to be undertaken to gather all the ripe crop.

Analysis of data

Analysis usually involves total crop per season, with perhaps, in addition, a division into top quality and the rest. The effect of seasons may be observed by looking for different patterns in the results of different treatments or varieties. This is often done by working out contrasts between seasons like those between treatments in Chapter 5. Really it is a matter of finding single degree-of-freedom effects that express important features. To take an example, if there are six seasons the total crop is given by

$$(+1 \quad +1 \quad +1 \quad +1 \quad +1 \quad +1)$$

i.e. in each plot the six crops are added to give a variate, which is then submitted to the analysis of variance in the usual way. However, there might be a biennial effect and the question arises whether or not it is the same for all treatments. In that case

$$(-1 \quad +1 \quad -1 \quad +1 \quad -1 \quad +1)$$

can be dealt with in the same way. Then perhaps someone suggests that some of the treatments are leading to a faster increase in crop than others. Since biennial effects are suspected, it would be better to work with two-year periods and

$$(-1 \quad -1 \quad 0 \quad 0 \quad +1 \quad +1)$$

might be used, as might

$$(-1 \quad -1 \quad +2 \quad +2 \quad -1 \quad -1)$$

to see if the increase in crop was progressing steadily or was slackening off. We should note, however, that though these contrasts would be orthogonal if they were applied to the treatments of an experiment of the kind considered at (5.6.6), there is not the same orthogonality here. The successive crops, unlike the treatment means, are associated, but not in any definable way. Consequently, it is not to be expected that they will all give the same 'error' variance. However, that does not matter if each is to be made the subject of a separate analysis of variance, following the approach suggested in Section 9.6.

10.4 Bivariate analysis and bivariate diagrams

There are occasions when two quantities should really be studied together. For example, the heights and spreads of plants are usually highly correlated, sometimes so much so that there is no need to study both because each tells the same story as the other. Suppose, though, that the experiment concerns irrigation and that plants are beginning to wilt where the supply of water is low. In that case the heights will decrease while the spreads will increase. Taking the two variates separately, the effect of water may not be significant, but taken together the two changes, i.e. in heights and spreads, may show up because they go against the prevailing positive correlation coefficient. To take another example; in general, plots that grow well will be found to crop well also, but what if the growth is a response to closer spacing and a need to find light? In that case the better growth on some plots could lead to less crop. The two effects may be non-significant when they are considered separately. Nevertheless there could be a marked effect when they are considered together. That is because the separate effects, which go in opposite directions, have to be seen against the positive correlation between the quantities (i.e. growth and crop) when competition is standardized. Such points have a special relevance in the study of intercrops, which will be considered in Chapter 11, but they apply in other situations also.

In dealing with an intercrop the usefulness of bivariate methods is obvious, the two variates being the yield of the two species. Sometimes the 'error' line shows little correlation between the two variates, but in practice it is hard to forecast the sign of the correlation. Some plots will be inherently better than others, and that will cause a positive correlation between the variates. On the other hand, the two species are in competition and that will cause a negative correlation. Either effect might dominate the other, or the two might approximately cancel. So, although there is no certain way of forecasting the degree or sign of the correlation, it would be most unwise to assume independence.

The problem then is this: there are two variates, a and b, which are to be analysed

	(i)	not separately as in Chapters 1 and 4,
and	(ii)	not with one serving to adjust the other, as in Chapter 8,
but	(iii)	together, giving equal weight to each.

To that end, a and b are transformed to two other variates, x and y, such that

(i)	x and y have a variance of 1,
(ii)	x and y are independent.

This is easily done. First, let

$$x = a/\sigma_A. \tag{10.4.1}$$

Now remove from b the component that could have been predicted from a. This leaves

$$b - \beta a.$$

Here β is the estimated regression coefficient of b on a. In (8.2.1) it is called

b but here the symbol has been changed to avoid confusion. It was mentioned at (8.3.5) that the sum of squares of such an adjusted variate is $S_{yy}(1 - r^2)$, where S_{yy} is the sum of squares before adjustment. Hence, here, the variance is $\sigma_B^2 (1 - r^2)$ and the standard error the square root of that amount. Dividing by that standard error gives

$$y = (b - \beta a)/(\sigma_B\sqrt{1 - r^2}) \qquad (10.4.2)$$

The transformation being known, it is an easy matter to find x and y for any plot or treatment, given the values of a and b. The values of x and y so found can be plotted against one another on a sheet of graph paper in the usual way, but that possibility will be examined in the next chapter. The task here is to describe a bivariate analysis of variance.

It will be supposed that there are eighteen plots in six randomized blocks of three treatments, A, B and C. It will further be supposed that treatment means are:

	A	B	C
a-mean	21	24	30
b-mean	57	63	51

and the analyses of variance and covariance (calculated as in Section 8.3) are as follows:

Source	d.f.	a^2	ab	b^2	
Treatments	2	7.00	− 6.00	12.00	(10.4.3)
'Error'	10	25.00	+ 10.00	32.00	
Stratum total	12	32.00	+ 4.00	44.00	

The standard error σ_A of a is $\sqrt{25.00/10} = 1.581$, so in this instance (10.4.1) gives

$$x = 0.6325a \qquad (10.4.4)$$

The regression coefficient of b on a is $+ 10.00/25.00 = + 0.400 = \beta$. Also, the square of the correlation coefficient,

$$r^2 = (+ 10.00)^2/(25.00 \times 32.00) = 0.1250$$

and the standard error of b is $\sqrt{32.000/10} = 1.7889 = \sigma_B$.
Hence, (10.4.2) is now

$$y = (b - 0.400a)/(1.7889 \times \sqrt{0.875})$$
$$= 0.5976b - 0.2390a \qquad (10.4.5)$$

In general we may write

$$x = \delta a, \qquad y = \theta b + \gamma a \qquad (10.4.6)$$

where, in this instance, $\delta = 0.6325$, $\theta = 0.5976$ and $\gamma = -0.2390$.

A digression

Although it is not an essential part of the calculations, we shall derive the sums of squares and products for x^2, xy and y^2, because they will show so clearly why the transformations at (10.4.6) are useful. First, a sum of squares for x^2 must equal

$$\delta^2 \times \text{(the corresponding sum of squares for } a^2).$$

Accordingly the analysis of variance for x^2 has 2.80 for treatments, 10.00 for 'error' and 12.80 for the stratum total. Similarly a sum of products for xy must be

$$a[\theta^2 \times \text{(sum of products for } ab) + \gamma^2 \times \text{(sum of squares for } a^2)].$$

Applying that result to the example, the sums of products for xy are -3.33 for the treatments and the stratum total and 0.00 for the 'error'. Finally, a sum of squares for y will be equal to

$$\theta^2 \times \text{(sum of squares for } b) + 2\theta\gamma \times \text{(sum of products for } ab) + \gamma^2 \times \text{(sum of squares for } a).$$

In the example this gives 6.40 for treatments, 10.00 for 'error' and 16.40 for the stratum total. Writing the whole as at (10.4.3), that is

Source	d.f.	x^2	xy	y^2
Treatments	2	2.80	-3.33	6.40
'Error'	10	10.00	0.00	10.00
Stratum total	12	12.80	-3.33	16.40

It appears that the transformation has achieved its objectives of giving two variates, x and y, such that each has a standard error of one, with a zero correlation between them. Nevertheless, as has been said, this is a digression, not needed except as a demonstration that all has gone well.

The calculation resumed

From this point it will be helpful to write the analysis of variance of (10.4.3) in a more general form similar to that at (8.5.4):

Source	d.f.	a^2	ab	b^2
Treatments	f	$D_{aa} - E_{aa}$	$D_{ab} - E_{ab}$	$D_{bb} - E_{bb}$
'Error'	e	E_{aa}	E_{ab}	E_{bb}
Stratum total	$e+f$	D_{aa}	D_{ab}	D_{bb}

The next step is to work out the quantity Λ, where

$$\Lambda = \frac{E_{aa}E_{bb} - E_{ab}^2}{D_{aa}D_{bb} - D_{ab}^2} \tag{10.4.7}$$

In this example, $\Lambda = 700/1392 = 0.5029 = (0.7091)^2$. The bivariate F equals

$$\frac{(1 - \sqrt{\lambda})(e - 1)}{\sqrt{\lambda}f} = \frac{0.2909 \times 9}{0.7091 \times 2} = 1.85 \tag{10.4.8}$$

with $2f$ and $2(e - 1)$ degrees of freedom, i.e. with 4 and 18. It does not appear that the treatment differences were significant at any important level, but perhaps that was not needed. The treatment means for x and y are readily found from (10.4.4) and (10.4.5), namely:

Treatment	a	b	x	y
A	21	57	13.3	29.0
B	24	63	15.2	31.9
C	30	51	19.0	23.3

The values of x and y can be plotted in the usual way with x measured along the horizontal axis and y along the vertical one. This will show that C does appear to stand away from the other two. It should here be explained that the bivariate F defined at (10.4.8) can be used for partitions of the treatment line just as for the line as a whole. In the present example, If there were good prior reason to regard C as possibly different from A and B, it would be permissible to partition at (10.4.3) thus:

Source	d.f.	a^2	ab	b^2
A $v.$ B	1	0.75	$+ 1.50$	3.00
AB $v.$ C	1	6.25	$- 7.50$	9.00
Treatments	2	7.00	$- 6.00$	12.00

(10.4.9)

If we are to apply the F-test to the contrast of [AB $v.$ C], we should first form the D-line by adding the line for the contrast to the E-line at (10.4.3), i.e. $D_{aa} = 6.25 + 25.00 = 31.25,$ $D_{ab} = - 7.50 + 10.00 = 2.50$ and $D_{bb} = 9.00 + 32.00 = 41.00$, which makes

$$\Lambda = \frac{700}{1275} = (0.7410)^2$$

so

$$F = 3.15$$

with 2 and 18 degrees of freedom. Significance is now higher, though it still has not attained the level of one in twenty.

If the treatment points are to be plotted on a bivariate diagram in the manner suggested, it would be a convenience to have a quantity corresponding to the least significant difference of univariate analysis. Here a quantity is found equal to

$$t\sqrt{K} \text{ Error m} - \text{s}$$

where t has its usual meaning and K is the constant defined at (4.1.1) and evaluated in various ways in Chapter 5. Then if two treatment means differ by more than that quantity, they are said to be significantly different. In bivariate analysis, a treatment point having been found, a circle can be drawn round it with a radius of

$$\frac{2KF'(e - 1)}{e} = L$$

(10.4.10)

where K is as for a univariate analysis and F' is the actual value of F with 2 and $2(e - 1)$ degrees of freedom for the significance level required. Then, if two points are so close that the distance between them is less than L, treatments can be said not to differ significantly. However, least significant differences need to be used with discretion in univariate analysis, and the same reservations apply in bivariate cases.

10.5 Fan trials

Spacing trials present special design difficulties. There are two in particular. One concerns the need for plots to be large if they are all to have the same area and each is to contain an exact number of rows.

For example, a comparison of inter-row spacings of 1.0 m, 1.5 m and 2.0 m requires a plot 6 m wide to accommodate respectively six, four and three rows. Another problem concerns guarding. Plants at different spacings give rise to different micro-climates. Further, they throw shadows of wind, rain and sun. A plot adjacent to one closely planted may be more sheltered and less moist and with less light than it would have been if it had a widely spaced neighbour.

For those reasons many people use fan trials. The idea is to plant a series of 'spokes' that radiate from a 'hub', which will ordinarily be outside the experimental area. An example is given in Fig. 10.1. There is a constant angle, θ, between adjacent spokes. On each spoke the distances of plants from the hub are the same, the innermost being at a distance D and the outermost at $D + L$. (Note that L is the length of the spoke in the sense of being the distance between the extreme planting locations. The end plants will each need further space to grow in.)

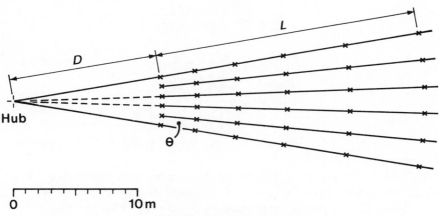

Fig. 10.1 Scheme of a fan trial

Fan trials are of many kinds. The chief distinction is between those intended to study (a) inter-row distances, or (b) the area that a plant needs for good development (A), or (c) rectangularity (R). The last needs a little explanation. By "rectangularity" is meant the ratio of the distance between plants within a row to the distance between rows. It will be seen that R and $1/R$ are the same: the difference is just a matter of the direction in which rows are taken, either along the spokes or across them.

Since plants on the outside spokes suffer less competition, only inside spokes can be used and, even with them, the end plants must be discarded. A plot consists of those plants on inside spokes that are the same distance from the hub. (In Fig. 10.1 there are four plants to each of the four plots.)

To return to kinds of fan trials, if the aim is to compare inter-row spacings, the plants are placed at a uniform distance apart along each spoke, and there are no special difficulties of design. If the intention is to compare areas, rectangularity being kept constant, each plot is an enlargement of its neighbour towards the hub, being C times longer and C times wider, as in Fig. 10.1. Finally, if the intention is to compare rectangularities, areas being kept constant, each plot is C times longer than its inner neighbour but only $1/C$ times as wide, the rectangularity being therefore changed by a factor of C^2. This last sort is rather unusual and will not be discussed further here.

The important case is the second, i.e. the one in which rectangularity is preserved but areas are changed. More specifically, let there be N areas, covering a range from A_1 to A_N. There will in consequence be $(N + 2)$ plants on each spoke. The dimensions of the fan can be worked out from four geometrical relationships, of which the first is a slight approximation. They are:

$$L = \frac{2(C^2\sqrt{A_N} - \sqrt{A_1})}{\sqrt{R}(C^2 - 1)} \tag{10.5.1}$$

$$2(N - 1)\log C = \log(A_N/A_1) \tag{10.5.2}$$

$$D = \frac{2\sqrt{A_1}}{\sqrt{R}(C^2 - 1)} \tag{10.5.3}$$

$$\theta \text{ in degrees} = 28.65\ R(C^2 - 1)/C. \tag{10.5.4}$$

The base of the logarithms in (10.5.2) is immaterial. In the example that follows the base will be 10, as is usual in most non-mathematical work.

To take an example, someone may want a fan to explore the range from $3\ \text{m}^2$ ($A_1 = 3$) to $15\ \text{m}^2$ ($A_N = 15$) with a constant rectangularity of 3 ($R = 3$

or 1/3). There is a constraint that L is not to exceed 32 m. (The example has been chosen for its awkwardness.) From (10.5.1) either

$$32 = \frac{2(3.873C^2 - 1.732)}{1.732(C^2 - 1)} \quad (R = 3)$$

or

$$32 = \frac{2(3.873C^2 - 1.732)}{0.577(C^2 - 1)} \quad (R = 1/3)$$

That is to say, C should be about 1.044 or 1.183 according to the chosen value of R. The first is rather small, so the second looks more hopeful. Note, however, that any change from 1.183 must be made cautiously. To use $R = 1/3$ and $C > 1.183$ will lead to $L > 32$.

From (10.5.2) several possibilities appear. In this instance, $(N - 1) \log C = 0.3495$ so the choice lies between

$N = 3$	$C = 1.495$
$N = 4$	$C = 1.308$
$N = 5$	$C = 1.223$
$N = 6$	$C = 1.173$

The last looks promising, though deceptively so. To raise C to 1.183 is, from (10.5.3), to increase A_N/A_1 and that will mean a larger value of C to satisfy (10.5.1), which will in turn require a higher value of A_N/A_1. Perhaps a solution can be found along those lines, but it might be better to retreat to $N = 5$, $C = 1.223$ and see what happens there. It appears from (10.5.3) that $D = 12.10$ m and $\theta = 3.87°$. Planting should take place at distances, $D, DC, DC^2, \ldots \ldots DC^6$, from the hub, i.e. at 12.10 m, 14.80 m, 18.10 m, 22.13 m, 27.07 m, 33.11 m and 40.49 m $(D + L)$. That puts L equal to 28.39 m $(= 49.49 - 12.10$ m), which is less than was intended. If C increases above 1.223, the value of A_N/A_1 will be increased. It could be argued that the ratio of A_N/A_1 of 5 to 1 is quite large enough so an alternative would be to reduce it and seek a solution for $N = 6$. One possibility is $A_1 = 3$ m^2, $A_N = 13.5$ m^2, $C = 1.625$, $D = 17.07$ m, $L = 31.91$ m.

Another useful expression gives the area of the mth plot. It is a generalization of (10.5.3). Because

$$A_1 = \tfrac{1}{2}D^2R(C^2 - 1),$$

$$A_m = A_1 C^{2(m-1)} = \left[\frac{D(C^2 - 1)}{2}\right]^2 RC^{2(m-1)} \tag{10.5.5}$$

Such then are the dimensions of the desired fan, but transferring them from a piece of paper to the field is not easy. The best way is to take one spoke as the base-line and to plot the positions of the end plants on all spokes with precision relative to that line. The task can be accomplished either by trigonometry or alternatively, the whole can be drawn carefully to scale on a large piece of squared paper with the base-line along one of the printed graduations. The important co-ordinates can then be read off. Once the end-points of the spokes have been marked in the field, there is no great difficulty with planting.

The fan will need to be replicated. Some people use complete circles. Certainly that avoids the difficulty of a single fan. If the wind blows into it, this funnelling effect can lead to damage at the narrow end; if the wind blows in the opposite direction, it is divided and the whole fan can be sheltered by the closely planted end. Another idea is to use fans in pairs, side by side, the narrow end of one adjoining the wide end of the other. A second pair at right angles to the first is valuable.

However the fans are disposed, the aim is to find the spacing that gives a maximum of characters like growth and cropping or a minimum of those like disease incidence. The appropriate statistical technique is therefore that of regression rather than the analysis of variance. Fans with different orientations may give different results, which is a reason for studying data from each fan separately, at least initially.

Some workers have found that crop-weights and plant-weights give closer regression relationships when in reciprocal transformation, i.e. when using $1/W$ rather than W. Also, it is better to transform the areas per plant (A_1, A_2, etc.) to plants per unit area (a/A_1, a/A_2, etc.) when seeking a quantity upon which to regress.

10.6   Systematic designs

Spacing trials are not the only sort where extreme treatments should not adjoin. Fertilizer trials are the same. If two treatments, one of high application and the other of low, come together on adjacent plots, there will be robbing as roots from the starved plants find the riches nearby and develop where there is fertilizer. The obvious solution is to leave a guard area between the two plots and to give it an intermediate level of fertilization, but that reduces the problem without eliminating it. Also it wastes space.

If there is only one factor, another possibility is to allot the treatments to plots within a block in ascending (or descending) order of level of application. In that way robbing is kept to a minimum. Further, if the plots are long and narrow and if they adjoin on their long sides, the experimenter can see the response surface before his eyes. There would, of course, have to be several blocks; otherwise the apparent response curve could be the result of a local trend. The only design problem remaining is the allocation of orders (i.e. ascending or descending) to the blocks. Some would randomize; others argue that randomization has been abandoned anyway and they would allocate the two orders alternately to successive blocks. If use is to be made of the method of analysis to be described below, the random approach is better.

The analysis of data is best approached in this way. First, we decide which features of the response curve are important. Here the likely answer is that we should consider linear and quadratic effects as described in Section 5.4. Others may want to carry on to later contrasts, like the cubic, while yet others may have ideas that are quite different. Whatever the answer, the next step is to calculate the desired quantities, q, for each block separately. The rest of the calculations are given in Section 9.6. If the 'error' sum of squares is $(b-1)s^2$, the variance of the mean value is s^2/b where b is the number of blocks. A mean of those values will give an estimate of the quantity under study. The sum of squares of that mean will be given by

$$s^2 = (q_1^2 + q_2^2 + \ldots + q_b^2) - (q_1 + q_2 + \ldots + q_b)^2/b.$$

The mean square will be $s^2/(b-1)$ and the standard error of the mean $\bar{q}$ will be the square root of $s^2/[b(b-1)]$, which is easily found and can be used either to show how well the mean $\bar{q}$ has been estimated or to carry out a t-test. (It is assumed that the null hypothesis implies that the values of $\bar{q}$ have a mean of zero.)

With two factors the situation is more complicated. Plots have to be small and nearly square, if not exactly so. The levels of one factor are applied in either ascending or descending order to the rows, and levels of the other factor are applied similarly to columns. The result is the growing of a response surface. Again the contrasts described in Chapter 5 can be used to estimate single degree of freedom effects, whether of main effects or interactions, and the replication in blocks will enable standard errors, t-values, etc. to be found. When randomizing there are four possibilities, because both rows and columns need to be assigned either an ascending or descending order. Again, the method of analysis is that of Section 9.6.

Serially balanced designs

A type of design intermediate between randomized and systematic has been used in studying powdery mildew, a fungal disease of the leaves of barley (Dyke and Shelley, 1976). It could be useful in other circumstances also. It is believed that the development of the disease in a plot of normal size may be substantially influenced by the treatment applied to a neighbouring plot; thus a plot downwind of an untreated plot will receive more spores than one downwind of an effectively sprayed plot. Similar considerations probably apply to experiments on many mobile diseases and pests of field crops. Most of the designs used in this work had four treatments, A, B, C, D, and used 38 plots in one line. They are constructed as follows:

Treatment A is tested in 9 situations:

BAB, BAC, BAD, CAB, CAC, CAD, DAB, DAC, DAD.

These, together with the other three treatments in the corresponding sets of situations, can be combined in a design such as

A, BCAD, ABDC, DBAC, ACBD, BDAC, DCAB, ABDC, BCDA, DCBA, B

(Commas indicate blocks, not breaks visible on the land.) This design has the additional property that, apart from the first and last, the plots fall into nine 'blocks' of four plots each, containing a replicate. The extreme plots are needed only as 'neighbours' and their yields need not be recorded. Although, of course, such a design is not fully randomized, it is one of a large sub-set (at least 1566 in number) of all possible randomizations.

This type of design does not include any treatment with the same treatment as its neighbour; to include these combinations would bring problems; for example:

(1) the design could not be divided into 'blocks' each containing a replicate of A, B, C, D;
(2) the larger source of spores from two or (three) adjacent unsprayed plots might appreciably influence plots at a distance.

The intended analysis ignores the division into 'blocks' (though this may be recognized in a 'post mortem' study of 'error' variances). The yields are swept for the effects of treatments applied 'direct' (i.e. to the plot under consideration) and successively for effects of treatments to the left-hand neighbours (e.g. B v. C v. D as neighbours of A), 8 d.f. in all; and similarly for right-hand neighbours. The sum of squares of the residuals with $35 - 3 - 8 - 8 = 16$ d.f. (which is based on the three-factor interaction) provides an estimate of 'error'.

10.7 Nearest neighbour methods

A long time ago, in 1937, Papadakis made a suggestion that seemed full of promise but even now few would feel certain about it. What he said was this: each plot has a total residual (Section 7.13) which indicates its fertility. Since good and bad land comes in patches, it should be possible to take each plot in turn and assess its potential performance, x, from the total residuals of its neighbours. Then when an analysis of variance was carried out on its actual performance, y, it should be possible to adjust by covariance upon x.

The difficulty with this suggestion comes from the mathematical complexities of adjusting y by a variate that is itself derived from y. Everything depends upon the correlation between the performance of adjacent plots, and that is a matter about which only the foolish dare to assert anything with confidence. Those who know about fertility patterns in fields will question almost any law supposed to be of universal application.

However, an illustration will show the method. It will represent data from a design without blocks but, if there had been any, they would have been ignored.

$$
\begin{array}{lll}
\text{A} \;\; 26 & \text{C} \;\; 31 & \text{B} \;\; 28 \\
\text{C} \;\; 29 & \text{A} \;\; 32 & \text{B} \;\; 28 \\
\text{B} \;\; 16 & \text{C} \;\; 21 & \text{A} \;\; 17
\end{array}
\qquad (10.7.1)
$$

The treatment means are A, 25; B, 24; C, 27.
Hence the total residuals are:

$$
\begin{array}{lll}
\text{A} \;\; +1 & \text{C} \;\; +4 & \text{B} \;\; +4 \\
\text{C} \;\; +2 & \text{A} \;\; +7 & \text{B} \;\; +4 \\
\text{B} \;\; -8 & \text{C} \;\; -6 & \text{A} \;\; -8
\end{array}
$$

In the absence of any special reason to the contrary it is usually best to estimate the potential performance of each plot from the total residuals of its neighbours, both in rows and columns, in so far as they exist, i.e. x is

$$
\begin{array}{lll}
\text{A} \;\; (+2+4)/2 & \text{C} \;\; (+1+7+4)/3 & \text{B} \;\; (+4+4)/2 \\
\text{C} \;\; (+1+7-8)/3 & \text{A} \;\; (+4+2+4-6)/4 & \text{B} \;\; (+4+7-8)/3 \\
\text{B} \;\; (+2-6)/2 & \text{C} \;\; (-8+7-8)/3 & \text{A} \;\; (-6+4)/2
\end{array}
$$

which is

$$
\begin{array}{lll}
\text{A} \;\; +3 & \text{C} \;\; +4 & \text{B} \;\; +4 \\
\text{C} \;\;\;\; 0 & \text{A} \;\; +1 & \text{B} \;\; +1 \\
\text{B} \;\; -2 & \text{C} \;\; -3 & \text{A} \;\; -1
\end{array}
\qquad (10.7.2)
$$

The figures at (10.7.2) show a clear fertility pattern from low potential at the bottom to high potential at the top.

It is now a question of adjusting y at (10.7.1) by x at (10.7.2). There is a point to be noted here. Because x is derived from y, the usual rules for finding error degrees of freedom in the analysis of covariance do not apply. If used, they will overestimate the true number by a quantity a which is difficult to estimate but lies between 0 and 1. It is therefore wise to play for safety and take a as 1. That means allowing two degrees of freedom for the regression instead of one.

In this instance, the calculations go like this:

Source	d.f.	x^2	xy	y^2
Treatments	2	0.89	− 2.33	14
Error	6	50.67	+ 88.00	266
Stratum total	8	57.56	+ 84.67	280

leading to

Source	d.f.	s.s.	m.s.	F
Treatment	2	42.28	21.14	0.75
Error	4	113.17	28.29	
Stratum total	6	155.45		

Such then is the method. How valid is it? Most authorities would agree that the analysis of data in the form just given leads to results not far from the truth. How effective is it? Here a lot must depend upon circumstances. With newly planted trees the variability has been brought over from the nursery, and there are no correlations between neighbouring plots to make use of. On the other hand, there are times when the variability is due chiefly to the effect of patchy soil and the method could well be very effective.

A study was carried out to compare the method of Papadakis with randomized blocks (Pearce, 1978, 1980).

The general conclusion was that the two methods were of approximately equal effectiveness, except where a mistake had been made in placing the blocks across fertility contours instead of along them. Then the method of Papadakis, which does not depend upon orientation, was better. Row-and-column designs were in the main better than the use of Papadakis, but, where they fail, they fail disastrously; whereas the nearest neighbour approach, which sometimes is ineffective, never does much harm. If there are no correlations between the performances of neighbouring plots, no advantage comes from the covariance adjustment and two degrees of freedom have been lost from 'error', but that is all. The method of Papadakis can at least be recommended as safe. That is not to say that it has no worrying features. It is, for example, quite unable to deal with a discontinuity in fertility like that caused by differential former crops, whereas if the position of the break is known, blocks can be formed accordingly. If, on the other hand, the position of the discontinuity is not known, a block design is equally unable to cope. In any case, blocks may be needed for purposes of administration.

There are several points still to be made. One concerns 'iteration'. The difficulty is this. From (10.7.1) the means of A, B and C are respectively 25, 24 and 17. After adjustment by covariance they are 24.6, 23.6 and 27.8. Should we not start again and calculate (10.7.2) afresh and go on round the cycle repeatedly until everything settles down? The question is a reasonable one. The analysis as it stands is inconsistent. It is based on certain values for the treatment means, which it then contradicts. Iteration has raised so many questions in the minds of the mathematicians that it is better avoided, at least for the present.

Others have argued that it would be better if the treatments could be dispersed more, so that two neighbouring plots were never treated alike. Some possible designs are called 'complete Latin squares'. The objectors are possibly right, but it is too early to say definitely.

It may be remarked that if anyone was designing an experiment with the intention of using Papadakis's method of analysis, there is a lot to be said for using long narrow plots, placed side by side so as to encourage a large correlation between adjacent plots. In that way there would be a single strip of plots, which were themselves placed across the strip. The mathematics of the one-dimensional model gives more confidence than that for the two-dimensional in which plots adjoin both at their ends and their sides. Also, it reduces difficulties about missing neighbours at the edges and corners. In the one-dimensional case only the end plots need be considered and it would not be difficult to add two extra plots to provide total residuals with which to assess x for the end plots in the experimental area, as was done in Section 10.6 with the serially balanced designs. The one-dimensional case could also be useful with 'contour blocks' which wind round a hill, giving plots that are admittedly all at the same altitude but very variable with regard to aspect.

Finally, there is a development associated with the name of Wilkinson, which is probably more widely used than that of Papadakis, but it will not be described in detail here because little has been published about it in practice. Essentially it consists in using moving blocks of three plots, the performance of the treatment on the middle plot alone being assessed, the block then passing on one plot for the assessment of the next 'middle treatment'.

10.8   Changing the treatments of an experiment

Sometimes the treatments are applied and their effect can be assessed soon afterwards. This happens, for example, when sprays are used to check the spread of a fungal infection on leaves. Sometimes too the plants are long-lived and will continue to develop well after the time that a single fertilizer application or a spell of irrigation has spent its force. In such circumstances the experimenter may wish to use the same plants for a second investigation. (With spraying experiments on trees, there could be need of repeated changes of treatments.)

There are three possibilities to be considered.

(a)   The treatments have had their respective effects and the plants have become uniform again. That could well be the case, for example, in a trial of insecticides. After a time rain will wash spray residue off the leaves and there will be a migration period during which a new generation of mites will disperse itself. Provided there has been no serious damage to the plants, either from sprays or insects, no special considerations apply if someone wants to use the plants for a further experiment.

(b)   There is a residual effect of the first set of treatments, but it is unlikely to interact with the fresh set of treatments to be applied. That is so, for example, when the first set of treatments is no longer operating, the passage of time having removed spray residues. There could still be different levels of insect population or disease infection or plant growth that would need to be allowed for.

(c)   The residual effects of the old treatments can be expected to interact with the new ones to be applied. To take an example, any fertilizer regime, if it is continued for long enough, will leave soil differences. A later experiment on the same plants, or even on the same site with different plants, may have to be designed with those former treatments in mind.

As has been said, Case (a) presents no special statistical problems. Case (b) is more difficult though not impossibly so. For example, suppose that the first experiment was in randomized blocks, like this:

I	A	B	C	D
II	A	B	C	D
III	A	B	C	D
IV	A	B	C	D

If there were four new treatments, a, β, γ and δ, they could be disposed in a Latin square. If there were only three, or if there were five, designs like those at (4.12.1) and (4.12.2) are available. The only difference lies in the two prior classifications of plots being by blocks and previous treatments instead of by rows and columns, but that is a change of name rather than a logical difference.

To take another example, if there had been five treatments, i.e.

Block	I	A	B	C	D	E
	II	A	B	C	D	E
	III	A	B	C	D	E
	IV	A	B	C	D	E

and someone wanted four new treatments, they could be applied using a design of Type O:TO (Section 4.11) like this:

Block	I	A a	B δ	C γ	D a	E β
	II	A γ	B a	C β	D δ	E γ
	III	A β	B β	C δ	D γ	E a
	IV	A δ	B γ	C a	D β	E δ

If there had been five new treatments, this would have been possible:

Block	I	A δ	B β	C a	D ε	E γ
	II	A β	B δ	C ε	D γ	E a
	III	A a	B ε	C γ	D δ	E β
	IV	A ε	B γ	C β	D a	E δ

It is of type O:OT (Section 4.11). There is no need to go on. An ingenious designer can often find a way. It is true that in all the designs illustrated the number of treatments in the second phase is not very different from the number in the first, but that is not a bad thing because it implies that the degree of replication also will be about the same. If a good choice was made for the first phase, little or no change in the second is to be desired.

The third case (c) can be the hardest. Where interactions between the two sets of treatments are to be expected, one possibility is to see whether the original plots can be split to take the new treatments. Sometimes a different situation arises. Suppose, for example, that an experiment is in progress and someone suggests that the treatment effects, already apparent, would not be there if the soil were irrigated. As a result, water is supplied to some blocks but not to others. The outcome is again a design in split-plots. (The original blocks will have become plots and the original plots will have become sub-plots.) It is true that there will only be a poor comparison of the irrigation treatments, but that will not matter if they have been introduced only to provoke an interaction.

With a 2^k design there is an easy way of adding another factor. If there is an even number of blocks, each containing a complete set of treatments, the additional factor can always be added by confounding an interaction, e.g.

Block				
I	(1)	A	B	AB
II	(1)	A	B	AB
III	(1)	A	B	AB
IV	(1)	A	B	AB

can readily become

Block				
I	C	A	B	ABC
II	(1)	AC	BC	AB
III	(1)	AC	BC	AB
IV	C	A	B	ABC

There is, however, the difficulty that the confounding of the highest-order interaction, here $A \times B \times C$, inhibits the addition of yet another factor if that should be needed. (The reason is simple. If a further interaction is to be confounded, it cannot be chosen so that both it and its generalized interaction with $A \times B \times C$ will be of high order.) In the example, which is of a small experiment, a fourth factor is unlikely. (Indeed, three seems rather a lot.) Nevertheless, with more plots it is better not to confound the highest-order interaction, if that can be avoided and if there is much chance of yet more factors being needed.

10.9   The size of an experiment

Experimenters sometimes ask how large their experiment should be and are bewildered when the statistician replies that he has no means of knowing. On the face of it the question is purely quantitative and people suppose that there must be a formula somewhere to give the answer. In fact, a number of considerations have to be taken into account and most of them are non-statistical.

We must start with the expression at (4.1.1). If we are interested in a certain contrast and if we need to estimate its value with a standard error, S, then $S^2 = Ks^2$, where K is a constant derived from both the contrast itself and the design adopted. (All this has been explained in Chapter 5.) Also, s is the estimated standard error of a single observation. It is usually determined by putting s^2 equal to the 'error' mean-square of the analysis of variance.

We must now ask how large S should be. If we are concerned solely with estimation, we probably know the answer to that question. Hence, assuming that we know the value of s, the problem is solved by proposing a design with an appropriate value of K. At least, it is solved if we can rely upon our estimate of s, but mostly we cannot. Some sites are more variable than others. Even if we do know what value of s is usually found, we may still be lucky or unlucky with our particular set of data. Also, we must be careful how we insert blocks (or rows and columns) because we can make things a lot better if we do it well, but we can make things worse if we do it badly. (We have already suggested in Section 10.7 that one advantage of nearest neighbour methods lies in their giving more consistent estimates of s.)

At this point we emphasize how important it is to keep a catalogue of standard errors. Whenever an analysis of variance is concluded, someone should make a record of the square root of the 'error' mean-square along with notes of location, plot size, block size and any attempts to reduce s by a covariance adjustment or similar device. (It is also useful to know the number of degrees of freedom upon which each value of s is based. If that is not recorded, a few high but badly determined estimates may be given undue weight.) As the catalogue lengthens, patterns will begin to appear. Further, if large values are followed up by a 'post-mortem', or at least by an evaluation of the residuals, errors of judgement will be disclosed and mistakes avoided for the future. Without such a catalogue the statistician cannot advise on the size of an experiment unless he has had considerable experience of that crop in those circumstances. Even then he can possibly only guess.

However, we will suppose that somehow we can make a fair estimate of our likely value of s. Turning to testing, we have first to ask how large the value of the contrast must be before it is regarded as important. The question is vital. We do not want to expend resources and energy on an experiment that shows a contrast to be significant if it is so small that no one is going to make changes to secure so trivial a gain. Equally we do not want to find a difference so large that it would revolutionize local agriculture if it could be relied upon, but is so poorly determined that we cannot be sure that it is really genuine. What sort of difference would we be interested in? We will suppose that we receive an answer to the effect that the value of the contrast should exceed some value, D. We next have to consider what significance level is called for. Perhaps the contrast is almost certain to exist and we need little confirmation to convince everyone; perhaps there are grave doubts about it and our evidence will have to be really strong. We shall probably end by following convention and decide on a significance level of $P = 0.05$ because people are very conservative in the matter. Now that we know P we can make a fair guess at t, which depends also on the number of degrees of freedom for 'error'. That enables us to design an experiment such that

$$D = tS = t(K)^{\frac{1}{2}}s,$$

i.e. such that

$$Ks^2 = D^2/t^2. \tag{10.9.1}$$

Unfortunately that is not the answer. We do not know s perfectly. We may indeed be able to estimate it without bias; in that case the actual figure may be above our estimate or below it. In fact, we have given ourselves a 50 percent chance of missing the contrast, even if it exists and its value does equal D. At this point we have to ask a further question. Supposing that the contrast does have the minimum value at which it becomes important, how ready are we to miss it? What probability, P', would we be willing to accept? The immediate response may be to insist that in such a case the contrast must be detected with certainty, but that is to set an impossible standard; also, it ignores the fact that we are talking about the critical value, i.e. the point at which people might begin to take note of it. A more reasonable response might be to take P' to be 0.1, but there is no universal answer that will satisfy everybody. Anyhow, the choice of P' finally identifies the problem.

Let us consider the situation carefully. If the true value of the contrast is D the estimates we obtain of it will be distributed about that value with a standard error of S. In deriving (10.9.1) we aimed at the middle of that distribution and arrived at a solution in which half the values lay above the point we hit and half below. What we want is to hit the distribution at a point such that 0.9 lies above and 0.1 below. That produces a situation akin to a one-sided test and leads us to aim not at D but at $(D - t'S)$, where t' has been selected for a probability of $2P'$. In fact, we want S such that

$$D - t'S = tS.$$

Hence (10.9.1) should be replaced by

$$Ks^2 = D^2/(t + t')^2. \tag{10.9.2}$$

To take an example, we may decide that s is likely to be about 10 and that we can expect to have about 20 degrees of freedom for 'error', the exact figure being known when the design has been chosen. We are given P as 0.05 and P' as 0.1 and we are told that D, the critical value of the contrast, is 20. How do we proceed? For 20 degrees of freedom t for $(P = 0.05)$ is 2.086 and t' for $(P' = 0.20)$ is 1.325. Hence we want a design such that

$$10^2 K = 20^2/(2.086 + 1.325)^2 = 34.4,$$

i.e., K should be about 0.344. Hence, if the contrast is a straightforward difference of two means, an orthogonal design with six replicates could be indicated. That makes K equal to 0.333, which is rather better than is required though not by much.

Several conclusions can be drawn from (10.9.2), of which the most important is the high cost of improving precision by increasing the replication. An experimenter may make a practice of using four replications. One day he decides to carry out a really precise experiment so he increases the number to five. In that way he will multiply the variance of a contrast by 0.8 ($= 4/5$) or thereabouts, and its standard error by the square root of that amount, i.e. by 0.89. He has therefore obtained an 11 percent reduction in standard error at the expense of doing 25 percent more work. It is true that he will have more degrees of freedom for 'error', but that may not be of great importance.

The formula at (10.9.2) also draws attention to the way in which K and s^2 should be considered together. In all our discussion of non-orthogonality we have had to face the fact that K for a non-orthogonal design is never less than K for one that is orthogonal with the same replication. (Sometimes non-orthogonality will permit unequal replication, which could be to the advantage of certain contrasts. This happens with supplemented balance and is a special case.) The reason for adopting a non-orthogonal design is almost always that it enables the blocking system to fit the land better in the hope that the reduction in s^2 will more than compensate for the increase in K.

If an experiment were intended to examine one contrast for one variate, the expression at (10.9.2) could be used to decide the design, but usually there are several contrasts and several variates and this can raise some difficult decisions. In most factorial experiments it is important to have good estimates of the two-factor interactions. If that is arranged, other contrasts may be determined with greater precision than is really required. To take another example, an experiment may be intended chiefly to determine increase in crop. Then someone wants to take insect counts as well and that variate will be much less uniform. On the other hand, small treatment effects will not matter, so perhaps that is all right, but what if someone wants to study the proportion of blossoms open at a certain time—this can be an awkward variate. Further, he insists that a small difference could be important. It may be necessary to say that the experiment is not designed for such precision and that the attempt had better not be made. This may cause disappointment at the time but that is better than disappointment when the data have been collected. Most experimenters are tempted to measure a lot of supplementary variates. On general grounds that should be encouraged, but it should not be taken to extravagant lengths. It does however provide an argument for being generous when the size of the experiment is decided. There is another reason too. As Chapter 12 will show, the loss of information from mishaps can be out of proportion to the degree of damage. If accidents are at all likely—and they are always possible—the experiment should not be of minimal size but should have some excess capacity.

Exercise 10A

A maize fertilizer trial was carried out at eight sites on the island of Antigua in the West Indies. The complete set of treatments was rather complex, but by selection of data it is possible to extract a 2^3 factorial design from each site with factors N (Nitrogen), P (Phosphates) and K (Potassium). The three-factor interaction was confounded, there being two blocks with Treatments (1), PK, NK and NP, the other two containing N, P, K and NPK. The data represent weight of good ears in kilograms from an area of 144 square feet.

At Site 3 (Thibou's Estate) the trial suffered damage from animals and is here disregarded. At the other sites treatment means were:

Site		(1)	N	P	NP	K	NK	PK	NPK
1.	Friars Hill	3.59	4.94	3.33	5.63	2.09	3.84	2.37	5.08
2.	Lower Friars Hill	2.55	4.49	3.26	5.17	1.30	5.15	1.75	5.56
4.	Wood's Estate	4.26	4.26	4.85	5.38	3.17	2.98	4.19	4.54
5.	Clare Hall	2.12	1.98	2.58	1.73	2.01	2.01	2.77	2.06
6.	North Sound	1.53	2.20	2.41	3.20	2.04	2.21	2.03	2.31
7.	Orange Valley	4.11	5.05	4.58	4.79	2.80	3.82	4.90	5.20
8.	Old Road	5.90	7.83	4.85	6.88	5.94	6.90	4.85	6.97

The respective error mean squares (s^2), each with six degrees of freedom, were:

1.	Friars Hill	0.5649	2.	Lower Friars Hill	0.2996
4.	Wood's Estate	0.5925	5.	Clare Hall	0.1405
6.	North Sound	0.2154	7.	Orange Valley	0.9903
8.	Old Road	0.9305			

You are asked to assess the effect of the three elements on maize yields in Antigua, noting especially any interactions of one element with another and of elements with sites.

Note: Anyone who examines the original data and works out the treatment means will find that they do not agree with those given above. What has happened is this. Since it has been assumed that there is no three-factor interaction, the computer has adjusted the treatment means to make the value of that interaction equal to zero, but it has done so in such a way that the values of the main effects and the two-factor interactions are unchanged. Thus, for Friars Hill the value of the three-factor interaction is

$$3.59 - 4.94 - 3.33 + 5.63 - 2.09 + 3.84 + 2.37 - 5.08 = -0.01$$

which is correct within the limits of rounding error, but other contrasts are unaffected. (Computers usually do that, so the warning may be helpful.) If the experimenter really believes that there is no three-factor interaction, the revised figures are an improvement because they make use of the additional information.

A warning should be given about the difficulties that arise if there could be an interaction, but the experimenter takes a chance and confounds it nonetheless. If the three-factor interaction may exist, difficulties arise whether the adjustments are made or not, because interpretation depends upon knowing about it and there is no way of finding out. On account of complexities of this kind, it is much better not to confound interactions if there is a reasonable chance of their existing. (The situation is different in an exploratory experiment, e.g., one with fractional replication, because then the aim is only to discover which factors interact. For that purpose it is enough to know about the two-factor interactions. Questions of interpretation do not arise.)

[Data from Andrews, D.F. and Herzberg, A. M., *Data: A Collection of Problems from many Fields for the Student and Research Worker* (1985), pages 339–46]

Exercise 10B

A set of experiments was conducted in England to study the fertilization of wheat. There were three sites, X, Y and Z. At each site two experiments were conducted. One was on land expected to supply little nitrogen from residues (N-index = 0); the other was on land expected to be rich in such residues (N-index = 1). The six experiments were carried out in three successive years, 1, 2 and 3, the later ones being always placed on fresh land and not on land occupied by an earlier experiment.

In each of the 18 experiments there were three blocks. Each block contained seven plots, one for each of seven levels of applied nitrogen, namely 0, 2, 3, 4, 5, 6 and 7 times the standard rate.

Among those seven levels there are six effects, (usually linear, quadratic, etc.) but you are here asked to consider only two less conventional ones, namely:

L: The effect of applied nitrogen at low levels, measured for present purposes by the difference in response between levels N_2 and N_0 in each block.

H: The same effect at high levels, here to be measured by the difference in response between levels N_7 and N_6.

Values of these effects are given in Table 10a. The data represent crops expressed in tonnes per hectare. Each involves data from two plots, not one, being a difference between N_2 and N_0 or N_7 and N_6 as the case may be. Consequently divisors of summation terms are not the number of figures involved from Table 10a but twice that number. You are asked to

Table 10a   Values of the effects, L and H, for each of three blocks of the 18 experiments in Exercise 10B

			L				H		
X	0	1	+ 1.42	+ 3.50	+ 2.82	——	− 0.38	+ 0.98	+ 0.07
X	0	2	+ 3.46	+ 2.65	+ 3.15	——	+ 0.63	+ 0.31	+ 0.02
X	0	3	+ 2.59	+ 3.00	+ 2.93	——	− 0.23	+ 0.09	− 0.06
X	1	1	+ 2.02	+ 2.06	+ 2.16	——	+ 0.03	+ 0.31	+ 0.24
X	1	2	+ 2.28	+ 2.48	+ 2.00	——	+ 0.17	− 0.05	− 0.05
X	1	3	+ 2.98	+ 2.85	+ 3.13	——	+ 0.08	− 0.28	+ 0.18
Y	0	1	+ 2.78	+ 2.89	+ 2.02	——	− 0.04	− 0.11	− 0.55
Y	0	2	+ 2.36	+ 2,43	+ 2.40	——	− 0.14	+ 0.25	− 0.09
Y	0	3	+ 2.15	+ 2.47	+ 2.05	——	+ 0.11	− 0.19	+ 0.47
Y	1	1	+ 2.57	+ 2.32	+ 1.10	——	+ 1.10	− 0.12	− 0.87
Y	1	2	+ 1.24	+ 1.67	+ 1.74	——	+ 0.17	+ 0.77	− 0.53
Y	1	3	+ 2.84	+ 2.80	+ 2.83	——	− 0.15	− 0.59	− 0.15
Z	0	1	+ 1.96	+ 1.86	+ 2.60	——	− 0.16	− 0.04	− 0.02
Z	0	2	+ 2.30	+ 1.81	+ 1.84	——	− 0.10	− 0.25	+ 0.05
Z	0	3	+ 2.38	+ 1.58	+ 2.05	——	− 0.08	—0.15	0.00
Z	1	1	− 0.63	− 0.23	− 0.11	——	− 1.42	+ 0.30	− 0.35
Z	1	2	+ 1.60	+ 0.71	+ 0.84	——	− 0.16	+ 0.02	− 0.37
Z	1	3	+ 1.54	+ 0.86	+ 1.24	——	− 0.16	+ 0.06	+ 0.21

[Data are presented by permission of the Agricultural Development and Advisory Service, Cambridge, who carried out the experiments.]

work out a complete analysis of variance for each variate and to write a careful interpretation.

Hint: The variates in Table 10*a* are in fact the effects under study. It is not necessary therefore to form differences between treatment means to evaluate them; that has already been done. (Indeed, the treatments no longer enter into the table of values to be analysed.) Hence, what in the ordinary way would be the correction term represents the sum of squares for the effect (L or H) itself. It should therefore be included. Further, in randomized block designs the 'error' is the interaction of blocks and treatments. Hence the 'error' sum of squares in these analyses can be found by adding the sums of squares for the block effects, each with two degrees of freedom, for the 18 separate experiments. Hence, the analysis of variance takes the following form:

Source	d.f.	s.s.	m.s.
Effect	1		
Sites (S)	2		
N-Index (I)	1		
Years (Y)	2		
S × I	2		
S × Y	4		
I × Y	2		
S × I × Y	4		
'Error'	36		
Stratum total	54		

Exercise 10C

An investigation is proposed for an area in which traditional farmers use neither fertilizers nor chemical weedkillers (herbicides). They fallow their land every third year, following the rotation:

Fallow—Cotton—Millet.

The fallow is believed to be necessary to restore fertility and to control weed-seeding, but no one knows how effective it is. Fertilizer and weedkiller have become available at reasonable prices. The Ministry suggest that they should be used to reduce the period under fallow, thus allowing an increase in the production of cotton. Outline the design of an experiment to test whether improvements can be made along those lines.

Exercise 10D

A series of experiments was conducted on a number of islands in the West Indies to investigate the fertilization of maize. The following data come from an experiment on Antigua in which there were many treatments. Here four have been selected. Treatment O, which was duplicated in each block, represented the usual fertilizer practice. Treatments N, P and K were the same except that dressings of nitrogen, phosphates and potassium respectively were applied at three times the usual level, the intention being to discover what would happen if radical changes were made in levels of fertilization. The complete experiment used a non-orthogonal design, but the data selected here make up an orthogonal block design with unequal replication.

The variate a represents the number of maize cobs per plot; the variate b represents their weight in pounds. Carry out a bivariate analysis of variance on x and y and assess the conclusions.

Block	I		II		III		IV	
Treatment	a	b	a	b	a	b	a	b
O	44	6.87	40	7.20	43	6.39	45	6.75
O	41	6.71	48	7.53	40	6.48	45	7.39
N	41	6.75	40	7.55	44	7.52	35	5.27
P	42	6.67	41	7.18	47	7.56	42	6.41
K	43	5.26	38	5.45	46	7.04	37	4.75

[Data: *A collection of problems from many fields for the student and the research worker* (1985), p. 346 (Experiment at Old Road)]

Exercise 10E

A fan trial is needed to cover the range of plot size from $A_1 = 1 \text{ m}^2$ to $A_n = 4 \text{ m}^2$ with square planting ($R = 1$). The length is not to exceed 20 m ($L = 20$). Determine the other dimensions to secure what is needed.

Exercise 10F

Analyse the data of Exercise 1F, ignoring rows and columns but using the method of Papadakis.

Exercise 10G

An experiment is to be conducted with four treatments, (1), X, Y and XY, interest being centred, as might be expected, on the two main effects and the interaction. There are no special constraints on the land, which lends itself readily to the use of blocks with four plots, so it is proposed to use a design in randomized blocks. In that case s^2 can be expected to be about 50. The question concerns the degree of replication required. It is intended to seek significances at the level $P = 0.01$. Taking D to be 25, the chance, P', of its being missed, supposing that to be its true value, must not exceed 0.05. How many replicates should be used?

Chapter 11

Intercrops and the problems they raise

11.1 The range of intercropping problems

There are many instances in which two or more crops are grown together in order to obtain some advantage. Perhaps the two species will call for water or nutrients at rather different times. On that account they will exploit resources better together than either can alone. Perhaps they benefit from different kinds of weather, so that in, say, a dry season the first will crop well, but in a wet one the yield will come from the second. Either way there will be food.

Intercropping has several variants. For example, the two species are not necessarily sown at the same time, but the second may be introduced before the first is harvested. That is called 'undercropping' or 'relay cropping'. Sometimes a leguminous species is grown as well as the main species, with the idea that it will improve future yields. This is called 'alley cropping', the main crop being in widely-spaced rows. A more intimate mixture, e.g. clover and barley, is often referred to as 'undersowing' or 'mixed cropping'. It is not to be expected that the same statistical approach will suit all problems.

It should be emphasized that diversified cropping is not necessarily intercropping. Anyone with a small area of land and a need for several crops, some to supply food and some to supply cash, will grow them intermingled, filling in gaps as may seem appropriate. Unless some benefit can be claimed for growing species in close association, the result should not be called intercropping.

Statistically there are several distinctions to be made. For example, if the two crops serve similar purposes, it does not matter if one dominates or even kills out the other. Where the two supply different needs, like a cereal and a pulse or a food crop and a cash crop, a balance between the two yields will often be essential.

An important difference is that between experiments in which the treatments, e.g. fertilization, are necessarily applied to both component

254

crops and those, like variety trials, in which a treatment is applied to one component only.

It should be noted that bivariate analysis (see Section 10.4) is not available unless it can be assumed that the correlation coefficient between the two yields is the same for all treatments. Where spacing is involved and in some other cases also, that could be a risky assumption.

11.2 Land Equivalent Ratios

The Land Equivalent Ratio is a measure of the extent to which more crop can be obtained from a piece of land by intercropping as compared with dividing it into two parts and growing a different sole crop on each. Used for that purpose it can be valuable, but it is not necessarily helpful in other contexts. It is calculated thus:

If a certain area of land is given over to an intercrop it may be expected to give m of the first crop and n of the second. If it were given over to the first as a sole crop, it could be expected to give a crop of a; if to the second, the crop would be b.

If we set out to produce the same yield as the intercrop, and to do so using sole crops, we should need an area of m/a of the first crop and n/b of the second. That makes a total of

$$m/a + n/b = \text{LER}, \tag{11.2.1}$$

the 'Land Equivalent Ratio'.

Suppose, however, that the intercrop does not yield as much of the second crop as we would have wished. If we want a ratio of r instead of n/m ($r > n/m$), we would need to supplement the intercrop with an area of the second crop grown sole. If we assigned a proportion θ of the land to the intercrop and $(1 - \theta)$ to the sole crop, we should get

    (i) θm of the first

and   (ii) $\theta n + (1 - \theta)\, b$ of the second.

We wish to choose θ so that

$$\frac{\theta n + (1 - \theta)b}{\theta m} = r$$

i.e. $\theta = b/(b - n + rm)$.

In that case the yields are:

(i) $bm/(b - n + rm)$ of the first

(ii) $bmr/(b - n + rm)$ of the second.

This gives an Effective LER (ELER) of

$$\frac{bm}{a(b - n + rm)} + \frac{mr}{(b - n + rm)} = \frac{m(b + ar)}{a(b - n + rm)} \qquad (11.2.2)$$

Note that if $r = n/m$, ELER = LER.

It could be that we are not concerned to obtain a given ratio between the crops so much as to obtain a given target, t, of the second crop, here called the 'staple crop'.

In that case, if we give θ to the intercrop and $(1 - \theta)$ to the staple, we shall get

$$\theta n + (1 - \theta)b = t$$

of the staple. We must therefore choose θ so that

$$\theta = \frac{b - t}{b - n} \quad \text{and} \quad 1 - \theta = \frac{t - n}{b - n},$$

since $n < t < b$, $0 < \theta < 1$. With that θ we get

(i) $m(b - t)/(b - n)$ of the first crop

(ii) $n(b - t)/(b - n) + (b(t-n)/(b - n) = t$ of the second.

That gives a Staple Land Equivalent Ratio (SLER) of

$$1 + \frac{b - t}{b - n}(\text{LER} - 1). \qquad (11.2.3)$$

It will be seen that SLER will exceed 1 only if LER does. Also any gain in SLER is only $(b - t)/(b - n)$ times the gain in LER.

If Land Equivalent Ratios need to be compared, provided both sole crops and all the relevant intercrops are represented in each block, the second method in Section 9.6 is available.

11.3 Bivariate diagrams as used with intercropping

We have two species, A and B, which we have grown in a range of conditions, e.g. in several seasons or at several sites or under different treatments. For each of these conditions we have values, a and b

respectively, for the two crops. Naturally they will be different for the various conditions, but we will assume that the standard deviations, σ_A and σ_B respectively, are constant over the whole. We shall also allow for the possibility that a and b are not estimated independently, i.e. that they have a correlation coefficient, ρ, which is not necessarily zero.

To form a bivariate diagram, we transform a and b to x and y, as described in (10.4.1) and (10.4.2). To examine our new variables more closely, x represents the crop of the first species expressed in terms of its own standard error. The second, y, represents that part of the crop of the second species that cannot be explained by the crop of the first, bearing in mind that the two are correlated. That also is expressed in terms of its own standard error. (The crop of the second species is in fact given by the ordinate of its point from the $0z$ axis described at the start of the next section.)

Bivariate diagrams are especially useful in the study of intercrops. First, we will take the two yields from the intercrop, either in a range of seasons, or at a range of sites, or more probably under a range of treatments, and then we will represent each by a point, surrounded by a circle with a radius of $1\sqrt{r}$, where r is the replication of the treatment concerned. A little care is needed here. Strictly speaking, field experiments estimate differences between treatment means, not the means themselves. As Chapter 5 showed, the variance of the difference between two treatment means is not necessarily

$$\left(\frac{1}{r_1} + \frac{1}{r_2}\right) s^2.$$

If it is not, the circles could cause some confusion and it might be better to omit them. Sometimes, in any case, it is better to put a circle of radius L, calculated from (10.4.10), round the point for the standard treatment. Points that lie outside the circle then indicate a treatment that differs significantly from the standard at the level used.

If there is reason to think that the correlation coefficient between a and b is not constant but depends upon the treatment, the bivariate diagram cannot be used, though an algebraic solution can sometimes be given. The situation is explored in the paper by Singh and Gilliver (1983).

11.4 Land equivalent ratios on a bivariate diagram

The diagram can be used to show LERs as in (11.2.1). First, though, we should see where sole crops go on it. If $a = 0$, $x = 0$, and the point lies up the y-axis. If, however, $b = 0$,

$$x = a/\sigma_A, \quad \text{as usual}$$

$$y = -a\rho/(\sigma_A\sqrt{1-\rho^2}).$$

It will be seen that $y/x = -\rho\sqrt{1-\rho^2}$, i.e. all sole crops of A will give points on a line, Oz, through the origin. That line also is shown in Fig. 11.1. The angle, Φ, is such that $\cos \Phi = \rho$. Consequently, if ρ is negative, the line will lie above the x-axis; if ρ is positive, the line will lie below it.

To return to LER's, any sole crop necessarily has an LER of 1. If the yield of each is plotted, one on Oy and the other on Oz, and a straight line is drawn between them, all points on that line will have the same LER. If now we think of the two sole crops as multiplied by α, we can plot these end-points and draw a line between them. All points on it will indicate an LER of a. Further, any point above the line or to the right of it will show

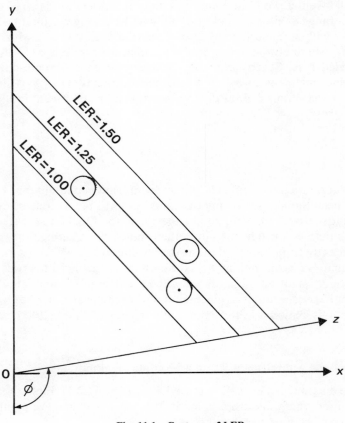

Fig. 11.1   Contours of LER

an LER greater than a, while all other points will indicate an LER less than a. This also is shown in Fig. 11.1.

It could be that we need a certain ratio between the yields of the two species, e.g. we might want the crop of the second to be r times that of the first. In that case $b = ra$. Since the regression coefficient can be written $\rho\sigma_B/\sigma_A$,

$$x = a/\sigma_A$$
$$y = a(r - \rho\sigma_B/\sigma_A)/(\sigma_B\sqrt{1 - \rho^2})$$

and y/x is a constant, i.e.

$$y/x = \frac{r\sigma_A - \rho\sigma_B}{\sigma_B\sqrt{1 - \rho^2}}$$

Consequently, for any r we can draw a line through the origin with that slope, and all points on it will give the desired value of $b/a = r$. Further, a line between the point for an intercrop and a sole crop will intersect that line in the ratio of θ to $(1 - \theta)$, as shown in Fig. 11.2. (The same is true of a line joining the points of two intercrops. That also is shown in Fig. 11.2.) We can still use the lines of constant LER to find the ELER of the combination of intercrop and sole crop or of two intercrops. Note that ELERs have been defined in (11.2.2).

Alternatively we might want a certain amount of one crop. Suppose we require that b shall equal t then, a now being undetermined,

$$x = a/\sigma_A$$
$$y = (t - a\rho\sigma_B/\sigma_A)/\sigma_B\sqrt{1 - \rho^2}).$$

As we vary a the point (x, y) will always lie on a line parallel to Oz and at a distance $t/(\sigma_B\sqrt{1 - \rho^2})$ above it. Again, we can find combinations of intercrops and sole crops with suitable values of θ by joining points and seeing where they intercept the lines just given. Contours for LER can be used in that case to show the SLER, as defined at (11.2.3).

11.5 Interactions in a bivariate diagram

Bivariate diagrams can also be used to show the form of interactions. Let the point for a standard treatment, O, be at (x_0, y_0) and let two modifications, A and B, give points at (x_A, y_A) and (x_B, y_B) respectively. What would we expect to happen if A and B were tried together? Supposing that the two modifications act independently, we can find the point by completing the parallelogram, i.e. we should expect

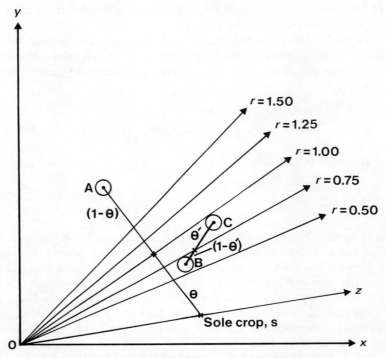

Fig. 11.2　Contours of equal ratio (r = second crop/first crop)

If it were required that Intercrop A be supplemented by a sole crop S to make $r = 1.00$, the proportion of AS that lies above the $r = 1.00$ contour gives (1–0), the proportion that needs to be given to the sole crop, the proportion of A that lies below $r = 100$ giving θ, the proportion that should be given to A. (Note that in this case it is the first crop that is being supplemented, not the second.) Similarly, if it were proposed to apportion land between Intercrops B and C to obtain $r = 0.75$, θ' should be given to B and (1–θ') to C.

$(x_A + x_B - x_0, \ y_A + y_B - y_0)$. If then we try them together and obtain instead the point $(x_{AB}, \ y_{AB})$, the displacement shows the additional effect brought about by their being in combination, i.e. their interaction. The approach is shown in Fig. 11.3.

Where the factors have more than two levels the diagram can become confusing, though usually its interpretation is clear enough. The method is this: if there are several factors, p in number, in the absence of an interaction between them the diagrams for $(p - 1)$ of them should be the same for all levels of the remaining factor. However, the standard errors of contrasts can vary so much that it is difficult to judge much by eye. It is better to explore the situation carefully by partitioning the treatment effects in the analysis of variance and testing each component separately,

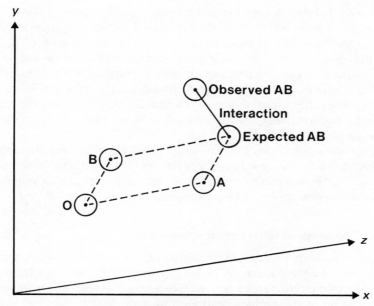

Fig. 11.3 An interaction

beginning with the highest-order interaction. The method of testing is quite simple. It has been given at (10.4.7). The only difference is that D_{aa}, D_{ab} and D_{bb} are no longer the sum of the 'error' and the treatment lines but of the 'error' and the component of treatments (main effect, interaction, etc.) that is under test. Once it is known what interaction is being sought, the diagram will help to show its form.

To take an example, with a 2^3 set of treatments, if there is no three-factor interaction the quadrilateral given by treatments (1), X, Y and XY should have the same shape as that given by Z, XZ, YZ, and XYZ. The difference in shape shows the form of the interaction.

11.6 Contours on the bivariate diagram

In assessing intercrops there can be different standards. Someone might want to consider monetary values in the current year, another biomass, and yet a third might be interested in protein. The best thing is to take contours of equal value. Thus, suppose someone proposed energy as a good basis of assessment. He has first to find conversion factors to change yields into energy and he suggests multipliers of C_A for the first species and C_B for the second. He now says that he wants the contour for E_1 units of energy. It can be found by asking what yield of each species would supply that need. If he used only the first he would need a crop of E_1/C_A. This would give a point on Oz. If, on the other hand, he were to get the required energy from the second species alone, he would need a crop of E_1/C_B), which is on Oy. A straight line joining them gives all combinations of the two species that give the required amount of energy. He could then draw further contours for E_2, E_3, etc. They will be straight lines parallel to that for E_1. When they are all drawn, it is a simple matter to assess the energy given by any treatment, the position of its point relative to the contours showing all that is needed.

If someone else comes along and says that he is interested in monetary value, M, then he will need other conversion factors, D_1 and D_2 instead of C_1 and C_2. He will therefore obtain different contours and he might well make a different choice of best intercrop.

11.7   The design of intercropping experiments

The preceding sections of this chapter show how diverse are the questions raised by intercrops. (Some of them indeed have no analogue at all with sole crops.) There is therefore greater danger of an imperfect appreciation of the problem leading to a poor design. That risk always exists, but with intercrops it is more likely to cause difficulties because the possibilities are more numerous.

The first question often is whether or not to include sole crops. Mostly experimenters include them, but if the object is to find the best cultural method for an established intercrop, they serve no useful purpose. The usual justification for including them is the need to show a good LER, but why? If the intercrop is really established, its LER must be good enough. If someone can improve it, the LER will supposedly be even better.

The opposite fault can arise if for any reason the sole crops are included. Given a range of fertilization levels for the intercrop and a need to find the LER for each, not only are the sole crops needed but they should also be represented at all levels. More usually the experimenter argues that he knows how to grow the sole crops and he will only introduce each at the level of fertilization that he would recommend. The argument may be sound, but it requires a sceptical examination on each occasion it is advanced.

Finally on the matter of sole crops, if they are needed only to establish the LERs, is it necessary to assign them to small plots and to randomize them? Would it not be easier to grow them in strips with blocks between the strips? After all, if they are only needed as a base-line to estimate a and b for (11.2.1), (11.2.2) or (11.2.3), they are not themselves the objects of study. Only if they are being studied for their own sake are all the sole crops needed in each block.

Other questions arise when one species dominates the other, usually on account of height but sometimes for other reasons. In such a case there could well be questioning whether it could not be grown in some other way, e.g. with wider spacing between rows, to allow more room for the other species. That can be a most useful enquiry, but if the aim is to find out what happens to the taller species using both configurations, i.e. if it is grown, say, at wider spacing than usual between rows but at closer spacing within them, what useful purpose is served at that stage by introducing the other species? When it has been found how to grow the first species to give as much space as possible to the second, then is the time to add it to the system.

It should also be borne in mind that a trial of configurations is not the same as an investigation of competition. If someone wants to know in a botanical sense whether A or B is the stronger competitor with X, then clearly A and B should be compared using the same configuration, but that is not the agronomic problem. If B is more spreading than A, in an intercrop it may well need more space, i.e. the rows should be further apart.

Finally, before starting to design an experiment some thought should be given to the method of dealing with the data. If the intention is to use a bivariate analysis (Section 10.4) it should be remembered that there must be a reasonable expectation of all treatments giving the same correlation coefficient between the two crops. If that is unlikely, as it would be in a spacing experiment, the task of analysis is going to be much more difficult. It will be impossible if there is not enough replication to estimate the correlation coefficient for each treatment separately.

Exercise 11A

An intercrop of maize and pigeonpea was tried out at three spacings (3, 6 or 9 plants per m^2). Yields, expressed in kilograms per hectare, were as follows:

Density	Maize (S)	Pigeonpea (S)	Maize (I)	Pigeonpea (I)
3	2679	988	1637	780
6	3398	1035	2205	672
9	3331	954	2400	768

(S indicates sole crop. I is a component of the intercrop.)

(a) Work out the LER for each density.
(b) Assuming that maize and pigeonpea were desired in a ratio of 2 to 1, find the ELER for each density.

(c)   Assuming that at least 900 kilograms of pigeonpea was required per hectare, work out the SLER for each density.

[Data from the Annual Report of the International Crop Research Institute for the Semi-Arid Tropics (ICRISAT) for 1976–7, p. 159.]

Exercise 11B

An intercropping experiment was carried out in four randomized blocks, I–IV. There were two strains of sorghum:

A   An early variety
B   A mid-season variety

and two strains of pearl millet

P   A short-stemmed variety
Q   A long-stemmed variety

Data were as follows:

Block		I	II	III	IV
AP	a	0.18	0.62	0.28	0.85
	b	1.95	1.70	2.12	1.49
BP	a	0.24	0.09	0.52	0.41
	b	2.99	4.24	3.15	3.13
AQ	a	1.59	1.81	1.12	2.12
	b	1.03	1.10	1.29	1.51
BQ	a	2.10	1.52	1.20	1.25
	b	2.10	2.63	2.42	1.69

The quantities a and b are respectively yields per plot of sorghum and millet.

Work out the bivariate analysis of variance with the treatments effects partitioned into two main effects and the interaction. Draw the bivariate diagram and offer an interpretation.

[Data published by permission of the International Crop Research Institute for the Semi-Arid Tropics (ICRISAT), where the experiment was conducted.]

Exercise 11C

An experiment concerned the time of planting of the cassava in a maize/cassava intercrop. The cassava was planted either at the time the maize was sown (0) or at 4, 8, 12 or 16 weeks afterwards. In half the plots melons were grown as well but in the other half they were omitted. Taking a as the yield of the cassava and b as the yield of the maize, the analyses of variance and covariance were as follows:

Source	d.f.	a^2	ab	b^2
Times of planting cassava (T)	4	4263	2790	6627
Melons (M)	1	17	35	71
Interaction (T × M)	4	882	262	212
'Error'	27	11 762	− 1362	1662
Stratum total	32	16 924	1725	8572

Treatment means were:

		T0	T4	T8	T12	T16
O	a	66.2	88.0	64.2	87.7	69.0
	b	61.0	57.2	41.9	52.1	30.2
M	a	84.0	79.2	60.2	93.0	65.2
	b	71.6	60.5	45.0	50.6	27.9

All figures represent crop in kilograms from a plot of 32 m². There were four randomized blocks, each of ten plots.

Calculate the bivariate analysis of variance and draw the bivariate diagram. Assess the results.

Note: There is an apparent inversion of Treatments T8 and T12 that no-one could explain. For present purposes there is no need to be worried by it.

[Data from S. C. Pearce and B. Gilliver. *J. Agricultural Science* (Cambridge), **91** (1978), p. 629.]

Exercise 11D

A 2^3 factorial experiment was carried out on an intercrop of sorghum (a) and pigeonpea (b). After transformation the treatment means were:

Treatment	x	y
$V_1P_1F_1$	0.86	4.26
$V_1P_1F_2$	2.21	1.80
$V_1P_2F_1$	1.24	5.59
$V_1P_2F_2$	2.83	4.12
$V_2P_1F_1$	3.26	2.76
$V_2P_1F_2$	8.39	-0.98
$V_2P_2F_1$	4.40	4.59
$V_2P_2F_2$	9.67	2.34

The two levels of Factor V were:

1 Local variety of sorghum
2 Introduced variety

Those of Factor P were:

1 Planting on the flat
2 Planting on raised beds

Those of Factor F were

1 Farmyard manure at 10 tonnes per hectare
2 Ammonium sulphate at 0.4 tonnes per hectare

There was no evidence of a three-factor interaction, but there was a significant interaction of V and F. Draw it on the bivariate diagram and derive the form of the interaction.

[Data from B. Gilliver and S. C. Pearce, *Experimental Agriculture*, **19**, p. 28.]

Exercise 11E

In Exercise 11C draw contours on the bivariate diagram to show calorific values of 30 000 MJ and 40 000 MJ per hectare. You may take a kilogram of maize to give 0.979 MJ and a kilogram of cassava to give 0.898 MJ. In order to obtain the greatest calorific value, would you plant cassava early or late?

Chapter 12

Defective data

12.1 The consequences of losing data

The analysis of data when some plots are missing is one of the classical problems in statistics and the subject has acquired a large literature. The development of completely general methods of analysis, e.g. the Kuiper–Corsten iteration, has made much of that work unnecessary, at least as far as block designs are concerned. Row-and-column designs raise further questions, chiefly on account of lost data causing the rows and columns to become non-orthogonal to one another. (They will therefore be considered separately in Section 12.5.)

It should be emphasized right from the start that there is always a price to be paid for lost data, just as there is for any other defect in the design of the experiment or for any other deficiency in the data. (This will have become apparent from a study of Chapter 4. In Exercises 4A and 4B it is indeed possible to derive analyses that are formally correct, but some standard errors of treatment differences are larger than they would have been if nothing had gone wrong.)

In the case of a block design the position is fairly well understood. To take an example, suppose that an experiment has been designed with four treatments in five randomized blocks, like this:

Block				
I	A	B	C	D
II	A	B	C	D
III	A	B	C	D
IV	A	B	C	D
V	A	B	C	D

Now suppose that the plot in Block I with Treatment A has been lost for some reason that has nothing to do with the treatment, e.g., the plants have not died from low fertilization nor from a disease that the treatment was intended to control. The plot is missing on account of some other cause unrelated to the treatment. Accepting that the data from the

267

remaining 19 plots can be satisfactorily analysed, how much has been lost?

The answer is that there has been a loss of information concerning the contrast between the treatment of the missing plot and other treatments in the damaged block. To be more specific, the contrast

$$
\begin{array}{cccc}
\text{A} & \text{B} & \text{C} & \text{D} \\
(+3 & -1 & -1 & -1)
\end{array}
$$

has suffered a loss of one of its effective replications, since Block I no longer has anything to say about it. That is to say, its standard error is not

$$
\sqrt{\frac{12 \times \text{Error mean square}}{5}}
$$

but

$$
\sqrt{\frac{12 \times \text{Error mean square}}{4}} \tag{12.1.1}
$$

(Note that $(+3)^2 + (-1)^2 + (-1)^2 + (-1)^2 = 12$.) There is now one contrast with an effective replication of four, namely $(3 - 1 - 1 - 1)$, and two others orthogonal to it, say $(0\ 2 - 1 - 1)$ and $(0\ 0 + 1 - 1)$ with five, a total of 14. Before, there were three orthogonal contrasts, each with an effective replication of five, a total of 15. That is to say, the loss of 1/20 of the data has led to a loss of 1/15 of the information; as usual the information loss is proportionately greater than the data loss.

The above would be helpful if $(+3 - 1 - 1 - 1)$ were a contrast of interest. Quite possibly it is, but not necessarily so. It could be that the four treatments form a factorial set, the contrasts of interest being $(-1 - 1 + 1 + 1)$, $(-1 + 1 - 1 + 1)$ and $(+1 - 1 - 1 + 1)$ as in Section 5.2. The general rule is that any contrast loses in effective replication by an amount ρ^2, where ρ is the correlation coefficient between the contrast concerned and the one that has suffered the direct damage, which in this instance was $(+3 - 1 - 1 - 1)$. Thus, for $(-1 - 1 + 1 + 1)$ $\rho^2 =$

$$
[(+3 \times -1) + (-1 \times -1) + (-1 \times +1) + (-1 \times +1)]^2/
$$
$$
[(+3)^2 + (-1)^2 + (-1)^2 + (-1)^2][(-1)^2 + (-1)^2 + (+1)^2 + (+1)^2]
$$

$$
= \frac{(-4)^2}{12 \times 4} = 1/3.
$$

It is the same for the other two contrasts of interest. It follows that each has a standard error of

$$\sqrt{\frac{12 \times \text{Error mean square}}{4\frac{2}{3}}} \qquad (12.1.2)$$

instead of

$$\sqrt{\frac{12 \times \text{Error mean square}}{5}}$$

The position now is that there are three contrasts, each with an effective replication of $4\frac{2}{3}$, making a total of 14 as before, the information loss still being 1/15. The same approach applies to data missing from block designs that are non-orthogonal.

It should be explained that the values calculated at (12.1.2) are sometimes approximate. In technical parlance they are exact only if the contrast of interest is an eigenvector of the coefficient matrix of the design achieved, but the ordinary practitioner does not need to bother about that. Always to accept the loss of ρ^2 in the effective replication is much more realistic than to pretend that nothing has happened. In the example given, exact methods show that the true effective replication is 4.62, which is much nearer to $4\frac{2}{3}$ than to 5.

12.2 Missing-plot values in a block design

The method to be described is the oldest and one that is still commonly used. In essence the idea is to fill each gap in the data with a figure that will give a zero residual for that plot. The fitted value then represents what the injured plot would have achieved according to the testimony of those that remain. There is the loss of a degree of freedom from the stratum total on account of each missing plot, with a similar loss from the 'error' line since the missing plots have been constrained to make no contribution to it.

The method will be illustrated using the following contrived data:

Block		I	II	III	IV		
Treatment	A	m	21	21	18	$60 + m$	
	B	13	15	19	13	60	
	C	12	14	17	13	56	(12.2.1)
	D	11	18	15	20	64	
		$36 + m$	68	72	64	$240 + m$	

Where it is possible to express the 'error' sum of squares using summation terms, there is no difficulty about writing down a formula for a residual. Here the design is in randomized blocks, so the 'error' sum of squares equals

Total term − block term − treatment term + correction term.

$$(12.2.2)$$

The four quantities derive respectively from the data, the block means, the treatment means and the grand mean. Following the form of (12.2.2), a residual equals

Datum − block mean − treatment mean + grand mean.   (12.2.3)

In the case of the missing plot, its residual equals

$$m - (36 + m)/4 - (60 + m)/4 + (240 + m)/16$$

so $9m - 4(36) - 4(60) + 240 = 0$ (12.2.4)
and $m = 16$.

It is instructive to analyse the data at (12.2.1) by sweeping, having first set m to 16. The block means are

I, 13;   II, 17;   III, 18   and   IV, 16.

Sweeping by them gives

A	+ 3	+ 4	+ 3	+ 2
B	0	− 2	+ 1	− 3
C	− 1	− 3	− 1	− 3
D	− 2	+ 1	− 3	+ 4

$$(12.2.5)$$

The sum of those values squared is 102 and the treatment means are: A, + 3; B, − 1; C, − 2 and D, 0. That gives residuals of

0	+ 1	0	− 1
+ 1	− 1	+ 2	− 2
+ 1	− 1	+ 1	− 1
− 2	+ 1	− 3	+ 4

$$(12.2.6)$$

The 'error' sum of squares is 46 with $(9 - 1) = 8$ degrees of freedom, one having been lost on account of the missing value. It will be seen that the missing plot is indeed giving a zero residual. So is another plot, but that is a coincidence.

It would however be a mistake to adopt 102, derived from (12.2.5), as the stratum total. Just as the missing plot must not contribute anything to the residuals, so it must have a zero deviation in order to contribute nothing to the stratum total. In (12.2.5) the value is + 3, so there is an overestimation of the stratum total and hence of the treatment sum of squares. It is necessary to find a new missing plot value, m', that will make the deviation zero. Since the total sum of squares for the stratum equals

$$\text{Total term} - \text{block term,}$$

m' should be such that

$$\text{datum} - \text{block mean} = 0$$

i.e.

$$m' - (36 + m')/4 = 0 \tag{12.2.7}$$

i.e.

$$m' = 12.$$

The deviations are found to be:

$$
\begin{array}{lcccc}
\text{A} & 0 & +4 & +3 & +2 \\
\text{B} & +1 & -2 & +1 & -3 \\
\text{C} & 0 & -3 & -1 & -3 \\
\text{D} & -1 & +1 & -3 & +2
\end{array}
\tag{12.2.8}
$$

(Block means are as before except for Block I, which now has a mean of 12 instead of 13.) The sum of squared deviations is 90 with 11 degrees of freedom, making the analysis of variance to be

Source	d.f.	s.s.	m.s.	F	
Treatments	3	44	14.67	2.55	(12.2.9)
'Error'	8	46	5.75		
Stratum total	11	90			

Some will wonder how the missing value can be both m and m', which are usually not the same. The answer is that the two values serve different purposes. The deviations represent the unexplained variation when treatments are ignored; the residuals represent the same variation when they are allowed for. On the testimony of the other plots, the missing value should be 12, supposing there to be no treatment effects, but 16 if there are.

In practice many people do not calculate m' at all, but use the sum of squared values in (12.2.5) instead of those in (12.2.8). Since that might increase the apparent significance of treatments with no possibility of decreasing it, the approximation will cause little harm if the value of F is plainly not significant or if it is so large that a small reduction will not change significance to non-significance. In those circumstances it may be permissible to avoid calculating m'. Sometimes, indeed often, no significance test is required, the aim being only to estimate means. In that case there is no need of m' because treatment means must obviously allow for treatment effects.

In general it is wise to calculate m and m' to one decimal place more than is needed for the data (see Section 1.9).

When several plots are missing, the method can still be used, the outcome being a set of simultaneous equations. For example, suppose that the datum for Treatment B in Block I was missing as well. Calling the two missing values m_1 and m_2, the data read:

Block		I	II	III	IV	
Treatment	A	m_1	21	21	18	
	B	m_2	15	19	13	(12.2.10)
	C	12	14	17	13	
	D	11	18	15	20	

Hence, by the same method as before,

$$m_1 - (23 + m_1 + m_2)/4 - (60 + m_1)/4 + (227 + m_1 + m_2)/16 = 0$$
$$m_2 - (23 + m_1 + m_2)/4 - (47 + m_2)/4 + (227 + m_1 + m_2)/16 = 0.$$

Simplifying these equations gives

$$9m_1 - 3m_2 = 105$$
$$- 3m_1 + 9m_2 = 53 \qquad (12.2.11)$$

and so $\quad m_1 = 15.3 \quad m_2 = 11.0.$

Turning now to the deviations, by the same method as for residuals it emerges that

$$m_1' - (m_1' + m_2' + 23)/4 = 0$$
$$m_2' - (m_1' + m_2' + 23)/4 = 0$$

Hence $\quad 3m_1' - m_2' = 23$
$\qquad\quad - m_1' + 3m_2' = 23$

so $\qquad m_1' = m_2' = 11.5.$

In this instance $m_1 = m_2$ because they refer to the same block, treatments being ignored, but that will not always be so.

The weakness of this method lies in the difficulty of finding the formulae for m and m' when the 'error' sum of squares cannot readily be found from summation terms. For that reason, it needs to be supplemented by some method of wider application.

12.3 Rubin's method for fitting missing-plot values

By contrast with the last method, the procedure suggested by Rubin (1972) is of completely general application. Conceptually it is very simple. Two parallel bodies of data are set up. The first of these, x, is called a 'pseudo-variate'; it has a datum of one for the missing plot and zero for all the others. The second, y, consists of zero for the missing plot and of the known values elsewhere, like this:

	x					y			
	I	II	III	IV		I	II	III	IV
A	1	0	0	0		0	21	21	18
B	0	0	0	0		13	15	19	13
C	0	0	0	0		12	14	17	13
D	0	0	0	0		11	18	15	20

$$(12.3.1)$$

Sweeping by blocks gives deviations of

A	$\frac{3}{4}$	0	0	0	-9	$+4$	$+3$	$+2$
B								
C	Not needed				Not needed			
D								

Sweeping now by treatments, the only residuals needed are those for the missing plot, namely, 9/16 and -9. (The first of these will be needed later, so it will be given a symbol, namely ψ. The corresponding deviation namely $\frac{3}{4}$, will be called φ.) The two missing plot values can now be found thus:

$m' =$ (deviation of y for the missing plot)/(deviation of x)
$\quad = -(-9)/(\frac{3}{4}) = 12$, and
$m = -$ (residual of y for the missing plot)/(residual of x)
$\quad = -(-9)/(9/16) = 16$.

It follows that any method that gives deviations and residuals, e.g. the Kuiper–Corsten iteration, provides a means of finding m and m'.

It may here be noted that the calculation of ψ is usually quite simple, because the ψ values for all plots must sum to the number of degrees of freedom for error. Since in the example all 16 plots have the same status (i.e. all blocks contain four plots, and all treatments are replicated four times, so there is no reason to pick on some plots as being different from the rest), there are 16 similar ψ values which must add up to 9. Hence each must equal 9/16. The argument holds not only for randomized blocks but for Latin squares, balanced incomplete blocks (Section 4.7), and lattices (Section 4.9). On the other hand, it breaks down when blocks were intended to be of unequal size, a case not considered in this manual, or when, as in designs with supplemented balance (Section 4.8), the replication was intended to be unequal. Even so, in those cases the evaluation of ψ is rarely difficult.

Similar to ψ is the deviation for the missing plot in the pseudo-variate, which has been written φ. (In the example, $\varphi = 0.75$.) The sum of φ-values over all the plots must give the degrees of freedom for the stratum total. If all blocks are the same size, all plots will have the same φ)-value, which must therefore be

(Stratum total degrees of freedom)/(number of plots).

In the example that gives 12/16, which is correct. The same argument applies for a row-and-column design.

The method can be extended to cover any number of missing plots, but the general case requires a matrix inversion. It will therefore be avoided here. The calculations are, however, quite simple when only two plots are missing.

The method is this. Set up a pseudo-variate for the first plot and find residuals. ψ_{11} and ψ_{12}, for the two plots that are missing. Then do the same for the second plot and find corresponding residuals, ψ_{21} and ψ_{22}. (It is no coincidence that ψ_{21} always equals ψ_{12}.) Next find $\kappa = \psi_{11}\psi_{22} - \psi_{12}^2$. Finally, it is necessary to fill the gaps in the data with two zeros and to find ρ_1 and ρ_2, the residuals for the two missing plots. Then the values sought are respectively:

$$m_1 = (\psi_{21}\rho_2 - \psi_{22}\rho_1)/\kappa$$
$$m_2 = (\psi_{12}\rho_1 - \psi_{11}\rho_2)/\kappa. \qquad (12.3.2)$$

The method will be illustrated by the example at (12.2.10). In the pseudo-variate for the first missing plot, $\psi_{11} = 9/16$ and $\psi_{12} = -3/16$; in that for the second, $\psi_{21} = -3/16$ and $\psi_{22} = 9/16$. Hence $\kappa = 9/32$. Filling in both gaps with zeros gives corresponding residuals of $-105/16$ ($= \rho_1$) and $-53/16$ ($= \rho_2$); hence from (12.3.2),

$$m_1 = \left[\frac{(-3)}{16} \times \frac{(-53)}{16} - \frac{(+9)}{16} \times \frac{(-105)}{16} \right] \frac{32}{9} = \frac{1104}{72} = 15.3$$

$$m_2 = \left[\frac{(-3)}{16} \times \frac{(-105)}{16} - \frac{(+9)}{16} \times \frac{-53)}{16} \right] \frac{32}{9} = \frac{792}{72} = 11.0$$

Obviously the calculations are very similar to what they were before. The choice between the two methods must depend upon convenience. The first way of calculating m_1 and m_2 needed the summation terms. It is therefore available only for orthogonal designs, whereas the second is completely general, provided a method is available for calculating residuals. Use of φ_{11}, $\varphi_{12} (= \varphi_{21})$ and φ_{22} will give m_1' and m_2', just as ψ_{11}, ψ_{12} and ψ_{22} give m_1 and m_2.

12.4 Use of the analysis of covariance with incomplete data

Given a computer program able to make adjustments by covariance, i.e. by the method set out in Sections 8.5 to 8.7, there is a simple method of analysing incomplete data. To take the example given in (12.2.1), it is sufficient to use the same data as at (12.3.1), the right-hand table, i.e. the known data with a zero for the missing plot, being taken to be y, the incomplete data to be analysed. The left-hand data provide x, the pseudo-variate by which y is to be adjusted. It is intended to adjust all values of y to a zero value of x. First, the summation terms are:

	x^2	xy	y^2
Total	1.0000	0	3998
Blocks	0.2500	9	3800
Treatments	0.2500	15	3608
Correction	0.0625	15	3600

This leads to the analyses of variance and covariance:

Source	d.f.	x^2	xy	y^2
Treatments	3	0.1875	0	8
'Error'	9	$0.5625 = \psi$	−9	190
Stratum total	12	$0.7500 = \varphi$	−9	198

Adjusting the analysis of variance of y^2 by the regression of y on x as in (8.5.4) gives

Source	d.f.	s.s.	m.s.	F
Treatments	3	44	14.67	2.55
'Error'	8	46	5.75	
Stratum total	11	90		

as at (12.2.9).

The one value of y that needs to be adjusted is that for the missing plot. Since x is being changed by -1, i.e. from $+1$ to 0, y has to be changed by $-b$, where b is the regression coefficient. That is, the zero value of y for the missing plot should become

$$- (\text{'Error' for } xy)/(\text{'Error' for } x^2)$$
$$= -(-9)/(0.5625) = 16 \text{ as at (12.3.3).}$$

If there are several missing plots, a separate pseudo-variate is needed for each. For example, for the problem given at (12.2.10), it would be necessary to use the variate, y, with two zeros, i.e.

Block		I	II	III	IV
Treatment	A	0	21	21	18
	B	0	15	19	13
	C	12	14	17	13
	D	11	18	15	20

and to adjust it by two pseudo-variates, w and x, like this:

Block		I		II		III		IV	
		w	x	w	x	w	x	w	x
Treatment	A	0	1	0	0	0	0	0	0
	B	1	0	0	0	0	0	0	0
	C	0	0	0	0	0	0	0	0
	D	0	0	0	0	0	0	0	0

The advantage of the method lies in its giving correct standard errors of treatment differences as well as a correct analysis of variance. Its disadvantage lies in requiring an additional pseudo-variate for each additional missing value. It is therefore limited by the capacity of the available computer program to adjust y by many variates.

12.5 Missing data in more difficult circumstances

With row-and-column designs the loss of data is more important than with block designs because it also gives rise to non-orthogonality between rows and columns. As a result, the loss of information can be more serious and more difficult to calculate. Clearly the Kuiper–Corsten iteration is not going to provide the ultimate protection that it does with block designs. The other methods are all available, but the preferred one must be use of the analysis of covariance because it gives correctly the standard errors of contrasts, which are otherwise rather elusive.

This still does not meet the need of someone who loses three or more plots from a row-and-column design. Also, to avoid a matrix inversion, we have not shown you how Rubin's method works with several missing values; for the same reason we have not gone beyond double covariance. There is, however, a method that can be used with any orthogonal design, whether in blocks or in rows and columns. It is rather laborious, but its advantage lies in its wide availability. We shall illustrate it using the data at (12.2.10).

The equations at (12.2.11) may be written like this:

$$m_1 = 105/9 + 3m_2/9 = 11.67 + m_2/3 \qquad (12.5.1)$$

$$m_2 = 53/9 + 3m_1/9 = 5.89 + m_1/3 \qquad (12.5.2)$$

In that form they are called 'leading equations' for m_1 and m_2 respectively.

We will start by choosing a likely value for one of the missing values. We might, for example, put m_2 equal to $(15 + 19 + 13)/3 = 15.67$, that being the mean value of other data from the same treatment. Then from (12.5.1), $m_1 = 16.84$; then from (12.5.2), $m_2 = 11.45$. Clearly we can continue the process, the two equations being taken in turn, like this:

Cycle	m_1	m_2
0		$15.67 = m_{20}$
1	$16.89 = m_{11}$	$11.52 = m_{21}$
2	$15.51 = m_{12}$	$11.06 = m_{22}$
3	$15.36 = m_{13}$	$11.01 = m_{23}$
4	$15.34 = m_{14}$	$11.00 = m_{24}$
5	$15.34 = m_{15}$	

The two equations have in fact 'led' us to the correct conclusion. (There will be no further advance because $m_{15} = m_{14}$.)

The method can be used for any orthogonal design whatever the number of missing plots. There are a few points to notice. One is that an equation will lead only if it is derived from an earlier one in which the highest coefficient is that of the appropriate unknown value. At (12.2.11) this was so for m_1 in the first equation and for m_2 in the second. The other point concerns procedure when there are three or more values, m_1, m_2, m_3, etc. to be found. (We shall assume for the sake of simplicity that there are only three.) First, approximations m_{20} and m_{30} are found for m_2 and m_3 in any way that seems reasonable. Then m_{11} is found from them using the first leading equation. Then m_{21} is found from m_{11} and m_{30}, then m_{31} from m_{11} and m_{21}, then m_{12} from m_{21} and m_{31}, and so on, i.e., each missing value in turn is found from the rest using the latest value for the other unknowns.

The last difficulty to be considered is that of missing sub-plots in a split-plot design. In fact the solution is very simple when, as is usually the case, each sub-plot treatment is represented once on each main plot. It arises because the sub-plot analysis can be regarded as the aggregation of the analyses given by a randomized block design on each of the main treatments. Thus, at (7.2.1) the analyses for the three variates separately are

	Source	d.f.	s.s.
Ladak	Cuttings	3	1.1792
	'Error'	15	0.3726
	Stratum total	18	1.5518
Cossack	Cuttings	3	0.6926
	'Error'	15	0.7200
	Stratum total	18	1.4126
Ranger	Cuttings	3	0.3012
	'Error'	15	0.1660
	Stratum total	18	0.4672

It will be seen that the 'Error' sum of squares at (7.3.2) was 1.2586, which equals the sum of the 'error' sums of squares in the component analyses, i.e. $0.3726 + 0.7200 + 0.1660$. Also, the sum of squares for treatments in the combined analysis at (7.3.2), i.e. $2.1730 = 1.9625 + 0.2105$, equals the sum of the treatment sums of squares in the component analyses, i.e. $1.1792 + 0.6926 + 0.3012$. It follows that if a sub-plot is defective, either by being missing or in one of the other ways to be considered, it is enough to isolate the component analysis, to deal with the difficulty as if the design were in randomized blocks, and finally to constitute the combined analysis from its components. (That is the explanation of Exercise 12A. The complete experiment was in split-plots. The data given are from one component.)

12.6 Approximate missing-plot values

There are several contexts, which will be described later, in which it is helpful to know the effect of choosing a wrong missing-plot value. There is in fact a simple rule. If $m + d$ is used when m would have been correct, the 'error' sum of squares will be increased by

$$\psi d^2. \tag{12.6.1}$$

Similarly, if $m' + d'$ is used instead of m' the stratum sum of squares will be increased by

$$\varphi d' \tag{12.6.2}$$

An example of the use of these results is afforded by the figures in Section 12.2. Fitting the missing plot value as $m = 16$ gave an 'error' sum of squares of 46, which is correct, but a stratum sum of squares of 102, which is wrong. It is overestimated because it should have been calculated using $m' = 12$ instead of $m = 16$. Hence $d' = 4$. Hence the overestimation equals $\varphi d'^2 = \frac{3}{4} (4)^2 = 12$, the true value being $102 - 12 = 90$, as given at (12.2.9). That calculation provides a ready means of judging the importance of the difference between m and m'.

12.7 Questionable data

Sometimes a plot is known to have suffered damage, and the question arises whether its datum should or should not be accepted for purposes of analysis. The decision can be a difficult one. The experimenter who discards every plot that is open to some criticism could well find himself with nothing left. On the other hand, it would be absurd to retain everything even when it was clear that the plot had been damaged severely by some mishap. Some procedure is needed for guidance with problems of that kind. It can be found by use of (12.6.1) and (12.6.2).

The following data will illustrate the method. They come from an experiment on Thibou's estate in Antigua, part of the series considered in Exercise 10A and similar to the one in Exercise 10D. The same general description applies. There were four treatments, O (duplicated), N, P and K, disposed orthogonally in four blocks. Goats had been observed eating the maize on the plot indicated by the asterisk and had been driven off. Had they done so much damage that the plot should be discarded?

The data, which represented crop weight per plot, were:

	O	O	N	P	K
I	2.10	3.20	3.69	3.16	1.27
II	2.18	4.20	2.02	2.01	3.91
III	2.57	3.01	3.25	3.92	2.87
IV	3.61	3.42	1.14	1.06*	3.05

The data should first be analysed as if there were no doubts about them. That gives:

Source	d.f.	s.s.	m.s.	F
Treatments	3	1.0206	0.3402	0.30
'Error'	13	14.9417	1.1494	
Stratum total	16	15.9623		

The missing plot value for the dubious datum is $m = 2.979$, which makes $d = 1.919$ (i.e. $2.979 - 1.06$). Since $\psi = 1 - 1/5 - 1/4 + 1/20 = 0.60$, from (12.6.1) the use of m instead of the observed value of 1.06 will reduce the error sum of squares by $\psi d^2 = 2.2095$. That will leave 12.5480 with 12 degrees of freedom and gives rise to another analysis of variance, namely,

Source	d.f.	s.s.	m.s.	F	
Due to the dubious plot	1	2.2095	2.3937	2.29	
Current 'error'	12	12.5480	1.0457		(12.7.1)
Former 'error'	13	14.7575			

It cannot be said that F is significant at any important level. However, since the goats can only have diminished the recorded crop and not increased it, this is really a one-sided test. Hence P can be halved. Even so, it still exceeds 0.05, but there is now quite strong evidence that the goats did in fact do appreciable damage. Since they were in fact observed eating, most people would omit the plot, but the decision really depends upon the assessment of damage made at the time. It could have appeared to be so serious that no statistical analysis was needed to justify the exclusion of the plot; it could have been so slight that no one bothered further about it. The significance level required to convince the experimenter that the goats had done important damage must depend upon the prior evidence. (The whole episode underlines the need for a diary in which events are recorded as they occur.) Here we shall assume general agreement that the plot should be taken out of the experiment.

The decision having been made, the next step is to find m'. It equals 2.805, so $d' = 2.805 - 1.06 = 1.745$.

Since φ for the damaged plots equals 0.8, the sum of squares for the stratum total, 15.9623, should be reduced according to (12.6.2) by $\varphi d'^2 = 2.4360$, which leaves 13.5263 with 15 degrees of freedom. Hence the final analysis is:

Source	d.f.	s.s.	m.s.	F
Treatments	3	0.9783	0.3261	0.31
'error'	12	12.5480	1.0457	
Stratum total	15	13.5263		

Regarding the doubtful plot as missing has increased the mean for Treatment P from 2.54 to 3.02 and that is important. In other respects everything is much as before, except that the results are more soundly based now that the ambiguity has been resolved.

In the example considered above there was a clear, objective reason for thinking that the datum might be wrong. The analysis at (12.7.1) measured the weight of evidence that the value observed was out of line with the others. Taken in conjunction with the prior evidence, that clinched the argument for excluding the plot. Much more difficult is the situation when a datum looks absurd but no one can suggest why it should be so.

Much care is needed. It should be recalled that if there are 60 plots and each residual is tested at a level of $P = 0.05$, it is to be expected that three will appear significantly large purely by chance. (The argument is not completely sound because residuals are not estimated independently, but it will serve.) The matter can be looked at more generally. Suppose there are n plots and each has a probability, p, of being rejected by some test. Then it has a probability of $(1 - p)$ of being acceptable; collectively the n plots have a probability of $(1 - p)^n$ of all being acceptable. That leaves a probability of $1 - (1 - p)^n$ that one or more will be wrongly rejected. To take an example, let $n = 60$; then

$$1 - (1 - p)^n = 0.05, \text{ say}$$

so $\quad (1 - p)^n \quad = 0.95$

and $\quad n \log (1 - p) = \log 0.95$

$$= \bar{1}.977\ 72 = -\ 0.022\ 28.$$

Hence $\log (1 - p) = 0.000\ 371\ 3$ and p is $0.000\ 832$ or about 1 in 1200. Hence, if each residual were tested at that level, there is one chance in 20 ($P = 0.05$) that one plot, or perhaps more, would be rejected even though nothing was wrong. The calculations will serve as a warning that data should not be rejected casually just because they look different. (Occasions do arise when a datum is so different from the rest that no one can believe in it, but they do not occur often.) Also there is no reason to adopt $P = 0.05$ as standard. If all data were checked carefully as they were recorded, the experimenter may be unwilling to believe that there was a mistake. He might be more easily convinced if there had been a rush that invited faults and left no time for checking.

When several data are suspect, there are two cases. In one, they are all suspected of the same defect, as when flood water has covered some plots and not others. It is then permissible to assign $x = 1$ to those subject to possible damage, and $x = 0$ to the rest. An analysis of covariance is then worked out on y, the yield being adjusted by x. Whether there is a significant reduction of the 'error' sum of squares or not, the adjustment can still be made, very little being lost if it is not needed. In the other case, each plot is suspected of a different defect, so the case for exclusion is separate for each. It is better to fit all by missing plot values and then to take the doubtful plots one by one, assigning each its observed value to see if that leads to a significant increase in the 'error' sum of squares. After each plot is dealt with, its missing-plot value is restored before another plot is considered. In that way a decision can be reached as to which values to reject and which to accept. (The procedure is not quite correct because, strictly speaking, the missing-plot values should be worked out afresh each time, but it will serve.)

12.8   Mixed-up plots

Another defect of data arises when there is doubt whether the yield of two adjacent plots has been correctly apportioned between them. That is to say, the total for the two plots, T, is known, but no one can be certain how much belongs to each. A similar difficulty arises when two samples become mixed.

In that case the recognized method is to ascribe T to one plot and 0 to the other. A pseudo-variate, x, is then formed in which the plot with T is assigned the value $+ 1$, the plot with 0 is assigned $- 1$ and all the others have $x = 0$. An analysis of covariance of y and x will give a valid analysis, but some standard errors will be increased, especially that between the treatments of the two plots involved in the muddle. One advantage of using covariance is the ability to give exact standard errors of contrasts.

Another method and one that is often simpler is this. Suppose that the two missing plot values are m_1 and m_2; then there is an amount, $T - m_1 - m_2$, which represents the discrepancy between actuality (T) and expectation ($m_1 + m_2$). It should be allocated to the first and second missing plots in the ratio of ($\psi_{22} - \psi_{12}$) and ($\psi_{11} - \psi_{12}$) respectively (see Section 12.3). Thus, to take the example at (12.2.10), $m_1 = 15.3$ and $m_2 = 11.0$. Suppose that the sum of yields from the two plots was in fact known to be 24.1, that is a discrepancy of -2.2. Since in this instance $\psi_{22} - \psi_{12} = \psi_{11} - \psi_{12}$, the discrepancy should be apportioned equally between the two plots, i.e. the quantity 1.1 should be subtracted from each missing plot value to give 14.2 and 9.9 respectively. The true sum of squares for the stratum total can be found in the same way by taking the discrepancy between T and ($m_1' + m_2'$) and apportioning it between the plots in the ratio of ($\varphi_{22} - \varphi_{12}$) and ($\varphi_{11} - \varphi_{12}$), where φ_{11}, φ_{12} and φ_{22} are deviations corresponding respectively to φ_{11}, φ_{12} and φ_{22}. If all blocks are of the same size, $\varphi_{11} = \varphi_{22}$, so this allocates half the discrepancy to each plot. Unfortunately there is no simple way from this point of finding the variance of a difference of treatment means.

12.9 Special problem with confounded designs

So far in this chapter it has been implicitly assumed that the design is not confounded. If it is, there will be a 'disconnection', i.e. some of the treatments will occur only in certain blocks while the other treatments occur only elsewhere. (There may be several disconnections, but that does not alter what follows.) In itself a disconnection is not serious, provided no one tries to estimate the contrast between the two parts, which has been lost. (To be more exact, it has been transferred to another stratum and could be recovered from there if needed, but in most instances for practical purposes it has indeed been 'lost'.) The special difficulty is that mishaps can create a disconnection where there was none before; they can also remove one. In a design as well connected as randomized blocks, only a disaster could bring about a disconnection but quite a minor accident could disconnect a simple lattice. Given an accident, the possibility has to be borne in mind. As to removal, a mishap of the kind considered in Exercise 4A could lead to the two sets of treatments becoming connected.

The Kuiper–Corsten iteration is always available for the analysis of the data themselves (Section 4.2), but when it comes to finding the variances (Section 4.3), if there is a disconnection the iteration should be applied in each part separately. There is no great difficulty in putting the distinct matrices together to generate a single covariance matrix of the kind used in Section 5.2.

The method, which is really very simple, will be illustrated by considering a 2^3 factorial set in four blocks with the three-factor interaction confounded, with treatments of two plots interchanged:

Block	I	(1)	BC	AC	AB
	II	A	A	C	ABC
	III	B	B	C	ABC
	IV	(1)	BC	AC	AB

It will be supposed further that Treatment (1) has been lost in Block I. In the first disconnected part, (1), BC, AC and AB, the covariance matrix is shown by the Kuiper–Corsten iteration to be:

$$
\begin{array}{cccc}
0.980 & -0.163 & -0.163 & -0.163 \\
-0.163 & 0.361 & -0.139 & -0.139 \\
-0.163 & -0.139 & 0.361 & -0.139 \\
-0.163 & -0.139 & -0.139 & 0.361
\end{array}
$$

For the second, A, B, C and ABC, it is

$$
\begin{array}{cccc}
0.625 & -0.375 & -0.125 & -0.125 \\
-0.375 & 0.625 & -0.127 & -0.125 \\
-0.125 & -0.125 & 0.375 & -0.125 \\
-0.125 & -0.125 & -0.125 & 0.375
\end{array}
$$

Taking the treatments in standard order, (1), A, B, AB, C, AC, BC, ABC, the two matrices just found can be combined. To show the method, elements marked * come from the first disconnected part and those marked § from the second. Elements that relate to treatments in different parts are set equal to zero.

$$
\begin{pmatrix}
0.980^* & 0.000 & 0.000 & -0.163^* & 0.000 & -0.163^* & -0.163^* & 0.000 \\
0.000 & 0.625\S & -0.375\S & 0.000 & -0.125\S & 0.000 & 0.000 & -0.125\S \\
0.000 & -0.375\S & 0.625\S & 0.000 & -0.125\S & 0.000 & 0.000 & -0.125\S \\
-0.163^* & 0.000 & 0.000 & 0.361^* & 0.000 & -0.139^* & -0.139^* & 0.000 \\
0.000 & -0.125\S & -0.125\S & 0.000 & 0.375\S & 0.000 & 0.000 & -0.125\S \\
-0.163^* & 0.000 & 0.000 & -0.139^* & 0.000 & 0.361^* & -0.139^* & 0.000 \\
-0.163^* & 0.000 & 0.000 & -0.139^* & 0.000 & -0.139^* & 0.361^* & 0.000 \\
0.000 & -0.125\S & -0.125\S & 0.000 & -0.125\S & 0.000 & 0.000 & 0.375\S
\end{pmatrix}
$$

In using such a matrix it is important to be clear what is confounded and what is not. If a contrast is to be unconfounded, its coefficients must sum to zero in each disconnected part separately. Thus, the particular effect of the interaction of A and B in the absence of C is confounded. Its coefficients are

$$(+1 \quad -1 \quad -1 \quad +1 \quad 0 \quad 0 \quad 0 \quad 0)$$

The two treatments, (1) and AB, in the first part both have coefficients of $+1$ and those in the second part (A and B) both have -1, so that contrast fails the test. If, however, someone wanted to know about the main effect of B, namely,

$$(-1 \quad -1 \quad +1 \quad +1 \quad -1 \quad -1 \quad +1 \quad +1)$$

there is no difficulty. The treatments in the first disconnected part, i.e. (1), BC, AC and AB, have coefficients respectively of -1, $+1$, -1 and $+1$ which sum to zero, as do the coefficients for the treatments in the second part.

Exercise 12A

An investigation was conducted on the growth of soya beans in nutrient solution. The following data have been extracted from those of a larger experiment. They give the dry weight of individual whole plants after 60 days for three concentrations of iron, using five randomized blocks.

	Fe 1	Fe 2	Fe 3
I	0.607	0.762	1.083
II	0.588	0.660	m
III	0.534	0.662	1.181
IV	0.555	0.674	1.123
V	0.449	0.601	1.061

Find m and m'. Complete the analysis of variance. Give the approximate effective replication of the linear and quadratic effects and assess their significance.

[Data from C. I. Bliss, *Statistics in Biology*, **2** (1970), p. 400.]

Exercise 12B

The following data are of interest because they come from the first paper ever published on missing data.

An experiment on sugar beet had five treatments arranged in a Latin square. One of the corner plots was trampled upon during the growing season and in consequence was discarded from the experiment. Data in pounds per plot were as follows, each plot having an area of 0.025 acres:

A	306	B	556	C	369	D	332	E	396
B	357	E	485	D	358	C	317	A	325
C	309	D	467	E	367	A	275	B	413
D	418	A	453	B	389	E	324	C	335
E	503	C	572	A	346	B	397	D	m

Analyse the data by at least two methods and check that you get the same results whichever method is used.

1 pound = 454 grams   1 acre = 0.405 ha.

[Data from F. E. Allen and J. Wishart, *J. Agricultural Science*, **20** (1930), pp. 399–406.]

Exercise 12C

We may ask ourselves what would have happened in Exercise 4A if the person responsible for the analysis of the data had been forced by lack of knowledge to regard all plots that had received a wrong treatment as missing. The data would then have read:

	A	B	C	D
I	14.7	m_1	12.5	14.2
II	m_2	17.1	13.3	15.0
III	15.4	17.6	15.0	16.7
IV	16.3	18.2	16.6	17.4
V	16.8	19.1	17.8	18.9

Find the missing plot values, m_1, m_2, m_1', m_2' and calculate the analysis of variance. Then study the data using the analysis of covariance and adjusting upon the two pseudo-variates. Check that you get the same analysis of variance. Then find the variances of estimation for the contrasts (i) between A and B, (ii) between A and C, (iii) between B and C. Compare them with the corresponding values in Exercise 4A and assess any gain from using all the data available.

Exercise 12D

An experiment was being conducted on six turnip variates using a Latin square, when thieves stole the crop of three plots in a corner. The remaining data were:

E	9.0	F	14.5	D	20.5	A	22.5	B	16.0	C	6.5
B	17.5	A	29.5	E	12.0	C	9.0	D	33.0	F	12.5
F	17.0	B	30.0	C	13.0	D	29.0	A	27.0	E	12.0
A	31.5	D	31.5	F	24.0	E	19.5	C	10.5	B	21.0
D	25.0	C	13.0	B	31.0	F	26.0	E	19.5	A	m_1
C	12.2	E	13.0	A	34.0	B	20.0	F	m_2	D	m_3

Data represent fresh weight of crops (including the tops) in pounds per plot, each plot being 15 ft square (1 pound = 454 grams; 1 foot = 0.305 m).

Use the method of leading equations to find values for m_1, m_2 and m_3.

[Data from A. A. Rayner, *A First Course in Biometry for Agriculture Students* (1969).]

Exercise 12E

In Exercise 4F a block was omitted because it contained two missing plots. We are now at stage when we can see how to deal with it. The additional data (i.e. those in Block III) are:

A	235	B	154	C	110
C	151	D	145	D	159
B	249	A	248	A	m_1
C	152	B	221	D	m_2

Analyse the complete data, missing plots included.

Exercise 12F

In Exercise 12B the plot that had earlier been trampled upon gave a yield of 279 pounds. Do you think that its rejection was justified?

Exercise 12G

The plot regarded as missing in Exercise 12A had given a datum of 0.710. That was regarded as so improbable that it must be wrong. Examine the situation.

Chapter 13

Writing the report

13.1 Introduction

Two questions must be considered before the report of a field experiment, or of a series of experiments, is written.

(1) Who is going to read the report immediately, and who may perhaps read it years later? Farmers? Extension workers? Fellow scientists? Administrators? The report should, as far as possible, be intelligible to all likely readers.

(2) What questions was the experiment designed to answer? Or, in other words, which contrasts were the main subject of interest? (Sometimes an experiment may give an unexpected, unplanned result. No hypothesis can be proved by the data that suggested it, but the wise can often take a hint, in this instance where to look in a future experiment.)

13.2 General

Estimates of treatment effects are almost always the most important results of an experiment; tests of significance, standard errors, etc. are less important. An estimate tells how much the yield is expected to be changed by using one treatment in place of another; an F-test or a t-test indicates the degree of confidence with which the estimate may be stated.

The magnitude of a treatment effect has to be seen in the light of the cost of making the change of treatment indicated. Extension workers seldom recommend to farmers a change of practice, e.g. a new variety, unless it is expected to increase crop by at least 5 percent. If the new practice is going to be costly, e.g. additional fertilization or increased seed rate, 10 percent may be a more likely critical figure. So for practical purposes, the question is not so much 'Can we detect any change in the value of the variate?' as 'Is the gain in excess of what would justify the change?' All this was touched on in Section 10.9.

In reporting on any experiment we should avoid making too much of differences that are too small to matter. Some minimum should be borne in mind. Sometimes one encounters an effect that appears to be large but is

289

so poorly determined that it cannot be regarded as proven. It should be reported only as a possible candidate for further investigation. The opposite also occasionally occurs, i.e., a small effect has a small standard error. In that case one should report it with the comment that the effect, though clearly established, is too small to be of much importance. A report like that, written with practical considerations in mind, will carry more weight than one that looks as if the writer had never stepped far from the statistics laboratory.

13.3 Presentation of tables of means, etc.

Tables of mean yields should be included in the report, and perhaps also tables of mean differences or of other contrasts. The report of any factorial experiment should include at least the 2-factor tables (or their equivalent, e.g. a table of differences), even if the relevant interactions are not significant. Each table should have attached standard errors ('SEs') or standard errors of differences ('SEDs'). There are times when the least significant differences ('LSDs') are needed, but this figure should be used with discretion. The general mean has no standard error.

13.4 Commenting on tables

When an interaction between two factors is found to be significant at the chosen level of probability (commonly 5%, or $P = 0.05$), some comment is needed on the effects of one factor at each level of the other. If an interaction with three or more factors is significant, we should try to detect an intelligible pattern in the results. For example, suppose an unconfounded 2^3 experiment gave the following results:

| Factor B | | 0 | | 1 | |
Factor C		0	1	0	1
Factor A	0	6	10	12	16
	1	7	10	14	26

SE (table entries) ± 1.0 (21 d.f.)

A suitable comment on the 3-factor interaction would be: 'Factor A had a positive effect on yield ($+10 \pm 1.4$ units) where both B and C were applied, but little or no effect (0, $+2$, $+1 \pm 1.4$ units) where B or C or both were omitted'. (Here ± indicates the standard error of a mean).

If the experiment is of a complex factorial design, there will be many separate treatment-contrasts; in an unconfounded 2^6 experiment, for example:

Main effects	6
2-factor interactions	15
3-factor interactions	20
4-factor interactions	15
5-factor interactions	6
6-factor interaction	1
Total	63

If there are in reality no treatment effects (imagine for example that the field workers had forgotten to apply the treatments!), about three of the 63 contrasts may be expected to exceed the 0.05 significance level. Further, one may well exceed the 0.01 level. So, if complex interactions (e.g. those involving three or more factors) were considered to be unlikely, it may be reasonable to dismiss one or two of the 42 such contrasts as the results of chance variation, even if they exceed the 0.05 level.

In such complex experiments the 'error' sum of squares may be far from homogeneous; some contrasts used to estimate 'error' may be high-order interactions, judged to have very small values. (In an experiment with fractional replication, such contrasts are the only ones available for estimation of 'error'.) Some may be of the nature of treatment × block interactions, and if each block contains replicate plots of one or more treatments, some are derived from plot differences within blocks. If some of the assumptions on which this pooling of 'error' contrasts is based turn out to be false, it may be necessary to examine the components separately. Occasionally an 'error' mean square can be greatly inflated by an unexpected interaction, either between several treatment contrasts, or between one treatment contrast and a block contrast, e.g., if the soils of different blocks are very different. Sometimes this phenomenon is indicated by several variance ratios being significantly *small*; this can be tested by entering the table of F with the reciprocal of the ratio, and with numbers of degrees of freedom interchanged. (With a row-and-column design it may indicate an interaction of rows and columns, leading to inflation of the 'error' sum of squares, a matter discussed in Section 10.8.)

13.5 Treatment contrasts

We should comment on the treatment contrasts of prime interest even if they are non-significant; if one is nearly significant, e.g. if it exceeds the $P = 0.10$ level, the fact should be mentioned. Also, we should be on the alert for simplifications, e.g. perhaps a complex interaction between two multilevel factors is dominated by the linear × linear component, with other components relatively small, even though some of them may be just significant.

We should remember too that an important and highly significant contrast may be overlooked if it is pooled with others that are not significant. For example, if the true response is exactly linear, and if there are six levels, a value of the linear contrast that is just significant ($P = 0.05$) when treated individually may need to be twice as large if it is to give a significant mean square for the five degrees of freedom for all the levels. Similarly, if the experiment compares many insecticides, all equally effective, with a single untreated control, the mean square for all treatment contrasts may be non-significant, even though the contrast 'nil versus treated' is highly significant.

13.6 Multiple variates

If two or more variates were recorded for each plot, e.g. weights of grain and of straw, or weights of harvests at different dates, several of them may show significant effects of one particular factor. We must be conscious that there are probably correlations between the different variates. Such correlations are often positive, for example, because plots on fertile soil give more grain and more straw than plots on poorer land; but negative ones may occur, even between yields of different fractions of one crop. For two variates, the method of bivariate analysis (see Section 10.4) allows correctly for such correlations.

If an analysis of covariance has been calculated, with a covariate ('independent variate') not affected by the treatments, the results may be used in the report. The nature of the analysis and the value of the regression coefficient, with its standard error, should be given. If it is believed that the covariate was affected by treatments, the analysis of covariance may be used, but only with the greatest caution. An example of misuse, often quoted, is the adjustment of yields by covariance with plant density in an experiment in which the treatments have produced different populations of plants. Covariance in such circumstances can, nevertheless, help to interpret the mode of action of the treatments, even though discretion is needed.

13.7 Graphs

Graphs are often helpful to the reader. They may be used to illustrate results given in tables. If one or more factors had many levels (e.g. 4 or 6), a graph will show the form of the response curve, and give the reader a chance to assess the position of any maximum (or minimum) values within the range of levels tested. The report may mention such estimates. To obtain them by strict mathematical methods is beyond the scope of this manual, but with reasonably well-determined response curves, curves drawn freehand are usually satisfactory for practical purposes. A graph may also be useful in assessing the value of a new material in relation to a standard one.

13.8   Miscellaneous

Most reports should include at least most of the following information: Design, plot dimensions, area harvested for yield, soil type, previous crop(s), location, standard error (s) per plot, degrees of freedom for 'error', coefficient of variation (CV) being s as a percentage of the general mean.

Exercise 13

The exercises in earlier chapters provide plenty of material for writing full reports, whether for research supervisors, other scientists, or farmers. Those at the ends of Chapters 6 and 7 are especially suitable, though Exercises 4A, 4F, 4G, 4H, 8C, 8D, 9A, 11B, 12D, 12E and 12F all present individual challenges.

APPENDIX

Confusing and Ambiguous Words

Several words and phrases are used by different writers in different senses. Often, but not always, it is possible to decide by considering the context which sense is intended. We discuss in this appendix some of the ones that are most likely to cause confusion.

(1) *Response*

Some writers use 'response' to mean the measurement made on any single unit, i.e. plot or sub-plot in a field experiment. We prefer 'observation', 'record', 'yield', or 'count' as appropriate. This leaves 'response to nitrogen fertilizer' to indicate a difference between means of treatments with and without nitrogen. The phrase 'response curve' follows naturally from this usage.

(2) *Effect*

In a 2^k experiment the word 'effect' is often used in the sense of 'main effect'. More generally, if (in any experiment) a factor is tested at two levels, the difference between the two relevant mean yields is called the 'effect' of that factor. Sometimes, however, the word 'effect' is used to indicate the deviation of the mean of one treatment from the general mean of all treatments.

(3) *Interaction*

In a 2^k experiment with r replicates the main effect of factor A is defined as follows:

$$(T_{A+} - T_{A-})/(r.2^{k-1}),$$

where T_{A+} and T_{A-} are the totals of the plots with the higher and lower levels of factor A. Each total has $r.2^{k-1}$ plots, and so the main effect is the difference between the two means.

Yates (1937) also used the same divisor $(r.2^{k-1})$ for all interactions, so that, for example,

$$\text{interaction } A/B = (T_{++} - T_{+-} - T_{-+} + T_{--})/(r.2^{k-1})$$

294

where T_{++} etc. are totals of $r.2^{k-2}$ plots each. Unfortunately, an alternative system has been proposed; in this, although the same divisor is used for main effects, a different one is used for two-factor interactions, another for three-factor interactions, and so on. Either option may be specified in Genstat output.

(4) *Control*

Since entomologists speak of the 'control' of a pest (e.g. by an insecticide), the use of the phrase 'control plot', meaning a plot *not* treated with insecticide or other experimental treatment, may be confusing. 'Nil plot' or 'untreated plot' is safer.

(5) *Residual*

This word has three senses:
(a)   = plot residual, as calculated, for example, by sweeping;
(b)   'residual effect' = effect of a treatment applied to an earlier crop on the plots of an experiment;
(c)   'residual herbicide' = weedkiller that remains active in soil for a prolonged period.

(6) *Error*
(a)   Mistake, as in 'gross error' of weighing.
(b)   In the statistical sense, referring to the unexplained component of a plot-yield, or of a sum of squares for unassigned variation (= 'residual' or 'error' sum of squares).

(7) *Sum of squares*

Sometimes used of 'raw' sums of squares, e.g.

$$x_1^2 + x_2^2 + \ldots + x_n^2$$

but also of 'corrected' sums of squares

$$(x_1 - m)^2 + (x_2 - m)^2 + \ldots (x_n - m)^2 \quad \text{(where } m = \text{mean).}$$

The difference between these two quantities, nm^2, should be called 'correction for the mean' (CFM), or 'correction term' rather than 'correction factor' because the word 'factor' suggests multiplication rather than subtraction.

(8) *Normal*

To avoid confusion with other uses of the word 'normal', the 'normal distribution' may be called the 'Gaussian' or 'Laplacian' distribution.

(9)   *Variance ratio*

Some tables of analysis of variance (ANOVA) include a column labelled 'F', others label the corresponding column 'variance ratio' or 'VR'. Strictly 'F' refers to a theoretical distribution; each tabulated value may (or may not) be a sample from an *F*-distribution.

(10)   *Parabolic*

Used as a synonym of 'quadratic'.

(11)   *Split-plot*

A synonym of 'sub-plot'.

Solutions to Exercises

1A For $e = +\frac{1}{2}$, the analysis of variance reads:

Source	d.f.	s.s.	m.s.	F
Treatments	3	340.000	113.333	19.17
'Error'	23	136.000	5.913	
Stratum total	26	476.000		

The residuals are:

0	+ 1	− 1	+ 2	+ 1	− 1	+ 3	− 1
0	+ 1	+ 3	+ 3	+ 1	+ 3	+ 2	− 2
+ 2	0	− 1	+ 1	− 1	− 6		
0	− 2	0	− 3	− 5			

The two low residuals ($- 5$ and $- 6$) suggest that the spray may have caused damage over a wider area than anyone had supposed.

1B For $e = +\frac{1}{2}$, the analysis of variance reads:

Source	d.f.	s.s.	m.s.	F
Treatments	5	444.434	88.887	23.48
'Error'	15	56.795	3.786	
Stratum total	20	501.229		

The residuals are as overleaf:

− 1.492	− 1.867	+ 2.183	− 1.167	+ 1.258	− 1.067
+ 1.083	− 0.517	+ 0.608	+ 0.833	− 0.242	+ 0.383
− 1.900	+ 0.850	0.000	+ 0.083	+ 0.633	+ 0.783
+ 0.825	+ 2.800	− 2.575	− 1.192	+ 2.808	− 3.117

The data were presented as kilograms per plot of 36 sq. metres, which calls for multiplication by 0.278 to convert to tonnes per hectare. That would be more generally understood, though other units might be preferred. It is better not to multiply the data themselves because that would lead to rounding errors, the likelihood of copying errors, and difficulty in applying the rule for determining e (Section 1.9). It is better to work with the data as they are on the field sheets and to use the multiplier to convert treatment means, standard errors, etc., at the end when the analysis is complete.

1C For $e = +\frac{1}{2}$, the analysis of variance reads:

Source	d.f.	s.s.	m.s.	F
Treatments	9	287.576	31.953	8.27
'Error'	27	104.362	3.865	
Stratum total	36	391.938		

The residuals are:

− 3.250	− 0.125	− 1.045	+ 3.345
+ 1.025	+ 2.175	+ 1.555	+ 2.645
+ 0.675	+ 1.125	+ 0.830	− 0.155
− 0.225	− 2.075	− 0.095	− 1.605
+ 1.650	+ 3.400	+ 0.705	− 0.280
− 1.925	− 0.775	+ 0.955	+ 1.345
− 0.675	− 2.000	− 1.145	− 2.855
− 0.125	− 1.275	− 1.545	− 1.405
+ 0.285	− 1.075	+ 1.400	+ 0.555
+ 2.575	− 0.075	− 1.645	− 1.580

There is no obvious pattern in the residuals to suggest that the blocks were formed badly. The matter will be studied further in Exercises 8E and 8F.

1D The residuals are:

+ 11.6	+ 48.8	− 21.7	+ 25.8	+ 32.9	+ 11.2	− 2.6	+ 20.7
+ 19.6	+ 2.6	+ 50.3	− 6.4	− 25.8	+ 19.9	+ 21.7	+ 6.4
− 20.7	− 16.2	− 11.2	+ 26.8	+ 69.9	− 13.6	− 11.6	− 26.8
− 69.9	− 19.9	− 32.9	+ 13.6	+ 16.2	− 50.3	− 19.6	− 48.8

Broadly speaking, the first row contains high values and the last contains low ones. It could be that the blocks would have been more effective if each had consisted of two rows and had extended across the whole area. The situation will be examined in more detail in Exercise 8G. It may be noted that the blocks actually used led to an 'error' mean square of 19.609. Using methods to be described in Chapter 4, it emerges that the alternative blocking system proposed above would have reduced that figure to 11.966. This gives a strong indication that the blocks could have been formed better, but the alternative analysis of variance should not be used in the interpretation of the present data. ('As the randomization is, so must the analysis be.') It could, however, be used as guidance if a future experiment were designed on the same site or in similar circumstances.

1E For $e = +\frac{1}{2}$, the analysis of variance reads:

Source	d.f.	s.s.	m.s.	F
Treatments	3	170.736	56.912	6.59
'Error'	6	51.834	8.639	
Stratum total	9	222.570		

The unit of cavans per hectare is no doubt well understood in some places, but for a scientific publication it is better to convert figures to units more widely understood. In any case, it is better not to convert the data themselves.

1F For $e = +\frac{1}{2}$, the analysis of variance reads:

Source	d.f.	s.s.	m.s.	F
Treatments	5	52.498	10.500	3.44
'Error'	20	60.949	3.047	
Stratum total	25	113.447		

It would be better to express results in litres per hectare and that requires a conversion factor of 89.9.

1G　For $e = -\frac{1}{2}$, the analysis of variance reads:

Source	d.f.	s.s.	m.s.	F
Treatments	4	53 068.4	13 267.1	13.88
'Error'	21	20 068.0	955.6	
Stratum total	25	73 136.4		

It is a pity that the plot size is nowhere stated. (The same comment can be made of a number of other exercises.)

2B　Block　I　　　　EBDAFC
　　　　　　　　II　　　　DFCBAE
　　　　　　　　III　　　FABECD
　　　　　　　　IV　　　AFECDB

2E　We suggest:

3	4	9	10	15	16	21	22	27	28	33	34	39	40	45	46
2	5	8	11	14	17	20	23	26	29	32	35	38	41	44	47
1	6	7	12	13	18	19	24	25	30	31	36	37	42	43	48
96	91	90	85	84	79	78	73	72	67	66	61	60	55	54	49
95	92	89	86	83	80	77	74	71	68	65	62	59	56	53	50
94	93	88	87	82	81	76	75	70	69	64	63	58	57	52	51

But do the field staff agree? Also, would it help to renumber the blocks?

3A　The variance of the mean is $25/64 = (0.625)^2$. The value of Z in Section 3.2 is therefore $(11.1 - 10.0)/0.625 = 1.76$, which raises no serious doubts about the null hypothesis that the mean is really 10.

3B　Note that nothing has been said about the form of the distribution. With 200 observations we can gauge if it is normal or nearly so; also their mean will come near to being normally distributed even if the observations themselves are not. We therefore note that the variance of the mean is $8/200 = (0.2)^2$, so Z equals $(4.77 - 5.00)/0.2 = -1.15$, which does not lead us to reject the null hypothesis.

If there had been only 20 observations there would have been even less evidence for doing so, and we would not know as much about the normality of distribution.

3C The variance of the mean is 8.4, so $Z = 1.38$. We have here a one-tail test because no one expects the soil conditioner to do harm, but there is little evidence that it has done good.

3D The variance of the mean is $49/100 = (0.7)^2$, so $Z = -4.29$. This is a two-tail test and the null hypothesis must be rejected, i.e. the two regions show a difference.

As in Exercise 3B the test can be relied upon only if the observations are normally distributed or if there are enough of them to give a normally distributed mean. Experience shows that the distribution of plant weights is usually skew (i.e. asymmetrical), so with only five observations neither condition holds.

3E From (3.3.1) the variance can be estimated by

$$s^2 = [(+1.2)^2 + (-1.2)^2 + (-0.3)^2 + (-0.8)^2 + (0.8)^2 + (+0.3)^2 + (-0.1)^2 + (+0.1)^2]/7 = 0.6229$$

with 7 degrees of freedom. (Note that $\bar{x}$, the mean, $= 0.4$.) The variance of the mean is therefore estimated as $0.6229/8 = (0.279)^2$ and $t = (0.4 - 0.1)/0.279 = 1.08$. Hence there are no grounds for rejecting the null hypothesis that the true mean is 0.1.

The actual values of t with 7 degrees of freedom and for $P = 0.05$ and 0.01 are respectively 2.365 and 3.499. Hence confidence limits for the observed mean are:

$$(P = 0.05) \quad 0.4 \pm (2.365)(0.279), \text{ i.e. } -0.26 \text{ and } 1.06$$
$$(P = 0.01) \quad 0.4 \pm (3.499)(0.279), \text{ i.e. } -0.58 \text{ and } 1.38.$$

3F The variance of the mean is $4.84/25 = (0.44)^2$ estimated with 24 degrees of freedom. Hence $t = (5.85 - 4.00)/0.44 = 4.20$, so the null hypothesis must be rejected. For $P = 0.01$, $t = 2.797$, so confidence limits are $5.85 \pm (2.797)(0.44)$, i.e. 4.62 and 7.08.

3G The ratio of the two variances (F) is $15.2824/8.0275 = 1.90$ with 10 and 15 degrees of freedom, so there is no objection to pooling. The result is a variance of

$$(10 \times 15.2824 + 15 \times 8.0275)/25 = 10.9295$$

with 25 degrees of freedom. The variance of the difference of means is therefore

$$10.9295(1/11 + 1/16) = (1.294)^2$$

so $t = (6.65 - 4.28)/1.294 = 1.83$ and the null hypothesis can be accepted.

For $P = 0.05$ critical value of t with 10 degrees of freedom is 2.228 and for 15 it is 2.131, so confidence limits for

> A are $6.65 \pm (2.228)(1.179)$, i.e. 4.02 and 9.28 and for
> B they are $4.28 \pm (2.131)(0.708)$, i.e. 2.77 and 5.79.

It will be seen that the two sets of limits overlap, though not by much.

3H   Mean difference is 2.65 with an estimated variance of $15.8307/11 = (1.200)^2$. The null hypothesis is that the difference is really zero, so $t = (2.65 - 0.00)/1.200 = 2.21$ with 10 degrees of freedom. That makes P approximately equal to 0.05, so more data are called for if a decision is to be made. The confidence limits ($P = 0.05$) are

$$2.65 \pm (2.228)(1.200) = -0.02 \text{ and } 5.23.$$

Zero is only just within the limits.

3I   The sum of squared deviations is

$$(18^2 + 21^2 + 12^2 + 16^2 + 25^2 + 20^2) - 112^2/6 = 99.33 = (n - 1)s^2$$

so χ^2 with 5 degrees of freedom is $99.33/15 = 6.62$, which is well within the upper and lower limits for $P = 0.025$.

3J   The value of χ^2 is also below the upper point for $P = 0.05$.

3K   For A, variance is 689.43 and for B it is 255.06. Hence $F = 689.43/255.06 = 2.70$ with 9 and 11 degrees of freedom. There is no reason to think that the two variances differ.

For A with 9 degrees of freedom critical values of χ^2 with $P = 0.025$ and 0.975 are 2.700 and 19.023. Also $9s^2 = 6204.9$, so σ^2 lies between 326.2 and 2298.1 with 0.95 confidence. Corresponding limits for B are 128.0 and 735.2.

3L
(a) $100 + 1.96\sqrt{10}$,   i.e. 93.8 and 106.2

(b) $100 + 1.96\sqrt{10/10}$, i.e. 98.0 and 102.0
(c) $100 + 1.96\sqrt{10/100}$, i.e. 99.4 and 100.6

If σ^2 were unknown, with (a) there would be no way of estimating s^2, but with (b) s^2 could be found from (3.3.1). With (c) the same method could be used, but s^2 would be so well known that little harm would result from using 1.96 instead of t for $P = 0.05$.

3M For A, $\bar{x} = 25.78$ and $s^2 = 13.4119$ with 8 degrees of freedom; for B, $\bar{x} = 28.24$ and $s^2 = 5.2525$ with 10. Hence $13.4119/5.2525 = 2.55$, which does not approach significance, so the two variances can be pooled to give $(8 \times 13.4119 + 10 \times 5.2525)/18 = 8.8789$ with 18 d.f.

The variance of the difference between the means is therefore
$$8.8789(1/9 + 1/11) = (1.339)^2,$$
so $t = (28.24 - 25.78)/1.339 = 1.84$ and there is no reason to think that the means differ.

3N For preparation A, the estimated probability of its proving effective is $172/250 = 0.688 = p_A$. For preparation B, it is $158/200 = 0.790 = p_B$. On the null hypothesis that there is really no difference between the preparations, $p = (172 + 158)/(250 + 200) = 0.733$. In that case the variance of the difference between p_A and p_B is $p(1 - p)(1/250 + 1/200) = (0.042)^2$.

Since $Z = (p_A - p_B)/0.042 = 2.43$, the two preparations differ at the level, $P = 0.05$.

Confidence limits ($P = 0.05$) are:

$$\text{A,} \quad 0.688 \pm 1.96 \sqrt{\frac{0.688 \times 0.312}{250}} = 0.631 \text{ and } 0.745$$

$$\text{B,} \quad 0.790 \pm 1.96 \sqrt{\frac{0.790 \times 0.210}{200}} = 0.734 \text{ and } 0.846.$$

For the confidence limits to be reduced from ± 0.06 (approx) to ± 0.03, i.e. halved, it would be necessary to take samples four times as large.

30 We here have a sample that probably follows the Poisson distribution with a mean of 4. The variance of a single observation will also equal 4 and that of a mean of 50 will be $4/50 = (0.283)^2$. Further, from a sample of that size its distribution will approximate to the normal. The confidence limits ($P = 0.05$) can therefore be set at

$$4 \pm 1.96(0.283) = 3.45 \text{ and } 4.55.$$

4A For $e = +\frac{1}{2}$, the analysis of variance reads:

Source	d.f.	s.s.	m.s.	F
Treatments	3	16.281	5.427	13.79
'Error'	12	4.722	0.393	
Stratum total	15	21.003		

For the intended design, which was orthogonal, K at (4.1.1) would have been $(1/5 + 1/5) = 0.4$ for all the contrasts mentioned. For the achieved design, K is 0.5 for A *versus* B, 0.425 for A *v.* C and 0.4 for C *v.* D. The 'error' mean square provides an estimate of s^2.

4B For $e = +1$, the analysis of variance reads:

Source	d.f.	s.s.	m.s.	F
Treatments	3	0.0333	0.011 1	5.63
'Error'	15	0.0296	0.001 97	
Stratum total	18	0.0629		

For a design in randomized blocks K would have been $(1/6 + 1/6) = 0.333$. With the design used K is 0.429 for A *v.* B, 0.440 for A *v.* C, 0.298 for B *v.* C and 0.333 for C *v.* D. The 'error' mean square of 0.001 97 provides an estimate of s^2.

4C For $e = +\frac{1}{2}$, the analysis of variance reads:

Source	d.f.	s.s.	m.s.	F
Treatments	4	186.800	46.700	11.82
'Error'	16	63.200	3.950	
Stratum total	20	250.000		

The residuals are:

$$+ 1.133 \quad + 0.333 \quad - 1.467$$
$$+ 1.800 \quad + 1.200 \quad - 3.000$$

− 0.533	+ 1.467	− 0.933
+ 1.000	+ 0.800	− 1.800
− 0.400	+ 0.600	− 0.200
+ 3.133	− 1.267	− 1.867
+ 2.267	− 0.133	− 2.133
+ 0.467	+ 0.667	− 1.133
− 0.467	− 0.067	+ 0.533
+ 1.200	+ 1.400	− 2.600

There is a strong tendency for the residuals in the last column to be negative. Probably two blocks of five plots in each column would have given a reduced value of s^2 in (4.1.1). That would also have avoided the non-orthogonality, which reduced an actual replication (r) of 6 to an effective replication (R) of 5. However, this is only a hint for the future.

4D For $e = +\frac{1}{2}$, the analysis of variance reads:

Source	d.f.	s.s.	m.s.	F
Varieties	12	327.891	27.324	1.22
'Error'	27	603.015	22.334	
Stratum total	39	930.906		

Here, where $R = 3.25$, the contrast between any two adjusted treatment means has a K equal to 0.615. Since $s^2 = 22.334$, the variance of any such contrast is 13.735, giving a standard error of 3.71. Since t for $P = 0.05$ and 27 degrees of freedom is 2.052, any difference between the adjusted means of a standard treatment and a new one should be regarded as significant $(P = 0.05)$ if it exceeds 7.6.

The adjusted means of the standard varieties are X, 23.8; 6, 29.3 and Z, 34.6. For the new varieties they are:

A	32.6	B	27.9	C	29.8
D	28.1	E	30.0	F	27.1
G	30.1	H	34.1	I	29.4
		J	30.4		

so none has been shown to yield more heavily than Y and Z. On the other hand, both A and H crop more heavily than X, which did not do very well. Was it perhaps introduced as a standard on account of some special property like disease resistance?

4E For $e = +\frac{1}{2}$, the analysis of variance reads:

Source	d.f.	s.s.	m.s.	F
Spray treatments	4	51.052	12.763	33.89
'Error'	8	3.013	0.377	
Stratum total	12	54.065		

Adjusted treatment means are:

A	B	C	D	O
4.68	3.35	2.65	8.23	4.48

For this design $R = 2.75$ and $R_o = 4.125$, so K for the contrast between O and one of the spray treatments is $(1/2.75 + 1/4.125) = 0.606$, making the variance $0.2285 = 0.478^2$. It appears then that the adjusted means for sprays B and C lie respectively 2.36 and 3.83 times the standard error below that for O. Also, the adjusted mean for D lies 7.85 times the standard error above. That provides a reservation about the use of one-tail tests. The spray substance itself may have done no harm, but how about the water with which it was formulated? (*Venturia* is a water-borne fungus.)

4F The design is in supplemented balance with $R = 13$ and $R_o = 351/43$, the supplementing treatment being A, so K for the contrast between A and any of B, C and D is 0.1994. Between any pair of B, C and D it is 0.1538.
For $e = -\frac{1}{2}$, the analysis of variance reads:

Source	d.f.	s.s.	m.s.	F
Treatments	3	13 305.7	4435.2	3.59
'Error'	41	50 643.1	1235.2	
Stratum total	44	63 948.8		

Adjusted treatment means are:

A	B	C	D
172.7	181.8	139.0	156.2

Here it should be recalled that we are dealing with yields, and the real object of the study was to try to alter fruit size. It is of interest, nevertheless, to note that B, in which only king fruits were removed, had no discernible effect on yield, whereas C in which fruit was removed from lateral branches, led to a loss of crop, $(172.7 - 139.0) = 33.7$ with a standard error of 15.7. Treatment D, in which both kinds of blossom would be damaged, was intermediate between B and C, though, of course, the general level of damage was not controlled and may well have been different from that for B and C.

With tree crops the presentation of yields as crop per tree (as has been done here) is usually more intelligible than crop per unit area. It is desirable though to give the density of planting, so that the figures can be converted to an areal basis if anyone wants them in that form.

4G For $e = -\frac{1}{2}$, the analysis of variance reads:

Source	d.f.	s.s.	m.s.	F
Varieties	15	15 070.6	1004.7	4.68
'Error'	9	1 931.4	214.6	
Stratum total	24	17 002.0		

For a contrast between two concurring varieties, $K = 5/4$; for other contrasts between two varieties, $K = 3/2$.

Adjusted means are:

A	140	B	160	C	183	D	150
E	145	F	157	G	164	H	186
I	168	J	111	K	202	L	206
M	141	N	191	O	181	P	179

Tillers per square metre of rice is a readily understood measure.

4H For $e = -\frac{1}{2}$, the analysis of variance reads:

Source	d.f.	s.s.	m.s.	F
Varieties	15	17 972.3	1198.2	4.62
'Error'	21	5 441.4	259.1	
Stratum total	36	23 413.8		

For a contrast between two concurring varieties, $K = 5/6$; for other contrasts between two varieties, $K = 11/12$.

Adjusted means are:

A	150	B	152	C	179	D	152
E	164	F	162	G	160	H	182
I	165	J	101	K	191	L	189
M	149	N	197	O	181	P	170

4I At (4.12.1), $R = 5/2$ and $R_o = 30/7$.
At (4.12.2), $R = 9/2$ and $R_o = 117/23$.

5A The treatment sum of squares is 982.15. The contrasts have been taken as:

$$
\begin{array}{llll}
(1) & (+3 & -1 & -1 & -1) \\
(2) & (0 & +1 & -2 & +1) \\
(3) & (0 & +1 & 0 & -1)
\end{array}
$$

From the rule at (5.6.8) they are orthogonal, as the following partition confirms.

Contrast	Value	K	Contribution
(1)	− 24.6	2.40	252.15
(2)	− 27.0	1.20	607.50
(3)	+ 7.0	0.40	122.50
			982.15

5B The contrast between the two varieties is

$$(+1 \quad +1 \quad +1 \quad +1 \quad +1 \quad -1 \quad -1 \quad -1 \quad -1 \quad -1)$$

What is left represents the variation of strains within a variety. That leads to the partition:

Source	d.f.	s.s.	m.s.	F
Between varieties	1	57.600	57.600	14.90
Between strains within a variety	8	229.976	28.747	7.44
Between strains	9	287.576		

Even after taking out the effect of varieties there are still considerable differences between strains.

5C It is always difficult to decide after the event what the experimenter had in mind. That is a good reason for always writing down the contrasts of interest at the time of inception.

Taking treatments in the order, S, M, C, D, O, there could well be interest in

$$(+1 \quad -1 \quad 0 \quad 0 \quad 0)$$

and in

$$(\ 0 \quad 0 \quad +1 \quad -1 \quad 0)$$

There is perhaps interest in

$$(+1 \quad +1 \quad -1 \quad -1 \quad 0).$$

Supposing that none of the above contrasts shows anything, the question will arise whether there was any effect at all of nitrogen. This would be shown by

$$(+1 \quad +1 \quad +1 \quad +1 \quad -4).$$

The conversion factor to tonnes per hectare is 0.0448.

5D This is an example of the way in which experiments sometimes form a cascade of treatments, each being a development of the one before. Here the idea was perhaps to study:

Nitrogen	(-1	$+1$	0	0	0	0)
Phosphorus	(0	-1	$+1$	0	0	0)
Lime	(0	-1	0	$+1$	0	0)
Potassium	(0	0	-1	0	$+1$	0)
Special mixture	(0	0	0	0	-1	$+1$)

If that was the idea, we suggest that a factorial design would have been better with, perhaps, D and F as supernumerary treatments. (By that we mean that they were added to the factorial set to provide special contrasts additional to those that would ordinarily be studied.)

The conversion factor to tonnes per hectare is 0.0953.

5E   Again, without guidance from the experimenter, it is not clear which contrasts were under study. Little and Hills (1978) point out that Treatment C involves an organic compound, all the rest being inorganic. Further, two of the others (A and B) are salts of ammonium; two (D and E) are metallic salts. That suggests the contrasts:

(1)	(− 1	− 1	− 1	− 1	− 1	+ 5)
(2)	(− 1	− 1	+ 4	− 1	− 1	0)
(3)	(+ 1	+ 1	0	− 1	− 1	0)
(4)	(+ 1	− 1	0	0	0	0)
(5)	(0	0	0	+ 1	− 1	0)

Since the propsed contrasts are in fact orthogonal, they could well be those intended. If so, the analysis of variance reads:

Source	d.f.	s.s.	m.s.	F
(1)	1	180.200	180.200	119.10
(2)	1	3.816	3.816	2.52
(3)	1	0.202	0.202	0.13
(4)	1	1.333	1.333	0.88
(5)	1	0.213	0.213	0.14
'Error'	20	30.256	1.513	
Stratum total	25	216.020		

There appears to be little difference in the effect of the various sources of nitrogen, but it is clearly important that the element be supplied.

The conversion factor to tonnes per hectare is 2.511.

5F   In Exercise 1E the contrasts of interest are:

(− 1	+ 1	0	0)
(− 1	0	+ 1	0)
(− 1	0	0	+ 1)

(The varieties are taken in the order R, X, Y, Z.) For each contrast, $K = 0.5$. The three contrasts give respectively the values:

$$+ 7.925, \qquad + 8.075, \qquad + 5.425.$$

The error mean square is 8.6390, so each has a variance of 4.3195. Dividing each value by its standard error, 2.0783, gives t-values of respectively

$$3.813, \quad 3.885, \quad 2.610.$$

Using the rule given at the beginning of Section 5.6, it will be found that the three contrasts contribute sums of squares of

$$125.611, \quad 130.411, \quad 58.861$$

respectively to the analysis of variance, each having one degree of freedom. This gives respective F-values of 14.54 ($= 3.813^2$), 15.10 ($= 3.385^2$) and 6.81 ($= 2.610^2$).

5G The initial partition reads:

Source	d.f.	s.s.	m.s.	F
L	1	76 0035	76 0035	6.87
Q	1	7 4405	7 4405	0.67
Departures	3	36 3890	12 1297	1.10
'Error'	15	165 8375	11 0558	
Stratum total	20	285 7705		

The line for departures, which was found by difference, does not look very interesting and the matter need not be pursued. Even if all the sum of squares for departures were due to one degree of freedom this would give an F-value of 3.29, which would be significant only at about $P = 0.1$, so the subject scarcely needs to be pursued. If anyone is interested in the further partition, the three remaining effects give:

Source	df.	s.s.
Cubic	1	11 3301
Quartic	1	9 0630
Quintic	1	15 9960
Departures	3	36 3891

5H   The contrasts are:

Linear	$(-7$	-3	$+1$	$+9)$
Quadratic	$(+7$	-4	-8	$+5)$
Cubic	$(+3$	-8	$+6$	$-6)$

5I   The contrasts are:

Linear	$(\quad -34$	-14	$+1$	$+16$	$+31)$
Quadratic	$(+1830$	-1242	-1747	-710	$+1869)$

6A   The first partition, which can be carried out using summation terms, reads:

Source	d.f.	s.s.
P	1	1638.40
K	3	2518.40
P × K	3	8.40
Treatments	7	4165.20

The further partition needs the following contrasts:

Main effect of K

L	$(-3$	-1	$+1$	$+3$	-3	-1	$+1$	$+3)$
Q	$(+1$	-1	-1	$+1$	$+1$	-1	-1	$+1)$
C	$(-1$	$+3$	-3	$+1$	-1	$+3$	-3	$+1)$

Interaction

L	$(-3$	-1	$+1$	$+3$	$+3$	$+1$	-1	$-3)$
Q	$(+1$	-1	-1	$+1$	-1	$+1$	$+1$	$-1)$
C	$(-1$	$+3$	-3	$+1$	$+1$	-3	$+3$	$-1)$

It is:

Source	d.f.	s.s.
P	1	1638.40
Linear K	1	2204.48
Quadratic K	1	313.60
Cubic K	1	0.32
P × Linear K	1	2.88

P × Quadratic K	1	1.60
P × Cubic K	1	3.92
Treatments	7	4165.20

Here again the data are presented after conversion from the field records. For reasons given above (Exercise 1B) this is not altogether wise. Conversion to tonnes per hectare requires further multiplication by 2.509.

6B The provisional analysis of variance obtained from summation terms reads:

Source	d.f.	s.s.	m.s.	F
Fungicide (F)	4	13 250.7	3312.7	64.11
Varieties (V)	2	5 762.1	2881.0	55.75
F × V	8	259.5	32.44	0.63
'Error'	28	1 446.9	51.675	
Stratum total	42	20 719.2		

There is, however, a clear structure among the treatments, namely, a factorial set of treatments with a supernumerary untreated control, which suggests the use of the following orthogonal set of contrasts of interest:

Substance (S)	(0	+ 1	+ 1	− 1	− 1)
Time of application (T)	(0	− 1	+ 1	− 1	+ 1)
S × T	(0	− 1	+ 1	+ 1	− 1)
Use of fungicides (V)	(− 4	+ 1	+ 1	+ 1	+ 1)

Taken in conjunction with two contrasts for the varieties, say, $(- 1 + 1 \quad 0)$ and $(- 1 - 1 + 2)$, this leads to a more detailed analysis of variance:

Source	d.f.	s.s.	m.s.	F
S	1	6900.7	6900.7	133.54***
T	1	1284.1	1284.1	24.83***
S × T	1	443.8	443.8	8.59**
U	1	4622.8	4622.8	89.46***
V	2	5762.1	2881.0	55.75***

V × S	2	0.6	0.3	0.01
V × T	2	143.3	21.6	0.42
V × S × T	2	35.8	17.9	0.35
V × U	2	79.6	39.8	0.77
'Error'	28	1446.9	51.675	
Stratum total	42	20 719.1		

We meet here a phenomenon that will become increasingly common, namely, occasions in which the sums of squares in a partition sum to a figure that is slightly wrong. Thus, here, $(0.6 + 143.3 + 35.8 + 79.6)$ $= 259.3$, not 259.5. That, of course, is due to rounding error and need cause no concern so long as the discrepancy is small.

To turn to interpretation, there is a marked effect of varieties, but no interaction of varieties with fungicide treatments, which may therefore be considered without reference to varieties. The four treatments in the factorial set averaged over varieties give means of

	4 times	10 times	
Copper oxychloride	40.0	45.0	(A)
Dithane	60.7	79.7	

Dithane has been more effective than copper oxychloride, especially when applied ten times. (The standard error of a difference of two means in Table A is 3.39.) The mean for the unsprayed control is 31.0, so the difference between this and the least effective treatment is 9.0, which is 2.65 times its standard error. It may be safely asserted that applying any of the four fungicide treatments gave better crops than doing nothing.

The conversion factor to tonnes per hectare is 0.247.

6C The preliminary analysis of variance reads:

Source	d.f.	s.s.	m.s.	F
Varieties (V)	2	882 917	441 458	2.99
Nitrogen (N)	4	39 621 078	9 905 270	243.52***
V × N	8	2 447 594	305 949	2.07
'Error'	42	6 209 863	147 854	
Stratum total	56	49 161 452		

The partition of the nitrogen effect into a linear and a quadratic effect has already been considered in Exercise 5I. The departures from quadratic form (i.e. the cubic and quartic effects) will have to be found by difference. The detailed analysis reads:

Source	d.f.	s.s.	m.s.	F
Varieties (V)	2	882 917	441 458	2.99
N, linear (L)	1	36 004 833	36 004 833	243.52***
N, quadratic (Q)	1	3 065 044	3 065 044	20.73***
N, departures (D)	2	551 201	275 600	1.86
V × L	2	723 240	361 620	2.45
V × Q	2	291 044	145 522	0.98
V × D	4	1 433 310	358 328	2.42
'Error'	42	6 209 863	147 854	
Stratum total	56	49 161 452		

It emerges then that there is a marked effect of added nitrogen; the response curve is not a straight line, but it is fairly well represented by a parabola. The varieties do not differ much and do not have any noticeable effect on the response curve, which is much the same for all of them. (The interaction V × D comes so near to significance at $P = 0.05$ that it perhaps deserves a mention, none the less. It is not clear what it means.)

6D The analysis of variance reads:

Source	d.f.	s.s.	m.s.	F
Fertilizer (F)	3	167.745	55.915	95.20**
Varieties (V)	1	19.220	19.220	32.72**
Infestation (I)	1	338.000	338.000	575.48**
V × I	1	3.645	3.645	6.21*
F × I	3	22.225	7.408	12.61***
F × V	3	0.705	0.235	0.40
F × V × I	3	0.330	0.110	0.19
'Error'	15	8.810	0.5873	
Stratum total	30	560.680		

All three factors enter into interactions of some sort, and some statisticians would insist that only a three-way table would suffice to show the results. We do, however, suggest an alternative. The effect of infestations is very great and it interacts with each of the other two factors. In those circumstances it would simplify interpretation to consider the results in two parts. For infested plots, the treatment means are:

	F_1	F_2	F_3	F_4	Means
A	20.4	22.6	29.4	22.7	23.88
B	19.1	21.3	26.9	20.8	22.02
Mean	19.75	21.95	28.35	21.75	22.95
Diff.	1.3	1.3	2.9	1.9	1.85

If this approach is to be followed, we should re-partition, thus:

Source	d.f.	s.s.	m.s.	F
Infestation (I)	1	338.000	338.000	
Fertilizer within I(F_I)	3	39.710	13.237	22.54***
Varieties within I(V_I)	1	3.062	3.062	5.21*
F × V within I($F_I \times V_I$)	3	0.248	0.083	0.14
Fertilizer within U(F_u)	3	150.260	50.087	85.28***
Varieties within U(V_u)	1	19.802	19.802	33.72***
F × V within U($F_u \times V_u$)	3	0.788	0.263	0.45
'Error'	15	8.810	0.5873	
Stratum total	30	560.680		

The sums of squares were obtained from two sets of summation terms, namely, S_{vF}, S_v, S_F and S_o, one worked out using only data from infested plots and the other only data from uninfested.

The revised analysis is quite easy to interpret. The only remaining question concerns the partition of the effect of Factor F, but here there is the cascade pattern noted in Exercise 5D and standard errors of treatment differences could well be most effective.

The conversion factor to tonnes per hectare is 0.0530.

6E   The partition gives:

Source	d.f.	s.s.	F
M	1	5184.0	57.26***
N	1	7267.6	80.27***

P	1	484.0	5.35*
K	1	9264.1	102.32***
M × N	1	169.0	1.87
M × P	1	1.6	0.02
M × K	1	900.0	9.94
N × P	1	196.0	2.16
N × K	1	1914.1	21.14*
P × K	1	169.0	1.87
N × P × K	1	4.0	0.04
M × P × K	1	10.6	0.12
M × N × K	1	1156.0	12.77**
M × N × P	1	33.1	0.37
M × N × P × K	1	39.1	0.43
'Error'	45	4074.2	MS = 90.537
Stratum total	60	30 866.1	

As to interpretation, the difficulty comes from the three-factor interaction, M × N × K. Of its two-factor components, only N × K appears to be of much importance, so it should be helpful to write out the table of means, thus:

	(1)	N	K	NK	
(1)	122.0	116.5	170.5	320.5	(A)
M·	177.0	265.5	233.5	341.5	
	149.5	191.0	202.0	331.0	

From the horizontal margin it is clear that N and K operating together are on average more effective than would be expected from their separate effects (331.0 against 191.0 + 202.0 − 149.5 = 243.5, a difference of 87.5). However, when this interaction is examined for the two levels of M separately, it emerges that it is marked in the absence of M (155.5) but scarcely exists (19.5) in its presence. Essentially the table at (A) sets out the conclusions relating to those three factors; its inclusion is essential to any report. The last factor, P, shows a difference of 22.0 which does not enter into any interactions, i.e. it does not depend in any way on the levels of the other factors. That also must be presented. The results are not complete without standard errors. Whether they are those of stated contrasts or of simple differences is a matter for local decision, though they should be pertinent to any discussion of results. Convention requires the presentation of the standard error of the means themselves, though nowadays some will object that field experiments do not estimate means but only contrasts between them.

7A Since the nitrogen factor is quantitative it will be divided into a linear and a quadratic effect. The analysis of variance reads:

Source	d.f.	s.s.	m.s.	F
Varieties (V)	4	6.4493	1.6123	5.04
'Error' i	12	3.8387	0.3199	
Stratum total i	16	10.2880		
N. linear (L)	1	6.4802	6.4802	293.89***
N. quadratic (Q)	1	0.0068	0.0068	0.03
V × L	4	0.0388	0.0097	0.44
V × Q	4	0.0659	0.0165	0.75
'Error' ii	30	0.6616	0.02205	
Stratum total ii	40	6.5917		

The following points could well be included in any report. (Note: the fact that varieties are different merely confirms what must have been assumed when they were introduced.)

(1) There is a marked effect of nitrogen, the response curve being virtually a straight line.
(2) The response to nitrogen is much the same for all varieties.

7B The analyses read:

Source	d.f.	s.s.	m.s.	F
Infection (I)	1	959.22	959.22	28.89*
'Error' i	3	99.61	33.203	
Stratum total i	4	1058.83		
Protectant (P)	3	421.60	140.53	7.29**
P × I	3	207.11	69.04	3.58*
'Error' ii	18	346.76	19.264	
Stratum total ii	24	975.47		

It is scarcely to be supposed that anyone wants to know that Factor I has had an effect, but the amount should be stated. Obviously it was introduced to see if it would provoke an interaction. Clearly it has done so. Consequently the essential table is the following:

Effect of Caresan compared with the control
Infected   14.6
Not infected   4.5

Effect of Panogen compared with the control
Infected   9.8
Not infected   2.2

Effect of Agrox compared with the control
Infected   1.2
Not infected   1.0

All these differences have a standard error of 3.10 because the variance is

$$19.264(\tfrac{1}{4} + \tfrac{1}{4}) = (3.10)^2.$$

(Note that all contrasts under study are between protectants within infection status. Consequently only the second analysis is involved.) It appears then that no protectant can be said to have led to an improved crop with oats that were not infected, but Caresan and Panogen did so when there was infection.

·The conversion factor to litres per hectare is 89.9.

7C It is not stated what contrasts were of interest, but it seems fair to regard A, B and C as one group with D and E in another. If that was the intention, reasonable contrasts are:

α	(+ 2	+ 2	+ 2	− 3	− 3)
β	(+ 1	0	− 1	0	0)
γ	(+ 1	− 2	+ 1	0	0)
δ	(0	0	0	+ 1	− 1)

The analyses of variance read:

Source	d.f.	s.s.	m.s.	F
α	1	514 332	514 332	13.30**
β	1	548	548	0.01

γ	1	22 743	22 743	0.59
δ	1	1976 247	1976 247	51.22***
'Error' i	12	462 998	38 583.2	
Stratum total i	16	2976 866		
Grasses (G)	3	298 350	99 450	5.99*
G × a	3	44 967	14 989	0.90
G × β	3	16 776	5 592	0.34
G × γ	3	41 676	13 892	0.84
G × δ	3	74 321	24 774	2.49
'Error' ii	60	995 390	16 589.8	
Stratum total ii	75	1471 480		

There is clearly a difference (a) between ABC as a group and DE as another. Since there are no discernible differences within the first group (β and γ) they can be regarded as a whole with a mean of 544. The principal difference lies in the second group, the mean of Treatment E being 913, in comparison with 468 for Treatment D. (In fact, the difference between making the final cut 84 after emergence as compared with 70 is extremely high and does perhaps provide the main conclusion.) There are no interactions with grass mixtures, so results can be presented without qualification in that respect.

Interpretation must depend upon the time of emergence, which is not given. If 30 October lies between 70 and 84 days after emergence, it would be clear that the date of final cut was of paramount importance. The results could then perhaps be best expressed by taking means for the final date of cutting, like this:

D	ABC	E
468	544	913

The standard error of the difference between D and E is 80.2. Between ABC as a group and either D or E it is the square root of

$$38\,583.2(1/36 + 1/12) = (65.5)^2.$$

Note that all contrasts under consideration relate to the first analysis.

The conversion factor to tonnes per hectare is 0.0224.

7D The analyses read:

Source	d.f.	s.s.	m.s.	F
Varieties (V)	2	1 905.5	952.8	1.64
'Error' i	10	5 799.1	579.91	
Stratum total i	12	7 7704.6		
N, linear (L)	1	19 096.1	19 096.1	107.43***
N, quadratic (Q)	1	430.2	430.2	2.42
N, cubic (C)	1	5.9	5.9	0.03
V × L	2	227.8	113.9	0.64
V × Q	2	4.7	2.4	0.01
V × C	2	126.7	63.4	0.36
'Error' ii	45	7 998.7	177.75	
Stratum total ii	54	27 890.1		

There is a marked effect of nitrogen, which appears to follow a straight-line relationship and to be the same for all three varieties.

7E The analyses read:

Source	d.f.	s.s.	m.s.	F
N	1	189.28		12.26**
P	1	8.40		0.54
K	1	95.20		6.17*
P × K	1	0.48		0.03
N × K	1	33.14		2.15
N × P	1	21.28		1.38
'Error'	12	185.29	15.441	
Stratum total	18	533.07		

There is a marked effect of nitrogen and a less well marked effect of potassium. There is some evidence that they interact, but it is not significant.

7F

(a)
I	(1)	d	bc	bcd
II	a	ad	abc	abcd
III	b	c	bd	cd
IV	ab	ac	abd	acd

A, B × C and A × B × C are all confounded.

(b)
I	(1)	be	cd	abc	abd	ace	ade	bcde
II	a	bc	bd	ce	de	abe	acd	abcde
III	b	e	ac	ad	bcd	cde	abce	abde
IV	c	d	ab	ae	bce	bde	abcd	acde

A × B × E, A × C × D and B × C × D × E are all confounded.

(c)
I	(1)	cd	abc	abd
II	be	ace	ade	bcde
III	a	bc	bd	acd
IV	ce	de	abe	abcde
V	b	ac	ad	bcd
VI	e	cde	abce	abde
VII	c	d	ab	abcd
VIII	ae	bce	bde	acde

The following contrasts are confounded in addition to those in (b): E, A × B, B × C × D and A × C × D × E.

8A The analysis of variance reads:

Source	d.f.	s.s.
Total regression of y on x	1	1806.5
Gain from using x_2 also	1	2440.2
Total regression of y on x_2	1	2471.7
Gain from using x_1 also	1	1775.0
Multiple regression of y on x and x_2	2	4246.7
'Error'	14	198.7
Total	16	4445.4

The partial and total regression coefficients are virtually the same because x_1 and x_2 are uncorrelated.

8B All four bodies of data lead to the relationship.

$$y = 3 + x/2.$$

Nevertheless, they correspond to very different cases:

(I) Here the regression line appears to be straight, but the values of y contain a large random component.

(II) Here the regression relationship is given by a curve and all the points lie close to it.

(III) Again the regression relationship appears to be straight, but there is little random variation apart from the one aberrant pair of values, (13, 12.74), which really requires further investigation.

(IV) Here everything depends upon one value of x that is different from the rest. A regression line, if straight, is fairly well determined, though it would be known better if there were more points with $x = 19$. There is, however, no way of judging from these data whether the regression line is straight or not.

8C Without a covariance adjustment, the analysis of variance of y reads:

Source	d.f.	s.s.	m.s.	F
Treatments	5	749	149.8	0.10
'Error'	15	23 433	1562.2	
Stratum total	20	24 182		

There is no evidence that the treatments are having any effect. The treatment means are:

A	B	C	D	E	O
285	268	275	270	277	280

After a covariance adjustment has been applied, the analysis of covariance reads:

Source	d.f.	s.s.	m.s.	F
Treatments	5	4359	871.8	3.15
'Error'	14	3881	277.2	
Stratum total	19	8240		

The treatment means are:

A	B	C	D	E	O
281	267	274	281	301	252

The adjustment has had two effects:

(a) It has explained much of the 'error' variation and has so reduced the estimated variance from 1562.2 to 277.2.

(b) It has shown that the treatment O (the control) had been assigned most of the best plots. Once this is allowed for, it becomes clear that it is rather an unproductive treatment.

8D To provide a check at an intermediate point in the lengthy calculations, we give the full analyses of variance and covariance.

Source	d.f.	x^2	xy	y^2
L	1	26 107	31 990	39 200
P	1	19 602	157 658	1268 028
L × P	1	36	546	8 256
'Error' i	9	168 543	60 952	434 947
Stratum total	12	214 288	251 146	1750 431
M	1	64 441	70 544	77 224
L × M	1	5 670	1 757	545
P × M	1	40 898	41 398	41 906
L × P × M	1	93 096	60 949	39 903
'Error' ii	12	337 844	196 772	263 583
Stratum total	16	541 949	371 420	423 161

Regression coefficients are: $b_i = +0.3616$: $b_{ii} = +0.5824$.
The adjusted analyses of variance are:

Source	d.f.	s.s.	m.s.	F
L	1	16 865	16 865	0.33
P	1	1 036 063	1 036 063	20.07
L × P	1	7 864	7 864	0.15
'Error' i	8	412 904	51 613	
Stratum total i	11	1 473 696		
M	1	14 201	14 201	1.05
L × M	1	415	415	0.03
P × M	1	6 741	6 741	0.50
L × P × M	1	382	382	0.03
'Error' ii	11	148 976	13 543	
Stratum total ii	15	168 612		

A covariance adjustment leads to non-orthogonality of contrasts that would otherwise be orthogonal. That is why the adjusted sums of squares do not add to the stratum totals.

As to conclusions, there is clearly a highly significant main effect of phosphate, but nothing else requires consideration. (It would, nonethe less, be wise in any report to give adjusted means for all main effects, whether significant or not.) The factor P, lies in the first analysis, so b_i applies, not b_{ii}. Hence, after adjustment of x to its mean, i.e. 703.9, the y-means are

$$(1). \ 617; \quad P, \ 998.$$

The difference (381) has a standard error equal to the square root of

$$51 \ 613(1/16 + 1/16 + (49.5)^2/168 \ 543)$$

i.e. 84.9, so it equals 4.48 times its own standard error.

If there had been any significant effects involving Factor M, b_{ii} and E_{xx} would have been taken from the second analysis. Also, interactions would have been most conveniently expressed in terms of the effect of M depending upon levels of L and P.

8E   After adjustment by the covariate, the analysis of variance read:

Source	d.f.	s.s.	m.s.	F
Treatments	9	276.33	30.70	8.16
'Error'	26	97.78	3.760	
Stratum total	35	374.11		

The 'error' mean square has been reduced from 3.865 to 3.760, which is not of much importance. On the other hand, K, according to (8.6.8), has been increased from 0.500 to 0.515, so the situation is little changed.

8F   After adjustment by $w = \sin \theta$ and $x = \cos \theta$, the 'error' mean square becomes 3.811 with 25 degrees of freedom. Again, nothing has been gained. There are in fact no grounds for supposing that the long, narrow blocks were badly chosen.

8G   The effect of the covariance adjustment is to reduce the 'error' mean square to 11.892.

9A   The means and ranges of the three treatments are as follows:

Treatment	Mean	Range
A	13.5	11
B	28.4	17
C	49.8	20

The ranges increase roughly with the square roots of the means, which indicates a square-root transformation, and that is not unreasonable. Taking square roots to two decimal places leads to this analysis:

Source	d.f.	s.s.	m.s.	F
Treatments	2	46.179	23.090	83.03***
'Error'	21	5.841	0.2781	
Stratum total	23	52.020		

There are clearly large differences between the treatments. Results are best expressed by squaring the means of the transformed variates, i.e.

A, 13.2; B, 28.1; C, 49.5

rather than the means of the untransformed variate as given above.

9B Here there is the complication of blocks, but again the simplest approach is to relate means and ranges, i.e.

Treatment	Mean	Range
A	13.8	17
B	13.5	21
C	10.0	18
D	7.3	18
E	24.2	38

The mean value for E is about twice that for A–D taken together, and the same can be said of the ranges. That implies a need for a logarithmic transformation. On the other hand, it is more reasonable in the present instance to expect a Poisson distribution (see Section 3.8), in which case the standard error (and hence the range) would vary, so the square root is the mean. Whichever transformation is used, there will be reservations, but either would be better than no transformation at all.

If these data stand in isolation, the cautious may take refuge in the method of Section 9.6. That is to say, the differences between Treatments, A, B, C and D are unimportant, whereas E does look successful. The six differences between F and the mean of the rest are:

I	II	III	IV	V	VI
+ 10.8	+ 16.2	+ 3.8	+ 24.2	+ 17.2	+ 7.2

That leads to an analysis of variance, thus:

Source	d.f.	s.s.	m.s.	F
Contrast	1	1050.73	1050.73	19.03**
'Error'	5	276.11	55.222	
Total	6	1326.84		

Critics may complain that information is being wasted, but at least the method is fairly safe.

If the data are part of a series, the other experiments will give a clue which transformation to choose.

9C   Again the first task is to relate means and ranges:

Treatments	Means	Range
A	5.0	12
B	24.8	61
C	16.8	44
D	8.6	27

In general the ranges are in much the same proportion as the square roots of the means. That suggests the need for a square-root transformation, However, discontinuity is serious, so the square root of $(y + 0.375)$ would be better.

The analysis accordingly reads:

Source	d.f.	s.s.	m.s.	F
Treatments	3	28.435	9.478	1.88
'Error'	21	106.096	5.0522	
Stratum total	24	134.531		

On the transformed scale the variety means are:

A, 2.05; B, 4.51; C, 3.52; D, 2.55.

The standard error of C difference between two treatments is 1.124. For 21 degrees of freedom and $P = 0.05$, $t = 2.080$, so a difference larger than 2.34 must be accounted significant at that level. There is no variety with a mean less than $(3.52 - 2.34)$, so none show any improvement. Even on a one-tailed test that remains better, but only just.

10A   This is a particularly awkward body of data because it exhibits both the features that raise difficulties of analysis. First, there are signs of strong interaction of sites with one of the factors, namely, nitrogen. At Friars Hill, Lower Friars Hill and Old Road it gives a marked positive effect; elsewhere the effect, if it exists at all, is negligible. (To anyone who knows Antigua the names will be meaningful, but clearly soil response to nitrogen differs from one part of the island to another.) Secondly, the various experiments gave widely different error mean squares, which implies the need to give a higher weighting to some (the more precise) than to others. Each of these features could be established by a formal test, but the exercise hardly seems necessary. (An analysis of variance could be used for the interaction of treatments and sites: Bartlett's test, explained in Section 9.6, for the homogeneity of variances.)

With this double difficulty the best course is probably to consider each site in isolation. There are enough data to estimate the three main effects and the three two-factor interactions for each of the eight localities, and this would give an indication of how to fertilize at each. If the values of those six quantities were marked on a map they might well show the responses to be expected in different areas.

If, on the other hand, there had been only a few observations at each site this procedure would not prove very informative. In that case the best procedure might well be to test each of the six effects against its own interaction with sites. Strictly speaking, that does no more than indicate whether or not each effect exists on average over the island as a whole, but that would be worth knowing and, in the absence of enough data at each site, is as much as can be expected.

10B The two analyses of variance read:

Source	d.f.	L		H	
		s.s.	m.s.	s.s.	m.s.
Effect	1	116.8544	116.8544	0.0138	0.0138
Sites (S)	2	7.9574	3.9787	0.3069	0.1534
Year (Y)	2	1.1751	0.5876	0.0470	0.0235
N-Index (I)	1	3.1896	3.1896	0.0370	0.0370
Y × I	2	1.6336	0.8168	0.0008	0.0004
S × I	2	1.7099	0.8550	0.0158	0.0079
S × Y	4	0.6641	0.1660	0.2141	0.0535
S × I × Y	4	0.9123	0.2281	0.3632	0.0908
'Error'	36	3.2087	0.08913	3.2627	0.09063
Stratum total	54	137.3051		4.2613	

To take L first, there is clearly a large effect. Its mean square is much the largest of any in the analysis and enables one to say, not just that there is an effect overall, but that there is one for all sites and years regardless of N-Index. The existence of other significant effects in the analysis shows, however, that its magnitude depends upon circumstances. For example, those for sites ($F = 44.64$) and N-Index ($F = 35.79$) are especially marked and show that the value of the effect varies markedly with those factors. For years, $F = 6.59$ and that also is significant, though one might have expected it to be larger. Further it appears to interact with both sites and years. Some might argue that all these effects would have been foreseen; consequently they require estimation rather than testing. That may well be so, but the analysis of variance needs to be calculated, and a preliminary survey of what it indicates does no harm, provided previous knowledge is not forgotten. (An experiment is rarely the sole source of information about the subject; it needs to be interpreted in the light of its predecessors.)

Estimation is, nonetheless, essential, whether there have been preliminary tests or not. Here the most important differences are associated with sites, N-Index and their interaction, so a table to show those effects should be helpful. It reads:

	X	Y	Z	Index means
Index = 0	+ 2.84	+ 2.39	+ 2.04	+ 2.42
= 1	+ 2.44	+ 2.12	+ 0.65	+ 1.74
Site means	+ 2.64	+ 2.26	+ 1.34	
Differences	+ 0.40	+ 0.27	+ 1.39	

There is an interaction. Though it is small relative to the main effects, it should, nonetheless, be looked at first. In general it may be summed up by saying that the effect of residual nitrogen (Index 1 compared with Index 0) is more marked when, as at Site Z, the crop is less good, supposedly on account of poor soil. Differences within the table have a standard error of 0.141. (It is found by taking 0.08913, multiplying by 4, dividing by 18, the number of data used to calculate each mean, and taking the square root. We recall that the figures in the table are themselves each the mean of two data, and a difference of two such quantities involves four data. That explains the use of 4 as a multiplier and not 2.) Here it should be remembered that the figures represent the effect of applied nitrogen ($N_2 - N_0$). On poor soil with good supplies of residual nitrogen, applications of that element have had little effect (0.65) compared with figures elsewhere in the table. (Perhaps there was some inhibition of cropping that had little to do with nitrogen, so, where there was already enough of that element, further supplies did no good. Questions of that sort can be decided only by those with local knowledge.) The interpretation of the main effects is obvious, but must be made with the interaction in mind.

The figures given say nothing about the effect of years, which was not very large anyway. Since no one can control the weather there is often little point in saying much about the year differences, unless one of the seasons was remarkable on account of drought or some similar feature. In this instance we have no information about that, but we do note that there was an interaction of years and N-Index, as follows:

	1	2	3
N-Index = 0	+ 2.43	+ 2.49	+ 2.36
N-Index = 1	+ 1.25	+ 1.62	+ 2.34
Year means	+ 1.84	+ 2.05	+ 2.35

The standard error is as before, since each figure is again the mean of 18 data. The result here is surprising and not easy to interpret. The figures suggest strongly that residual nitrogen had little effect in the third year, the effect of applied nitrogen being much as usual. Could it have rained hard at the beginning of the season so that residual nitrogen was leeched out? Again, more intimate knowledge of all the circumstances would be a help.

Turning to the other variate, the 'error' sum of squares was much the same as for L, but there is no suggestion of anything being significant, not even the effect itself ($F = 0.0138/0.090\,63 = 0.15$). There is therefore in a sense nothing to interpret, but it would still be wise to set out means and standard error as for L.

10C Any suggestions for the design of a rotation experiment with different lengths of rotation will be criticized by someone, but here is one approach.

First, we can compare the three-year rotations:

I	F	C	M	...
II	C	C	M	...
III	C	M	M	...
IV	X	C	M	...

(We are assuming that it is possible to grow cotton after cotton.) Next we can add the six-year rotations, including one year's fallow, like this:

I/II	F	C	M	C	C	M	...
I/III	F	C	M	C	M	M	...
I/IV	F	C	M	X	C	M	...

These latter rotations require six phases, but I–IV require only three. We can economize a little by associating plots that differ in phase by three years, thus:

Year	1	2	3	4	5	6	7	8	9	10	11	12	13	14	15
I/II	F	C	M	C	C	M	F	C	M	C	C	M	...		
I/III	F	C	M	C	M	M	F	C	M	C	M	M	...		
I/IV	F	C	M	X	C	M	F	C	M	X	C	M	...		
I	F	C	M	F	C	M	F	C	M	F	C	M	...		
II	C	C	M	C	C	M	C	C	M	C	C	M	...		
III	C	M	M	C	M	M	C	M	C	M	C	M	...		
IV	X	C	M	X	C	M	X	C	M	X	C	M	...		
I/II	[F	C	M]	F	C	M	C	C	M	F	C	M	C	C	M	...
I/III	[F	C	M]	F	C	M	C	M	M	F	C	M	C	M	M	...
I/IV	[F	C	M]	F	C	M	X	C	M	F	C	M	X	C	M	...

The ten treatments may be arranged in one randomized block, or preferably more. Useful information on yields of cotton as affected by previous cropping will be obtained in years 2, 4, 5, 8, 10, 11, etc. and on millet in years 3, 5, 6, 8, 9, 12, etc. A little information about the new crop, X, will be found from years 4, 7, 10, etc. For completeness of information and to guard against the mishaps of season (e.g. a failure of millet in year 6), it would be wise to start replicate blocks one year later and two years later, so as to give all six phases in each year. It would also be desirable to split the plots, perhaps into four sub-plots each, so as to add the factors of weedkiller and fertilizer, each at two levels.

10D The analyses of variance and covariance read:

Source	d.f.	a^2	ab	b^2
Treatments	3	36.30	+ 7.017	5.193
'Error'	13	144.50	+ 22.631	5.583
Stratum total	16	180.80	+ 29.648	10.776

Hence $\cos \theta = 0.635$, $\theta = 0.50°$.

Transformations are:

$$x = + 0.300a$$
$$y = - 0.395a + 2.525b.$$

Bivariate $F = 3.62$ with 6 and 24 degrees of freedom.
Treatment means are:

	a	b	x	y	Distance from O
O	43.2	6.92	12.97	0.36	—
N	40.0	6.77	12.00	1.28	1.34
P	43.0	6.96	12.90	0.56	0.21
K	41.0	5.62	12.30	− 2.01	2.46

For the contrast between O and any other treatment, $K = (1/8 + 1/4)$ $= 0.375$, so L in $(10.5.1) = 1.32$ for $P = 0.05$.

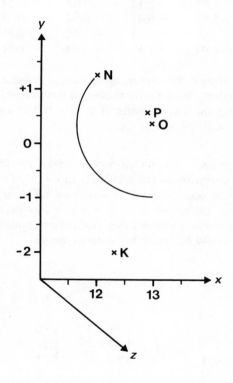

Compared with 0, a heavy dressing of nitrogen had led to small decreases both in number of cobs and their weight, which together are just significant $(P = 0.05)$. (Note that y indicates weight of cobs after an adjustment for their number. If that adjustment is omitted, the value for n is slightly less than that for 0.) A large application of potassium has led to the same two effects, but more marked in both cases. Using two-univariate analysis of variance, the effect of potassium on crop weight comes through clearly, but nothing else does.

10E We suggest $C = 1.061$, $N = D = 15.9$, $\ominus = 3.39°$.
$L = 18.4$.
It is a little on the short side since L could go to 20.

10F The Papadakis covariate is:

+ 0.72	+ 1.80	− 1.48	− 0.66	− 1.35	− 2.19
+ 1.30	− 0.85	− 1.12	− 3.40	− 2.39	− 3.11
+ 1.41	− 0.85	− 2.12	− 2.48	− 3.51	− 1.92
+ 0.21	+ 1.67	− 0.43	− 0.42	− 0.28	− 1.82
+ 3.92	+ 1.68	+ 2.14	+ 0.77	+ 0.88	+ 0.41
+ 1.86	+ 3.90	+ 1.67	+ 2.28	− 0.06	+ 0.77

As a result of using it, the 'error' mean square is reduced to 5.516 with 28 degrees of freedom. Without local control it was 8.582 with 30 degrees of freedom. Using the Latin square (Exercise 1F) it was 3.047 with 20 degrees of freedom.

10G We first guess $r = 6$, which would make $f = 15$, $t = 2.947$ and $t' = 1.753$. The expression at (10.9.2) leads to $r = + 7.07$. Taking $r = 7$, f becomes 18, t becomes 2.878 and t' becomes 1.734, so r, the required replication, is now estimated as 6.81, which is less than the figure of 7 proposed. Nevertheless, we advise that replication should not be minimal. Eight replicates would be better but nine excessive.

11A

Density	3	6	9
LER	1.38	1.30	1.53
ELER ($r = \frac{1}{2}$)	1.37	1.21	1.36
SLER ($t = 900$)	1.16	1.11	1.15

11B The transformations are:

$$x = 2.81a$$
$$y = 2.62b - 0.37a.$$

Treatment means are:

	a	b	x	y
A P	0.48	1.82	1.36	4.93
Q	0.32	3.38	0.88	8.93
B P	1.66	1.23	4.66	3.85
Q	1.52	2.21	4.26	6.36

The bivariate F for all treatments is 12.89 with 6 and 16 degrees of freedom. For the main effect of sorghum varieties, the main effect of millet varieties and the interaction, the bivariate F had values of 13.88, 11.32 and 0.97, respectively.

Looking at the means of x and y, those for sorghum are:

	x	y
Early	1.12	6.93
Mid-season	4.46	5.10

The mid-season variety has given more sorghum with some loss of millet, having proved a strong competitor.

For millet the means are:

	x	y
Short-stemmed	3.01	4.39
Long-stemmed	2.57	7.64

The long-stemmed variety has given more millet, but there may be a slight loss in the yield of sorghum. However, judging from the invariate analysis of x, that is not significant.

11C The transformations are:

$$x = 0.0479a$$
$$y = 0.0155a + 0.1340b.$$

Consequently the treatment means for the eight treatments are:

	T0		T4		T8		T12		T16	
	x	y	x	y	x	y	x	y	x	y
O	3.17	9.20	4.22	9.03	3.08	6.61	4.20	8.34	3.31	5.12
M	4.02	10.90	3.79	9.34	2.88	6.96	4.45	8.22	3.12	4.75

It is a simple matter to plot those points on a bivariate diagram.

After transformation the analyses of variance and covariance become:

Source	d.f.	x^2	xy	y^2
Time of planting cassava	4	9.7793	21.0722	131.6072
Melons	1	0.0390	0.2373	1.4243
Interaction	4	2.0233	2.3362	5.1067
'Error'	27	26.9820	− 0.0153	27.0080
Stratum total	36	38.8237	23.6304	165.1462

It will be seen that the two 'error' sums of squares do not exactly equal the 'error' degrees of freedom, nor is the 'error' sum of products exactly equal to zero, but that is the result of rounding. If the bivariate analysis is to be obtained precisely, more decimal places are needed in the coefficients of the transformation. However, although the bivariate analysis lies at the heart of the method, it is not always necessary to calculate it. The mean values of x and y can be found without it, while the values of the bivariate F are better found from the analyses of variance and covariance of a and b, i.e. as given in the Exercise, because to use x and y would be to incorporate the rounding errors already noted.

To consider the interaction first, Λ equals

$$(11\ 762 \times 1662 - 1362^2)/(12\ 644 \times 1874 - 1100^2)$$

which equals 0.7869, showing the bivariate F to be equal to 0.83 with eight and 26 degrees of freedom. That is clearly not significant, so the correct procedure is to examine the two main effects. The bivariate F for the melons is 0.69, so again there is no sign of any effect. Hence it may be concluded that the interplanting of melons has had no discernible effect, so anything gained from their crop has been obtained without loss of cassava. The last bivariate F is that for the main effect of time of planting cassava. It equals 11.60 with 8 and 26 degrees of freedom. Clearly that gives strong evidence of an effect, and the tables show that there is advantage to the cassava in planting it early.

11D

The means for the combinations of V and F are:

	x	y
V_1F_1	1.05	4.92
V_1F_2	2.52	2.96
V_2F_1	3.83	3.60
V_2F_2	9.03	0.68

In the absence of an interaction, V_2F_2 would be expected at the point
$$(3.83 + 2.52 - 1.05, \ 3.60 + 2.96 - 4.92)$$
i.e. at (5.30, 1.64). It is in fact, at (9.03, 0.68), displaced by a distance equal to the square root of
$$(9.03 - 5.30)^2 + (0.68 + 1.64)^2 = 3.85^2$$
The following diagram shows the form of the interaction:

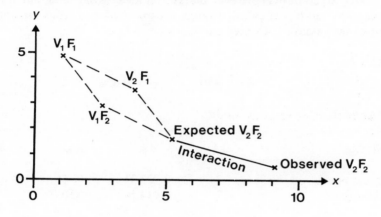

It appears V_2F_2 has given much more sorghum than would be expected from the performance of the other treatments and has done so without having had much effect on y.

11E To take the contour for 30 000 MJ first, this calls for 96 MJ per plot of 32 m². We will start with $a = 60$. In that case the maize will be contributing 58.74 MJ, leaving the cassava to provide 37.26 MJ, so b must equal 41.49 MJ. Hence $x = 2.874$ and $y = 6.490$. Another point is that for $a = 75$, $b = 25.24$, $x = 3.592$, $y = 4.531$. The simplest way of drawing the contour is to put a straight line between the two points just found. If the equation of the line is needed, it is

$$(x - 2.874)/(3.592 - 2.874) = (y - 6.490)/(4.531 - 6.490)$$

or

$$x + 0.367y = 5.25.$$

Turning to the contour for 40 000 MJ, corresponding points are given by:

$$a = 60, \quad b = 77.13, \quad x = 2.874, \quad y = 11.265;$$
$$a = 75, \quad b = 60.77, \quad x = 3.592, \quad y = 9.306.$$

This leads to the equation

$$x + 0.367y = 7.00.$$

It will be noted that $5.25/7.00 = 30\,000/40\,000$.

Once the contours have been marked on the bivariate diagram, it will be apparent that higher calorific values for the combined crops are obtained when the cassava is planted early.

12A

$$m = 1.130 \qquad m' = 0.624.$$

The analysis of variance reads:

Source	d.f.	s.s.	m.s.	F
Treatments	2	0.723 31	0.361 66	174.63***
'Error'	7	0.014 50	0.002 071	
Stratum total	9	0.737 81		

The damaged contrast is $(-1 -1 +2)$, so the approximate effective replications of treatments for study of the linear, $(-1 \quad 0 +1)$, and quadratic, $(-\frac{1}{2} +1 -\frac{1}{2})$, effects are respectively 4.25 and 4.75.

The linear effect is estimated as 0.569 and its variance is 0.002 071 $(2/4.75) = 0.0312^2$. It is therefore very highly significant. The quadratic effect is estimated as -0.159 with a variance of 0.002 071 $(1.5/4.97) = (0.0250)^2$, so the figure for Fe2 is significantly below the mean of the other two.

12B Essentially there are three main methods:

(a) The fitting of missing-plot values, whether by the method of Section 12.2, by Rubin's method or in any other way.
(b) The use of covariance.
(c) By the Kuiper–Corsten iteration. However, in this text we have not

shown the extension to row-and-column designs, so that is not available in this instance.

(a) *Missing-plot values*

$$m = 464.3 \qquad m' = 441.6.$$

The analysis of variance reads:

Source	d.f.	s.s.	m.s.	F
Treatments	4	21 828	5457	5.05
'Error'	11	11 898	1081.6	
Stratum total	15	33 726		

(b) *Covariance*

The analyses of variance and covariance read, m having been put equal to zero, like this:

Source	d.f.	x^2	xy^2	y^2
Treatments	4	0.16	− 59.76	43 159
'Error'	12	0.48	− 222.88	115 387
Stratum total	16	0.64	− 282.64	158 546

Adjusting y by x gives the analysis of variance at (a). Further, $222.88/0.48 = 464.3 = m$, so means, etc., will be the same by either method.

The conversion factor to tonnes per hectare is 0.448.

12C

$$12m_1 + m_2 = 202.4$$
$$m_1 + 12m_2 = 187.2$$

Hence $m_1 = 15.68$ and $m_2 = 14.29$.

Further, $m'_1 = 13.80$ and $m_2 = 15.13$, so the analysis of variance reads:

Source	d.f.	s.s.	m.s.	F
Treatments	3	15.1211	5.040 4	10.78
'Error'	10	4.6738	0.467 38	
Stratum total	13	19.7949		

Using covariance, setting $m_1 = m_2 = 0$, the analyses of variance and covariance read:

Source	d.f.	w^2	x^2	y^2
Treatments	3	0.15	0.15	37.286
'Error'	12	0.60	0.60	297.099
Stratum total	15	0.75	0.75	334.385

Source	d.f.	xy	wy	wx
Treatments	3	− 0.23	− 1.99	− 0.05
'Error'	12	− 10.12	− 9.36	+ 0.05
Stratum total	15	− 10.35	− 10.35	0.00

From the 'error' line the partial regression coefficients are − 14.29 ($= − m_1$) and − 15.68 ($= − m_2$). From the 'stratum total' line they are similarly − 15.13 and − 13.80. It will be found that if y is adjusted by both w and x, the resulting analysis of variance will be that given above.

For the three contrasts the value of K from (8.7.2) become respectively 0.545, 0.467 and 0.400. Since s^2 is 0.467 38, the respective standard errors are 0.505, 0.467 and 0.432. Using the methods of Exercise 4A, the values of K are respectively 0.500, 0.425 and 0.400, so, as far as the damaged treatments were concerned, it was helpful to have data from all the plots, even if some of them involved a mistake.

12D   The equations for the missing-plot values are:

$$10m_1 + m_2 - 2m_3 = 270.8$$
$$m_1 + 10m_2 - 2m_3 = 175.4$$
$$- 2m_1 - 2m_2 + 10m_3 = 148.4.$$

They convert into three leading equations:

$$m_1 = 27.08 - 0.1m_2 + 0.2m_3$$
$$m_2 = 17.54 - 0.1m_1 + 0.2m_3$$
$$m_3 = 14.84 + 0.2m_1 + 0.2m_2.$$

We will start by putting m_2 and m_3 equal to their respective treatment means. The iteration proceeds thus:

Cycle	m_1	m_2	m_3
0	—	18.80	27.80
1	19.64	24.36	23.64
2	29.37	19.33	24.58
3	30.06	19.45	27.74
4	30.08	19.48	24.75
5	30.08	19.48	24.75

12E Although the complete data could be analysed using the Kuiper–Corsten iteration, it is easier to use the method of covariance. (There is no simple way of expressing a residual, so missing-plot values will not be found easily.)

It is therefore proposed to put $m_1 = m_2 = 0$. The effect of this is to add 78 350 to the stratum total sum of squares in Exercise 4F and $+ 27.0$, $+ 168.0$, $- 43.0$ and $- 152.0$, respectively, to Q_A, Q_B, Q_C and Q_D. With the enlarged design $\lambda = 52$, $\lambda_o = 36$, $R = 16$, $R_o = 144/13$.

Two pseudo-variates are needed, one for the plot missing from Treatment A(w) and the other for the plot missing from D(x). Both give a stratum total sum of squares of 11/12, being zero in all blocks except 111. The values of Q are:

	Q_A	Q_B	Q_C	Q_D
w	$+ 0.75$	$- 0.25$	$- 0.25$	$- 0.25$
x	$- 0.25$	$- 0.25$	$- 0.25$	$+ 0.75$
y	$+ 119.3$	$+ 433.7$	$- 333.3$	$- 219.3$

Accordingly the analyses of variance and covariance are:

Source	d.f.	w^2	x^2	y^2
Treatments	3	9/144	$-3/144$	22 991
'Error'	52	123/144	$-9/144$	119 308
Stratum total	55	132/144	$-12/144$	142 299

Source	d.f.	xy	wy	wx
Treatments	3	-1454	$+944$	$-3/144$
'Error'	52	-13746	-16194	$-9/144$
Stratum total	55	-15200	-15200	$-12/144$

It will be noticed that the sums of squares and products for the covariates w and x have been expressed as fractions and not in decimals, as were the effective replications, R and R_o. Since the fractions are exact, whereas the decimals would involve rounding, there are advantages in doing so.

The resulting analysis of variance for y adjusted by w and x reads:

Source	d.f.	s.s.	m.s.	F
Treatments	3	24 059	8020	6.51
'Error'	50	62 790	1231.2	
Stratum total	53	86 849		

The treatment means, after adjusting all values of w and x to zero, are:

A	B	C	D
182	187	139	157

Standard errors of contrasts can be found in the usual way from the expression at (8.7.2). It can be generalized, if desired, in the same way that (8.6.7) was generalized to (8.6.10).

12F The value of 279 shows a discrepancy from m of 185.3. All plots will have the same value of ψ, which must therefore equal $12/25 = 0.48$. Hence, if 279 were used instead of m, the 'error' sum of squares would be increased by $0.48(185.3)^2 = 16\,481$. Hence the analysis of variance reads:

Source	d.f.	s.s.	m.s.	F
Discrepancy	1	16 481	16 481	15.24**
'Error'	11	11 898	1 081.6	
Total	12	28 379		

The discrepancy is too large to be explained as chance ($P < 0.01$).

12G The discrepancy is $(1.130 - 0.710) = 0.420$. All plots must have the same value of ψ, namely $8/15$, so the sum of squares for the discrepancy is $(8/15)(0.429)^2 = 0.094\,08$. The analysis of variance therefore reads:

Source	d.f.	s.s.	m.s.	F
Discrepancy	1	0.094 08	0.094 08	45.43***
'Error'	7	0.014 50	0.002 071	
Total	8	0.0108 58		

The discrepancy is clearly significant ($P < 0.001$).

Suggestions for Further Reading

General There are many books on crop experimentation, though some of the best are now rather out-of-date. Among recent publications are those of Preece (1982) and Pearce (1986a).

Chapter 1 The method of sweeping derives from the paper of Wilkinson (1970). The concept of strata was advanced by Nelder (1965a,b). On precision of measurement we mention the papers of Yule (1927), Preece (1981) and Riley *et al.* (1983).

There is an interesting historical survey in the paper by Kempton (1984), which also considers some alternatives to traditional methods.

Chapter 2 The law of environmental variation given by Fairfield Smith (1938) has been widely used to decide questions of plot size and shape, but not always with happy results. A recent paper by Brewer and Mead (1987) goes into the matter in some detail, besides giving a useful survey of the literature.

Chapter 3 There are many texts that advocate using multiple comparisons as if that represented accepted wisdom. In fact, ever since the methods were introduced, they have occasioned dissent. Papers that put the case for the other side are those of Chew (1976), Little (1981), Bryan-Jones and Finney (1983), Pearce (1983b) and Perry (1986).

Chapter 4 In essence this chapter is an attempt to take some established mathematical results and to make them accessible to those who may have occasion to use them. The underlying results are mostly to be found in the book by Pearce (1983a) in Sections 3.5, 5.2, 5.3, 5.8, 6.1, 6.2, 6.6 and in Example 6C. There is also the paper of Pearce (1987).

Supplemented balance has been studied by Pearce (1960a), Beckhofer (1969) and by Beckhofer and Tamhane (1981). Lattice designs were developed by Yates (1936a).

Chapters 5 and 6 The idea of contrasts is a very old one, though only recently has it begun to play much part in the general theory of statistics. Special cases, however, have been studied extensively. Thus, polynomials to a high order were presented a long time ago by Fisher and Yates (1938).

As to other partitions, the first paper on the analysis of variance (Fisher and Mackenzie, 1923) dealt with a factorial design. The two classic publications of Yates (1935, 1937) remain useful to this day, not least for their treatment of confounding.

Chapter 7   Designs with split plots have a reputation for being rather mysterious; it is hoped that this chapter will have dispelled some of the darkness. Much of the difficulty comes from teachers making an early distinction between blocks and plots and then having to minimize it. That is where an understanding of strata helps (Nelder 1965a,b). Single replication experiments have been considered by Kempton (1984). Fractional replication was developed by Finney (1945, 1946, 1950).

Chapter 8   Considering that the analysis of covariance was developed in an agricultural context by R. A. Fisher over fifty years ago, there is surprisingly little about it in the literature, though it is used by many people as a standard technique and many computer packages facilitate its use. A complete number of *Biometrics* (Vol. 13, Part 2, 1957) was dedicated to it; then, to commemorate the 25th anniversary, a further group of papers was published in Volume 38, Part 2 (1982). Volume 8, Part 8 (1979) of *Communications in Statistics* was similarly dedicated to the subject. Useful accounts of the method have been given by Bliss (1970, chapter 20) and Finney (1962). The paper of Preece (1980) expresses some necessary warnings. That of Wishart (1934) gives the modern form of the technique. The data of Exercise 8C have been studied by a number of authors, the remarks of Cox (1958) being especially illuminating.

Local control by covariance on pseudo-variates was suggested by Federer and Schlottfeldt (1954) and taken further by Outhwaite and Rutherford (1955). The use of Fourier functions was suggested by Dyke *et al.* (1982).

Chapter 9   It would be a pity if some of the earlier papers were overlooked, especially that of Cochran (1938a). Hoyle (1973) has given a useful bibliography. Corrections for discontinuity were investigated by Anscombe (1948). The paper by Box and Cox (1964) shows how powerful transformations can be at stabilizing variance. The method of Section 9.6 is very old (Tharp *et al.*, 1941).

Chapter 10   On the subject of series of experiments there are some established classics, notably the papers of Yates and Cochran (1938) and the relevant passages in the book by Cochran and Cox (1950). For rotation experiments useful papers are those of Yates (1954), Patterson (1964) and Preece (1986). The last contains a short bibliography.

On experiments with long-term crops there are the two editions of the book by Pearce (1953, 1976); each contains material lacking in the other. Sources of variation were investigated by Pearce (1960b). Those interested in long-term experiments with annual species will find much of value in the paper of Patterson and Lowe (1970).

Multivariate methods go back to Wilks (1932) and were taken further, among others, by Rao (1952). Pearce and Gilliver (1978, 1979) pointed out the special interest of bivariate methods.

Fan trials owe much to the paper by Nelder (1962). A bibliography was given by Pearce (1976). The papers by Freeman (1964, 1969) and Cleaver *et al.* (1970) show how useful systematic designs can be. Serial balance was investigated by Dyke and Shelley (1976) and by Jenkin *et al.* (1979).

Nearest neighbour methods again have a large literature, starting with two papers by Papadakis (1937, 1940) and one by Bartlett (1938). More recent work has been set out by Bartlett (1978) and Wilkinson *et al.* (1983); with both, the discussion contains much of value. Mention should also be made of the papers by Besag and Kempton (1986).

An introduction to the changing of treatments has been given by Freeman (1959).

Chapter 11   Among general papers on the statistical aspects of intercropping experiments, the following should be mentioned: Federer (1979), Mead and Stern (1980), Mead and Riley (1981), Pearce and Edmondson (1983, 1984).

The use of bivariate analysis of variance has been considered by Pearce and Gilliver (1978, 1979) and by Gilliver and Pearce (1983).

Land Equivalent Ratios were considered by Mead and Willey (1980) and have been taken further by Riley (1984) and by Reddy and Chetty (1984).

The paper by Oyejola and Mead (1982) considers the behaviour of Land Equivalent Ratios in the analysis of variance.

Chapter 12   Missing data also have a large literature; it goes back to the paper by Allen and Wishart (1930). More recent papers are those of Rubin (1972) and of Pearce and Jeffers (1971). Recently Pearce (1986) has examined the consequences of a range of data defects.

References

Allen, F. E. and Wishart, J. (1930)   A method of estimating the yield of a missing plot in field experimental work. *Journal of Agricultural Science*, **20**, 399–406.

Andrews, D. F. and Herzberg, A. M. (1985)   *Data: A Collection of Problems from Many Fields for the Student and Research Worker*. Springer-Verlag, New York.

Anscombe, F. J. (1948)   The transformation of Poisson, binomial and negative binomial data. *Biometrika*, **35**, 246–54.

Anscombe, F. J. (1973)   Graphs in statistical research. *American Statistician*, **27**, 17–21.

Bartlett, M. S. (1938)   The approximate recovery of information from field experiments with large blocks. *Journal of Agricultural Science*, **28**, 418–27.

Bartlett, M. S. (1978)   Nearest neighbour models in the analysis of field experiments. *Journal of the Royal Statistical Society*, **B40**, 147–74.

Beckhofer, R. E. (1969)   Optimal allocation of observations when comparing several treatments with a control. Pages 463–73 of *Multivariate Analysis*, Vol. 2. Academic Press Inc., New York.

Beckhofer, R. E. and Tamhane, A. C. (1981)   Incomplete block designs for comparing treatments with a control: General theory. *Technometrics*, **23**, 45–57.

Besag, J. and Kempton, R. A. (1986)   Statistical analysis of field experiments using neighbouring plots. *Biometrics*, **42**, 231–52.

Bliss, C. I. (1967)   *Statistics and Biology*, Vol. I. McGraw-Hill Book Company, New York.

Bliss, C. I. (1970)   *Statistics and Biology*, Vol. II. McGraw-Hill Book Company, New York.

Box, G. E. P. and Cox, D. R. (1964)   An analysis of transformations. *Journal of the Royal Statistical Society*, **B26**, 211–43.

Brewer, A. C. and Mead, R. (1987)   Continuous second order models of spatial variation with application to the efficiency of field crop experiments (with Discussion). *Journal of the Royal Statistical Society*, **A149**, 314–48.

Bryan-Jones, J. and Finney, D. J. (1983)   On an error in "Instructions to Authors". *HortScience*, **18**, 279–82.

Campbell, R. C. (1967)   *Statistics for Biologists*. Cambridge University Press.

Clarke, G. M. (1980)   *Statistics and Experimental Design* (2nd edn). Edward Arnold, London.

Cleaver, T. J., Greenwood, D. J. and Wood, J. T. (1970)   Systematically arranged fertilizer experiments. *Journal of Horticultural Science*, **45**, 457–69.

Cochran, W. G. (1938a)   Some difficulties in the statistical analysis of replicated experiments. *Empire Journal of Experimental Agriculture*, **1**, 157–75.

Cochran, W. G. (1938b)   Problems arising in the analysis of a series of similar experiments. *Journal of the Royal Statistical Society, Supplement* **4**, 102–18.

Cochran, W. G. and Cox, G. M. (1950)   *Experimental Designs*. John Wiley & Sons, New York.

Corsten, L. C. A. (1958)   Vectors: a tool in statistical regression theory. *Medelingen Landbouwhogeschool*, **58**, Wageningen.

Cox, D. R. (1958)   *Planning of Experiments*. John Wiley & Sons, New York.

Dagnelie, P. (1981)   *Principes d'Expérimentation*. Les presses agronomiques de Gembloux, Belgium.

349

Dyke, G. V. (1987)   *Comparative Experiments with Field Crops* (2nd edn). Charles Griffin & Co., London.

Dyke, G. V. and Shelley, Christine F. (1976)   Serial designs balanced for effect of neighbours on both sides. *Journal of Agricultural Science (Cambridge)*, **87**, 303–5.

Dyke, G. V., Smith, G. L. and Yeoman, D. P. (1982)   Fourier series and response curves. *Journal of Agricultural Science (Cambridge)*, **98**, 119–22.

Eden, T. and Fisher, R. A. (1929)   Studies in crop variation. VI. Experiments on the response of the potato to potash and nitrogen. *Journal of Agricultural Science*, **19**, 201–13.

Federer, W. T. (1979)   Statistical designs and response models for mixtures of cultivars. *Agronomy Journal*, **71**, 701–6.

Federer, W. T. and Schlottfeldt, C. S. (1954)   The use of covariance to control gradients in experiments. *Biometrics*, **10**, 282–290.

Finney, D. J. (1945)   The fractional replication of factorial experiments. *Annals of Eugenics*, **12**, 291–301.

Finney, D. J. (1946)   Recent developments in the design of field experiments. III Fractional replication. *Journal of Agricultural Science (Cambridge)*, **36**, 184–91.

Finney, D. J. (1950)   The fractional replication of factorial experiments—a correction. *Annals of Eugenics*, **15**, 276.

Finney, D. J. (1962)   *An Introduction to Statistical Science in Agriculture*. Munksgaard, Copenhagen.

Fisher, R. A. and Mackenzie, W. A. (1923)   Studies in crop variation. II. The manurial response of different potato varieties. *Journal of Agricultural Science*, **13**, 311–20.

Fisher, R. A. and Yates, F. (1938)   *Statistical Tables for Biological, Agricultural and Medical Research*. Oliver & Boyd, Edinburgh.

Freeman, G. H. (1959)   The use of the same experimental material for more than one set of treatments. *Applied Statistics*, **8**, 13–20.

Freeman, G. H. (1964)   The use of a systematic design with a tropical crop. *Biometrics*, **20**, 713–20.

Freeman, G. H. (1967)   The use of cyclic balanced incomplete block designs for directional seed-orchards. *Biometrics*, **23**, 761–89.

Freeman, G. H. (1969)   The use of cyclic balanced incomplete block designs for non-directional seed-orchards. *Biometrics*, **25**, 561–71.

Gilliver, B. and Pearce, S. C. (1983)   A graphical assessment of data from intercropping factorial experiments. *Experimental Agriculture*, **19**, 23–31.

Gomez, K. A. and Gomez, A. A. (1976)   *Statistical Procedures in Agricultural Research with Emphasis on Rice*. The International Rice Research Institute.

Hoyle, M. H. (1973)   Transformations—an introduction and a bibliography. *International Statistical Review*, **41**, 202–23.

Jenkin, J. F., Bainbridge, A., Dyke, G. V. and Todd, A. D. (1979)   An investigation into inter-plot interactions in experiments with mildew on barley, using balanced designs. *Annals of Applied Biology*, **92**, 11–28.

Kempton, R. A. (1984)   The design and analysis of unreplicated field trials. *Vortrag Pflanzenzuchtung*, **7**, 219–42.

Kuiper, N. H. (1952)   Variantie-analyse. *Statistica*, **6**, 149–94.

Lanczos, C. (1957)   *Applied Analysis*. Pitman, London.

Lester, E. (1980)   Multidisciplinary Activities, *Rothamsted Experimental Station, Annual Report for 1979*, 17–25.

Little, T. M. (1981)   Interpretation and presentation of results. *HortScience*, **16**, 19–22.

Little, T. M. and Hills, F. J. (1978)   *Agricultural Experimentation, Design and analysis*. John Wiley & Sons, New York.

Mead, R. and Riley, J. (1981) A review of statistical ideas relevant to intercropping (with discussion). *Journal of the Royal Statistical Society*, **A144**, 462–509.

Mead, R., Riley, J., Dear, K. and Singh, S. P. (1986) Stability comparison of intercropping and monocropping systems. *Biometrics*, **42**, 253–66.

Mead, R. and Stern, R. D. (1980) Designing experiments for intercropping research. *Experimental Agriculture*, **16**, 329–42.

Mead, R. and Willey, R. W. (1980) The concept of 'Land equivalent ratio' and advantages in yields from intercropping. *Experimental Agriculture*, **16**, 217–18.

Nelder, J. A. (1962) New kinds of systematic designs for spacing experiments. *Biometrics*, **18**, 283–307.

Nelder, J. A. (1965a) The analysis of randomized experiments with orthogonal block structure: Block structure and the null analysis of variance. *Proceedings of the Royal Society*, **A283**, 157–62.

Nelder, J. A. (1965b) The analysis of randomized experiments with orthogonal block structure: Treatment structure and the general analysis of variance. *Proceedings of the Royal Society*, **A283**, 163–78.

Outhwaite, Anne D. and Rutherford, A. (1955) Covariance analysis as an alternative to stratification in the control of gradients. *Biometrics*, **11**, 431–40.

Oyejola, B. A. and Mead, R. (1982) Statistical assessment of different ways of calculating land equivalent ratios (LER). *Experimental Agriculture*, **18**, 125–38.

Papadakis, J. (1937) *Méthode statistique pour des expériences sur champ*. Bulletin No. 23 de l'Institut pour l'Amélioration des Plantes, Salonique (Grèce).

Papadakis, J. (1940) Comparison de différentes méthodes d'expérimentation phytotechnique. *Revista de Argentina Agronomica*, **7**, 297–362.

Patterson, H. D. and Lowe, Bridget I. (1970) The errors of long-term experiments. *Journal of Agricultural Science (Cambridge)*, **74**, 53–60.

Pearce, S. C. (1948) Randomized blocks with interchanged and substituted blocks. *Journal of the Royal Statistical Society*, **B10**, 252–6.

Pearce, S. C. (1953) *Field experimentation with fruit trees and other perennial plants*. Technical Bulletin 23 of the Commonwealth Bureau of Horticulture and Plantation Crops.

Pearce, S. C. (1960a) Supplemented balance. *Biometrika*, **47**, 263–71.

Pearce, S. C. (1960b) A method of studying methods of growth. *Biometrics*, **16**, 1–6.

Pearce, S. C. (1965) *Biological Statistics: an Introduction*. McGraw-Hill Book Company, New York.

Pearce, S. C. (1976) Second edition of Pearce (1953).

Pearce, S. C. (1978) The control of environmental variation in some West Indian maize experiments. *Tropical Agriculture (Trinidad)*, **55**, 97–105.

Pearce, S. C. (1980) Randomized blocks and some alternatives: A study in tropical conditions. *Tropical Agriculture (Trinidad)*, **57**, 1–10.

Pearce, S. C. (1983a) *The Agricultural Field Experiment: a Statistical Examination of Theory and Practice*. John Wiley & Sons, Chichester and New York.

Pearce, S. C. (1983b) The monstrous regiment of mathematicians. *The Statistician*, **32**, 375–8.

Pearce, S. C. (1986a) Experimental design: the first sixty years. *Tropical Agriculture (Trinidad)*, **63**, 95–100.

Pearce, S. C. (1986b) Defective data in the analysis of variance. *Journal of Applied Statistics*, **13**, 139–48.

Pearce, S. C. (1987) Some simple algorithms for the analysis of variance with non-orthogonal block data. *Journal of Applied Statistics*, **14**, 53–9.

Pearce, S. C. and Edmondson, R. N. (1983) Historical data as a guide to selecting farming systems with two species. *Experimental Agriculture*, **18**, 353–62.

Pearce, S. C. and Edmondson, R. N. (1984) Experimenting with intercrops. *Biometrics*, **40**, 231–8.

Pearce, S. C. and Gilliver, B. (1978) The statistical analysis of data from intercropping experiments. *Journal of Agricultural Science (Cambridge)*, **91**, 625–72.

Pearce, S. C. and Gilliver, B. (1979) Graphical assessment of intercropping methods. *Journal of Agricultural Science (Cambridge)*, **93**, 51–8.

Pearce, S. C. and Jeffers, J. R. N. (1971) Block designs and missing data. *Journal of the Royal Statistical Society*, **B33**, 131–6.

Perry, J. N. (1986) Multiple-comparison procedures: A dissenting view. *Journal of Economic Entomology*, **79**, 1149–55.

Preece, D. A. (1980) Covariance analysis, factorial experiments and marginality. *The Statistician*, **29**, 97–122.

Preece, D. A. (1981) Distribution of final digits in data. *The Statistician*, **30**, 31–60.

Preece, D. A. (1982) The design and analysis of experiments. What has gone wrong? *Utilitas Mathematica*, **21A**, 201–44.

Preece, D. A. (1986) Some general principles of crop rotation experiments. *Experimental Agriculture*, **22**, 187–98.

Rao, C. R. (1952) *Advanced Statistical Methods in Biometric Research*. John Wiley & Sons, New York.

Rayner, A. A. (1969) *A First Course in Biometry for Agriculture Students*. University of Natal Press, Pietermaritzburg.

Reddy, M. N. and Chetty, C. K. R. (1984) Staple land equivalent ratio for assessing yield advantage from intercropping. *Experimental Agriculture*, **20**, 171–7.

Riley, J. (1984) A general form of 'Land Equivalent Ratio'. *Experimental Agriculture*, **20**, 19–29.

Riley, J., Bekele, I. and Shrewsbury, B. (1983) How an analysis of variance is affected by the degree of precision of the data. *Bulletin in Applied Statistics*, **10**, 18–43.

Sibbesen, E. and Anderson, C. E. (1985) Soil movement in long-term field experiments (in two parts) I. A model for approximating soil movement in one horizontal dimension by repeated tillage. II. How to estimate the two-dimensional movement of substances accumulating in the soil. *Experimental Agriculture*, **21**, 101–17.

Smith, H. F. (1938) An empirical law, describing heterogeneity in the yields of agricultural crops. *Journal of Agricultural Science (Cambridge)*, **28**, 1–23.

Steel, R. G. D. and Torrie, J. H. (1978) *Principles and Procedures of Statistics: A Biometrical Approach* (2nd edn). McGraw-Hill Book Company, New York.

Tharp, W. H., Wadleigh, C. H. and Barker, H. D. (1941) Some problems in handling and interpreting plant disease data in complex factorial designs. *Phytopathology*, **31**, 26–48.

Wilkinson, G. N. (1970) A general recursive procedure for analysis of variance. *Biometrika*, **57**, 19–46.

Wilkinson, G. N., Eckert, S. R., Hancock, T. W. and Mayo, O. (1983) Nearest neighbour (NN) analysis of field experiments (with discussion). *Journal of the Royal Statistical Society*, **B45**, 151–211.

Wilks, S. S. (1932) Certain generalizations in the analysis of variance. *Biometrika*, **24**, 471–94.

Wishart, J. (1934) Tests of significance in the analysis of covariance. *Journal of the Royal Statistical Society, Supplement* 3, 26–61.

Yates, F. (1935) Complex experiments (with discussion). *Journal of the Royal Statistical Society, Supplement* 2, 181–247.

Yates, F. (1936a) A new method of arranging variety trials involving a large number of varieties. *Journal of Agricultural Science (Cambridge)*, **28**, 556–80.

Yates, F. (1936b) Incomplete randomized blocks. *Annals of Eugenics*, **7**, 121–9.

Yates, F. (1937) *The design and analysis of factorial experiments.* Technical Bulletin 35 of the Imperial Bureau of Soil Science.

Yates, F. (1954) The analysis of experiments containing different crop rotations. *Biometrics*, **10**, 324–46.

Yule, G. U. (1927) On reading a scale. *Journal of the Royal Statistical Society*, **90**, 570–87.

Index